DATE DUE

CONFEDERATE MINDS

CIVIL WAR AMERICA *Gary W. Gallagher, editor*

CONFEDERATE

The University of North Carolina Press · Chapel Hill

MICHAEL T. BERNATH

MINDS

The Struggle for
Intellectual Independence
in the Civil War South

© 2010
The University of North Carolina Press
All rights reserved

Designed by
Jacquline Johnson
Set in Arnhem Blond
by Keystone Typesetting
Manufactured in the
United States of America

The paper in this book meets the guidelines for permanence and durability of the Committee on Production Guidelines for Book Longevity of the Council on Library Resources.

The University of North Carolina Press has been a member of the Green Press Initiative since 2003.

Library of Congress Cataloging-in-Publication Data
Bernath, Michael T.
  Confederate minds : the struggle for intellectual independence in the Civil War South / Michael T. Bernath.
    p. cm. — (Civil War America)
  Includes bibliographical references and index.
  ISBN 978-0-8078-3391-9 (cloth : alk. paper)
  1. Southern States—Intellectual life—19th century. 2. Confederate States of America—Intellectual life. 3. Southern States—Civilization—19th century. 4. American literature—Southern States—History and criticism. 5. Regionalism—Southern States—History—19th century. 6. Group identity—Southern States—History—19th century. 7. Nationalism—Southern States—History—19th century. 8. Nationalism—Confederate States of America—History. 9. Nationalism—United States—History—19th century. 10. United States—History—Civil War, 1861–1865—Social aspects. I. Title.
    F214.B47 2010
    973.7'13—dc22
    2009052889

14 13 12 11 10   5 4 3 2 1

For Cathy

CONTENTS

ILLUSTRATIONS

ACKNOWLEDGMENTS

This book has been nearly ten years in the making, and I have had the help of many along the way. At Harvard, where this project began, I was blessed with a supportive network of mentors and friends. William Gienapp fundamentally shaped my approach to both the study and the teaching of history. Due to his untimely death, he was able to read only three chapters of my first draft, but I hope that he would have been pleased with the final result. In retrospect, the timing of Drew Faust's arrival at Harvard seems almost providential. No scholar's work has influenced me more, and I could not have hoped for a better mentor. James Kloppenberg and Gary Gallagher improved my work immeasurably through their many suggestions.

I am grateful for the opportunity to have presented portions of this book at meetings of the Organization of American Historians, Southern Historians in New England, Harvard Nineteenth Century American History Workshop and at the Boston Athenaeum. Michael O'Brien, Bill Harris, Bob Bonner, Donald Fleming, Jack Thomas, Chandra Manning, Lisa Laskin, Tom Coens, Yonatan Eyal, Dara Baker, and Bob Brugger all offered helpful feedback at various times. I would also like to thank my colleagues at the University of Miami's Department of History for their support and encouragement. I owe tremendous debts to Richard Godbeer, my readers for the University of North Carolina Press, George Rable and Steven Stowe (who thankfully agreed to unmask themselves at the end of the process), and an anonymous reader, all of whom helped me to revise and condense my lengthy manuscript into a book. I stand amazed at the time and attention that these busy scholars devoted to my work. I cannot imagine more generous, more insightful, or more helpful readers.

Research and writing require travel, resources, and, above all, time, and my work would not have been possible without the aid of a number of generous fellowships and grants. During my graduate career, two year-long fellowships from the Whiting Foundation and the Charles Warren Center permitted me to devote myself exclusively to writing. Research grants from the Harvard History Department, the Warren Center, and a Harvard Merit Fellowship allowed me to travel south and granted me the time required to sit hunched in front of a microfilm machine for weeks and months at a time. A Caleb Loring Jr. Fellowship from the Boston Athenaeum provided unfettered access to that remarkable institution's unparalleled collection of Confederate print literature. At Miami, I have been fortunate to receive two Max Orovitz Summer Awards in the Arts and Humanities, and I would also like to thank the College of Arts and Sciences for providing subvention funding for this book.

In my research, I have called upon the aid and goodwill of numerous institutions and librarians, and invariably my calls have been answered. My greatest debt is to the Harvard Library system, and I wish to thank the staffs at Widener, Houghton, Government Documents, Gutman, Baker, and Andover-Harvard Theological libraries for all their help over the years. Alison Scott at Harvard never flinched at any of my acquisition requests and now has assembled one of the finest collections of Confederate periodical literature to be found anywhere. At the Boston Athenaeum, I would like to thank Stephen Nonack and Mary Warnement for all their help throughout this process as well as Patricia Boulos for her assistance in securing the images for the book. I would also like to thank the staffs and research librarians of the North Carolina Collection and Rare Book Collection in Wilson Library at the University of North Carolina at Chapel Hill; the Rare Book, Manuscript, and Special Collections Library, and the Divinity School Library at Duke University; the South Carolina Historical Society; and the Georgia Historical Society. Here at the University of Miami, William Walker, Craig Likness, and Chella Vaidyanathan went above and beyond the call of duty in helping to facilitate my research, to the point of acquiring a complete microfilm copy of the Confederate Imprints collection.

The University of North Carolina Press has made the road to publication as smooth as possible. I would like to thank David Perry, Ron Maner, Zach Read, David Hines, Dino Battista, and Ellen Bush. I especially want to thank my copyeditor, René Hayden, who smoothed my prose and spared me from embarrassing mistakes.

Finally, I would like to thank my family for all of their encouragement and especially my mother, Mary Bernath, for serving as my on-call proofreader. To my wife, Cathy, who has lived with this book for as long as I have, I am forever grateful for her patience, her critical eye, her good humor, and her unflagging support. This book would not have been possible without her.

CONFEDERATE MINDS

INTRODUCTION

This book examines Confederate cultural nationalism during the Civil War. It explores the rise and fall of a cultural movement among white southerners dedicated to liberating the South from its intellectual "vassalage" to the North and to creating an autonomous and distinctly Confederate national culture. In the years leading up to the war, southern nationalists had continually decried the South's dependence on northern print literature, but they were unable to convince southern readers to shun northern importations and support their own native productions. Secession dramatically altered the situation, however. Separate nationality and the coming of the war provided southern cultural nationalists with a new sense of purpose and urgency as well as a unique opportunity to actually achieve their long-cherished goal of southern cultural autonomy. With the Confederate reading public shut off from northern publishers and at last awakened to the dangers of northern culture, these nationalists found a receptive audience for their ideas and a captive market for their literature. As a result, the Confederacy witnessed a period of dramatically accelerated literary and cultural production during its short life. At its birth, the Confederacy lacked many of the cultural prerequisites for true nationhood, but Confederate writers, editors, publishers, teachers, and ministers were determined to write and publish their own books, periodicals, and textbooks, train their own teachers, and educate their own children, all amid the distractions and shortages of civil war.

1

In the eyes of southern nationalists, this movement, this struggle for Confederate intellectual independence, was a vital component of the larger war effort. Independence won on the battlefield would be meaningless so long as Confederates remained intellectually and culturally dependent upon the North. Until southerners produced and consumed their own native literature, they could never achieve true independence, nor could the Confederacy be a complete nation. Recognizing the inherent weaknesses of Confederate nationalism as it existed at the start of the war, Confederate thinkers and writers made a conscious and concerted effort to foster nationalist sentiment through the development of an autonomous Confederate culture free from the pernicious and corrupting influences of the North. Guided by the romantic ideal that a nation was defined by the unique "character" of its people as expressed through their literature, their religion, and their education—in short, their culture—Confederate nationalists sought to bolster the Confederacy's claim to nationhood by providing the intellectual and cultural foundation necessary to sustain it.

Historians of the United States have begun to elbow their way into the larger discussion of the rise of nationalism in the modern world. Often ignored, or at best mentioned in passing by the canonical works in the field, the American experience did not seem to fit established models.[1] Recent scholarship, however, has shown that the construction of American nationalism was both real and powerful, and that the similarities and contrasts between New and Old World nation-building are extremely important.[2] In regard to the mid-nineteenth century, where many of these latest studies have focused, there has been particularly excellent work done on the rise of nationalism in the northern states before, during, and after the Civil War.[3]

There have been similar developments in the scholarship surrounding that other, albeit much shorter lived North American nation, the Confederacy. Long after Drew Faust urged scholars to take Confederate nationalist ideology seriously, and even longer after David Potter provided us with a sophisticated model for understanding the rise and fall of southern nationalist sentiment, Confederate nationalism has finally assumed a central, if contested, place in Confederate and Civil War studies.[4] Historians have moved beyond debating whether Confederate nationalism existed and, if so, whether it was legitimate (an ahistorical and unanswerable question) to analyzing its substance. Recent scholarship, particularly that of Gary Gallagher, Robert Bonner, and Anne Sarah Rubin, has broadened our understanding of the role and nature of Confederate nationalism and challenged us to reconceive its sources, symbols, and duration.[5] But even apart from these focused discussions, Confederate nationalism has emerged as an important concern in studies of soldiers and campaigns, state and national politics, local southern communities and subregions, ordinary southern men, women, and even children. In surveying this literature, the reader will encounter many different definitions of nationalism ranging from the literal to the highly abstract. This range of meaning, appropriately enough, probably corresponds well with the actual range of understanding of nationalism as held by different groups of Confederates themselves. While some studies have relied on keyword searches through letters, diaries, and other primary documents for terms such as "country," "nation," "patriotism," and "duty" to locate nationalist sentiment, others have equated Confederate nationalism with support for the war, support for the government, faith in particular military figures or bodies, steadfastness in military service, or defiance in the face of the enemy. Conversely, the waning of support for, or even outright resistance to, the war effort, the government, or the armies, a soldier's decision to desert, or a civilian's acceptance of occupation have been seen as evidence of the weakness or incompleteness of Confederate nationalism.[6]

Confederate nationalists, however, had their own definitions. During the war, southerners thought deeply and wrote extensively about the meaning and requirements of nationhood. After all, they faced the difficult task of actually building a nation, and they needed to come to grips with what this would entail. Inevitably we today view Confederate nationalism within the context of Confederate defeat. Since we already know the end of the story, historians are predisposed to analyze the weaknesses of Confederate nationalism as a cause or at least contributing factor to the Confederacy's ultimate demise. But Confederates at the time, of course, did not know that their nation was doomed. Their viewpoint was forward looking, even millennial. They expected the Confederacy to survive and thrive, and thus it was incumbent on them, as their new nation's founding generation, to determine the meaning of their independence. It is the writings and activities of these Confederate nationalists that I examine in this book. They believed that southerners and northerners were distinct peoples and that the Confederacy was an organic nation arising from the fundamental differences between them. This conception of nationalism goes beyond simply supporting the war or the government, as demonstrated by the fact that some of the most fervent Confederate nationalists were also the most vitriolic critics of Jefferson Davis and his conduct of the war. These Confederates knew or thought they knew what nationalism was, why it was important, what it required, and how to go about constructing it. At the most basic level, they believed that nationality—

true and enduring nationality—must be rooted in culture. As a result, they launched a comprehensive campaign immediately following secession to build and bolster the self-supporting and uniquely southern culture that their vision of Confederate nationhood required.

This book traces the development of this movement by focusing on the activities, accomplishments, and failures of a diverse but coherent group of white southerners whom I have labeled "Confederate cultural nationalists." Composed of writers, critics, editors, publishers, educators, ministers, artists, poets, musicians, actors, playwrights, theater managers, doctors, scientists, philosophers, lawyers, and political theorists, cultural nationalists shared a common commitment to the cause of Confederate intellectual independence and saw themselves, each within their own spheres, as contributing to a larger national struggle. A conscious and explicit, if not formal, connection existed between the members of this movement, and a mutual network of support and encouragement grew up among them as the war progressed. The names of some of these Confederate cultural nationalists will be familiar to anyone who has studied nineteenth-century southern intellectual and cultural history—George Bagby, James De Bow, Henry Timrod, Paul Hamilton Hayne, William Gilmore Simms, Augusta Jane Evans, J. H. Thornwell, Benjamin Palmer, and George Fitzhugh among others—but most are far less well-known or even anonymous. They were editors of literary journals, publishers of textbooks, and pseudonymous contributors to weekly family newspapers. Most of them were not great thinkers themselves, and I have refrained from labeling them "intellectuals" as much as possible, even though they certainly did take ideas seriously and expressed those ideas in print (one possible definition of "intellectual"). Primarily, they were facilitators of culture, dedicated to constructing a southern cultural infrastructure capable of supporting and disseminating the great Confederate intellectual awakening they were sure would now arise. They provided the vision, created the framework, and served as the leaders and driving force of the struggle for Confederate intellectual independence. Most important, they wrote and published what the rest of the Confederacy read, and it was their agenda that was emblazoned on the pages of the Confederacy's books, newspapers, periodicals, textbooks, and pamphlets and imbedded within its fiction, poetry, history, humor, drama, and sermons.

There was nothing obscure about the campaign for Confederate intellectual independence. It was conducted in public. Indeed, it had to be. Its success depended upon the mass production and home consumption of a native print literature. This literature was both the measure of progress and the means of dissemination for Confederate cultural nationalism. South-erners spoke openly about the meaning and requirements of nationhood, and it is this public discourse that I examine here. Far more than simply the pet project of a select few thinkers, this campaign involved an entire nation of writers and readers, all of whom had important duties to fulfill in advancing their young country toward true independence and cultural sustainability. My research has endeavored to encompass the entirety of Confederate litera-ture, to discover what Confederates actually produced during the war, and what ideas were publicly circulated.

In the past, historians of the Confederacy have been hampered by the incompleteness of the available holdings of Confederate print literature, es-pecially its periodical literature. In compiling his bibliography of Confeder-ate belles lettres in 1941, historian Richard Harwell noted with regret that "an adequate critical evaluation of the whole literature of the Confederacy and of its effect on the people of the South must await the day when Southern librarians and historians have succeeded in locating more adequate files of these Confederate periodicals."[7] That day has now come. Digital cataloging and extensive microfilming have made it possible to survey Confederate peri-odical literature in a systematic and reasonably comprehensive manner, and this study is in large part the result of such an undertaking. Along with the aid of the invaluable and now expanded *Confederate Imprints*, there has never been a better time to study the content, significance, and underlying agenda of Confederate print culture.[8]

Structurally, the book is divided into four chronological parts. The first part focuses on the initial "call to arms" that arose in the days following secession as Confederate cultural nationalists attempted to convince the public of the necessity of southern cultural autonomy, both as a nationalistic imperative and as a protective measure to prevent the further infiltration of dangerous northern ideas. The second part discusses the organization and development of this movement for intellectual independence during the first year of the Confederacy's life; it traces the birth of Confederate literature, especially its periodical literature, and the initial efforts to promote Confed-erate educational independence. The third part deals with the middle years of the war, which witnessed the high-water mark of Confederate culture. An impressive array of new and self-consciously Confederate periodicals, text-books, poetry, fiction, historical works, children's literature, humor, soldiers' literature, and even theatrical works, appeared and flourished during this period, exceeding the expectations of even the most sanguine. Given this rapidly proliferating print literature, hopeful cultural nationalists believed they were witnessing the long-awaited southern renaissance that had been heretofore suppressed by northern cultural dominance. The last part examines the final year of the war and its aftermath. Worsening hardships, bleak military prospects, and an increasingly frank appraisal of the inadequate quality of the literature produced up to that point compelled cultural nationalists to scale back their expectations and adopt a more gradual approach. Recognizing that southern society was not yet capable of producing or appreciating the great national culture they envisioned, they focused their energies on preparing future generations for eventual autonomy. Even during the dark final days of the war, these cultural leaders continued to carry on the struggle for their dying nation's intellectual independence. In the end, Confederates proved no more able to win their intellectual independence than their political freedom, though they had struggled mightily for both. The failure of cultural nationalists, the way in which they failed, and the reasons why they failed reveal much about the nature and limitations of the Confederate nationalist project as a whole.

A FEW QUALIFICATIONS ARE in order. The ideas and dreams of Confederate cultural nationalists were not born out of a vacuum. As I discuss, the desire for Confederate intellectual independence grew directly out of antebellum southern cultural nationalism. As John McCardell and others have shown, rising sectional tensions during the 1840s and 1850s led a group of southern activists to warn of the dangers of northern influence and the necessity of a separate southern culture.[9] Thus, the campaign for Confederate intellectual independence represented the realization of these earlier hopes and demands.

Apart from these studies of southern cultural nationalism, there has been a recent sea change in the field of southern intellectual history. The massive surveys of antebellum southern thought by Michael O'Brien and by Elizabeth Fox-Genovese and Eugene Genovese, as well as other more specifically focused works, have revealed a far more extensive intellectual landscape than was previously thought could have existed. Forever banishing Henry Adams's famous dismissal that "strictly, the Southerner had no mind. . . . he had no intellectual training; he could not analyze an idea, and he could not even conceive of admitting two," these historians have shown conclusively that the southern states were home to a fertile and remarkable cosmopolitan intellectual life.[10] Challenging the long-held view that the antebellum obsession with defending slavery stunted the southern mind, inhibited creativity, and transformed the South into a stagnant and isolated intellectual backwater, recent scholarship argues that southern thought ranged widely and that southern thinkers were very much aware of, and intimately connected with, broader intellectual and international trends.[11] To their great credit, these scholars have effectively reintegrated the South back into mainstream American intellectual history.

But while there can be no doubt that the Old South had a "mind," it remains a question whether that mind had much of an audience or influence within southern society. The frustration of the members of Drew Faust's "sacred circle" of southern intellectuals was real, and southern thinkers, writers, and publishers constantly bemoaned the lack of status accorded them by their society, the inability to make a living by one's pen, and the seeming refusal of southern readers to support them even as they dedicated their efforts to defending the southern way of life.[12] A book's southern imprimatur doomed it to obscurity and the Old South was a mass grave of promising periodicals that had withered and died for want of support. Thus, though recent scholarship has revealed the richness of antebellum southern thought, little has been said to challenge the long-standing perception that these thinkers were unappreciated by southern society and largely unread by southern readers.

Poet Henry Timrod expressed well the frustrations of many of his peers when in 1859 he called "the Southern author the Pariah of modern literature." "In no country in which literature has ever flourished has an author obtained so limited an audience," he complained in the short-lived, Charleston-based *Russell's Magazine*. "In no country, and at no period that we can recall, has an author been constrained by the indifference of the public amid which he lived [the South], to publish with a people who were prejudiced against him [the North]." It was not that southern literature did not exist, he maintained. Rather, it was "the fate of that literature" that was "a reproach to us." Timrod did not believe that mediocre literature should be supported simply because of its author's birthplace, but he scolded southerners for their "stolid indifference" toward even their most gifted writers. It was this public indifference, and not any deficiencies in southern intellect, he argued, that explained the seeming absence of a vigorous native southern literature.[13]

Thus, even if the southern mind was thriving during the antebellum years, it did not seem so to most southerners at the time. It was this perception of past inadequacies that drove Confederate cultural nationalists to campaign for a national literature. To be clear, when talking about the state of southern culture in the pages that follow, I am speaking about the perceptions of contemporary southern observers and not necessarily the reality of antebellum southern intellectual accomplishment. Certainly, when Confederate papers like *Southern Field and Fireside* spoke of the long-standing "lethargic stupor that broods over our literary energies," they expressed a widely accepted truism.[14]

FINALLY, IT IS IMPORTANT to specify what this book examines and what it does not. My focus is the print literature that was produced and circulated in the Confederate States of America. I do not deal with pro-southern writers or publications outside the Confederacy, nor do I discuss the literature of the occupied South. I am concerned with Confederate nationalists, those southerners who believed in the cause of their nation and fervently desired Confederate independence. As such, unionists are not included in this study except as the objects of Confederate scorn. Also, when referring to "southerners" as a group I do not mean to obscure differences or to assert homogeneity. Instead, I want to show how Confederate nationalists spoke of southerners and imagined them as a people.

While this book takes Confederate literature as its source and subject, it is not intended to be a literary history of the Confederacy. Rather, it examines the nationalist agenda that motivated the production and shaped the perception of native southern literature. My primary interest lies in what Confederates themselves thought about this emerging national culture, why they felt it was important, and what they hoped it would become. Likewise, Confederate music, while not ignored in this study, does not receive the specialized attention it deserves. It remains for future historians equipped with the proper analytical tools to fully mine its rich depths.[15]

It is also essential to emphasize that the southerners in this book are white. Understandably, slaves and southern free blacks did not contribute to the struggle for Confederate intellectual independence. While race and slavery were omnipresent in the minds and everyday lives of Confederate nationalists, the national culture they envisioned was an exclusively white one.

As one would expect, there were clear class dimensions to this intellectual struggle as well. It was a movement of the educated and the literate, and its leaders were drawn entirely from the middle and upper classes. That said, the unique conditions created by the war would soon bring their literature before the eyes of a much larger and more economically diverse audience than southern publishers had ever reached before. Hunger for war news combined with the increasing aggregation of people both within the armies and on the home front brought the printed word to an unprecedented number of southerners. Even the illiterate could have Confederate literature read to them in the camps and in the ever-growing towns and cities. Still, while the conditions of war may have softened class lines when it came to the consumption of native print, there is no disguising the fact that Confederate cultural nationalists—those who wrote and published Confederate literature—were not yeoman farmers.

But while class barriers were significant and the racial divide absolute, Confederate cultural nationalists were enthusiastically inclusive when it came to gender. Indeed, they had to be. Southern women would serve as important producers and vital paying consumers of this emerging Confederate national culture. Also, as we will see, Confederates quickly realized that their hopes for educational independence and finding a supply of native teachers for southern schools of necessity rested largely on female shoulders.

The struggle for intellectual independence was not a sideshow to the Confederate war effort, cultural nationalists passionately argued. Just as political and military leaders worked to secure southern nationhood in their spheres, these cultural leaders would guide southerners to independence in theirs. Indeed, cultural nationalists considered their efforts to be the more fundamental, as they would endow the military and political struggle with its true meaning. By demonstrating the existence of their own unique national culture, they would prove the distinctiveness of the southern people and thereby legitimate their desire for a separate national existence. If successful, the campaign for intellectual independence would vindicate Confederate nationalism as a whole by rooting it to the strongest and most enduring foundation possible.

PART ONE

NOW Is the Time

CHAPTER ONE

AN INTELLECTUAL CALL TO ARMS

With secession and the formation of the Confederacy, the southern states embarked on their ill-fated attempt at separate nationality. For four years, the Confederacy fought a long and bloody war in an effort to secure its political independence. However, while the fighting raged at the front, there was another war being waged behind the lines. This war would be fought on the pages of the Confederacy's periodicals and newspapers, in its books and textbooks, from its pulpits, podiums, and theatrical stages, in its songs, poems, and literary productions, and in its classrooms and schoolhouses. During the Confederacy's war for political independence, southerners attempted to escape from the South's "intellectual vassalage" to northern culture and to create an autonomous culture of their own. Finally free from the North, southerners suddenly had to write and publish their own books and textbooks, edit and sustain their own periodicals, teach their own children, train their own teachers and clergymen—all amid the distractions, hardships, and shortages of a cataclysmic and all-absorbing war.

Confederate thinkers recognized that any struggle for political independence would necessitate a cultural transformation. As Charles Smythe observed in the preface to his 1861 grammar textbook for Confederate children, "The political revolution in which we are now engaged makes necessary an intellectual one."[1] Almost immediately upon secession, Confederate editors, publishers, writers, teachers, and clergymen alerted the southern populace to the deeper meaning of the impending struggle. "The present occasion is by no means a purely military one," William Falconer instructed the readers of the *Southern Literary Messenger*, "at most it is but a mixed one, in which the intellectual, by far, preponderates over the physical."[2]

True independence, these cultural nationalists agreed, could be achieved only by establishing the Confederacy's intellectual and cultural autonomy. As a group of twelve prominent southern educators insisted in a published address to the people of North Carolina, "intellectual must precede or sustain political independence."[3] So long as the South depended upon the North for its higher culture, it would forever remain a province of the United States regardless of its military victories or nominal political status. "Whatever the achievements of our brave soldiers upon the battlefield; whatever the terms upon which peace shall be finally established, the victory will be incomplete until we shall have secured our Literary Independence," *Southern Field and Fireside* warned a month following the firing on Fort Sumter. "Now, we think, is the time to battle for this—to arouse the South to contest with the pen as well as with the sword, the championship of the North."[4] The editor of the *New Orleans Daily Delta* went even further: "The destiny of the South will be but a crude and unfinished attempt, an unmeaning, inconsequential projection into time and space, unless along with her political independence she achieves her independence in thought and education, and in all those forms of mental improvement and entertainment which by a liberal construction of the word, are included in literature."[5] In order to be permanent and meaningful, the separation between North and South had to be cultural as well as political. Otherwise, the Confederacy would be a mere shell of a nation, possessing its political independence in name but remaining intellectually enslaved to its hostile neighbor to the north.

Recognizing the far-reaching cultural implications of secession and civil war and the incompleteness of the Confederacy's claim to true nationhood, Confederate cultural nationalists embarked on a crusade to free the South from its intellectual "thralldom" to the North and lay the foundations upon which a true Confederate national culture could be built. "This is a war of *Independence*," emphasized Calvin Henderson Wiley, superintendent of North Carolina schools and the leading advocate for southern educational independence. "Its battles are to be fought in the open field, in the school room, in the council chamber, by all the arts and appliances which make a people self-supporting, and keep alive and active in their midst the benign and invigorating influences of religion, law, education and domestic thrift," he declared in a public letter.[6] Confederate writers, publishers, and teachers had a special duty to fulfill, one that was as crucial to the Confederacy's ultimate independence as shouldering a musket. For, as George Bagby proclaimed in the *Southern Literary Messenger*, "Political and intellectual independence are inseparable synonyms. To achieve the one, we must achieve the other."[7]

Hence, even before hostilities had commenced, Confederate nationalists issued an intellectual call to arms alerting writers and readers alike to the great task that lay before them. "It is the duty of the South to trample under foot those mental shackles which have so long disgraced her," President William Peck announced to the assembled crowd at Greenville Masonic Female College in July 1861.[8] Likewise, editor George Bagby impressed upon his readers the preeminent nature of this cultural struggle. "A subject people are to be rescued from the dominion of fanatics," he declared. "Until this is accomplished, perish all minor matters."[9]

Not only did the South have to break free from northern intellectual domination, but, more important, it needed to begin producing and supporting its own native productions. "We must . . . see and think for ourselves," Charles W. Howard demanded in the pages of the *Southern Cultivator*. "We are not to follow, but lead—not to imitate, but originate."[10] As the blind editor of the *Southern Literary Companion* in Newnan, Georgia, dictated to his editorial assistant in January 1861, "The South is bound by every principle of honor, duty and self-respect to have a literature of her own, and the only thing which is necessary to induce her sons and daughters to make a united effort for this purpose, is to demonstrate to them the fact that we are able of ourselves to build up and maintain a literature of the highest order and merit."[11]

This project could not wait for a more tranquil moment. "RIGHT NOW is the time to begin the work of Southern Independence in fact as well as theory," proclaimed "twelve North Carolina educators."[12] This call for cultural self-sufficiency would have to rise above even the din of war. "The war needs attention—must have it," the *Southern Cultivator* admitted, "but not our whole attention. We are bound to lay the foundation of our own future greatness and independence *now*. If we would be a great people, we must have something more than cotton bags at our command."[13]

This challenge, this intellectual call to arms, that ran through the pages of southern periodicals and pamphlets and thundered from podiums and pulpits in the early months of the Confederacy's life operated on two levels: general and specific. At its broadest, it called upon the entire literate population of the Confederacy to free itself from northern culture and support its own native productions. A successful war for intellectual independence would require "the enlistment of the mind and heart of all ages, of both sexes, of every class of the people—and the continual aid, in their proper places, of all those energies and appliances, moral and physical, which, under God, constitute and preserve the vitality and power of a nation."[14] The entire population, not just able-bodied males of military age, had to be mobilized for war. This mobilization, however, would be a mustering of consciousness, a widespread commitment on the part of southerners to assert their autonomy and prove to themselves and the rest of the world that the Confederacy was in fact a true nation. This was the patriotic duty of those who remained on the home front—a separate but essential struggle in which they could engage from the comfort of their own firesides. "Then let us who stay at home while our braver brothers are on the tented field, or in the halls of state, battling with the manifold difficulties of our position, be up and doing, achieving something for the happiness, elevation, and glory of our common country," Professor A. B. Stark urged the readers of the *Home Circle*, a Nashville-based Methodist magazine.[15] As this agenda for intellectual independence began to form and articulate itself in the early months of the war, it became clear that this would not, and could not, be a movement solely of elites and self-proclaimed intellectuals.

More specifically, however, the intellectual call to arms targeted the would-be creators of this new Confederate culture. Not only would the Confederate people need to purge themselves of all things northern and support southern publications, but southern writers would need to produce a literature worthy of their patronage. Hence, editors, publishers, teachers, writers, scientists, artists, actors, musicians, and ministers had a crucial role to play, and existing southern periodicals at the beginning of the war were not slow to call on these classes of men and women to fulfill their patriotic duty. "The South hath need of those of her sons and daughters whose minds nature has endowed largely with her choicest gifts, and who have improved their endowments by study and thought," the *Charleston Courier* declared. "This numerous class should feel the duty they own, and set about its performance."[16] "All classes of men must now wake up," the religious weekly *Banner of Peace* agreed. "The men of art and science must furnish a thousand handiworks."[17]

Before Confederate nationalists could focus their attention on building a self-sufficient publishing industry or creating a new periodical, educational, and religious literature, southerners first needed to free themselves from the products of northern culture. Until the South was no longer flooded with inexpensive northern print, native publications would have little chance of success. "For more than a half century," William Peck grumbled, "the Southern mind has ignominiously truckled to the North in all matters, especially those appertaining to Education and Literature."[18] The roots of this dependence were not difficult to discover. In the years prior to the war, southerners, with the exception of a small but passionate group of southern nationalists, had been content to allow the North to supply their print literature. While southerners devoted their energies and resources to staple crop production, the North had built a commercial and manufacturing society, which included a large and increasingly profitable publishing industry. Southerners saw no harm in availing themselves of the conveniences and products offered by their fellow countrymen to the north, and publishers in New York, Boston, and Philadelphia were only too happy to supply them with all of the books and periodicals they could desire. By mid-century, the northern print industry had the equipment, distribution networks, experience, and capital to manufacture superior products at inexpensive prices, so much so that any upstart southern publishing concern had little chance of matching northern quality, quantity, or price.

Likewise, in the years leading up to the Civil War, southerners largely looked to the North to supply their teachers and textbooks, and even sent their sons and daughters to northern colleges and universities for their higher education. Teaching, as a profession, was not highly esteemed (or lucrative) in the antebellum South, and few self-respecting southerners desired to pursue a career in education. Consequently, southern parents hired the many young, well-educated northerners who flocked to the South seeking employment as teachers and private instructors. Soon, C. H. Wiley and his fellow southern educators lamented, "we began to look to the people of these States for supplies of everything except the raw produce of the soil."[19]

The results of this dependence were predictable. Unable to compete, southern literature was often strangled in the crib. Although many southern magazines were founded during the antebellum period and efforts were made to publish southern books and write southern textbooks, most of these endeavors died prematurely. As a result, Charles Wallace Howard complained in December 1860, "we have no State Literature—very few books by native authors, and we are flooded by periodicals from other [northern] States and countries, while the few established by our own people drag out a precarious existence, if indeed they are permitted to live beyond infancy."[20] This "monopoly of the book and magazine trade by the North," another Confederate writer declared, had prevented "the growth of our literature in the past," and, he warned, "will conduce to the same result in future" unless southerners took immediate steps to prevent it.[21]

Any southern writer who wished to live by his pen had to seek northern publishers and produce work acceptable to northern tastes. Unlike their northern competitors, struggling southern periodicals were simply unable to pay most of their contributors, and consequently the South's would-be professional writers sent their best work north. Meanwhile, southern editors filled their columns with donated pieces that were often of inferior quality. "We have frequently heard it urged, as an excuse for supporting Northern periodicals, that they were superior in point of merit to those published at home," one writer in the *Southern Teacher*, an educational periodical from Montgomery, Alabama, conceded in May 1861. "Admit this to be true, whose is the fault? and why is it the South is unable to equal the North? The cause is patent to every one that will not close his eyes; the North has had the support that belonged to the South, not only Southern pay, but our star contributors." While northern editors bought up the South's best talent at bargain prices, southern journals "were but mere starvelings, dependent for contributions on those who deemed it a sufficient gratuity to read their names in print, or the devotion of a few, with whom sectional pride was superior to every other motive."[22]

The North, however, was not solely to blame for the underdeveloped state of southern letters. Most galling of all was the fact that the southern people themselves had encouraged this state of dependency by consistently and persistently patronizing northern publications over southern ones, and while native authors struggled and southern periodicals died due to lack of support, northern books and journals enjoyed large circulations in the South.[23] "Week after week," the *Southern Home Journal* complained, "thousands of copies of magazines . . . containing the insidious and destructive poison of Northern sentiments, were purchased and read by citizens of the South, while their own journals were left, if not to perish, to languish and live out a sickly and miserable existence."[24] Although southerners could and clearly did decry the omnipresence of northern culture, there was no avoiding the painful fact that "there was no law to bind us to take Northern teachers and their books. *This* yoke of bondage was not imposed, but voluntarily assumed."[25] To their shame, southerners had "eagerly paid tribute" to the North, "not merely a tribute of the purse . . . but the tribute of the mind, the tribute of intellect, the tribute of the god-like brain!"[26]

Not surprisingly, this state of dependence had bred a sense of superiority in the North. Northern assumptions about the backwardness of southern culture were not difficult to understand, Confederate observers were forced to admit, and these airs of superiority explained, in part at least, recent northern policies toward the South. Southerners should not be surprised that northerners had "latterly assumed to dictate to us our political character," Calvin Wiley told them, "for a people who are expected to educate our children, to furnish them with their literature, and to supply us with every manufacture that requires skill or science, will inevitably put on airs of superiority, and take to themselves a kind of guardianship of the whole community who are thus dependent."[27] The Confederacy would have to assert itself intellectually if only to disabuse the North of its self-inflated importance. Looking to the future, an anonymous New Orleans pamphlet writer expressed his hope that the war would finally secure "our release from that literary, financial and commercial vassalage which has . . . emboldened [northerners] to imagine that, as compared to themselves, we were an inferior race."[28]

These northern slights to southern intellect became a rallying cry for Confederate writers in the early days of the war. "Shall we, for one moment, give countenance to the charges slanderously preferred against the slaveholding States of America, of being inferior in moral and intellectual resources, and necessarily dependent on other communities for teachers, for schools, for literature, for thought, for mental and religious light?" a group of militant southern educators demanded.[29] Confident that southerners could produce their own literature and teachers, if only they set their minds, pens, and resources to it, Confederate cultural nationalists appealed to sectional pride and anti-northern animosity to awaken the southern "mind" and "prove [the South's] inferiority to no land under Heaven."[30]

By allowing others to write their books, teach their children, and, in some cases, preach their sermons, southerners had permitted the North to set the intellectual agenda of the nation as well as to establish the standards of taste. Only now, as secession and war brought the evils of northern culture into stark relief, did southerners realize the consequences of their decades of intellectual, educational, and literary neglect. As Robert Ruffin Barrow conceded in an 1861 pamphlet, "We, by our course, justified the criticism of the French traveler [who observed] 'that without the North the South would not know how to read.' Stinging, yet true! The viper that we have warmed into life in our bosoms has at last stung us."[31]

In addition to discouraging southern productivity, the dominance of northern print literature had allowed abolitionists to launch bitter denunciations of southern slave society, to which southerners had little means to respond. As A. S. Worrell complained in the preface to his 1861 textbook, *The Principles of English Grammar*, southerners had foolishly "allowed the North the *chief means of shaping national bias*—THE PRESS."[32] Using the press, northern "fanatics" had decried the horrors of slavery and vilified southern slaveholders. Consequently, northern society and Europe saw the South through the eyes of its harshest critics. "For many years past, God has permitted us, as a people, to be deeply humiliated," Bishop Stephen Elliott told the assembled congregation of Christ's Church in Savannah in June 1861. "We have been systematically slandered and traduced, in public and in private, at home and abroad, in a way such as no free and independent people has ever before so quietly submitted to." Employing "the lecture-room, the forum, the senate chamber, the pulpit," northern and European fanatics "have vied to express their abhorrence of our social life and their contempt for ourselves. The grave statesman, the flippant poet, the sentimental novelist, the critical reviewer, the witty satirist, has each in turn singled out our homes as the targets of his falsehood."[33]

Although southern journals throughout the antebellum period had devoted themselves to defending southern society and especially slavery, their limited range and often short life spans prevented their words from having much impact north of the Mason-Dixon line or across the ocean. "Certainly such literature as [the South] was able to claim for her own, intrinsically rich and vigorous as much of it may have been, was woefully inadequate to cope with the literature arrayed against her," the editor of the *New Orleans Delta* complained. With nearly all of northern and European literature "openly or insidiously hostile" to her interests, the South was "at a fearful disadvantage in the controversy she was compelled to maintain before the tribunal of public opinion."[34]

Yet, while they resented these northern insults, years of cultural dependence had left a legacy of self-doubt in the minds of many southerners and an unspoken fear that perhaps they were not capable of sustaining themselves intellectually. Secession, cultural nationalists eagerly predicted, would cure southerners of this lack of confidence. As one contributor to *De Bow's Review* complained in July 1861, prior to the war "the true [southern] gentleman was educated at a Northern college, wore clothing made at the North or imported by the North, employed a Northern teacher, male or female, listened to a Yankee parson, and read Northern books, magazines and newspapers. We have been Yankee imitators and worshipers until now." During the antebellum period, the South had allowed itself to remain in "a state of pupilage, and never learned to walk alone." Secession and war, however, would change all that and force southerners to live "without Yankee nursing."[35] As one

Virginian bluntly put it, "The idea of Southern inferiority has become so deeply rooted that it has become part of our nature; and nothing but the struggles of the revolution now in progress will pluck it out of our hearts."[36]

Secession would force the Confederacy to become intellectually self-sufficient. "Self-dependence" was the watchword of cultural nationalists as they called on southerners to support the cause with their pens and their wallets as well as their rifles. "We are about to take our destiny into our own hands—to throw ourselves upon our own resources—to assume the place of a Nation among the powers of the earth," the *Southern Cultivator* declared in January 1861. "We shall be at liberty, and in a position, to *develope our resources*, to foster our industries; and to elevate and improve our people."[37] No distinction was made here between agricultural, industrial, and intellectual resources. The production of native books and periodicals was hailed as no less vital to the cause than the production of gunpowder. In order for the Confederacy to survive as an independent nation, not just during the war but in the future, it would have to become a whole country, not just a one-dimensional agricultural region. From a cultural perspective, this vital need for autonomy meant that "it is time for us to patronize our own newspapers, our own schools and colleges, our own institutions of every kind, and to leave our enemies and traducers to the devices and desires of their own hearts," soon-to-be Confederate general Daniel Harvey Hill explained in the pages of the *North Carolina Presbyterian*.[38] "We have played squire to the North Knights of the quill, long enough," *Southern Field and Fireside* declared. "From this time, we must foster Southern publications, encourage the development of Southern talent, and furnish the means, at home, for the expression of Southern mind, or sink below the level to which we have been accustomed to feel ourselves entitled."[39]

Much of this rhetoric was not new. Southern thinkers had been decrying the South's dependence on the North for decades. Numerous attempts had been made and innumerable appeals to the public had been issued to encourage the development of an indigenous southern literature. During the 1840s, and especially the 1850s, a group of committed southern cultural nationalists had published journals, held conventions, written books, and founded schools, all in an effort to alert the southern public to the dangers of their intellectual dependence and the need for a uniquely southern culture.[40] Although these thinkers did manage to produce a fair body of writing and attract some historical attention, they failed to generate much interest among their own people. For the most part, they were a loosely connected group of alienated southern writers and editors who wrung their hands and cried into the void about the failure of southern society to appreciate and support them. Despite their efforts and heartfelt appeals, they were unable to convince the southern public at large to stop buying northern books, hiring northern teachers, reading northern periodicals, or sending their children to northern schools. For all of its passion and fire, the movement for southern cultural nationalism in the antebellum period was primarily characterized by frustration and failure, as a seemingly indifferent public consistently ignored the cries and protestations of its advocates.

Secession and the coming of the war, however, promised to alter the situation dramatically. The war presented southern cultural nationalists with a tremendous opportunity to finally liberate the South from northern intellectual dominance and accomplish what they had always claimed they could: create and sustain a southern intellectual culture. The antebellum experience had convinced many southern observers that nothing short of forced separation, and perhaps even war, could break the stranglehold of northern printers on southern readers. The need for southern "social, commercial and literary independence" had "often been urged on the Southern people, and they have often resolved to establish it," the *Southern Presbyterian* noted following Lincoln's election. "But it seems to us wholly impracticable, not to say impossible, so long as the North and South continue politically one. . . . As long as the Union exists as it does at present, the Southern people will *buy* from the North whatever they can get cheaper there than any where else."[41]

Regional loyalty alone had proven insufficient to cure the South of its addiction to northern goods, and it was doubtful that even the increased tensions between the North and South caused by the Republican victory in November would alter the situation, unless the South seceded. "We have great respect for what is called Southern patriotism," Reverend A. A. Porter, editor of the *Southern Presbyterian*, assured his readers. "We believe it is genuine, fervent, heroic, and capable of any needful self-sacrifice. But, 'there is a great deal of human nature in people,' and one principle of it is, to consult its interests. While the Union exists this will naturally and necessarily control the great majority every where. For they will justly feel and judge that there is a grievous inconsistency, so long as North and South are one, in acting as if they are foreign and foes." Southern patriotism had always been an abstract concept, and one that was applied selectively and unevenly. The southern public had failed to grasp the inconsistency of denouncing northern fanaticism and seething under northern insults while at the same time continuing to buy northern books, read northern newspapers, assign northern textbooks, and hire northern teachers. Secession, cultural nationalists predicted, would lay bare this inconsistency and create a united front among the Confederate people in all matters political, social, economic, and intellectual. Without secession, southern writers argued during the winter of 1860–61, intellectual independence, or even parity, would remain an impossibility. "If the Union stands," Porter concluded, "we do not think there is any hope for the South to struggle against the preeminence of the North in these respects." If southerners decided to remain in the Union, "we must make up our minds humbly to accept a subordinate, *provincial* position."[42]

If even political separation could not break the mental shackles that bound the South to the North, then war would necessarily force the southern people to perform their duty. As the acting editor of the *Southern Literary Messenger* observed sarcastically in September 1861:

> Southern patriotism never was proof against Northern newspapers and picture magazines. If the angel Gabriel had gone into the very heart of the South, if he had even taken his seat on the top of the office of the Charleston Mercury [the preeminent fire-eating secessionist newspaper] and there proclaimed the immediate approach of the Day of Judgment, that would not have hindered the hottest secessionist from buying the New York Herald and subscribing for Harper's Magazine. Southern patriotism is, and has always been, a funny thing—indeed the funniest of things. It enables a man to abuse the Yankees, to curse the Yankees, to fight the Yankees, to do everything but quit taking the Yankee papers. Nothing less than a battery of 10-inch Columbiads can keep Southern patriotism away from Yankee papers.[43]

Happily for cultural nationalists, the war promised to provide, literally, the necessary heavy artillery.

The war would serve as the vehicle for both the Confederacy's political and intellectual independence. Southern nationalists eagerly embraced the war and even the hardships that it would bring in the expectation that hostility and bloodshed would permanently break the South's addiction to northern culture. "I, for one, will applaud the cause that shall annihilate this curse of Southern genius, even though that cause should be the trump of civil war, whose clarion note is reverberating throughout the civilized world," William Peck declared.[44] Conceding that war was not an ideal environment for contemplation and intellectual endeavors, Confederate thinkers nevertheless insisted that only now could the South hope to break free from its mental vassalage to the North. It was now, "while the smoke of war [still] tinges our horizon, and the din of arms resounds in our borders [that] it becomes us . . . to nourish and develop the arts and tastes of peace."[45] Once peace returned (with a Confederate victory of course), the North would once again flood the South with cheap print literature unless the Confederacy established its own periodicals, its own publishing houses, and its own educational and religious literature to fend off these unwelcome foreign intruders. The writers, editors, and educators of the Confederacy had to act immediately. They could not allow themselves to be sidetracked by the political and military tumult swirling around them. As C. H. Wiley and his fellow North Carolina educators demanded of the southern people in July 1861, "If we are ever emancipated from thraldom to foreign influences, we must have our own authors and our own publishers; and when, we ask, could be a better time to begin the experiment of independent thought and action?"[46]

Sensing their opportunity, southern (now Confederate) cultural nationalists took up their cause with renewed vigor. During the antebellum years, calls for southern cultural autonomy had been loudest during periods of demonstrated weakness—when a notable southern magazine failed for want of support or when a new northern textbook arrived in southern classrooms tinged with the poisons of abolitionism, for instance. Now, however, Confederate cultural nationalists approached their project from a position of perceived strength coupled with a new sense of optimism. The changed conditions brought about by secession and war would provide a singular opportunity to establish the Confederacy's cultural self-sufficiency, and it was an opportunity that Confederate nationalists were determined to exploit.

The first and most important benefit of the war would be the severing of supply lines between northern publishers and southern readers, and the banishment of northern teachers and textbooks from southern soil. Wartime animosity, the discontinuance of mail service between the North and South beginning in June 1861, and the Union blockade of southern ports would all work to place the Confederate reading public on a forced fast. Although breaking southerners' addiction to northern literature would be painful, Confederate writers assured them that it was for their own good. "In nothing, perhaps, for a while will Southern people feel the change of our relations with the North, more than in the matter of books and periodicals," the *Southern Christian Advocate* observed in the summer of 1861. "They have so persistently cultivated their dependence upon Northern publishers—so constantly ignored the claims of Southern authors and publishers, that in respect to book writing and book making, we have to begin almost at the foundation."[47]

But at least the stoppage of northern trade now would allow southerners to lay those foundations.

Even the Union blockade, which by the latter part of 1861 was beginning to make itself felt by depriving southerners of much needed supplies and revenue, served a beneficial purpose.[48] "The *blockade* will make us very independent at the South, and thank God for it," James De Bow editorialized. "Our people need but this spur."[49] T. O. Summers, editor of the Nashville-based *Quarterly Review of the Methodist Episcopal Church, South*, "devoutly hoped" that the "Lincoln blockade—which in some respects has already proved like certain guns which do more mischief at the breech than at the muzzle—will assist us in correcting the evil" of southern literary dependence. "We shall be blockheads indeed if we do not profit by his insane policy."[50]

With the northern literary floodgates closed, a dearth of print literature in the South would create demand for home productions. Necessity, Confederate cultural nationalists predicted confidently, would spark a cultural renaissance in the South. Southern readers would be forced to turn to native authors and publishers for their books, magazines, and newspapers. "For we must read," observed a contributor to the Augusta *Weekly Constitutionalist*, "and having thrown off the yoke of subjugation to the North, we will no longer depend on her for literature, and, per consequence, must have it made at home."[51] Southern authors and publishers now had a captive audience of readers ready and willing to buy southern productions. "Now that we are cut off from the religious papers published in Northern States, is it not the time to make a successful effort to place our Diocesan organ on *a permanent basis*?" a "friend" of the struggling Charleston-based *Southern Episcopalian* asked hopefully.[52] Likewise a group of educators in North Carolina rejoiced at the dwindling supply of available northern textbooks. "At a superficial glance this want [of books] would seem to be an additional discouragement to our schools; but it is obvious to us, and must be to every reflecting mind, that if we meet it with the proper spirit, nothing could be more fortunate for us."[53]

In sharp contrast to the antebellum years, when southern editors and publishers had desperately appealed in vain for public support, now, they expected, southern readers would eagerly lavish money and attention on their literary men and women, thus giving rise to a vibrant native literature. "This will require, we presume, but a short while, after the public shall have settled down in the determination to be free from the North," *Southern Field and Fireside* projected optimistically. "The demand for home publications will bring the supply."[54]

While the forced isolation of the South was the most tangible immediate consequence of the war from the perspective of cultural nationalists, it was not the only reason that gave them hope for success in their quest for intellectual independence. A second encouraging sign was the growing receptivity that cultural nationalists found among the broader Confederate public. Prior to the war, southern cultural nationalism had been the pet project of a small group of southern thinkers. For all their dire warnings and fiery appeals, they had little influence on mainstream southern society or its reading habits. The need for intellectual independence and a uniquely southern literature resonated at the margins of most literate southerners' consciousnesses, if it existed at all. While many may have been sympathetic in the abstract, few appreciated the sense of urgency in the appeals of cultural nationalists and fewer still were willing to change their day-to-day reading habits.

The coming of the war, however, had changed public perceptions considerably. In addition to reinvigorating those already devoted to the cause of southern intellectual independence, the war also made their demands seem much more relevant and their warnings about the dangers of northern culture seem much more plausible to a larger Confederate reading public. Suddenly, hitherto-ignored southern writers found themselves able to command public attention. *Southern Field and Fireside* was amazed by the rapid transformation of public sentiment following secession. "A few months ago we should have hesitated before attempting to say any thing relating to Southern Literature; now we introduce the matter with confidence. Current events have taken off the threadbare suit which so long banished our favourite from good society, and arrayed it in habiliments which render it not only presentable, but welcome to the very best circles."[55]

Secession, war, and separate nationality had removed the blinders that had kept southerners content with their northern-produced goods. "The shackles that have too long bound the South to Northern intellect and enterprise are dropping off one by one," editor James Ells reported with glee in January 1861, and, as a consequence, he wrote a few months later, "We are glad to believe that a better day is coming for the development of Southern Literature. . . . The public mind is working up to the subject."[56] "The people of the South are beginning at last to awake to the importance of cultivating a healthy and conservative literature in their midst—a literature suited to their tastes, character and institutions," the *Southern Home Journal* likewise rejoiced; finally, "the people in alarm become sensible of their negligence and indifference. It is not yet too late . . . to do some good."[57] With northern trade suspended and the Confederate populace awakened to the need for southern self-sufficiency, Confederate cultural nationalists ironically found their greatest chance for success at the very moment that their new country was desperately fighting for its life.

Emboldened by patriotic duty, encouraged by newfound support among the southern people, and dramatically aided by the interruption of northern trade, southern cultural nationalists entered the Civil War with a renewed commitment to their cause. Of course, these changed circumstances also meant that cultural nationalists would have to practice what they had been preaching for decades. Rather than simply complain about southern dependence on the North, they now actually would have to produce a "literature" worthy of southern patronage. They had always claimed that they could match and even exceed the quality of northern productions if only they were given a fair chance. Now that chance had come, and it remained to be seen if Confederate writers, publishers, educators, editors, and ministers were up to the task.

In making their case to the southern public, Confederate cultural nationalists explicitly linked their project to the war itself. Whereas prior to secession, southern thinkers had based their appeals primarily on southern pride and regional identity, Confederate writers now portrayed intellectual independence as a nationalistic imperative, and emphasized the concrete wartime and future benefits to be gained from escaping northern dominance.

On the most pragmatic level, the outbreak of hostilities mandated that southerners stop supporting their enemies financially. It was one thing to buy northern publications during the antebellum years when the old Union was still intact, but it was quite another to send badly needed money to the enemy during a life-and-death struggle for national existence. Northerners, cultural nationalists argued, were fighting this war in order to keep the South as an intellectual and commercial tributary and to prevent it from developing its own resources: "They justly regard this as a struggle on our part not for a merely nominal existence as a political organism, or for the supremacy of arms; but they know that the real principle at stake is that of moral, social, intellectual and industrial equality, and they conceive that its maintenance will be to them an irretrievable disaster."[58] As such, it would be madness, not to mention treason, for southerners to continue buying northern products. "We must not give 'aid and comfort' to our enemies in any conceivable shape or form," the *Columbus (Ga.) Times* passionately demanded.[59] That "artery of our life-blood, which flows northward to nerve the arms and strengthen the hearts of our deadliest foes" must be stanched, agreed a Virginian in *De Bow's Review*.[60]

Confederate nationalists insisted, furthermore, that strong home support for native cultural institutions would demonstrate the internal strength of southern society to the outside world. This argument found its most vocal advocates within the organization of North Carolina educators led by C. H. Wiley, and its mouthpiece, the *North Carolina Journal of Education*, which from the very beginning of the war stressed the need to preserve the South's (and particularly North Carolina's) educational system "as an illustration to the world of the civilization of the people of the Confederate States, and of their right and ability to assert and maintain their freedom and independence." The Confederacy had to show its internal stability during this time of war, urged Wiley and company, by supporting its schools, its churches, its publishers, its periodicals, and its literature. Otherwise, military triumphs "will be comparatively barren if we suffer society to become disorganized, our institutions of beneficence to languish and perish, and the light of religion and virtue which now irradiates our homes and sanctifies our hearths, to be extinguished."[61]

The maintenance of existing cultural institutions and especially the creation of new ones would send a strong message to the North about the Confederacy's determination to achieve its independence, thus undermining northern morale and commitment. Allowing southern schools to close, churches to sit vacant, and periodicals to die would only confirm northern taunts and strengthen northern resolve. "Panic and confusion at home are the most effective allies of a foreign foe seeking our destruction," Wiley advised in May 1861, "while nothing more discourages an insolent invader, than the spectacle of a people fighting for their independence and still refusing to be terrified into the abandonment or neglect of a single domestic interest."[62] Every dollar given in support of Confederate literature or education was a blow struck against the Yankee invaders.

INTERNATIONAL CONCERNS FURTHER SPURRED a desire to establish the Confederacy's intellectual independence, particularly during the opening months of the war. Recognizing that foreign intervention could be the deciding factor in determining the outcome of the conflict, Confederate writers insisted that the South had to fight a war of international opinion in addition to that on the battlefield. Foreign recognition would be determined by European perceptions of southern society, and those perceptions would be shaped exclusively by their northern enemies unless southerners immediately began to write and circulate their own views. "It is a little singular that the leading statesmen of Europe have actually no definite idea of Southern independence, apart from revolt and rebellion against the general government," Madame V. E. W. McCord observed in *The Aurora*, a monthly "Ladies' Book" from Memphis. "The scarcity of southern books in Europe, and the total want of a circulating journal of any kind, may account for this fact; while . . . there is scarcely a town in Germany, Holland, France, and even in Russia, that the [New York] Tribune and Herald are not translated weekly, for the instruction of the people in American matters."[63] Now that Europe's attention was focused on America and particularly the South, Confederates had a chance to present their own story on the world stage. "The institutions of no people have ever been more misrepresented; and no people ever had a more glorious opportunity of acting out their true character before the fixed and interested gaze of all mankind," Wiley and his colleagues urged.[64] But to demonstrate this character to the world, the Confederacy would have to write and publish its own books, pamphlets, and periodicals in order to enlighten Europeans as to the true nature of southern society.

Slavery was, of course, the sticking point. In order to gain international recognition and support, Confederates needed to convince an abolitionist-minded world of the benevolence and benefits of their much maligned peculiar institution. To do this, they would have to assert themselves intellectually, to make their case boldly and confidently in order to refute their numerous critics. There was some doubt, even among Confederate nationalists, whether southerners were prepared for the difficult task of undoing the damage wrought by abolitionist writers. In discussing the controversial, and ultimately rejected, proposal to reopen the African slave trade in the early days of the Confederacy, one contributor to the *Southern Literary Messenger* reacted with frustration to southern reservations about what Europeans might think. "Here the want of a genuine autonomy makes itself felt," he fumed. "The people of the Southern States have so long been under the moral dominion of the North and of England; have been so broken by their denunciations and execrations; and have grown so accustomed to that tone of superiority, assumed by them, that they seem to a great extent to have lost a spirit capable of asserting itself."[65] But assert themselves they must. Southerners could no longer allow the North to carry on a one-sided diatribe against the South and its institutions. In fact, some Confederate thinkers pointed out, southerners were the only people truly qualified to write on the subject of slavery and, consequently, it was their responsibility to educate the rest of the world. "Conscious that we are not, in any sense, an inferior people, and firmly convinced that our own position on the subject of slavery is the right one, we contend that it is but strict justice to ourselves to think and write on some subjects for other nations."[66]

Not all Confederate writers were willing to go so far, at least not yet, and many recognized that so long as the war and the blockade continued, Confederate thought would have a very limited reach beyond.its borders. But even if Confederate literature would be primarily for domestic consumption in the present, wartime isolation would give southerners time to prepare their response to the international abolitionist crusade. By presenting a complete picture of southern life and showcasing southern culture, Confederate writers could counter northern propaganda as well as demonstrate to the world the virtues of southern society.

A Confederate renaissance, it was predicted, would blossom as soon as southern culture was brought out from the shade of the northern canopy. But Confederate nationalists worried that peace might come too soon and that they would not have enough time to erect adequate cultural defenses before the resumption of trade with the North would again threaten to cast the South into darkness. The Confederacy was living on borrowed time. The North Carolina State Educational Association predicted that "the establishment of our independence, will be followed probably, by an influx of foreigners, and at all events by a free intercourse with foreign nations; and that thus the mind and heart of the South will be brought in direct contact with the pernicious modes of thought which have infested Northern society with a thousand destructive *isms* from which we are happily exempt."[67] The war would provide a much needed respite from such people and their ideas, but it was incumbent upon Confederates to erect intellectual barriers during that time to keep these corrupting influences out in the future. "We should be equipped with a full and efficient system of moral agencies of our own, when this day of trial comes," the association advised, "and prepared rather to impress our own modes of thought on others than passively to receive from them."[68] The war, in other words, was a preparatory period, a staging ground to muster the Confederacy's intellectual forces to meet and repulse foreign ideas once peace returned. While Confederate writers, editors, publishers, teachers, and ministers enjoyed an exclusive audience during the war, they would have to fight fire with fire when the war ended and northern publishers again had access to southern markets.

BINDING TOGETHER ALL OF these wartime arguments for Confederate intellectual independence was a powerful nationalist ideology. As author A. S.

Worrell succinctly declared in the preface to his grammar textbook, *"Every independent nation must furnish its own literature."*[69] Southern nationhood necessitated far more than simply a declaration of secession and an army. It also required a separate culture with all the necessary trappings and outlets. "We are now treading the path to independence," the *Charleston Courier* explained in calling for an autonomous southern literature. "We have begun a new career; unbounded prosperity and glory, such as our fathers never dreamed of in the wildest flights of their imagination, invite and stimulate our efforts and energies. We have risen to the dignity and importance of a nation. We must respect the claims of our nationality, and go forward in the performance of the high duties it makes incumbent."[70]

Much of this desire for intellectual independence was premised on nineteenth-century romantic notions of what it meant to be a true nation. To the romantic mind, a nation was defined not by territory, military might, politics, or economics, but rather by the unique and recognizable "character" of its people, as most often exhibited through its cultural and literary productions.[71] As "Sybil" told the readers of *Southern Field and Fireside*, "In all ages of the world has it been seen and felt, that those nations, as well as individuals, who wield most influence are those who have attained superiority in science and literature.—No matter how *brave* a people may be—how much they may be *feared*—they will not be *respected* unless they possess the attribute of intellect cultivated and refined."[72] A nation was identified by its culture, and that culture, in turn, had to be recognized as unique and as possessing merit. And it was precisely on this vital point, Confederate cultural leaders correctly perceived, that the Confederacy was at its weakest in terms of its claims to legitimate nationhood. "We must manufacture, at any cost, our own literature," Virginian George Fitzhugh pleaded, "for until we do, we shall have no Thought of our own, and, of consequence no national character whatever."[73] The stakes could not be higher. As one contributor to *Southern Field and Fireside* declared, "Henceforth we are to have a literary name and fame of our own. It *must be so*, or we must fail to secure and maintain the position among the enlightened nations of the earth, to which our talents, statesmanship and resources entitle us."[74] The Confederacy needed to prove that it was indeed a real nation and not merely a disgruntled and rebellious province, and this could be accomplished, the cultural nationalists believed, only by demonstrating the unique character of the Confederate people through their literature, their art, their schools, and their religion.

Historians are not the first people to point to the inherent weaknesses of Confederate nationalism. At the beginning of the war, Confederates themselves recognized that the concept of Confederate nationality was incomplete at best. It lacked many of the cultural and intellectual supports necessary to sustain it. Confederate nationalists firmly believed that the southern people possessed a distinctive national character, and they were anxious to show it. The struggle for cultural autonomy, then, would serve a number of vital functions simultaneously. First, intellectual independence was a fundamental requirement for nationhood, as no independent nation could be beholden to a foreign power, and certainly not one as openly hostile as the United States. Second, the emergence of an original national culture would prove the legitimacy of southerners' desire for separate nationality. It would justify secession and ennoble the cause for which southerners fought and died. Born out of explicitly nationalistic impulses, the struggle for intellectual independence, if successful, would retrospectively vindicate the entire nationalist project. Finally, an authentic Confederate national literature imbued with proper southern values and illustrative of true southern character would serve as the primary means for the dissemination of nationalist sentiment within the southern populace at large. It would unite the Confederate people culturally and bind them to the national cause, while at the same time demonstrating to the world the viability of the Confederacy as a nation. If all went according to plan, this quest to secure the Confederacy's claims to nationhood by strengthening and accelerating its cultural development would act as a self-fulfilling prophecy. Confederates would prove to themselves and the rest of the world that they were a true nation with all the requisite and demonstrable cultural and intellectual components.

Galvanized by this patriotic imperative, Confederate thinkers resolved, in South Carolina professor John McCrady's words, "that we will not be *provincials* in the world of intellect and of civilization."[75] Across professional lines, writers, editors, publishers, teachers, ministers, artists, poets, musicians, actors, playwrights, theater managers, doctors, scientists, philosophers, lawyers, and political theorists came together to forge an agenda dedicated to achieving the Confederacy's intellectual and cultural independence. Through a variety of media, these groups would continue to beat the drum even during the darkest days of the war. It was their consciously nationalistic purpose that enabled these Confederates to unite behind a common project in a way that had never been possible before.

Prior to the conflict, some southern activists had attempted to excite such sentiments, but to little effect. The need for a southern regional literature was often admitted, but few southerners felt any sense of urgency in bringing these changes about. The war provided this sense of immediacy and necessity—and with it a broader constituency. Secession had transformed southern nationalism from an abstract concept into a potent force, and in so doing had breathed new life into what had been a stagnant movement. Now that southerners finally had their own country, there could be no denying that the South needed a national culture. Nor could there be any delay. Determined to strengthen and shape the Confederacy into a true nation, Confederate writers and readers embarked on a quest to liberate the South intellectually as well as politically. Secession and war compelled southerners to start down a road often contemplated but never journeyed, with southern writers and readers advancing together—if not arm-in-arm, then at least not as far apart as they had been but a few months earlier.

The campaign for southern cultural nationalism did not end with secession. Those who had agitated for southern intellectual self-sufficiency during the antebellum years did not simply sit back with an air of self-satisfaction when disunion came. Rather, secession and the war represented a turning point in the quest for an autonomous southern culture. Frustrated by repeated failures in the antebellum years to convince southerners to buy southern magazines, read southern books, hire southern teachers, matriculate at southern schools, and assign southern textbooks, Confederate cultural nationalists saw the coming of the war as their golden opportunity. During the year following secession, they issued an intellectual call to arms to the Confederacy's writers and readers, arguing that necessity, self-interest, and above all, patriotic duty compelled them to action. Although many of the reasons given for the necessity of southern intellectual independence were not new, secession endowed them with a new sense of relevance, immediacy, and hope for success. Furthermore, the outbreak of war had changed the intellectual landscape considerably and provided new justifications for the immediate attainment of Confederate intellectual and cultural self-sufficiency. True independence and national legitimacy required that the Confederacy become a complete nation in the cultural sense, with its own unique literature and its own recognizable character. By the fall of 1861, Confederate cultural nationalists had defined their problem, identified their enemies, mustered their intellectual resources, and marshaled their support. Their agenda was set. They had thrown down the intellectual gauntlet. It now remained to be seen if the southern people would accept the challenge.

CHAPTER TWO

THE CONFEDERATE CRITIQUE OF NORTHERN CULTURE

Before southerners could build a Confederate intellectual and literary culture of their own, they first had to detach themselves from the North. Thus, during the first year of the war, southern writers spent as much time attacking northern culture and decrying the pernicious influences of northern literature and education as they devoted to erecting an alternative southern culture. Attacking the North had been a favorite pastime for many southern writers during the antebellum period, but secession and the outbreak of war understandably prompted an intensification of southern criticism. Confederates attempted to distance and distinguish themselves from their northern adversaries as much as possible by constructing elaborate, novel, and, at times, outlandish arguments for the necessity of secession and separate southern nationality. Arguing that northerners and southerners were culturally distinct peoples, Confederate thinkers maintained that the United States had been merely the unnatural (or at best outmoded) conglomeration of two separate nations.

Confederate cultural nationalists had a ready arsenal of extended metaphors to prove their point. Many sought to portray the old Union as not a nation in itself, but rather the womb from which true nations were born. Eminent Presbyterian divine Benjamin M. Palmer declared his "profound conviction that the separation of this country into two governments was in-

35

evitable: simply because, from the beginning, two nations have with us been in the womb—and the birth, however long delayed, must come at length."[1] "The gestative period is passed," another writer agreed, "the days of our glorious old mother, the Union, are fully accomplished; and the whole country is in the agonies and convulsions of delivery."[2] Political theorist George Fitzhugh described the separation of North and South as "a natural operation; the Union has served its purposes, and expires in gentle euthanasia. The apple is ripe, and drops from its parent-stem."[3] Whereas these men saw disunion as a natural process, one contributor to *Southern Literary Messenger* depicted secession as an unpleasant but necessary surgical procedure. The North was a cancer and the continued health of the South demanded its immediate removal. "Let us cut it off; for the time has fully come for us to do so."[4] In what surely must be the most elaborate, if bizarre, metaphor in southern writing about secession, South Carolina fire-eater Leonidas W. Spratt likened the two sections to "twin lobsters in a single shell, if such a thing were possible, the natural expansion of the one must be inconsistent with the existence of the other. Or, like an eagle and a fish, joined by an indissoluble bond—which, for no reason of its propriety, could act together, where the eagle could not share the fluid suited to the fish and live—where the fish could not share the fluid suited to the bird and live—and where one must perish that the other may survive, unless the unnatural union shall be severed."[5] Whatever their chosen imagery, these writers agreed that the North and South were in fact two separate nations with unique cultures and characters whose distinctiveness had been hitherto concealed under the deceptive blanket of Union.

While these two nations had coexisted, albeit with tension, for the past eighty years, recent developments in the North had brought the matter to a head. Not only did the North and South have separate cultures, but northerners had become increasingly imperialistic and fanatical. Not content to allow their southern brethren to cultivate their own culture in peace, northerners sought to impose their own misguided notions on others by exporting their ideas and their people. These northern incursions not only undermined southern cultural development, but also exposed the South to an increasingly degraded, foreign, and dangerous culture. Only complete and immediate separation could save the South from fatal infection.

Southern critics saw themselves as uniquely positioned to judge the qualities and, more importantly, the dangers of northern culture. After all, they read Yankee books, subscribed to Yankee periodicals and newspapers, studied under Yankee instructors, attended Yankee schools, and even vacationed at Yankee resorts. No one could accuse southerners of not knowing their enemy. As one columnist in the *Southern Presbyterian* responded angrily to a recent circular letter by a group of twenty-six northern clergyman suggesting that tensions between the two sections resulted from southern misunderstanding of northern attitudes: "If ever one people understood and knew another people, we of the South understand and know the people of the North thoroughly well. We have, all our lives long enjoyed every facility for making their acquaintance, and have studied them under circumstances most favorable to a thorough and unbiased knowledge of them. . . . There is not a shade of opinion among them on religion, or morals, or on politics, with which we are not perfectly familiar."[6]

While the extent to which Confederates were indeed familiar with every "shade" of northern opinion is debatable, they certainly had more firsthand knowledge of northern society than did northern critics of southern slave society. Using this one-sided relationship with northern culture to their advantage, Confederate critics embarked on an impassioned and highly partisan attack on northern character, religion, politics, education, and literature. For the most part, these arguments were not new. Southern thinkers had been leveling similar charges against northern culture for years. What was new, however, was the urgency and scope of these attacks. In response to the secession crisis, Confederate thinkers reorganized and refocused arguments that had been in circulation for decades in order to present the southern people with a wide-ranging cultural justification for separate Confederate nationality. In the antebellum years, these critiques of northern culture had surfaced piecemeal at different times, from different thinkers, and in different forums. Now, however, they were presented to the southern public all at once as one comprehensive indictment. Coupled with a new clarity of purpose and a new confidence in the receptivity of the southern people to their ideas, Confederate cultural nationalists launched an all-out assault on northern culture and its agents of dissemination.

THE OVERARCHING SOUTHERN COMPLAINT leveled against northern culture was its inherent fanaticism. Armed with what southerners saw as self-righteousness gone mad, northern reformers carried every idea and impulse to excess and, worse still, sought to impose those excesses on others. Not surprisingly, New England was invariably singled out as the source of this evil, fanning the flames of northern fanaticism from the pulpits, podiums, and printing houses of Boston. The *Church Intelligencer*, a weekly Episcopalian paper from Raleigh, for instance, knew of "no other people so ready, and predisposed, as [New Englanders] are, to push an idea to its extremest terms, force it to its extremest applications, and, with what is to us a most fearful self-complacency, balance themselves on its outermost edge. They will do worse than that. They will try to persuade, or force, all others to stand there with them."[7] Greatly exaggerating the influence of these northern radicals, Confederate critics charged that fanaticism had engulfed nearly the entire northern population, creating a condition akin to mass insanity. "It is very evident to many of those who are at all conversant with the details of life at the North, that the people of that section are, whether from the effects of climate acting upon the idiosyncrasy of race, or from some other cause, wonderfully predisposed to insanity," one anonymous contributor to the *Southern Literary Messenger* opined in May 1861. "Beside those who are recognized and confined as insane, an incredible number of that population not deemed to be stricken with any mental disorder, are nevertheless mad to [a] certain extent."[8] For whatever reason (and southern writers had many working theories), a rapidly increasing proportion of the northern population had taken leave of its senses and, worse still, had invaded the South with its people, its reforms, and its ideas.

This extremism was fueled by an unwavering faith in the righteousness of northern intentions. Dazzled by their own intellectual and moral magnificence, northern reformers could do no wrong, and this conviction, southern critics argued, was precisely what made them so dangerous. Zealot reformers had to eradicate every perceived evil immediately, with no thought given to potential consequences and no consideration granted to alternative viewpoints. "Under this specious cry of reform," Reverend Benjamin Palmer complained to his New Orleans congregation, these northern crusaders demanded "that every evil shall be corrected, or society become a wreck—the sun must be stricken from the heavens if a spot is found on his disk."[9] Clothed in the impermeable armor of good intentions, northern reformers could not be dissuaded from their various quests. What the *Southern Cultivator* called "the fanatical, pseudo-philanthropy of the Northern people," southerners found to be a meddlesome and disruptive force that could not be stopped with reason, obstruction, or even violence.[10]

The fanaticism of northern culture manifested itself most concretely in the innumerable reform societies, religious and philosophical movements, and utopian projects that sprang up throughout the North during the antebellum period, especially in New England. Collectively, southerners referred to these movements as the "isms" of the North and regarded them with a mixture of fear, bewilderment, and mocking amusement. These "isms" included abolitionism, agrarianism, womanism (also called woman's-rightism), Fourierism, Owenism, free-loveism, free-soilism, transcendentalism, perfectionism, vegetarianism, animal magnetism, socialism, spiritualism, Mormonism, Matthiasism, Millerism, Mesmerism, unitarianism, universalism, Tompkinism, agnosticism, and even atheism.[11] Utopian communities of all sorts were highly suspect both for their strange communal behavior and for the sexual promiscuity and blurred gender divisions that were said to thrive within them. At best, the existence of these "isms" demonstrated the deteriorating moral fabric of northern society as cherished institutions, cultural norms, and religious traditions were challenged and flaunted on a daily basis. At worst, these "isms" threatened to further radicalize northerners and incite them to carry their heretical beliefs and practices southward.

In either case, Confederate critics argued that the fact that these "isms" thrived in the North and did not exist in the South (with the notable exception of temperance reform) was proof of the distinctiveness of the two cultures and of the moral superiority of the latter. One Alabamian explained matter-of-factly: "The reason why these 'isms' do not flourish in the South, is owing to several causes—chief among which are, we are a *different race* [from northerners], speaking the same language [but] in a *different manner*. We are guided by loftier impulses and nobler sentiments."[12] As James De Bow proudly proclaimed in the pages of his influential journal, "Adhering to the simple truths of the Gospel, and the faith of their fathers, [southerners] have not run hither and thither in search of all the absurd and degrading isms which have sprung up in the rank soil of infidelity. . . . They are not for breaking down all the forms of society and of religion, and of reconstructing them; but prefer law, order, and existing institutions, to the chaos which radicalism involves."[13]

The innate conservatism of the southern people had acted as their saving grace by keeping them rooted against this tide of fanaticism. Unlike in the North, where "there [was] faith about nothing—speculation about all things," southerners continued to "accept as true the faith of our fathers, believe in the authority of the Bible . . . heed and respect the lessons of history, ancient and profane, and pursue no Utopias that promise to change man's nature, his social habitudes, and his inequalities of condition, because we believe in nature and in nature's God."[14] Southerners, cultural nationalist Atticus Haygood argued, benefited from "a peculiar *balance* about the Southern mind, that will effectually shield us from the wasting influences of the various 'Isms,' that like monstrous *fungi*, have grown out from Northern character. . . . We Southerners are easily humbugged about some things, but we cannot so readily lay down the faith of our fathers."[15] Over and over again, southern writers invoked this "faith of our fathers" and southern fidelity to it as clear indicators of southern conservatism and continuity. Grounded in their past, devoted to their religious faith, firmly attached to their existing institutions, and harboring no illusions about the perfectibility of man, southerners, these writers argued, represented the last bastion of rationality and common sense remaining on the North American continent.

WHILE CONFEDERATE CRITICS CONDEMNED all the "isms" of the North, they singled out certain movements as especially offensive. Cultural nationalists were quick to use these examples to expose the great gulf that had grown up between the two sections. The nascent women's rights movement, for instance, was deemed both a brazen affront to common decency, and particularly compelling proof of the degraded state of northern society. With increasing frequency and boldness, women in the North had reached beyond their prescribed sphere of influence (the home) into the hitherto male public sphere. They sought entrance into the professions, aspired to the pulpit, wrote racy fiction and inflammatory tracts, and delivered speeches at reform society meetings, lyceums, and even political rallies. Some of these radical women went so far as to demand political rights equal with men's. In the southern view, these actions not only challenged the existing male-dominated order, but, even worse, degraded the purity and virtue of the female sex. Sullied by contact with a world outside their proper sphere, these women were unsexing themselves while at the same time dragging the virtuous female ideal through the mud. "Abjuring the delicate offices of their sex, and deserting their nurseries," northern women now "stroll over the country as politico-moral reformers, delivering lewd lectures upon the beauties of free-love and spiritualism, or writing yellow back literature, so degraded in taste, so prurient in passion, so false in fact, so wretched in execution, and so vitiating to the morals of the mothers in the land, as almost to force them to bring [up] daughters without virtue and sons without bravery."[16] Thus, the women's rights movement not only demonstrated the decline of northern society, but necessarily portended its further precipitous decline with each subsequent generation.

Southerners who wished to speak out on women's issues, even in a limited way, had to distance themselves carefully from the northern fanatics. As one writer arguing for the expansion of female education in the Confederacy was quick to point out, "We are in favor of women's rights in the highest, noblest sense. . . . But for that pestilent doctrine, springing latest-born and ugliest from the foul embrace of Yankeeism and infidelity, we have no sympathy. . . . Those creatures in the Northern States who appear in the pulpit, at the bar, on the lecturer's stand and on the arena of politics, are not *women*; they are horrible abortions, nondescripts, utter perversions of human nature."[17] Southern womanhood stood in stark contrast to these unsettling "creatures" in the North and remained the model of virtue, restraint, and proper decorum. "Our women are all conservative, moral, religious, and sensitively modest, and abhor the North for its infidelity, gross immorality, licentiousness, anarchy, and agrarianism," George Fitzhugh boasted.[18] Even higher education did not seem to have the same pernicious effects on the minds and habits of southern women as it evidently did on their northern sisters. While educated southern women, in Fitzhugh's view, were often "less reserved, less oversensitive, less prudish than formerly," they remained "none the less feminine." Their education did not lead them to question or challenge social roles, but instead reinforced the existing order. "They confine themselves exclusively to the pursuits and associations becoming their sex, and abhor the female lecturers and abolition and free love oratrixes, and Bloomers, and strong-minded women of the North." Southern women, unlike their northern counterparts, used their intelligence to better accomplish their necessary and proper tasks and did not corrupt their gifts by meddling in a world for which they were not suited.[19]

Confederate critics noted with satisfaction that unlike many northern women, southern women had eschewed political debates during the antebellum years and had not sought to overstep their bounds. The passions of the secession crisis, however, had recently induced women to speak out in favor of the southern cause. In fact, many observers noted, women often led the popular movement for secession by cajoling their sometimes reluctant husbands to the polling places and secession conventions. As Fitzhugh wrote of his own native Virginia, "The men of our State had neither the sense to understand the crisis nor the firmness to meet and grapple with it. The secession of Virginia is the work of her women." Whereas such direct involvement with political issues would have been condemned as a Yankeeism during the antebellum period, southern secessionists now welcomed female support with open arms. By an interesting twist of logic, Fitzhugh reasoned that because southern women had maintained their purity and innocence by not intermingling with politics, their endorsement of secession proved the righteousness of the Confederate cause. "We recollect no occasion, except the present, when they [women] have interfered with or discussed political movements. Now, they and the clergy [the other segment of white southern society culturally prohibited from the political realm] are the staunch-est champions of the Southern cause. That cause must be pure and righ-teous whose most zealous upholders are the most peaceful, benevolent and pious portion of society."[20] By remaining outside the political world, south-ern women saw clearly the fundamental issues involved in secession and thus could lend their unsullied voices to the Confederate cause.

WHILE SOUTHERNERS SAW THE northern women's rights movement as a perversion of nature and an affront to southern womanhood, they viewed the rise of "agrarianism" as a dire threat to their property, their rights, and their very lives. Confederates demonstrated no very precise understanding of what agrarianism actually meant, but they were certain that it was dangerous. For southern writers and political theorists, agrarianism could be anything from the equal distribution of land and property, to communal property, to the abolition of property, to class war, to mob law, and chaos. To archconserva-tive, antidemocratic southern political thinkers, agrarianism was a blanket term covering all the evil tendencies of the past thirty years, including a dramatic expansion of suffrage rights, an influx of foreign immigration, and an increased political pandering to the mob. The term was southern short-hand for any and all of the "leveling" tendencies of northern society which sought to remove the natural and necessary divisions between men. What-ever their working definition, southern writers agreed that the threat of agrar-ianism was very real and that a cabal of northern fanatics and political dema-gogues were seeking to destroy the right of property and the rule of law in the United States.

Unlike many of the other northern "isms," which could be dismissed as small social and religious movements without any real power, agrarian-ism reared up as a lethal combination of fanaticism and politics. Working through the party systems and political machines of the North, agrarian fanatics sought to "inaugurate enforced equality and 'Free Lands.' "[21] "Very soon," one contributor to the *Southern Literary Messenger* gloomily predicted in January 1861, "King numbers [the mob] will reign supreme." With "learn-ing and political experience . . . already at a discount," men of inferior educa-tion, rank, and character had risen to national political prominence as evi-denced by the recent Republican victory.[22] With such men in power, there was nothing to stop northern demagogues from carrying out "their wicked pur-pose to bind a noble and free people hand and foot to the swift-rushing chariot of agrarianism, whose goal is anarchy, and whose only arrest is in the bayonet-power of a military despotism."[23]

For archconservative Confederate political theorists, the rise of agrarianism was the inevitable and long-predicted result of the worst tendencies of democratic politics.[24] As Mississippian J. Quitman Moore wrote with much rhetorical flourish:

> Radical, levelling, and revolutionary—intolerant, proscriptive, and arbitrary—violent, remorseless, and sanguinary—[the democratic principle's] course has been tending constantly downward, from the promulgation of the doctrine of "natural rights" and the theory of social and political equality, down through all the contrivances of party craft, and all the schemes of demagogical art, as expressed in the laws of universal suffrage—abrogation of entails—popular judicatures—State repudiation—to that latest fledgling of the prolific harpy nest, that, under the name of "popular sovereignty," perches itself upon the battlements of the Constitution, and battens on the sores and corruptions of the body politic.

This "revolution" had been progressing covertly since the founding of the nation, Moore argued, only now to be exposed by "the designs and delusions of fanaticism and demagogism."[25]

It was universal suffrage that these conservative critics most deplored, both as an evil in itself and as the all-powerful tool of northern agrarianism. "Where is the thinking man, who now believes that universal suffrage is not subversive of all free institutions?" one southern writer demanded in the January 1861 issue of the *Southern Literary Messenger*. Such a comment might seem strange, considering that the South itself was not immune to the democratizing influences of the era and that suffrage rights had been greatly expanded in the southern states as well as in the North. Slavery, however, was the trump card. Anticipating charges of hypocrisy, this anonymous writer explained that the southern states "have, or many of them have, universal suffrage, it is true. But it is universal suffrage for only one half the population. With them the whole menial and nearly all the labouring population have no votes. While we have slavery, we shall never have universal suffrage." In the North, the laboring classes enjoyed voting rights, thereby giving a voice to the dangerous and discontented. In the South, the existence of slavery permitted universal white manhood suffrage without the dangers of agrarianism. So long as the South remained attached to the North by the bonds of Union, however, it too could be dominated by the fickle will of the northern mob. Without separation, southern critics warned, it would not be long before the rapacious agrarians of the North turned their greedy eyes and ill-gotten political power on the riches of the South. As Lincoln's inauguration neared, how could southerners continue to "cling to the Union, when the government of that Union is in the hands of wild agrarians, whose policy is to be most destructive to all that the South holds dear?"[26]

Not only would secession free the South from northern agrarianism, it would also hasten the downfall of northern society. Without the conservative counterbalance of the southern states, the North would quickly spin into chaos, Confederate critics confidently predicted. "I look upon the people of the North as perfectly incapable of self government," Alabama lawyer William Falconer wrote, arguing that northern society would have torn itself apart years ago "had it not been for the conservative influence which the South exerted till recently."[27] For his part, George Fitzhugh believed that the North's agrarian impulses would lead immediately to anarchy and ultimately to military despotism. Indeed, in Fitzhugh's mind, a military dictatorship would be "a great improvement in Northern affairs, and the sooner it comes about the better. Military despotism is far preferable to Northern democracy, agrarianism, infidelity, and free love."[28]

But whatever the North's future fate, southern commentators were confident that the rise of agrarianism over the previous thirty years and its recent intensification, evidenced by Lincoln's victory, represented a serious threat to southern property and way of life. Agrarian fanatics had incited the northern mob against the South, leaving southerners no alternative but secession and war.

WOMAN'S-RIGHTISM WAS PROFOUNDLY troubling and agrarianism inherently dangerous, but no other northern "ism" outraged or offended southerners so much as abolitionism. For southern thinkers and religious leaders, abolitionism flew in the face of God, history, reason, experience, science, and common sense, and could be explained only by northern ignorance, infidelity, or insanity. It was the presence and perceived strength of the abolitionist movement in the North that brought northern and southern cultures into starkest relief and, for southerners, demonstrated unequivocally the fanatical excesses to which northern society was prone.

Southern writers, politicians, and ministers had been waging an active campaign against the northern antislavery movement for the past thirty years. Many historians have thoroughly examined the southern response to abolitionism and the rise of proslavery thought in all its forms, and there is no need to retread that ground here.[29] For the purposes of this discussion, it is important to examine how southern nationalists seized on abolitionism to underscore cultural differences between the two sections and make a case for secession and, if necessary, war. For these southerners, abolitionism epitomized and magnified all the evil tendencies of northern culture and the very real dangers that the unchecked growth of "isms" posed. While some "isms" like transcendentalism, Mormonism, or vegetarianism in no way immediately threatened the South, the disruptive and heretical ideas spawned and spread by these movements could only cause trouble. Abolitionism functioned for southern nationalists as the archetypal "ism," as definitive proof of the extremes to which such misguided thinking could lead.

At their most charitable, southern critics maintained that abolitionism, like the other northern "isms," stemmed from ignorance. While all the "isms" shared an unrealistic and overly optimistic view of human nature and the perfectibility of man, abolitionists compounded their folly by trying to meddle with a system about which they knew nothing, to liberate a race of slaves with whom they had no familiarity and for whom they felt no genuine sympathy. While most southern writers, save a few diehard proslavery extremists, willingly conceded that the southern slave system was not without its faults and abuses, they believed that southerners alone could fix these problems, and they deeply resented northern interference. This view was especially prevalent among the South's religious leadership, many of whom had desired for years to enact reforms such as the legal recognition of slave marriages and the abolition of antiliteracy laws, but had been reluctant to act for fear of providing abolitionists with fresh ammunition. So long as the institution was under attack from without, southern would-be reformers remained silent in order to present a united front against a hostile foe. "We do not pretend that our system of labor is free from its defects,—that our laws are altogether righteous, or our practice all that a Christian could desire," the Charleston-based *Southern Episcopalian* admitted. "We believe that there are many and important points in which each and all might be improved; but we are certain that the pretensions of Northern fanatics to regulate our domestic slavery, are presumptuous, and their remedies of the most pernicious tendency."[30]

Abolitionists simply did not know what they were talking about. "The North has no conception of the negro, or of his true relation to the white race," one typical 1861 southern pamphlet explained.[31] Unlike white southerners who had lived with "the negro" for generations, the abolitionists did not know or care what was in the best interests of the slaves themselves. As fiery author and minister Joseph C. Stiles explained, "The *social and religious improvement of the man of color*, his *all-in-all*, awakens comparatively no interest . . . in the Northern mind, while his personal freedom, which it were murder to put into his hands to-day, the man of color must have, though it cost the instant overthrow of universal social order."[32] While this view of the slaves' inability to survive without the protection of slavery was premised upon racist and transparently self-serving beliefs about black inferiority, southerners of this period were not much given to introspection. Rather, they firmly believed that experience, proximity, Christianity, and reason taught them that they knew what was best for their slaves, and they were equally certain that northerners, who had no direct contact with slaves or slavery, did not.

Ignorance, however, was the least of northern abolitionists' faults, according to southerner writers, for they also acted in defiance of God. The southern religious defense of slavery had a long history.[33] Voluminous biblical evidence and a firm conviction that a providential God would not allow human bondage to continue and flourish if it existed contrary to His will had convinced southern theologians that slavery was a divine institution. They argued that white southerners were God's chosen people who had been entrusted with the care and safekeeping of their slaves. From this position, it was a short jump to the conclusion that those who opposed slavery and actively sought its abolition acted against God's express wishes. The impact of this infidelity, southern divines argued, stretched far beyond the abolition debate. By questioning divine law and disputing biblical truth, abolitionists threatened to undermine the sanctity of God's word and unleash a wave of atheism concealed beneath the deceptive cloak of humanitarianism. Hence, the southern struggle against abolitionism was not merely a fight to preserve slavery, but a noble attempt to uphold the power and authority of true Christianity. "The abolition spirit is undeniably atheistic," Presbyterian New Orleans divine Benjamin Palmer warned his congregation, and by fighting against it, southerners joined an age-old struggle against an ancient and diabolical adversary. Here, in the United States, "among a people so generally religious as the American," the "demon" had concealed himself behind the "old threadbare disguise of the advocacy of human rights," but Palmer urged southerners not to be fooled.[34] The South stood as the last remaining bulwark against this tide of infidelity. "If we fail, and the North succeeds, the Bible will be falsified; Christianity now tottering to its fall in free society will perish from the earth," warned one columnist in *De Bow's Review*.[35] "This spirit of atheism, which knows no God who tolerates evil, no Bible which sanctions law, and no conscience that can be bound by oaths and covenants, has selected us for its victims, and slavery for its issue," Palmer exclaimed.

"To the South is assigned the high position of defending, before all nations, the cause of all religion and of all truth."[36]

Some, like Joseph Stiles, still held out hope that Christianity would redeem the abolitionists "and rectify the consciences of the North," but most southern thinkers concluded that by 1860, the North had been "abolitionized" beyond the point of return.[37] The spirit of abolition, they argued, had infected and corrupted nearly every aspect of northern culture and society. As Virginia State Attorney General J. Randolph Tucker grimly explained, "Church and State are saturated with Abolition. Literature teems with it—the schools resound with denunciations of the slaveholder—and the highest seats of learning succumb to its omnipotent dominion." With the victory of the sectional Republican party in November, the infection of abolitionism had evidently spread so far that there was little further need to distinguish friend from foe in the northern states. Even the North's staunch conservatives, from whom southerners had always received support and sympathy, had fallen silent due to their dwindling numbers and fear of the fanatical mob. "A very few larger minded men respect and esteem our civilization. Not one man in ten, as I sincerely believe," Tucker observed sadly.[38] George Bagby, editor of the *Southern Literary Messenger*, thought that even this estimate was too charitable. Convinced that abolitionism had seeped into the minds of nearly every resident of the free states, whether they were aware of it or not, Bagby no longer saw any reason to draw distinctions between members of the abolitionist movement and the general northern population. Given these new realities, he wrote, the term abolitionist required redefinition: "An Abolitionist is any man who does not love slavery for its own sake, as a divine institution; who does not worship it as the corner stone of civil liberty; who does not adore it as the only possible social condition on which a permanent Republican government can be erected; and who does not, in his inmost soul, desire to see it extended and perpetuated over the whole earth, as a means of human reformation second in dignity, importance, and sacredness, alone to the Christian religion."[39] Thus, essentially every northerner, in Bagby's eyes, was at least a tacit abolitionist. While most commentators were not willing to go so far as Bagby, they, like him, believed that abolitionism had overtaken northern society, to be followed shortly by atheism and anarchy.

Abolitionism, then, was the ultimate "ism." It encapsulated and clearly displayed all the evils to which the northern mania for fanaticism could lead. For Confederate cultural nationalists, the presence of abolitionism in the North demonstrated irrefutably the cultural divide between the two nations and exposed the very real dangers posed by northern ideas. While all the "isms" were unsettling and in some cases directly threatening, abolitionism proved conclusively the extent of northern fanaticism and the insane and destructive forms that it could take.

BY 1861, THIS FANATICISM, in all its guises, had evidently saturated northern society to such an extent that most southern commentators simply gave up trying to reason with northern critics. So deeply had the "isms" and the radical thinking they engendered seeped into the northern consciousness that there was little worth saving. "The disease is in the Northern mind, and it is neither transient nor acute, but deep-seated and chronic," J. Randolph Tucker told the readers of the *Richmond Examiner* while writing under the incongruous pseudonym "Bland."[40] There was no "hope for a change of public sentiment at the North," another columnist agreed; the sooner southerners accepted the fact, the better. "The [northern] people are bred, born and educated to their levelling views. Their religion fosters the tenacity with which they cling to these views. And, above all, they are utterly unable to resist the temptation to carry out these views."[41] Confronted with a foreign and hostile culture gone mad, Confederate nationalists assured their readers that only one option remained: separation. As one writer asked in the days following Fort Sumter and Lincoln's call for troops, "can we consent to form one society; one indivisible consolidated people with a population evidently deranged, when we have the means of avoiding it? . . . Can we consent to trust the government under which we live to the direction of men more or less insane?"[42] To such questions, clearly, there could be but one answer.

Confederate critics were not content simply to catalog the symptoms of northern decay. They delved deeper into northern culture to diagnose the underlying causes of the disease—seeking to explain what made northerners so susceptible to fanaticism. The "isms" were merely the most visible signs of illness, and Confederate thinkers wanted to root out the sources of the corruption, both in order to differentiate themselves from northerners and, if possible, to prevent the infection from spreading southward. Some southern writers simply attributed the northern penchant for fanaticism, and the South's seeming resistance to it, to climate and lifestyle, arguing that unlike northerners "we are not thrown together in heated houses and populous cities; but, on the contrary, spend much of our time, the year round, in the sunny fields, on horse-back, in the more active pursuits of life."[43] On a more penetrating level, however, other critics directed their cultural analysis toward the failures of northern religion, the dangers of northern education, and the innate deficiencies of Yankee character.

These often elaborate critiques appeared mainly in the Confederacy's self-consciously highbrow periodicals such as *De Bow's Review*, the increasingly politicized *Southern Literary Messenger*, and, to a lesser extent, prominent religious and educational journals such as the *Southern Presbyterian Review*, the *Quarterly Review of the Methodist Episcopal Church, South*, and the *North Carolina Journal of Education*. Unlike the daily and weekly papers, these monthly and quarterly journals welcomed essays of greater length and complexity. While denunciations of northern "isms" were widespread, and attacks on northern literature nearly universal across the spectrum of the Confederate periodical, newspaper, and publishing industry, these more in-depth and quasi-scholarly critiques of northern culture were restricted largely to the pages of the South's preeminent intellectual journals. While not as widely circulated as many of the weekly papers, these journals did set the tone for the early Confederate attack on northern culture, and their arguments helped to establish the underpinning for the larger struggle for Confederate intellectual independence.

ACCORDING TO MANY CONFEDERATE critics, much of the blame for the North's susceptibility to fanaticism lay with the northern religious establishment's complicity in, and even encouragement of, such misguided and destructive notions. Rather than acting as an example of moral and religious conservatism, northern Protestantism had become a breeding ground for fanatics. Abdicating its religious and moral duty, the northern priesthood had prostituted itself "to a level with a blackguard" by entering "the secular field of politics, in the spirit of a beer-house bully."[44] "The business of a preacher, as such, is to expound the Word of God," James H. Thornwell, the most respected and influential Presbyterian divine in the South, reminded his fellow clergymen in November 1860. "He has no authority to expound to senators the Constitution of the State, nor to interpret for judges the law of the land. In the civil and political sphere, the dead must bury their dead."[45] By speaking out on political and social issues, of which abolition was only the most flagrant example, northern ministers had violated the essential division between secular and sacred. By degrading themselves to the level of the demagogue, northern clergymen had lost their claim to the moral conscience of the people. "The cloak of the philosopher" and the frock of the priest were simply "too scant to hide the burly form of the partisan."[46]

By ceding their moral authority, northern clergymen had paved the path to infidelity and atheism. In the spiritual vacuum of the North, wayward Christians freely questioned biblical truth and divine law—especially when it came to slavery—and substituted, with their ministers' blessing, the philosophy of human rights, the "idolatry of a flag and a demoniacal worship of a Union," in place of God.[47] As Episcopal Bishop Stephen Elliott told his Savannah congregation, in the forthcoming struggle with the North, the Confederacy was "fighting to drive away from our sanctuaries the infidel and rationalistic principles which are sweeping over the land and substituting a gospel of the Stars and Stripes for the gospel of Jesus Christ."[48]

Hypocritical as it might seem for these southern clergymen to denounce their former colleagues for engaging in secular matters in the very same sermons in which they themselves sought to vindicate political secession and catalog northern violations of the national compact, Confederate ministers vehemently denied any double standard. Unlike northern clergymen who actively and eagerly engaged in the political sphere, southern ministers assured their congregations that they did so only with the greatest reluctance. During the secession crisis and the months leading up to Fort Sumter, it was customary for southern clergymen to offer extended explanations, bordering on apologies, for speaking out on the issues of the day. Particularly while the matter of secession was still being debated, southern divines agonized over the propriety of taking sides. "It is, indeed, difficult to say, in every case, where, precisely, Church power ends, and the power of the State begins," Reverend John D. Adger later wrote to the subscribers of the *Southern Presbyterian Review*, and he refused to stipulate "how far the individual Pastor, in his pulpit, may go in manifesting his sympathy with the old Government or the new."[49]

Others, like James Thornwell, believed that despite the risks involved, the times called for strong spiritual leadership. "During the twenty-five years in which I have fulfilled my course as a preacher . . . I have never introduced secular politics into the instructions of the pulpit. It has been a point of conscience with me to know no party in the State," he began his influential sermon to the assembled congregation in Columbia, South Carolina. Now, during the height of secessionist passions following Lincoln's election, Thornwell felt compelled to offer guidance at the risk of transgressing "the limits of propriety" and merging "the pulpit into the rostrum." Still, he chose his steps very carefully, and there were lines he promised not to cross. In cases relating to "a change in the government, in which the question of duty is simply a question of revolution," Thornwell maintained that "the minister has no commission from God to recommend or resist a change, unless some moral principle is immediately involved." During times of political unrest, the clergyman may rightfully "expound the doctrine of the Scriptures in relation to the nature, the grounds, the extent and limitations of civil obedience; but it is not for him, as a preacher, to say when evils are intolerable, nor to prescribe the mode and measure of redress. These points he must leave to the State itself." However, once "a revolution has . . . been achieved" (and by the late November date of Thornwell's sermon, secession was a foregone conclusion in South Carolina), "he can enforce the duties which spring from the new condition of affairs."[50]

Once war with the North seemed unavoidable, the situation became much more clear cut. "The invasion of our soil by armed hordes of abolition fanatics, under the usurped authority of Lincoln, puts the question of defense above all party," the editor of the *North Carolina Christian Advocate* reasoned. "Self-defense is no less a law of religion than of nature; and we hope to be enabled to recognize this law, in these columns, without abating the claim of the paper to be a religious journal."[51] Southern clergymen quickly and effortlessly recast the conflict as a religious struggle in which the righteous Confederates squared off against the godless fanatical northern hordes. Given their faith in the divine sanction of slavery, ministers showed little hesitation in taking sides once the fighting started. They assured southerners that God clearly favored the Confederacy. As early as January 1861, the Columbia *Southern Presbyterian* predicted that if war did come, "it will be a religious war. It will be a cause to die for. . . . And if ever a people might look for Divine protection in a conflict, it will be the South."[52]

According to secessionists like George Fitzhugh, the southern clergy, like southern women, had maintained their purity by refusing to intermingle in worldly affairs prior to the war. Consequently they, unlike their former colleagues to the North, were in a position to provide strong moral leadership once the war came. It is debatable to what extent southern clergymen did in fact avoid political questions during the antebellum period, and questionable as to why abolitionist sermons qualified as corrupting political action whereas proslavery sermons did not. The South's men of the cloth nevertheless assured themselves and their congregations that there was a profound difference between their behavior and that of their northern counterparts, indicative of the larger cultural divide between North and South.

The strongest evidence that Confederate critics could muster for the degraded state of religious leadership in the North and the purity of southern

Christianity was the simple fact that infidelity and fanaticism flourished in the northern states, while they had yet to obtain even a foothold in the South. The strength and orthodoxy of southern Christianity offered a stark contrast to the North's many "isms" and served as indisputable proof of the righteousness of southern slave society and the Confederate cause. "If our theory be not true," one contributor to *De Bow's Review* asked rhetorically, "how comes it that faith predominates with us, and infidelity, in its every form, rages elsewhere?"[53] George Fitzhugh agreed: "There is no infidelity in our Confederacy. Religion is universal. It binds us together, and makes us one patriotic and moral people."[54] In the South, religion worked to unite all Christians, whereas in the North, it served only to divide them into factions and "isms." For the South, institutionalized Christianity was a source of strength, a conservative bulwark against the corrupting influences of the secular world. For the North, the failure of religion to uphold its sacred charge had enabled and even encouraged the rise of fanaticism. Having immersed themselves in the putrid waters of politics and social reform, northern clergymen could no longer provide proper spiritual leadership. All the pious South could do for the North was pray. "Let us pray *for the North*, even for those who are most hostile to Southern institutions and Southern interests," the *Southern Presbyterian* advised. "Let us repay good for their evil."[55]

WHILE NORTHERN RELIGION MISLED the spirit, northern education actively corrupted the mind. For decades, smug northerners had pointed to their magnificent public educational systems and the relative lack of public schools in the South as clear proof of northern superiority. Although a few southern states, most notably North Carolina, had established rudimentary state-supported school systems during the late antebellum period, universal public education was still a long way off—a fact that many northerners saw as indicative of the general cultural stagnation of southern slave society. However, with the rise of sectional tensions, southern critics had turned the tables on northern schoolmasters by arguing that, far from a blessing, the northern system of education was a primary cause of cultural deterioration and a leading culprit in the proliferation of "isms."

Confederate critics conceded that "education is more general at the North than at the South," but this, they countered, was precisely the problem.[56] "We will admit that New England is crowded with free schools; and here, conscientiously, we must stop to say that in *this* . . . we recognize the curse of New England Society, and the great revolutionary element of the North." Realizing that such a statement would appear "paradoxical," Edward Pollard, the newly appointed and often controversial associate editor of the Richmond *Examiner*, went on to explain:

> We believe that the education of the New England common school is carried out to that point where learning is dangerous, and where it bears no better fruits than presumption, disrespect to superiors, a vain passion for reform, infidelity, and the agitations of revolution. It is this imperfect education of the people in the North which we see deluging them with all the vices of the smattering of schools; causing men to run to extremes; begetting irreverence in everything; generating "isms;" populating the mind with all sorts of crudities, and . . . making "human stupidity vocal."[57]

Other southern writers joined with Pollard to condemn the Yankee system of education for teaching the masses just enough to unsettle their minds, question their betters, and undermine their institutions. "Nothing," these writers agreed, "is more to be dreaded than a community half-educated, and who consider themselves learned." They firmly believed, and often cited, Alexander Pope's famous maxim that " 'A little knowledge is a dangerous thing.' "[58]

The vaunted schools of the North, these critics charged, provided merely the appearance of erudition. Northern teachers recklessly exposed their students to a broad range of topics and ideas without any attention paid to comprehension or appropriateness. Hence, the education that northern teachers championed and northern children received was superficial and deceptive, "the knowledge imparted is a mere smattering; the accomplishments mere tinsel gloss."[59] "It is impossible for one mind to know everything thoroughly," one Virginian reasoned in *De Bow's Review*, "and, as the Yankee nation claims to know every science and teach every art under the sun, it must be that, where the streams of knowledge are so broad, they are very shallow."[60] Exposed to new and potentially unsettling ideas without the benefit of adequate understanding and taught to automatically question accepted truths without thought of the consequences, the northern masses were left in a dangerous state of half-education, possessing only enough knowledge to render them discontented, but not enough to grant them restraint, wisdom, or foresight. With such an education, the northern people were primed for fanaticism, and "isms" swam in the wake of the northern schoolmaster.

What was worse, these "isms" had turned the northern classroom itself into an insidious instrument of indoctrination. As always, abolitionism was the prime culprit. Through a network of abolitionist teachers and textbook authors, it had quietly seeped into every aspect of northern education. Many northern textbooks, one southern critic claimed, "already are crammed full of the most incendiary abolition doctrines," and he was certain that the abolitionists would not stop there. "The idea of 'publishing tables of anti-slavery sines and co-sines,' is not by any means improbable or inconsistent with that insane spirit of fanaticism which proposes to employ *all* means to compass its ends."[61] While Reverend George Naff found the rantings of abolitionists to be generally "harmless in their original expression, in shrieking lectures or acrimonious essays," he warned that when such passages were "deliberately culled out" for inclusion in school books, "to be read and committed to memory by the young, as the formatives of taste and opinion, they become evil, perverted for mischief, or wickedness overlapping and multiplying itself."[62]

While most Confederate critics believed in the benefits of widespread education if properly conducted, they were equally convinced that northern education was misguided and dangerous. They refused to be deceived by Yankee appearances of learnedness and they rejected that "thrasonical notion . . . that machines, and school books, and Yankee smartness, and Yankee trade, constitute the excellence of refinement, and the strength and ornament of society." By trumpeting their education and their seeming intellectual accomplishments, northerners pointed to false indicators of civility and culture. "You exhibit your material wealth, you parade your ingenuity, you insult us with the babblement of your schools, you vaunt over our heads a rotten and phosphorescent literature, you even sneer at us over self-assertions of your puritanical virtues. False virtues—poor hypocrisies!" Edward Pollard shouted in April 1861.[63]

Southern critics argued that the only way to evaluate the relative merits of northern and southern education was to examine their results, and, not surprisingly, these comparisons invariably demonstrated the clear superiority of the latter. While northerners may have had the edge in terms of *"school-learning,"* when it came to *"public intelligence—*that intelligence which contributes to the interests of the State, which is peculiarly the aid of *civilization,"* southerners stood head and shoulders above their northern neighbors. Arguing that *"the order and security of the State and mutual justice between its citizens"* were the true markers of civilization and the proper goals of education, Pollard predictably concluded that the South had the "vastly superior" system, especially in view of the "barbarism, savagery, and wild and reckless revolution" that the North "has given to the world." While southerners were taught to respect law, order, and their proper and necessary place in society, northerners, through their abolitionist education, learned to destroy rights, violate laws, and "preach the divine right of murderers."[64] Far from the embodiment of culture and civilization, northern education was a curse on northern society and a threat to children everywhere.

TO CONFEDERATE OBSERVERS, THE failings of Yankee religion and education revealed much about the underlying character of the northern people. The concept of "character" was central to nineteenth-century nationalism. It was the essence of a people, that innate and distinctive combination of values, proclivities, customs, and history that set one group apart from another. Character was fundamental. It unconsciously shaped every aspect of society and culture. Ultimately, then, it was a question of character—Yankee character and southern character—that was at the heart of all these differences, and Confederate writers were eager to bring to light the deficiencies in northern character that made them so naturally predisposed to fanaticism. Although the most abstract of the Confederate critiques of northern culture, the critique of northern character served as a convenient catch-all: it neatly explained all the evil tendencies of the North while at the same time establishing the more ambitious nationalist argument that northerners and southerners were in fact two distinct and utterly incompatible peoples. In this view, the apparent differences between the North and South were only the most obvious indicators of a much more fundamental division. Those who thought that northern fanaticism was the cause of disunion simply were not looking deep enough. It was unfortunate, Alabamian William Falconer told his fellow Confederates in July 1861, that "the common style of opinion" blamed the troubles between the two sections on "that which is known by the general name of *fanaticism*, on the part of the Northern people, and an insane philanthropy for the negro. This is measurably true; true, at least, so far as it goes, but then it contains the error of giving the *effect* for the *cause*." "Transient [Republican] politico-party success" and agitation over slavery were merely flashpoints for conflict, Falconer assured his readers, and northern fanaticism was only the most visible sign of the inherent characteristics of the Yankee race.[65]

In their critique of northern character, Confederate writers fielded two contradictory arguments. On the one hand, nativist-minded critics charged that the deterioration of northern society stemmed from the heterogeneity of its population. A free-labor system combined with a welcoming immigration policy had attracted the "heterogeneous spawn of European civilization" to northern shores.[66] As a result, the North was not composed of one people, but rather, was made up of an unsettled and dangerous mix of different peoples with different traditions and ideas. "The weakness of the North proceeds entirely from its various and incongruous population," George Fitzhugh maintained. "Her people have no opinions or objects in life in common," and as a consequence, he predicted, what remained of the Union would soon tear itself apart "into three or four independent states or nations."[67]

The damage caused by this "incongruous" population stretched beyond the realm of politics. A mixed population had degraded northern culture and prevented its true expression from rising above the cacophony. In fact, given all of these fragmentary and competing segments, Fitzhugh denied that "Northern people have any taste, elegance, or refinement" at all. The only tastes or rather "sensual appetites" that the Yankees had were "for beefsteak, ale, pumpkins, collards, and *saur-kraut*," he snorted.[68] With no harmony of people or thought, northerners had no identifiable character. Instead, northern culture went in all directions at once, resulting in the proliferation of "isms" at the expense of producing anything of substance or lasting value.

The southern population, on the other hand, was homogeneous and united, or so its spokesmen maintained. Southern economic development, especially slavery, had discouraged foreign immigration, and as a result the population had maintained its purity and its traditions. As one southerner proudly explained to his incredulous friend from Boston, "In manners and customs, we are more homogeneous than you of the North. Our slavery has operated as an effective though indirect barrier to that deluge of foreign emigration, which, among you, has compromised the process of social crystallization. We are less changed than you, since the days of George Washington."[69] This homogeneity had protected southerners from the disruptive social and cultural forces that had overtaken the North and it provided the basis for a true southern nationality. "The Southern people, now, are fused into a common mass; all speak the same language, have the same manners and customs, the same moral notions, the same political opinions; emphatically, they are one people," Fitzhugh rejoiced.[70] Likewise, editor James De Bow, in celebrating the birth of the Confederacy in February 1861, predicted that the South's "homogeneous population, little admixed [as it was] with those of foreign blood," would be its greatest source of strength as a nation. "This homogeneity will keep us a unit for as long a period as any government can be kept such, and much longer than the governments that surround us."[71] Whereas the North's heterogeneity doomed it to division, faction, and civil strife, the Confederacy's undiluted population assured a united and glorious future for the southern nation.

THE OTHER PRINCIPAL EXPLANATION for the weaknesses and proclivities of Yankee character stemmed from a racial argument—compelling to southerners despite its inaccuracy—that northerners, as a people, were descended from a common, inferior stock. The intolerant Yankees of the North were the direct descendents of the Saxon-blooded Puritans, whereas Confederates traced their lineage to the noble and aristocratic Norman cavaliers. This line of argument, which implicitly maintained that northerners had a homogeneous, albeit inferior, racial background, directly contradicted southern denunciations of the North's heterogeneity, but no one seemed to notice. In fact, many of the same critics who launched the most vehement attacks against the North's mixed population were also the leading proponents of the Norman versus Saxon interpretation of the Civil War. Like Ralph Waldo Emerson, it would seem, Confederate writers were not beholden to that "hobgoblin" of a foolish consistency.

This belief in southern racial superiority was not new. A certain segment of the southern gentry had been celebrating their noble Norman ancestry for generations. The coming of war, however, suddenly provided a new utility for these romantic racial ideas.[72] The Civil War, in this light, was simply the most recent manifestation of an age-old struggle between two bitterly hostile peoples. According to southern commentators, America, at the time of its colonization, had attracted two distinct groups of settlers, and the characteristics and motivations of these original groups had set the tone for the societies that would follow. "The higher classes of English, the Norman race, even Frenchmen and Italians, were of Roman ancestry—they, and the Huguenots, Jacobites, and Spaniards, all of Roman or Mediterranean ancestry, settled the Southern States of America. Hence the generosity, chivalry, and high sense of honor, of the Southern people," George Fitzhugh believed.[73] While the forebearers of southerners hailed from salubrious sunny climes which inculcated a natural civility and refinement, the ancestors of the Yankees, "the Saxons and Angles," came from "the cold and marshy regions of the North; where man is little more than a cold-blooded, amphibious biped."[74] The Norman settlers had been motivated by "romance, love of adventure, love of danger, honor, and religion," whereas "animal, brutish motives brought the amphibious men of the North to America."[75] With such divergent motivations and racial backgrounds, it was only natural that these diametrically opposed peoples would give birth to two hostile cultures. As Mississippi political theorist J. Quitman Moore explained, "Cavalier and Roundhead no longer designate parties, but *nations*, whose separate foundations were laid on Plymouth Rock and the banks of James river." Thus "the causes of the present convulsions in America" were rooted in "the irreconcilable character of the Courtier and Puritan."[76]

Having confidently asserted these racial links, amateur southern ethnologists found it an easy task to attribute all the negative stereotypes associated with the Saxons to their alleged descendents. Some critics even traced the tendencies of the Yankees back to their primordial German roots. The Yankees, William Falconer explained, "have ever been, and are still, impudent, ferocious, meddling, fanatical, half superstitious, and half religious, after their own peculiar fashion. . . . The highest type of Northern character is to be found in some of the German nations, whom we find to be steeped in fanaticism, and infidelity, and a certain sort of transcendental religion; always engaged in tumults, wars and revolutions, and ever have the worst and meanest governments in Europe."[77] By descending into chaos and fanaticism, northerners were simply following the path set by their progenitors. No great culture or lasting government could be constructed from such base materials.

Other southern writers, not willing to delve so deeply into the ancient past, instead linked present-day Yankee behavior to their more immediate English Puritan ancestors. It was from the Puritans that the Yankees had inherited their fanaticism, extreme intolerance, penchant for persecution, and drive for tyranny. Fleeing from religious persecution in their native country, the Puritans, who "were in their hearts tyrants," only sought a new location in which to set up a tyranny of their own. Thus, William Archer Cocke instructed his readers, the Yankees were and had always been "bigoted, intolerant and persecuting."[78] Likewise, Fitzhugh noted with pride how "favorably" the southerners' Norman roots "contrast with the Puritans of the North, who begun by persecuting people who would not conform to their faith, and are ending by having no faith at all—whose religious convictions were too strong in the beginning, and whose infidel convictions are now as obtrusive and intolerant as their former religious bigotry."[79]

This racial difference also helped to explain why slavery existed in the South but had never thrived in the North. While writers such as George Fitzhugh, William Falconer, J. Quitman Moore, and William Cocke took great pains to assure their readers that the conflict between the two sections was far more fundamental than simply a disagreement over slavery, they nevertheless believed that the presence or absence of slavery, though not the direct cause of strife, was a telling indication of white racial difference. "I yet do not agree that *slavery per se* was at the bottom of this dissimilarity and variance," Falconer maintained. Instead, he argued that the distribution of North American slavery was "the result of other and higher differences, having their beginning far back in the annals of time." Conveniently ignoring the presence of transplanted northern slaveholders in their own midst, these writers declared that northerners were now, and had always been, racially incapable of holding or controlling slaves. They lacked the temperament, patience, benevolence, wisdom, and commanding presence to manage them. Slavery simply "did not nominally belong to them, or that latitude," and any subsequent moral or religious qualms were merely rationalizations designed to conceal northern racial inadequacies.[80]

The rise of "isms" and the increasing instability in the North were not aberrations, but rather the inevitable course of any civilization founded by such people. According to these southern ethnologists, when compared to the noble and native southerner, northerners were "ethnologically deficient," neither knowing "how to conduct good government among themselves, nor how to deport themselves as a people, towards another people." In surveying the whole of northern culture and character, Falçoner concluded that "we have then, to treat them to some extent, as an *inferior race*."[81]

The Norman versus Saxon dichotomy enjoyed a certain degree of popularity during the initial years of the war.[82] Its attractiveness as an explanation for northern behavior rested primarily on its simplicity, which more than made up for its inaccuracy. These alleged racial differences neatly explained all the evils of northern society and recast the complicated issues and emotions surrounding the war into a basic primal struggle. The Civil War, in this view, was "*a contest for the supremacy of race*" between "Norman and Saxon— Cavalier and Puritan" that would once and for all answer the "unsettled question on this continent."[83] The divide between northerners and southerners was fundamental, and the conflict between them inevitable. For, as George Fitzhugh explained matter-of-factly in September 1861, "People of different races, or different national origin [like northerners and southerners], always hate each other, and fight each other, too, if they can get a chance, simply because it is natural to do so."[84] Although fanciful and often contradictory, the southern critique of Yankee "character" offered a compelling and all-encompassing explanation for the downfall of northern society and the rise of sectional tensions. Such arguments offered a measure of certainty to a people confronted with the prospect of a long and bloody war against their former countrymen.

Despite these profound differences, had the Yankees been content to keep their degraded culture to themselves, conflict might have been postponed. For southerners, the fanaticism of the North would have been simply a cautionary tale, something to be studied and pitied, certainly—but not feared. However, northerners had repeatedly demonstrated their determination to export their fanatical notions across the Mason-Dixon Line and thus directly threaten the tranquility and sanctity of the South. If the "isms" of the North were the symptoms, and northern religion, education, and character were the sources of disease, then northern literature was the primary means of infection. Through their print literature northern fanatics had unleashed their dangerous ideas—that "most nefarious of the products of a prolific source of evil"—on an unsuspecting reading public.[85] Emblazoned on the pages of innumerable pamphlets, surreptitiously placed within the columns of newspapers and periodicals, and, worse still, carefully hidden within seemingly innocent children's textbooks, northern fanaticism sought to infect southern readers. Constantly barraged by fanatical northern notions, it was only a matter of time, southern thinkers warned, before these foreign ideas began to take root in southern soil.

Confederate critics used the term "literature" in its broadest possible sense, encompassing all exportable facets of northern culture high and low, including books, novels, pamphlets, histories, sermons, lectures, poetry, music, drama, fine arts, scientific papers, medical journals, religious tracts, newspapers, periodicals, and textbooks. All these forms of literature could, and in the opinion of many southern critics, did serve as carriers of the contagion that had corrupted northern society and now threatened to do the same in the South. Employing literature as a weapon, northern writers and editors had used their print monopoly to launch an all-out assault on southern values and institutions. Instead of the binding cultural force that it might have been, American literature had been "perverted from its good offices, drawn away from its duties" to become "a ready instrument of discord for the use of the agitator."[86] "Literature ought not to be sectional," the *New Orleans Crescent* lamented, "but the North has made it so."[87]

To make matters worse, southern exposure to these agents of infection was far from casual. Through the mail and a network of northern booksellers, subscription agents, clergymen, and teachers, "our land has been deluged with Northern periodicals," one southern woman grumbled in a letter to *Southern Field and Fireside*.[88] "The post-office has become the vilest nuisance," George Fitzhugh agreed in March 1861. "It does little more than transport and infest the South with Yankee lying circulars, Yankee lottery schemes, Yankee pictorial papers and reviews, and Yankee gift-books" as part of an insidious campaign to "swindle, demoralize, sensualize, and abolitionize the South."[89] Even so ardent a cultural nationalist as Atticus Haygood found himself unable to escape from the pervasiveness of this "foreign" literature. In his own "not very large library . . . the proportion of Southern to Northern and English books, is about 10 to 100. This is not choice, but dire necessity," he observed gloomily. "Some of these books, such as our circumstances render indispensable to us, are sadly defiled with abolitionism. No Southern author has yet supplied their place. God speed the day when they can!"[90]

Throughout the entire war, but especially at its beginning, Confederate writers and editors bombarded their readers with dire warnings about the dangers that Yankee literature posed to themselves, their children, and their nation. As Professor A. B. Stark cautioned his audience of young ladies from the Port Gibson Collegiate Academy, excepting "a few histories and a few short poems, all Northern literature is full of the poison of fanaticism, and ought to be hurried away with palpitating heart into the pit that shall swallow all that is false and vicious."[91] Confederate critics attacked northern literature on a number of different levels simultaneously. Focusing on content, style, and taste, they exposed the many dangers that lay concealed beneath attractive covers and elegant print. Breaking northern literature down into its constituent parts, Confederate critics excoriated northern periodicals, books, histories, and textbooks in turn, stripping away their deceptive veneer to reveal a rotten core.

NORTHERN PERIODICALS AND NEWSPAPERS were of particular concern. The power of the press, Confederate writers warned, could not be overestimated. "The tone of the public mind is at this era of the world's history almost entirely directed by the periodical press," *De Bow's Review* noted in December 1860. Indeed, in the North, these "immense newspaper establishments have become almost a ruling power."[92] With northern periodicals and newspapers now actively employing this awesome might against southern interests, it was madness, Confederate critics implored, to continue to patronize and ingest their falsehoods. Northern periodicals like *Harper's Weekly*, *Frank Leslie's Illustrated Newspaper*, Bonner's *Ledger*, *Godey's Lady's Book*, the

Home Journal, and *Peterson's Ladies' National Magazine* enjoyed large circulations in the South while at the same time espousing increasingly antisouthern views, especially in the wake of secession. C. M. Irwin and Samuel Boykin, the new editors and proprietors of the struggling Macon-based Baptist weekly, *Christian Index*, admonished their readers to remember "that the Northern periodicals which many of you have been supporting have all turned against you." With the true sentiments of the northern press now fully revealed by the secession crisis, they hoped that southerners would "make up [their] minds at once" and shift their patronage to native publications, particularly "a Southern and a Georgian enterprise" like the *Christian Index*.[93]

But even apart from the recent hostilities, northern periodicals simply were unsuited to a southern audience, critics contended. Whatever their merits, northern magazines and newspapers spoke to the realities of northern society and, as such, they had little relevance for southerners. Particularly when it came to agricultural literature, the exasperated editor of the *Southern Cultivator* argued, northern journals, though "excellent papers in their way, and worth many times their cost to those to whose meridian they are adapted," were "entirely *foreign to our circumstances and wants*." With its unique system of commercial agriculture based upon slavery, "*the South must look at home*" for such literature.[94] What held true for southern agriculture also applied to the other branches of periodical literature. The stark divide between northern and southern cultures and the increasing animosity between them rendered northern literature incompatible with Confederate tastes and development. "It seems to us that the radical difference" between northern and southern "political, moral and religious sentiments ought to prevent the Southern people from bestowing their patronage upon Northern publications," editor I. N. Davis of the *Southern Literary Companion* declared in words echoed by nearly every southern editor during the secession winter. "Every idea which [northerners] advance and every sentiment which they express are tinged with their peculiar views."[95]

The most "peculiar" views to be found in the pages of northern periodicals of course related to slavery. Through "the frenzied witchery of Abolition Editors," the North had been thoroughly abolitionized and an irrational hatred of southerners had been implanted in the heart of every "New England boy." But even more distressing was the fact that southerners had "freely extended" their support to these same northern periodicals whose "every column was charged with poison for our children and our servants, and whose every issue was filled with insult and falsehood."[96] In this self-destructive "rage after foreign productions," southerners unthinkingly had sent "their money away from home to patronize those who are inimical to their institutions and unfriendly to their best interests."[97]

Abolitionism, be it subtle or overt, was the most serious charge leveled against northern periodical literature, but it was not the only one. In their campaign to break the South's dependence on northern periodicals, critics attacked the triviality and sensationalism of the northern press nearly as often as they condemned it for crusading against slavery. The trashy fiction, lowbrow humor, gossip columns, and lurid crime stories featured regularly in northern papers and magazines degraded the taste and undermined the morals of southern society, these critics charged.[98] As one reviewer in *De Bow's Review* complained, "the Harpers and Leslies, the Bonners and Godeys, have swamped our reading community with deleterious trash, unworthy of perusal, and obnoxious in sentiment."[99] Atticus Haygood likewise blamed the "humbugging Bonner and his 'Ledger,'" *Frank Leslie's* "exhibit of buffoonery, prize-fights and 'horrible murders,'" as well as the *New York Tribune*, *New York Times*, "and many others," for rendering "the *Union of our Fathers* no fit place for a Southerner to live."[100]

Resentful of the public's appetite for such trash over struggling southern periodicals of superior merit, some Confederate editors also directed their barbs at southern readers. Dripping with sarcasm, the acting editor of the esteemed *Southern Literary Messenger* threatened to give the reading public (and especially the female reading public) what it apparently wanted, announcing that "arrangements have been made to combine in the *Messenger* all of the most trashy, contemptible and popular features" of northern pictorial journals:

We shall have nothing but pictures. We shall have nothing but the latest news and the fashions. Diagrams of baby clothes, worked slippers, edgings, frills, cuffs, capes, furbelows, furaboves, and indeed all of the most interior and intricate feminine fixings, shall be supplied in much profusion. We shall pay particular attention to wood-cuts, representing bonnets, cloaks, *basquines*, *robes de* all sorts, &c. We shall furnish every month not less than 1800 different photographic views of the proper way to do up the back hair. We shall devote eleven-ninths of each number to crochet work and fancy pin-cushions. Meantime we shall devote our entire space to riddles, charades, acrostics and questions in arithmetic. But the greater part of the magazine shall be given to little dabs of light literature *a la* Fanny Fern [and other frivolous northern writers]. . . . We shall, in a word, satisfy, and if possible satiate the depraved taste of Southern patriotism.[101]

Most editors, fearful of alienating their readers, refrained from making such direct accusations. But many genuinely believed that northern periodicals had degraded southern taste by catering to the baser human appetites and providing trivial amusements. Southern readers would have to be reeducated to appreciate the noble literature that Confederate writers and editors intended to provide them.

NORTHERN BOOKS WERE NO better. While Confederate cultural nationalists poured much of their vitriol on the mass-circulated middle and lowbrow periodicals of the North, they were no more impressed by the supposed accomplishments of northern high culture with its acclaimed authors, artists, and philosophers. Southerners, they argued, had been duped into accepting the literary merit of the North's celebrated writers. While they begrudgingly admitted the skill of a few northern authors, most often Cooper and Irving, Confederate critics adamantly maintained that the North had no more than its proportionate share of talent; to them, most northern writers were merely articulate spokesmen for fanatical causes whose status had been artificially inflated. While the power of the northern print industry assured that these authors enjoyed a wide circulation, and a network of sycophantic northern editors continued to laud their accomplishments, southerners, Confederate critics argued, needed to look beyond this propaganda and see these figures for who they really were.

Northern literary dominance had corrupted southern taste by providing false models for literary excellence. With its often overly elaborate language, its alternation between extreme sentimentality and lurid sensationalism, and, most of all, its questionable morality, northern literature, by virtue of its ubiquity, had lowered the standards of literature. As one columnist in *De Bow's Review* complained, "Time that should have been employed by our reading people in acquainting themselves with the literary treasures in which the English language so richly abounds, has been wasted in delving among the rubbish of the Yankee press."[102] Works of great literature, the *North Carolina University Magazine* informed its alumni, "do not excite the baser desires of the heart; but affect the generous principles of man; while many of the vaunted bards of the *favored* North, clothed in 'gilt and blue,' conceal beneath the tinsel rottenness and nourish within the seeds of moral degradation."[103]

Many of the North's most acclaimed and bestselling authors were also dyed-in-the-wool abolitionists who used their prominence to advance an anti-southern agenda. Blinded by northern assurances of the literary greatness of these works, southerners purchased and ingested the books of some of the South's most insidious enemies. "Our minds have been fed by the writings of a [E. D. E. N.] Southworth, [William Cullen] Bryant and [Henry Wadsworth] Longfellow, and many others who have leveled their keenest arrows at the South and its principles, while we have continued to pour gold into their ungrateful grasps," Mrs. B. M. Z. groused in *Southern Field and Fireside*.[104] According to the *Southern Home Journal*, "Southern Generosity" actively funded such abolitionist writers as Henry Ward Beecher, W. C. Bryant, William Godwin, John Greenleaf Whittier, George William Curtis, and "others of like ilk."[105] George Bagby of the *Southern Literary Messenger* took aim at Ralph Waldo Emerson, whose mind was "like a rag-picker's basket—full of all manner of trash" and whose books only served to "illustrate the utter worthlessness of the philosophy of free society." While Emerson never completely embraced the abolitionist movement, nevertheless his was precisely the kind of dangerous thinking that had led to the moral disintegration of northern society, Bagby charged. For the public good, he suggested that Emerson be placed in "perpetual confinement, with plenty of pens, ink and paper. Burn his writings as fast as they come from his table, and bury the writer quietly in the back yard of the prison as soon as he is dead. If, in early life, the speculative lobes of his brain had been eaten out with nitric acid, EMERSON would have made a better poet than any New England has yet given us. As it is, he is a moral nuisance. He ought to be abated by act of Congress, and his works suppressed."[106]

Of course, Harriet Beecher Stowe had a special place reserved for her on this southern enemies list. Since the publication of *Uncle Tom's Cabin* in 1852, southern writers and editors had conducted an unremitting campaign of condemnation against this most flagrant and famous example of northern literary abolitionism.[107] By 1861, however, southern critics were careful not to limit themselves to Stowe. They endeavored to expose all the South's literary foes, many of whom were far more subtle and therefore even more subversive. Nearly all of the alleged literary lights of the North, they argued, were by sentiment or action opposed to the institution of slavery and the South, and therefore must be stricken from Confederate libraries and bookshelves. By attacking the North's most prominent authors, Confederate critics hoped to shatter the myth of Yankee intellectual superiority and show southerners that "we have been not only dupes in politics and trade, but likewise dupes in literature." Recent political events had revealed the Yankees' "true character" and "now that the screen has been removed and the wires exposed, like an urchin let behind the scenes after a puppet show, we feel that we have been cheated by ingenious contrivance to get our pennies."[108]

LIKEWISE, THE APPROPRIATION OF American history by northern historians had long irritated southern observers, and now that separate nationality, and hence a separate history, had been formally achieved, it was also time to banish these skewed historical works. Yankee historians had advanced northern interests at the expense of the South and states' rights, Confederate critics charged. "From the very formation of the late Federal Union, [northern historians] began a systematic perversion of the facts of history, both in order to magnify their own merits and to enslave the South by falsely interpreting the constitutional compact entered into between the States."[109] Passing off assertion as historical fact, northerners had bent American history to their will. Always minimizing southern contributions and exaggerating northern accomplishments, these history writers actively perpetuated the myth of northern superiority and foisted a false history upon southerners.

In the hands of northern historians, the history of colonial America had become the glorious story of the New England Puritans. The founding of Jamestown and the growth of the southern colonies received barely a mention. It was not surprising, Madame V. E. W. M'Cord of Memphis complained, that early American history was full of Bradfords, Winthrops, Cottons, and Mathers, "whose names have [come] down to us in the shining pages of the histories" written by the very "descendants of that Puritan race of Plymouth Rock notoriety."[110] Likewise, southern critics resented northern accounts of the American Revolution that focused on the early events and battles in New England and virtually ignored southern contributions and sacrifices. One disgusted reviewer for the *Southern Literary Messenger* observed that a recent northern history book "takes up forty pages in describing the Pequod war, and [only] six in giving an account of the Southern campaigns of the revolution."[111] Significantly, most northern history books presented slavery as an aberration, placing the blame for its continued existence squarely on southern shoulders. Little mention was made of the fact that northern colonies also had permitted slavery and that much of the slave trade was carried out by northern merchants and northern ships. Nineteenth-century abolitionists, southern critics charged, had rewritten American history to suit their fanaticism.

In order to reclaim their true past and chronicle their new national history,

Confederates needed their own historians to counter the misrepresentations and half-truths of the Yankee version of American history. The necessity for such southern scholarship was immediate. Confederate historians and chroniclers were required not only to correct the historical record, but also to present the world with a true picture of southern society. The southern historian, the *North Carolina University Magazine* urged,

> has an honorable part to perform and one of the most delicate character, in ages to come his pages must set forth the excellencies of our institutions, the soundness of our principles and the success of our system: he will have to repel the slander and abuse of foes, shield the names of the departed from vile aspersion and award to each his due meed of praise. His volumes will have to replace those which deny our prowess, blacken our motives, strip us of the glories earned in the dark hours of the Revolution and on the plains of Mexico, and which even cast a reproach upon the fame of Washington.[112]

The injury inflicted upon the South by northern history was great, and it would take a concerted effort on the part of truehearted southern historians to undo the damage. While other northern books and periodicals were more transparently biased, northern history books cleverly concealed their sectional agendas behind dry scholarly text and assurances of historical truth. Southerners had to be wary of all of the products of northern pens, Confederate critics warned, for dangerous and foreign ideas had infiltrated even the most seemingly innocent and incorruptible of works.

MOST INSIDIOUS OF ALL was the Yankee textbook. Hostile to the South and its institutions, northern textbook authors and teachers worked to corrupt southern society from within, or so their critics charged. By neglecting the education of their children, southerners had foolishly "placed the education of the young—the moulding of thought and opinion—in the hands of our enemies" and permitted those most antagonistic to southern interests direct access to the minds of the rising generation.[113] Throughout the antebellum period, one Confederate writer complained, "there [had] been a disposition at the South to rank teaching among the *menial* employments, and hence fit for Yankees only." As a result, the South had been "overrun by Yankee teachers of every grade, from the professor down to the common-school teacher."[114] In schoolrooms, northern textbooks were ubiquitous and little was done to prevent dangerous ideas from seeping into southern minds.

While southern parents looked on, northern educators bombarded their children with carefully concealed anti-southern propaganda intended to destroy the southern way of life by striking at the young and impressionable.

Unlike much of Yankee culture, which traveled mainly through the mail, the dangers of northern education had been imported in person by the numerous northern teachers and tutors employed throughout the South. While northern authors and newspapermen had but distant contact with their southern readers, northern teachers, both secular and religious, journeyed deep into the heart of the South, bringing their heresies directly to southern children. "With the same cool impudence that Satan entered the garden of Eden, have Northern school-masters, ministers of the Gospel and Sunday-School teachers, been entering the abodes of peace and quietness at the South," one Confederate "Octogenarian" complained in the early days of 1861.[115] Looking back on the antebellum years, Confederate cultural nationalists had no doubt that northern teachers had "labored diligently to pervert the minds of the young" and that "the great and prevailing vice in our [educational] system . . . has been and is now, to a great extent, *Yankeeism*."[116]

Even otherwise well-meaning northern teachers could not help but spread the sentiments of their culture. They simply could not be trusted. As editor Charles Wallace Howard of the *Southern Cultivator* explained, "even among the good, well-educated and well-principled Northern female teachers who have come among us, their early habits of thought have been so different from our own on many subjects, particularly the subject of slavery, that their influence over their pupils has been, perhaps unconsciously to them, to unsettle their minds and unnecessarily disturb them as to a condition of things which we believe to be right."[117] Northern teachers were foreigners, instilled with foreign sympathies, and as such, were innately unsuited to educate southern children. "If the South is determined upon one thing more than another, it is never again to entrust the education of its children to Yankee teachers," editor George Bagby declared after hostilities had commenced. "The subjugation of the mind to that vicious system of pernicious principles, which is summed up in the word 'Abolitionism,' is far more to be dreaded than the subjugation of the soil by force of arms."[118]

The hiring of northern teachers and the even more "suicidal" practice of sending children off to northern schools not only exposed southern sons and daughters to the evils of northern culture, but also greatly strengthened the perception of northern intellectual superiority and undercut efforts to encourage southerners to enter the teaching profession. With southern parents showing so little confidence in native southern education, southern schools struggled, and would-be southern teachers sought other means of employment. "So far was this miserable subserviency carried, that many seemed to consider it a species of heresy to contend that the Southern born could be educated upon Southern soil," President William Peck of the Greenville Masonic Female College in Georgia sadly observed. "And as for contending that the Southern teacher was the equal of the Northern; oh! that was abominable nonsense!"[119]

Thankfully for Confederate nationalists, secession and the coming of the war had cut off the supply of northern teachers and closed the doors of northern schools to southern scholars. With northern teachers fleeing the South for friendlier climes, Confederates now would have to turn to southern teachers and southern schools for their educational needs. Shut off from the North and now fully awakened to the dangers of northern culture, southerners, cultural nationalists hoped, had realized their preeminent responsibility to educate their own children and would no longer look to the North for guidance. "It would insult every true Southern man and woman to assert that such a foolish and ruinous policy will ever again be encouraged," Peck maintained. But it was certainly not to their credit that it took the outbreak of war and "no less a spirit of evil than ABRAHAM LINCOLN" to awaken southerners to their responsibilities and their own self-interest.[120]

While secession had purged the South of northern teachers and sealed the doors of northern schools, northern textbooks and school primers remained. "We have expelled the whole brood of [northern teachers] from our borders, and are fast eradicating the false sentiments and ideas which they introduced and labored so assiduously to impress upon the minds of the young," one Virginian wrote with satisfaction in the early summer of 1861. But the task was only half done. "They have left behind them a legacy of school books. Let us complete the work by banishing them, too, from our land."[121] Confederate children had to be protected "from the infectious character of those plague-spots which are so often found in our school books of Northern production," the newly installed associate editor of the Atlanta-based *Educational Repository and Family Monthly* demanded.[122] For the good of society as well as for the future of the southern nation, Confederates had to "cease to supply our schools with text-books from a section so corrupt and inimical as the so-called United States."[123]

In their campaign to free the South from northern textbooks and encourage the production of native southern ones, Confederate cultural nationalists found much to criticize in the content and tone of the most popular northern schoolbooks of the day. Such books were produced haphazardly with an eye toward making money, critics charged, and, as a result, their handsome appearances and well-executed illustrations masked serious defects and slipshod pedagogy. Apart from this inherent poor content quality, commentators also objected to the near total exclusion of all things southern. Northern-produced compendia of American literature, for instance, "seem[ed] studiously to ignore the *existence of Southern authorship* and *Literature*," griped President William A. Rogers of Georgia's Griffin Female College.[124] Likewise, American history textbooks from the North overwhelmingly focused on northern history and the development of northern society. Even the examples and place names in mathematical word problems always came from the North. Southern writers complained that the effect of these exclusions was to undermine southern confidence, retard the growth of southern culture, and bolster the myth of northern superiority. Through their biased selections, the northern "horde of compilers" had skewed these textbooks so dramatically as to render them irrelevant for southern children.[125]

The most serious charge leveled against northern schoolbooks was that they carried the seeds of northern fanaticism and secretly sought to subvert the principles of southern society—especially the institution of slavery. Northern authors, Confederate critics insisted, had launched a campaign of indoctrination against the children of the South. Through carefully selected examples, reading passages, and tone, northern textbooks corrupted the educational process by agitating sectional issues.[126] In his review of northern schoolbooks for the *Quarterly Review of the Methodist Episcopal Church, South*, President George E. Naff of Soule Female College in Murfreesboro, Tennessee, condemned northern educators for introducing "questions of a political, theological, or sectional character" into the sacrosanct realm of the classroom. Such an underhanded, dishonest, and cowardly attempt to "foist the peculiar dogmas of one section, sect, or party upon the unadvised and unsuspecting children of another, should be regarded as an act of gross fraud, a species of base cunning deserving the execration of every honest man," Naff thundered.[127] Tinctured by "the most dangerous and incendiary doctrines in morals and politics," these books consciously tried to contaminate "the youth of the South with the [same] foul miasma that taints the Northern atmosphere."[128]

For proof of this abolitionist educational conspiracy, southern parents were told to look no further than the most popular northern texts already in circulation. Within books in "every branch of education," from math, to history, to grammar, to even Latin, Confederate cultural nationalists felt the presence of the abolitionists. Antislavery sentiment was to be found in the "examples for analysis, short sentences in the primary readers," and, most flagrantly, in the "pictures, caricatures, chairs, whips, and all the parapher-nalia of cruelty" that abolitionists had "artfully inserted" into their school-books.[129] In his own field of moral philosophy, Professor R. H. Rivers com-plained that "for many years, the institutions of learning in the South have been without a suitable text-book. . . . Most of the philosophical writings of American authors are exhibitions of fanaticism, rather than of sound logic or scriptural truth, when they discuss the subject of slavery."[130] So diaboli-cal and pervasive had these abolitionist intrusions become, that only con-certed and immediate action by Confederate educators and parents could extract their poisons from southern schoolrooms. As G. B. Haygood, editor of the *Educational Repository and Family Monthly*, urged in May 1861, "The protection of our section, our children, and ourselves, so imperiously de-mand that the streams which flow through our schools should be thoroughly purified."[131]

Confederate critics generally preferred to attack the northern textbook in-dustry as a monolithic entity rather than taking the time and effort to cite spe-cific examples or identify specific texts. Some books were deemed so offen-sive and so blatantly corrupt, however, that they received special attention and served as archetypal examples of this Yankee conspiracy. Charles Dexter Cleveland's massive *Compendium of American Literature* was one such work. In the early days of the war, Cleveland's book, along with his earlier and slightly less offensive *Compendium of English Literature* and *English Litera-ture of the Nineteenth Century*, were singled out as flagrant examples of the northern attempt to spread the gospel of abolition in the guise of education. Originally published in Philadelphia in 1858, and significantly expanded the following year, Cleveland's book appeared to be what it claimed: a com-prehensive compendium of American literature. On careful examination of its 784 pages, however, southern critics found that not only were southern authors woefully underrepresented but that much of the book was filled with the writings of the North's most fanatical abolitionists.[132] Although Cleve-land's book had been a favorite target for southern critics since its pub-lication, the secession crisis inspired a pointed reexamination of his com-pendium. In the first half of 1861, *De Bow's Review, Home Circle*, the *North Carolina Journal of Education*, and the *Quarterly Review of the Methodist Episco-pal Church, South* all ran scathing reviews of Cleveland's work with the avowed purpose of alerting Confederate parents to the dangers of northern textbooks and the need to establish the Confederacy's intellectual and educational independence.[133]

Unlike most northern authors, his attackers conceded, Cleveland was at least forthright about his true motives.[134] Whereas the abolitionist agenda of most northern schoolbooks was implicit and subtle, the "virulent Abolition character" of this book was so blatant "no unbiased mind" could miss that Cleveland's "leading motive . . . was the dissemination of the author's own peculiar sentiments . . . of cherished and uncompromising hatred to the domestic slavery of the American States."[135] Indeed, Cleveland proudly admitted in the preface to the 1859 edition that he had selected these particular passages in hopes of convincing Americans, and "especially the youth of my country," that "the founders of our Republic . . . were always and earnestly on the side of Freedom as opposed to Slavery; and that most of our wisest and best men and ablest writers—poets, essayists, historians, divines—down to the present day, have taken the same high Christian ground."[136]

With such an openly avowed purpose, Cleveland's book was an easy target for southern cultural nationalists. "We open 'American Literature;' and lo! the death's-head and cross-bones, the sweeping broadside, the haggard-visaged pirates, with pike and cutlass, are upon us!" Naff exclaimed. "The spirit of John Brown hovers near. Here are his principles! Here are his abettors!"[137] The reviewer for *De Bow's Review* likewise suggested that the volume might be more accurately titled " 'A Compendium of Abolitionism.' "[138] These critics were appalled that Cleveland had inserted such abolitionist writers as James Wilson, John Quincy Adams, John Mitchell Mason, William E. Channing, William Jay, Albert Barnes, George B. Cheever, Richard Hildreth, Elizabeth Margaret Chandler, John G. Whittier, Andrew Peabody, Harriet Beecher Stowe, Henry Ward Beecher, and many others of like ilk into the pantheon of American literature by placing them alongside true luminaries like Jefferson, Madison, Poe, Cooper, and Irving.[139]

So obvious was Cleveland's abolitionist agenda that Confederate critics had no fear that his book would gain widespread acceptance in the South. However, they warned that such a book was not an aberration, only the most clumsy example of a growing conspiracy. "That such a book as this can circulate in the South, is, of course, impossible," one Virginia educational reformer admitted. "But there are many others less open in their teachings, and, therefore, more to be dreaded."[140] Through their attack on Cleveland, Confederate critics and educators hoped to issue a wake-up call to their fellow southerners by showing them in the starkest possible terms the ever-present dangers of northern textbooks and the need to establish a pure educational literature of their own. At the conclusion of his thirteen-page indictment of Cleveland's work, George Naff implored all southerners "to be ever vigilant, ever on the alert for books that come from Northern book-makers and Northern press[es], and to frown down, write down, condemn and spurn every one containing this covert abolitionism and incendiarism. . . . Let us, by a proper watchfulness, defeat the diabolical designs of these unscrupulous fanatics, and, by a hearty support of our own literature, presses, and writers, do away with all dependency on those who would ruin us."[141]

BUT WHAT ABOUT THE damage already done? Having discredited northern teachers, rejected northern educational methods, and exposed the dangers of northern textbooks, Confederate writers attempted to assess the impact of these agents of fanaticism. The effect that northern textbooks and teachers had on southern students was difficult to determine, but all agreed that it must be unhealthy. Speculation concerning the damaging consequences of northern education was complicated by the fact that many of the most ardent southern cultural nationalists had themselves been taught by these same northern teachers and textbooks, and, in some cases, had even attended northern schools with no discernable harm. As William Peck mused in view of his own northern education:

> It is a subject of wonder to me that so many of those of the South, who were educated at the North, have become true and faithful citizens at home. . . . Day after day, for years, [the southerner] drew his learning from books tainted with abolitionism from preface to finis; hourly he heard the principles, laws and institutions of his home reviled, jeered, sneered and fleered at, made the laughing stock or scorn block of the learned or unlearned. . . . I do not exaggerate, but speak from personal knowledge; I passed through the ordeal of four years heat unscathed; for when I entered it I was past redemption, in the grievous sin of loving my own native South more than Yankee soil, and Yankee principles.[142]

His own personal experience notwithstanding, Peck and others agreed that they could not rely indefinitely on the personal fortitude of each southern child to resist the evils of northern culture. It certainly was of no benefit to the student to be continually bombarded with ideas antithetical to his religion, society, and culture, and it was only a matter of time, southern thinkers feared, before the fanatical ideas of the North began to take root. The ultimate survival of the new southern nation required that Confederates be "educated in the same principles, trained in the same ideas, inspired with the same sentiments" so as to become "thoroughly one in every thought and feeling and sympathy."[143] Clearly such a vital and weighty task could not be left in the hands of the South's enemies.

If many of the charges brought against northern literature seem vague, shallow, overgeneralized, and overstated, it is because they were. In truth, the Confederate attack on northern culture was more caricature than critique. Only rarely did Confederate critics direct their barbs at particular works or authors, preferring instead to indict Yankee culture in its entirety. When they did cite specific examples, only the most extreme, like Cleveland's anthology, would do. These flagrant cases were presented to southern readers as typical of the sentiments of the Yankee press. Indeed, the Confederate critique of northern culture was built primarily on forceful assertion rather than thoughtful analysis. With independence declared and war looming, this was no time for nuance or equivocation, and southern nationalists saw no need to indulge in subtlety. For instance, one writer told the readers of the *North Carolina Presbyterian* that the dangers of Yankee culture, and specifically "the influence of evil teachers," were simply "too well known through our country . . . to call for any investigation."[144] The political situation required absolute clarity and, as such, the case against the North was painted in the starkest possible terms.

Even if not particularly penetrating or original, the Confederate attack on northern culture served important purposes. Confederate critics may have been drawing upon longstanding complaints, but they had adapted them to new circumstances. The terrifying vision of Yankee fanaticism with which they bombarded southern readers made northern culture easier to vilify and dismiss, providing a cultural justification for secession and southern independence. The message was clear, making up in forcefulness what it lacked in accuracy. From podiums and pulpits, in pamphlets and periodicals, Confederate cultural nationalists demanded that the South be immediately purified, that "every vestige of Yankeeism . . . be purged away."[145]

In large part, this task of freeing the Confederacy from northern literature would fall on individual southern readers, and cultural nationalists in the days following secession reveled in the growing public sentiment against northern publications and those who purchased them. By May 1861, James Gardner, editor and owner of the *Weekly Constitutionalist* in Augusta, perceived "a general disposition on the part of our people to repudiate Northern literature."[146] Likewise, the *Columbus (Ga.) Times* was pleased to report "that the publications issued from Black Republican, Abolition establishments are fast losing their circulation in the South. Packages after packages are being returned."[147] The attack on northern literature seemed to be having the desired effect and now, with the assistance of the Union blockade, Confederate cultural nationalists hoped that southerners would cease to be "derelict in [their] duty" and would devote themselves wholeheartedly to ridding their land of pernicious foreign influences.[148]

The critique of northern culture served another important purpose as well. In cataloging the evils and deficiencies of northern literature, Confederate cultural nationalists constructed a foil against which the purity, originality, and distinctiveness of a future Confederate national literature could be judged. In effect, they established the parameters and requirements for Confederate intellectual independence, albeit in negative terms. The picture they painted of northern culture and literature, accurate or not, was the polar opposite of the culture that these nationalists intended to create. Therefore, it was less important that their critique present a fair or even truthful assessment of northern culture, than that it be useful in establishing what Confederate culture must not be.

DURING THE FIRST YEAR of the Confederacy's life, Confederate cultural nationalists constructed a two-pronged argument to convince the southern people of the need for intellectual independence. On the one hand, they offered the positive argument that true Confederate independence required an autonomous and vibrant southern culture. They maintained that until the South wrote and published its own books and taught its own children, it could not be a complete nation. The unfettered expression of the southern mind would reveal to the world the virtues of southern society, would serve to unite the Confederate people culturally, and would solidify their claims to nationhood. Confederate thinkers coupled this positive nationalist argument with a powerful attack on the corrosive influences of northern culture and literature. Inspired by the intense anti-northern sentiment brought on by the secession crisis and approaching war, Confederate cultural nationalists seized their opportunity to finally and forcefully awaken southerners to the cultural dangers surrounding them.

These two intertwined arguments—positive and negative—collectively constituted the conceptual basis for the Confederate struggle for intellectual independence. During the early days of the war, Confederate nationalists alerted the southern public to the massive project that lay before them. The nationalists' agenda was comprehensive and their mission clear. The South had to be freed from northern cultural dominance, and more importantly, it had to produce and support its own uniquely Confederate intellectual and literary culture. Now that the ultimate objective had been articulated and the rationale for the struggle provided, what remained was the daunting task of actually providing the Confederacy with its own print literature, written by native authors, published by native presses, and purchased by native readers —all while engaged in a devastating civil war.

PART TWO

We, as a Nation, Spring into Existence: 1861–1862

CHAPTER THREE

THE BIRTH OF CONFEDERATE LITERATURE

Breaking free from northern culture was only the first step. The task of actually producing and sustaining a native-born Confederate literature would prove far more difficult. The Confederacy lacked many of the basic material resources required to support a large-scale publishing industry. Practical printing needs such as paper, ink, typeface, presses, and the ability to maintain them were constantly and increasingly in short supply as the war progressed. With most of the able-bodied white men serving in the ranks, printers struggled with a lack of manpower. The unsettled condition of the Confederacy, combined with encroaching Union armies, the blockade, inflation, and unreliable mail service compounded the difficulties faced by publishers. Nevertheless, intrepid editors were determined that the Confederacy would have a literature, and resourceful publishers were equally determined to furnish the means necessary to provide it. "Now that the Gordian knot has been cut which has so long curbed the free flights of native genius . . . let us stand proudly forth, like Paul before Agrippa, and speak for ourselves, through the pure channels of a native and unshackled literature," *Southern Field and Fireside* cried.[1] Fully aware of the obstacles they faced, Confederate cultural nationalists eagerly undertook the challenge of presiding over the birth of a new national literature. There could be no half-measures or hesitation. Now that their dearest wishes had been answered, there also could be no excuses. As one subscriber to the *Educational Repository and Family*

Monthly declared in March 1861, "If in the present state of affairs we cannot be induced to make a better than *wordy* effort at literary emancipation, I think we had better have our ears bored to the Northern door-posts, and resign ourselves to perpetual subordination and dependence."[2]

The task before them was immense. There were "two grand divisions of literature, the literature of knowledge and the literature of power," Professor A. B. Stark explained to the readers of the *Home Circle*, and "both are needed to complete the sphere of our intellectual wants." The "literature of knowledge" included newspapers, periodicals, histories, encyclopedias, and "popular treatises of every kind." It was the "lower" and "easier to produce" of the two. It required "sound judgment, good memory, industrious research, and capacity for work," but not necessarily the "creative powers of imagination and pure reason." Stark likened the writer of such literature to a harvester in a field of blackberry bushes. "He must squat and gather the fruit, regardless of scratches and soiled hands and torn breeches. He cannot make fruit grow, but he can gather it; he cannot originate great thoughts, but he can put them into suitable forms for the use of the people." This literature of knowledge could be produced quickly, provided the proper patronage, and would serve to educate and refine both its readers and writers.[3]

A true southern "literature of power" would take more time to develop. It would be that "higher form of literature which influences the hearts and actions of men through the deepest agencies which teaches . . . by throwing our passions into peculiar channels, and determines the character of our lives mysteriously and radically by directing the course of our feelings." It was the exclusive domain of "true poets, whether they voice their thoughts in eloquent prose or in rhythmical verse." Unlike the literature of knowledge, the literature of power did not seek to "teach us any new fact," rather it brought "into the full light of consciousness feelings and thoughts that already exist in the heart and mind of every man."[4]

While his terminology was uniquely his own, Stark had hit upon a vital distinction that would remain at the heart of the struggle for Confederate intellectual independence from beginning to end. Confederates needed both an ephemeral and a transcendent literature to make their independence and nationality complete. The former was a pragmatic necessity, the latter a romantic nationalistic imperative. A native everyday literature would replace northern publications, free the South from dangerous influences, and establish southern self-sufficiency. It would contribute to cultural independence by forever ending the southern addiction to northern print literature. The romantic requirements for nationhood, however, could be realized only through the production of a transcendent and timeless literature. Stark alone termed this a "literature of power," but other cultural nationalists spoke of a "high," "refined," "polite," or "national" literature while signifying essentially the same thing. The "power" that such a literature was thought to possess was to force its way abroad and compel others to recognize its merits and the unique national character that flowed through it. It was the production of this higher type of literature, this exalted, nation-affirming literature, to which Confederates had to aspire and upon which the realization of their true nationality depended. Such a literature would dazzle the world with its originality, debunk the lies of northern fanatics, and forcefully and irrefutably demonstrate the virtues of southern slave society.

Cultural nationalists frankly recognized that the Confederacy was not yet prepared to produce its "literature of power." When it came to everyday literature, however, they were confident that "we can at once assume complete independence" by meeting the reading needs of Confederate citizens.[5] It was clear to all that the periodical press would be the engine driving this movement for Confederate intellectual independence, especially in the beginning. Periodicals had a number of distinct advantages. Unlike books, novels, textbooks, and schools, which would take time and money to create, periodicals could be produced and distributed quickly and cheaply. Nearly every southern town of any significance already had at least one newspaper press, and often several. There was nothing to prevent Confederate newspapers and periodicals from asserting their independence immediately and beginning the work of providing the Confederacy with its own literature. Equally important, there was now no excuse for the southern people not to support their own native papers and magazines. "We must have a periodical literature," the editor of the *Charleston Courier* demanded. "The need is great and it is felt. Forced from our dependence on the North, we must see to it, that we meet this pressing demand with cheerfulness, earnestness and liberality."[6] While cultural nationalists were certain that Confederate intellectual development would proceed rapidly now that southerners were free from northern interference, they conceded that this progress had to be made in stages. The establishment of a self-sufficient periodical press was the first. A well-edited and amply supported periodical literature would serve as the training ground to "prepare the way for more serious undertaking, both by disciplining Southern writers, and by preparing the people to appreciate *books made at home*."[7]

At the outbreak of the war, the South was not without periodicals and newspapers. In fact, the 1860 census reported that in the eleven southern states of the future Confederacy, there were 844 newspapers and periodicals with an annual production of 103,041,436 copies.[8] However, these numbers should not obscure the fact that many of these journals, and especially the literary publications, were poorly supported and managed to survive only on a day-to-day basis. Secession, it was hoped, would change all that, and Confederate periodicals devoted what little resources they had to meeting the new demands placed upon them. Although often on financially shaky ground, existing southern periodicals were well-positioned to take advantage of the changed conditions that separate nationality presented.

While all Confederate newspapers and periodicals, by the very nature of their existence, furthered the cause of Confederate intellectual independence, some served it more directly and forcefully than others. The Confederacy's daily papers as well as its small town weekly and tri-weekly papers were primarily and understandably concerned with reporting the news of the day, especially war news. In these exciting times, Confederate citizens craved every scrap of information, confirmed or not, that the papers could provide about battles and troop movements. While sympathetic to the cause of Confederate cultural nationalism, the editors of these publications did not have the time or column space to devote much attention to such matters. It was left then to the Confederacy's magazines, journals, and literary, educational, agricultural, scientific, and religious papers to actively advance the struggle for Confederate cultural autonomy, and they did so eagerly. While the dailies confined themselves to news items, casualty lists, and critiques of the management of the war, the weekly, monthly, and quarterly press provided longer essays, serialized fiction, political treatises, poetry, and reflective editorials.

The editors of these papers and magazines were fiercely and explicitly committed to the achievement of Confederate intellectual independence and saw themselves as contributing directly to the larger war effort. As such, they felt they had special claim to the patronage of southern readers and would-be, should-be subscribers. "Literary journals of a high order must be sustained at the South, if we would have an actual and not a merely nominal independence of the North," the acting editor of the esteemed *Southern Literary Messenger* argued, with not a little self-interest.[9] Weekly newspapers of lesser intellectual pedigree also had a crucial role to play. Before the war, southern families had relied on northern periodicals for most of their light reading and religious instruction. Now, however, the secular and religious "family" papers of the South would have to fulfill the recreational reading needs of an entire nation. "Whatever may be the results of the war, the time is far distant when *Southern* families generally will welcome to their homes *Northern* newspapers of *any* class," one such religious weekly reported with glee. These family papers contained light fiction, inspirational passages, poetry, sermons and denominational news (in the religious press), home tips, children's sections, agricultural advice, lengthy editorials, as well as summaries of the news of the day. They were designed to enlighten and improve southern home life, and their weekly visits were intended to "aid in the formation of the character of a family."[10] With such direct access to the home and the minds of the rising generation, it was vital that such literature be pure, instructive, and above all southern.

THE TWO MOST PRESTIGIOUS journals in the Confederacy were the *Southern Literary Messenger* and *De Bow's Review*. Published in Richmond and New Orleans respectively (although *De Bow's* would soon relocate its publication office to Charleston), these two journals were the standard bearers for high southern intellectual culture. Their monthly issues were impressively sized, ranging from 80 to 130 pages each, and as a consequence, they featured the lengthy articles, stories, and political treatises that the smaller weekly papers were simply unable to carry. Since its founding in 1834, the *Southern Literary Messenger* had actively sought to advance the cause of southern letters by encouraging and printing the work of native authors. While the *Messenger's* editors found themselves unable to avoid the political questions that dominated antebellum southern life, especially the issue of slavery, they had attempted to maintain an overtly literary character both in their editorial columns and in their selection of contributed pieces. With the ascension of the talented and fiery George W. Bagby to the editorship in 1860, however, the venerable journal took on a decidedly political and sectional tone. Following a very brief medical career, Bagby had made a name for himself as a newspaper correspondent and writer of humorous and satirical essays for various magazines, especially the *Southern Literary Messenger*. While previous editors had broached political issues with reluctance, the thirty-two-year-old Bagby saw no reason to differentiate between literary and political matters. An ardent southern nationalist, he did not hesitate to call for Virginia's secession and the establishment of a southern confederacy.[11] His primary aim, however, and the one that ran throughout the pages of his editorials, was the cause of southern literary and cultural independence. Bagby was determined that the South become its own nation with its own pure, enlightened, and indigenous literature, and that the *Southern Literary Messenger*, as the most respected literary journal in the South, take the lead in its creation.[12]

For his part, James Dunwoody Brownson De Bow had never shied away from political controversy. Since launching *De Bow's Review* in 1846, he had dedicated his journal to the development of southern agriculture, the defense of slavery, and especially the industrial, commercial, and manufacturing independence of the southern states. De Bow also sought to alert his readers to their intellectual, literary, and educational subservience to the North, and included southern fiction, poetry, history, and literary criticism in his issues. With his stable of contributors, including George Fitzhugh, J. Quitman Moore, and Dr. Samuel Cartwright, De Bow transformed his fledgling journal into the preeminent forum for southern political and proslavery thought. Not surprisingly, De Bow rejoiced at secession and vowed to continue the fight for southern, now Confederate, agricultural, commercial, industrial, and intellectual independence.[13]

While the *Southern Literary Messenger* and *De Bow's Review* were the two most esteemed southern journals, they were by no means the only ones fighting for Confederate intellectual independence during the early days of the war. Nor were they necessarily the most influential. The *Messenger* and *De Bow's* appealed almost exclusively to an elite group of highly educated southern readers, and as a consequence were not to be found in most southern homes.[14] Most readers lacked the time, interest, and fortitude necessary to parse the long and complex political arguments that appeared regularly in *De Bow's* or the intricacies of the *Southern Literary Messenger's* literary criticism. While these two journals did to some extent set the tone of Confederate intellectual discourse, they rarely had direct contact with the bulk of southern readers.

Other more middle-brow periodicals sought to cater to the literary needs of a more widespread audience.* *Southern Field and Fireside* was perhaps the

*A Note on Confederate Readership: Estimating readership for Confederate periodicals is tricky business. Subscription numbers are often unavailable or incomplete, and even when available, these figures are useful only to a point. It was common practice for multiple individuals and neighboring families to share subscriptions. Oftentimes, entire congregations would share a single subscription to a denominational paper or religious journal. Therefore, it is impossible to know how many readers each issue reached. The problem of estimating readership is greatly complicated by the realities of army life during the Civil War. Within the army, a single issue could be read by scores or even hundreds of men. Periodicals, especially the religious papers, sent thousands of free copies into the ranks, and this makes determining the actual readership of a paper impossible. Suffice it to say that readership was many times greater than subscription numbers indicate, especially during the war, and that even journals with relatively small subscription lists and print runs could reach a large number of Confederate readers and exert significant influence. For information on the subscription numbers of these periodicals, see the endnotes throughout this section.

best of the literary family papers at the start of the war. Printed weekly in Augusta, Georgia, *Southern Field and Fireside* was produced in a newspaper format of eight large pages. As the name implied, it focused on both entertainment and agriculture, and each issue contained a literary, agricultural, and horticultural section. The literary, however, was by far the primary emphasis. Founded in 1859, and owned by the cantankerous and politically powerful James Gardner, *Southern Field and Fireside* was explicitly dedicated to the creation and improvement of a uniquely southern literature. Under the literary editorship of James Nathan Ells at the time of secession, the paper eagerly printed native fiction and poetry alongside editorials denouncing southern intellectual dependence.[15]

Other literary papers included the *Southern Literary Companion* of Newnan, Georgia, edited and owned by blind former attorney, I. N. Davis Sr., the *Southern Home Journal* of Union Springs, Alabama, and the *Georgia Literary and Temperance Crusader* of Atlanta.[16] More sizable were the two "ladies' books" of the South: the Methodist *Home Circle* of Nashville and *The Aurora: A Southern Literary Magazine* of Memphis.[17] These monthly journals printed fiction, poetry, pedagogical essays, religious literature, as well as home and garden items. Though advertised as "ladies' magazines," there was little that was strictly feminine about the contents and much that actively promoted southern cultural nationalism.

At the time of its birth, the Confederacy also had a number of educational journals. Although often poorly supported, these periodicals continued to speak for the cause of education reform and southern educational independence. Their primary concern remained the desperate need for native southern textbooks and native southern teachers. The most important of these journals was undoubtedly the *North Carolina Journal of Education*. Published monthly in Greensboro, North Carolina, and edited by J. D. Campbell, the *Journal* ostensibly spoke for the interests of North Carolina educators and served as the mouthpiece of the State Educational Association of North Carolina and the Superintendent of North Carolina schools, Calvin H. Wiley. In a larger sense, however, the *Journal* represented the preeminent pedagogical forum in the Confederacy and the staunchest advocate for Confederate educational independence. Despite its title, it enjoyed a circulation throughout all the southern states, and it attempted to speak for all southern teachers.[18] Other education journals of note included the Methodist-affiliated *Educational Repository and Family Monthly* from Atlanta, the monthly *Southern Teacher* from Montgomery, and the weekly *Educational Journal* from Forsyth, Georgia.[19] There were also a few university magazines, such as the *North*

Carolina University Magazine and the *Virginia University Magazine*, but these were quickly discontinued when most of the men of the colleges marched off to war.

Although seemingly an unlikely candidate, the *Southern Cultivator* also played a major role in the campaign for Confederate intellectual independence. The premier agricultural magazine in the South, the *Cultivator* sought to address all issues that affected the lives of southern planters including politics, education, and literature. Thus, alongside lengthy articles on proper manure techniques, Dennis Redmond and his fellow editor Charles Wallace Howard ran columns devoted to the management of the war, the need for southern literature, and the evils of northern textbooks. The *Cultivator* dedicated a surprising amount of space to the publication of original southern poetry, usually war-related. Founded in 1843, and published monthly in Augusta, the *Southern Cultivator* was the Confederacy's oldest, strongest, and intellectually most impressive agricultural journal.[20]

Other miscellaneous secular periodicals contributed to the struggle for Confederate intellectual independence as well. A number of weekly general newspapers ostensibly dedicated to war news and politics also took a strong interest in the fostering of native southern literature. Many of these papers were weekly summations of their daily versions, but they also included longer, more reflective editorials on broader cultural issues. The *Weekly Constitutionalist* is a good example. Owned by James Gardner, it was composed primarily of stories from the previous week's issues of the Augusta *Constitutionalist*, Gardner's daily paper. But he also used the weekly edition to campaign for Confederate cultural self-sufficiency, both in his own editorials and through his selections of reprinted articles from other southern literary journals. Not coincidentally, Gardner's ownership of *Southern Field and Fireside* greatly contributed to his personal desire to bring attention to the cause.

The Confederacy also contained a number of medical journals, including the *New Orleans Medical and Surgical Journal*, the *Savannah Journal of Medicine*, and the *Southern Medical and Surgical Journal* in Augusta. Straightforward and technical, they contained a mix of original and reprinted material. However, with secession, the journals' editors and contributors voiced an increasing desire to foster an expressly southern medical and scientific community with its own native literature.[21]

Lastly, the vital role of the southern religious press in the struggle for Confederate intellectual independence must be recognized. Both in its reach and sheer volume, the religious press dwarfed its secular counterpart. Like the secular journals, religious periodicals ran the gamut from highbrow monthly and quarterly reviews, to middlebrow weekly family newspapers, to specialized journals dedicated to particular issues. Unlike the secular press, however, the religious papers were further subdivided by denomination. Denominational newspapers and magazines primarily served as official organs for a region, synod, or diocese. They contained denominational news, reported on conventions and meetings, reprinted important sermons, and covered theological debates. In effect, they bound the scattered churches of the South into religious communities.[22] Church members were expected and indeed implored to support their own denominational papers, and congregations often had collective subscriptions. At the same time, these papers sought to be all-in-one family newspapers. Although primarily concerned with religious and denominational matters, they did not neglect the secular world, and they usually carried some social and political commentary, poetry, short fiction, as well as news summaries of the week's events, especially during the war. As one writer to the *Southern Presbyterian* explained, "We think a religious paper ought to be pretty nearly something like a real, good Christian—a fair reflection of Christian life and character as it ought to be here upon earth—*religious in everything*, but not *all* religion."[23] What was more, all these papers recognized the need for Confederate intellectual independence and actively fought for its attainment. Now free from the North, the South would have to produce its own religious as well as secular literature, and these denominational papers were determined to provide it.

The Presbyterians offered a range of periodicals designed to meet the religious, intellectual, and entertainment needs of their brethren. The most respected Presbyterian journal, and for that matter, the most respected southern religious journal, was the *Southern Presbyterian Review*. Published quarterly in Columbia, South Carolina, and ranging from 150 to over 200 pages in some issues, the *Review* was edited by a distinguished association of Presbyterian ministers. It published notable sermons and essays from eminent Presbyterian divines such as James H. Thornwell and Benjamin Morgan Palmer. It carried on spirited denominational and sectional debates with other prominent northern religious journals, especially the *Princeton Review*. During the secession crisis and war, it also sought to bring a larger religious perspective to the meaning of the conflict and to elucidate God's purposes for the Confederacy. It generally shied away from commenting on day-to-day political and military affairs, however, and instead focused on broader, more intellectual issues.[24]

Given its lofty character, the *Review* failed to attract much of a readership beyond an elite group of clergymen and religious scholars, even among Presbyterians. The more general Presbyterian reader was better served by the weekly family newspapers. The best Presbyterian weeklies were the *Southern Presbyterian* in Columbia, the *North Carolina Presbyterian* in Fayetteville, the *Central Presbyterian* in Richmond, and the *Christian Observer*, soon to be relocated to Richmond.[25] These four papers provided their readers with a wealth of thoughtful religious, social, and political commentary, and, taken as a whole, were the most broadly intellectual of the Confederate religious newspapers.[26]

The Methodists, for their part, matched the Presbyterians publication for publication. They too had a respected and intellectually impressive quarterly, practically, if unimaginatively, titled the *Quarterly Review of the Methodist Episcopal Church, South*. Published in Nashville and edited by T. O. Summers, the *Quarterly Review* was not as strictly theological as its Presbyterian counterpart, containing articles on education reform, Shakespeare, and Thomas Carlyle in addition to reprinted sermons and denominational matters. Like the *Southern Presbyterian Review*, on which it was modeled, the *Quarterly Review* was intended for the clergy and religiously minded intellectuals. The Methodist Church also supported a host of weekly family papers. It developed a virtual franchise of *Christian Advocate* weeklies throughout the southern states including the *Southern Christian Advocate* in Charleston, the *Richmond Christian Advocate*, the *North Carolina Christian Advocate* in Raleigh, and the *Christian Advocate* in Memphis.[27] These papers were regionally based and primarily focused on denominational matters, though they also contained original poetry and occasional social and literary commentary. The Methodists also produced more specialized journals like their *Sunday-School Visitor* as well as the aforementioned *Home Circle* and the *Educational Repository and Family Monthly*.[28]

Although their church membership was smaller than either the Presbyterians or the Methodists, southern Episcopalians boasted some impressive periodicals of their own. Their premier organ was the monthly *Southern Episcopalian* published in Charleston. Like its sister journals, the *Southern Presbyterian Review* and the *Quarterly Review of the Methodist Episcopal Church, South*, the *Southern Episcopalian* aimed above the heads of many readers, and, despite its often excellent articles, struggled to support itself. The Episcopalians had weekly papers as well. The *Church Intelligencer* in Raleigh was the accredited organ of the bishops of Texas, Louisiana, Mississippi, Alabama, Florida, Georgia, South Carolina, North Carolina, Tennessee, the missionary bishop of the South-West, and the University of the South in Sewanee, Tennessee. Edited by T. S. W. Mott, the *Intelligencer* was not intended to be "a religious journal *exclusively*, but a scientific and literary one" as well, publishing short fiction pieces, original poetry, literary criticism, and general book reviews in addition to its religious articles.[29] The other Episcopalian weekly paper of note was the *Southern Churchman*. Printed in Alexandria at the start of the war but soon relocated to Richmond, the *Churchman*, under the editorship of D. Francis Sprigg, contained a mix of religious, secular, and literary material.[30]

Not to be outdone, the Baptists produced a large number of weekly newspapers befitting the size of their denomination in the South. Taken as a whole, the Baptist papers were the most strictly religious of the Confederate denominational papers, often eschewing worldly and political matters. There were exceptions, however. The Atlanta-based *Landmark Banner and Cherokee Baptist*, renamed the *Banner and Baptist* in July 1861, became increasingly literary-minded as the war progressed. Some other important Baptist weeklies included the *Biblical Recorder* in Raleigh, the *Christian Index* in Macon, and the *Religious Herald* in Richmond.[31] *Dayton's Monthly* was the Baptist answer to the Methodists' *Home Circle*. Published in Nashville, the magazine, as its title suggested, was owned and edited by A. C. Dayton, and it contained a mix of religion, poetry, moral lessens, and educational articles.

THIS SURVEY OF EARLY Confederate periodicals is by no means complete. There were other smaller literary papers, many other general weekly papers, and scores of other religious denominational papers. However, the journals listed here represent the most important publications in terms of setting the intellectual tone for the Confederacy and guiding the struggle for cultural autonomy. Significantly, most of these periodicals either enjoyed or aspired to national circulation within the Confederacy. They spoke, or attempted to speak, to the entire country. Although their foci and audiences differed, these periodicals were firmly committed to the cause of Confederate intellectual independence and they were determined to provide their readers with a uniquely southern literature, be it literary, educational, agricultural, scientific, or religious.

At the outbreak of war, Confederate periodicals not only shared common aspirations, but also suffered from common difficulties. Separation from the North may have opened new possibilities and given cultural nationalists new reasons for hope, but it also created some very real logistical obstacles. The onset of war added further challenges, and many periodicals and publishers who had barely managed to scrape by during the antebellum years found themselves unable to adapt. Having finally attained some degree of stability for the *Educational Repository and Family Monthly*, editor W. H. C. Price worried about his magazine's fate on the eve of Georgia's secession: "the future was beginning to brighten up before us; our feet . . . becoming firmly fixed, when the political horizon became so suddenly overcast. As we now write, we cannot see our way clearly for the coming year. . . . All we can do is to walk steadily and steadfastly on, with stout heart, working hands, and unflinching faith in God."[32]

Secession had cut off southern readers from northern publishers, but it also had cut off southern publishers from northern printing supplies. At the beginning of the war, the Confederacy lacked many of the basic resources necessary to carry on a campaign for literary self-sufficiency. While in the short term they could rely on their existing stocks of northern-produced paper, ink, typeface, and printing presses, it was apparent to all that Confederates would need not only to write their own literature, but also find a means of mass producing it.

The supply of paper remained a constant worry for Confederate publishers and largely dictated the size, shape, frequency, and appearance of Confederate publications. The South did have a few paper mills of its own at the start of the war, and more would be built during the Confederacy's short life, but they never were able to keep up with demand, either in terms of quantity or quality. Except for those fortunate few blessed with a reliable local paper mill, Confederate publishers were at the mercy of distant suppliers, unreliable transportation systems, and, later, invading Union armies when it came to securing paper for their next issue. Periodicals were often forced to delay printing, reduce their size, or limit the frequency of publication. To conserve paper, editors packed as much as they could onto each page by using smaller typeface, much to the chagrin of contemporary readers and future historians. In nearly all cases, the physical appearance of Confederate periodicals suffered as a result of substandard paper. Nevertheless, many editors joined *Southern Field and Fireside* in pledging that even if "the robe worn by our welcomed weekly visitor be less brilliant for a season, as warm a heart as ever will claim a place around the Southern fireside."[33] Ink, too, was hard to obtain. Although a number of ink producers like Taylor & Baptist in Richmond sprang up in the wake of secession and publishers devised ingenious methods of concocting their own out of whatever happened to be lying around, southern-made ink was much inferior to what printers were used to working with and Confederate print quality suffered seriously as a result.[34]

Pictures and engravings were among the first things sacrificed following secession. By the mid-nineteenth century, American magazines and newspapers routinely provided intricate engravings and even color picture plates in their issues. Illustrated newspapers, most notably *Harper's* and *Frank Leslie's*, enjoyed large and ever-growing circulations in the North and South in the years leading up to the war. Southern periodicals, too, had included pictures, but these were almost always commissioned from northern engravers. Consequently, when war came, southern publishers could not provide the detailed images that their readers had come to expect. As W. S. Perry, the general subscription agent for *The Aurora* noted in May 1861, "Our patrons will see that we have no embellishments in the present number, and we presume that it is unnecessary for us to assign the reason." He promised, however, that publishers Hutton & Freligh were in the process of obtaining their own engravers "from whom we will be enabled to obtain anything in that line hereafter."[35] While a number of Confederate publishers did manage to establish their own engraving operations and the Confederacy would see the advent of its own illustrated newspapers and magazines, inferior paper and ink prevented their pictures from ever approaching the quality or intricacy that had become the standard in the North.

An even more serious problem was the Confederacy's lack of printing press manufacturers and type foundries. While some publishers, like the enterprising Evans & Cogswell in South Carolina, had the foresight to begin frantically importing printing presses and binders immediately following secession, most printers had to rely on their old and jury-rigged presses for the duration of the war.[36] Typeface wore out with use, and Confederate printers were forced to either smuggle new type through the blockade at great expense or use other less popular letters in place of broken ones. Clearly, these stopgap measures could not continue if the Confederacy hoped to achieve complete self-sufficiency. For this reason, the celebration of the Confederacy's first stereotyped edition of the New Testament, printed in Nashville in the fall of 1861, was somewhat muted. Although, for the first time, the printing plates had been manufactured in the South, the type for the plates had to be smuggled in from Philadelphia.[37]

Of course, the limited supply of paper, ink, presses, type, and other printing necessities meant that prices for these items increased dramatically. This problem would only get worse with time, especially with the rapid depreciation of Confederate currency in the later years of the war. Subscription-dependent periodicals particularly suffered as a result. Unable to predict price increases, publishers were locked into outdated subscription rates for the duration of the term. Although they would increase subscription prices and reduce the length of subscription periods, especially later in the war, periodical publishers were never able to keep up with inflation.

Beyond the shortages of printing supplies, the war presented other difficulties for Confederate publishers and periodicals. For those rare southern journals of national (U.S.) circulation, namely the *Southern Literary Messenger* and *De Bow's Review*, secession and their support for it had cost them a significant number of subscribers.[38] More generally, however, secession cost southern newspapers and magazines the bulk of their advertising revenue. Even though northerners did not often read southern periodicals, they did advertise heavily in their pages, and southern publishers had come to depend upon this vital, if foreign, source of funds. As sectional tensions mounted, northern advertisers began to withdraw their support, and, with secession, northern money stopped flowing entirely. Between January and May of 1861, for instance, the advertising section of the *Southern Teacher* was reduced by a third, and other journals found their ad space shrunken to almost nothing.[39] Although Confederate businesses, booksellers, and manufacturers would provide some advertising revenue, they were never able to fill the gap left by the absence of northern money.

The most significant wartime obstacle for publishers, however, apart from chronic supply shortages and the always erratic Confederate mail service, was a lack of manpower. With so many of the South's white able-bodied males in military service, Confederate publishers and periodicals struggled to find experienced printers, typesetters, engravers, editors, and assistants. In some cases, as with the *North Carolina University Magazine*, publication had to be suspended completely when the staff and student body marched off to war.[40] Others were left to make do with insufficient staffs composed of the elderly, infirm, and inexperienced.

Often the most fervent of Confederate nationalists, some southern editors could not resist the call of battle themselves. "From our own SOUTHERN FIELD AND FIRESIDE a gallant spirit goes forth to prove in another arena, and seal, if Heaven so decree, with his life blood, his devotion to the best interests of the South," James Gardner wrote of departing literary editor James Ells. "He resigns the pen for the sword."[41] Likewise, by May 1861, George Bagby found Richmond to be "in such a fever of excitement that it is impossible for one endowed with human sensibilities not to participate in it."[42] It came as no surprise when the *Southern Literary Messenger* announced a month later that its editor had "left 'for the wars.' "[43] Like Bagby, W. H. C. Price, editor of the *Educational Repository and Family Monthly*, found himself so "shifted from my moorings" by recent political events that he was "unable any longer to do any kind of justice to the editorship of so important a journal as ours."[44] For his part, James De Bow was too old to enter the ranks, but he did immediately offer his services to the Confederate Government. Working for the Treasury Department, De Bow moved to Richmond in order to organize the Confederate Produce Loan Agency. Meanwhile, his magazine relocated its printing establishment to Charleston with his brother, B. F. De Bow, placed in charge of the business department. Still, James De Bow never ceased to be the editor of *De Bow's Review*, and although his attention may have been divided, he continued to write his fiery editorials and champion the cause of Confederate intellectual and economic independence.[45] While this departure of experienced editors certainly posed a problem for Confederate periodicals at the beginning of the war, it should be noted that many of these soldier-editors returned to their desks after a brief taste of life in the field. Due to his "infirm health," Bagby was discharged from the army in September 1861, and James Ells later resumed his literary duties, though for the *Banner and Baptist*.[46] Still, the war did significantly reduce editorial and printing staffs, made hiring new employees difficult, and certainly distracted the attentions of those who remained.

GIVEN THESE MANY OBSTACLES, it is no surprise that Confederate periodicals struggled to maintain their size, quality, and publishing schedules. A significant number of southern journals failed to adapt to the changed conditions caused by secession and war and would suspend publication before the end of 1861. For those who survived, their ability to endure despite these hardships became a badge of honor, inspiring a renewed commitment to the cause of Confederate intellectual independence. "During these war times, the Messenger comes tardily to its subscribers," its acting editor wrote in September 1861. "When the Editor, the type setters and the pressman are gone to 'fight the battles of their country;' when paper is scarce and printing ink is mean, we feel not so much regret in appearing late in the day, as pride in being able to appear at all."[47]

Fully cognizant of the difficulties they faced, Confederate editors and publishers were determined to provide their new nation with a literature, whatever the cost. "Had we consulted our present comfort and interest, it is probable that we, too would have suspended ere this," editor and proprietor Dennis Redmond of the *Southern Cultivator* admitted in December 1861, "but our pride is deeply involved . . . we have 'enlisted for the war,' and so long as we can procure a scrap even of 7 by 9 paper to print on, so long will the Cultivator be issued—and so long will we employ our best efforts for the good of the cause to which we are devoted."[48] The obstacles could be overcome, Redmond and his fellow editors believed, if the public granted southern journals the patronage that they deserved and that patriotic duty demanded.

For those southerners who could not be induced to support Confederate literature through simple patriotism, shame would compel them to do their duty. During the first year of the war, Confederate editors and writers used a combination of stirring appeals and vicious tongue-lashings to win new subscribers. "None of you will admit that the Southerners are *mentally inferior* to the Northern people," Ella Swan chided in *Southern Field and Fireside*. "You would feel insulted did any one tell you they were; still you have united with the entire North in supporting a literature at war with your dearest interests."[49] The only way to show the world that southerners were not "intellectual pigmies" and to counter this stigma of mental inferiority was to cultivate the South's many "intellectual treasures." "Bestow but the fostering hand of Southern patronage upon the effort to bring out these resources," editor James Ells promised, "and another phase of Southern Independence will shine forth."[50]

While such calls for support might increase sales for a time, cultural nationalists knew that they alone would not secure the public's lasting affection. In order for the Confederacy to win its intellectual independence and forever break free from its addiction to northern literature, it would have to produce a literature worthy of patronage in its own right. Publishers could not rely on the blockade and sectional animosity indefinitely. Southern readers would again return to northern books and periodicals unless the quality of southern productions was elevated to the point where foreign publications held no allure. Confederate patriotism would give a much needed boost, but it would be only temporary. Ultimately, Confederate literature would have to sink or swim on its own merits.

With this in mind, Confederate editors and publishers struck a deal with the southern public. If southerners would grant them their patronage, they in turn would provide a literature worthy of their support. "Let the people, by a wise and generous patronage, make our papers what they ought to be; and let the papers themselves see to it that they deserve patronage," the *Southern Christian Advocate* demanded.[51] For "if we do our part, we shall not be compelled to solicit subscriptions by the worn out appeal to Southern patriotism," the *Southern Literary Messenger* pledged.[52] In effect, Confederate cultural nationalists were asking for a leap of faith. As W. S. Perry, the general subscription agent for *The Aurora*, explained in May 1861, "all we want now, is that liberal support from the South that has been so long extended to the North: and then, if we don't publish a better Magazine in twelve months, for the South, than they ever sent us from the North, we will resign our position and quit the field. Try us, one time."[53] With the generous and active support of southern readers, Confederate writers and editors promised to soon "rival in letters the most polished nations of the globe" by creating an authentic southern literature, "a literature not like that of the North, remarkable chiefly for the fecundity of its abortive issues, but having its marks in the aptest use of language, in the highest standards of excellence, in the purest models of taste."[54]

Having fanned the flames of Confederate cultural nationalism, southern editors wanted to reap the rewards. This was their chance to place their journals on a firm financial footing and take advantage of the stoppage of northern trade. "Let us now show our independence of Yankeedom by rallying around our own institutions, supporting liberally our own literary enterprises —in particular, let the good effects of the blockade be seen in the increased patronage of our Quarterly Review," solicited the editor of the *Quarterly Review of the Methodist Episcopal Church, South*.[55] Likewise, the proprietors of the venerable *Southern Literary Messenger* hoped "to avail ourselves of the splendid opening which the pending Revolution secures to every Southern enterprise." "Now that Northern journals have become, as long ago they should have been, contraband articles at the South, . . . there is no reason," as far as the editor could see, "why the support of the Messenger should not be ample and liberal."[56]

In soliciting this "ample and liberal" support, Confederate periodicals consciously situated themselves within the broader struggle for intellectual independence. Editors told their readers that by subscribing, they would vindicate Confederate nationalism and strike an effective blow against the Yankees. "We are yet laboring and striving, pleading and begging our countrymen to come up to the measure of their duty, awake to their true interests, shake off their vassalage, and maintain their independence," G. B. Haygood of the *Educational Repository and Family Monthly* implored. "Will they do it? We shall see."[57] *Southern Field and Fireside* was perhaps the most vigorous in this respect. Under the banner "ENCOURAGE HOME LITERATURE," it placed advertisements in other southern periodicals presenting itself as the exemplar of this new Confederate literature.[58] "An enterprise like THE FIELD AND FIRESIDE has a strong claim on the patriotic sentiment of every Southern man," editor James Ells told his readers, and he warned that failure to support it would have dire cultural consequences. "If not sustained, the result will but add one more theme for the jeers of our Northern enemies over what they are pleased to designate the inferiority of the South in intellectual culture, in enterprise, and in public spirit."[59]

More specialized journals relied on direct appeals to the interests of their own particular demographic, professional, or religious affiliations. Realizing that much of the public's attention was absorbed by war news and the papers that covered it, these editors struggled valiantly to retain readership and to convince their subscribers of their journal's own unique contribution to the fight for independence. Confederate religious journals felt particularly disadvantaged in vying for readers during wartime, and they appealed to their subscribers for support in the name of denominational pride. Noting that one "secular paper" recently boasted an average acquisition of one hundred new subscribers a month, the *Richmond Christian Advocate* urged devout Methodists to follow suit. "Is there nothing in this suggestive to Christians? Church papers struggle for an existence; but the love of news is making secular papers rich. Let us, in these times of patriotism, when a word about the state of the country is paid for eagerly in spite of hard times, see what can be done in the way of Church patriotism."[60] Ministers were urged to solicit subscriptions, ministers' wives and daughters were promised commissions for finding new female subscribers, and congregants were browbeaten to support their religious papers individually, or, at the very least, to contribute for a group subscription.[61] "Do not think that you can quit and that it will not be noticed," the Methodist *Educational Repository and Family Monthly* warned wavering subscribers. "We know every one of you."[62]

THE MOVEMENT FOR CULTURAL autonomy, however, was far more than simply the self-interest of southern editors and publishers wrapped in a Confederate flag. Admittedly opportunistic, these men and a few women nevertheless had loftier goals than mere personal gain, though they certainly would not have refused the chance to profit had it presented itself. They were ardent nationalists, and the opportunity that they saw was to advance the general cause of Confederate intellectual independence. Of course, their own periodicals needed to be sustained in order to carry on this fight, and the achievement of Confederate cultural autonomy would depend ultimately upon the establishment of a profitable periodical press that could afford to liberally pay its staff and contributors. Still, Confederate editors did not enter their profession in order to get rich. In fact, many editors were not paid at all, and those who were supposed to be compensated rarely saw the money promised them. In asking for increased patronage, these editors and owners sought the means to continue the fight for independence, and many of them were so determined that the Confederacy would have its own literature that they exhausted their own personal fortunes in order to continue publishing until the last possible moment. Having never received his promised pay for his services as editor, treasurer, and general agent of the soon-to-be-suspended *Educational Repository and Family Monthly*, G. B. Haygood found compensation in the knowledge that he and his staff had "labored diligently and earnestly, by day and by night, in a great and good cause—the cause of our country and of our beloved South—in trying to persuade our people to assert their literary independence, rid the South of obnoxious books, and offer them a Journal unequalled in its department in the North or in the South."[63] Editors only asked that the public sustain them in this essential battle. They would fight on until they ran out of paper, determined that if their journals "shall go down, the blame will not rest on us."[64]

Editors demonstrated this common cause by encouraging the efforts of other, seemingly competing, Confederate newspapers and magazines, and they urged their readers to do the same.[65] For instance, the *Southern Teacher* celebrated *Southern Field and Fireside* "as the harbinger of what the South can, and will do. We heartily commend it to the patronage of our readers."[66] Even though competing journals often directly threatened their own self-interest, southern editors welcomed all comers to the field of Confederate literature, and they did so for avowedly nationalistic reasons. The reaction of the struggling *Church Intelligencer* to the revival of the *Southern Churchman* in December 1861, was typical. Although worried about losing readers, the *Intelligencer's* editor concluded: "Well, the Confederacy is broad, and there is room enough for us all, and work enough to be done. Let us pursue our work, each in his own line, and according to his own convictions of truth and duty; and instead . . . of biting and devouring each other, let us strive rather to lend to each other a helping hand."[67]

Later in the war, when supplies became especially tight, it was not uncommon for publishers to share paper, ink, and other printing needs with their neighbors so that they could continue publishing. While relations between the editors of the daily political papers, especially in Richmond, would eventually reach the height of acrimony, a strong camaraderie formed between editors of the literary, educational, agricultural, and religious journals across the South. The secular papers urged readers to support the religious, the agricultural journals endorsed the literary, and everyone rallied to the cause of the educational press. And so Confederate editors explicitly and publicly linked all of the various and perhaps seemingly unrelated efforts of their peers, and endorsed them as equal co-contributors to the same nationalist campaign.

Apart from printing positive notices and glowing reviews, southern editors also expressed approval of their literary comrades in another, more subtle way. By reprinting and excerpting the articles and editorials of others in their own pages, Confederate editors tacitly commended the work of their rivals and visibly demonstrated the common sense of purpose that existed across the spectrum of the Confederate periodical press. Whenever a new editorial appeared, urging southerners to support native publications, attacking northern culture, or predicting future Confederate cultural magnificence, it was quickly copied and reprinted throughout the Confederacy. Editors of the literary journals scoured the pages of the South's daily and weekly papers for fodder in their fight for intellectual independence and singled out like-thinking editors, writers, and periodicals for praise. In part, this practice of reprinting articles arose from the need for additional filler material now that editors were cut off from the northern papers and news agencies, but it also served to document the breadth and development of the movement for Confederate intellectual and cultural independence. So long as proper credit was given, editors welcomed other papers to pick and choose from their columns, thereby further demonstrating the good will that existed between members of the Confederate periodical press.

Content was the most important challenge that these would-be creators and purveyors of a new Confederate literature faced. In order to achieve intellectual self-sufficiency and live up to the demands of Confederate nationalism, they needed to fill their periodicals and books with the products of native southern pens. "Every civilized nation must have its literature," Atticus Haygood explained, "and if ours be such as shall teach a wise philosophy, and a pure morality to our children, it must be *native-born*. Nothing else can reflect our principles or defend our character." A virtuous and well-supported Confederate literature "would do more to set us right before the world, than all other things whatever."[68]

Confederate cultural nationalists felt confident that the South possessed the necessary, albeit underdeveloped, talent to produce such a literature. As H. Hinkley declared in a letter to the *Southern Cultivator*, "Thousands of minds that are now in the rough, need but the culture and *direction* to make them shining ornaments of worth to their country and the age."[69] Spurred on by revolution, separate nationality, and war, "Southern Genius shall break the Northern chain which has hitherto bound it," *Southern Field and Fireside* agreed. "Full well we know this fair land has poets, and essayists, and novelists within her borders, whose powers and talents will be developed by the circumstances of the hour."[70] "New thoughts" arising from this "new national life" would spark a renaissance in the Confederacy, and it was incumbent on those who lived in such times to aid this rising Confederate culture.[71] "We are entering upon a new era—we live in historic times, and many things are to be thought of and to be done," Atticus Haygood told his readers. "Old forms are passing away—new ideas are being struck out . . . and new duties devolve upon us all."[72]

Momentous historical events inevitably spawned "periods of great intellectual activity," these nationalists assured themselves. For, as Professor A. B. Stark explained, "When the minds and passions of men are aroused by these political upheavals, they must manifest and body forth themselves in some form."[73] Neither Stark nor Haygood had any doubts about how these heightened passions would manifest themselves in the Confederacy. "Great moral, or political, revolutions nearly always inaugurate new eras in literature," Haygood intoned. "We are now in the midst of great revolution—we are to be 'a peculiar people,' and our literature ought to bear the impress of our distinctive characteristics. It must, then, *be created; and never was there a more glorious prospect than is now inviting Southern talent.*"[74] Breathing the rarefied air of their new nation and confronted with daily examples of unprecedented heroism and valor on the battlefield, Confederate writers and poets could not help but be inspired to excellence. Far from inhibiting the production of literary works, the war would now, and especially in the future, serve as the defining national experience around which a true Confederate literature could be built, a literature "worthy of the heroic age in which we live, and of the rich heritage we enjoy."[75] As ancient wars and conquests had stirred the muses of great epic writers, the Civil War would provide themes and inspiration for generations of Confederate authors.

But the importance of this national literature was such that it could not wait until the war was won. The nation and its literature had to be born of the same labors, and Confederates could not allow wartime hardships to distract them from the intellectual struggle. "It may be urged that our people are engrossed with objects of more vital and sacred importance; that it is well to see that we have a country, before we concern ourselves for its literature. This is a dangerous and unworthy conclusion," a writer in *Southern Field and*

Fireside cautioned. "Must literature be neglected, and every fireside denied the cheering visit of monthly or weekly periodicals, because Lincoln refuses to send them to us? Must the gardens of poesy no longer send forth their cheering fragrance, because we have no Yankee fingers to twine wreathes from their redolent borders? Such admissions are libels upon a people emulating each other in labours and sacrifices worthy of a Spartan age, in the great cause of independence."[76] While conceding that the Confederacy's true intellectual potential would be realized only after the excitements of war had passed, A. B. Stark rejected any suggestion that it was "premature to speak of a *national* literature in the South."[77] Indeed, according to the editor of the *New Orleans Delta*, failure to "employ every instrumentality appertaining to the production of a vigorous, healthy, native, loyal and beneficent literature" during the war would be "to manifest a fatal hesitation—to throw away a magnificent future" and to doom the Confederacy "to dwell amid the defilements and abominations of a detested past, and famishing in arid plains, to feed upon apples of ashes."[78] Confederate writers and editors were determined to exploit the rare opportunity that the war presented to advance and shape the development of southern literature. "There is a great awakening and arousing of the public mind on all subjects," the *Southern Presbyterian* reported, "and now, while the iron is hot, is the time to strike."[79]

Confederate cultural nationalists were convinced that separation from the North would spark a tremendous literary outpouring in the South, but they were equally certain that this new Confederate literature would require careful supervision and guidance in order to reach its full potential. Proper models and carefully edited and critiqued forums needed to be established in order to ensure that this new literature would take the shape that it should. Presiding over its birth, editors and publishers needed to provide the proper trellises upon which a Confederate literary culture could grow and ultimately thrive. That said, cultural nationalists articulated no clear vision of what this pure Confederate literature might actually look like. Beyond demanding that it be uniquely southern, virtuous, original, and free from corrupting northern influences, they offered very few details when it came to predicting the actual shape, content, and style of this great future literature. For instance, the *Southern Christian Advocate* envisioned Confederate periodical publications that would be "instructive, models of good taste, a prime means of home education, enemies of vice, promoters of virtue, never venal, always pure, truthful, generous, high-minded and patriotic," but gave few practical suggestions on how to bring this about.[80] When it came to higher forms of literature—the "literature of power"—the proposed guidelines were even more vague. But this was not cause for immediate concern. At the moment of birth, no one could predict the shape a man's life would take, and so it was with a national literature, A. B. Stark assured southerners. "What will be the peculiar form and distinctive spirit of Southern literature it is impossible to foresee—indeed, to foretell its features would be to create it." Extrapolating from the "character of the people and their country," Stark confidently expected Confederate literature to be "high-toned, and noble, and free, and natural, and religious, perhaps wild, and irregular, and eccentric"—in short, the polar opposite of northern literature.[81] Cultural nationalists might not have had a definite idea of what their future Confederate national literature would be, but they had strong feelings about what it must not be.

While the great authors of the Western world could provide valuable models, they could only serve as a base from which to launch this new Confederate literature. In speculating as to the possible form and ultimate merits of their future national literature, Confederate critics put great stock in the racial and cultural ties that bound southerners to the Old World, particularly England. Stark, for one, hoped that Confederate authors would pick up where the great "English bards and philosophers" had left off. Since "the greatest works of England were done . . . *before* our fathers came to America," southerners could rightly claim that "the glories of English history are ours." But "here, stimulated by new ideas, new circumstances, new interests, and new affinities," these English "thought-germs," if "judiciously cultivated by the impulsive Southern sons of those stern old fathers," would "swell, and burst, and germinate, and grow, and blossom, and fructify in a most wonderfully significant manner."[82] Other commentators worried that too close an identification with English models would restrict the true intellectual potential of Confederate culture, and instead urged southerners to incorporate "as many elements as possible" into their literature—"Greek, Roman, Hebrew, Christian, English, French, Spanish and Italian." Otherwise, "we shall be mere imitators of the English."[83] But whatever their chosen inspirations, all agreed that Confederate literature must not be a mere imitation of earlier forms, and that the unique character of the southern people and their peculiar institutions would give rise to a completely new literary culture.

Of course, southerners had their own models and authors to follow, and these antebellum writers were paid due respect. Confederate cultural nationalists celebrated vigorously the work of such southern literary lights as William Gilmore Simms, Paul Hamilton Hayne, Edgar Allan Poe, Augusta Evans, John R. Thompson, James Barron Hope, John Esten Cooke, St. George Tucker, Nathaniel Beverly Tucker, Augustus Baldwin Longstreet, James Thornwell,

William Caruthers, Thomas Chivers, Philip Pendleton Cooke, John Pendleton Kennedy, William Tappan Thompson, William Wirt, Hugh Legaré, and of course such brilliant southern political theorists as Jefferson, Madison, and Calhoun.[84] "Too much praise cannot be awarded to these noble men and women who have spent their strength in the attempt to elevate the intellectual character of our people," the *Charleston Courier* reverently observed.[85] Impressive as these accomplishments were, however, they represented only a taste of what was to come. If the South had managed to produce such writers and thinkers while laboring under a debilitating vassalage to the North, just imagine, Confederate critics urged, what the future portended. The South already had some "writers of great depth and marked originality of thought; we have artists world-known; we have scholars of profoundest learning and most varied research; we have physicists among the foremost in the world; we have colleges and universities with princely endowments." However, these were "but preparations for something of greater value—but rude scaffoldings to be used in building our magnificent temple—but foresplendors of the brightness and the glory to come in the near future. How bright is the dawn of our day! What will its noon be? Who can tell?"[86]

While earlier writers could provide guidance and inspiration for future authors, Confederate literature could not be mere imitation of old forms, even old southern ones. Furthermore, separate nationality had breathed a new intellectual atmosphere into the South, and many of the themes that drove antebellum southern thought were no longer pertinent. In particular, the twin ideological pillars of proslavery and states' rights that had so dominated southern public discourse during the antebellum years had lost much of their urgency. Separated from their northern intellectual sparring partners, Confederate thinkers no longer had anyone with whom to argue these hitherto divisive issues. Confederate editors and critics quickly realized that it was pointless to carry on these debates in an environment of virtual consensus and instead urged abandoning these tired arguments in favor of exploring new intellectual terrain.[87] In September 1861, the *Southern Literary Messenger* announced that the "arguments on secession and on slavery" were "exhausted" and that "to attempt longer to uphold our cause by reasoning or by ridicule, is a senseless misuse of time."[88] During this period of rare opportunity, the mental powers of the Confederacy could not be wasted fighting battles whose time had passed. Publishing in August 1861 what would have been a typical antebellum proslavery article on Thomas Jefferson, the Declaration of Independence, and slavery, James De Bow inserted a note for the benefit of future contributors: "We consider the discussion of the slavery question as properly closed, and endeavor now to avoid more than an occasional reference to it in the pages of the Review. Let us away with all abstract reasonings, and go to work in developing the great political and industrial future which is before the South. The negro, except in his relations to these, is clearly used up." By making this startling pronouncement in what had been the primary forum for southern proslavery thought, De Bow hoped that "our friends will take the gentle hint, and oblige us and our readers by devoting, hereafter, the same thought, ability and labor which they have given to this topic to others which require attention and in which laurels may yet be earned."[89] As they had discarded the old Union, so too southern thinkers had to abandon the old arguments in order to assist in the Confederacy's quest for intellectual independence.

Of course, the topic of slavery did not disappear from Confederate intellectual discourse during the war. So central was the institution that nearly every facet of southern life, cultural or otherwise, was profoundly influenced by its presence, and the entire Confederate nationalist project was fundamentally and unapologetically rooted to the preservation of slavery and the white racial order it upheld.[90] At the same time, however, traditional proslavery treatises praising the virtues of human bondage and responding to abolitionist attacks did recede largely into the back pages of Confederate periodicals. The continued presence of slavery in the South was no longer in dispute, and while slavery received a great deal of discussion and debate as it related to the war and the Confederacy's divine purpose, the proslavery diatribes that characterized the antebellum years seemed antiquated in this new Confederate nation.

Instead, secession allowed southerners to discuss slavery and its shortcomings in ways that had never been possible before. Although many southerners had misgivings about the practice, if not the existence of slavery, and recognized its abuses during the antebellum years, the need to present a united front against abolitionist assaults often prevented these concerns from being aired publicly. So long as slavery remained under attack from without, there could be no reform from within. However, now that secession had cut off the abolitionist press and freed southerners from the obligation of constantly defending the institution, reforms—such as the recognition and protection of slave marriages and the elimination of anti-literacy laws—could be openly considered and safely advocated.[91] "We are now in a position to examine this matter," Charles Wallace Howard of the *Southern Cultivator* wrote in April 1861. "Prior to our separation from the North, such an inquiry might not have been prudent."[92] As early as February, the *Southern Presbyterian* expressed its hope that now that disunion was an established fact, "the South . . . can give her attention to certain abuses of slavery which demand her own action." Under the old Union and subject to "ignorant and self-righteous meddlers, who could not leave us to do our own duties and to bear the responsibility of our own sins, there was a natural disposition to yield in nothing to them, which prevented the amelioration, in certain respects, of the slave's condition."[93] Slavery, then, could, and indeed had to continue to receive scrutiny, but it would be a different kind of scrutiny and for different purposes than before the war. Confederates needed to move beyond the anti-abolitionist tirades of the antebellum years and instead focus on fostering the internal development and growth of their nation and its social institutions.

Likewise, antebellum political discussions of states' rights and the right of secession would have to be scaled back dramatically, and perhaps abandoned altogether, now that secession was accomplished. Confederate nationalists recognized the threat that the continued advocacy of a strong states' rights ideology posed to the survival of their new nation, and while admitting that such ideas had served a beneficial purpose in facilitating the creation of the Confederacy, they believed that these arguments had now outlived their usefulness. For the time being, William Falconer conceded, the idea of separate state secession and the doctrine of states' rights, though "objectionable in many respects," must still be "treated with much leniency, as having been, if not the only, at least the most direct method of inaugurating the new [Confederate] regime." In "the future time," however, they "must be ignored." States' rights ideology "was doubtless an unrecognized agent of good in the past, still we know it to be a destructive principle in the science of government, and hostile to all ideals of *permanency*."[94] Now that the Union was broken and the true southern nation allowed to emerge, there was no need to endlessly debate the right of secession or the sovereignty of the states. "These and all former issues are now dead, and swallowed up in events of mightier moment," political theorist J. Quitman Moore declared in *De Bow's Review*.[95] As Dennis Redmond of the *Southern Cultivator* bluntly told his political contributors, "We really have no time to waste in 'talking over' questions already settled."[96]

To some extent, of course, these calls to abandon the old debates represented wishful thinking. Committed proslavery ideologues, like Dr. Samuel Cartwright of New Orleans for instance, continued to extol the virtues of slavery and to attack abolitionists just as they had before the war.[97] States' rights ideology did not disappear, and soon, as nationalists feared, would work to undermine the integrity and military capabilities of the Confederacy, especially in such states as Georgia and North Carolina. However, there was a definite change of trajectory within Confederate periodicals. Editors expressed impatience and sometimes refused to print articles that merely rehashed old sectional arguments. Confederate literature could not be simply a continuation or imitation of antebellum southern literature, these cultural nationalists believed. Changed national circumstances demanded new forms of thought and literary expression.

ACCORDINGLY, SOUTHERN PERIODICALS HAD to alter their focus in order to provide proper forums for this emerging Confederate literature. No matter how established or specialized at the time of secession, southern journals and newspapers were forced to reevaluate their mission and decide what role they would take in the struggle for their nation's independence, political and intellectual. With southern guns trained on Fort Sumter and Virginia teetering on the brink of secession, George Bagby announced a modification in the *Southern Literary Messenger*'s editorial policies. In the face of such momentous events, he shifted the journal's focus and now actively solicited essays on political theory and current affairs as well as works of pure "literature." He "cordially, earnestly invited" Confederate thinkers to make the *Messenger* "their medium of swaying the intellects of men and the destinies of the country."[98] Dennis Redmond also acknowledged a change in his magazine. While maintaining that "it is not the mission of the *Southern Cultivator* to enter into a discussion of what is generally termed *politics*," he also believed that "in the present crisis, no true Southern man or friend of the South can occupy neutral ground."[99] Five months later, he told his readers that if they found the *Cultivator* "strongly tinctured with articles and suggestions bearing on the present state of our country, they must not deem us at all forgetful of our special 'mission' as Agricultural journalists. We cannot, if we would, shut our eyes to the perils that surround us. . . . Let the rifle, the revolver and the trusty 'double-barrel' be no less familiar to our hands than the peaceful implements of Agriculture."[100] Other Confederate magazines and newspapers followed suit, altering their content and editorial policies in order to bring themselves in line with the new political, military, and intellectual realities facing their fledgling nation.

Secession and the coming of the war presented a unique dilemma for the Confederacy's religious press. Because religious papers were expected to avoid secular issues and focus instead on saving men's souls, religious editors were torn between their desire to rally support for the southern cause and their duty to walk a higher path. For instance, in December 1860, even in radical South Carolina, Reverend A. A. Porter of the *Southern Presbyterian* felt compelled to restrain his own secessionist sympathies, at least in print. "All we are authorized to do is to remind [the readers], the dangers which impend over their country, and the general principles and spirit of religion which ought to control their action," but he could not utter "an opinion in favor of union or disunion."[101]

Once war erupted, however, these same editors quickly found rationalizations to allow them to openly support the war and their new nation while at the same time maintaining a decidedly religious perspective. The war, they argued, transcended the political and secular sphere. At heart, it was a moral and religious conflict for Confederates. Theirs was God's cause and southerners could not forget that they were fighting "in defence of religion as well as civil rights." The coming conflict would "enlist the holiest sympathies of all our Christian people" and "appeal to every sentiment of piety as well as patriotism."[102] For this reason, religious editors were allowed, indeed compelled, to offer guidance. "There is a right and there is a wrong side to the case," Porter now felt comfortable exclaiming. "We think the South has the right side, and we must say it."[103]

Casting aside many of the accepted divisions between secular and sacred, Confederate religious editors shifted their focus in order to lend their voices and direct support to the cause of Confederate independence. Porter, for one, dismissed any concern that the war "may get too strong a hold upon our attention" to the exclusion of religious matters. Indeed, "properly presented and properly regarded, [the war] cannot receive too much consideration."[104] For, as he bluntly told one disgruntled reader, "if religion has nothing to say or do *in regard to the present war*, if it has not *much* to say in regard to it, we must confess that we are laboring under an immense delusion."[105]

Other religious editors adopted similar lines of reasoning to defend their involvement in the war and the issues surrounding it.[106] It should be noted, however, that there were differences in the degree to which the various denominational papers engaged with the secular world. In general, the Presbyterians were the most eager to delve into issues and debates not strictly religious, and were also the most vigorous in defending their right to do so. As the acknowledged intellectual leaders of southern Christianity, Presbyterian divines and editors believed that it was their duty to offer guidance to their newborn nation in all matters, political, intellectual, social, and of course religious. The Episcopalians and Methodists attempted to strike a balance between the secular and sacred, and continued to express reservations about straying too far from the fold. For the most part, the Baptist papers remained the most strictly religious, and while they too commented on the religious meaning of the conflict and worried about the moral well-being of the soldiers in camp, they generally refrained from trying to sway public opinion on secular matters. But whatever the degree or comfort level of their involvement with secular affairs, the Confederate religious papers, like the secular press, adapted to the new conditions presented by war. They remolded themselves into more effective and focused instruments designed to foster a native Confederate literature and assist in the struggle for Confederate independence. A new era of Confederate literature was dawning in the South, southern editors promised their readers, and they would be there, ready to encourage and guide this national literature at the moment of its birth.

Confederate editors, having prophesized a new era of southern intellectual greatness, having argued for the highest standards of quality and taste, having urged Confederate thinkers to abandon the tropes of the past, and having altered their own publications to better facilitate this birth of Confederate literature, now called upon southern writers to rise to the occasion and fill their newspapers, journals, and books with a literature befitting their new nation. The editors and publishers of the Confederacy could not create a national literature by themselves, and now, having established the parameters of the mighty project that lay before them, they turned to the aspiring writers, poets, and artists of the Confederacy to bring their grand vision to life. All southerners had a national duty to support the development of Confederate culture through their generous patronage, but southerners of talent had a special responsibility to actively participate in this national intellectual awakening. "Surely the pen has its mission as well as the sword," James De Bow urged, "and we trust that our scholars and writers will not, in such an exigency, prove wanting."[107] In the emerging Confederate nation "there is work to be done—there *is* Southern talent for the work; and there are themes worthy of its highest efforts. There is room for every order of mind," Atticus Haygood beckoned.[108]

In order to best serve their nation, "our men and women of education and attainments" must not allow themselves to become entirely absorbed in the exciting events of the military struggle.[109] "The mind cannot, and should not, be chained down to the consideration of war, and its bloody themes, alone," *Southern Field and Fireside* advised. "We cannot all engage in war and war pursuits"—there were other important services to be rendered.[110] Patriotism demanded that those with the requisite mental capabilities engage simultaneously in two concurrent struggles: one military and one intellectual. The distractions of war were no excuse to shirk the responsibility incumbent upon those who would have the Confederacy achieve true independence and a complete nationality.

Distinction and honor could be found in intellectual pursuits as well as on the field of battle, these cultural nationalists promised. In the emerging Confederate nation, authorship would become a path to social prominence. Unlike in the antebellum years, when southern authors labored in obscurity for an unappreciative public, Confederate writers would receive a very different reception, or so it was hoped. "In our age and country," Professor Stark maintained, "literature presents the most inviting field to a man ambitious of fame, or to a man humbly desirous of usefulness, because if he speaks what lies in the domain of *truth* and *reality*, he speaks to the whole world."[111] "Is not this a great age to live in?" the *Banner of Peace* asked budding southern authors. "Behold the work—the chance for good—the margin even for distinction."[112]

Implicit in these arguments was the assumption that authorship would become a viable profession in the new Confederacy, something it never had been in the antebellum South. Writers had to be able to dedicate themselves exclusively to their craft and this meant that they had to be paid, and paid well. In order to produce an admirable national literature, southerners could no longer rely on the scribblings of amateurs. "But one asks—'are there not plenty of writers at the South, who will write without pay?'" The *Southern Christian Advocate* answered:

Yes—such as they are. But in a leading monthly we want something besides the compositions of a boarding-school miss—something better than the tentative efforts of the fledgling sentimentalist—something wiser than the lucubrations of the unreading wiseacre, who has just unearthed an idea, that the student will know has been exploded and buried for centuries— something with more of genius and power in it, than the "hurried lines which I have not time to copy," that, halting on unequal feet, might have limped on to local notoriety in the columns of the village paper.[113]

"The greatest difficulty in our way hitherto, has been that we have not allowed our scholars and authors to make *literature a profession*," Atticus Haygood opined.[114] Great literature could not be squeezed out between harvests, court dates, and legislative sessions. It required the long, uninterrupted labor of the mind, and therefore, the *Southern Teacher* argued, "the successful writer is as much entitled to pay as the lawyer or doctor."[115]

While some suggested that the Confederate government itself take an active role by sponsoring promising writers through pensions and official positions, most believed that increased patronage on the part of the Confederate people would be the surest means of elevating authorship to the status of a profession.[116] In order to promote and sustain this new Confederate literature, southern publishers and periodicals needed the means to pay their authors. As they attempted to increase their own subscription lists in order to achieve the financial stability necessary to pay for contributions, Confederate editors encouraged native writers to send their best work now, on the promise that improved quality would in turn increase patronage and secure future payment.[117] The war years then presented Confederate writers with the opportunity not only to advance the national cause of cultural independence, but also to stake their own claim as a true and vital profession within southern society.

Nor were these new opportunities open solely to the Confederacy's talented "sons." Its "daughters," too, could take an active role in the creation of a new Confederate literature. Confederate cultural nationalists recognized that, with most of the men serving in the ranks, women would be the primary paying consumers of southern newspapers, periodicals, and books. While soldiers certainly read newspapers and magazines, and did so eagerly, the unreliability of mail service, the movement of armies, the practice of passing a single issue between dozens and perhaps hundreds of readers, plus the fact that many Confederate papers, especially the religious ones, sent thousands of free copies to the camps, meant that financial support for Confederate print literature had to come from home. But in this fight for Confederate intellectual independence, women would be more than simply silent consumers. "Woman must act an important part in building up a national literature," A. B. Stark told his mostly female audience. "She must be not only an appreciative reader and encourager of worthy books, but also an enthusiastic producer. She will infuse into the printed thought that is to control and shape our lives and moral being those high qualities and deep religious impulses which belong peculiarly to her. . . . Daughters of the South, sisters, we expect your earnest cooperation and refining influence in performing the great work that lies before us."[118] Through writing and teaching, southern women could fulfill their patriotic duty and make a meaningful contribution to the Confederate cause.

Given their privileged status, upper-class slaveholding women in particular were urged to take an active role in ushering in this new Confederate literature.[119] "You have schools inferior to none in the world," Stark reminded his wealthy listeners; "you have the means to purchase ample libraries, and every other facility; you enjoy in many cases immunity from the necessity of household labors; you have the high privilege of speaking the truth without regard to profit or present acceptance. If, with these advantages, you fail to send out many volumes replete with moral and religious instruction, you will be utterly inexcusable."[120] While prohibited from the battlefield by their sex, southern women could engage in a related intellectual and cultural struggle, helping to bring meaningful and lasting independence to their young nation.

Female authors had not been absent from the pages of antebellum southern literature. Indeed, some of the most celebrated writers in the South were women. But never before had literature written specifically by women been so enthusiastically solicited or so publicly embraced. Seizing the opportunity that the war presented to female authors for recognition and publication, "Sybil," writing in *Southern Field and Fireside*, exclaimed: "Happy am I to feel that *our* country—our beloved Southern Confederacy, though in its infancy, is by no means inferior" in terms of literary talent, "thrice happy and thankful am I to feel and know that *our* sex are reaping so rich a benefit from this fact." Pointing to recent contributions by authors Mrs. Du Bose, Miss Bacon, Miss Kendall, Miss Thigpen, Mrs. H. T. Jones, Miss M. Louise Rogers, and Mrs. Mary McCrimmon, she applauded these women for "putting forth every effort to awaken an interest in the public mind to the necessity of giving earnest support to 'Southern Literature,' " and she called on other southern female writers to do the same.[121] In this fight for intellectual autonomy, all southerners, of both sexes, had a part to play, and those blessed with intelligence and talent were duty-bound to place their gifts in the service of the Confederate nation.

ARMED WITH THESE APPEALS, Confederate editors set to work actively soliciting original contributions for their own journals. In the momentous times of the early Confederacy, there were momentous issues to discuss, and all capable Confederate minds were encouraged to join the national discourse. "What will be the destiny of the newborn nation? Can that destiny be shaped for good? Can it be shaped at all? Ought we attempt to shape it? If so, then surely the attempt should be made in good earnest now while the nation is in a plastic state. . . . These are grave questions," the *Southern Literary Messenger* stressed, and it invited "thinking minds throughout the Confederacy to discuss them freely, seriously in the columns of this magazine. The last experiment at a great Republic which the world will ever see, is now beginning to be made. . . . An hour so momentous was never recorded in the annals of human history."[122]

Editors could no longer cut and paste articles from northern papers, even if they had so desired. Both national pride and the blockade dictated that the Confederate press fill its columns with native material. Before secession, the front page of the *Southern Christian Advocate* had been composed primarily of "selections" from elsewhere, mainly the North. Now, its editor demanded, *"why might not this page be wholly original?* Why might not our readers become our writers?"[123] The *Southern Presbyterian* agreed: with their separation from the North complete, "It is exceedingly desirable and important that the habit of writing for the press should be cultivated by our Southern ministers and people." Thus, native works were always to be preferred over foreign. "We could easily fill our columns from other papers and from books, and with excellent matter too," editor A. A. Porter explained. "But we desire the *Southern Presbyterian* to reflect the thoughts and spirit of the times, and to be a medium through which our readers will have an interchange of living opinions and sentiments. For this reason we prefer to insert an original communication" even if it be "inferior in every [other] respect."[124]

Confederate editors encouraged this "habit of writing" by offering prizes and occasionally promising outright payment for native contributions of true merit. The North Carolina State Educational Association offered "very liberal Premiums" of twenty-five dollars apiece for the best essays written by southern teachers on such subjects as: "The Art of Reading the English Language," "The Claims of English Orthography and Orthoepy," "The Propriety and Importance of Employing more Female Teachers in our Common Schools," and "The Standard of Moral Character in Teachers."[125] *Southern Field and Fireside* promised $100 for the best "Tale" written by a Confederate author. In the end, the judges decided to split the prize between Emma Miot of Ellisville, Florida, for her story "Our Little Annie," and Clara Dargan of Columbia, South Carolina, for her tale "Helen Howard." The winning stories were featured as lead pieces in *Field and Fireside*.[126] Some periodicals, like the *North Carolina Presbyterian*, claimed to pay "liberally for our regular correspondence," but it is unclear to whom, how often, or how much.[127] These and other financial incentives were but the first inklings of what the future promised, Confederate editors assured their contributors. Additional and larger prizes, and even direct payments did become more common during the later years of the war, but it is notable that even at the very beginning of the

Confederacy's quest for intellectual independence, Confederate editors and publishers attempted to cultivate original southern writing. They endeavored to improve literary quality by not only appealing to patriotic duty, but also by actively promoting the professionalization of authorship in the South.

FOR THEIR PART, CONFEDERATE writers responded enthusiastically, flooding the offices of southern periodicals with essays, stories, sermons, and especially poetry. Even if they never completely realized their goal of obtaining enough new material on a weekly or monthly basis to publish an entirely original product, Confederate periodicals could claim that they contained more contemporary southern writing than their antebellum forebearers. In March 1861, the *Southern Presbyterian* noted with approval the rapidly increasing number of original articles and other contributions arriving daily through the mail.[128] Likewise, in September, it gave *Southern Field and Fireside* great pleasure "to announce that during the past fortnight we have received a large accession to our list of contributors . . . whose gems of poesy, pearls of thought, golden dreamings, and flashes of wit, will materially aid in retaining for our enterprise the distinction of 'the favourite home paper.'" These new contributors had "taken up the Pen most willingly—determined that our loved sunny clime shall, while throwing off the yoke of Abolition tyranny, free herself from the shackles of Northern literary bondage."[129]

While prestigious journals like *De Bow's Review*, the *Southern Literary Messenger*, and the *Southern Presbyterian Review* had the luxury of enlisting established southern writers to fill their columns, other Confederate periodicals were not so fortunate. Instead, they relied on a growing number of occasional or first-time writers who recently had taken up their pens in the service of their new nation. These writers often left their essays unsigned or used pseudonyms or initials, and, though not as polished as the experienced southern essayists, they lacked none of the latter's devotion to the cause of Confederate intellectual independence.

Many of the contributions from new Confederate writers came in the form of verse. Poetry was commonplace in the columns of all southern magazines and newspapers, and it seemed a particularly fitting medium to capture the passions of the times. Editors encouraged their readers to invoke their poetic muses, and Confederates in turn responded with enthusiasm, if not always with talent. Battles and even skirmishes, generals and lesser officers, individual regiments, flags, parades, and countless other war topics received their own odes, and often multiple ones. Individual soldiers who had fallen in battle were commemorated publicly in verse.

Cultural nationalists particularly stressed the need for a Confederate national anthem. "In this glorious dawn of the history of our Confederacy, is it not singular that the poetic muse is so crippled in her efforts to introduce an anthem worthy of such times?" Joan of Columbia, South Carolina, challenged the South's poets.[130] To this and other such calls, amateur Confederate poets responded with an ample supply of potential candidates. More prominent figures, too, contributed their voices, and the journals and papers of the Confederacy eagerly printed and reprinted the poems of William Gilmore Simms, John R. Thompson, Henry Timrod, Paul Hamilton Hayne, James R. Randall, A. B. Meek, Dr. William H. Holcombe, Susan Archer Talley, Dr. Francis O. Ticknor, and John C. McCabe.

Throughout the war, editors expressed amazement at the sheer volume of native southern poetry that continually flooded their offices and crested at moments of particular excitement such as the secession crisis, the battle of First Manassas or the death of Stonewall Jackson. "It would surprise some folks to see what piles of *blank* verse accumulate in our office in a month," the editor of the *Richmond Christian Advocate* noted. "No poets in Virginia?—We know better. Not a day of poetry, eh? Ask the editors."[131]

Cultural nationalists had reason to be pleased with the enthusiasm with which their intellectual call to arms was being met. They pointed to the increasing number of southern contributors, and especially first-time contributors, as evidence of the growing determination on the part of Confederates to assert their intellectual and cultural independence. Even if most editors could not yet fill their periodicals entirely with original material, the number of contributions and native contributors was increasing at an impressive rate, and this "free offering of so many minds" warranted "the expectation that a vigorous fruitage will surely follow such efflorescence."[132] Galvanized by patriotism, southerners who had never before considered writing for an audience now took up their pens resolved that the Confederacy would indeed have its own homegrown literature.

At the same time, this increase in contributions presented a significant challenge for cultural nationalists. While hailing the rise of native authorship, they also recognized the risks that such amateurish and hastily written productions posed to their ultimate objective of intellectual independence. The editor of the *Southern Christian Advocate* explained the dilemma thus: "We hope now for a perfect flood of original articles—only, that the waters shall not rise so high as to become *very* muddy."[133] In order to achieve true cultural autonomy, Confederate literature needed to be not only native-born, but also of sufficient quality to supplant foreign productions and merit international recognition. To this end, Confederate editors and critics attempted to temper their enthusiasm and retain critical standards as they decided what to print and what to return.

In defending their right to do so, Confederate cultural nationalists evoked the memory of the Young America literary movement of the 1830s and 1840s which had struggled to win international recognition for American (mainly northern) culture and literature in the face of dismissive European critics.[134] The parallels between their own struggle for intellectual independence and that of the Young America movement, in which some southern writers like William Gilmore Simms had actively participated, were not lost on Confederate thinkers. In fact, one contributor to *De Bow's Review* linked the two movements directly. Recalling Sydney Smith's famous dismissive question of 1820, "Who reads an American book?" which had become the rallying cry for the Young America movement, this Confederate writer suggested that the "old taunt . . . may be revived, with the change, 'Who reads a Southern book?' "[135] Cultural autonomy could be won only by pursuing the highest quality in Confederate literary productions. Only then would the rest of the world read a southern book, and only then would it recognize the Confederacy as a true nation.

For this reason, Confederate editors struggled to balance their desire to encourage new and inexperienced writers with their obligation to maintain the high critical standards necessary to legitimize Confederate literature. Generally, they preferred to err on the side of inclusiveness, but they did so with reservations. As the *Southern Christian Advocate* explained, "while we may not expect young and unpracticed writers, at once to develop the highest talent for composition, and we may not, therefore, always require as perfect articles as we could select; yet we do not desire to make the paper, a mere field for experimental composers."[136] The Episcopalian *Church Intelligencer* in Raleigh also opened its columns to new southern writers, but not without strict guidelines. Before the war, its editor had refrained from printing poetry which had "not previously run the gantlet of public opinion." In response to southern independence, however, the *Intelligencer* now resolved to become an active "cultivator of [southern] literary taste and literary talent." To this end, editor T. S. W. Mott announced that "we will not, in future, decline *all* original poetry," but, he added, "it must be remembered . . . that the office we sustain is a high and responsible one, and we intend to discharge it to the best of our ability and *judgment*, without fear, or regard to the favor of any one."[137]

As they waded through piles of lackluster contributions in search of native prose and poetry worthy of publication and representative of southern genius, Confederate editors expressed their impatience at poor writing, sloppy thinking, and amateurish compositions, and they were not shy in letting their contributors know that such productions were simply not up to the mark. In surveying the content of Confederate periodicals during the summer of 1861, the editor of the *Southern Christian Advocate* found little to commend. "The stories are barren in invention, lamely developed, slip-shod, sometimes puerile, in style—the poetry, prose set in unmeasured lines—and often poor prose at that—the wit often coarse, clownish, and flavored with Ethiopian rather than with Attic salt." He urged writers and readers alike to elevate their literary tastes—for writers to strive for a higher standard and for readers to demand more of native publications.[138] Fed up with sorting through insipid prose and maudlin poetry, George Bagby lashed out at their overeager but unpracticed authors. "Dare we hope for pardon if we announce the fact, hitherto unsuspected, that THE MESSENGER is a magazine, and not a scrap-basket for the reception of paper which has been scribbled over?" He singled out the Confederacy's aspiring poetesses for a particularly harsh rebuke: "Highly cultivated and eminently benevolent young ladies may save much postage if they will remember this fact. Weak little compositions, by turns pious, pathetic, and romantic, which might pass muster at a female school exhibition, are not, as a general thing, desirable for magazines. Such tender and sentimental trash had better be burned. When written on blue paper, the flame is particularly pretty." Plenty of bad poetry, he admitted, "has been printed in THE MESSENGER, but not because we felt much morbid anxiety to print it," and he announced it was "high-time a close stop" was put to such contributions. "It would be well, therefore, for all young people, of the 'thou hast wounded the spirit that loved thee' species, and all older folk who dabble in meaningless sonnets, odes, and the like, henceforth to retain their vapid oozings" or at the very least to relegate them to the "corners of the country newspapers."[139]

Not surprisingly, such rebukes were not always appreciated by hopeful Confederate writers taking their first reluctant steps into the public domain. "Three Sisters of South-Western Virginia" took sharp exception to Bagby's criticism and chastised him for discouraging female authors at the very moment when they most needed encouragement:

Cheerfully they send forth their loved ones to fight the battles of the South; lovingly they toil day and night for them; tenderly they nurse the sick and wounded, and they are called "Heroines," for doing what their *patriotism* and *womanly hearts* suggest; but when some of them, not aware that the Messenger was not a "scrap basket," unwittingly "wasted their postage," by sending some "weak little compositions, by turns pious, pathetic, and romantic," the Editor taking it for granted that the minds of all Southern ladies were of the same calibre, *politely* excluded . . . all articles written by ladies, thereby effectually crushing the budding genius of at least *three*, who, imagining themselves "highly cultivated and eminently benevolent young ladies," were about to make extensive preparations, such as purchasing a supply of "blue paper," etc., for the purpose of contributing to the interesting columns of the Messenger; but now preferring to witness, themselves, the "pretty flame" which blue paper makes, they have determined to burn all compositions over which so many precious moments have recently been wasted.[140]

In a similarly sarcastic vein, one disgruntled writer from South Carolina composed a lengthy poem, "To the Poetical Editor of the [Southern] Presbyterian." Resentful that her submissions had been rejected in the past, "Incognito" attacked the editor's literary standards and went so far as to question his age, intelligence, experience, manhood, patriotism, and physical appearance: "I wonder if he's handsome, / Or wrinkled bald and wan?" She further wondered:

> If he could bravely fight?
> And if he hates the Yankees,
>   And glories in the right.
>
> But this can scarce be doubted
>   Of one who haileth from
> The land of the Palmetto,
>   The great secessiondom.
>
> Will he smile upon their efforts,
>   And whisper "try again,"
> To those who plume their pinions
>   For Poesy's domain?
>
> And when our rhymes are rugged,
>   Will he sweetly smooth them o'er?
> Or with a vastly awful frown
>   Vote doggerel a bore.

And last, not least, I wonder
    If he's noble, good and true,
And who, Oh! tell us *who* he is,
    The echo answers *who*![141]

But Confederate editors held their ground. As the nation's self-appointed arbiters of taste, they staunchly defended their patriotic and professional duty to uphold literary standards. If they "had been annoyed as we have been by trash, they would not blame us for adopting the only method within our power of getting rid of such annoyance," George Bagby told the three sisters. His object had been "simply to impress upon the minds of Southern writers the propriety of giving" their work "that finish and elaboration of thought and style . . . without which no article should ever be admitted into the more pretentious and more permanent columns of a magazine." He assured the sisters, however, that their future contributions would receive due consideration and that "if the sense be only half as sound as their hand-writing is beautiful," their work would "most assuredly be printed."[142] The poetry editor of the *Southern Presbyterian* made no such reply to "Incognito's" biting poem, but he did display his sense of humor by printing it.

Throughout the war, Confederate editors would continue to defend zealously their right to judge southern works by the highest possible standards. It was not enough that an essay or poem flowed from a southern pen. It also had to bring credit to a burgeoning Confederate literature. In reality, of course, editors, desperate to fill their columns, were unable to maintain these lofty critical standards. Much of what was printed in the Confederacy's papers and journals was of mediocre literary quality at best. Still, not everything that aspiring Confederate authors wrote made it into print, much to the editors' credit. Though often forced by necessity to print lesser works, Confederate editors and critics were quick to point out the shortcomings of such pieces and continually encouraged southern writers to do better. Determined to guide the development of Confederate literature as well as preside over its birth, they performed the crucial, if sometimes unpopular, role of challenging and chastising native authors in order to ensure the proper growth of a virtuous, self-sufficient, and creditable national literature.

DESPITE HARDSHIPS AND DISAPPOINTMENTS, Confederate cultural nationalists had reason to be hopeful by the end of 1861. They marveled at how much the Confederate people had accomplished in such a short period of time amidst the most distracting conditions imaginable. By July 1861, A. B.

Stark was even prepared to exclaim that "we, as a nation, spring into existence from the head of Liberty, full panoplied, intellectually, religiously, morally, politically, and materially, a nation full-grown, with strength and energy, with thews and brains, to enter gloriously on the highest career of civilization and intellectual greatness."[143] While Stark clearly overstated the case, his enthusiasm was shared by others across the Confederacy. While not yet "a nation full-grown," the Confederacy was a nation growing. It had boldly taken its first steps toward true intellectual and cultural independence, and all expected still greater things to come.

CHAPTER FOUR

THE CAMPAIGN FOR CONFEDERATE EDUCATIONAL INDEPENDENCE

As southern editors, writers, and critics orchestrated the creation of a Confederate literature, southern educators set to work within their own field to advance the cause of Confederate independence. A true, virtuous, and above all independent Confederate education was universally heralded as a vital—perhaps the vital—requirement in the struggle for intellectual independence, as well as the most effective safeguard of the sanctity of southern character and the future prosperity of the southern nation.[1] "We are urged by every conceivable motive to give our sons and daughters a *Southern* training and education," the *Southern Presbyterian* explained, for "if we are to preserve our own institutions, our own ideas, our own manners and customs, our own style and character of society, and our own *type* of Southern men and women, we must educate our own children."[2] Worried that the war would derail efforts to strengthen southern education and destroy what modest gains had been made during the antebellum years, Confederate cultural nationalists of every stripe urged southerners to contribute their pens, money, and children to the cause. "We have a future as well as a present," the *Southern Cultivator* reminded its readers, and that future depended on the proper education of their children.[3] Southerners could not allow the internal life and institutions of the Confederacy to die or even lie dormant during the war years. As J. D. Campbell, editor of the *North Carolina Journal of Education*, asked in October

1861, "If, while we are fighting for national independence and the maintenance of our just and inalienable rights, we should permit those interests,
which alone can make freedom worth possessing, to languish and even perish, through neglect; what will we have gained, when we shall have brought
the war to a successful close?"[4]

Literary and educational independence were prerequisites for southern
intellectual autonomy. But while all Confederate cultural nationalists recognized the link between the two and portrayed them as coequals in the larger
struggle, there was a definite divide between the literary nationalists and the
educational reformers. The editors and writers agitating for the development
of a Confederate literature voiced their support for the cause of Confederate
education and enthusiastically celebrated the arrival of each new southern
textbook, but they generally left the business of maintaining schools, training teachers, approving curricula, raising funds, calling conventions, and
writing textbooks to the educators themselves. Although part of the same
larger project as that of the literary nationalists, the campaign for Confederate educational independence generally involved different people, different
publishers, and was centered in different places.

While the literary nationalists were often vague when it came to plans of
action, believing that southern letters would flourish of their own accord once
freed from northern competition, Confederate educational nationalists had
concrete goals and immediately pressing needs. Southern educators recognized at once that the coming of the war presented both a tremendous opportunity and a dire threat to the cause of Confederate education. The South was
now finally free of northern teachers and the importation of corrupt northern
textbooks, but the war also threatened to draw southern teachers and students out of the classroom into the ranks, as well as divert essential state and
municipal funds to the war effort. While the cause of literary independence
could advance at its own pace and build public support over time, Confederate children needed teaching now, "war or no war," as the *Charlotte Democrat*
bluntly declared.[5] Confronted with the departure of northern teachers, the
likely departure of southern teachers and students for the battlefield, a desperate shortage of acceptable schoolbooks, underdeveloped—and, in some
southern states, completely undeveloped—school systems, as well as a distracted population, educators had to act immediately or risk losing the cause
of Confederate educational independence at its very inception. In order to
meet the crisis, Confederate teachers and educational reformers quickly issued public statements, speeches, pamphlets, and articles designed to impress upon their countrymen the vital importance of education to their na-

tion's future and to remind southern educators of their patriotic duty during this time of war. "All is lost, if we permit our children to grow up in ignorance," A. B. Stark warned his Mississippi audience. "On the question of Southern school-books the time for discussion is gone by; we must now act. The logic of facts is irresistible, and has closed the discussion."[6]

While the movement for Confederate literary independence had many important editors, writers, and publishers in its service, it did not have any one clear leader. The struggle for Confederate educational independence, by contrast, did have such a spokesman in the person of Calvin Henderson Wiley. Superintendent of Common Schools for North Carolina, Wiley was the most prominent educational reformer in the South and one of the staunchest advocates for Confederate intellectual independence following secession. Throughout the 1850s, Wiley had campaigned tirelessly for the necessity of common schools, native southern teachers, and southern-authored textbooks, and had even written a textbook himself, *The North-Carolina Reader*. When North Carolina seceded, Wiley immediately set to work to free the South from northern dominance by establishing its own homegrown and self-supporting system of education. Although his official authority extended only to the borders of his state, Wiley's influence and his words reached the entire Confederacy. Along with a cohort of likeminded North Carolina educators and publishers, Wiley spearheaded the struggle for Confederate educational independence and made North Carolina the epicenter for southern educational activism and textbook publishing.[7]

In pamphlets, circulars, letters, and articles, Wiley rallied teachers to the cause and sought to convince the southern public at large to lend its vigorous support to native education. "We are fighting for *Independence*," he reminded the County Superintendents of North Carolina in an open letter, and while "our brave troops are doing their part . . . there is an allotted task for every one who remains at home." In this time of crisis, teachers had to "stand manfully by our trust, knowing the precious hopes, the inestimable interests committed to our keeping."[8]

Wiley and other southern educators of like sympathies constructed a multipronged justification for a uniquely Confederate education. Their primary argument centered on the demands of nationalism and the ultimate sustainability of Confederate independence. Their summer 1861 "Address to the People of North Carolina" effectively served as the manifesto for the campaign for educational independence, not just in North Carolina, but for the entire Confederacy. In it, Wiley and eleven other prominent North Carolina educators publicly resolved:

That as this is a struggle for national existence and independence, it is to be maintained and carried on, under Providence, to a successful issue, not only by legislative acts and by force of arms in the field, but, also, in the school room, at the fireside, and by all those moral agencies which preserve society, and which prepare a people to be a free and self-governing nationality; and that, considering our former dependence for books, for teachers and for manufactures on those who now seek our subjugation, it is especially incumbent on us to encourage and foster a spirit of home enterprise and self-reliance.

Wiley and his colleagues sought to "impress on the mind of the public" that the forthcoming war required far more than just military service. As southerners prepared to march off for the battlefield, they had to remember that "the contest in which the Confederate States of America are engaged is not a war growing out of questions of commerce or political complications—it is a struggle for national existence and independence, and involving . . . all that can affect the life of a civilized people."[9] As such, southerners had to constantly strive to ensure that southern culture and civilization, and not just the Confederate army, continued to be supported and provisioned.

Education, these advocates argued, was the key to true independence as well as the surest means of instilling Confederate nationalism in its broadest and most sustainable sense. "It is essential to our independence that we think for ourselves," the members of the North Carolina State Educational Association resolved at their annual meeting in November 1861. Now that southerners had their own nation, they had to cultivate all their resources, especially their mental resources. "It should be remembered that a country which cannot be sustained by its own energies and productiveness can be subdued or ruined," a committee on the "General Interests of Education in our Country" warned. "It is in the School Room that the mind of the State is prepared for special usefulness in the development of its material and moral resources, and for their skilful application to its support and defence."[10] With the stakes so high, the *North Carolina Journal of Education* called upon all patriotic southerners to "arouse ourselves; let us assert and maintain our entire independence, in all that relates to education . . . let us prepare and publish our own text books, and train up our children to feel that they are to be citizens of a country that is the most independent on earth—independent of all except Him who is the Ruler of the universe."[11]

A second, related argument supporting the development of Confederate education hinged on international and northern perceptions of southern society. By sustaining their schools and teaching their children even in the face of war, Confederates would demonstrate to the world the viability of the Confederacy as a nation as well as convince northerners of the southern resolve to be free. The war and the international attention it attracted would grant southerners a rare opportunity to showcase the virtues of southern civilization and refute the many misrepresentations of their abolitionist critics. "[Europeans] are doing now what we have long asked the civilized world to do: they are examining for themselves the state of our civilization," Wiley and his eleven colleagues observed. "It cannot be doubted that they will judge of our self-sustaining ability by that moral courage which triumphs over present difficulties by grasping with a tenacious hold the hopes of the future."[12] Northerners too, Confederate educational advocates warned, were carefully scrutinizing not only Confederate military capabilities, but also the state of southern society. Any sign of weakness or decay, such as the abandonment of educational interests, would only strengthen northern resolve. "Our Northern foe does not expect to conquer us merely by force of arms," Wiley argued in November 1861, but rather, "with the calculation which is his leading characteristic, he is looking anxiously for the drying up of the springs of our domestic life, or for such a social disorganization as will cripple us more than the loss of a battle in the field."[13] In their war for independence, southerners could ill afford to ignore the perceptions of outsiders, as European intervention, and especially the northern will to fight, could very well determine the outcome of the conflict. The best means of demonstrating the strength of southern society, these educators argued, would be through a widespread commitment on the part of the Confederate people to educate their children and break free from northern educational dominance despite the hardships of war.

In adapting their arguments to wartime realities, Confederate educators and advocates emphasized both the opportunities and dangers that the war presented to the cause of education and the future of southern youth. On the one hand, the war would allow southerners finally to free themselves from northern teachers and textbooks, and hopefully to bring southern teachers, publishers, and textbook authors the respect and patronage they had always lacked. On the other hand, however, the war, with its violence, heartache, and chaos, threatened at best to delay, and at worst to corrupt the moral education of southern children. Throughout the conflict, educators, religious leaders, and parents worried that the experience of war would undermine religious values and lead to the moral decay of southern society, unless immediate steps were taken to meet the challenge. The northern hordes were not the only enemy threatening to overrun the Confederacy. Strong moral and religious leadership would be required to protect southern children from that inevitable and omnipresent handmaiden of war: moral turpitude. "The minister, the parent, the teacher, and every other laborer in the moral vineyard, will find this foe encroaching upon the very grounds where he has been stationed for defence," the cosigners of the "Address to the People of North Carolina" warned. "In the minds and hearts of our younger children there is a citadel, whose possession, by good or bad principles, is to be decisive of our future fate."[14] Charged with the protection of this citadel, the members of the North Carolina State Educational Association urged their fellow Confederate teachers to use their "own peculiar weapons to defend the homes made sacred by the blood of our brave and patriotic troops from an invasion of that ignorance, vice and confusion, which are the fit and effective allies of those who seek our subjugation."[15]

There was no clear dividing line between secular and religious instruction in the South. Nor was there any perception that there should be. Wiley, a devout Presbyterian and future ordained minister, certainly believed that education's primary goal was to advance the cause of Christianity, and he proudly advocated "universal education as a means of vastly economizing and expanding the agencies for spreading the Gospel."[16] In their writings, educational advocates seamlessly merged this divine purpose with their nationalist agenda and used it to reinforce the drive for Confederate educational independence. Fostering Confederate nationalism and protecting southern children from moral depravity were the express missions of southern education, Wiley and other educational leaders argued, and the advancement of that mission was a cause all truehearted Christian southerners were duty-bound to support.

All of these arguments, of course, hinged on "anticipations of the future," to borrow the title of Edmund Ruffin's prophetic secessionist novel.[17] Education was the only means to ensure the future greatness of the Confederate nation, according to the educational reformers. Having dearly bought their independence with their fortunes and their very lifeblood, Confederates could not allow their glorious legacy to be bequeathed to a generation of uneducated moral delinquents. While all agreed in the ultimate value of an educated populace, Confederate educational advocates discovered an even more immediate justification as they attempted to rally the public to their cause: safeguarding the accomplishments of the present generation. In this war, Confederates saw themselves as fighting and dying for such noble causes as republicanism, political self-determination, freedom from tyranny, Christian virtue, and the preservation of a divinely ordained slave society. Without the right education, the rising generation would be ill-equipped to appreciate or defend these all-important ideals. "It cannot be expected that the under-standings of the very young will grasp the great principles at stake in our controversy with the North," Wiley's twelve North Carolina educators ex-plained, "and while they are in the midst of the more entertaining excite-ments of war, and out of view of its sterner realities, there is great danger that their minds will become dissipated, and that they will acquire habits which it will be difficult to eradicate, and which may unfit them for those great and solemn trusts which will soon be devolved upon them."[18] Even though their struggle for independence had barely begun, Confederates needed to take action to ensure that its legacy was protected and its ideals upheld in the future. Without a strong commitment to the proper education of their chil-dren, the war, even if successful, would be a pointless endeavor.

Having established the rationale for Confederate educational independence and demonstrated the self-interest and patriotic duty of every southerner to support it, Confederate educational advocates turned their attention to the trying business of providing southern children with an education during a time of war. Southern textbooks had to be written, published, and distrib-uted. Southern teachers had to be recruited, trained, and paid. Teachers and students alike somehow had to be persuaded to remain in the classroom as the tumult of war spiraled around them. Southern schools had to be main-tained, improved, and in some cases created. In short, the infrastructure of education had to be assembled, and quickly, if the Confederacy were to have any chance of establishing its own educational independence.

At the war's outset, and indeed throughout its entirety, the production of southern textbooks was deemed "our first intellectual necessity" by Confed-erate cultural nationalists.[19] The supply of teachers and the maintenance of schools were important concerns that would attract growing attention as the war progressed, but textbooks remained the focal point of the movement for Confederate educational independence. Nearly everything else "we may buy in ordinary times in the markets of the world, exactly suited to our wants," *Southern Field and Fireside* argued, but textbooks "can only be per-fectly adapted to our necessities by those of congenial habits of thought and like principles with ourselves."[20] True independence required a native edu-cational literature. "There is a large class of text-books which every inde-pendent nation, if it would maintain its independence, must have written and published by its own citizens," the twelve North Carolina educators explained. What was more, "the Southern States of America, distinguished by a peculiar social system [slavery], and one obnoxious to the phariseeism of the world, are especially called on to think in such things for themselves, and to see that their children are instructed out of their own writings."[21]

There were a number of reasons, ranging from the practical to the ideological, why the production of textbooks received the preponderant attention that it did. In the first place, it would be difficult to overstate the importance of textbooks in nineteenth-century classrooms. At a time when qualified teachers were few and those who did teach often showed little inclination for pedagogical innovation, it was the textbook that set the curriculum and structured the school day. In fact, schools often listed in their advertisements the titles of the textbooks used rather than the names of the teachers employed. With the classroom experience so centered on the textbook, it was no wonder that Confederate educational reformers focused on obtaining suitable books. The entire project of Confederate educational independence hinged on the ability of Confederate writers, teachers, and publishers to write, approve, and publish native textbooks, and to do so quickly.

The need was urgent. Southern schools were rapidly exhausting their supply of serviceable books. Already, by the summer of 1861, "the want of books" had become "an immediate, practical and pressing" concern.[22] At a July 1861 meeting of North Carolina teachers in Raleigh, the English textbook committee reported that "so far as we have been able to ascertain, there are not books enough within reach to supply our schools, except for a very few months."[23] The Confederacy was running out of books, and southerners had no choice "but to turn our attention to the publication of school-books, or to consign our children to ignorance and vagrancy until the close of the war."[24] Of those few books still available in the Confederacy, most were unusable, or at least unpalatable, due to the changed political climate. Northern teachers had been driven from the South, it was true, but their books remained. Always viewed with suspicion, northern textbooks became even more offensive once the war began, not only for the alleged fanaticism contained within, but also because their continued presence underscored the depths of southern dependence on the North. Given wartime animosity and the desire to establish the Confederacy as a self-sufficient nation, southern educators agreed that they could not in good conscience continue to use these foreign publications.

Another consideration that attracted these nationalist-minded educational reformers to textbook production was the truly national audience that these books could reach. Teacher training, school reform, and education budgets were necessarily local or state matters. There was no national Confederate system of education, nor was one desired. For commercial as well as patriotic reasons, however, textbooks would be geared and marketed towards the Confederacy as a whole.[25] Confederate textbooks would have titles like *The Confederate Primer*, *The Dixie Speller*, and *Our Own School Grammar*. Textbooks offered the opportunity to shape the education and perhaps the collective consciousness of an entire country, and as such, drew the immediate interest of Confederate cultural nationalists.

There was another, certainly less publicized, reason why the efforts of wartime educational reformers focused on textbook production. Their obsession with textbooks effectively obscured a tacit admission that gains in other important areas of educational development, namely teachers and schools, would be difficult, if not impossible during the war. With so many young men departing for the front, there was no avoiding the painful fact that many schools, and nearly all colleges and universities, would have to suspend classes, or at least carry on in a drastically diminished capacity. New teachers would be difficult to recruit. Families, facing the uncertainty of the times, might be forced to remove their children from the classroom. State and municipal funding, always precarious, certainly could not be counted on. In short, whether they admitted it or not, the immediate situation facing Confederate educators was bleak. It would be a struggle to maintain education at existing levels, let alone pursue the expansion required for true educational independence. Textbook production, however, could be implemented during the war in spite of the hardships. Even a reduced student population needed textbooks, and an independent Confederacy would need an extensive native educational literature when peace returned. The establishment of a native textbook industry, then, would be the first step, and an important one, toward Confederate educational self-sufficiency.

While nationalism, wartime isolation, and simple necessity required that the Confederacy produce its own schoolbooks, the question remained of how best to encourage "our practical working men" to write and publish them, and ensure that, once produced, these books found a receptive audience and lucrative market.[26] Confederate educational advocates had no doubt that "we have Southern material, and literature and talent enough, to manufacture *all* our text-books," but they feared that the Confederate people, distracted by war and accustomed to northern-produced goods, would not offer the immediate support required to encourage these fledgling efforts.[27] During the antebellum years, southern readers had developed an unfortunate prejudice "against everything of Southern production." Only textbooks with "the *im-*

primatur of the Harpers or the Appletons" attracted "the attention of the Southern man," a contributor to *De Bow's* complained bitterly.[28] As a result, at the start of the war, there was "scarcely a school book published at the South," noted the *Southern Christian Advocate*.[29] Discouraged by lack of public support, antebellum southern writers and publishers had seen little reason to continue their unappreciated efforts. The indifference of the public and the despondency of authors and publishers had combined to create a cycle of lethargy in the realm of southern educational literature. As one "young teacher" from Granville, North Carolina admitted, "we are all, to some extent, to blame; our scholars and men of letters for not originating and publishing, and we, the people generally, for not patronizing and sustaining them."[30]

Confederate educational advocates promised that the war years would be different, however. Patriotism would awaken the public to the need for native productions and reinvigorate authors and publishers. Wherever patriotism did not reach, necessity would fill in the gaps. Even so, educators and editors debated the most effective means of encouraging the rapid production of new textbooks, and of convincing authors and publishers to embrace the opportunities presented by the war. Some teachers' associations and periodicals began offering small cash prizes for estimable educational writing.[31] Others argued that the task of providing the South with its own educational literature was of such importance that direct government assistance was called for, through subsidies, investment incentives, tax and duty exemptions, or, at the very least, strict trade barriers to guarantee exclusive markets for southern publishers.[32]

Most educational leaders, however, recognized that such proposals were either too limited or too unrealistic. Beset by war and restrained by long-standing southern hostility to expansionist government, the state or Confederate governments could not be expected to play the leading role in encouraging the creation of an educational literature.[33] The impetus for textbook production, Confederate writers agreed, must come from home demand. In addition to patriotism, profit, or at least the promise of eventual profit, would be the lure that would rekindle the interest of southern writers and publishers. "Bounties will not stimulate a healthy production," Wiley's group of North Carolina educators concluded; "this always has and always will depend on consumption." The southern people alone had the necessary resources to finance the creation of a Confederate textbook literature, and the war and the blockade would provide exclusive access to this lucrative market for ambitious and quick-acting textbook publishers. As Wiley and his colleagues urged, "The first literature that pays, in any country, is that for educational purposes, as this is a prime necessity wherever there are schools; and hence our school system is to be the patron which is to call into life a new and essential business at the South."[34] Leading by example, the members of the North Carolina State Educational Association pledged, "to encourage the production of Southern Text Books, by buying such as are at all suitable to our wants, in preference to those of *all* other Countries, whatever the difference in price and mechanical execution."[35]

Textbooks were big business, or at least they were for northerners, and there was no reason why southern publishers could not now capitalize on a captive and sympathetic Confederate market. For instance, the northern-published *McGuffey Readers* were "the most widely read books in nineteenth-century America" after the King James Bible.[36] The publishers of Noah Webster's ubiquitous *Elementary Spelling Book* claimed to be printing 1.5 million copies a year by 1857.[37] A sizable portion of the sales of these and other northern textbooks had come from the South, and "having enriched them, having placed in their hands the wealth which they are now using to compass our ruin and subjugation," there was no reason why Confederates could not now channel these much-needed funds toward home production.[38]

Textbooks had a number of distinct advantages over other forms of book literature from the perspective of publishers. For one, the demand for textbooks was steady and widespread. Children needed schoolbooks, war or no war. The same could not necessarily be said for novels, poetry, biographies, histories, or the other branches of popular book literature. During these exciting times, southern readers wanted up-to-date reports on the progress of the war—something books simply could not provide. As a consequence, Confederate publishers devoted most of their initial efforts to the production of newspapers, periodicals, published speeches, sermons, tracts, sheet music, and pamphlet literature. Although native authors did manage to produce a few quasi-book-length and politically timely works during the first year of the war such as James Lyons's *Four Essays on the Right and Propriety of Secession*, Harrison Berry's seemingly incongruous *Slavery and Abolitionism, as Viewed by a Georgia Slave*, and T. W. MacMahon's *Cause and Contrast: An Essay on the American Crisis*, these were exceptional, and in any case, were more akin to extended pamphlets than books in their own right.[39]

Textbooks were different. Prompted by patriotism and assured that the public would now buy their books, Confederate writers and publishers immediately set to work to provide their new nation with its own textbook literature. In June 1861, J. D. Campbell of the *North Carolina Journal of Educa-*

tion was delighted to report that native authors were "already at work, and we expect to see *North Carolina* books ready for our children to use, during the present year."[40] Campbell was right. During the year following secession, schoolbook production soared, and not just in North Carolina. The Confederacy's first geography textbook appeared so quickly that the late-seceding states of Virginia, North Carolina, Tennessee, and Arkansas were still shown as part of the United States.[41] Over the course of the war, Confederate publishers produced well over 100 different textbooks with at least eighteen titles appearing in 1861 alone.[42] Printers from all over the Confederacy eagerly entered into the textbook trade. In 1861, textbooks were issued by publishers in Richmond, Greensboro, Charleston, New Orleans, Athens, Savannah, Atlanta, Macon, Memphis, and Nashville. Most of these were already established printers, but some, like Sterling & Campbell (soon to become Sterling, Campbell, & Albright), were new companies dedicated exclusively to the production of Confederate textbooks. Some of these books, such as Richard H. Rivers's *Elements of Moral Philosophy*, Epes Sargent's *The Standard Speller*, and Richard Whately's *Elements of Logic* and *Elements of Rhetoric*, were republications of earlier works now seeking a wider southern audience, but the majority of textbook publications were new. Of the books that appeared in 1861, most were intended for the education of young children, including four spellers, four primers, three grammars, one arithmetic, and one geography. There were a few books geared toward older students as well, including three works of philosophy, one book of French, and one chemistry textbook.[43]

In their prefaces and introductions, the authors credited nationalistic motives for their efforts and consciously situated their works within the larger struggle for Confederate independence. Charles Smythe, in the preface to his *Our Own Primary Grammar*, explicitly linked the creation of a southern educational literature, and the publication of his book in particular, with the "intellectual" revolution that southern independence mandated. Having undertaken this project "at our own risk and under great disadvantages," Smythe called upon southern "friends of education" for "aid and encouragement."[44] A. S. Worrell offered two reasons for writing his new grammar: "first, *that every independent nation must furnish its own literature*; and second, *that none of the works hitherto presented to the public are perfect*."[45] Likewise, Reverend Allen M. Scott grandiosely boasted of his new book that "for the first time in the history of our beloved South, a new Grammar, written by one of her own sons, printed by a Southern house and in a Southern city, goes forth to battle with critics and instruct the young."[46] Clearly, the calls of the cultural nationalists had not fallen on deaf ears. Textbook authors attributed their own efforts to the inspirations of nationalism and sought to attract patronage by appealing to those same sympathies within the Confederate public at large.

That said, there did not seem to be much that was uniquely "southern" about the content of these new Confederate textbooks. Generally, they followed models established by the popular schoolbooks of the day, if they did not copy the text directly. In many cases, the only thing that differentiated these textbooks from their northern competitors was the removal of northern place names and the substitution of southern ones in the reading passages and word problems. But even these seemingly small revisions were hailed as progress towards educational self-sufficiency. If the content was not entirely original, cultural nationalists maintained, its compilation was, and more to the point, it had been assembled by truehearted southerners. These books were "safe" for southern children because any poisons hidden within northern textbooks had been carefully screened by watchful southern eyes. In addition, the sale of these books rewarded ambitious Confederate publishers and encouraged the future growth of a vibrant and ultimately original southern textbook literature.

Early Confederate textbooks were not entirely devoid of original material or political content, however. Given their audience and limited vocabulary, spelling books and primers for young children were not ideal vehicles for political discourse or the dissemination of nationalist ideology.[47] Nevertheless, some Confederate textbook authors could not resist commenting on the present struggle. At the end of the "Promiscuous Exercises" section of *The Principles of English Grammar*, A. S. Worrell took up the issue of secession directly by asking if the southern states had had a right to secede—"a question of no little importance." He told his young readers that "nearly all the Northern States violated the plain letter of the Constitution in their efforts to abolish or circumscribe slavery; for the Constitution, which the States all agreed to live under, was a *slave* Constitution." In a somewhat loaded question, he further asked, "Was it *wrong* for us to separate from a people who would not regard their obligations to us? who were using their utmost energies to destroy our *equality*, our *property*, our *respectability*, and take upon *themselves* the management of *our own* property, and thus make us their *slaves*?" Not surprisingly, Worrell concluded that "no sane man, unbiased by prejudice, can say that it was. . . . *Secession* or *ignominious submission*, was our only remedy. The States that seceded, therefore, did *right*."[48] While Worrell's was the most extensive justification of the southern cause to be found in the pages of Confederate textbooks in 1861, other authors, in their prefaces, introductions, and occasionally within the lessons themselves, expressed

similar sentiments and affirmed their commitment to Confederate independence.[49] But whether explicitly stated or not, all Confederate textbooks, by
very virtue of their wartime southern publication, self-consciously advanced
the cause of Confederate cultural nationalism, and authors and publishers
appealed to the public for support in precisely these terms.

Recognizing the importance of a native textbook literature, editors across
the Confederacy hailed enthusiastically the arrival of these books and urged
their readers to taste these first fruits of cultural independence. The *North
Carolina Journal of Education* rejoiced at the publication of Charles Smythe's
Our Own Primary Grammar, declaring it to be "a harbinger of that true independence which we all should desire to achieve for our Country and without
which, a mere political independence will be but a name. We must think for
ourselves, we must write and publish our own books, especially those from
which our children are to imbibe their earliest modes of thought."[50] Likewise,
the *Educational Repository and Family Monthly* celebrated the arrival of John
Darby's chemistry book as "the first text-book, we believe, that has been
issued from the Confederate States, bearing the imprint of Southern houses
alone," and George Bagby of the *Southern Literary Messenger* declared the
newly issued *Confederate Primer* and *First* and *Second Confederate Spellers* to
be vast improvements over "the clap-trap publications of Yankee land."[51]

But even in their praise, editors and educational leaders were careful to
maintain critical standards. After all, it was not enough that a book be written
and published in the South, it also had to be of merit. At a meeting of North
Carolina teachers in Raleigh on July 9, 1861, the Committee on Classical
Textbooks cautioned against "hasty publication" and urged instead "that an
earnest effort be made to bring the works to the highest standard of modern
philological research."[52] Only superior textbooks could permanently supplant northern competitors. For this reason, Confederate reviewers emphasized the pedagogical virtues of these new books as well as their southern
origins. For instance, after voicing some mild criticisms of Smythe's new
grammar, the *North Carolina Journal of Education* concluded that "so far as
we have been able to examine this first North Carolina school book, that has
made its appearance since commencement of the war, we are much pleased
with it, and consider it equal, if not superior to any English Grammar for
beginners that we have ever examined."[53] Bagby also particularly stressed the
"strictly philosophical and progressive plan" of the *Confederate Primer* and
Spellers in asserting their superiority over corrupt northern works.[54]

Other books did not fare so well under critical scrutiny. For instance, *Southern Teacher* had hoped to recommend a series of reading books written be-

fore the war by "a Southern teacher of the city of Charleston, and . . . prepared expressly for the use of Common Schools in the South." Their southern pedigree, however, was not enough to merit their endorsement. "We have examined them with some care," the reviewer explained, and while "we have no doubt at the time they were written, they were regarded as works of superior merit," there were now "several series" available "in many respects far superior to these."[55] Throughout the war, editors and commentators continued to offer a mix of encouragement and constructive criticism for the ever-growing number of Confederate textbooks that flowed from southern presses. Although the reviews were almost always more encouraging than critical, the idea that textbooks needed to be approved before attaining a general circulation remained strong. Some teachers' groups and educational journals even attempted to provide formal frameworks by which books could receive official endorsements.[56] But whether it came from teachers' associations or from editorial reviews, the message was the same: Confederate textbooks had to be both southern-produced and of sufficient pedagogical value to merit their use in the classroom. Inferior or slapdash textbooks, though they certainly existed in the Confederacy, were condemned on the grounds that true educational independence required books that not only had been purged of northern fanaticism, but also upheld the highest educational standards.

WHILE TEXTBOOK PRODUCTION ABSORBED much of the attention of educational reformers in 1861, other aspects of Confederate education were not neglected. Maintaining southern schools and finding qualified teachers to staff them were significant challenges facing southern educators, administrators, and parents, and these issues immediately entered the public discourse on the future of Confederate education. While Confederate educational advocates hoped that a native textbook literature would blossom and flourish during the war, their primary concern when it came to schools was simple survival. With older male students departing for the front, and younger ones of both sexes being called home, with state funding in jeopardy and teachers in short supply, it was an open question whether the Confederate States could maintain the modest schools they had, let alone expand them. Closure was not an option. Even a short suspension would prove disastrous to the future of the southern nation, educational advocates warned. "If our fields are laid waste and our homes burned down, we can re-build the one and replant the other, and in a short time wipe out every trace left by the enemy," the *Greensborough Patriot* explained, "but if your school-houses are shut up, even for a few years, and our common school system broken up, it will take many long and weary years to regain the position which we now occupy."[57]

Forced to cut their losses, educators rallied to preserve those schools whose students, by age or gender, could not be called into battle. "If it is deemed expedient to suspend our higher male seminaries," the *Southern Presbyterian* conceded reluctantly, "by all means let us keep the common schools of the country, those at which the masses of the rising race must be educated, in successful operation."[58] Wartime hardships might prevent southern schools from offering the full range of services expected in peacetime, but they could not cease to function entirely, for the future of the Confederacy depended upon a rising generation "train[ed] up" in "learning, virtue, and religion."[59] "Whatever the circumstances of the country, there will be children at home who can only be usefully employed in study," and it was to these children that educational leaders directed their immediate attention.[60]

First, Confederate educational reformers needed to find competent teachers to run the schools and teach the children. The quality of Confederate education hinged largely on the ability of southerners to produce qualified teachers from among their own population, and to do so in sufficient numbers as to ensure that southern children would be instructed solely by true-hearted southerners. Educational advocates faced three major wartime challenges when it came to teachers. First, they would have to persuade current teachers to remain at their jobs and not allow the war to distract them from their important work. Next, educational leaders would have to recruit a large number of new teachers in order to meet the demand created by the departure of northern instructors. Finally, they would have to establish professional standards and teachers' colleges in order to guarantee that all Confederate teachers had the intellectual, pedagogical, and moral qualifications necessary to guide the future development of the nation.

Finding enough willing and capable southerners to staff the various schools and academies of the Confederacy would be difficult. The South had never been able to muster a sufficient number of native teachers. Northern teachers and private instructors, both male and female, had found ready employment in the southern states performing the tasks that self-respecting southerners refused to do themselves. As already discussed, northern interlopers were constant targets of southern suspicion, but the fact remained that southern education, such as it was, depended upon these northerners for its day-to-day operations. While secession had removed these potentially disruptive pedagogical influences, it also created a tremendous teacher shortage in the

South. At the beginning of the war, there were simply not enough teachers to go around.

To make matters worse, the war threatened to pull many southern educators out of classrooms and into the ranks. The first order of business, then, was to convince these men to stay at their posts. Confederate teachers had their own unique patriotic duty to fulfill, educational reformers intoned, and "however ready they may be to march forth at their countries call," they had "an equally important part to perform, at the head of the little army which they are leading to less bloody conquests in the field of science."[61] Indeed, so vital were these teachers to the future of the Confederate nation that the *North Carolina Presbyterian* urged "every community to throw obstacles in the way of their going to war; since the military service of the country will not gain as much from their enlistment as the interests of education will lose."[62] Despite the general rush to battle, the southern people had to make a concerted effort to retain their educators, by affirming the importance of their teachers, dissuading them from abandoning the schoolhouse for the camps, and later, when it became necessary, exempting them from compulsory military service.[63]

But even if all the eligible teachers had decided to remain in the classroom (and they did not), there still would not have been enough to fill the gaps left by departing northerners. Southerners would have to recruit new teachers out of their own ranks if their children were to receive even a remedial education. Concerned writers and educators had complained for decades about the difficulty of persuading southerners to pursue careers in education. Teaching was not a high paying profession in the South, but more than this, it was not a respected profession. In general, southern men and women of education and refinement did not become teachers. Apart from a dedicated few, the task of teaching was left to northern visitors and southerners without means or prospects. Most southerners who taught viewed their employment as temporary, not as a vocation. Southern educational reformers had long known the solution to this problem. " 'Is it hard to command a Southern Lawyer, Doctor or Minister?' " editor W. S. Barton asked. " 'No!' 'Why not?' 'Because the profession is honorable.' The way is plain, make the profession honorable and there will be no want of teachers. It is the degradation attached to it, that causes hundreds to avoid it."[64] The way may have been "plain" to Barton and others during the antebellum years, but they had few practical ideas on how to actually raise the social standing of teachers and "make the profession honorable."

Independence and war, however, promised to do just that. Confederate nationalism would bring a new sense of dignity, importance, and patriotic sacrifice to the profession of teaching. For those who could not fight due to age, infirmity, temperament, or gender, teaching offered a way to contribute directly to the national cause. Furthermore, with the departure of northern teachers, southerners simply had no choice but to undertake the education of their own children. "The necessity for Northern teachers may have been unavoidable, to a very considerable extent, up to the present," *Southern Teacher* admitted, "but it must cease now forever. There is but one way to remedy the evil, and that is to train up teachers at home."[65]

Thus, it was hoped, a combination of patriotism and necessity would persuade southerners to become teachers in the service of their country and induce the Confederate public to accord them the esteem they deserved. But issues of decorum and class consciousness would have to be overcome first, in order to make this sort of public employment palatable to members of the respectable classes. Indeed, class concerns were inseparable from the story of antebellum southern education in general.[66] Many of the complaints leveled against the "half educated and incompetent teachers" employed throughout the South were objections to the class and character of those reduced to teaching, more so than objections to their pedagogical qualifications.[67] The native Confederate education that its advocates envisioned required a different type of teacher—one whose social standing, refinement, and moral virtue would inspire students. In order to attract these southern men and women, changes would have to be made. For instance, during the antebellum years, school masters often traveled door-to-door and town-to-town seeking employment. Respectable southern men and women could not be expected to participate in this kind of public pandering. If the Confederacy wished to recruit first-rate teachers, a more discreet system, one "adapted to the native impulses and characteristics of the Southern mind," would have to be implemented. The public had no right to assume that self-respecting southerners would simply accept the same degraded roles as northern itinerants. Allowances would have to be made. "If the public expect Southern educated gentlemen, much less Southern educated ladies, to thrust themselves forward, and stand candidates for place before the public gaze, as is the custom of our Northern friends, they will be mistaken, and fail to secure what they want, and what we have an abundance of the very best material to supply," President George Naff of the Soule Female College in Murfreesboro warned. "Some means must be devised by which place can be sought and obtained at a smaller sacrifice of modesty than is usual."[68] Naff's suggestion was to use educational journals, and the *Educational Repository and Family Monthly* specifically, as placement agencies. The journals would provide advertisement space for teachers seeking positions and schools seeking teachers, and would also privately forward applications between the parties.[69]

Naff had hit upon a problem that had continually hampered efforts to recruit southern teachers in the past and would likely discourage their participation in the future. In order to attract the type of people that would elevate perceptions of southern education, accommodations would have to be made to the class-based and often gender-based sensibilities of reluctant potential teachers. During the course of the Confederacy's short life, the exigencies of war would cause ground to be given on both sides. Teaching did become an accepted wartime employment for many southerners, especially women, who in the past never would have considered undertaking such work. For their part, these new female teachers were forced to modify their rules of etiquette, expand their spheres of acceptable activity, and enter into gainful employment, albeit with pronounced ambivalence.[70] It is notable, however, that Confederate educational activists at the very beginning of the war recognized these formidable class-based barriers to teacher recruitment and formulated proposals to circumvent them.

While obtaining the right sort of southerners to serve as teachers would ensure that children had proper role models in the classroom, these new teachers still would have to be trained in order to possess the pedagogical skills required to be effective instructors. Thus, the quality of southern education could be assured only through the creation of schools and colleges specifically dedicated to teacher training.[71] Establishing such schools would professionalize teaching and help boost the social standing of educators. If education was indeed on par with other respected professions, then surely it too required specialized schools to train its practitioners. "It is just as impossible to educate teachers for the profession of teaching, without Schools of this character, as to prepare young men for the practice of Medicine without Medical Colleges," the *Southern Teacher* argued in May 1861. "It is a wide mistake to suppose that Colleges are sufficient for this purpose. . . . The young graduate of the Literary College learns the art of teaching only from practice, and enters upon its duties ignorant of the first step to be taken. He is just as unprepared for the duty before him as he would be for the science of Surgery."[72]

At the beginning of the war, at least two "normal schools" existed in the South, one in Charleston and one in New Orleans, but this was hardly sufficient to meet the educational demand.[73] According to the *Southern Teacher*, it was no coincidence that "the gallant State of South Carolina was not only first to resist Northern aggression, and to lead the way to the formation of the Confederate States," but was also the first "to found an institution for the education of her own teachers." The two actions were born out of the same desire to overthrow northern tyranny and establish southern political and intellectual independence. Now, as with secession, it was time for the rest of the South to follow South Carolina's bold example and for "every State at once [to] take steps for establishing Normal Schools of a high order."[74]

In common with grandiose schemes to create great new Confederate universities or dramatically expand southern common schools, many of these improvements would have to wait until peace returned.[75] Predictions that "the day is not distant when every Southern State will have a well endowed Normal College" seemed quite unrealistic so long as the Confederacy was devoting its attention, resources, and lifeblood to winning the war.[76] Still, normal school proposals were not simply idle fantasies. As the war progressed, demand for qualified teachers was such that, despite the obstacles, Confederates did take strides toward providing their teachers with a professional education. Some normal schools were indeed founded during the war, often as separate departments of existing schools and colleges. Some even offered free tuition in order to encourage women, in particular, to enter the profession.[77] For now, however, educational reformers focused their attention on cataloging the immediate, as well as long-term, needs of Confederate education. They hoped that by drawing the public's attention to the South's dire lack of qualified teachers, reformers could set the agenda that would guide Confederate educational development through the war years and beyond.

The primary advocates pushing this agenda were the teachers' associations and organizations. Some of these groups, like the North Carolina State Educational Association and the Educational Institute of the Methodist Episcopal Church, South, had been founded during the late antebellum years, while others like the Educational Association of the Confederate States of America and the Educational Association of Virginia would grow out of the war itself.[78] The educational journals of the Confederacy were in effect teachers' organizations created by groups of concerned educators, and some, like the *North Carolina Journal of Education* and the *Educational Repository and Family Monthly*, were the official organs of formal educational associations.[79] There were also smaller, usually county-based, educational associations composed of local teachers addressing mostly local concerns. These were especially active in North Carolina.[80] Besides these organizations and editorial boards, there were numerous informal and temporary teachers' groups that came together to author textbooks or issue public statements at various times during the war.[81]

These groups—formal and informal—served a number of purposes. First and foremost, they represented the interests of the South's teachers. They advocated the creation of teachers' colleges; petitioned for higher wages, better working conditions, and job security; lobbied for state educational support and teacher draft exemption; and strove to gain the respectability that the teaching profession deserved and, for its future, required. They also worked to maintain morale by continually reminding southern teachers of their vital role in the war. Finally, these associations effectively spearheaded the general campaign for educational independence, pushing for native textbooks and better schools. They tried to keep educational issues front and center in the public's eye, even during the darkest days of the war.

The largest and best organized of the teachers' organizations was the North Carolina State Educational Association. It was also the most comprehensive in its goals and articulate in its message. Composed of prominent North Carolina educators, led by the indefatigable Calvin Wiley, and publicized through the *North Carolina Journal of Education*, the association immediately took the lead in agitating for wartime educational reform and Confederate intellectual independence. The association "endeavor[ed] to lead the public mind . . . to just views in regard to the true elements of national strength," all the while encouraging "teachers and others of kindred occupations never to despair of the Republic, but to stand at their posts through every storm and trial, supporting and animating each other, and determined that neither the United States or any other Power shall force us to the abandonment of these moral agencies, the want of which will leave us in the end dependent on our enemies for books, for schools, for teachers, and for all the influences that make and direct society."[82]

Though state-based, the ideology of the association was strongly nationalistic. At their meeting in November 1861, the members resolved to "discountenance and frown on all insinuations that the people of the Confederate States are not able . . . to maintain their Independence against any human power." They promised to encourage the production of native textbooks by purchasing and assigning only works by southern authors and publishers. They offered "premiums" for essays on various pedagogical topics in order to encourage teachers to contribute articles to the educational journals and hopefully inspire them to undertake textbook authorship. They pleaded for the maintenance of southern schools, and the need to create new and better ones on par with the North and Europe. In short, they endorsed the entire campaign for Confederate educational independence and vowed to constantly strive, prod, and agitate for its attainment.[83] While representing North Carolina teachers, the association did not restrict itself solely to their particular interests. Rather, it attempted to speak for the educational concerns of all southerners.

The best way to mobilize teachers and attract public attention, advocates believed, was through teachers' conventions. By assembling in one place, teachers could demonstrate their unity as a profession. At these conventions, they could formulate wartime educational agendas, affirm their commitment to the Confederate cause, approve new textbooks, track teacher shortages and other immediate needs, as well as generate publicity through newspaper and magazine coverage. While some local teachers' associations already conducted monthly meetings, there was a perceived need for a national or at least a regional southern teachers' conference to address broader educational policies and objectives. For this reason, numerous calls went forth in 1861 to bring together a large body of teachers to deal with pressing wartime concerns. S. E. Goetzel, a publisher and bookseller from Mobile, called for a "*Convention of Southern Teachers*, to take into consideration the subject of school-books, and recommend a series which shall thence be adopted throughout the Confederacy."[84] More ambitiously, "an esteemed correspondent" for the *Educational Repository and Family Monthly* proposed "a general Convention of educators in the South" to be assembled in Atlanta in July "for the purpose of taking concerted action in regard to the supply of our school books."[85] While all recognized the utility of such meetings, logistical and transportation problems created by the war effectively thwarted many of these early efforts to bring teachers together.

As was often the case, North Carolina was the notable exception. North Carolina educators staged not one, but two major teachers' meetings during the first year of the war as a result of the determination of Calvin Wiley, the help of preexisting teachers' networks and associations, and the state's relative insulation from the fighting (excepting its coast). On July 9, 1861, Wiley assembled a group of college and seminary teachers in Raleigh to discuss the newborn Confederacy's dire need for schoolbooks. After hearing reports detailing the lack of acceptable books in the South, the attendees formed committees to address the textbook needs of common schools—basic primers, grammars, and spellers—as well as the production of more advanced works in the fields of mathematics, natural sciences, English, Latin, and Greek. They also created a committee on college textbooks. Significantly, these teachers proceeded to pass resolutions in favor of convening a national convention in order to construct a comprehensive educational strategy for the country as whole.[86] Most important, the ideas discussed at this meeting were committed to paper by Wiley and published soon thereafter as the influential "Address to the People of North Carolina."

This July "Meeting of Teachers" was essentially a brainstorming session for educational leaders struggling to meet the new challenges presented by separation. In order to formulate a wartime educational agenda and energize the teachers of North Carolina, and of the rest of the Confederacy by extension, a larger, more inclusive and more official convention was required. With this in mind, Wiley and his supporters set to work to organize the Sixth Annual Meeting of the State Educational Association following the July meeting. Despite the obstacles created by war and the unsettled condition of the country, the organizers were determined to hold their annual convention as usual and to assemble as many teachers as possible for the proceedings. The meeting would take place on November 19, 1861, in Greensboro. The organizers did all they could to encourage North Carolina teachers and other "friends of education" to participate. Delegates could attend the meeting free of cost, and railroad companies agreed to provide half-price fares. "Never was there a time when teachers, authors, and friends of education could labor with better prospects of immediate usefulness to the State," the *North Carolina Journal of Education* urged. "We cannot but hope that our educators will be fully impressed with a sense of their obligations, and rise to the dignity of the crisis in which they are placed."[87] Inspired by this charge, approximately sixty members of the Association made the trip to Greensboro. Though "not as large as usual," the number was impressive given the circumstances, and more than enough to proceed with drafting a plan of action.[88]

The overall message of the meeting was one of dedication to the national cause and determination to advance the struggle for educational independence during the war. Significantly, members debated not only the course of North Carolina education, but also the general educational interests of the country as a whole.[89] Wiley and his fellow participants knew that their actions and words would reach beyond the borders of North Carolina, and much of their rhetoric was directed toward a national audience. The printed proceedings of this meeting appeared complete in the *North Carolina Journal of Education* and were excerpted in newspapers across the Confederacy. The proceedings, along with the earlier "Address to the People of North Carolina," represented the key founding documents of the movement for Confederate educational independence. Together they served as both ideological underpinning and plan of action for education reform, not just in North Carolina, but for the entire Confederacy.

Beyond its message, the fact that southern educators managed to stage a major teachers' convention in the midst of war showed their determination to play an active role in the development of an autonomous Confederate culture. This meeting, as well as the other teachers' conventions held throughout the war, demonstrated the cohesion and patriotism of the teaching profession as well as its willingness to assume a leadership position in the struggle for Confederate intellectual independence. Rather than allow educational issues to fall by the wayside during the war, teachers, through their associations and conventions, continued to push for an expanded Confederate educational system with its own books, its own teachers, and its own schools that would equal in merit and excel in morals that of their northern enemies.

All this attention to Confederate education—both in terms of who should be taught during the war and who should do the teaching—forced a dramatic reconceptualization of southern female education. While the quality and availability of education in general was very uneven throughout the antebellum South, it had been particularly so when it came to women. The daughters of wealthy planters were well served by the numerous academies and female colleges that sprang up before the war, but these were often only available to the rich.[90] The majority of young southern women received a haphazard education. Even many of those southerners who insisted on seeing that their sons obtain a full education saw little point in providing their daughters with an equivalent level of schooling.

For those fortunate few who were permitted to pursue education beyond the primary level, the content, duration, and purpose of their instruction differed from that of their brothers. For many southern ladies, education was primarily an adornment, a mark of class. "The accomplished lady of the day seems to be of no further practical utility to the world than to contribute to the amusement of her friends," Professor R. N. Price complained to readers of the *Home Circle*. "She is little more than a striking and attractive article of parlor furniture; she is a mere creature of fancy—a butterfly, that flutters a while in the social breeze, exhibiting her pretty colors for the amusements of amateurs, then pines and dies, feeling that she has adequately answered the ends of her creation!"[91] While academic subjects were certainly taught, the focus of female education remained on cultivating proper morals and social graces. The southern gentleman wanted a wife who would "minister to his wants and pleasure," one writer in *De Bow's Review* observed. He did not necessarily want a highly educated wife, just an adequately educated one.[92]

Growing up in this environment, southern girls had absorbed many of these values. The proper goal of young southern ladies was marriage, preferably as soon as possible, and they were often averse to remaining in school too long for fear of wasting time and perhaps even hurting their chances of obtaining the best match. That "our women marry too early" was a constant complaint of educational reformers. "A vicious public sentiment has stamped the character of a woman who remains unmarried, either from choice or necessity, with something of disgrace. Hence it is that young women yet in their early teens, chafe at the restraints of the school and sigh to launch forth upon the ocean of life." Rushing into marriage with their minds and bodies yet "undeveloped," young southern women resigned themselves to intellectual immaturity.[93]

But the coming of the war gave reformers new hope. Secession and war had altered, or at least unsettled, southern society, and educational advocates perceived immediately that these years could provide a window of opportunity to enact long overdue reforms. "The time . . . is auspicious," wrote one eager columnist in *De Bow's Review*. "The beginning of our career as an independent nation, a career destined, we believe, to be prosperous beyond all comparison in the annals of history, ought to be signalized by the beginning of a nobler, loftier career for women."[94] There were a number of reasons why the war years were believed to be "auspicious" for the cause of southern female education. For one, the unprecedented situation on the home front forced Confederates to focus their attention on the role and status of women in southern society. With most of the able-bodied men away from home, and even more to go as the war continued, southern society became progressively feminized. Women were forced to assume an increasing number of what had been considered "male" roles and responsibilities.[95] They managed plantations, undertook wage labor, conducted business, and in innumerable other ways entered into the public sphere. The congregations to which ministers preached, the audiences before which orators spoke, and the readership upon which editors and publishers depended were largely female. This was especially so when it came to the Confederacy's schools. With young men marching off to fight, and many of the South's male academies, seminaries, and colleges forced to close, the focus of Confederate intermediate and higher education would necessarily turn to its remaining female schools and students. During the war, then, southerners would have little choice but to confront the practices and inadequacies of female education, and reformers were anxious to convert this newfound attention into support for meaningful change.

The interest in female education was also driven by the Confederacy's desperate need for teachers and a growing awareness that only by attracting large numbers of women to the profession could southerners hope to keep their schools running. With northern teachers gone, male southern teachers leaving for the front, and no ready supply of educated southern men to take their place, the large-scale employment of female teachers was the only viable option. Indeed, in some ways, women teachers were believed to have advantages over their male counterparts. The maternal instinct and supposed moral superiority of women recommended them as instructors for children, especially the very young. While southern women had served as teachers during the antebellum years, they had never been actively recruited as a sex. Wartime conditions, however, now necessitated such gender-specific recruitment. The departure of male teachers presented southern women with "a glorious opportunity of usefulness," Calvin Wiley told them in January 1862.[96] "Patriotism calls them to the school room," editor J. D. Campbell likewise prodded. "Ladies, it is a *duty* that you owe your State, in this her time of trial; think of it, act upon it."[97]

If women were to become the primary teachers of southern children, it was only logical that they themselves be properly educated. In urging Confederate women to "come to the rescue" and "*volunteer* in this warfare against *ignorance* and *vice*," educational advocates also "charge[d] them to look well to their armor, to see that they spare no efforts to prepare and equip themselves thoroughly for the great work that is before them."[98] Thus, the growing demand for female education reform went hand-in-hand with efforts to recruit native teachers. The skewed education of the antebellum years could not adequately prepare women for the vital roles they would be called upon to play. In the interest of the Confederacy's future, "thousands of select female minds" had to be "thoroughly cultivated."[99]

Sensing their opportunity, educational advocates and other cultural nationalists produced a spate of articles, pamphlets, and speeches designed to rally women to the Confederate cause and, in turn, to alert the public to the new nation's obligation to provide a proper education for its women. Proponents of reform were quick to point out that shortcomings in female education could not be blamed on the Yankees, however much they were responsible for other evils plaguing southern education. As one anonymous contributor to *De Bow's Review* explained in a remarkable article, it was not "Yankeeism," but rather a "belief, unexpressed though it may be, that the female mind is so inferior to the male that it does not deserve the fostering care of Government" that had prevented southern female education from "occupying that rank to which it is entitled."[100]

In making their case for reform, advocates attacked long-standing notions about female intellectual inferiority and insisted instead on the existence of a mental equivalency between the sexes. "Female intellect differs from male intellect in kind, not in degree," Professor Price instructed the readers of the *Home Circle*.[101] While upholding some conventions about the differences between the male and female mind—with the male geared toward reason and the female toward sentiment—reformers nevertheless rejected the idea that one was superior to the other or more deserving of educational advantages. There may be separate male and female spheres, Price admitted, but "it remains to be proved that a high order of mental development is less necessary in the one sphere than in the other."[102] "The desire of knowledge is naturally as strong in women as in men, and its gratification accompanied with a pleasure just as exquisite," the writer in *De Bow's* maintained, and therefore "that system of society is wrong which condemns woman to comparative ignorance."[103]

Such arguments were not new. Proponents of female education had been making their case in these terms since long before the war. However, the war itself provided a new twist to these old arguments. Given the staunch support of southern women for secession and the Confederate cause, and in view of the duties they would be called upon to perform during the war, reformers argued that women deserved to share directly in the benefits of independence. The new nation would owe much to its women, and educational leaders urged them to collect on this debt by insisting on significant reform. "The wisdom of Government interfering at all in education may be questioned," one writer admitted, "but surely if it interferes at all it is but just that the female sex should share, to some extent, in its bounty."[104] In recognition of the contributions of Confederate women, "who, with a prescience and a zeal surpassing that of men, urged on the present revolution, and who are now devoting all their energies and industry to clothe the soldier, to heal his wounds, to tend on him in sickness, and to relieve the wants of his family," George Fitzhugh heartily applauded the increased attention paid to female education and he exhorted his countrymen to give women their due.[105] In fact, one commentator even suggested that the strong support for secession displayed by southern women might have been unconsciously rooted in "an instinctive perception of the great advantages which would result to their sex from Southern independence." But whatever the reason, "the part contributed by her in throwing off a hateful and despotic sectionalism has not been a slight one; and in the advantages resulting from the political revolution she ought to share largely."[106]

This contention—that women had earned the right to a proper education through their support of, and service to, the Confederacy—had important advantages over the more abstract arguments about the equivalency of the male and female minds. In the conservative Old South, where gender roles were staunchly upheld as a matter of pride, demands for educational equality on the basis of intellectual equivalency smacked of Yankee fanaticism. However, when framed as a right earned through patriotic devotion and service, such demands seemed far less radical and disruptive to the social order. Sensing this, wartime advocates for female education reform were careful to always couch their appeals in the most overtly patriotic terms possible.

But convincing the Confederate public to support these initiatives was only half the battle. The young women themselves had to be willing to take advantage of the new opportunities presented by Confederate independence. Responsibility for the present state of female education lay with both sexes. "If he is to blame for asserting the inferiority of woman she is to blame for assenting so readily to the imputation and contentedly accepting the rank of an inferior creature." It was the fault of women themselves "for not making a better use of such educational advantages as are within [their] reach, limited as they are," and for accepting "the notion that the fruit which grows upon the higher branches of the tree of science is to them forbidden."[107] Thus, while public support was essential, "the reform in the system of education, to be complete, must begin with [young women]." Southern daughters had to resolve to remain in the classroom. "They must be willing to undergo the labor and toil of a thorough training." To that end, they had to "postpone a few years the period of marriage." The war would help with this: with the men away, women would be prevented from marrying young, and thus would be forced to focus on their studies. The war was a period of unprecedented opportunity to change attitudes and approaches toward female education, so long as the women themselves were willing to take advantage of it. "She has but to will it and the result will follow."[108]

Confederate proponents of female education reform were vague about the details. Exactly how southern female education was to be improved, how a proper curriculum was to be constructed, or how these proposed new and better schools were to be funded remained murky. For now, however, advocates focused their energies on convincing southerners of the importance of female education. They demanded that the education of women receive equal attention to that of men, and they sought to convince young women to seize every new opportunity presented them. The unique conditions imposed by war gave reformers hope that now was the time to push for these long contemplated changes, and they developed new arguments to convince southern women and the public at large that women deserved a rigorous and broad education.

The first year of the war witnessed hurried activity in the field of southern education. Driven by necessity, lest an entire generation of young southerners be lost to ignorance and vice, Confederate educational advocates rushed to identify the Confederacy's many shortcomings when it came to the education of its children. Educational leaders and teachers' associations bombarded the Confederate public with a flurry of articles, speeches, and pamphlets in an effort to highlight the reforms made incumbent by secession and separate nationality. Through a series of novel arguments, these advocates directly linked the cause of Confederate education to the successful prosecution of the war and the ultimate attainment of Confederate independence.

Such appeals seemed to be having the desired effect, and Confederate educators saw heartening signs during the year following secession. True, the war had created severe difficulties for the South's meager educational institutions and school systems, but the Confederacy's educational needs had been quickly cataloged and, more encouraging still, efforts were already underway to meet those needs with native southern books and truehearted southern teachers. Like the literary nationalists, Confederate educators had enlisted in the struggle for intellectual independence. While the enormity of the challenges before them necessitated an incremental approach, they nevertheless shared the same grand vision as their fellow cultural nationalists, and they anticipated eagerly the day when the Confederacy would be "the most independent [nation] on earth—independent of all except Him who is the Ruler of the universe."[109]

PART THREE

A Stride without Parallel in the
Progress of National Intellect: 1862–1864

CHAPTER FIVE

THE HIGH-WATER MARK

Just as the Confederate military effort charged to its symbolic high-water mark amid a copse of trees on Cemetery Ridge, so too did the struggle for Confederate intellectual independence dangle the prospect of success before the eyes of hopeful cultural nationalists. Between 1862 and 1864, the movement for Confederate cultural autonomy experienced its heyday, as southerners witnessed a dramatic expansion and remarkable diversification of native cultural productions. New and impressive periodicals appeared by the score. Books and textbooks flowed from presses across the Confederacy. Confederate literature expanded to include new genres, giving rise to Confederate belles lettres, humor magazines, illustrated periodicals, juvenile literature, histories, medical journals, soldiers' literature, and even theater. What was more, this expansion was driven by an increase in demand from the southern public. Confederate periodicals and books attained enormous circulations by antebellum standards. Whereas before the war, southern editors and publishers had pleaded for patronage, now the problem became finding enough paper and printing supplies to keep up with demand.

The tone of Confederate literature changed as well. During the first year of the war, Confederate editors had focused much of their attention on assigning blame for southern cultural deficiencies. Now their primary concern was obtaining the right native literature to fill their columns. To the amazement of cultural nationalists, their project seemed to be advancing at a pace that even they, in their wildest flights of fancy, could not have predicted. Given the underdeveloped state of southern publishing, increasing shortages of supplies and manpower, a rapidly depreciating currency, and a devastating war, it is a startling, almost unbelievable, fact that by the end of 1862, the Confederacy had just about entirely cast off its age-old dependence on northern publishers and was now able to satisfy domestic demand with its own products.[1]

No one was more surprised by the rapid development of Confederate print culture than its strongest advocates. Even the generally gloomy George Bagby of the perennially underappreciated *Southern Literary Messenger* could not contain his amazement. Marveling at the instant success of a number of new Confederate literary magazines, not to mention recent additions to his own subscription list, Bagby announced at the end of 1862 that "indications are not wanting . . . of an upward and onward movement in literature." By February 1863, he saw "the salutary results of our liberation from Yankee bondage . . . already developing themselves, in the field of Literature, upon a scale surpassing the anticipations of the most sanguine." "In the briefest imaginable space of time," he boasted, "literary enterprise in the South has taken . . . a stride without parallel in the progress of National Intellect."[2]

Nor was Bagby alone in his excitement. There was a general feeling among cultural nationalists that they were indeed witnessing the first stirrings of an intellectual and cultural renaissance in the South. In January 1864, the *Richmond Enquirer* noted with satisfaction that "notwithstanding the many drawbacks incident to a long and bloody war, *Literature* has grown apace in the Confederacy, and our people have at last become to rely exclusively on the exertions of Southern authors and publishers for intellectual entertainment and amusement."[3] "A Southern book, at one time, was a dreg in the market, now it immediately springs into popularity and is eagerly sought after," the new and enormously successful *Southern Illustrated News* reported with glee.[4] Likewise, Confederate humor magazine *Southern Punch* was delighted to find that "instead of Yankee pictorials, spread out in 'gorgeous array' " at southern newsstands, "one now sees the Southern literary papers and periodicals displayed for sale."[5] One columnist for the *Chattanooga Rebel* sought to encapsulate the rise of this new national Confederate literature within extended metaphor:

> "The house that is building," says an apt old proverb . . . "looks not as the house that is built." Nay, truly, but yet through the mass of rubbish, the piles of brick, the heaps of mortar, the scaffold poles, the hod-carries, and

the clouds of dust, we frequently get some notion of the edifice, which completed, is destined to crown this confusion and tumult. So is it with this Southern literature of ours. . . . The voice of its workmen is drowned in rolling drums; its stout foundation only faintly rises from the material . . . and we lose sight of the noble temple, amid so much smoke and noise of the elements. But trust our word for it, the building is going up slowly and surely, with the events of a revolution, the most gigantic on earth, for its base, and the sufferings and glories of a people for its pillars of life and light and inspiration.[6]

While there was some disagreement as to this building's state of completion, there was a definite consensus that "the first step in the establishment of a literature of our own has . . . been taken."[7]

Cultural nationalists heralded this burgeoning literature and the warm reception it received as evidence of the crystallization of true Confederate nationality. Eminent poet Henry Timrod, who in January 1864 took a job as assistant editor of the *Daily South Carolinian* in Columbia, certainly saw the rise of a wartime southern literature in these nationalist terms. "It must be confessed," he wrote in one of his first editorials, "that, until this war, the nationality of the Southern mind was never complete." The war had been "necessary to isolate us completely, and to define more sharply the boundaries of our national idiosyncrasy. . . . We are now a people to ourselves, while the very rim of our skirts is free from the contagion of Yankee influence."[8] Joseph Addison Turner, longtime southern cultural nationalist and cantankerous editor of the weekly journal *The Countryman*, agreed with Timrod's assessment. The wartime surge in the production and consumption of native literature indicated that southerners were coalescing into a nation. "The South [has become] Southernized at last."[9]

The war experience had transformed southerners into a people ready and willing to embrace their native culture, or so Confederate nationalists claimed. As one editor remarked in December 1862, "In very truth, the war, if it has not taken from us at once and entirely the habits of our whole existence in the past, has so altered and modified them that they are no longer the same. . . . [W]e have, insensibly, to a great extent, but certainly, undergone an extraordinary change."[10] "The people of the Confederate States are now as the heated iron," the *Southern Presbyterian* exclaimed. "Probably their minds and hearts were never so much awakened and alive as they are at this moment. War and revolution have quickened and aroused them in a wonderful manner. They are accessible to thoughts and feelings to which formerly they would have opposed the unyielding resistance of an utter indifference and apathy."[11]

Regardless of whether a national spiritual awakening or simple wartime necessity was driving this change, Confederate publishers, editors, and other cultural nationalists resolved to strike while the iron was hot and take advantage of the unique and possibly profitable opportunities that these altered circumstances presented. The obstacles facing such new endeavors were formidable but would-be publishers and newspapermen nevertheless believed that the opportunities outweighed the risks. As the new proprietors of the *Southern Illustrated News* explained in their first issue in mid-September 1862, "The times are in some respects inauspicious, but in others happy for such an undertaking. We labor under some material disadvantages, arising out of the existence of the blockade . . . but none, we confidently believe, that may not be overcome by energy."[12] Committed to the cause of Confederate intellectual independence and determined to exploit the advantages offered by their wartime isolation, publishers eagerly crowded into the Confederate marketplace.

Leading the charge, as they had during the early days of the war, were the Confederacy's literary papers and magazines. But the journals and editors enjoying unprecedented success in the middle years of the war often were not the same ones who had issued the intellectual call to arms in 1861. The disruptions and hardships of war had silenced many of the voices who had presided over the creation of the movement for Confederate cultural independence. Gone were the *Educational Repository and Family Monthly*, the *Home Circle*, *The Aurora*, and *Southern Teacher*, as well as other important journals like the *Quarterly Review of the Methodist Episcopal Church, South*, the *Southern Episcopalian*, *Dayton's Baptist Monthly*, the *Georgia Literary and Temperance Crusader*, the *New Orleans Medical and Surgical Journal*, the *Southern Medical and Surgical Journal*, and the *North Carolina University Magazine*.[13] In their place arose a new generation of avowedly Confederate periodicals. Born out of the war experience, these new papers and journals were consciously and explicitly dedicated to advancing the cause of Confederate intellectual and cultural independence. In general, the new periodicals were better organized and better financed than their antebellum forebearers. The unique conditions imposed by war and separate nationality attracted new men and money to the business of southern publishing. These new entrepreneurs, editors, and writers pledged to produce periodicals of such quality, originality, and popular appeal as to permanently supplant northern publications.

THE FIRST MEMBER OF this new generation of Confederate literary periodicals made its appearance in late 1861. Hutton and Freligh's *Southern Monthly* was an impressively sized journal similar in style to the earlier *Home Circle* and *The Aurora*. Published in Memphis, the new magazine was launched in September 1861. Believing "the present condition of the country" to be "propitious to the cultivation of Southern periodical literature," its proprietors invited the best writers in the Confederacy to help them create a new national literature.[14] In their opening editorial, Hutton and Freligh conceded that both the magazine and the Confederacy as a whole had a long way to go before they would be able to offer Confederate readers a vehicle truly worthy of their future literature. But if their magazine was not yet "as able as Blackwood, nor as handsome as Harper," at least "it is *ours*, made here at home by Southern men for Southern use, free from poison, and promising of growth."[15]

In tone and content, the *Southern Monthly* shared many similarities with the preexisting journals of the day. It too denounced northern literature, condemned southern intellectual dependence, cataloged the failings of the past, and fretted over the unwillingness of southerners to support native productions.[16] There were some things, however, that set the new magazine apart from antebellum periodicals and provided glimpses of what was to come. For one, the *Southern Monthly*, while not "fortune-making," was financially "self-sustaining"—perhaps "the first Southern Magazine that ever could truthfully make the assertion."[17] As the number of subscribers increased, so too did contributions from Confederate writers, giving "an inkling of the vast numbers throughout this Confederacy who feel attracted to literary pursuits."[18] While many of the submissions were not of the quality "exactly calculated to establish the reputation of a Magazine," the editors were greatly encouraged by the enthusiasm of contributors and the sheer volume of articles and poems submitted.[19] They were especially impressed by the "several novels of more than ordinary merit" that had been "placed in our hands."[20] One of these serialized novels, "Idlewild: A Tale of West Tennessee" —"a Southern novel, and a good one" in the opinion of the editors—was published starting in December 1861.[21] This, and other contributions by Confederate authors meant that the editors could fill their columns exclusively with native southern literature, and the financial health of their journal meant that they could begin paying authors for their work—something that most other southern journals simply could not afford. "We are beginning to pay contributors," Hutton and Frelish proudly announced in February 1862, "not as highly as we could wish, nor as amply as they deserve; but still we are paying, and if our present ratio of increase in sales and subscriptions continue, we will soon be able to pay more, to pay as well as Northern publishers paid. When we have reached that point, we will have reached the goal of our ambition, for the Magazine will then be a practical fosterer of Southern talent at home, and a representative of it abroad."[22]

For all its apparent success, the *Southern Monthly* did not live very long. Memphis, as it turned out, was not a safe location from which to launch a new magazine. As the Union army advanced through Tennessee following the fall of Fort Donelson, Hutton, Frelish, their staff, and their printing press fled to Grenada, Mississippi. In April, they promised "to keep beyond the reach of Lincoln's stretching arm," vowing that the *Southern Monthly* "will cease but with the Confederacy that gave it birth."[23] But it was not to be. Although they did manage to produce one more issue in May, the magazine did not long survive its relocation.[24] While short-lived, the *Southern Monthly* was a harbinger of things to come. Its success, its large pool of contributors, and its determination to pay authors paved the way for future, better geographically situated Confederate literary journals. With the demise of this, the first truly Confederate periodical, it would be left to others to carry on the fight for intellectual independence.

FAR LONGER-LIVED WAS Joseph Addison Turner's remarkable weekly paper, *The Countryman*. "Independent in Everything—Neutral in Nothing," *The Countryman* was edited, assembled, and printed on Turner's large plantation, Turnwold, nine miles outside Eatonton, Georgia.[25] Strongly opinionated, often witty, more often caustic, and occasionally humorous, *The Countryman* was one of the best written and certainly one of the most entertaining journals to appear during the Confederacy's life.

History mainly remembers Joseph Turner for his decision to employ the thirteen-year-old Joel Chandler Harris as compositor and "Countryman's Devil" in March 1862, thereby launching the young writer's career as well as providing much of the background material for Harris's later tales; but Turner was a powerful force in his own right, and one of the best and most outspoken editors in the Confederacy.[26] Turner already had tried his hand at publishing four failed magazines and three volumes of his own poetry before the war. Deeply embroiled in rising sectional tensions, he became so antinorthern and so proslavery during the 1850s that not even *De Bow's Review* or the *Southern Literary Messenger* would print his articles.[27] Not to be dissuaded, Turner published his writings at his own expense, but still failed to garner much of an audience. Despite presiding over a successful plantation with over one hundred slaves, a hat factory, and a private distillery, Turner's main passion remained the creation of a "separate and distinctive Southern literature." "From my youth up, I have hated yankees," Turner wrote in January 1864. "I wish to see our people in their manners, customs, laws, letters, religion, art, science, agriculture, and commerce—free, independent, *Southern* ANTI-YANKEE."[28] A thigh bone infection at the age of seven had rendered him lame and thus unfit for military service, but, following secession, Turner resolved to place his fortune and his pen in the service of his country's struggle for independence.[29]

In launching his new endeavor, Turner's aim was "to fill my Little Paper with Wit, Humor, Anecdotes, Essays, Poems, Sketches, Agricultural Articles, and Short Tales. I do not intend to publish any thing that is dull, didactic, or prosy."[30] While *The Countryman* would not long remain a "Little Paper," it did largely live up to Turner's promises. Editorials and opinion pieces were the driving force of the paper, but it also prominently featured excerpted and original southern literature, poetry (often Turner's own), essays, and general miscellany. Turner, his brother, William Wilberforce Turner, and, as the war progressed, Joel Chandler Harris wrote most of the material that appeared in each issue, but other writers contributed work as well. All submissions were subject to Turner's exacting standards and he claimed to decline "19 communications out of 20."[31] In the interest of guiding the proper development of Confederate literature and maintaining the reputation of his journal, Turner zealously policed his columns and maintained probably the strictest editorial regime to be found anywhere in the Confederacy.

The Countryman was also notable, indeed unique, for its hostility to the sectarian press and organized religion in general. In his columns, editorials, and reviews, Turner carried on a campaign of unrelenting criticism against the southern religious press. By his own admission, Turner was "no church-member, and never expect[ed] to be one," and while he generally thought "it much better for men to be God-worshipers than Devil-worshipers," he had nothing but contempt for what he saw as the "religious bigotry" and general hypocrisy of the Christian sects and their leaders.[32] Branded an infidel by some, Turner and his paper kept up a constant skirmish with the religious press, and he took great delight in highlighting the failings and hidden motives of its allegedly pious editors.[33] He dismissed the universal mantra of the Confederate clergy that the war and especially its reverses were God's way of

punishing the South for its sins. "We don't believe one word of it," he told his
readers, refusing to accept that "we are greater sinners than the yankees."[34]
He was especially enraged by "the constant cries of those mendicant editors
of sectarian journals" who solicited donations and subscriptions in order to
pay for proselytizing literature for the soldiers. Their "unceasing utterance is

that of the horse leech—'Give! Give!'" Turner wrote in disgust in September 1863, and he accused religious editors of "extending their circulation, and enhancing their own interests" under the guise that "it is all for the poor soldier!"[35] Still, for all of Turner's sparring with the denominational press, his religious views did not seem to damage the fortunes of his paper. He was respected, even by many religious leaders, for his brutal honesty, and if his views were somewhat unorthodox, at least they were held in earnest.

First published on March 4, 1862, as a modest four-page journal, *The Countryman* quickly attracted the notice of the Confederate press and, more importantly, Confederate readers. By September, Turner's new venture had become a "pecuniary success," a success made all the more remarkable by the fact that a subscription at the time cost only one dollar.[36] In just six months and without the transportation, distribution, and supply advantages enjoyed by the city journals, *The Countryman* had attained an impressive circulation of 2,000 subscribers.[37] More impressive still, this was a truly national circulation with readers in Virginia, North Carolina, South Carolina, Georgia, Florida, Alabama, Mississippi, Louisiana, Texas, and Tennessee; there were even subscription orders from Union-held Kentucky and Missouri.[38] By April 1863, *The Countryman* had "almost too many subscribers for the present unfavorable times, and its list is steadily increasing"—a problem that no antebellum southern journal ever had the good fortune to face.[39]

An even more telling indication of *The Countryman*'s success was the fact that, while many Confederate periodicals were forced to reduce dimensions as a result of paper shortages and other war-related hardships, Turner doubled the size of his paper twice during the war. By September 1862, *The Countryman* had grown to eight pages, and by July 1863, Turner was thinking of expanding again.[40] After a number of delays, the paper reached sixteen pages starting in January 1864.[41] Remarkably, Turner managed to keep *The Countryman* at this enlarged format, albeit with a few interruptions, throughout the rest of the war.

THE FALL OF 1862 marked a turning point in the struggle for intellectual independence. Not only had *The Countryman* hit its stride, reaching an impressive size and national circulation, but other new Confederate periodicals were entering the field, determined to advance the southern nation toward cultural autonomy. Launched three weeks apart in Richmond, the *Southern Illustrated News* and the *Magnolia Weekly* were the exemplars of this new generation of Confederate periodicals. They immediately assumed a leadership role in guiding the growth of Confederate literature, and the *Southern*

Illustrated News, in particular, convincingly demonstrated the opportunities for success that the war now offered.

The brainchild of Richmond publishers E. W. Ayres and W. H. Wade, the *Southern Illustrated News* was the great success story of Confederate periodical literature.[42] Well-organized and well-financed, Ayres and Wade envisioned a weekly pictorial paper that would permanently supplant *Harper's Weekly* and *Frank Leslie's Illustrated Newspaper*. This would be no small feat. The northern illustrated papers had been a constant thorn in the side of southern cultural nationalists, both because of the large circulations they enjoyed in the South, and because of the complete inability of southern publishers to compete. The South simply lacked the means, not to mention the experience, to produce intricate illustrations, and no startup southern endeavor had any chance of vying for public attention. However, now that the blockade had put a stop to these northern intrusions, the ambitious Ayres and Wade decided that the time was right to introduce the South's first illustrated paper.

The obstacles to such an undertaking were considerable. An illustrated journal, even with rudimentary illustrations, required better paper and ink than was generally available during the war. It also needed artists and engravers to produce the illustrations, as well as a host of writers to fill its columns. However, with "great toil of mind and body, lavish expenditure, ceaseless energy and not a little 'Southern pluck,'" the necessary paper, ink, and personnel were found or improvised, and what could not be obtained from within the Confederacy was smuggled through the blockade. "Lavish expenditure" was the key, and was what set this endeavor apart from previous southern literary journals. "Having put our hand to the plough, we were determined not to look back," Ayres and Wade recalled. "Expense was not considered. A certain sum of money had been devoted to the undertaking, and every cent of it was to be sunk before the first thought of abandoning the enterprise should be entertained. . . . No stone was left unturned to insure success."[43]

In tone and content, the *Southern Illustrated News* was literary, employing the most distinguished writers in the Confederacy, but unlike older literary journals such as the *Southern Literary Messenger*, it catered explicitly to a popular audience. "We propose to issue an Illustrated Family Newspaper," Ayres and Wade explained, "acceptable alike to the lawyer, the merchant, the minister, and the mechanic—to the rich and the poor." While "devoted to literature, to public instruction and amusement, [and] to general news," the paper was also devoted to the war, for it "would, in no true sense, be a literary organ of the South if it ignored in its columns the Great Revolution." "The literature of the time," they insisted, "must of necessity be deeply colored with the crimson tint of war."[44]

The primary purpose of the paper, the very reason it was founded, was to be a "champion for the intellectual independence of the South."[45] "We have not entered upon this enterprise for mere pastime or for amusement," Ayres and Wade wrote in their fourth issue, "but we have turned our little bark loose upon the rough, and, at times, tempestuous billows of public opinion, for the purpose of forever chasing out the catch-penny papers of Yankeedom." Both "native here, and to the manor born," they refused to "believe that the people of the South will ever again welcome a Northern periodical into their households . . . and it is for the purpose of filling the hiatus created by the expulsion of these worthless sheets, and to supply them with a good literary journal, that we have started upon the present undertaking."[46]

Though an "illustrated" paper, the words, not the pictures, were the selling point of the *Southern Illustrated News*. The illustrations, especially at the beginning, were crude and infrequent productions. While the quality would improve as the war progressed, the pictures never approached the level of detail or sophistication commonly found in northern papers. Each issue generally featured a portrait on its front page, usually of a Confederate general. As James McCabe remembered after the war, "Some of the portraits were admirable likenesses—others horrible caricatures."[47] The "portrait" of Stonewall Jackson that appeared on the cover of the first issue certainly fell into the latter category, as it bore no resemblance to its alleged subject.[48] Ayres and Wade frankly admitted that the illustrations "were not of a character to please us," but they promised improvement in the future.[49] "In good times, we shall have paper as white as a Yankee's cheek when he sees a Confederate bayonet, and pictures as pretty as Burnside's army before it was defeated." But in the meantime, in lieu of elegant illustrations, they pledged "to have the very best reading matter that Southern genius can produce."[50]

To this end, Ayres and Wade aggressively recruited the best writers and poets that the Confederacy had to offer. Eminent southern authors William Gilmore Simms, Henry Timrod, Paul Hamilton Hayne, James Barron Hope, John R. Thompson, George Bagby, John Esten Cooke, James McCabe, Susan Archer Talley, and Margaret Stilling all contributed to the *Illustrated News* and their names were proudly listed at the head of each editorial page. It was largely on the strength and fame of its contributors that the *News* staked its reputation and sought to win subscribers. In order to showcase "the best capacities of the Southern mind," Ayres and Wade attracted their literary luminaries the same way the northern journals did: "not by *begging* contri-

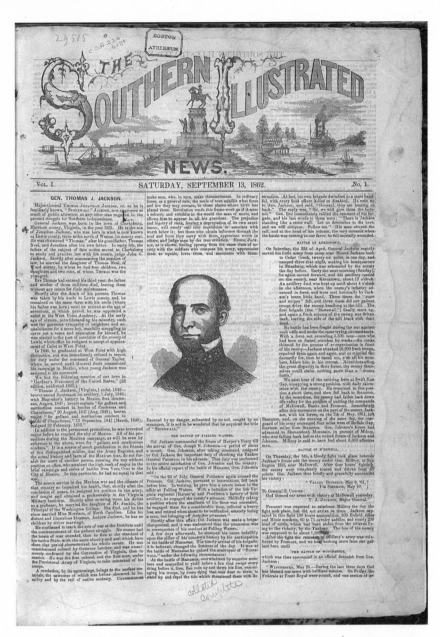

The South's first illustrated newspaper, the *Southern Illustrated News* soon boasted a circulation surpassing "that of any other paper in the Confederacy, not excepting even the most successful daily." The quality of its illustrations would improve as the war progressed. The first issue bore a crude portrait claiming to be Stonewall Jackson. One year later, the *News* again honored Jackson with a far more recognizable likeness. Boston Athenaeum.

SOUTHERN ILLUSTRATED NEWS

Vol. II.   RICHMOND, SATURDAY, AUGUST 29, 1863.   **No. 8.**

Recollections of Stonewall Jackson.

Our readers are doubtless aware that we have recently issued from our presses a memoir of this great and good man. The book will be read by thousands, still there will remain many who will never have an opportunity of perusing its pages. For the benefit of such of our readers we make a few extracts from the work. The "Dispatch" of this city has truly remarked, "that the people can never be tired reading even the slightest unveiling of this mysterious man, whom they almost worshipped."

"JACKSON IS DEAD."

"Seldom have words penetrated more deeply to the heart of a great nation. The people of the Confederate States had begun to regard this immortal leader as above the reach of fate. He had passed unhurt through such desperate contests; his calm eye had surveyed so many hard fought battle-fields, from the commencement of the combats to their termination, that a general conviction of the hero's invulnerability had impressed every heart—no one could feel that the light in those eyes of the great soldier would ever be quenched. But that Providence which decrees all things wisely at last sent the fatal bullet; and the South is called upon to mourn the untimely death of one who seemed to his countrymen the chosen standard bearer of liberty. After the battle of Chancellorsville and while the wound of the famous soldier attracted to him the warmest sympathy and drew forth the earnest prayers of many thousands for his recovery, the journals of the land contained many notices of his services and genius, and his death was alluded to as a calamity too frightful to be contemplated. Well has one of those journals in speaking of Lee and Jackson said: 'It is an honor to breathe the air they breathe. Together, they make up a measure of glory which no nation under Heaven ever surpassed. Other great leaders we have, to whom unstinted praise is due and everywhere gladly accorded; but the rays of their fame converge and accumulate but to add to the dazzling splendor that illuminates the names of Lee and Jackson.

"'The central figure of this war is, beyond all question, that of Robert E. Lee. His, the calm, broad military intellect that reduced the chaos after Donelson to form and order. But Jackson is the motive power that executes, with the rapidity of lightning, all that Lee can plan. Lee is the exponent of Southern power of command; Jackson, the expression of its faith in God and in itself, its terrible energy, its enthusiasm and daring, its unconquerable will, its contempt of danger and fatigue, its capacity to smite, as with bolts of thunder, the cowardly and cruel foe that would trample under foot its liberty and its religion.

"'Jackson was no accidental manifestation of the powers of faith and courage. He came not by chance in this day and to this generation. He was born for a purpose. In this conviction, he reefs serenely, awaiting the healing of his wounds; willing once more to hear the wild cheers of his men as he rides to the front; or, if that be denied him, content to retire from the field, a maimed, humble, simple Christian man. Civil honor, were it the highest gift of the country, could not add one cubit to the stature of his glory.

"'Even should he die, his fiery and unquailing spirit would survive in his men. He has infused into them that which cannot die. The leader who succeeds him, be he whom he may, will be impelled, as by a supernatural impulse, to emulate his matchless deeds. Jackson's men will demand to be led in "Stonewall Jackson's" way.' The leader who will not or cannot comply with that demand, must drop the baton quickly. Jackson's corps will be led forever by the memory of its great chieftain.

"'Alas! the termination of his wound was fatal. The great soul has passed away from us: and we are left without his sagacious counsels, his splendid powers of execution; his unerring judgment, and that intuitive genius for war which made him, in his sphere, the first of living leaders, and ranked him with the greatest who have lived in all tide of time."

HOW HE GOT THE NAME OF "STONEWALL."

'Twas at the first battle of Manassas, when the Southern leaders "saw with irrepressible anguish the exhaustion of the troops, the waning fortunes of the day, and the countless reserves which the enemy hurled incessantly upon their thin and weary lines. Among these was the heroic General Bee, in command of the 4th Alabama and some Mississippians, who were nearly worn out by the terrible ordeal through which they had passed. Bee rode up and down the lines, cheering on the men, and beseeching them, by all they held dear, not to give way, when he met Jackson, and said, in the bitter despair of his heart, "General, they are beating us back!" The face of the stern, silent soldier betrayed no answering emotion. The keen eye glittered for an instant; the lips opened; and in the curt, peculiar tones of the speaker he said, "Sir, we will give them the bayonet!" Bee seemed to gather new inspiration from the words; he galloped back to the remnants of his command, and frowning to Jackson, called out to his men: "There is Jackson standing like a stonewall! Let us determine to die here, and we will conquer. Follow me!" to which the country had gained a splendid victory against enormous odds; and although he did not then know it, Jackson had gained a name with which he is forever inseparably identified. When the heroic Bee exclaimed, "There is Jackson standing like a stonewall," he unconsciously employed a term which thenceforth clung to Jackson more closely than his baptismal appellation. From that hot day of battle, the leader of the men of the Valley was known as "Stonewall Jackson,—his command as the "Stonewall Brigade." Many are ignorant and few recall the fact, that the great soldier was christened "Thomas Jonathan." His veritable christening in the popular mind was on that evening of Manassas when Bee, about to surrender his great soul to his Maker, baptised him, amid blood and fire, "STONEWALL JACKSON!'

PERSONAL APPEARANCE.

The outward appearance of the famous leader was not imposing. The popular idea of a great general is an individual of stiff and stately bearing, clad in splendid costume, all covered with gold lace, and decorations, who prances by upon

LIEUT. GEN. T. J. JACKSON.

Entered according to the act of Congress, in the year 1863, by ATERS & WADE, in the Clerk's Office of the District Court of the Confederate States for the Eastern District of Virginia.

butions, but by *paying liberally for every line that appears in its columns.*"[51] By paying contributors "with a spirit of liberality heretofore unknown in the South," they signaled that the *Illustrated News* would be different from the amateurish and poorly supported productions of the past.[52]

Ayres and Wade launched their ambitious journal on September 13, 1862, and were soon rewarded for their efforts. The success of the *Southern Illustrated News* was phenomenal, and unparalleled in the history of southern publishing. "The career of the 'Illustrated News' has been upward and onward from the very start," its owners proudly announced in January 1863. "The first number more than paid for itself, and each succeeding number has given a better account of itself than its predecessor."[53] By April, they claimed a readership of "more than *one hundred thousand respectable and honorable* residents of the Southern Confederacy."[54] At the close of the first volume in late June 1863, their readership was "largely in excess of what we had dared to hope it would be, in our most sanguine imaginations at the outset of the undertaking," and by the end of the second volume six months later, they reported that their circulation had "gone on steadily increasing, until it now surpasses that of any other paper in the Confederacy, not excepting even the most successful daily."[55]

The rest of the Confederate press reacted to the success of the *Illustrated News* with a mix of jubilation and envy.[56] The paper even attracted attention outside the Confederacy in the form of a contemptuous notice in *Frank Leslie's Illustrated Newspaper*—much to the delight of the *News*'s proprietors.[57] At home, editors who had struggled at subsistence levels for years looked on this upstart's success with amazement. The *Southern Literary Messenger*'s George Bagby, who incidentally was also a paid contributor for the *News*, marveled that the new paper after little more than a month already had "a circulation quadruple that obtained by THE MESSENGER after twenty seven years."[58]

THE *MAGNOLIA WEEKLY*'S RISE to prominence was neither so immediate nor so smooth as that of its crosstown counterpart. Under the proprietorship of Charles Bailie, the Richmond literary weekly, originally titled *The Magnolia: A Southern Home Journal*, first appeared on October 4, 1862, as a modest four-page journal. When Bailie died unexpectedly two months later, William A. J. Smith and Oakley P. Haines bought the struggling paper for $50, and installed Haines as editor.[59] More ambitious than its previous owner, Smith and Haines quickly reshaped the magazine in order to broaden its appeal and circulation. The young journal was rechristened the *Magnolia*

Weekly in March 1863, and expanded to eight full pages.[60] When Haines's poor health forced him to retire and sell his stake in the magazine in June 1863, Smith appointed the able James D. McCabe as the new editor.[61]

Despite the numerous ownership and editorial changes, the mission of the *Magnolia* remained consistent.[62] It was a purely literary magazine. In content and tone, it was slightly higher-brow than the *Southern Illustrated News*. Its literary pieces were generally longer, and it was less concerned with miscellany and war news. Above all, the *Magnolia* was dedicated to the cause of Confederate intellectual independence, and its primary goal was to aid in the creation of a distinctly southern literature. "We are 'heart and soul' interested in the cause of the Southern *literary* independence," James McCabe declared.[63] Confederates needed "a popular literature of our own," one that was "as far removed in style from that of our invaders as it is possible for it to be," and it was the *Magnolia*'s stated mission "to bring out the literary sunshine of the land, to encourage established genius to still greater efforts, and stimulate the pens of the unknown and obscure to adventures upon which laurels may be won."[64]

The editors prized originality above all else, and made it the selling point of their journal.[65] The rationale for doing so was explicitly nationalistic. Confederate critics, Bailie, Haines, and McCabe all argued, had to be ever vigilant in order to prevent southern literature from following corrupt northern models. "Southern literature has yet to be established, but must first be purified, before it can adorn," Haines declared in one of his final articles. "To purify, elevate and encourage it is our purpose, and we shall give up our all, our means, our labor, and our influence to accomplish it."[66] While they welcomed aspiring Confederate writers, or "the pens of the unknown" as Haines put it, the editors focused much of their attention on encouraging the "established genius" of the Confederacy. Following the model of the *Southern Illustrated News*, the *Magnolia Weekly* prominently advertised the names of its better-known contributors in order to gain new readers and affirm its literary credentials. Like the *Illustrated News*, the *Magnolia* attracted its star writers by paying them "liberally."[67] Such luminaries as Simms, Hayne, Hope, Cooke, Talley, Stilling, A. J. Requier, William Archer Cocke, Edward Joynes, Henry L. Flash, John C. McCabe, W. Gordon McCabe, M. Schele De Vere, Clarence Russell, and Augusta Washington contributed to the *Magnolia*'s columns. Simms, for instance, published his lengthy "Benedict Arnold: The Traitor" in twelve installments in the *Magnolia* between May and August 1863.[68] Professional writers in the Confederacy were starting to find native venues for their wares. Their reputations as established authors secured

THE MAGNOLIA WEEKLY

A HOME JOURNAL OF LITERATURE & GENERAL NEWS.

VOL. I.   RICHMOND, VA., MARCH 21, 1863.   No. 24.

Written for the Magnolia Weekly.

The Beechwood Tragedy.

BY M. J. H.

CHAPTER I.

THE slanting rays of an October sun last making beneath the western horizon, fell over and around a handsome mansion, situated upon a fine eminence, commanding the north bank of the Chickahominy river, about ten miles above its junction with the James. And through the parted curtains, a few bright beams, a farewell smile from the departing day god, gleamed like a golden benediction over the polished brow and glittering hair of a beautiful girl, who sat, deeply absorbed on a piece of embroidery, just inside the parlor window. Near the centre of the room sunk in a luxurious lounge, was a youth but little her junior, his well defined features giving like carved ivory, against the dark velvet lining of the chair; and his thin white fingers turning abstractedly the leaves of a book open upon his knee, while his large, pensive eyes were fixed with a look of interest and tender admiration upon the bowed face of the fair girl...

Magnolia Weekly. Boston Athenaeum.

these journals' legitimacy, while the success of these new periodicals provided authors with at least some money and, more importantly, a home reading audience.

While not as meteoric as that of the *Southern Illustrated News*, the success of the *Magnolia Weekly* was impressive. When Haines and Smith bought the journal following Bailie's death, it had a circulation of about two hundred readers, only seventy of whom were "regular subscribers."[69] Under new ownership, however, the magazine thrived. By the end of January 1863, it had amassed a sufficient readership to justify doubling its size and making other improvements "so as to render it literally *an ornament* to the rising periodical literature of the south."[70] By the time that McCabe assumed the editorship in July 1863, the *Magnolia Weekly* enjoyed "a liberal support" and was on its way to becoming "one of the best established journals of the South." McCabe only regretted that its founder, Charles Bailie, had not "lived to see the result of his experiment."[71]

Together, the arrival of the *Southern Illustrated News* and the *Magnolia Weekly* marked an important milestone for Confederate cultural nationalists. While *The Countryman* was primarily the idiosyncratic mouthpiece of its eccentric editor, the *Illustrated News* and the *Magnolia* represented the mainstream of the Confederate popular press. In the timing of their arrival, in their format and editorial policies, and in their explicit dedication to the cause of Confederate intellectual independence, these two new Confederate journals provided the models for future periodicals. Having shown the Confederate public and Confederate publishers what native journals could accomplish given the proper organization, dedication, and patronage, they called on others to follow in their footsteps and expand the boundaries of Confederate literature. "Pitch in," the *Magnolia Weekly* called, "the more the merrier."[72]

AND THERE WERE MORE.[73] At about the same time that the *Illustrated News* and the *Magnolia* appeared, A. G. Horn in Mobile launched his own literary weekly, the *Gulf City Home Journal*. Circulating mainly in Alabama, Mississippi, and Georgia, it, like the other members of this new generation of Confederate periodicals, was dedicated to building up "a Southern literature which shall achieve our literary independence of the North while our armies are working out our political."[74] In Raleigh, the late-arriving *Illustrated Mercury* presented yet another new entry to the growing field of Confederate literary papers. Launched in April 1864, and owned by William B. Smith, the eight-page *Mercury* was modeled on the *Southern Illustrated News*. To fill his columns, Smith appealed to all "the *Literati* of the South" to produce a "high toned *Polite Southern Literature*," for which, he promised, "we are willing and expect to pay the very best prices."[75] Smith's invitation was answered, and the results were impressive. In a remarkably short period of time, he compiled one of the best literary magazines in the Confederacy.

Also deserving mention was Felix G. De Fontaine's *Daily South Carolinian* from Columbia. Though not technically a literary paper, it became a strong advocate for Confederate cultural independence following the installation of poet Henry Timrod as assistant editor in January 1864.[76] With Timrod writing most of the editorial material, the *Daily South Carolinian* and its weekly digest *The Portfolio* took a decidedly literary turn.[77] Writing about "Southern Nationality" in one of his first editorials, Timrod promised that "it will be one of the objects of this journal to encourage the expression of our peculiar nationality in all the departments of life, but especially in those of literature and art."[78] Although military affairs, politics, and wartime morale were the subjects of many of Timrod's articles, this "Laureate of the Confederacy" nevertheless managed to infuse the *Daily South Carolinian* with a good deal of literary material and to lend his voice to the cause of Confederate intellectual independence.

OF COURSE, NOT ALL upstart Confederate literary periodicals were as successful as the *News*, *Magnolia*, *Countryman*, or *Mercury*. Many never made it out of the planning stages. Others never made it past the first issue. Of the latter, *Smith & Barrow's Monthly Magazine* was particularly noteworthy. Making its much delayed debut in May 1864, and published by William A. J. Smith and H. C. Barrow, co-owners of the *Magnolia Weekly*, the short-lived, but lengthy (nearly one hundred pages) magazine was decidedly highbrow, far more so than the popular literary papers. The stated purpose of the magazine was to elevate the literary and cultural taste of the Confederate public, to encourage the future production of higher works of literature and art, and "to add our efforts to those of the laborers already a-field in the good work of rearing the fabric of our Letters."[79]

As it turned out, it was not lack of public support, but rather an ownership dispute between the two proprietors that put an end to this promising journal.[80] But while failed literary periodicals like *Smith & Barrow*'s or the similarly fated *The Bohemian* were not notable for their success, they did speak to the larger ambitions of cultural nationalists.[81] These were intended to be literary journals of the highest order—on par with the best that the North and Europe had to offer. They sought to guide Confederate cultural development from the top by providing a venue for long essays and literary works by the South's most distinguished thinkers. The appearance of these magazines in late 1863 and early 1864 underscores the optimism within the movement for Confederate intellectual independence during this period, while their failure speaks to the difficulties imposed by the war, and, as we will see, perhaps to the limits and ultimate fate of the project as a whole.

THERE WAS ALSO AN entirely new type of Confederate literary periodical that appeared during this time: the "eclectic" magazine. *The Record of News, History and Literature*, *The Age*, and the *Weekly Register* were intended to replace northern journals like the *Eclectic Magazine*, *Living Age*, and the *Albion*, as well as to provide a documentary record of the war. For the most part, the material appearing in these journals was not original. Rather, it was selected from official government and military documents, speeches, public correspondence, Confederate periodicals and newspapers, and European— mainly British—journals. Selections of native literary works were also included in order to highlight and preserve the burgeoning wartime literature of the South.

Launched in June 1863, *The Record of News, History and Literature* was edited by the ubiquitous John R. Thompson and was published weekly in Richmond by West & Johnston. The paper was successful, reportedly reaching "a popularity almost without precedent" by December 1863.[82] In January 1864, however, *The Record* was absorbed by another new arrival, *The Age*.[83] Published in Richmond by Ernest Lagarde & Co. and edited by William M. Burwell, *The Age* was an impressively sized monthly of approximately eighty pages adorned with an ornate frontispiece that Burwell described accurately as "one of the best in that line, got up since the war."[84] Like its predecessor, *The Age* was eclectic, reprinting articles and serialized fiction from British magazines, as well as running original editorials, essays, and reviews. It was more overtly literary than *The Record* had been, and its larger size permitted the inclusion of lengthier essays and works of fiction. Burwell and Lagarde managed to produce consecutive issues through April 1864, when wartime disruptions forced them to suspend until January 1865. Although *The Age* lived through just five issues, it totaled over four hundred pages and boasted some of the finest content and print quality to be found in the Confederacy. Finally, the *Weekly Register* in Lynchburg was a more modest and less literary paper modeled on the old *Nile's Register*. It commenced in early 1864.

Collectively, these eclectic journals represented an interesting development within the rising generation of Confederate literary periodicals. Unlike the other papers, they were not obsessed with printing only original southern works. Rather, they sought to use the writings of insiders and outsiders to guide the proper cultural development of the Confederacy.[85] In this struggle for intellectual independence and international recognition, carefully selected eclectic magazines could play an important role, their editors argued, by "seeking to contribute to the sacred cause of Southern independence, all that can be copied from the literature, the arts or good example of others."[86]

While these newborn Confederate periodicals attracted much attention and many readers, the older established southern magazines and papers were not silent. *De Bow's Review*, the *Southern Literary Messenger*, *Southern Field and Fireside*, the *Southern Literary Companion*, the *North Carolina Journal of Education*, and the *Southern Cultivator* all managed to survive the first year of the war in varying degrees of health.[87] These journals and their editors remained fervently committed to the cause of Confederate cultural nationalism and they now hoped to reap the rewards of their labors. During the middle years of the war, they attempted to adapt themselves to the growing demand for native print literature, and, in some cases, they too shared the success enjoyed by the new Confederate literary papers.

The winter, spring, and summer of 1862 were especially difficult for Confederate publishers. Stockpiles of northern supplies, particularly paper, were exhausted, and new Confederate production and distribution networks had yet to be solidified. Faced with shortages, many periodicals scaled back production. *Southern Field and Fireside* issued as only a half sheet for nearly all of 1862, and *De Bow's Review*, the *Southern Literary Messenger*, and the *Southern Cultivator* resorted to bimonthly editions in order to conserve resources. Still, Dennis Redmond resolved, in a sentiment echoed by the other editors, that "in some form or other—covering greater or less surface—THE CULTIVATOR SHALL GO ON, so long as we feel that it is doing good to the country and is acceptable to our people."[88] Having long agitated for southern cultural autonomy, these journals were determined to see the fight through.

Not surprisingly, given New Orleans's exposed military position, *De Bow's Review* fared the worst. Having completed his official duties in Richmond, De Bow returned to New Orleans in early 1862, only to witness the fall of his city to Farragut's forces on April 25th. Fleeing across the country, he relocated his journal to Columbia, South Carolina, and issued a quadruple edition after a suspension of over four months. While vowing "never to give up the ship," De

Bow recognized that the forced move had crippled his magazine. Cut off from "more than half of our subscribers" in the now unreachable Louisiana and trans-Mississippi West, he was compelled to suspend, and published no issues at all in 1863.[89] *De Bow's Review* was not dead, however. It would appear again in 1864.

The other journals, less precariously situated (for the time being) in Georgia, North Carolina, and Virginia, managed to survive and even thrive during the middle years of the war. Even with its comparatively small readership, the *North Carolina Journal of Education* somehow continued to operate. Rising paper costs forced editor J. D. Campbell to resort to bimonthly issues in 1863, but the *Journal* still led the charge for school reform, southern textbooks, native teachers, and the cause of Confederate educational independence generally.[90] Likewise, the *Southern Cultivator* showed extraordinary resilience. Despite the editor's constant complaints that southerners in general and the planter class in particular were "culpably, remiss in . . . supporting and building up a Literature of Agriculture for the South," the *Southern Cultivator* continued to publish throughout the war, even though it was compelled to print bimonthly issues starting in March 1862.[91] Indeed, the *Cultivator*'s much publicized financial straits were somewhat deceptive. It was true that Redmond had to deal with increased supply costs and a depreciating currency, but so did the other editors of the Confederacy. The main reason why the *Cultivator* struggled was that, unlike the other proprietors, Redmond staunchly refused to increase his subscription rates beyond "the old peace price" of one dollar.[92] When he finally did raise his prices during the latter half of 1863 (and still only to a modest three dollars), the prospects of the magazine improved immediately. In January 1864, he resumed monthly editions, and later that year, he even briefly experimented with turning the *Cultivator* into a weekly. While the wartime circulation of the *Cultivator* is difficult to gauge, the fact that the journal was never suspended, and even expanded and improved itself, points to a certain degree of success and financial security, even if Redmond himself was loath to admit it.

Of all the established southern periodicals, *Southern Field and Fireside* underwent the most dramatic transformation during the war. Throughout 1862, the weekly paper went into a steep decline. Not only had paper shortages cut it down to half size, but the content suffered as well. The paper became less literary, and instead filled its columns with gossip, humor, short quips, and "interesting facts." The header no longer contained the illustrations it once had, and the shabby general appearance of the paper bespoke its ill health. However, in the late fall of 1862, at the same time that the *Southern*

The improved "New Series" of *Southern Field and Fireside*. Boston Athenaeum.

Illustrated News and the *Magnolia* made their first appearances in Richmond, and that the military prospects of the Confederacy seemed to be brightening, James Gardner resolved to halt *Field and Fireside*'s deterioration by refashioning it to take advantage of rising home demand for popular literature. Following the November 15 issue, he suspended publication until the first Saturday of January 1863, "for the purpose of making some changes in the form of the paper, by which it will be enlarged and improved in appearance." "There will be no relaxation of effort to make the paper a creditable exponent of Southern letters," Gardner assured his faithful subscribers, "rather—as the political skies seem to reveal some gleams of promise—we shall pursue with renewed vigor the path marked out for the paper, as an organ of a pure literature."[93]

True to his word, *Southern Field and Fireside* was reborn with the new year.[94] The new format was in every way an improvement. The journal returned to its original eight-page length (though the physical size of those pages remained smaller than before the war), paper and ink quality improved, and the illustrated header reappeared. In May, Gardner hired artist and engraver Alfred Maurice, and *Field and Fireside* began to carry ornate maps, portraits, and illustrated scenes.[95] In terms of content, the expanded size enabled editor S. A. Atkinson to run longer works of native fiction and poetry, as well as more substantial essays and editorials. Taking its cues from the new literary papers, *Southern Field and Fireside* also paid some of its contributors in an effort to attract the highest quality work and even secured "a series of sketchy romances from the pen of that brilliant and popular novelist—W. Gilmore Simms."[96]

Gardner was rewarded for his efforts. The "New Series" was "received with so much favor" that by late February 1863 its circulation was "increasing with unprecedented rapidity."[97] Even the burning of the vital Bath Paper Mill in South Carolina, which forced Gardner to suspend briefly and then resort to printing half sheets for a time, did not dampen the popularity of the weekly.[98] With its large readership and national circulation, *Southern Field and Fireside* was among the most important periodicals in the Confederacy, and it continued to be so even after Gardner sold his interest to Stockton & Co. in 1864.[99] While its exact circulation during the war is unknown, a note to subscribers in March 1864 revealed that there were some 13,000 subscriptions about to expire in that month alone.[100] In its success, format, and the timing of its rebirth, *Southern Field and Fireside* might well be classed among the new Confederate literary papers that appeared during this period. For those willing to invest the resources, brave the supply difficulties, and strive to produce a superior product, the middle years of the war represented a time of great opportunity to capitalize on the growing demand for native literature.

As for "the Nestor of the Southern periodical press," the *Southern Literary Messenger* under the editorship of George Bagby continued unabated, and even managed to take advantage of new opportunities.[101] Like all Confederate periodicals, the *Messenger* suffered from printing delays and inferior supplies. Starting in July 1862, dwindling paper stocks forced proprietors MacFarlane and Fergusson to resort to bimonthly issues. Bagby himself found the "distractions of the times" so great that it was "impossible to perform [my] task in a manner at all satisfactory."[102] Still, through it all, he consistently managed to put together a very creditable journal filled primarily with native fiction, thought, and wartime commentary. The *Messenger* struggled through most of 1862, but by the fall its fortunes began to improve. In December, Bagby reported that the magazine was now "gathering in dollars at a very agreeable rate."[103] Much of this popularity, it seems, was the result of a new regular contributor. In March, Bagby had introduced historian Robert R. Howison's serialized "History of the War."[104] By October, Howison's history had "awakened such an interest in THE MESSENGER, that we are now able to sell nearly our whole edition in [Richmond] alone."[105] The war and the public's appetite for accounts of it had brought some measure of prosperity to the long-struggling journal. By January 1863, increased readership as well as a more reliable supply of paper enabled the *Messenger* to resume its regular monthly appearances.

Despite this success, Bagby believed that the *Messenger* could be doing better—much better. He blamed the failure of the magazine to live up to its true potential not on supply shortages or public indifference, but on the proprietors' refusal to fully adapt to the changed conditions brought about by the war. Having learned firsthand during the antebellum years the dangers of placing "too much confidence in the Southern demand for literature," owners MacFarlane and Fergusson were reluctant to make changes or invest in improvements. Instead, they continued to base their appeals for patronage primarily on the magazine's age and past reputation. Bagby was of a different mind. He argued that the success of native magazines, and that of the movement for Confederate intellectual independence generally, rested on the ability of southern publishers to provide their readers with superior products that would supplant northern productions by virtue of their merit as well as their patriotism. He advocated following the lead of the new Confederate literary papers to "make THE MESSENGER, both externally and internally, far more inviting than it has heretofore been; to pay for contributions; to advertise liberally; . . . to enlist the best and brightest talent in the land; and, while upholding a lofty standard of literature, so to enliven and invigorate the old magazine, as to enlist favour and attract the admiration of all classes of society." For this reason, he heartily welcomed the sale of the old magazine in January 1864 to Wedderburn and Alfriend—"young gentlemen brimful of energy and ambition, with abundant means, and, above all, imbued with correct opinions in regard to the proper mode of developing a literary journal" — even though Bagby himself would no longer be at the editorial helm.[106] He left predicting (incorrectly, as it turned out) great success and prosperity for the *Southern Literary Messenger* and its new owners.[107]

Bagby's frustration with the *Messenger*'s proprietors was telling of the new publishing environment that the war had created. Even though the journal did achieve some success during the middle years of the war and certainly enjoyed the good will of the Confederate press, the longtime leader of southern intellectual discourse had been eclipsed by the new Confederate literary papers. Bagby knew why. Through their complacency, the *Messenger*'s owners had allowed other, more ambitious publishers to take the lead in the movement for cultural self-sufficiency and to reap the profits therein.

AS FOR THE RELIGIOUS periodicals, there were simply too many to recount their fortunes on a case-by-case basis. In general, though, the story of the Confederate religious press was characterized more by perseverance than prosperity. There was no religious equivalent to the *Southern Illustrated News*. In fact, the proliferation and popularity of Confederate secular periodicals directly threatened the survival of the religious journals. With the public hungry for war news and light entertainment and literary magazines ready to provide both, religious papers struggled to compete. But while they may not have enjoyed the same heights of success as their secular counterparts, the religious journals did not die off during these years. In fact, they entered the final year of the war stronger than they had been in 1862. While many editors were forced to reduce the size of their papers at various times, and a few had to suspend briefly, almost no religious papers were discontinued during this middle period. Some new papers were even born, and several others resumed publication.

Editors and religious leaders continued to emphasize the necessity of a vibrant religious press to the Confederacy's struggle for political and intellectual independence. The widespread circulation of religious papers would help maintain the moral compass of southern society in the chaotic days of the war and would foster true, faith-based patriotism. "The *country*, at a time like this, needs the influence of the religious press as it never needed it before," A. A. Porter of the *Southern Presbyterian* wrote in March 1862. "We say the country, in distinction from the Church, which of course always needs it. But *our country now needs it.* We are in the midst of a terrible revolution, demanding patriotic sacrifices of the truest and purest kind. The basis of any such patriotism as this must be a religious basis."[108] For the good of their souls, their church, and their country, religious editors strove to keep their denominational papers alive, and it was their determination, more than anything, that enabled so many of them to survive throughout the war. "Let no one suppose *The Southern Presbyterian* is *going to die*," Porter defiantly declared when paper shortages forced him to resort to a half sheet in April 1862.[109] "We intend, the Lord willing, to keep the 'Old Richmond' afloat while there is a Stonewall to whip the Yankees, a city in which we can print the paper, paper to print on, and a dollar to pay the printer," James Duncan of the *Richmond Christian Advocate* pledged, even as the Seven Days' Battles raged nearby. "As to our own support, we live on faith, and find it very good living."[110] Even when there was no longer a Stonewall to whip the Yankees, the Confederate religious press would continue to live on faith and dutifully send out its weekly issues.

While all Confederate periodicals, secular and religious, suffered from supply and labor shortages, rising costs, erratic mail service, and encroaching Union armies, the religious press had unique problems with which to contend. Almost all the religious papers sent free issues to the soldiers, and this practice, though it greatly expanded readership and helped to spur revivals in the ranks, also imposed tremendous financial burdens on the publishers and paying subscribers. "We *give* away to the soldiers hundreds of copies per week . . . and yet we have hundreds of applicants in the army for the paper which we cannot supply," the Methodist *Richmond Christian Advocate* reported in June 1862.[111] For their part, the men in camp greatly appreciated these visitations from the religious press. One soldier told the *Southern Presbyterian* that the papers did far more good and attracted far more attention than traditional tracts. "There is something fresh and attractive about a newspaper," he explained, "and in camp it is considered a prize and is handed from one to another. It seems to be a part of us—contemporaneous—breathing the same air we breathe, buffeting the same waves that beat against our breasts, and we look into it as in a mirror, to see reflected some of our own feelings."[112]

Religious papers now reached larger audiences than ever before, but unlike the secular papers, they did not profit from their expanded circulations—

quite the opposite. In fulfilling their religious mission to spread the word of God among the soldiers, the denominational papers ensured that they would be perpetually strapped for cash. Religious papers were never intended to be profit-making endeavors, but they still needed to maintain at least subsistence levels of income. Subscription prices and donations would have to pay for free issues, for while the editors might be willing to live on faith, the printers and paper suppliers were not. For this reason, Confederate religious editors constantly bombarded their readers with appeals for money, reminding them of their patriotic and religious obligation to look after their soldiers' spiritual well-being. They called in all debts and rescinded the long-standing policy of allowing delinquent subscribers to remain on the lists. "We can carry no *dead heads*," the *North Carolina Presbyterian* warned. "We need money."[113] The *Richmond Christian Advocate* "in the most modest, genteel, sweet, amiable, delicate, beautiful and touching manner" reminded those "people who owe us money that we positively are fully prepared to receive it!"[114]

Such appeals did manage to raise some money, as did hiking subscriptions rates, but rarely was the revenue enough to cover the increased costs of production or pay for the extra soldiers' editions. Often unable to secure a sufficient supply of paper and even more often unable to afford what was available, nearly all Confederate religious papers resorted to half sheets, at least for a time. "No one grieves over this more than we do," A. A. Porter assured the readers of the *Southern Presbyterian*. "But we must submit to imperative necessity. . . . Soldiers in war times often have to be content with *half rations*, but they ought not for that to desert their banner."[115] A few journals were even forced to suspend entirely until a suitable supply of paper could be found or additional funds raised.[116]

But things were not as bleak as they sometimes appeared. Despite the shortages and half sheets, the southern religious press wielded more influence and reached more readers than it ever had before. That many of these new readers received their papers for free created serious challenges, but it also provided an opportunity to introduce native southern literature to an ever-widening segment of the population. There were more tangible successes as well. Some religious papers actually managed to increase their number of paying subscribers. The Episcopalian *Church Intelligencer* made its "weekly visit to about twenty-eight hundred families and single individuals, comprising, on a moderate calculation, some six or eight thousand readers."[117] The newly revived *Christian Advocate* in Raleigh already had amassed a circulation of 5,000 within eight weeks of its resumption in April 1863.[118] Likewise, the *Southern Presbyterian* reported "large additions to our subscription list," and by Spring 1863, had a weekly run of 7,000 copies.[119] The *North Carolina Presbyterian* had as many as 10,000 readers and editor James McNeill reported in April 1863 that his subscription list had "never been so large as it now is."[120] The *Southern Christian Advocate*, recently relocated from Charleston to Augusta, was reported to have a circulation of between 10,000 and 15,000.[121] These were impressive numbers, especially considering that most religious papers drew upon a regional, not national, subscriber base.

To everyone's amazement, the *Southern Presbyterian Review* continued on at nearly the same dimensions and quality of content as before the war. The fact that this venerable quarterly could survive seemingly unaffected by the swirling conflict was hailed as a triumph by religious and secular editors alike. "We are glad to find the *Review* . . . looking so vigorous and healthy," the *North Carolina Presbyterian* wrote in January 1863. "It exhibits less signs of the blockade than almost any publication we see. Intellectually there is certainly no blockade."[122] The *Review* even managed to lengthen its subscription list during these middle years, though these gains were largely offset by the loss of Confederate territory (and therefore subscribers) in the West.[123] Still, the *Southern Presbyterian Review*'s success was measured by its perseverance, not its profitability. As the intellectual standard-bearer for the Confederate religious press, the *Review*'s regular appearances and continued high quality served as an inspiration for the other denominational papers.

There were other hopeful signs for the religious press in the middle years of the war. Many of the papers forced to resort to half sheets returned to their full size.[124] Those compelled to temporarily suspend, like the *Southern Lutheran* and the *Southern Presbyterian*, soon resumed, and some journals that had been suspended since the first year of the war, like the *North Carolina Christian Advocate* and the *Southern Churchman*, were revived. There were even a few new faces to appear during these years, including the *Confederate Baptist* in Columbia, the *Nazarene Banner* in Atlanta, the *Watchman and Harbinger* in Greensboro, and the *Southern Observer* in Selma. That the success of the Confederate religious papers did not match that of the secular journals is not surprising. Their primary purpose had never been making money or catering to the public taste. Still, they managed to continue publication and expand their readership, even if much of it was non-paying. The survival of a native religious periodical press was deemed essential to the larger struggle for Confederate independence, and religious editors and publishers were determined to keep their papers alive for the duration of the war. For Confederate cultural nationalists, the resilience of these religious papers coupled with the proliferation and vitality of the secular press meant that their campaign for intellectual independence was working.

The fortunes of the literary and religious periodicals were only a part, albeit an important part, of the high-water mark of Confederate cultural productivity. As they rejoiced at the success of these journals, cultural nationalists were equally encouraged by the expansion of Confederate literature in other forms. During these hopeful middle years, Confederate print culture demonstrated a remarkable breadth as well as depth, which nationalists considered yet another indication of the maturation of the movement for cultural autonomy.

Book publishers assumed an increasingly prominent role in the struggle for intellectual independence at this time, and they facilitated the growth of Confederate literature in new directions. Like periodical publishers, southern book publishers eagerly sought to capitalize on the opportunities created by the war to supplant northern competitors. They too believed that they were actively participating in the fight for Confederate independence, and were striking an effective blow against northern dominance through their activities. As Texan textbook publisher Edward Cushing succinctly declared: "The South has made *heroes*; let us also make *books*."[125] And they did. The Confederacy had no lack of publishing houses, including West & Johnston (Richmond); Ayres & Wade (Richmond); A. Morris (Richmond); George L. Bidgood (Richmond); J. W. Randolph (Richmond); Nash & Woodhouse (Richmond); Macfarlane & Fergusson (Richmond); W. Hargrave White (Richmond); James E. Goode (Richmond); Ritchie & Dunnavant (Richmond); Smith, Bailey & Co. (Richmond); Geo. Dunn & Co. (Richmond); Evans & Cogswell (Charleston and Columbia); Branson & Farrar (Raleigh); Strother & Co. (Raleigh); Sterling, Campbell, & Albright (Greensboro); S. H. Goetzel (Mobile); A. G. Horn (Mobile); Burke, Boykin & Co. (Macon); J. J. Toon & Co. (Atlanta); J. H. Seals & Co. (Atlanta); Blackmar & Brother (Augusta); Hill & Swayze (Griffin, Ga.); H. C. Clarke (Vicksburg); and E. H. Cushing & Co. (Houston), as well as many more smaller presses. Besides dedicated book presses, newspaper and periodical publishers also had the capability to produce books, and did so with some frequency.

The most successful and respected of these Confederate publishing houses was West & Johnston of Richmond. It published a broad range of books and shorter pamphlets, including novels (both original southern and reprinted European works), military manuals, dramas, histories, poetry, music, political essays, children's literature, and textbooks. The paper and print quality of their productions were some of the best to be found in the Confederacy, and their books were widely distributed throughout the southern states. As the *Southern Illustrated News* gleefully noted, prior to the war "southern authors [had] looked to the Harpers, the Appletons, and others of a like character, to publish their books for them—now they rely upon those enterprising merchants, Messrs. West and Johnston."[126]

West & Johnston and the other Confederate publishers discovered that a captive reading audience translated into brisk business, and they continued to expand their operations and increase their number of titles as the war progressed. Before Columbia fell to Sherman's forces in 1865, publisher Evans & Cogswell had seventy-six printing presses, twenty-five ruling and binding machines, and 344 employees, all housed within a "gigantic" newly built brick building "covering exactly two acres of ground."[127] The success of these firms meant that southern publishers finally could afford to pay authors, and pay them well. Now able to match and even exceed (albeit in Confederate scrip) what northern publishers had paid, Confederate publishers moved their country another step closer toward cultural self-sufficiency. As publisher Hill & Swayze advertised in 1863: "The popular plea heretofore with writers, in justification for finding a market at the North for their productions, was, that Southern publishers would not pay an encouraging price for their labors. The time for that excuse is now past. Our house is *one* that will pay more than ever was paid by any house in the North, and will do more to encourage Southern literature than was ever done at the North. . . . Writers, come forward, and take a place in our ranks."[128] For southern publishers to pay writers more than a pittance was a remarkable turn of events. Looking over a list of recent books by West & Johnston in February 1863, George Bagby marveled: "Now, if in the January of 1861, any man were to have told the Appletons, or the Harpers, that, in 1863, a Southern publishing house would make such announcements . . . he would have been scoffed at! Nay, but were he to have stated, that such a house would pay to Southern authors, in 1862, $5000 for their writings, he would have been regarded as demented; yet, Messrs. WEST & JOHNSTON, in that year, have paid to such over $15,000—more than *all* the publishers of the North ever paid any one year to Southern writers!"[129] Even taking into account the depreciation of Confederate currency, such numbers were impressive.

The establishment of each new publishing house, and even the publication of each new book, were celebrated as triumphs for the cause of Confederate independence. Joseph Turner, for instance, declared the formation of Burke, Boykin & Co. in late 1862, to be "a *splendid* victory" and an important step toward banishing northern "abolition literature" from the South forever.[130] As they surveyed the growing strength of the Confederate book industry during these years, cultural nationalists rejoiced that "we will no longer be compelled to read the trashy productions of itinerant Yankees, whose books, as a general thing, are as worthless as their hearts are black; but will, in future, have Southern books, written by Southern gentlemen, printed on Southern type, and sold by Southern publishing houses."[131]

The efforts of these publishers enabled Confederate print literature to expand and diversify. In its books, periodicals, and even on the stage, Confederate literature broadened to encompass new forms of expression, filling the large gaps left by the expulsion of northern literature in all its various iterations. Soon, it was predicted, Confederate publishers would be able to meet all of the South's professional, educational, and entertainment needs. Once this was accomplished, the Confederacy would be finally free from the North's cultural bondage.

THE PRODUCTION OF CONFEDERATE fiction and poetry surged during this period.[132] "Southern Independence has struck the lyre as well as unsheathed the sword," William Shepperson grandly declared in the preface to his large volume of compiled Confederate poetry in 1862.[133] Southern writers, with emotions stirred by the momentous events swirling around them, set their pens in motion to the beat of the drums of war, flooding Confederate periodicals and publishers with their poems and stories. "We observe the press now plied with a degree of activity hitherto unexampled, and writers yet 'to fame unknown,' are constantly entering upon the various fields of literary labor, with the promise of ultimately creating for us a national literature marked by all the distinctive characteristics of the Southern temperament," Samuel Davies exclaimed in the *Southern Literary Messenger* in October 1863. Southern men, and especially women, who would never have considered writing for publication before, now rushed their often hastily composed lines off to the nearest paper or literary journal. The "disposition" to write "was perhaps never so strongly and so generally felt as it is at the present time," Davies mused. "We have, as it were, newly discovered the immense treasures of intellectual wealth, which have so long lain hidden in the Southern mind, and we are eagerly hastening to draw it forth."[134]

Not surprisingly, most of the poetry and fiction produced during the war was about the war. As George Bagby explained, "The country craves literary food with an insatiable hunger, for it has fasted long. But no namby-pamby, everyday fiction will appease that craving. Light reading is eagerly desired, but it must smack of war, for all our wishes, hopes, and fears—every breath we breathe by day or night—

> All thoughts, all passions, all delights,
>   Whatever stirs this mortal frame,
> All are but ministers of *War*,
>   And feed his *horrid* flame."[135]

Much of this flood of imaginative writing was channeled into literary journals and even daily papers. Poetry was everywhere. As one literary historian has noted, poetry in the Confederate South enjoyed a popularity "probably unprecedented and almost certainly never to be equaled thereafter."[136] By virtue of its ubiquity, if not its literary merit, Confederate poetry reached a broad national audience and both shaped and reflected public perceptions of the war. As William Shepperson observed at the time, "Through the Poet's Corner in the newspaper," these poems "sped their flight from and to the heart and mind of the people. They showed which way the wind was blowing." Even during the darkest days, "they bravely sing above the storm, soaring so high that their wings are brightened by the sun beyond the clouds."[137] Inundated with verse, editors found it increasingly difficult to balance their desire to encourage the growth of Confederate literature with their obligation to police the quality of native productions. Although they repeatedly expressed frustration at the volume of bad poetry arriving daily at their offices, Confederate editors continued to find more than enough serviceable original southern material to fill their columns. They were encouraged by the enthusiasm, if not always the skill, of these burgeoning Confederate poets.

Periodical editors had more to choose from when it came to fiction as well, and, in fact, stories and serialized novelettes became the main selling point for many Confederate literary papers. A review of the contents of the *Magnolia Weekly* during this period reveals a large number of war-related pieces such as "The Aid-de-Camp: A Romance of the War"; "Nellie Graves: A Story of the Present War"; "Played Sick; or, Furloughed for Ten Days"; "The Story of a Refugee"; "The Old Scout, or, Ben Phelps's Adventure in the Yankee Fleet"; "Until Death Do Us Part. A Story of this War"; "Forcing the Pickets: A Reminiscence of the Present War"; "The Fatal Spring: A Peninsula Episode"; and "Sam Simpkins' First and Last Night as Sentinel."[138]

In order to further accelerate the production of Confederate fiction and secure the highest quality native writing for their columns, the major literary weeklies held a series of competitions with large cash prizes for the best new novels. Southern periodicals had held similar competitions before, but never with such high stakes. The *Magnolia Weekly* offered $500 "to the Author of the best Romance," and in December 1863 awarded it to Charles P. J. Dimitry for his novelette "Guilty, or Not Guilty?"[139] In 1864, *Southern Field and Fireside* promised $750 for the best story and $250 for the best poem submitted by May 1.[140] Not to be outdone, the *Southern Illustrated News* awarded Mary Jane Haw of Virginia $1,000 for her prize-winning romance, "The Rivals, A Tale of the Chickahominy."[141] Tempted by these impressive rewards, Confederate writers, male and female, soldier and civilian, rushed their creations to the offices of the South's literary journals before the ink was dry. For a contest ending in January 1863, for instance, *Southern Field and Fireside* received 17 new novelettes for consideration.[142] Such competitions benefited writers and publishers alike. In addition to printing the winning story or poem, the editors could also pick and choose from among the runners-up to fill their columns.

While the literary papers absorbed the brunt of this tide of Confederate imaginative literature, books also played an important role. There were volumes of Confederate poetry and a significant number of authentic Confederate novels. Cultural nationalists recognized that periodical literature was fleeting and that works of true merit or true profitability needed to be presented and marketed in a more durable form. As William Shepperson explained, "the newspaper can give only an ephemeral life to 'thoughts that breathe and words that burn.' The book embalms if it does not immortalize."[143]

Notable only for its early arrival, the first book of poetry to be published in the Confederacy was Theophilus Hunter Hill's *Hesper and Other Poems*.[144] When the slim volume appeared in 1861, Confederate critics rightly heralded it for what it portended rather than what it accomplished.[145] Other books like William Shelton's *Confederate Poems*, Cornelia J. M. Jordan's *Flowers of Hope and Memory*, Margie Swain's *Mara: or, A Romance of the War*, John Hewitt's *War: A Poem . . . founded on the Revolution of 1861–1862*, Joseph Martin's *Smith and Pocahontas*, James Rogers's *Lafitte*, R. Lynden Cowper's *Confederate America*, and Joseph Turner's *The Old Plantation* would follow Hill's, as would an immense amount of broadsheet poetry.[146]

A particularly notable book was William Shepperson's *War Songs of the South*, published by West & Johnston in 1862. Under the pseudonym "Bohemian," Shepperson culled original poems from various Confederate newspapers, magazines, and broadsides, and compiled them into a single volume. His reasons for doing so were explicitly nationalistic. Believing that "these newspaper waifs have played no unimportant part in the actual drama which surrounds us" and "that their wealth of patriotic sentiment is too precious to be lost," he "gleaned through the fields of newspaper literature" in order to document this emerging Confederate national culture.[147] Of the 110 poems he selected, many were penned by familiar figures such as Hayne, Holcombe, Hope, Randall, Simms, Stilling, Talley, Thompson, Ticknor, Timrod, and Tucker, but there were many others by obscure or anonymous southern poets. By gathering these poems in one place, Shepperson attempted to demonstrate to the world and his fellow countrymen that a Confederate national literature was indeed rising out of the flames of war.

Further adding to this burgeoning book literature were the Confederate novels. The general popularity of novel reading in the mid-nineteenth century, combined with the need for distraction on the home front as well as in the camps, ensured that native novels would enjoy instant popularity, if only authors and publishers could supply them quickly. Many of the novels and novelettes that appeared during the war were simply the serialized fiction of the literary magazines finding its way into book form. The owners of the *Magnolia Weekly*, the *Southern Illustrated News*, and *The Illustrated Mercury* reissued such works as James McCabe's *The Aid-de Camp*, Mary Jane Haw's *The Rivals*, and W. D. Herrington's *The Captain's Bride, A Tale of the War*. *Southern Field and Fireside* launched its own series of novelettes in 1863.[148] But there were new stand-alone books as well, including Alexander St. Clair Abrams's *The Trials of the Soldier's Wife: A Tale of the Second American Revolution*; Napier Bartlett's *Clarimonde: A Tale of New Orleans Life, and of the Present War*; Jane T. H. Cross's *Duncan Adair: or, Captured in Escaping. A Story of One of Morgan's Men*; the reissue of Mary E. M. Davis's *The British Partizan: A Tale of the Olden Time*; Sally Rochester Ford's *Raids and Romance of Morgan and His Men*; Richard Malcolm Johnston's *Georgia Sketches*; Ebenezer W. Warren's proslavery novel *Nellie Norton: or, Southern Slavery and the Bible*; the anonymous *The Step-Sister*; and, the best-selling Confederate book of all time, Augusta Jane Evans's *Macaria; Or, Altars of Sacrifice*.[149] Nathaniel Beverly Tucker's 1836 novel *The Partisan Leader*, which had predicted the dissolution of the Union, civil war, and the establishment of a southern nation, was rediscovered, republished, and was now embraced as part of Confederate literature. In marketing the book, West & Johnston simply extended its title: *The Partisan Leader: A Novel, and an Apocalypse of the Origin and Struggles of the Southern Confederacy*.[150] Many of these novels enjoyed substantial success —most notably *Macaria*—and several were issued in multiple editions.[151]

Taken as a whole, the quantity of Confederate poetry and fiction was impressive (leaving aside for the moment the question of quality). By the middle years of the war, southern authors and publishing houses could meet most of the literary and entertainment needs of the reading public, at least for those fortunate enough to live still within reach of booksellers and Confederate mail service. Wartime literature was intended for immediate consumption, and most critics recognized that there was little here that would live through the ages. Still, in this flurry of activity, they hoped they had seen the beginnings of a true national literature, and they confidently expected greater things to come.

CONFEDERATE LITERATURE ALSO BEGAN to include works of history during this period. Southerners, of course, had written history before the war, including a good many state histories, but the conflict imparted a new sense of purpose to southern historians, not to mention a new subject.[152] That native history writing would be an important priority for cultural nationalists was not surprising. Having complained for years that biased northern historians had hijacked American history and perverted it to their own fanatical ends, Confederate historians and cultural leaders wanted to seize control of their new nation's history at the outset. While Confederate writers managed to produce a few scholarly works on non-southern topics, most notably D. F. Jamison's 600-page *The Life and Times of Bertrand Du Guesclin: A History of the Fourteenth Century*, most of the books, articles, and pamphlets focused on very recent southern history and especially the war.[153] With historic events occurring daily around them and southern readers hungry for accounts of the war, Confederate historians saw little reason to look beyond their immediate surroundings.

In chronicling their struggle for independence, by cataloging incidents of southern bravery and exposing northern atrocities, Confederate historians attempted to create a shared heroic history that would bind the southern nation together. "We are in the midst of a revolution unparalleled in the histories of nations, and in times like the present, our surest and best monitor for the future must be derived from the indisputable facts and incidences of past and daily occurring events," Henry W. R. Jackson declared at the start of his *Confederate Monitor and Patriot's Friend*, itself an odd mix of original essays and historical pieces combined with selected articles, reports, and poems taken from Confederate periodicals.[154] While cultural nationalists were aware that "contemporaneous history may always be erroneous, because it is necessarily partial, [and] incomplete," they did not deem this a sufficient reason to abstain from writing it.[155] The publisher of *The War and Its Heroes*, a collection of biographical sketches immortalizing the Confederacy's great military leaders, casually brushed aside such objections: "That the work is incomplete is a fact which requires no apology, the struggle itself being incomplete."[156] Undaunted by their lack of historical perspective and the incompleteness of their sources, Confederate writers proceeded to churn out a spate of military histories, unit histories, biographies, battle accounts, and personal and compiled reminiscences.[157] The death of Stonewall Jackson in particular sparked an entire cottage industry, with some of the most prominent Confederate authors, including John Esten Cooke, James McCabe, and later Robert Lewis Dabney, paying homage to the Confederacy's great martyr with competing volumes about his life.[158]

The two most ambitious Confederate historians were Edward A. Pollard and Robert R. Howison. In 1862, both men began writing their own comprehensive histories of the war. Remarkably prolific, Pollard authored eight books during the course of the war (and many more after it), in addition to serving as the associate editor of the *Richmond Examiner*.[159] For each year of the conflict, he wrote a lengthy volume.[160] His practically, if not imaginatively, titled *The First Year of the War*, arrived in Confederate book stores in 1862. Pollard was a committed Confederate nationalist, and his writings constantly emphasized the legitimacy of the Confederate nation and the righteousness of its cause. "The war," he believed, had revealed "not discordant States, but two distinct nations, in the attitude of belligerents, differing in blood, in race, in social institutions, in systems of popular instruction, in political education and theories, in ideas, in manners."[161] Pollard's love for the southern nation, however, did not extend to its chief executive. In his mind and in his books, the Confederacy had two enemies threatening to destroy it: the hated Yankees and the nearly as hated Jefferson Davis. Pollard freely inserted his political opinions into his historical narrative and consequently his books were as much extended diatribes against Davis as accounts of the war.

Not surprisingly, Pollard's books provoked a great deal of controversy. In reviewing *The Second Year of the War*, the editor of the Baptist *Religious Herald* of Richmond objected to "certain passages, written in obvious disregard of the Divine injunction, 'Thou shalt not speak evil of the ruler of thy people.'"[162] The newly installed editor of the *Southern Literary Messenger* (and future Davis biographer), Frank Alfriend, complained that "Mr. Pollard appreciates and applies well the secret of the superior vantage ground possessed by those who assail others for failure or malfeasance in matters in which they themselves are encumbered with no responsibility."[163] For staunch Davis supporters, like Alexander St. Clair Abrams, Pollard's politically motivated rabble-rousing was more akin to the "practice of the demagogue" than to that of the historian.[164]

Other reviewers had quite different reactions to Pollard's work. George Bagby, who not coincidentally was also no admirer of Davis, celebrated Pollard's harsh treatment of the President and his pet generals as evidence of the Confederacy's determination to maintain freedom of thought during the war. "Only a Southerner," he gushed, "would have had the courage, while a war of dimensions unparalleled in military annals was yet undecided, to handle the President, the administration, and the leading generals, with the absolute freedom of a historian living in another age and in a foreign country." He believed that Pollard's *First Year of the War* was "more convincing proof of Southern mettle and Southern freedom than any victory we have achieved. It will astonish European nations by its boldness, and open the eyes even of the Yankees by its perfect candour."[165]

But whether they agreed with his opinions or not, Confederate readers bought Pollard's books. Indeed, the fieriness of his writings and the controversy surrounding them guaranteed brisk sales. *The First Year of the War* passed through three editions, as did *The Southern Spy*, subtitled "Letters on the Policy and Inauguration of the Lincoln War." In April 1864, Frank Alfriend admitted that Pollard's "writings have been more widely circulated and more generally read during the past two or three years than those of any author of his day and country."[166] Clearly, Pollard had tapped into a great public demand for Confederate popular history. His focus on southern honor, northern depravity, and Davis's culpability ensured a lively, if rather skewed, version of the war that proved highly seductive for both contemporary readers and generations of southerners afterward.[167]

More balanced in his political opinions, more deliberate in his approach, and generally more concerned with adhering to the historical record, Robert Howison presented a much denser, but far less entertaining narrative. Unlike Pollard, he did not use the events of history to underscore Davis's ineptitude or arrogance. Like Pollard, however, Howison was a Confederate nationalist, and he left no room for doubt as to who were the heroes and who the villains. For Howison, there was no questioning the Confederate cause. In the first installment of his "History of the War" in the March 1862 issue of the *Southern Literary Messenger*, he flatly declared before embarking on a lengthy justification of secession that "the South was *right* in this controversy" and that "the world has never seen a revolution founded on higher principles or a broader basis of reason than she may claim herein."[168] For the North, he had nothing but vitriol, and much of his time was spent documenting the atrocities of its soldiers and the criminality of its leaders. "Never since the inhuman wars among the degenerate successors of Alexander of Macedon, has the world seen a more fiend-like and atrocious spirit than that exhibited by the Northern States in commencing this war on the South."[169] In his recounting of the aftermath of the First Battle of Manassas, Howison claimed that numerous handcuffs and nooses intended for southern rebels were found among the captured Union baggage. He invariably portrayed the Yankees as subhuman demons with whom southerners shared no similarities and certainly no lasting bonds. Purported personal letters found among the northern dead were "so full of foul obscenity, brutal oaths and fiendish malice against the South, that they could not be published without shocking the decency of public opinion." He was particularly delighted to report that "the letters *from Northern women*, were full of obscene allusions and inquiries, giving a glimpse into the putrid fountains whence they flowed, and furnishing renewed cause of joy that the South had cut loose the bonds which once bound her to the society that could hold such women!"[170] Clearly, Howison's version of the war was no less partisan than Pollard's. The difference was that Howison's barbs were directed toward the North while Pollard fought on two fronts.

Howison's history proved extremely popular. As already discussed, his monthly contributions were credited for the *Southern Literary Messenger*'s increased circulation. His articles were almost always the lead piece in each issue. Howison's history moved glacially, however. After 24 installments and 350 double-columned, micro-printed pages, he got only as far as Fort Donelson.[171]

Collectively, Howison, Pollard, and the other Confederate historians played an important role in the struggle for intellectual independence. George Bagby mentioned the work of Howison and Pollard specifically as evidence of the intellectual "regeneration" taking place in the Confederacy.[172] These popular historians were writing the first pages of a Confederate national history, a shared narrative of heroism and sacrifice to bind the southern people together.

CIVIL WAR MIGHT SEEM an unlikely time and subject for humor, but Confederates nevertheless produced an impressive volume of humorous and satirical writing. Nor were the contributions of the humorists, caricaturists, and satirists deemed unimportant to the struggle for Confederate cultural independence. "WHERE ARE OUR HUMORISTS?" the *Southern Monthly* had demanded in October 1861. "Why shall the effervescence of the soul, the sparkling bubbles of wit and humor cease to rise, because the Northern glass has been shivered wherein they were wont to shine?"[173] Besides supplanting these northern writers, Confederate humor could also provide psychological release from the strains of war. "In these sad times," the *Magnolia Weekly* observed, "all the fun that can be started is needed."[174]

Humor had always occupied a prominent place in southern newspapers and magazines, and it continued to do so throughout the war. Even the high-toned *Southern Literary Messenger* regularly featured the contributions of southern humorist Harden E. Taliaferro under the pseudonym "Skitt," and editor George Bagby himself was a humorist of no small ability.[175] Not surprisingly, the focus of such writing changed during the war, and the conflict itself became the subject. The cowardice of northern soldiers, the crudeness of their manners, and especially the ineptitude of their generals and politicians became the preferred fodder for Confederate humorists. Abraham Lincoln, predictably, was a favorite target. But Confederate humor also looked inward. Before the war, southern writers had poked fun at the cracker culture of poor whites, the way they talked, and their peculiar superstitions. Slaves and slave dialect were also popular subjects for jest. During the war, Confederate humorists relied on these same characters, only now poor whites reported from the front as soldiers, offering frank, if crude, appraisals of the conduct of the war, the experience of "skummagin" against the Yankees, and the general disruptions of southern society caused by "Militeer Needcessity."[176] In the hands of these writers, fictitious slaves became the unwitting spokesmen for the absurdity of Lincoln's emancipation efforts.[177] Humor also enabled Confederates to complain about the war without seeming unpatriotic.[178] Davis, his generals (especially Braxton Bragg), speculators, impressment, shortages, starvation, refugees, and inflation were all fair game. Humorist Jeffrey M'Lory Northrop, for instance, writing for the *Richmond Examiner*, suggested that food shortages could be easily overcome if the people would simply eat Confederate currency as it was the cheapest possible food. "If Confederate notes will pass in no other way, they certainly will in this, and I need not say how happy the effect would be upon the finances of our distracted country."[179]

So fruitful were these subjects and so great the demand for them that specialized humor publications began to appear during the middle years of the war. There were even a few book-length works like *The Camp Jester or, Amusement for the Mess*, George Bagby's *The Letters of Mozis Addums to Billy Ivvins*, and Augustus Baldwin Longstreet's *Master William Mitten: or, A Youth of Brilliant Talents, who was Ruined by Bad Luck.*[180] Humor remained primarily the domain of the periodicals, however. In addition to the regular appearance of humorists in the daily newspapers and literary magazines, the Confederacy witnessed the birth of no less than four new Confederate journals dedicated exclusively to this genre.

Launched in August 1863 and published monthly in Griffin, Georgia, the *Bugle-Horn of Liberty* was a self-proclaimed "Humorous Paper, Devoted to Fun, Fact and Fancy."[181] Publishers Hill & Swayze attained an instant reputation for their journal by securing the services of the Confederacy's favorite humorist and Georgia cracker, Bill Arp (aka Charles Henry Smith).[182] Arp's first, and as it turned out only, contribution, "Dodgin Around—Melankolly Reflekshuns," appeared in the September issue.[183] The *Bugle-Horn of Liberty* did not live very long, but not for the reasons one might expect. In October, it ran a series of captioned engravings caricaturing Confederate General John Hunt Morgan and his exploits.[184] Not amused, enraged convalescent soldiers from the nearby Confederate hospital in Marietta descended on the offices of Hill & Swayze and "rode the editor of the 'Bugle Horn of Liberty' on a rail," thus permanently halting the paper.[185] Clearly, there were limits to what Confederate humorists could satirize. Unpopular officers like Bragg and Pemberton were fair game, but the editor who skewered a revered general did so at his own peril.

Not to be dissuaded, other Confederate humor magazines appeared soon thereafter. The monthly *Confederate Spirit and Knapsack of Fun* was published in Mobile by H. C. Clarke starting in the late fall of 1863. It was composed primarily of military, dialect, and racial humor. For instance, the May 1864 issue contained the racist cartoon "Miscegenation: or, the 'Free American of African descent' enjoying his long-lost 'Freedom,'" which depicted a demonic ex-slave with two white women in his arms.[186] It is difficult to determine how long *Confederate Spirit* lasted, for there are very few surviving issues, but it published at least six numbers and probably more. Even more elusive is *Hard Tack*, "an illustrated comic monthly" published in Atlanta by John Seals & Co. No copies of this magazine seem to have survived, but, from what can be gleaned from the notices in the literary periodicals, it was launched in May 1864.[187]

Far more successful (and better documented) was the weekly *Southern Punch* in Richmond which made its first appearance on August 15, 1863.[188] Edited by John Overall, the former editor of the New Orleans *Daily Delta*, this "hearty, laughing disciple of Momus" was modeled directly on the "world-renowned" *London Punch*. But while mimicking its English namesake in

The cover of *Southern Punch*, the Confederacy's "hearty, laughing disciple of Momus." Boston Athenaeum.

form, Overall assured his readers that this Punch was a "genuine Confederate," preferring "the Virginia mint julep and the mixed drinks of the Cotton States, to Brown Stout and Cheshire cheese."[189] Above all, "Punch hates anything Yankee," and Overall pledged that its first priority would be eliminating "Yankeeism at home," for "every blow dealt that monster, is a blow in the right direction."[190]

Punch's eight pages were filled with original fiction and humorous stories, poetry (mostly by Overall himself), jokes, quips, and funny anecdotes, as well as bitter denunciations and editorials against the Confederacy's enemies, both internal and external. Speculators, in particular, were a favorite target. *Punch*'s comedy relied mainly on racial and dialect humor with a dose of anti-Semitism thrown in. The physical appearance of *Southern Punch* was impressive. It was well illustrated, including numerous political cartoons. These were quite intricate by Confederate standards, and they targeted Lincoln, Yankees, speculators, and draft dodgers.[191] Many of them dealt with slavery and emancipation, often contrasting the benevolent treatment of slaves in the South with the harsh conditions experienced by contrabands under their new, uncaring Yankee masters.[192]

Punch quickly found readers. "Already a success" after its first month, Overall reported in October that the paper was "steadily pushing itself into popular favor" and gaining new subscribers even from "remote localities in the far South." It also enjoyed a substantial circulation in the army.[193] Despite "almost insurmountable difficulties of publishing such an illustrated weekly in these days of blockaded ports and invaded borders," Overall claimed, with some exaggeration, that "Punch is the greatest hit of the times."[194] Bolstered by this success, *Southern Punch* continued publication through at least February 1865, and even toyed briefly with the idea of doubling its size in the late summer of 1864.[195]

Admittedly, much of the humor produced in the Confederacy was not all that funny, certainly not to the modern reader, and probably not even to many contemporaries. In reviewing the first issue of *Southern Punch*, the *Gulf City Home Journal* found it more "satirical than funny, sharp than witty."[196] Still, this did not especially bother Confederate cultural nationalists. Such humor was almost always fleeting, and it was not surprising that Confederate humorists produced little of lasting value. Much more heartening to cultural nationalists was the fact that such books and periodicals were being produced and were proliferating rapidly, as they represented an extension of Confederate literature into yet another genre, making another step toward freeing the South from its dependence on the North. For Joseph Turner, the arrival of *Southern Punch*, and by extension the rest of Confederate humor literature, "mark[ed] an era in our nationality. As provinces of the yankee Government, we would never have produced anything like Punch. New York, Boston, and Philadelphia absorbed all our art, and all our literature, as they drained us of all the proceeds of our cotton, tobacco and rice. But thank God all that is over now. The appearance of Punch is a land-mark which clearly indicates the progress of our nationality. It is decidedly Southern, and it is more than refreshing to see it so."[197] Historian Frank Mott in *A History of American Magazines* notes with some derision that the founding of *Southern Punch* was "probably the height of publishing optimism," but this is precisely the point.[198] It did mark the height of optimism and not just for *Punch*'s owners. Rather, it and the other humor magazines, all appearing at nearly the same moment, contributed to the general feeling of excitement and accomplishment that characterized these middle years. Confederate cultural nationalists believed that their movement was coming of age, and they rejoiced at what this proliferation of humor writing signified for their cause.

CONFEDERATE ADVANCES IN THE field of scientific literature were more modest. There were a few books, most notably Francis Porcher's *Resources of the Southern Fields and Forests*, as well as medical manuals and a few works of applied science on the likes of how to manufacture saltpeter.[199] More significantly, the Confederacy produced an important medical journal during these years. Much of the credit for the creation of the *Confederate States Medical and Surgical Journal* belongs to the *Southern Illustrated News*. Starting in October 1863, the *Illustrated News* began chastising the Confederate Surgeon General, the Confederate Government, and the medical profession as a whole for allowing wartime medical advances to go undocumented, while northern doctors churned out volumes publicizing their findings for the world to see. "This is simply disgraceful, not only to the surgeons themselves, but to the whole country," the *News* fumed, "and, more than all things else, will justify and confirm in European eyes, the sneers of the Yankee at 'Southern ignorance' and the 'barbarism of slaveholders.' "[200] Here was another opportunity for Confederates to assert themselves intellectually. Deeming the efforts of the Surgeon General's Office woefully insufficient, the *Southern Illustrated News*, flanked by the editors of the *Richmond Enquirer* and the *Richmond Whig*, called for the immediate creation of a national Confederate medical journal.[201]

Under such pressure, the *Confederate States Medical and Surgical Journal* was willed into existence in January 1864. Managed "under the auspices of the Surgeon-General," edited by Dr. James B. McCaw, and published by Ayres and Wade (the very men who had called so vigorously for its creation), the journal was an impressively sized and well-illustrated compilation of Confederate case histories, official medical reports, and reprinted European medical articles.[202] But the new journal had a nationalist as well as a medical agenda. "Amid the din of war's wild alarms, when the shock of opposing armies is felt around us, while a new-born nation struggles for its breath, even then the calm, peaceful voice of Science is heard," Dr. McCaw wrote in his "Salutatory." "Let all who love her heed the call. The medical men of the South have had their part to play in the terrible drama"[203]

The new journal was a surprising success. Already by May, it had "attained a larger circulation than was ever reached before by any Southern medical periodical, and promise[d], in the future, to surpass the most sanguine expectations of its friends." New subscriptions "flowed in rapidly," as did "contributions of a useful and instructive character."[204] In fact, the magazine was so flush with both subscriptions and contributions that it doubled its size in September 1864, at a time when the fortunes of most Confederate periodicals were deteriorating rapidly alongside those of the Confederacy as a whole.[205]

The establishment of this new medical journal was seen as yet another important step toward lasting Confederate independence. Ambitious cultural nationalists expected Confederate thinkers to distinguish themselves in the sciences as well as the arts, and they recognized that a vibrant scientific and medical literature could bolster their case for national legitimacy and international respectability. Granted, the gains made in these areas were small, but in the fledgling efforts of their scientific literature, Confederate cultural nationalists saw great promise for the future.

GIVEN THE EXTENT OF the Confederacy's military mobilization and the sheer number of men serving in the armies, it was only natural that publishers would seek to provide this enormous audience with its own reading material. Effectively, all Confederate literature was soldiers' literature in that it was read widely by troops in the field. The tedium of the camps and the massing of large numbers of men in the same place meant that the printed word passed eagerly through the ranks. The literary and humor magazines had many readers in the army, and the religious papers, as already discussed, sent free copies to the troops. But there was also a subset of Confederate literature aimed expressly at the soldiers, including books of stories like *The Camp Follower* and *The Camp Jester* aforementioned, as well as specialized soldiers' papers. These papers were usually denominationally based, though they carried such seemingly secular titles as *The Soldier's Visitor, The Soldier's Paper, The Soldier's Friend, The Army and Navy Messenger, Army and Navy Herald,* and *The Army and Navy Messenger for the Trans-Mississippi Department.*[206] Because these papers passed quickly from hand to hand and often were distributed for free, they easily attained large circulations. The first issue of the *Army and*

Navy Messenger, for instance, ran 10,000 copies.[207] In truth, these papers were little more than extended tracts with some news, poetry, and morally uplifting anecdotes added for spice. Most of what appeared in Confederate soldiers' literature was reprinted from elsewhere. For instance, the selections in *The Camp Jester* had been "drawn heavily" from *Southern Punch* and "culled from the luminous pages of the 'Confederate Knapsack,' and 'Bugle Horn of Liberty.' "[208] Still, even if there was little that was original in its content, Confederate soldiers' literature did contribute to the struggle for intellectual independence in a limited way. Simply by reaching so many soldiers, these papers exposed thousands of new southern readers to the products of Confederate presses, accustomed them to the presence of native writers, and laid the basis for a future home market for Confederate literature.

CHILDREN'S LITERATURE WAS ONE of the fastest growing segments of Confederate print culture during the war's middle years.[209] Much of this was driven by the tremendous demand for textbooks, but Confederate publishers also began to supply young southerners with recreational reading. Books and booklets like Edward Boykin's *The Boys and Girls Stories of the War*, *Uncle Buddy's Gift Book for the Holidays* and the slightly revised Confederate version of Francis Goulding's *Robert and Harold; or the Young Marooners on the Florida Coast*, in addition to short volumes of poetry like Ebenezer Starnes's *Rhymes, Serious and Humorous, for my Children*, and *For the Little Ones* by a "lady of Savannah," were intended to entertain children on the home front as well as to provide moral guidance in these times of uncertainty.[210] The Confederacy also produced no less than seven periodicals geared specifically toward young readers, namely the *Child's Index*, the *Children's Guide*, the *Children's Friend*, the *Child's Banner*, the *Portfolio*, the *Sunday School Paper for the South*, and the bizarrely titled *Deaf Mute Casket*.[211] With the exception of the *Casket*, they were explicitly religious in nature.[212] All these papers (the *Casket* included) focused on the moral development of southern children. Their stories, anecdotes, and poems emphasized obedience to God and parents, the rewards enjoyed by those who lived a virtuous life, and the dire consequences for those who did not.

In addition to helping southern youth walk the straight and narrow path, Confederate publishers had two main objectives in creating these new children's books and periodicals. First, they wanted to supplant northern juvenile journals and the ubiquitous Sunday school papers with their own native southern products. "Since we have been engaged in repelling our wicked invaders, you have been deprived of the neat and interesting papers you used to get from the North," Samuel Boykin told the young readers of the *Child's Index* in September 1862. "We thought we'd try to supply their places, and furnish you with a paper printed and edited at the South, and designed for Southern children." While Boykin admitted that Confederate publications lacked the "handsome" appearance of the northern papers, "We know the patriotic little folks of the South had rather have yellow looking paper, and less handsome pictures, than to have us trade with our enemies."[213]

Whether or not they preferred the yellow-looking paper, southern children, or rather their parents, were more than willing to buy it. Already, by September 1862, the circulation of the *Children's Friend* was approaching 4,000 subscribers. By January 1863, it had over 6,000. Six months later, its circulation was still "increasing every day" with new subscribers from "all over the Confederacy" and from "all denominations of Christians."[214] The *Child's Index* grew from 4,000 subscribers in February 1863, to 11,000 in November, 12,000 by May 1864, and finally to as many as 15,000 by that December.[215] Clearly, there was strong demand for children's literature, and Confederate publishers, freed from competition with the North, were eager to meet their young readers' needs.

The second goal of the publishers, editors, and writers of this juvenile literature was to instill Confederate nationalism within the rising generation of southerners. In addition to conventional stories and cautionary tales about God and family, they wrote about the war and the righteousness of the Confederate cause in language that children could understand. They attempted to inspire patriotic devotion through tales of Confederate heroism and sacrifice, as well as to incite hatred through accounts of Yankee cruelty and cowardice. Sometimes, authors spoke directly to their readers about the war and its meaning, as Samuel Boykin did in his "Editor's Monthly Letters" in the *Child's Index*. In the first issue, he wrote: "War is horrible, children, most horrible because it causes so much suffering and sorrow and distress. . . . But it is a great consolation to know that we are fighting in a just cause; that is, to save our country from ruin. We are but trying to drive wicked invaders from our land."[216] "We are fighting for the right to govern ourselves in our own way," he explained simply. "The Yankees want us to live under their government and be governed by them. . . . They would take away our slaves, and deprive us of our houses and lands, and money, and deny us all the rights we claim for ourselves, as freemen."[217] Slavery was spoken of freely and defended vigorously. "Our slaves belong to us," Boykin assured his readers in October 1863. "The Bible authorizes us to hold them as such, and the Yankees have no business interfering in the matter."[218]

Edward Boykin's pocket-sized *Boys and Girls Stories of the War*, 1863.
Boston Athenaeum.

More frequently, however, such sentiments were couched within the stories and poems that these new books and papers carried. The *Index* printed poignant war fiction like Mrs. Boykin's story "Nellie Lester" about Yankee atrocities, Boykin's "The Raid" about Nathan Bedford Forrest's heroics, and Mrs. M. J. Mallary's "A War Picture (Founded on Fact)."[219] *The Boys and Girls Stories of the War*, as its name suggested, contained original war tales: "The Story of a Refugee," a heroic account of pious Stonewall Jackson defeating evil Yankee General Milroy; "The Mountain Guide," the story of a Yankee-hating faithful slave who guides Confederate troops through the mountains; and "The Brave Editor," a celebration of a patriotic newspaper editor during the battle of Chancellorsville.[220] Among its miscellany of original and reprinted tales, poetry, games, anecdotes, and conundrums, *Uncle Buddy's Gift Book* also included war stories. "The Young Confederate Soldier" was the unlikely account of an adolescent southern boy named, appropriately enough, "Johnny," who by chance captures six Union soldiers. Having "given the boys a story," Uncle Buddy also provided one for the girls entitled "Helen Norcross, or, The Two Friends." While Helen dutifully knits socks for Confederate soldiers, her disobedient friend Alice decides to go out and play instead. Upon reaching the street, she is immediately run over by an out-of-control horse and buggy. Battered and bruised, Alice regains consciousness at home and promises to change her ways, obey her mother, and perform her duty.[221]

There were also many war-related poems intended for children. For instance, "Willie's Political Alphabet," in *For the Little Ones*, was an A to Z list of patriotic names and topics. "A" was "for the Army," "B" "for the Banner, the 'flag of the free,' / For Beauregard, Bartow, Bethel, and Bee! / And C's for the 'Southern Confederacy' brave, / Our bold little ship, all afloat on the wave!" "D" was for Davis, and "L" for Lincoln—"oh, woe to his crown!" "M" was for Manassas, "our glory, our pride," "R" for Rebels, and so on.[222] Nor was this the only such alphabet poem. Another "Confederate Alphabet" appeared as a broadside publication and, though similar in form, its tone was quite different. While "Willie's Political Alphabet" was concerned primarily with extolling the Confederacy and its heroes, this poem focused on attacking its enemy. For instance, "E" was "for [the American] Eagle transformed to a Crow," and "F" "for the [Union] Flag spreading ruin and woe." "Y" was "for Yankees, that self-esteemed nation," while "Z" was "for Zero, their true valuation."[223]

While one may question the literary merit of these poems and stories, their message was unmistakable. That such writing was didactic was to be expected, as all nineteenth-century children's literature read much the same way. Frivolous reading was frowned upon, and everything that a child read was supposed to have some instructive value. But Confederate children's literature also had a strong and rather transparent political agenda: to actively promote Confederate national identity and patriotic loyalty. Confederate children needed to be "fitted to take the place of those who are now pouring their life blood to secure our freedom, and preserve that freedom to the latest generation," and literature for them was intended to prepare these young southerners to defend their nation when the time came.[224]

Even more vital in this regard were the textbooks. The primacy of native textbook production to the plans of cultural nationalists has already been discussed above. Their commitment to providing the Confederacy with its own educational literature only strengthened as the war progressed. This "unanimity" on the necessity of Confederate schoolbooks was "an outgrowth of that determination which possesses the true Southern mind, to secure a real independence," *The Age* explained in January 1864. "The universal desire is for a separate and distinct nationality. This, of right, we ought to have."[225] Driven by such nationalist impulses as well as public demand, textbook production exploded during the middle years of the war, reaching its peak in 1864. Schoolbooks became the fastest-growing and most profitable segment of a rapidly proliferating Confederate literature. Confederate publishers, from Virginia to Texas, discovered "a vast and exceedingly lucrative field" open before them.[226]

It was quite lucrative. W. G. Clarke & Co., publishers of Adelaide De Vendel Chaudron's series of reading and spelling books, reported in June 1864 that demand for her *First Reader* was "almost unexampled" and that the original edition was already "exhausted without filling the orders on hand."[227] In order to keep pace, *The First Reader* passed through two editions as did *The Second Reader*. By 1865, *Chaudron's Spelling Book* had been issued five times, with a total of 40,000 copies in print. Nor was this an exceptional case. Richard McAllister Smith's *Confederate Primer* passed through four editions and his *Confederate Spelling Book* through five.[228] Branson, Farrar & Co. sold out two editions of 10,000 copies each of Marinda Branson Moore's *The Geographical Reader*, and her *Dixie Primer* and *First Dixie Reader* were each issued at least three times.[229] E. H. Cushing's *New Texas Spelling Book* sold out of its 12,000 copies in just five months, and a second edition of another 12,000 within six. He is estimated to have sold over 54,000 copies of the three books in his "New Texas Series" in just two years.[230] Robert Fleming's *Revised Ele-*

mentary Spelling Book, appearing in 1863, was reissued eight more times that year with a total print run of 40,000 copies.[231] Clearly, Confederate textbooks had become big business.

Cultural nationalists and educational reformers hailed this influx of new Confederate textbooks "as presage of our deliverance from our humiliating vassalage . . . to those who, no longer permitted to use us for selfish purposes, are seeking to exterminate us from the earth."[232] Confederate textbook writers and publishers had proven that they could provide their country with its own educational literature. "A new day has dawned," the *Southern Illustrated News* rejoiced. "The last Yankee school-book for Southern consumption has been printed."[233] Confederate textbooks not only had become more numerous, they also had become more "southern." Although many books still mirrored and in some cases directly copied standard northern works (especially Noah Webster), Confederate authors increasingly sought to insert new material about the South, the war, slavery, and the hated Yankees that would set their work apart from, and indeed render it antithetical to, the Yankee schoolbooks of the antebellum years. Cultural nationalism was the primary motivation driving Confederate textbook authors as they attempted not only to produce their own educational literature, but to make that literature distinctly southern. William Bingham, for instance, presented his *Grammar of the Latin Language* as "an auxiliary, however feeble, in establishing Southern literature and intellectual independence."[234] Incensed at the "many infections" and "omissions" to be found in northern texts, John Rice produced his *System of Modern Geography* in 1862, in order to "make us feel independent, and furnish the schools of the Confederate States with a geography, compiled by a Southern man, published upon our own soil—one that would approximate justice to ourselves, our institutions and our country."[235]

Textbook authors promoted Confederate nationalism through a number of means. At a minimum, all place names and other proper nouns now had to be recognizably southern, but more ambitious authors found other ways to impart a southern flavor to even the most primary of schoolbooks. In his *New Texas Reader*, for instance, Edward Cushing presented a "large number of original articles" on Texas and southern history "with the view of inspiring our youth." These mainly involved battle scenes of heroic Texans fighting Yankees or Mexicans, but they also covered general Confederate military topics such as Stonewall Jackson and the CSS *Virginia*. Cushing included an article on Lincoln's first inauguration which, not surprisingly, blamed Lincoln for the war and placed on his head "the blood upon a hundred gory fields, the ashes of ten thousand desolated homes, the groans and tears of innumerable wives, mothers and sisters, and the faded glory of his nation's flag and honor." "The memory of this wretch will . . . survive the lapse of time," the *New Texas Reader* promised, "and stand out in all its original blackness, as the greatest tyrant, and the meanest creature, that ever cursed a nation, or disgraced the name of man." Immediately following this article, Cushing ran an account of Jefferson Davis's inauguration which contrasted the simple and subdued dignity of the man and the occasion with the over-blown pomp and garishness of Lincoln's ceremony.[236]

Even math and spelling books could help bolster national fidelity and emphasize the differences between North and South. In his *Elementary Arith-metic*, Lemuel Johnson quizzed students: "If one Confederate soldier can whip 7 Yankees, how many soldiers can whip 49 Yankees?"; or "7 Confeder-ate soldiers captured 21 Yankees and divided them equally between them; how many did each one have?"; or "If one confederate soldier [can] kill 90 yankees, how many yankees can 10 confederate soldiers kill?"[237] Marinda Branson Moore's *Dixie Speller* also spoke directly and extensively about the war, albeit in far less celebratory tones. For instance, she included this poem written from the perspective of a young Confederate boy:

> This sad war is a bad thing.
> My pa-pa went, and died in the army.
> My big broth-er went too, and got shot. A bomb shell
> took off his head.
> My aunt had three sons, and all have died in the army.
> Now she and the girls have to work for bread.
> I will work for my ma and sis-ters.
> I hope we will have peace by the time I am old enough to
> go to war.
> If I were a man, and had to make laws, I would not have
> any war, if I could help it.
> If little boys fight, old folks whip them for it; but when
> men fight, they say "how brave!"

But though she clearly deplored the war, Moore left no doubt that the evil Yankees were to blame, maintaining and seeking to impart a grim Confeder-ate patriotism in her books.[238]

Certain northern works, it was discovered, could be refitted for Confeder-ate service. Robert Fleming, for instance, took Noah Webster's classic spell-ing book and, with some creative editing and key insertions, transformed it into a stridently pro-Confederate and proslavery book. As with nearly all

Confederate reprints of northern works, the proper names were changed to reflect southern places and events, but Fleming went further in his *Revised Elementary Spelling Book*, rewriting some of Webster's sentences and adding others. For instance, whereas Webster defined "Despotism" as "tyranny or oppressive government," Fleming altered it to read: "Despotism is a tyrannical, oppressive government. The administration of Abraham Lincoln is a despotism." Determined that "the people of these Confederate States of America will not henceforth withhold from their school-books, the teachings of the Scriptures" on the subject of slavery, Fleming not only removed all instances of real or imagined abolitionism from Webster's work, but inserted his own proslavery passages and lengthy biblical justifications. He also added facts and statistics about the various states in the Confederacy, including their dates of secession, and concluded the work with a biographical sketch of the Confederacy's greatest hero, Stonewall Jackson. Thus, while much of the content remained the same as Webster's original, Fleming altered the tone significantly in order to champion Confederate nationalism and the southern way of life.[239] The public rewarded him for his efforts: the *Revised Spelling Book* was a runaway best seller.

Of course, southern authors could pack only so much Confederate nationalistic propaganda into spellers, readers, primers, grammars, and arithmetics. These books were dedicated primarily to teaching young children how to read, write, and add, and their lessons, for the most part, reflected these goals. Not so with the geographies: by the very nature of their subject, geography writers had more latitude (pun intended) to express their political opinions and advance an explicitly nationalistic agenda. Since northern texts had largely ignored, or at least underrepresented, the southern states, Confederate writers had a responsibility to correct these past wrongs. For instance, while much of John Rice's *System of Modern Geography* was a "compilation, made up from the best authorities at hand," he greatly expanded the southern sections and reduced the northern ones so as to make his book "*the only work in existence that approximates doing justice to the country now composing the Confederate States of America*; its actual conditions and resources having been studiously concealed by every *yankee* work."[240] Marinda Moore's *Geographical Reader, for the Dixie Children* was an original work, likewise dedicated to demonstrating the greatness of the Confederacy, the righteousness of slavery, the vileness of the Yankees, and the unjustness and barbarity of the war they continued to wage against the South.

Both authors sought to instill national pride by lauding the Confederacy's political system, cataloging its resources, celebrating its wartime achievements, and predicting still greater accomplishments to come. The Confederacy was "*the best example of a republican government in the world*," Rice declared. "Under the influence of slavery, which is the corner stone of her governmental fabric, and an indomitable spirit of self-reliance in the hearts of the people, the Confederate States has just commenced a career of greatness."[241] "This is a great country!" Moore readily agreed, a greatness further demonstrated by its continued and determined resistance to Yankee tyranny. "We were considered an indolent, weak people, but our enemies have found us strong, because we had justice on our side."[242] To prove their point, Rice and Moore offered lengthy descriptions of the political, social, agricultural, material, and intellectual geography of each of the Confederate states, optimistically including Missouri, Kentucky, New Mexico, and Arizona. While Moore's account was an impressionistic survey of the individual states and their contributions to the war effort, Rice provided a systematic breakdown of each state's geographical position, its natural features, products, population, chief cities, manufactures, commerce, educational institutions, and internal improvements. Still, by emphasizing Confederate geography and showing the collective strength of the southern nation through its constituent parts, both of these textbooks served the same nationalistic purpose.

Invariably, these authors portrayed the North as a foreign and hostile country that bore little resemblance to the "high minded and courteous" South.[243] In retaliation for decades of perceived slights in northern geography books, coverage of the northern states was reduced drastically and what remained was peppered with negative comments. The Yankees, according to Rice, were "a keen, thrifty, speculating, ingenious people; money-loving and money making, without much restraint as to means, *success* being the all absorbing object." In recent days, he added, "infidelity, and a reckless puritanical fanaticism is fast robbing the people" of whatever "ennobling traits of character" they may have had. The government established by the sacred U.S. Constitution had been "overthrown" in the North, "and despotism reigns supreme in the hands of a political anti-slavery party."[244] Moore was somewhat more generous when it came to Yankee character, calling them "ingenious, and enterprising . . . noted for their tact in 'driving a bargain.' They are refined, and intelligent on all subjects but that of negro slavery, on this they are mad." As for northern politics, she too blamed the "Abolitionists" for the war. She told her readers that Lincoln was "a weak man" who had lost "thousands of lives" and "exhausted nearly all the strength of the nation, in a vain attempt to whip the South back into the Union."[245] Most important, both Rice and Moore sought to impress on Confederate children that the Yankees were their bitter enemies, intent on destroying their homes, looting their country, and killing their fathers and brothers.

Rice and Moore defended slavery vigorously. They both subscribed to the standard pseudo-scientific racial theory of the day that divided man into five races: "the Caucasian, or White race; the Mongolian, or Yellow race; the African, or Black race; the Malay, or Brown race; and the American, or Red race."[246] From this, they launched into a spirited defense of the institution of slavery as it existed in the Confederacy. In the South, Rice explained, the black race had been "brought and humanly [*sic*] reduced to their proper normal condition of slavery." He rejoiced that slavery had been "expressly recognized" in the Confederate constitution, "*as it is in the Word of God*," and that its practice was "universally approved of by the people."[247] Moore also defended the institution by arguing that slaves were "generally well used and often have as much pocket money as their mistresses. They are contented and happy, and many of them are christians." In "Lesson IX," she included this question and answer exercise:

Q. Is the African savage in this country?
A. No; they are docile and religious here.
Q. How are they in Africa where they first come from?
A. They are very ignorant, cruel and wretched.

Interestingly, Moore admitted that slaves were "sometimes mistreated" and urged "all the little boys and girls [to] remember that slaves are human, and that God will hold them to account for treating them with injustice." Still, she believed that "the negro" was an inferior race and that white southerners were right, divinely right, to hold them in bondage. She scoffed at northern attempts to enlist emancipated slaves in the army, maintaining that "the negro is too cowardly for a soldier."[248] Such declarations in support of slavery and black inferiority certainly were not surprising, but they did highlight the differences between these new Confederate textbooks and their northern forebearers. Northern geographies often had little to say about the South except when lamenting slavery. In contrast, Confederate textbooks placed their preponderate attention directly on the South while actively defending the righteousness of its peculiar institution.

Taken as a whole, Confederate cultural nationalists liked what they saw in this new and ever-growing crop of Confederate textbooks. New titles appeared and sold out with amazing rapidity, and it seemed as if the South had finally freed itself from its dependence on northern textbook publishers. What was more, these new textbooks were increasingly southern in their tone and outlook. By printing and privileging southern history and geography, by treating the North as a foreign country, by cataloging incidents of southern heroism and Yankee cowardice, by lionizing the military heroes of the Confederacy, and by actively defending the institutions of the South—especially slavery— textbook authors created an educational literature designed specifically to foster Confederate nationalism in southern children. Not all Confederate textbooks were explicitly political in their content, but even those which did not stray beyond the ABCs were hailed for helping break southern dependence on the North. While the importance placed on native schoolbooks was not new, the scale of production and the expanding range of Confederate textbooks during these middle years further fed the hopes of cultural nationalists. They considered the success and proliferation of native textbooks and juvenile literature during this period to be some of the strongest indications yet that Confederate cultural autonomy was within reach.

FINALLY, THE SOUTHERN STAGE had its own role to play in this high-water mark of Confederate culture. This was the "halcyon time for theatre in the South."[249] Swelling urban populations provided Confederate theater managers with large and appreciative audiences. Business was booming. Nearly every major Confederate city had its own theater, and Richmond, the "Broadway of the Confederacy," had three.[250] Of course, there had always been some theater in the antebellum South, particularly in New Orleans, but these productions generally had been run by northern managers, acted by northern actors, and written by northern or European playwrights. In the wake of secession, these theaters closed, the companies disbanded, and the actors and managers fled north. In their place arose new Confederate theaters with Confederate managers, Confederate actors, and quite often Confederate plays.

Brushing aside the vociferous objections of religious leaders who denounced the theater as both immoral and inappropriate during time of war, secular-minded cultural nationalists heartily endorsed the idea of native theater, if not always the quality of the productions themselves.[251] They eagerly welcomed this new and unexpected venue for the transmission of Confederate culture, and they immediately sought to bring it within the fold of the movement for intellectual independence. The timing of this "regeneration" of theater in the South was no coincidence, nationalists argued. It grew out of the same cultural impulse that had given life to the new Confederate periodicals and driven the rapid proliferation of native print literature. As Charles Bailie explained in *The Magnolia*, following secession "all thought of the arts had ceased, and the Drama, with one swoop of the mighty hand of revolution, became 'a thing that was.' " By the fall of 1862, however, Confederates were learning to "maintain ourselves as a nation" and as "the general mind has become gradually more tranquil . . . the people have begun to look around them for those enjoyments, those recreations, and means of entertainment to which they had been accustomed before their country's call, for a vindication of its rights, attracted them." It was incumbent upon Confederate editors, writers, and theater managers to ensure that these new "means of entertainment" be distinctly southern. "We must have native talent," Bailie demanded. "If we have Drama, it must be 'native and to the manner born.' We have already commenced the foundation of a literature. So let it be with the drama."[252]

Having embraced theater as yet another accomplice in the struggle for southern cultural autonomy, Confederate nationalists sought to guide its proper development and at the same time bring legitimacy to this somewhat morally suspect form of entertainment. For instance, Henry Timrod contributed one of his finest wartime poems to mark the opening of the New Richmond Theater on February 9, 1863 (the old one had burned to the ground on New Years Day 1862).[253] Timrod's poem celebrated the theater in the most romantic of terms. It was a place where:

Shut for one happy evening from the flood
That roars around us, here you may behold—
    As if a desert way
    Could blossom and unfold
  A garden fresh with May—
Substantialized in breathing flesh and blood,
    Souls that upon the poet's page
    Have lived from age to age,
And yet have never donned this mortal clay.

.   .   .   .

Bid Liberty rejoice! Aye, though its day
Be far or near, these clouds shall yet be red
With the large promise of the coming ray.
Meanwhile, with that calm courage which can smile
Amid the terrors of the wildest fray,
Let us among the charms of Art awhile
    Fleet the deep gloom away;
Nor yet forget that on each hand and head
Rest the dear rights for which we fight and pray.[254]

More telling still was the amount of coverage that the Confederate press devoted to theatrical productions and new Confederate plays. The *Magnolia Weekly*, *Southern Field and Fireside*, the *Southern Literary Messenger*, *Southern Punch*, the *Gulf City Home Journal*, the *Bugle-Horn of Liberty*, and the *Confederate Spirit and Knapsack of Fun* all had either specific drama sections or regularly featured reviews of new plays and performances, as did many of the daily papers. The *Southern Illustrated News* even secured eminent man of letters John R. Thompson to serve as its drama critic. Nearly every performance was announced in the Confederate press, and nearly as many were reviewed. The theater critics were often harsh, castigating actors, managers, writers, and audience members by turn and sometimes all at once. But they continued to write about the theater—and write extensively—and in so doing brought a certain degree of respectability to the genre as a whole, even as they eviscerated the previous night's performance. Through their often scathing reviews, they attempted to raise the level of expectations for native theater. They pushed Confederate writers and theater managers to produce a dramatic literature truly worthy of their new nation and its lofty intellectual aspirations.

The theaters in Richmond, Augusta, Savannah, Atlanta, Wilmington, Montgomery, Mobile, and Selma presented Shakespearean tragedies and comedies, as well as other stock pieces and English plays smuggled through the blockade—along with a good deal of much lower-brow fare. But they also produced a substantial number of original Confederate works. For instance, of the 400 odd plays and "farces" presented in Richmond during the war, more than sixty were original productions.[255] Invariably, these Confederate plays took the war as their subject, thus appeasing the public's appetite and guaranteeing a certain degree of popularity. The dual motivations of nationalism and profit compelled theater managers to actively solicit native works, much to the delight of cultural nationalists. Alfred Waldon, manager and patriarch of the Augusta theater company "Thespian Family, or The Queen Sisters," offered $500 in premiums for new three-act dramas ($300 for the best and $200 for the next best). Waldon stipulated that the plays "must be written by Southern citizens, and purely southern in their sentiments."[256] The *Southern Literary Messenger* advised Richard Odgen, manager of the New Richmond Theater, that the only way "to ensure really good original plays, is to pay—not high—but very high prices for them. If Mr. Manager Ogden desires to immortalize himself as the founder of the Southern Drama—which ought to be as high as the character of the people—let him offer $10,000 or $20,000 for the best Southern play."[257] While Ogden never paid so much, he did actively encourage the production of original Confederate works and featured them regularly on his stage. In fact, the *Magnolia Weekly* later credited him for fostering "Southern dramatic authorship to a greater extent than was ever done before."[258]

With Confederate audiences and theater managers clamoring for native drama, Confederate playwrights churned out new plays at an amazing pace. Most of these were unpublished, bearing titles like "None but the Brave Deserve the Fair," "The Roll of the Drum; or, The Battle of Manassas," "The Scouts; or, The Plains of Manassas," "The Maiden's Vow; or, The Capture of Courtland, Alabama," "Our Cause; or, The Female Rebel," "The Virginia Cavalier," "The Rebel Spy," "Miscegenation; or, A Virginia Negro in Washington," and "King Linkum the First."[259] John Hill Hewitt alone wrote over 20 unpublished plays which were performed in Richmond, Augusta, and Savannah.[260]

Of the published plays, the best known and most extensively reviewed was James McCabe's *The Guerrillas*.[261] Full of "blood and thunder," this inaccurately self-proclaimed "first original [Confederate] drama" was an exciting war tale of capture, escape, and revenge with all the stock characters one would expect: the daring Confederate guerrilla (Arthur Douglas), his steadfast and equally heroic wife (Rose), their staunchly loyal slave (Jerry), and not one, but two bloodthirsty and lecherous Yankee officers (Colonel Bradley and General Fremont).[262] Following the brutal murder of his family and the burning of their mansion by Colonel Bradley's men in western Virginia, Arthur Douglas swears revenge and launches a guerrilla campaign against the Yankees. In addition to condemning northern barbarity, McCabe's play actively promoted Confederate nationalism and attempted to bolster southern confidence in the institution of slavery. For instance, when Arthur offers Jerry his freedom in gratitude for protecting Rose from the evil Bradley, Jerry refuses: "If you'se tired of old Jerry, jist take him out in de field and shoot him, but don't send him away from you; don't set him free." Jerry's submissiveness did not extend to all whites, however, for he hated the Yankees as much as any truehearted white southerner. In bayoneting a Union soldier to death, Jerry reasons, "don't make no difference. He ain't nothing but a Yankee." In the final climatic battle, Rose kills Colonel Bradley as Jerry defeats General Fremont in a sword fight. McCabe was able to cast a slave in this heroic role because Jerry never forgets his place within the racial order. He continually expresses his love for his white masters and his contentedness under slavery. Jerry, like Arthur and Rose, is ready and willing to fight and die for the Confederacy and the southern way of life. As Rose, in the face of torture, defiantly tells General Fremont, "We are proud of that which you call treason. Go back . . . to those that sent you, and tell them that they can never conquer the South. You may kill every man and boy in our land, but you will then have to meet the women; and woe to you when that day comes."[263] Opening on December 22, 1862, at the Richmond Varieties (Franklin Hall), *The Guerrillas* was "enthusiastically received by the public, and had a successful run for an entire week."[264]

Other published plays, like William Russell Smith's coarse parody of Lincoln, *The Royal Ape*, J. J. Delchamps's *Love's Ambuscade; or The Sergeant's Stratagem*, Joseph Hodgson's *The Confederate Vivandiere; or, The Battle of Leesburg*, and the anonymous farce *Great Expectations; or Getting Promoted*, enjoyed varying degrees of success. In terms of literary quality, Confederate plays ranged from the forgettable to the truly abysmal with *The Guerrillas* ranking near the top and *The Royal Ape* very near the bottom. Apparently, however, a play's literary merits did not greatly affect its profitability. G. W. Alexander's "abominable" *The Virginia Cavalier*, for instance, was the "greatest hit of the Confederate Stage."[265] So long as the work was fiercely patriotic and focused on the war, theater managers had no trouble filling the seats.

Still, it was a start, and cultural nationalists and theater critics viewed the growing number of original Confederate plays and the increasing popularity of native theater as hopeful signs, even as they gritted their teeth through each evening's performance. As an explicitly popular form of entertainment with a questionable moral compass, theater was a more unruly animal than the other forms of this burgeoning Confederate literature, but cultural nationalists were determined to bring it under control. By actively encouraging native theatrical writing, while at the same time harshly criticizing those works which failed to live up to the mark, cultural nationalists hoped to foster a uniquely Confederate theatrical literature that would be acceptable to southern tastes and expressive of southern character, transforming drama in the South "from an exotic into a flower of native growth."[266]

During the middle years of the war, Confederate literature expanded in all directions at once. In a remarkably short period of the time, southerners had broken free from their longtime "vassalage" to the North and found themselves capable of supplying their own cultural needs. New Confederate literary magazines appeared by the score and quickly became some of the strongest advocates for intellectual independence. Confederate book production soared, and ambitious writers, publishers, and theater managers opened up entirely new venues of literature. Backed by strong public demand, publishing became a profitable endeavor in the Confederacy. Confederate periodicals and books reached circulations that would have been unthinkable before the war, and editors and publishers could finally afford to pay native authors for their work. The success and proliferation of Confederate publications during this period was all the more remarkable considering the tremendous logistical obstacles that stood in the way. Overcoming shortages of every kind, inflation, inexperience, and wartime disruptions, Confederate publishers nevertheless continued to expand their production and offer their readers a wide variety of new and self-consciously Confederate books and periodicals.

As they looked about them, Confederate cultural nationalists saw all of their predictions, and even some of their wildest dreams, coming true. A Confederate national literature was emerging, a strong market for native publications had developed, and corrupt northern works had been banished from southern borders. Even if these new Confederate works lacked the polish of northern productions, this was only a temporary inconvenience. Once the war ended, Confederate publishers could devote the resources necessary to match the outward appearances of northern and European publications. For now, however, what was between the covers was more important than what was on them, and Confederate cultural nationalists were delighted by this dramatic expansion of native writing. The campaign for Confederate intellectual independence, it seemed, was on the brink of success. Southerners had learned to supply themselves with their own literature, a literature geared to their own tastes, values, and needs. Before their hopeful eyes, cultural nationalists saw the Confederacy solidifying into a real country in the truest cultural sense, and they felt that its intellectual independence, if not yet an accomplished fact, was certainly on the not-too-distant horizon.

CHAPTER SIX

SEARCHING FOR A CONFEDERATE "LITERATURE OF POWER"

The predictions of the cultural nationalists had come to pass. The unique wartime conditions within the Confederacy had indeed proved to be a fertile, if not ideal, environment for the creation of a native Confederate literature. "The first step" to true cultural autonomy had been taken, the *Richmond Enquirer* announced in January 1864. "Let peace come when it may, the *literati* of Yankeedom will find no mean competitors in the learned men scattered throughout the Confederacy."[1] But it was only the "first step." To their credit, Confederates had managed to produce their own popular literature, one suited to their day-to-day needs. They had created what A. B. Stark had called in 1861, a "literature of knowledge." This utilitarian, if ephemeral, literature included newspapers, magazines, pamphlets, textbooks, and popular histories, as well as light fiction, drama, and poetry. Prior to the war, these types of publications had come almost exclusively from the North and served as the primary conduits for dangerous ideas. Breaking their dependence on northern publishers and creating their own popular literature in such a short period of time in the middle of a war was no small feat for southerners, and cultural nationalists enthusiastically applauded their impressive gains. But for its intellectual independence to be complete, the Confederacy also needed a transcendent literature, what Stark had termed a "literature of power," those works of true merit and originality that would embody southern character, crystallize Confederate nationality, and win the admiration and respect of the world.[2]

Written by the Confederacy's "true poets," this great literature would showcase the virtues of southern society and forever banish all doubts about the stultifying effects of slavery. "We must convince the world, by actual demonstration, that we can write and print and publish as good books as any other nation on the earth," Mary McCrimmon explained in the *Southern Christian Advocate*.[3] "So great a people as we claim to be, should have a language calculated to convey true ideas of our habits, tastes, and rules of etiquette," textbook author Marinda Branson Moore agreed. "If we would be truly great, we must rise above the lower stratum of intellectual atmosphere."[4] Confederate cultural nationalists were convinced that such a literature was absolutely essential to the success of their project and the future of their country. At the same time, they were equally certain that what had been produced thus far during the war was not up to the mark. Hence, even as they rejoiced at the tremendous strides made by Confederate writers, editors, and publishers during the first half of the war, they continually pushed for improvement. "The support which has been accorded literary enterprizes since the beginning of the war, is encouraging, and justifies the hope that we may be able to perform all that the warmest friend of our literature can desire," the *Magnolia Weekly* noted in November 1863. "Still we must not be satisfied with what is now being done. We must do more. We must make our literature something of which we may be proud."[5]

Confederate critics realized then what literary historians have concluded since: that with the exception of a few poems, mostly by Henry Timrod, there was little to be found in Confederate literature that would stand the test of time. Surveying the quality of what Confederate writers had produced, cultural nationalists conceded that there was some truth to the contention that "the present revolution has developed only a kind of hot-house literature, which will sink into insignificance, when the storm that called it forth shall have subsided."[6] "In all periods of excitement, especially of war, the tone of current literature naturally adapts itself to the prevailing sentiment," and so too had it in the Confederacy. Much of Confederate literature was indelibly marked by the passions and events of its immediate surroundings, and this, while serving a public need for patriotic expression, also dated such works and limited their lasting influence. "Most of the productions which have as yet emanated from 'Confederate pens' bear the stamp of instability, we fear, too deeply, for them to escape the common doom of war-time literature," one critic concluded. "Too many are following in the beaten track of tale and song whose glory rests upon the issues of the moment" to have any hope of achieving more than "ephemeral repute."[7]

Confederate writers had not even produced a worthy national anthem—"Dixie," of course, was ineligible due to its northern origins. "Good and bad poems were written," Henry Timrod observed, "but none, with the exception of 'My Maryland', and that only for a little time, touched the heart of the people so deeply as to become one of its representative songs."[8] "Nearly three years have elapsed since the birth of our nation, and we have produced but a very few respectable ballads, not one of which can be called 'National,' " an exasperated James McCabe wrote in October 1863.[9] Timrod, too, was embarrassed. "Surely, in the present situation of their country, struggling for its liberties against over-powering odds, and isolated from the rest of the world—a situation more full of pathos and grandeur than anything in Greek or Roman story," he reasoned, Confederate poets (presumably including himself) "ought to find inspiration enough to draw forth the utmost capacity of their genius" and write songs that will "stir the heart more than the roar of a thousand patriot cannon!"[10]

Even more troubling than the impermanence of this war literature, however, was the fear that southern writers and editors might still be treading the paths set by the "blue and yellow covered literature" of the Yankees.[11] In replacing corrupt northern literature with a literature of their own, Confederates needed to guard against following familiar, but dangerous, models. Sensational tales, prurient drama, gossip columns, indecent humor, and frivolous novels must not be allowed to become part of Confederate popular literature, and nationalist-minded critics were quick to condemn any writer, editor, publisher, or theater manager who presented such trash to the public. Frank Alfriend of the *Southern Literary Messenger* warned of the "calamity" menacing Confederate society "in the insidious growth of a spurious literature whose noxious fruits, once permitted to reach maturity, will render the mental soil barren to the culture of the bloom and beauty of the health-giving and life-inspiring productions of True Learning and Genuine Virtue." Such a literature was "more to be dreaded than even absolute ignorance."[12] In reacting to the appearance of a "Gossip Column" in *Southern Field and Fireside*, one outraged critic demanded: "Are such things to go before the world as part of our literature? Do we reflect on the fact that the columns of journals and newspapers are considered a true and exact reflex of the opinions, customs, manners, and general characteristics of the people among whom they are published? My God! Is THIS miserable excrescence of Yankeeism to become a feature of Southern literature?"[13]

Still, despite these shortcomings and missteps, critics saw promise in the wartime literary outpouring. Henry Timrod devoted his first editorial in the *Daily South Carolinian* to this subject. "The great and troubled movement through which we are passing has stirred the Southern mind to an unwonted activity." True, he admitted, "No preeminently great man . . . has arisen amid the turmoil, but the people are beginning to think with an independence which they never evinced in their former provincial position." Freed from the North, southerners had produced "more novels, histories, and poems . . . within the last two years than within any previous ten." Even if many of these "have been of merit sufficiently indifferent," Timrod maintained that they "all tend to show that a new era of intellectual energy is dawning upon us." In fledgling literary efforts, he detected "the national mind struggling to find fit and original expression." That there were still "traces . . . of imitation in everything that we do" was not surprising, considering the extent and duration of the South's intellectual dependence on the North and the short amount of time that had passed since secession, "but it is something that we have commenced to speak for ourselves." Timrod remained confident that "our literature shall yet be peculiarly our own. At present, perhaps, it is like Milton's lion, not yet freed from earth, and 'pawing to get free,' but it will soon shake off every trammel, and trust to its native strength alone."[14]

Of course, the complete realization of this intellectual potential would have to wait until peace returned, and cultural nationalists frankly recognized that "it remained for the future, with its great calm, enriched with a brilliant retrospect, to glen over the fields of the past, and build up a characteristic and substantial literature."[15] "Complete success" might be impossible while the conflict continued, Professor Edward Joynes conceded in 1864, "yet seeds sown now, in the eager and earnest minds of our people, will take deeper root and bear surer fruit, than if postponed to a later day, when once more purely material enterprises shall absorb their attention." Indeed, he warned, "if the foundations that are to secure our intellectual and moral independence of the North be not laid now, under the impulses of this revolution, they will probably never be laid at all, and that independence never be won."[16]

In order to lay those foundations, native writers and readers required guidance. Having proven that the Confederacy could indeed sustain its own print literature, Confederate cultural nationalists needed to ensure that this "exertion of the giant intellect of the South" was channeled in the right directions.[17] "Our Republic is yet in its infancy; but all should watch the rapid growth of the young Oak, and see that no rancorous weed grow up around and graft itself with the parent stem," John R. Thompson advised in December 1863. "The literature of a newborn Republic like ours should be jealously guarded."[18] To this end, the focus of cultural nationalists changed during the middle years of the war. The quality of Confederate literature increasingly became their primary concern, rather than the mere origin of its production. In the past, cultural nationalists had always used such words as "originality," "quality," and "character" to define their project, as if the meanings of these terms were self-evident. Now, however, as native literature began to thrive, they attempted to clarify these concepts in order to better guide young southern writers. Through their essays, criticisms, and editorial decisions, cultural nationalists sought to steer the development of Confederate literature, to shun imitation—especially of the North—and to create a national literature that would exemplify southern character, elevate southern taste, and demonstrate to the world the cultural legitimacy of the South's desire for independence.

Confederate cultural nationalists were confident that they would know such a literature when they saw it. Above all, they knew what this literature must not be. It could not be an imitation of others. There was only "one way to be a truly national writer," Timrod counseled in January 1864, "and that is by being a truly original writer. . . . The man of original genius draws his matter from the depth of his own being; and the national character, in which, as a unit of the nation, he shares, finds its utterance through him without his will."[19] Other commentators agreed with Timrod's romantic definition. Originality should be prized above all else for only an original native literature could be "a true reflection of Southern manners, customs, and mind."[20] It had to be "so Southern that there would be no mistaking it. A Yankee would throw up—the whites of his eyes to read it."[21]

It was essential that Confederates "discountenance all imitation" and write "in utter independence of all foreign models." Imitation of the North, in particular, had to be avoided at all costs.[22] Given the South's past literary dependence, this was "a most powerful *habit* to contend against," but the dictates of nationality demanded that southerners be unrelenting in their efforts "to crush it out forever."[23] They must be "ever watchful, and see to it, that the literature about to be formed is genuinely Southern, and not a disgusting off-shoot—a loathsome rehash—a miserable aping of the worst-form of yankee mannerism."[24] Originality was the key to intellectual independence, and whatever form their national literature was to take, cultural nationalists knew that it could "in no way resemble the Yankee abortion."[25]

The unsettled conditions created by war, cultural nationalists predicted, would help southerners forever break from northern models and encourage them to explore new intellectual ground. "Originality, energy and self-reliance, are what we have never shown until the pressure of circumstances calls them forth, and nothing has ever done this so effectually as war," Samuel Davies observed in October 1863.[26] Additionally, the "general upheaval of the surface of society" caused by the ongoing "revolution" had allowed new voices to rise to prominence. "The crust is broken," the *Confederate Baptist* noted, "and they who have been hitherto consigned to obscurity, emerge into activity and splendor." The war created new avenues for social advancement —primarily military, but also intellectual—and in so doing had brought new men and women to the fore. "It is well that society should be exposed to these periodical agitations," the *Baptist* philosophized. "Cliques are broken up, charmed circles are disenchanted of their pernicious spell, and a field is opened for the genius of the nation to enter the lists, and win the prize. Revolution is the death of old fogyism, the antagonist of the defunct past, and the beneficent patron of the future."[27] The dramatic expansion of southern authorship during the war was a clear indication of the benefits resulting from such disruptions, and cultural nationalists were confident that this infusion of new people and new ideas into the public intellectual sphere could only bode well for the creation of a unique national literature.

But "old fogyism," as it was called, would be a problem, and cultural nationalists worried about the resistance with which new authors and new literature might be met in certain corners. Hesitantly, some even began to speak out against southern conservatism. This was an unexpected development. Conservatism had always been a point of pride and a saving grace for southerners. The Confederacy itself was founded upon avowedly conservative principles. Secession, Reverend William A. Hall instructed audiences in Petersburg and Richmond, was "a remarkable historic protest against philosophic infidelity and disorganizing wrong." The Confederacy's birth marked the dawning of a worldwide *"Period of Conservatism"* that would sweep aside the "extremes of individual authority."[28] Theorist George Fitzhugh likewise saw the formation of the Confederacy as the beginning of "a great conservative reaction." As he told the readers of the *Southern Literary Messenger*, secession was "a solemn protest against the doctrines of natural liberty, human equality and the social contract, as taught by Locke and the American sages of 1776, and an equally solemn protest against the doctrines of Adam Smith, Franklin, Say, Tom Paine, and the rest of the infidel political economists who maintain that the world is too much governed."[29] The extent to which the Confederacy did indeed uphold these philosophical ideals is debatable, but it is true that conservatism was a badge of honor for many southerners and had been for a long time.

Cultural nationalists had no quarrel with these conservative principles. In fact, they celebrated them as one of the Confederacy's great strengths and the potential basis for a truly original national literature. What they objected to was blind adherence to the past and suspicion of new ideas. This type of conservatism advocated "the defence of things as they are, because they are. . . . Memory it has, but no Hope. It reads History, but has no Prophecy. . . . Its language always is, 'the old is better'—a maxim very precious to wine-drinkers and conservatives." Under the old Union, when southerners had been forced to defend themselves constantly against northern fanatics, this type of thinking was understandable, even laudable. It had kept the country in balance and enabled it to survive for as long as it did. But now "we are the South no more," argued one contributor to *Southern Field and Fireside*. "Our sectional position has been changed into an independent position. South meant the antithesis to North, but to us there is no North now." As such, the old knee-jerk reactionary brand of southern conservatism had to be abandoned for the Confederacy to grow intellectually. "Conservatism does infinite harm when you organize it as a system," this writer warned. "It is only one element, a good and potent element; and the moment you forget this, you pervert it from it uses." By "repressing their aggressive energy, binding them down to hereditary ideas and usages," continual conservatism could cause a people to develop a "chronic resistance to innovation. It deadens their aspirations; it converts them into petrefactions. And this was precisely the harm that conservatism did us in the old Union."[30]

Now that the South was its own nation, "active and aggressive ideas" were what was needed.[31] "O, for a bold original thinker . . . and the exodus of literary charlatans from the realms of authordom," called *Southern Punch*.[32] This did not mean, of course, that the Confederacy should follow the North in its descent into fanaticism and madness. "Conservatism must not yield to Radicalism; no, not an inch, not a hair's breadth," *Southern Field and Fireside* explained. But there must also be "Progress."[33] Such direct assaults on southern conservatism were relatively rare. Still, this type of thinking was implicit in the calls for an original native literature. In order for the Confederacy to realize its intellectual potential and produce the transcendent literature that true independence required, southerners would have to overcome past suspicions, embrace new ideas, and even accept dissenting opinions.

AS TO WHAT CONSTITUTED proper subjects for this original Confederate literature, cultural nationalists and literary critics were quick to establish some guidelines as well as to dispel a few misconceptions. For one, a national southern literature, they argued, was not necessarily literature about the South. "It would be quite possible for a Southern poet to write a hundred odes to the Confederate flag, or for a Southern novelist to fill his books with descriptions of Southern scenes, and yet to be un-Southern in every respect," Henry Timrod explained. An author's "southern-ness" was revealed through his independence of foreign models and by the sentiments, values, and, above all, ineffable character that spoke through his work. It was not required that "all his trees should be palmettos, and all his fields white with cotton."[34]

Of course, this was not to say that southerners should not write about the South. After all, to produce great literature authors needed to know their subjects intimately. Many critics echoed George Bagby's fictional "Uncle Flat-back" who urged Confederate poets to focus on "the things we common people most care about—the scenes and sounds of home, far in the depths of the uncontaminated country, where the little that is yet unpolluted by Yankee ideas and customs still remains."[35] But Confederate writers could not feel restricted to such topics; "if they are led by some inner inspiration, and not by the mere caprice of choice, they may find, even amid the Arctic ice, or the luminous seas of the tropics, spots upon which they may plant, never to be taken down, the flag of their country's genius."[36]

As for the war itself, there was some disagreement as to its immediate utility as a subject for great literature. Some believed that the passions of war would quickly solidify themselves in verse and prose and thus create an instant southern literature of great inspirational power and emotional depth. Other, more patient, critics had no doubt that the collective experience of war would provide a common national heritage, a new pantheon of southern heroes, and the primary inspiration for a great southern literature *in the future*. All realized that they were living the stuff of epic literature and fully believed, as Professor Edward Joynes did, that "the war . . . will be the basis upon which the distinctive civilization of this people will be founded here-after. . . . Its experiences, recollections, and traditions; the impulses, the energies, the passions and aspirations it has called into being, will be impressed with controlling force upon every mind, and will inspire the thoughts and the sentiments, the literature and the ambition, of the present and future generations, with ever increasing influence."[37] "We are *making* the materials for the drama, and for future songs and fiction," William Gilmore Simms explained, but the composition of those great works "must be left to other generations, which, in the enjoyment of that peace and independence for which we are now doing battle, will be able to command the leisure for those noble and generous arts by which nations best assert their claims to independence, and secure a proud immortality for fame!"[38] In the interest of aiding this future war-inspired literature, *Southern Punch* only half-jokingly suggested that Confederate generals make a conscious effort to select fields of battle with "euphonious and sonorous names," for which "the ballad writers will not only thank you, but serenade you all the way down the vista of time."[39]

In the short term, however, most critics thought it best for writers of serious literature to avoid the war. There was no sense in "dallying with the record before it is complete." Anything written while the cannon still thundered was bound to suffer from lack of perspective, overly excited passions, incomplete information, and "exaggeration." The war's true significance was not yet known, and peace, time, and reflection would be required before southern authors could begin to profitably mine its depths. What was more, while the drama was unfolding daily, any fictional account would pale in comparison to the majesty, tragedy, and heartache of the real thing. For these reasons, Confederate critics advised eager southern authors to wait before embarking on writing the great novels and epic poems of the war. Popular literature, of course, would continue to focus almost exclusively on the conflict, but for those seeking to assist in the creation of a Confederate "literature of power," critics recommended that for the time being they avoid the actual, and instead "plant their bantling thoughts amidst the gardens of the purely ideal."[40] The war would become the central theme and chief inspiration for Confederate literature in the future, but for now, southern authors would be wise to choose other, less immediate, subjects.

Beyond simply stressing the importance of originality and the need for an illustrious national literature, there were a number of ways in which cultural nationalists tried to actively encourage the production of such literature and guide its development. One approach was to highlight the southern literary tradition as it existed, lauding its past triumphs and celebrating its authors. The dominance of northern print literature had blinded southerners to their own literary achievements, and cultural nationalists, turned literary historians, were determined to rectify this wrong. Their point was not to prove that the Confederacy already had a national literature, but rather to provide glimpses of what a future Confederate literature based on past accomplishments might look like, as well as to point aspiring writers toward helpful (and safe) models. The South had never wanted for talent or intelligence, these writers argued, only the means, support, and appreciation needed to produce and sustain a native literature.

Such praise of past southern writers and thinkers was not uncommon in the early years of the war or indeed before it, but starting in mid-1863, these southern literary histories became more systematic as well as more pointed. Confederate literary magazines began to run long and often serialized explorations of antebellum southern thought, as well as many shorter essays to the same purpose. On July 4, 1863 (the day Vicksburg fell, and the day after Pickett's Charge), the *Southern Illustrated News* proudly presented Paul Hamilton Hayne's long "finely wrought" poem, "The Southern Lyre," in which "one of the most graceful and imaginative of the poets of our sunny land sings the praises of his brother minstrels, with a felicity of epithet, a wealth of imagery, and a generous appreciation, that commend his verses to the acceptance of everybody."[41] In October, essayist and constitutional historian William Archer Cocke commenced his seven-part "Sketches of Southern Literature" in the *Magnolia Weekly*.[42] *Southern Punch* ran a series of articles on southern literature, including the three-part "An Hour Among the Southern Poets."[43] Appearing later, but clearly driven by the same impulse, James Wood Davidson's serialized "Litterateurs of the South," first appeared in the June 11, 1864 issue of *The Illustrated Mercury* and ran, in weekly installments, through the beginning of September.[44]

These wartime surveys of southern literary history had a definite and quite explicit purpose. In order to produce a great national literature, southerners, as a people, first needed to rid themselves of any residual feelings of intellectual inferiority that still lingered from decades of northern cultural dependence, and this parading of southern literary luminaries was intended to do just that. As Paul Hamilton Hayne lyrically proclaimed at the start of his poem:

No longer shall the darksome cloud
Of Northern Hate and Envy shroud
The radiance of our Poets proud.

They come, a glorious Band, to claim
The guerdon of their poet-fame—
Their brows with heavenly light aflame![45]

Once the achievements of their writers were laid bare before the eyes of Confederate readers, printed in the pages of their own native periodicals, and blessed by their own native critics, "who," *Southern Punch* asked, could "sneeringly assert that this brilliant South of ours has contributed little to literature?"[46]

By flooding the South with their literature and restricting the access of southern writers to the means of publication, the Yankees had created the illusion that southerners were an intellectually backwards and unproductive people. They taunted the South that "literature sickens and poesy dies in a land of slavery."[47] For decades beset by "American" literary anthologies from which "all Southern effusions" had been excluded, "it is not remarkable that Southern readers should be ignorant of Southern writers," the editors of the *Southern Illustrated News* conceded.[48] Constantly told of "our barrenness in the belles-lettres" by Yankee arbiters of taste, "not a few among ourselves have accepted it as truth, in all its length and breadth, and sought in various ways to apologize for it."[49]

Now, thankfully, all that was over, and it was time for southerners to reclaim their literary treasures. The "true character and excellence" of a literature was determined not by the "number of its authors, nor the bulk of their books," as northerners would have them believe. Rather, William Cocke argued, such qualities were measured "by the choice spirits among them, who soar with eagle pinion far above the flight of their innumerable coveys, whose wings, ladened by the ink in which they have dabbled, can only perch from branch to branch, or hurdle on the earth, with no aspiration, or capacity to bathe their plumage, high up in the pure cerulean atmosphere where exalted genius delights to dwell."[50] While the Yankees certainly could claim a far larger covey of the flightless, fluttering, and sputtering, it was the South, these Confederate critics insisted, where the "choice spirits" resided, even if they had gone unrecognized by their own people. When properly evaluated, "Our literary history is equally as brilliant, and far purer than that of the North," the *Magnolia Weekly* announced.[51] Cocke was even more categorical: "From the days of the Revolution of 1776, to the present day, the literature of the Southern States, in history, in poetry, in philosophy, [in] science, in theology: as manifested on the pages of its newspapers and magazines, and as illustrated by the talents, the taste, and the learning of its professors, has surpassed, in every respect, except quantity, that of the North, even as the sun surpasseth in glory the twinkling of the countless stars."[52]

To support these grandiose claims, cultural nationalists confronted their readers with a southern literary cavalcade. In "The Southern Lyre," Hayne memorialized over twenty southern poets, living and dead. Varying the number of lines and stanzas devoted to each in accordance with their importance, he praised the work of Edgar Allan Poe, William Gilmore Simms, Henry Timrod, Washington Allston (both as poet and painter), Edward C. Pinckney, Richard H. Wilde, Henry J. Jackson, Albert Pike, William J. Grayson, William Crafts, Alexander B. Meek, brothers Philip Pendleton Cooke and John Esten Cooke, James R. Randall, John R. Thompson, James Barron Hope, Augustus Requier, Henry L. Flash, and Severn Wallis. Of himself, Hayne, out of modesty, did not speak, but the editors of the *Southern Illustrated News* were quick to add three stanzas of their own composition celebrating this "Petrarch of the Land."[53] Notably (in fact Hayne footnoted it), "The Southern Lyre" did not include any of the "many gifted female poets of the South."[54] Still, even with such a significant and regrettable omission, "many will be surprised, perhaps, in reading the poem, at the length of the list," the editors noted with satisfaction.[55] Hayne had provided a valuable service to his young nation. An ode to the great southern poets of the past and present written by one of their own spoke with great authority, and revealed a literary tradition that many Confederates were unaware they possessed. While some might quibble with Hayne's selections, the heroic language with which he celebrated his poets and the clearly nationalistic message he imparted through his work refuted forcefully any notions of southern intellectual inferiority. Hayne's plaudits invited future Confederate poets to build on the accomplishments of their forebearers.

Other writers, expressing similar sentiments, presented similar sets of names in their essays and reviews. Beyond the poets cited in common with Hayne, cultural nationalists evoked other great southern thinkers and authors, including William Wirt, Hugh Swinton Legaré, John C. Calhoun, John Marshall, the Tuckers (St. George, George, and Nathaniel Beverly), Charles Gayarré, William Caruthers, George Fitzhugh, Sergeant Prentiss, Thomas Grimké, Abel Upshur, Thomas Dew, James Thornwell, Albert Bledsoe, John Pendleton Kennedy, A. B. Longstreet, Philip Barbour, William Preston, William Trescot, William Shepperson, Edward Pollard, and Howard Caldwell. Of southern female authors, only Augusta Jane Evans received mention with any frequency, but she was almost always mentioned. Sometimes these names simply appeared in lists following or preceding claims of southern intellectual superiority or literary accomplishment, as if just the names themselves were sufficient to prove the point. Other commentators delved a little deeper in order to extol the merits of these writers. The author of "An Hour Among the Southern Poets" in *Southern Punch*, for instance, focused his attention specifically on the work of Poe, Requier, Philip Cooke, and A. B. Meek.[56] In any case, the point was less to critique than to introduce Confederate readers to the luminaries of their shared, if unappreciated, literary tradition.

The most comprehensive of these surveys, by far, was William Archer Cocke's "Sketches of Southern Literature." In fact, Cocke's was less a survey than a southern intellectual inventory. He divided literature into categories (theology, history, biography, linguistics, political and constitutional theory, slavery, science including the science of race, fiction, poetry, translation, art, and periodicals) and then proceeded to name every southern thinker and writer (arranged by state) who belonged in each. In all, he compiled a list of over 110 of these "choice spirits." For good measure, he also enumerated all the universities and colleges as well as all the state libraries and historical societies to be found in the Confederacy. Quantity, if not the ultimate measure of a nation's literature, clearly, did matter. Cocke's strategy was to wash away all doubts about southern intellectual capabilities with a flood of names.

As he moved from genre to genre, Cocke explained why southern literature was superior to northern in each. In theological literature, for instance, whereas northern writers were "controversial, litigious, covetous, forsaking the Bible for politics; plunging into the vortex of 'free thinking;' tampering with truth, and so mixing doctrines of faith with misapplied theories of moral and physical philosophy, as to become tainted with an infidelity," the "literature of the Southern pulpit" had remained "pure, healthy and conservative."[57] On the subject of slavery, which qualified in Cocke's view as a separate literary genre, southern thinkers had again shown their preeminence. In the North, discussions of slavery spawned "silly novels, low and vulgar sermons . . . and miserable verse." In the South, by contrast, slavery was "the foundation of a profound political and sociologic philosophy," attracting "some of the most logical, and cultivated minds to be found in the various fields of our literature."[58] When it came to fiction and poetry, southern authors may not have been as "prolific" as the Yankees, Cocke conceded, but "we can refer with satisfactory pride, to the superiority in talent, and taste, everywhere conspicuous on the pages of Southern romance, and in the realms of Southern poetry."[59] And so it went. In every category of intellectual endeavor and by every measure except that of quantity, southerners had "surpassed" their northern rivals. The Confederacy boasted an impressive literary tradition, Cocke had shown, one of which southerners should be duly proud.

Striving for comprehensiveness, Cocke had little time to discuss the merits of each author's work. Some figures, however, were deemed of such importance as to require special commendation. The work of Calhoun, for instance, "will stand an enduring monument of political and philosophical literature, without an equal in this country or in England." Legaré "was the most elegant and accomplished scholar the South has yet produced. The North has not had his equal." George Fitzhugh was "the Briarian son of Southern literature," and, "In Romance, this country has produced North nor South, no writer equal to South Carolina's distinguished son," William Gilmore Simms.[60] Cocke provided little evidence and only snippets of literary criticism to support these claims, and instead relied mainly on assertion. But this was not surprising. In canvassing southern literary history, Cocke's goal was to highlight the South's great thinkers and demonstrate the breadth, not the depth, of southern intellectual accomplishment.

More probing was James Wood Davidson's "Litterateurs of the South" in *The Illustrated Mercury*. Davidson focused only on the Confederacy's most acclaimed writers, and devoted entire articles or multiple articles to each.[61] In surveying their work, Davidson's tone was generally celebratory, but tempered with criticism. Augusta Jane Evans was "a patriot in the broadest sense. . . . Her pen is constantly active in our cause; and her voice is never silent, nor her hands idle, whenever a soul or a body can be strengthened by their ministrations." But Davidson found her *Macaria* to be too "*learned*," replete with too many obscure references.[62] As for Fitzhugh, Davidson placed him "one step in advance of the front rank in the Southern line of battle" in the slavery debate, but noted that his "genius is polemic.—His organ of Destructiveness is large."[63] Davidson praised Hayne's poetry, but not for the reasons often given and he blamed the "injudicious efforts of over-partial friends" (most likely Simms and Timrod) for "trying to foist upon the public mind the idea that he [Hayne] is distinguished for Classical attainments."[64] As for Simms, Davidson admired his prolificness and praised his fiction and drama, but found his poetry wanting. Simms's poems were "*prosaic*; excellent things, many of them, in their way, but not poetically excellent." Davidson conceded that the basis for this judgment was incomplete as "we have not read *all* of his books," but, he added sardonically, "in justice to ourselves we desire to say we do not intend to do so."[65]

The tone of Davidson's "Litterateurs of the South" reflected the increasingly critical edge to be found in much of late war Confederate commentary, but the articles' primary purpose was to affirm the existence of a vibrant southern literary tradition.[66] By treating these authors as serious figures deserving serious critical consideration, Davidson helped to further their reputations, even as he criticized their work. It should also be noted that his criticism never outweighed his praise. These litterateurs, he insisted, deserved the respect and gratitude of their nation for advancing the cause of native letters and bringing intellectual respectability to the South.

Still, for all their assertions of southern intellectual superiority and all of their praise of past literary accomplishment, Confederate critics adamantly maintained that a true Confederate national literature had yet to emerge. Having unearthed a proud literary tradition for all to see, these writers did not want southerners to rest on their laurels. The South may have had a praiseworthy literary past, they argued, but the Confederacy did not yet have its own unique literature. "Literary men . . . we have produced, but *not* a literature," the *Southern Monthly* had observed in 1861.[67] The reason was simple. Prior to the war, "The South had no distinctive and separate existence, and consequently could have no literature of its own. Its literature, like its constitutional rights, was absorbed by the grasping, over-seeking, never-contented North."[68] A national Confederate literature had to be born out of the Confederate experience, and nothing produced while the old Union was intact could rightly represent the new nation.

But more than this, these critics insisted that what had been produced in the past, great as it was, had not achieved that level of quality or originality that true intellectual independence required. The southern literary tradition was the basis, and a good one, for a Confederate national literature, but it was only the beginning. "We have yet to complete these elegant literary structures," William Cocke reminded his readers. More, much more, was still to be done, and he could not "with self-satisfaction" conclude his survey of southern literature "without remarking to Southern authors, and Southern readers, that while we have the foundation, and the material for a distinct national literature, its temples are yet to be erected, with care, caution, and long and continuous labor."[69] Likewise, even as he praised the abilities of southern poets and claimed their superiority over their northern counterparts, Samuel Davies was quick to qualify: "We do not, of course, mean to affirm that our poetry, in general, has attained to perfection, or that it is entirely faultless in the best of its present examples." What southern poetry had, Davies argued, was promise.[70] The past showed what native writers could accomplish in the face of northern contempt and southern indifference. It was impressive, but it remained for future Confederates to realize the full potential of the southern mind. Paul Hamilton Hayne probably explained it best in the final stanzas of "The Southern Lyre."

The storm must break—the spring-time come!
No longer drowned by trump and drum,
Truth's voice shall waken Christendom!

Then, with the war-clouds rolled afar,
And all undimmed our natal star,
Mankind SHALL know us—AS WE ARE!—

A People liberal, noble, brave,
And courteous to the feeblest slave
Trembling at fourscore o'er his grave;

Unmoved 'mid Battle's wild alarms—
Supreme in will—sublime in arms—
Yet cultured, open to the charms

Of Beauty! from whose genial Lyre
Hath poured full oft a strain of fire,
To rise in future Ages higher!

Unshackled by the Northman's rule,
Freed from the Bigot's canting school,
The maxims of the knave and fool,

The Genius of this youthful Land,
Like some rare blossom, will expand,
Upflowering to the Fair and Grand!

Then, Art will build her stately Fane,
And Song resound from Height to Plain,
Re-echoing to the Heights again!

Till, in the ripened time, shall rise,
With deep, divinely-thoughtful eyes,
And brow whereon the Destinies

Placed, even at birth, a shadowy crown,
The Poet whose august renown
Will smite the haughtiest natures down

To homage!—from whose "golden mouth,"
(Fit well-spring for a World in drouth,)
Outspeaks the Shakespeare of the South![71]

While the past would inspire Confederate writers, criticism would guide and chide them toward greatness. Criticism, properly employed, had a vital role to play in the struggle for Confederate intellectual independence. It would refine southern thinking, temper southern writing, and unearth true talent and originality, while at the same time drive out any pretenders or, worse still, Yankee imitators. Through the establishment and "rigid enforcement of enlightened critical rules," Confederates had a duty to "regulate our literature according to the principles of good taste and sound morality."[72] But it must be native criticism to which this new literature was subjected. As with everything else, Confederates would have to learn to "criticize without regard to foreign models."[73] It was the responsibility of editors and critics to prevent this emerging national literature from going astray. "Criticism, if it be just, will injure no one," explained one correspondent to the *Gulf City Home Journal*. "It is the crucible into which is cast the crude ore of letters, and none but the pure metal which passes unscathed through the fiery ordeal, has a right to immortality."[74] Southern literature had to be made to survive on its own merits and endure internal and ultimately external scrutiny. "Let every tub stand upon its own bottom," the *Chattanooga Rebel* declared. "We in the South must learn to judge of merit for itself alone."[75]

With watchful eyes, judicious editors, publishers, and critics would oversee the steady elevation of the southern reading public's literary taste, until "the proper relation between our literature and the requirements of the public mind" was achieved. Ultimately, the creation of an original Confederate literature would depend upon the ability of southern readers to appreciate it. "Good literature will be produced and encouraged wherever the public taste is capable of rejecting the opposite," Samuel Davies explained.[76] The "blue writing," "*fast* literature," "spurious literature," and Yankee "froth and bombast" that cultural nationalists deplored could be banished permanently only if southern readers refused to read it.[77] Thus, thoughtful native criticism would simultaneously promote two objectives. On the one hand, it would encourage Confederate writers to strive for excellence, and, on the other, it would educate southern readers to appreciate the type of literature that their intellectual independence required.

In the meantime, however, critics would have to tread carefully. As they strived to "bring out the genius of the country," all shared editor Oakley Haines's desire of "keeping down the pretenders and cutting off the dead weights which would oppress our scheme."[78] But given the fragile nature of these fledgling literary efforts, there was a danger that too harsh critical standards or excessively high expectations might cut off the living with the dead. Editors recognized that "a large proportion of our writers are mere beginners in the pursuit of literary honours, and cannot, therefore, be expected to give such evidences of disciplined and well-digested learning as might be required by the highest standards of taste and education."[79] These "maiden efforts" required at least some "INDULGENCE," *The Countryman* argued. "We should be very careful to give countenance to those who take upon themselves the hard task of becoming pioneers in the formation of a literature that shall be peculiar to our section, and characteristic of our people."[80] For this reason, Samuel Davies called upon those "who are qualified for the office of critic" to refrain from "testing too severely these first fruits of our national literature." In tending to these early literary seedlings, "Some weeds must necessarily flourish, else in plucking them up, we may destroy the delicate plants we wish to cultivate."[81] Such was the dilemma facing Confederate editors and critics. As they attempted to nurse this Confederate national culture to health and guide its development, they had to balance their desire to encourage native writers with their responsibility to critique their work. As the war progressed, however, they came to use the rod with increasing liberality.

"The trials of the Editor of a literary periodical are not sufficiently considered by the public," the *Magnolia Weekly* complained in January 1864.[82] Charged with upholding the literary reputation of their nation as well as that of their own journals, Confederate editors rejected much of what southern writers sent them. "We may as well state at the outset, that the standard upon which we have fixed, and by which we shall measure all poetical contributions to our columns, is high," Henry Timrod told all would-be contributors. "To that standard we shall adhere, without reference to any other considerations than those of merit or demerit."[83] "Besieged" with submissions of indifferent quality, hasty composition, and, at best, uncertain writing ability, editors pleaded with their writers to withhold all but their best work.[84] The Confederacy's amateur poets were by far the worst offenders both in terms of quantity (too much) and quality (too little). The *Christian Advocate* (Raleigh) had to "beg" its contributors to "send us no more poetical effusions, until, if they are real poets, they have pruned them thoroughly, or have submitted them to good judges, and they have recommended their publication."[85] George Bagby of the *Southern Literary Messenger* was far less diplomatic. "We are receiving too much trash in rhyme," he vented in July 1863. "What is called 'poetry,' by its authors, is not wanted. Fires are not accessible at this time of year, and it is too much trouble to tear up poetry. If it is thrown out of the window, the vexatious wind always blows it back."[86] "Those 'little articles' about 'Spring-time,' 'The Rainbow,' 'Falling Leaves,' 'Baby's Shoes,' 'Grandma's Pet,' and the thousand other subjects which have been treated of in every school girl's composition from time immemorial, we do not want even as *gratuitous contributions*," the *Southern Illustrated News* announced a month later. "We want good poetry—all that has the ring of the genuine metal, but none other."[87]

Despite such tough talk, even a casual glance through the pages of the Confederacy's literary journals reveals volumes of poetry and prose of questionable merit. The desire to cultivate native authors as well as the simple necessity of finding enough material to fill their columns led to a certain degree of leniency on the part of editors. "We do admit into the columns of our journal, sometimes, articles from young writers, for their encouragement, which do not contain the merit we would require in articles from the pens of older writers," Joseph Turner of *The Countryman* conceded. "We are satisfied that we have been too indulgent at this point: but then 'our failing leaned to virtue's side.' "[88] Still, these "indulgent" editors were not blind to the shortcomings of their less-gifted contributors and often signaled to their readers which pieces in the current issue were truly commendable and which ones still needed work.

Nor did these nationalist-minded editors restrict their critical scrutiny to just their own columns. Acting as the literary policemen for the nation, their jurisdiction extended over the entirety of Confederate print culture. "At this moment, when the minds of all men and women are naturally pre-occupied with bulletins and battles," it might seem a strange time to pursue literary criticism, the *Southern Illustrated News* admitted, "but the new books must be acknowledged."[89] And they were. Nearly every book, textbook, song, pamphlet, theater production, and major sermon printed or performed during the war received notice and often a review in the Confederate press. While at least as celebratory as they were critical, these notices effectively inventoried the progress of the campaign for intellectual independence, and southern critics carefully monitored this new literature for any signs of moral weakness, sloppy construction, or, worst of all, Yankee imitation.

A few examples should suffice. One critic writing for the *Magnolia Weekly* in

October 1863, condemned the entire genre of Confederate popular history as a "ludicrous spectacle." Regardless of their popularity or profitability, "We cannot for one instant admit the claim of these works to respectability," this writer scolded. Contemporary histories, especially during time of war, were hopelessly flawed and incomplete, and could in no way enhance a nation's intellectual reputation. "Where is the information contained in them, gained!" he demanded,

> From what source do they derive their authority! These are questions which, we confess, we cannot answer. We know very little of our own official history, and absolutely nothing of that of the enemy.—The operations of our armies are still shrouded in mystery. We know very little, with certainty, concerning the plans of our Generals, and nothing of their motives —nine-tenths of their reports remaining, as yet, unpublished. Of the plans and motives of the enemy we know still less—we must simply *guess* at them. The injunction of secrecy still rests upon a large part of the proceedings of Congress; the financial history of the country is very imperfectly known; its diplomatic history shrouded in total darkness; the motives for the actions of the authorities still unexplained—in fact there are thousands of questions undecided, and scarcely an incident is clear and unmistakable. While we know so little concerning ourselves, what do we know concerning our enemies! Absolutely nothing.

Writers like Pollard and Howison, the critic continued, were deluding themselves if they thought their work would "live" after them. "They may rest satisfied that no matter how honest and earnest are their efforts, future generations will regard them as worthless and without authority." Historians of the war should desist until the "momentous issues" were decided, the facts known, and a degree of historical perspective gained. The critic urged Confederate historians to continue their explorations of other periods but found little of worth and much that worked against southern intellectual aspirations in the growing body of wartime historical literature.[90]

Given the vital role that textbooks were believed to play in the inculcation of national character, reviewers scrutinized these new offerings with particular care. A. G. Horn of the *Gulf City Home Journal*, for instance, nitpicked his way through Adelaide Chaudron's *First Reader*, finding such minor infractions as failing to capitalize the first letter of a sentence in a reading example and using the "Websterism [Yankee] abhorrent" "*ax*" instead of "*axe*." Small points, Horn conceded, but "a faulty example should never be placed in a child's hands, as first impressions are difficult to eradicate."[91] *The Age*'s treatment of *Smith's English Grammar* was far harsher. *Smith's Grammar* was a northern book "revised and improved, and adapted to the use of the schools in the Confederate States." According to the preface, these revisions consisted "chiefly in changing the imperfect sentences in which 'answers' were frequently given, into complete affirmations where ever practicable; and using Confederate instead of foreign names in the 'examples.' "[92] *The Age*, however, thought that this was hardly sufficient, and that no amount of revision, and certainly not these superficial changes, could make this corrupt Yankee book acceptable. Believing "there is nothing more subversive to the interests of our national education and literature . . . than the reproduction, by Southern publishers, of Yankee-text books," the reviewer savaged *Smith's Grammar*. With a nearly line-by-line analysis, he carefully documented all the grammatical and pedagogical errors. Having picked the book to pieces, finding it wanting in all areas, and even dangerous in some, the review concluded that "it would have been difficult to select from the mass of crude, false and silly grammatical publications of our enemies, a more despicable production for our use, than the one before us."[93] *The Age*'s meticulous and devastating critique of *Smith's English Grammar* was meant to serve as a warning for other Confederate publishers who also might be tempted to cash in on a lucrative market by reproducing or minimally revising dangerous northern texts.

Songs and sheet music also were subject to critical oversight. In noticing new songs, Confederate editors ferreted out any whose southern origins were questionable. Some songs circulating in the Confederacy came straight from northern pens; others simply had had their lyrics adapted to southern climes. Stressing the need for originality, some Confederate critics rejected such popular songs as "Dixie," "Bonnie Blue Flag," and "When this Cruel War is Over" as "confounded, stupid, horribly sounding doggerel trash."[94] Despite its southern lyrics, the popular "Who Will Care for Mother Now," the *Magnolia Weekly* revealed, "is merely a reprint of a *Yankee war song*—the words being made to suit the South."[95] Southerners must be wary of the songs they sing, cultural nationalists warned. "We have no desire to see these Yankee effusions palmed off upon the people as Southern productions. If we cannot compose our own music, for Heaven's sake, let us not steal that of the Yankees."[96] Even some authentic Confederate songs were criticized for not being original enough. *Southern Punch* disparaged the popular "God Save the South" for its clear imitation of "God Save the Queen," and the *Magnolia Weekly* in turn found too close a resemblance between Professor de Coeniel's "Confederate Anthem" and "God Save the South" to "accept it as an entirely original production."[97] Every component of Confederate culture needed to be original, and editors and critics watched carefully for any hint of foreign intrusion.

Confederate theater was the focus of constant critical attention, for there was much to criticize. Amateur actors who routinely forgot their lines, drunken audience members, military officers in the company of prostitutes, unscrupulous theater managers, and the many surrounding disreputable drinking houses were but a few of the complaints lodged against Confederate theaters.[98] Still, drama was part of a nation's literature and, if "properly represented," a powerful agent for good.[99] Thus, it was essential for cultural nationalists to watch over the development of the Confederate stage and steer it in wise directions. They called on the nation's theater managers to help them elevate and refine southern theatrical tastes by presenting plays, especially native plays, of a high moral and literary order. Far too often, however, managers disappointed such hopes by staging comedies and dramas of "the clap-trap sensational order" that appealed solely to the "groveling herd."[100] This brand of lurid drama was yet another carryover from Yankee cultural domination, the critics charged. "We very well know that in New York, and other Northern cities, this catering to the imagination and tastes of the wicked and depraved, is made a special feature in the entertainment put forth at the lower theatres, but that it should be attempted in Richmond, we were not quite prepared for it," the *Magnolia Weekly* wrote in disgust.[101] What the Confederacy needed instead was "legitimate drama, devoid of all the loathsome and abominable isms of Yankeedom."[102]

Ultimately, the salvation of Confederate theater rested on the ability of native writers to create an original dramatic literature that would capture the emotions, guide the morals, and exemplify the character of the Confederate people. For this reason, new Confederate plays were particularly scrutinized, and if deserving, celebrated. Plays like J. J. Delchamps's *Love's Ambuscade*, G. W. Alexander's *Virginia Cavalier*, and James McCabe's *The Guerrillas* received mixed reviews from the Confederate press.[103] Most critics, though not all, found William Smith's Lincoln parody, *The Royal Ape*, to be simply beyond redemption. The *Talladega Watchtower* declared it "not fit for any gentlemen's library, much less to grace a lady's boudoir," and that "the most licentious of the yellow-covered [Yankee] literature is not worse."[104]

The Royal Ape aside, cultural nationalists applauded what Confederate playwrights were attempting to do, if not always what they actually produced. Even more so than the other genres of Confederate literature, drama was a true infant and one that required as much encouragement as discipline. With this in mind, *Southern Punch* advised its fellow journals not to be too harsh when judging these first productions. "Under the most disadvantageous circumstances, the Southern stage has got along in such a way as to astonish the Yankees, who did not dream that theatricals could flourish in the midst of carnage and in the face of the blockade," *Punch* reminded them. "All this sort of enterprise deserves encouragement; and, for one, we feel like according it."[105] While other critics may not have always followed *Punch*'s inclination toward leniency, all shared a fundamental belief in the importance of drama as a literary form and worked to mold it through their criticism into a genuine expression of southern character and a legitimate component of a Confederate national literature.

The periodical press also criticized itself. An extensive exchange network developed among editors across the Confederacy, and everyone knew what everyone else was printing. It was essential that the periodical press remain on target, and it was the editors' job to draw attention to anyone who stepped out of line. Some of this sniping was no doubt the result of personal animosity (as was certainly the case between the editors of the Richmond daily papers), but much of it was motivated by a patriotic desire to foster a strong Confederate periodical literature. For instance, when *Southern Field and Fireside* introduced a "gossip column," long viewed as one of the most indecorous features of the Yankee press, *The Countryman* objected on strictly nationalistic grounds. "This in a Southern literary journal!" which had "professed to cut loose from yankees, and yankeeisms!" the outraged *Countryman* sputtered.[106] Other editors joined in the condemnation, and by February 1864, William W. Turner expressed his "very great gratification at the fact that the odious, abominable, and yankee-like feature of a 'gossip column'" had been removed from *Field and Fireside*, thereby no longer marring "the fair appearance of what we are now proud to recognize as a truly Southern journal."[107]

Editors and critics also faulted their peers for failing to adequately enforce literary standards. "Uncle John" in the *Magnolia Weekly*, for instance, castigated Confederate editors for saddling the public with "abominable" poetry. "Who reads such trash I should like to know?" he demanded. "Not one in a hundred; and the Editors know this, yet will persist in filling up their columns with it. It's a downright swindle." "For the sake of our Southern literature," he called (jokingly) upon the Confederate Congress to "pass a resolution that no matter pretending to rank as Poetry, shall be published, until approved as such by a committee of competent judges."[108] Another critic accused editors of "puffing," that is lavishing "the most indiscriminate praise upon everything of which they are the recipients." By not being harsh enough in their reviews of new southern books, editors undermined the "independence of the press" and performed a disservice to their nation's struggle for cultural self-sufficiency. This "custom" of puffing might have "originated among the Yankees, (where everything mean and contemptible seems to flourish,) but is now as common in the South, as it is there," and it had to stop immediately. Editors needed to "preserve" their "independence and honesty" if they were to guide their nation toward a truly original literature. Simply praising all Confederate productions because they were Confederate did not advance the cause. Progress would require negative reinforcement and censure, and it was the editors' duty to provide it.[109]

The most common complaint that editors leveled against each other, however, was that of appropriation without attribution. With their network of exchanges and the need to fill their columns with interesting material from around the Confederacy, it was a common and accepted practice for editors to reprint articles, stories, poems, and editorials from other journals. Editors were also expected to give due credit to the original source, but this they did not always do. While such pilfering had always been a problem, North and South, the new emphasis on originality arising from demands for Confederate cultural autonomy had raised the stakes and made editors even more zealous in the guardianship of their intellectual property. Editors competed for native contributors, and it was a matter of pride, not to mention business interest, to run an "original" southern story or a poem that was exclusively "Written for the *Magnolia Weekly*," for instance. For this reason, editors decried literary theft, when lifted from their own journals, and chastised the guilty. They demanded that their "brothers of the *steal* pen and *steal* scissors" render "unto Caesar the things that are Caesars."[110]

When the *Magnolia Weekly* published Ethel Deen's "original" poem, "A June Vigil," only to learn that the same poem had appeared in *Southern Field and Fireside* a week earlier, editor James McCabe was furious. Concluding that the author must have sold the poem to both papers in breach of honor and professional etiquette, McCabe publicly denounced Deen and took steps to prevent any such future occurrences. Only a letter from Deen herself, which McCabe published, and an explanation from *Southern Field and Fireside* that she had submitted the poem during the paper's suspension at the end of 1862 and, receiving no response, had assumed understandably that her work had been rejected, defused McCabe's indignation and returned Deen to the list of the *Magnolia*'s acceptable contributors.[111] Originality, and proper credit for it, were serious and sometimes contentious issues among editors who were determined that their own efforts in building up a national literature be explicitly acknowledged.

More serious still were instances in which foreign literature, worst of all northern literature, appeared in Confederate literary journals masquerading as original southern work. The *Atlanta Intelligencer* discovered that a purportedly original story entitled "An Unprofitable Guest" in the *Magnolia Weekly* was in fact a northern reprint. "We saw the very same article, divested of the commencement, three years ago, in a yankee literary paper." Likewise, *The Countryman* discovered similar instances of falsified authorship in *Southern Field and Fireside*, the *Southern Literary Companion*, and *Southern Punch*. In fact, Turner recognized a recent article in *Punch* from an 1850 issue of *Graham's Magazine*.[112] In October 1863, the *Magnolia Weekly* informed the *Savannah News* and the *Chattanooga Rebel* that the new "southern" poem which they had recently published with great fanfare was in fact written by Sir Edward Bulwer-Lytton and provided the page number from Bulwer-Lytton's works where the original could be found.[113] Not all cases of plagiarism were discovered at the time. Historian Alice Fahs has found that four war romances printed in the *Southern Illustrated News* were in fact reprints from *Harper's Weekly*.[114]

These incidents seem to have been the result of unscrupulous contributors looking to cash in on the literary journals' new willingness and ability to pay for native writing. "When will Southern men leave off such a despicable way of obtaining money and notoriety," the *Atlanta Intelligencer* demanded.[115] The *Magnolia Weekly* ferreted out "a very aggravated case of plagiarism" from among its own contributors in which money also appeared to be the motive. Only the "young man's poverty, and the fact that he is the sole support of a widowed mother" prevented the *Magnolia* from exposing him publicly, but the editor promised no similar consideration "to any who may hereafter be induced by our leniency in this case to follow in his footsteps."[116]

Even if these were relatively isolated instances, plagiarism was a serious and potentially crippling offense, requiring the condemnation of all true-hearted Confederates. To reprint foreign literature as original work belied southern claims to intellectual independence and undermined the legitimacy of Confederate nationality. "How disgraceful are these things, and how contemptible they make us appear in foreign eyes, for all these contrabands are given to the winds, and we know not where they may be wafted," one writer fumed in the *Gulf City Home Journal*.[117] Joseph Turner agreed. These instances of plagiarism were "discreditable, not to say disreputable" to "Southern letters, and Southern literary journals. We cannot help feeling mortified—neither can any other man who has the reputation of his country at heart. The worst feature of the case is, that we have given even the yankees just cause to laugh at us—*even* the *yankees!*"[118] There was no way to completely safeguard the Confederate press from these literary deceptions, but they could be combated through constant vigilance. It was the responsibility of the editor and critic to protect their own columns from this manner of fraud as well as to expose it in others when found.

Cultural nationalists also monitored the Confederate literary public to gauge their commitment to the cause and correct them when they went astray. For instance, when a Richmond bookseller began advertising the sale of northern books and periodicals during the summer of 1863, the *Southern Illustrated News* was quick to act. This "outrage upon public morals" threatened "to weaken the barrier which secession has erected between us and the Yankees" and restore "that literary bondage . . . which so degraded us in times past in the eyes of the world." To patronize this traitorous bookseller or even permit him to offer his pernicious wares was a betrayal of the Confederate cause. National pride and "fair play" demanded that Confederate publishers be protected from northern competition as they struggled "to build up a literature of our own, free from the cant and fanaticism, the sickly sentiment and dangerous doctrines of the Northern school of writers." To allow northern literature to reenter the Confederacy could undo the impressive gains that southerners had made since the beginning of the war. As for Mr. Starke, the guilty bookseller, the *News* reminded authorities that "there was a time when the traffic in incendiary anti-slavery publications was a statutory offence, and we are not aware that the war has changed the law in this particular."[119] As military necessity demanded fidelity on the part of the Confederate populace, so too did intellectual necessity mandate continued support for the development of a Confederate national literature.

CRITICISM IN THE CONFEDERACY served both as a means of encouragement and as a disciplinary tool, and its often inconsistent application during the war reflected these dual roles. Still, and most important, Confederate criticism was purposeful. Driven by a consciously nationalist agenda, it was designed specifically to aid in the creation of an original Confederate literature. All commentators recognized that southern literature needed refinement before it could take its rightful place on the world stage as an exemplar of southern character, vindicator of southern slave society, and debunker of Yankee lies. To this end, Confederate editors and other cultural nationalists attempted to cultivate inexperienced native writers, to push them in certain directions and away from others. At the same time, they sought to elevate the literary taste of the southern public as a whole. The ultimate success of their plan required that Confederate readers learn to be discriminating patrons, and these nationalist-minded critics intended to show them how.

Such concerns made education even more central to the plans of cultural nationalists as the war progressed. Education—a proper native education—would broaden the intellectual awakening already underway and prepare the southern populace to appreciate and support an exalted national literature when it came. Education was one of the "*foundation* works" through which southern character would be instilled and upon which "the future of our Country" depended.[120] "Among all the interests and influences which comprehend the character and welfare of a people, there is no one more important than that of EDUCATION," Edward Joynes argued in a public letter. "This embraces the very sources of the national life, and, conceived in its moral as well as intellectual aspects, it may almost be said to be omnipotent in its influence upon national character." While education was "important at all times, and for all peoples," it was "especially so for the South and at this time," as Confederates grappled with the meaning of their independence.[121]

The relationship between education and an original national literature was a direct one, as both were intimately connected with national character—education in its "foundation" and literature in its expression. As such, Confederate cultural nationalists had great faith in the power of education to shape and promote native literature. "Now is the time for inaugurating a purely national literature," *Southern Field and Fireside* declared in April 1863, but "it must have its beginning with us, as with all people, in the schools."[122] William Archer Cocke agreed. The literary achievements of a people were directly proportional to their educational standards. As he reminded his fellow Confederates in the final installment of "Sketches of Southern Literature," "The character of a nation is governed in many respects by the educational taste of the existing generation; its literature is the reflex of that character; if it be pure, strong and powerful will be its tendency to elevate and purify the moral tone of the body politic; if driveling and corrupt, equal is its tendency to undermine the social fabric."[123]

A proper native education complete with southern schools, southern teachers, and guided by southern textbooks would benefit both the producers and consumers of this future Confederate literature. For southern writers, native education would provide discipline, encouragement, and proper morals. By reading southern textbooks and literary anthologies, they would be exposed to models worthy of their admiration and emulation, and from southern history books and geographies they would imbibe their nation's character and learn to hold their collective past in reverence. For the larger Confederate populace, education would raise "the standard of general intelligence," elevate literary taste, instill a sense of nationalism and cultural pride, and thereby create an environment in which native literature would flourish.[124] This "moral elevation of the masses" would also immunize them from the poisons of northern literature and safeguard Confederate society from these foreign intrusions in the future.[125]

WHILE CONFEDERATE NATIONALISTS OF every stripe celebrated education's awesome transformative power and urged all patriots to "do all they can to advance the cause of education in our country," it was left to the Confederacy's teachers to actually devise and implement a native system of instruction for southern children.[126] The story of Confederate education during these middle years, and indeed throughout the entire war, was one of unflagging determination in the face of severe adversity. Nearly everything that educational advocates had feared in 1861 had come to pass as a result of the increasingly devastating conflict. School closings, teacher shortages, and budget shortfalls threatened to undo the modest gains southern states had made during the antebellum years, and the army continued to swallow entire classes of would-be students. The war absorbed the attention of all, and, as Edward Joynes admitted, "the boy, who studies now anything else, must be 'either more or less *than boy*.' "[127]

And yet the fight for Confederate educational independence continued, and its leaders showed no signs of capitulating, either to internal obstacles or to external enemies. Motivated by patriotism and an unflinching belief in the vital importance of their contribution to the war effort, Confederate educators continued to battle for the hearts and minds of the nation's youth. Textbooks streamed from southern presses. New teachers, specifically female teachers, were recruited aggressively. Teacher organizations remained active, and indeed proliferated as the war progressed. Educational advocates recognized that while the war raged, theirs must necessarily be a losing battle, but it was nevertheless essential that they fight a stubborn delaying action until peace and stability returned. For his part, Calvin Henderson Wiley vowed that the schools of his state would continue to operate so long as one teacher and one student remained. He firmly believed that North Carolina's undying commitment to education would be its "crowning glory" when the history of the war was written. No doubt "the future historian of this stirring age" would celebrate the achievements and sacrifices of these noble educators and marvel "that in the darkest hour of the Confederacy, when every nerve and muscle of the country were wrought to the highest tension in a terrible and unexampled struggle for existence and independence, North Carolina still supported a vigorous and beneficent system of free and public schools."[128]

Now was the time to act while educators had the attention of the public and perhaps the sympathetic ear of the legislatures. By presenting the cause of education in the strongest possible patriotic light and linking it directly to the struggle against the North, educational leaders hoped to shake southerners out of their educational lethargy. As Professor Joynes argued, "All the energies of the people are now concentrated upon the one object of securing their independence; and whatever will contribute, in any way, to confirm and perpetuate that independence, will awaken an interest and a support on the part of the people, which they would never hereafter accord to any object, upon its own merits alone."[129] Highlighting the opportunities for reform created by the war, Calvin Wiley not only managed to safeguard state money for the North Carolina common school system, but also introduced new legislation for the creation of "graded schools" (high schools) as well as "normal schools" to train teachers. The bill authorizing normal schools passed in 1862, and the graded schools legislation, introduced in 1863, passed both houses by the end of 1864. While neither of these ambitious plans could be implemented during the war, they laid the foundation for a complete public school system once peace returned.[130]

While inspired by such hopes, educators were even more driven by the fear of what would happen if they did nothing. If they allowed the war to halt completely all education in the South, it would inflict "a most grievous and permanent injury" upon the nation that would "descend most heavily upon our children and children's children, and would outlast all the other calamities which this war will entail upon her."[131] Even a "comparatively brief" interruption, Henry Timrod warned, would be "very nearly tantamount to depriving a whole generation of all literary culture," leaving little hope for lasting intellectual independence.[132] One "Teacher" writing for *The Countryman* put it even more starkly: "Unless *we know*, unless *God tell us* that we, the Southern people, will all be slain in this war, it is our duty to provide for the education of our children; for they are to take charge of this government and conduct it successfully, or allow it to fail ignobly, after it shall have been established by their fathers."[133]

Of course, for the older male students of military age, there was little to be done except mourn their loss from the classroom. "Almost an entire generation of our young men, since the beginning of this war, have passed from childhood to manhood, and entered the field of strife, in great measure without even the ordinary advantages of intermediate education," Edward Joynes observed sadly.[134] Educational advocates lamented the "vast amount of seed corn" that had been "ground" by the war machine or allowed "to grow wild among the brambles of ignorance."[135] All dreaded the lasting impact that this loss would have on the future of the Confederacy, as "there can be no doubt, that we must expect a lamentable deficiency with regard to literary and scientific culture, on the part of the generation now growing up."[136]

This regrettable but unavoidable consequence of war required that the younger children who remained be educated all the more rigorously. Teachers and parents could not allow the primary schools to sit vacant. Across the Confederacy, many parents had withdrawn their children from school due to monetary concerns, need for home labor, or general wartime uncertainty, but it was a patriotic imperative, educational advocates declared, that the children return to the classroom at once. "Something must be done to arrest and turn back the tide of ignorance which is about to sweep over the land," the *Magnolia Weekly* demanded. "It is positively frightful to think of the vast number of children who are growing up in intellectual darkness, to which they have been consigned by the mad folly of their parents."[137] "Those parents who can, even by a sacrifice, continue the education of their children, are under weighty obligations, not only as parents, *but as patriots*, to do so," another columnist urged. The wheels of education must continue to turn so that the generation of young men now being lost to ignorance and often death in the defense of the Confederacy would be replaced by a "rising generation" of educated men and women capable of upholding their nation's dearly won independence.[138]

As he often did, Calvin Wiley coupled these abstract arguments with a more immediate one. Recognizing the impact of home front morale on the willingness of soldiers to fight, he argued that one way to keep the troops in the ranks was to keep their children in the classroom. "Whatever tends to render home desirable increases the heroism and determination of those who defend it; and with a very large portion of the brave soldiers of the Confederacy the only stake in this struggle is the moral and social condition in which it is to leave their families."[139] Ensuring that southern children continued to receive a proper education would strengthen soldiers' commitment to the cause, he reasoned. Keeping the schools open would not only safeguard the Confederacy's future but would aid the present military struggle as well.

WITH SO MUCH AT stake, Confederate educators pledged to fight on, whatever the obstacles. Native textbooks, those "stepping stones to a pure native literature," remained the first priority for educational advocates, and the spate of new Confederate textbooks that appeared during these middle years represented their greatest triumph.[140] Having proven that schoolbooks could indeed be written, printed, and profitably marketed in the South, cultural nationalists needed to protect them from any possible foreign influence or competition. In particular, the practice of republishing northern textbooks, even with southern revisions, had to be stopped. "How does it present our character for consistency in the eyes of the civilized world," educational leaders asked, "to see alongside the same bulletin that proclaims a glorious victory over our foe, won at the cost of our most precious blood and the anguish of heart of our mothers, wives and sisters, the advertisement of a reprint of Webster's spelling book, or some other successful Yankee speculation?"[141] Such "subversive" publishing practices deserved "the ban of public opinion, and the active condemnation of every patriot," the editors of *The Age* declared. "By it we are in danger of losing this golden opportunity of throwing off the incubus of the New England system of education. It continues upon us the hold of the Yankee; it tightens his grip upon our throat. It discourages native authorship, and is a direct and powerful contribution to the cause of the enemy."[142] Still, despite these fears, substantial gains had been made, and cultural nationalists, while cautious, were greatly heartened by the rapidly expanding Confederate textbook industry.

Finding enough competent teachers to staff southern classrooms and assign these native textbooks was another matter. As the war progressed, teacher shortages became increasingly severe. In order to keep the remaining teachers at their posts, the Confederate government exempted male teachers and professors from the draft when it enacted conscription in April 1862.[143] Initially, all teachers with at least twenty students were exempt from Confederate military service. The additional requirement of at least two years teaching experience was added in October 1862 to discourage draft dodgers from entering the profession. As with all occupational exemptions, the exemption of teachers was controversial, albeit less so than it was for some other groups.[144] Despite a few challenges, the teacher exemption was upheld throughout the war.[145]

The granting of exemption status was intended to impress upon all teachers, and not just males of military age, the vital role that they were expected to play in this war. Their mighty task was "to carry forward successfully this revolution, in their own sphere, and to establish this bulwark of independence for our people henceforth."[146] Educational activists and cultural nationalists had always emphasized the awesome responsibility entrusted to teachers, but exemption made it official, visibly binding teachers to their nation's cause. As F. H. Johnston, C. W. Smythe, and J. D. Campbell sternly reminded their fellow teachers in July 1863, "It becomes you to weigh well the obligations under which [the State] has thus placed you, that you may make a proper return. She has not released you as a favor, but has assigned to you a special duty, to watch with unwavering fidelity over the interests of her children."[147] It was the "peculiar duty" of teachers to anticipate their nation's future needs even as "our brave brothers in arms" battled for its present day survival. Vital issues of national character, proper morals, and cultural development had to be considered and acted upon by these "appointed Cultivators and Guardians," for "unless *they anticipate*" these future concerns, they "will be but too late regarded by other men." The Confederate government's validation of the importance of their work hopefully would foster "a just *esprit du corps*, a deep sense of professional duty, a lofty professional pride, and the highest standards of professional ambition and distinction" among Confederate teachers, whether they were eligible for exemption or not.[148]

But even if all the male teachers eligible for exemption remained, there still would not be enough teachers to meet the demand. What was more, with nearly all the college-aged young men now serving in the ranks, where would the Confederacy find its future teachers? To anyone surveying the demographic makeup of the Confederate home front, the answer seemed obvious. "Hitherto we have looked to the North for [teachers], but that can be done no longer; we must now depend upon ourselves," the *Southern Presbyterian* reasoned in June 1863. "Neither can we look to our sons; for they, too, even those of tender years, turning from their books to the battle-field, have offered themselves upon their country's altar; and should they be spared to return again to their homes they will be poorly prepared for the work of teaching." The simple process of elimination dictated that "it is to our daughters . . . we must look, and to them alone, as the future instructors of our youth."[149]

The challenge for southern nationalists was convincing educated women to teach. Wartime hardships and financial necessity did much of the necessary prodding, but educational activists also relied on patriotism to call women to service. Such appeals had been heard since 1861, but as the war dragged on and fears of an uneducated rising generation mounted, cultural nationalists became increasingly aggressive in recruiting female teachers. "Why should not our educated ladies now respond to the call made upon them?" Calvin Wiley demanded. "They *all* desire to contribute something to the cause of Southern Independence; and in the preservation of the order, morality, and intelligence of Society there is a wide and most important field."[150] Editor J. D. Campbell believed that Confederate women needed only be "convinced that patriotism calls them to the school room, and there will soon be more than one applicant for every school in the State."[151] By the midpoint of the war, such appeals seemed to be having some effect as more and more southern women, driven either by patriotism or necessity, were taking up the business of teaching.[152]

The push for Confederate women to play an expanded public role as their nation's teachers intensified demands that women receive a rigorous education themselves. "Tis not dolls and playthings we now need, but noble, earnest, working women," the *Southern Presbyterian* announced.[153] Unlike most male colleges, female schools remained open during the war and parents were urged, in the name of patriotism, to advance the education of their daughters to the highest possible level. Beyond improving the general standards and expectations of female education, educational advocates also wanted aspiring teachers to undergo specialized professional training. "Young ladies must be prepared to teach," J. M. M. Caldwell explained in April 1863. "Special instruction must be given them by an enlarged course of study, and by lectures on various subjects connected with their proposed profession."[154] Remarkably, Confederates took steps toward establishing such female teacher training even as the war raged—a testament to the perceived importance of this project. A few female colleges successfully added a "teacher's department" to train young women for the profession, and many more such "normal" schools and departments were in the works when the Yankees overran them.[155]

TEACHERS' ORGANIZATIONS CONTINUED TO lead the way in the campaign for educational independence. Holding conventions, issuing circulars, approving new textbooks, proposing legislation, and encouraging teacher recruitment and training, they worked to bring public attention to the cause of education and exhorted southern educators to remain steadfast in times of difficulty. Ardent nationalists, the leaders of these associations constantly reminded their members and the public of the vital role that education played in the struggle for Confederate independence. Textbook production—both the encouragement of native works and the condemnation of Yankee ones— was the salient issue for the various teachers' organizations, but they also discussed the larger struggle for cultural autonomy. For instance, at their 1862 annual meeting, North Carolina educators staged a formal debate on the essential question of "Can there be political, without intellectual indepen- dence?" The outcome can be surmised by the pledge that all members subse- quently took "to use their efforts to achieve the intellectual independence of our Confederacy."[156]

These educational associations persevered, and even gained strength, dur- ing the war. Not surprisingly, the State Educational Association of North Carolina was the most active. Meeting in Greensboro in November 1861, Lincolnton in October 1862, Lexington in August 1863, and Charlotte in November 1864, the North Carolina association was Confederate education's most powerful voice and diehard advocate.[157] But North Carolina was no longer alone. In May 1863, concerned educators in Richmond and Petersburg formed the Educational Association of Virginia (the forerunner of the current Virginia Education Association), and held their first and only convention in Petersburg on December 29, 1863.[158] More significant still, 1863 also wit- nessed the creation of a new national teachers' organization: the Educational Association of the Confederate States of America. The Association was sum- moned into existence by Wiley and his North Carolina cohort who issued a much reprinted resolution following their October 1862 meeting in Lincoln- ton, calling for a "general convention" of Confederate teachers "to take into consideration the best means for supplying the necessary text books for schools and colleges, and for uniting their efforts for the advancement of the cause of education in the Confederacy."[159] The meeting was to convene on April 28, 1863, in Columbia, South Carolina. In order to promote attendance, conference organizers persuaded the presidents of six different southern railroads to provide either free or half-price passage for teachers.[160]

About seventy delegates from six states (Virginia, North Carolina, South Carolina, Georgia, Alabama, and Louisiana) attended the three-day conven- tion. After organizing themselves into a permanent body and drawing up a constitution, each delegation reported on the educational conditions in its state and the status of textbook production in particular. Having assessed the progress that had been made, determined what still needed to be done, and appointed committees to investigate further, the members of this new national association "collectively, and individually" pledged: "1st. To endeavor to lead the public mind . . . to just views in regard to the true elements of national strength. 2d. To regard all classes of schools as identified in their general interests; and to watch over our State educational systems with sleepless solicitude. 3d. To encourage our own citizens by every means in our power, to prepare and publish suitable text-books for our schools; and in all cases where such books are of equal merit with foreign works, to give them the decided preference."[161]

The conference was well publicized and newspapers throughout the Confederacy carried accounts of its proceedings. Confederate President Jefferson Davis himself officially endorsed the Association's activities in a public letter. The "object" of the convention, he declared, "commands my fullest sympathy, and has, for many years, attracted my earnest consideration. It would be difficult to overestimate the influence of primary books in the promotion of character and the development of mind. Our form of Government is only adapted to a virtuous and intelligent people, and there can be [no] more imperative duty of the generation which is passing away, than that of providing for the moral, intellectual and religious culture of those who are to succeed them."[162] Other dignitaries such as North Carolina governor Zebulon Vance and Professor Edward Joynes also sent letters of support in lieu of attendance. The convention was considered a major success, and the fact that educators were able to form such an organization and convene a national meeting in the midst of war spoke to the importance placed on the development of native education.

When they adjourned on April 30, members voted to reconvene in Atlanta in early September 1863. The misfortunes of war, however, forced the meeting's postponement.[163] The Educational Association of the Confederate States of America would assemble once more before the Confederacy collapsed. On November 9, 1864, the day following the North Carolina Educational Association's convention, the national organization convened for the last time in Charlotte. Not surprisingly, most, but not all, of the delegates came from the host state. Nevertheless, choosing to meet during the darkest days of the war demonstrated the determination of Confederate educators to carry on their fight to the very last. Ultimately, the Association was significant more for what it symbolized than what it accomplished. It showed that educational independence was a national movement driven by the desire to establish Confederate cultural autonomy, and not simply the project of individual states or a handful of leaders.[164]

CONFEDERATE CULTURAL NATIONALISTS BELIEVED that education was the key to lasting intellectual independence and the foundation of an authentic southern literature. While the movements for literary and educational independence developed along different tracks and through different media, literary nationalists and educational leaders saw their projects as inextricably linked, and their goals as identical. The native education they envisioned would refine and reinforce southern character, instill proper moral values, train the next generation of Confederate writers, thinkers, and artists, and create a cultural environment capable of appreciating the great national literature of the Confederacy when it came. The state of Confederate education was seen as vital to the larger struggle, and concerns about textbooks, teachers, and schools resonated far beyond their seemingly limited sphere.

To legitimate its nationality, the Confederacy required a means of cultural expression capable of exhibiting the unique virtues of southern character and the richness of the southern mind. The creation of an exalted national literature would banish all doubts about the backwardness of southern slave society and bring respectability to the new Confederate nation. Surveying the state of Confederate literature at the midpoint of the war, cultural nationalists realized they had not yet attained the level of quality or originality required for national greatness, and they took action to encourage its development. To a large extent, their project still rested on the principle of exclusion, and their efforts focused mainly on removing foreign carryovers and condemning imitation. But once this pruning was complete and the proper trellises erected, they believed that a purely and unmistakably southern national culture would grow and flower. The coming of this transcendent literature, this "literature of power," would mark the final step toward intellectual independence and the realization of a complete and culturally sustainable Confederate nationality.

PART FOUR

Are We a Highly Civilized People?: 1864–1865

CHAPTER SEVEN

ARE WE A HIGHLY CIVILIZED PEOPLE?

Confederates would never take the essential final step toward intellectual independence, and their great national literature would remain an indistinct and distant dream. As their country spiraled toward oblivion, cultural nationalists tried to keep the cultural struggle alive. The shortages and hardships faced by publishers multiplied and compounded, threatening to undo the gains made toward establishing a self-sustaining southern print culture. What was worse, Confederates were forced to confront the ugly truth that the quality of what they had produced thus far was woefully insufficient. A southern renaissance had not been born with the Confederacy as everyone had confidently expected. Instead, Confederate literature presented itself as the rough-hewn product of immature and inexperienced writers, lacking the originality, polish, and power that intellectual independence required. As Appomattox approached, Confederate cultural nationalists began to publicly ask themselves, as *Southern Punch* did in early 1864, "Are we a highly civilized people?"[1] Were Confederates capable of intellectual independence? As their country contracted around them and the armies of Grant and Sherman loomed, these once-confident advocates of southern cultural autonomy, "more in sorrow than in anger," were forced to answer that "it is to be feared we are not."[2]

Or rather, they were not yet a highly civilized people. In the face of mounting hardships and an increasingly frank appraisal of the inadequate quality of

249

Confederate literature, cultural nationalists reconceived their project, scaled back their expectations, and adopted a more far-sighted approach. The Confederacy was not yet ready for intellectual independence, they now admitted. The raw material was there, they were certain, but it could not be developed overnight. One day, they promised (but there was substantial disagreement as to how many days and generations would have to elapse), Confederates would seize their true independence and dazzle the world with their cultural achievements, but not today, and probably not with this generation. Thus, during the final days of the war, Confederate nationalists adopted a new plan of action focused on taking gradual steps toward the same ultimate objective. Culturally speaking, Confederates may not be a highly civilized people now, but with guidance, preparation, and time, they could be. It would be left to future Confederates, perhaps still unborn, to complete the revolution and finish the work started by the heroic war generation. The Confederacy would win its political independence soon, they assured themselves, but the fight for cultural autonomy would have to continue long after the war.

The physical and logistical obstacles faced by publishers during the last year of the war were truly staggering, and the fact that Confederate print literature continued to be produced at all said much about the determination of these southerners to keep the nationalist struggle and their enterprises afloat. By this point, inflation was spinning out of control, removing all hope of profitability and threatening the viability of the Confederacy's publishers and periodicals. The price of printing supplies as well as labor costs had skyrocketed to astronomical levels and continued to climb on a daily basis. In the summer of 1864, the *Fayetteville Observer* enumerated some of its recent exorbitant supply costs:

> Not being able to procure suitable qualities of glue and molasses to make "composition rollers," for our presses, we ordered some from Nassau, through a friend in Wilmington. The cost is $1,582,88, for a barrel of molasses, and a keg of 44½ pounds of Irish glue, of which, $775 is for the freight of the barrel and keg! The freight is required in advance, at Nassau, so, that if the vessel had been lost, we should have lost that, as well as the goods. Fortunately, the ship arrived safely, a day or two ago. Before the war, the articles would have cost us $40. Inferior articles here, now, would cost about $3,000.[3]

And so it was with everything that printers required. The *Floridian & Journal* reported purchasing twenty pounds of printer's glue for $500 (plus $16 for shipping) which in "ordinary" times would have cost no more than $8. The *Confederate Union* complained that paper now cost $150 a ream, up from the prewar price of $2.50. In February 1864, the *Southern Christian Advocate* noted with dismay that the price of paper had jumped more than 25 percent in just one week.[4]

In the vain hope of keeping pace with inflation, the Confederate press frantically raised its prices and reduced the length of subscriptions. The *Richmond Christian Advocate*, for instance, increased its annual rate from $5 to $8 in April 1864. By October, it cost $15 and by January 1865, $20.[5] Between May and October 1864, the *Southern Presbyterian* quadrupled its rates.[6] In May 1864, Joseph Turner raised the price of *The Countryman* from $5 a year to $5 for four months, and in July, reduced the term to just three months.[7] And so it went with the rest of the Confederacy's newspapers and magazines. By 1865, few publishers accepted subscriptions longer than six months, and many insisted on much shorter terms. All were charging anywhere from ten to thirty times the prewar rates.

Hemorrhaging money, Confederate editors had long abandoned the hat-in-hand approach to announcing their rate increases and now showed little patience for complaints from subscribers. "Don't fuss about the subscription price," editor James Duncan bluntly told his readers, "if the [Richmond Christian] Advocate is worth keeping up at what it costs to publish it, keep it up; if it is not worth it, let it go down."[8] Editors repeatedly pointed out that compared to everything else in the Confederacy, their prices were quite reasonable, and in fact had decreased in relative cost. The $10 subscription price of the *Southern Cultivator* was "nominally high," its editor admitted in February 1865, "but the planter cannot complain of that. He gets a year's subscription for far less gold, less silver, less wheat, less corn, less cotton, less butter, less bacon, less lard, less wood, or any other product, whatever, than he ever did."[9]

Still, no matter how quickly they raised their prices or shortened their subscription periods, the proprietors of the Confederate press could not keep up with inflation; their journals and their own personal fortunes suffered as a result. A. A. Porter of the *Southern Presbyterian* estimated that "we cannot publish even our half sheet at current rates, without an outlay of at least *ten thousand dollars* per year, beyond the income of the paper."[10] Strapped for cash, literary journals now found it difficult, and in most cases impossible, to make good on their promises of payment for contributions, reversing one of the most encouraging literary developments of the war.

But inflation was not the only danger threatening the survival of southern publishers. Shortages persisted, especially of paper, though by 1864 publishers seemed to have less trouble locating a source for their materials—provided they could afford them—than finding a way to safely and reliably transport them. Missed paper shipments often forced Confederate periodicals to delay publication or issue half sheets. It was not uncommon for hard-pressed editors to borrow from their neighbors when transportation networks failed them; and all southerners were urged to send their cotton rags to needy publishers. Even when they could get it, the quality of paper as well as that of other vital printing materials like ink and glue remained primitive, and the appearance of Confederate publications continued to suffer as a result.

The difficulty in obtaining supplies underscored another major obstacle confronting Confederate publishers during this final year: the Yankees. As invading Union armies moved ever deeper into Confederate territory, they cut rail lines and roadways, depriving Confederate publishers of access to vital materials. With large sections of the Confederacy now in Union hands or otherwise cut off from mail access, southern periodicals could not reach many of their readers. As Grant's army inched ever closer to Richmond in the summer of 1864, the *Christian Observer* found itself separated from "more than half of our subscribers."[11] In April 1864, the *Southern Cultivator* ran a list of the Confederate towns with paying subscribers rendered inaccessible by the "encroachments of the enemy." The list included fifteen towns in Georgia, five in Alabama, thirty-seven in Tennessee, eighty-four in Mississippi, twelve in Louisiana, two in Virginia, two in Florida, six in Arkansas, and twenty-eight in Texas.[12]

But even for those subscribers still within Confederate lines, the general disruption of Confederate mail ensured that deliveries would be erratic or at best tardy. The *Christian Observer*, for instance, knew of "a subscriber in Mississippi, within our lines, to whom the 'Observer' has been mailed regularly, every week" but who "had received *only one number* in three months!"[13] The increasing unreliability of the mail combined with an ever-shrinking sphere of Confederate influence limited the reach and threatened the financial survival of the Confederacy's struggling periodicals. The breakdown of the postal system also severely hampered the exchange network that had developed among Confederate journals, whose editors, especially those outside the big cities, were hard-pressed to obtain reliable information.

Yankees could do worse than disrupt the mail. Those publishers caught in the direct path of invading Union armies either had to flee, or risk being destroyed or shut down by northern authorities. A number of journals uprooted when their situations were rendered untenable by real or threatened Union advances. "Compelled by stress of war to retreat," the *Southern Cultivator* relocated from Augusta to Athens at the end of 1864. Likewise, new owners William B. Smith and J. H. Bryahn Jr. decided to move *Southern Field and Fireside* from Augusta to Raleigh and merge it with *The Illustrated Mercury* in November. The *Southern Presbyterian* fled Columbia for Augusta, and the *Southern Christian Advocate*, which had previously moved from Charleston to Augusta in 1862, announced another relocation to Macon during the very last days of the war.[14]

For those who stuck it out and remained when the enemy approached, their fates differed. The newspapers of Atlanta did not fare well. As *The Countryman* reported in the wake of the city's fall to Sherman, "The offices of the old establishments are pretty thoroughly 'done for.' The Register office is represented by a pile of blackened brick. It was burnt to the ground, a month ago. The [Southern] Confederacy office has had its flag staff cut away by a shell, and has received several tokens of attention through its front. The Intelligencer office is thoroughly used up, powder-stained, and bullet-riddled. The Appeal building is also shot through and through."[15] Others, like the *Child's Index* in Macon, were spared at the last minute. As editor Samuel Boykin told his young readers:

> Well, children, we have come to see you again after quite a delay. But no doubt you forgave the delay. You know how near the Yankees came to our town; and we suppose you know that such an event would stop all business, and especially all printing. So it did. We thought at one time that our office would be destroyed, and your paper stopped altogether. But such was not the case. God did not let the Yankees take our city, though they tried, [and] as soon as they passed by, we put up our presses, which we had taken down in order to carry them away, and went to work again.[16]

When the Yankees came to Joseph Turner's Turnwold plantation, they took slaves, mules, horses, Turner's gold watch, his saddles, and much of his silverware, but they inexplicably left his press and printing supplies untouched.[17] Still, even when northern men did not stay to occupy the region, as in Turner's case, the chaos they left in their wake was not conducive to the regular publication of periodicals or the free expression of ideas. Immediately following the departure of Sherman's troops, Turner refrained from printing the details of his experience: "The truth is, we don't know, just now, whether we are a subject of Joe Brown, Gov. Logan, Jeff Davis, old Abe, or the king of Dahomey." But "judging from the airs which the colored gentry give themselves, about now, we would suppose we belonged to the last-named scion of an imperial race."[18] Once it became clear that the Yankees were gone, Turner regained his fire and filled his columns with accounts of northern depredations and atrocities during Sherman's March.[19]

The proximity of the enemy, combined with serious manpower shortages in Confederate armies, created another unanticipated obstacle that greatly hindered the southern press during the final year of the war. Over their vociferous objections, Confederate editors, printers, and their staffs were repeatedly called into the service of the state and—temporarily at least—forced to exchange "the pen and the composing stick . . . for the musket and cartridge box."[20] Starting in the late spring of 1864, these unpredictable stints of military service began to disrupt the regular operation of the Confederate press, especially weekly and monthly periodicals. The *Southern Illustrated News*, the *Magnolia Weekly, Southern Punch*, the *Southern Literary Messenger, The Age*, the *Southern Cultivator*, the *Central Presbyterian*, the *Christian Observer*, the *Richmond Christian Advocate*, the *Religious Herald*, and the *Child's Index*, among others, suffered serious delays, lengthy suspensions, and general declines in quality as a result of their staffs being ordered to the trenches. Outraged editors accused the Confederate and state governments of attempting to overthrow the freedom of the press, and they steadfastly maintained that their services to the nation far outweighed any benefit that their paltry numbers could contribute on the battlefield.

This continuing controversy over the role and rights of the press during wartime involved two overlapping issues: the status of the press's exemption from the Confederate draft, and the authority of state and local officials to suspend the press in the name of local defense. Editors, printers, and a portion of their staffs had been exempted from Confederate conscription since it was implemented. During the final year of the war, however, that exemption status came under repeated attack as critics accused newspapers and magazines of harboring unnecessarily large numbers of otherwise eligible men; others, like President Jefferson Davis himself, simply wanted to do away with such exemptions entirely. Editors remained ever-wary of any attempt on the part of Confederate authorities to control the press or abridge its free speech by sending newspapermen off to the front or by placing the papers and their staffs under direct government jurisdiction through a detail system. "There is a threatening look in Mr. Davis' eye," Henry Timrod warned in November 1864, "his fingers are obviously itching to bury us all under military rule."[21] Still, the exemptions held, if just barely, throughout the war, and the Confederate press successfully managed to fend off all efforts at the national level to interfere with its regular operations.[22]

While newspapers and journals were safe from Confederate conscription officers, they were still vulnerable to the whims of their local and state governments. In Virginia, most notably, Governor Smith began to "set aside" the "Privileges of the Press" in the summer of 1864, by periodically closing the offices of Richmond's religious and literary papers and ordering their employees to the trenches anytime real or rumored Yankees threatened.[23] The legality of such actions was debatable, and the Richmond press howled at this "first instance, in the history of the South, of the forcible suppression of newspapers."[24] The fact that there were no Yankees at the gate (at least not yet) made the governor's decrees seem all the more tyrannical, and their uneven application made them all the more odious. Fearing the political power of the daily papers, the governor left them untouched, closing only the offices of the weekly and monthly press. As *Southern Punch* bitterly complained, following a two week forced suspension in June 1864, "the religious papers . . . and the young champions of a new Southern Literature—weeklies and monthlies, that have striven with might and main to put an end to our literary vassalage to Yankee *litterateurs* and publishers, were compelled to succumb to a militia 'military necessity' which is on all hands pronounced the greatest farce of the day."[25] The theaters were also closed for a time. The governor's singling out of Richmond's cultural institutions along with its literary and religious publications directly threatened the cause of Confederate intellectual independence by silencing its strongest advocates, cultural nationalists feared.

The Confederacy's editors responded with a combination of reasoned argument and vituperative attack. On the most pragmatic level, they argued that the actual number of able-bodied newspapermen exempted from service was so small that their addition to the army "would not be felt for a moment."[26] The *Southern Cultivator* pointed out that at the price of "not merely 'abridging' but *utterly destroying* the freedom of the press," the Confederacy would gain "less than half a regiment of men."[27] Available statistics seemed to bear out these assertions. In Alabama, according to one 1864 report, of the 5,066 men exempted from service, only 163 were editors or printers.[28] Another report, commissioned by the Confederate House of Representatives in February 1865, likewise found that out of the 67,000 men "on this side of the Mississippi River" who had obtained official exemptions only 795 were editors or newspaper employees. Of all the exemption classes, only insane asylum managers and nurses, apothecaries, and mail contractors could claim smaller numbers, Joseph Turner noted.[29]

But while adding a handful of newspapermen to the ranks would make no difference in the military struggle, editors argued that the consequent loss of the newspaper and periodical press would be a public calamity which "would be regretted from one end of the Confederacy to the other."[30] It was not simply a question of numbers. "We have in The Countryman office only one, or at most two, able to do military service," Joseph Turner explained. "But if we had twenty, we are doing that amount of good for the country, that it would never do to suppress our journal for the want of hands. The cause of liberty, of patriotism, of morals, of religion—of right over wrong—and of the country, would suffer too much, by such an untoward event."[31] "To suppress a machine that operates so well, for the purpose of putting a few soldiers into the army," Timrod argued, "would be like cutting an elephant into pieces in order to scare an enemy with the bits."[32]

With the survival of their journals thus threatened, Confederate editors launched a vigorous counteroffensive to defend the freedom of the press, highlight its many contributions to the war effort, and assert its vital role in the struggle for southern independence. "Count its many services to mankind, and compare them with the services of every other existing institution, and it will be found that no one of them, not even the pulpit itself, has been more widely beneficial in its actions and influence," Timrod insisted.[33] The press was a nationalizing force which formed "a kind of bond of union—a common medium of the interchange of ideas, and next to our organized armies are the most powerful engines within our country for the attainment of its independence."[34] Given the indispensable role that the press played in the political, intellectual, and cultural life of the nation, it was vital, editors argued, that they be allowed to carry on their work unimpaired. As *Southern Punch* concisely put it, "Exemption from conscription is not a privilege but a right."[35]

For any politician, general, or conscription agent who refused to recognize this sacred right, editors promised that their crimes against southern liberty would not go unrecorded. "Mark this, ye Sir William Berkleys of 1864, the Press of the South will be an avenging Nemesis when this war is over," *Southern Punch* warned Confederate senators as they debated a new conscription bill in February. "The press builds up and pulls down, and woe to him who butts his head against its steaming engine. The fate of the bull that attacked the locomotive will be the fate of that man."[36]

These threats of a future reckoning aside, there was little that editors could do to stop state and local officials from commandeering their staffs. Apart from Confederate defeat itself, nothing disrupted the literary and religious press so much as this compulsory military service. Journals like the *Southern Illustrated News*, the *Magnolia Weekly*, and *Southern Punch*, which had appeared with clockwork regularity throughout the war, were now suspended for weeks at a time.[37] Between May 7 and July 23, 1864, the *Magnolia Weekly* published only two issues. By December, "almost constant employment on military duty" had forced the owners to resort to a half sheet for the remainder of the war.[38] After its April 1864 issue, *The Age* did not appear again until January 1865.[39] Some, like *Southern Punch*, tried to make up for labor deficiencies by hiring women as temporary workers, as "these fair beings, at least, [were] not in the power of official Moguls."[40] Still, new workers were hard to find and could not in any case make up for the experience and expertise lost to the militia.

Confederate publishers and periodicals had labored under tremendous difficulties throughout the war, but the final year introduced new obstacles and intensified existing hardships. For some, the strain proved too much to bear, and a number of the Confederacy's oldest and most distinguished voices fell silent as a result of ever-worsening conditions. The *Southern Presbyterian Review* published its last wartime edition in April 1864. Crippled by the continued appropriation of its printers and staff by Richmond authorities, the venerable *Southern Literary Messenger* issued no more numbers after June.[41] Phoenix-like, *De Bow's Review* rose from the ashes in July, only to disappear again until after the war.[42] The *North Carolina Journal of Education* ceased publication after its July issue. The *Gulf City Home Journal*, the *Church Intelligencer*, and the *Southern Presbyterian* were suspended as well, though the latter two would resume again before the war was over.[43] For the surviving members of the Confederate press, the final year of the war was a period of constant struggle characterized by delays, suspensions, and reduced dimensions.

Yet the fight for Confederate intellectual independence endured. Despite the hardships and disruptions, Confederate nationalists continued calling for cultural autonomy and their words continued to find their way into print. The obstacles imposed by the final year of the war exacted a heavy toll on the monthly press, and the loss of the *Southern Literary Messenger* was particularly lamented, but the weekly literary and religious papers survived and their editors refused to allow the Yankees or Confederate officials to derail their cause. The *Richmond Enquirer* marveled at the tenacity with which the *Southern Illustrated News* and the *Magnolia Weekly* clung to life despite the "unprecedented demands from the military authorities":

> By spasms . . . they have burst out into the light, enfeebled, it is true, at times by the absence of most of their respective corps—contributors, printers, engravers, editors—delving in the mud of the trenches or standing guard around the prisons and bridges of this devoted city. Here and there, through Spring, Summer and Fall, we get a glimpse of transitory evidence that they did not quite expire under the blight of the cold, wanton and arbitrary curse which came on their heads that bright May day, when the din of bells and the rush of men, and the insolent outrages of armed guards wrote down a whole page of folly and fury for anybody's history of Richmond who may choose to transcribe it now or hereafter.[44]

As daunting as the difficulties were, the Confederate press proved to be remarkably resilient. As historian Henry Stroupe noted with amazement in his study of the religious press of the South Atlantic states, the Confederacy entered the year 1865 with a net loss of only three religious papers from what these states had had in 1860.[45] In terms of literary periodicals, the Confederacy still boasted a net gain.

Nor were the periodicals the only survivors. The *Southern Illustrated News* proudly reported that "notwithstanding the attack made by the conscript gatherer, the drama yet lives in this city."[46] Confederate book publishers also showed no signs of slackening, and, in fact, issued more books and textbooks in 1864 than in any previous year. In his research into Confederate belles lettres, historian Richard Harwell discovered that the production of such works continued to accelerate throughout the war, reaching its peak in 1864. Remarkably, he projected, if the number of books produced in the first three months of 1865 had been "increased proportionately over a full year" they "would surpass even the figure for 1864."[47]

In the face of nearly overwhelming difficulties and shrinking personal fortunes, the "Quill-Drivers" of the Confederacy hardened their resolve and reaffirmed their commitment to the cause of cultural independence.[48] "We repudiate any other thought than final triumph and the attainment of perfect national independence, and the continued and prosperous and (we hope) useful existence of the [Christian] Index," Samuel Boykin declared in March 1864.[49] "Our journal, it is true, has felt the storm," the editors of the *Southern Cultivator* conceded in January 1865, "but only to strike its root deeper into the sustaining soil."[50] The new owners of *Southern Field and Fireside* likewise resolved that "no obstacle, however formidable, over which an unflagging energy or ordinary human power can have control, will deter us." "We have measured the distance. We shall do what we propose." Even when Sherman threatened to take their home city of Raleigh in March 1865, they promised that "no time shall be lost in resuming it at some other point. The paper shall not be stopped."[51]

But some Confederate periodicals did more than simply hang on. While the general trajectory of southern periodical literature during that final year was one of decline, it was not universally so. Some editors expanded their papers as well as introduced new features and flourishes.[52] Periodicals which had been suspended managed to resume production, and, more improbably still, a few new journals were introduced even as the Confederacy itself teetered on the brink of annihilation.

Having been reduced to half sheets, a number of weekly papers, including the *Christian Index*, the *Southern Presbyterian*, the *Southern Churchman*, and the *Baptist Banner*, regained their full size in the waning days of the war.[53] "There being no longer any danger of an advance of the enemy, into this section of the country, we have determined to bring back our large press," the *Southern Literary Companion* announced following the departure of Sherman's troops in November 1864.[54] Other editors found sufficient resources to expand their journals beyond their original size or increase the frequency of their issue. In September 1864, publishers Ayres and Wade made good on their promise to double the size of the *Confederate States Medical and Surgical Journal*, and, in January 1865, congratulated themselves that their circulation had "surpassed any reasonable expectation."[55] "In order to supply in some measure, the want of Sabbath School books," in 1864 the Presbyterian *Children's Friend* began issuing "twice a month instead of once a month as heretofore."[56] More daring still was the *Southern Cultivator*'s transformation from a monthly into a weekly journal in November 1864. "The present may not, perhaps, be considered a very favorable time for the expansion of our publishing department," editor and owner Dennis Redmond conceded, "but, with the means and resources at our command, and the liberal support which we confidently expect from the public, we have no fear of the result." After a "fair trial," the *Cultivator* returned to its monthly format in 1865, but its dramatic, if temporary, expansion evinced a surprising degree of optimism at such a late date in the Confederacy's life.[57]

No editor showed more ambition or defiant perseverance in the face of mounting hardships than Joseph Addison Turner. *The Countryman*'s continued expansion and its strict adherence to high critical and typographical standards defied logistical possibility, it seemed. Although occasionally reduced to a half sheet, *The Countryman* seems never to have missed an issue during the entire war. Even amid the chaos of Sherman's March, Turner continued to churn out his weekly edition. In January 1864, he expanded his paper to sixteen full pages, making *The Countryman* the longest weekly paper in the Confederacy. At the end of July, he announced a further expansion, not in pages, but in the amount of printed material. By adopting an even smaller typeface, he added "what is equivalent to ten more pages of reading matter," making the paper "virtually" twenty-six pages long. More remarkable still, Turner maintained these dimensions throughout the rest of the war. Modeling his expanded paper on the late *Niles' Weekly Register*, Turner boasted that "The Countryman has the same number of pages with that journal, uses the same sized page, is printed in the same type, and is modeled after that most useful publication ever issued in America." But *The Countryman* surpassed the venerable *Register* in one important respect, "to wit, a department of elegant literature, rejecting the style of Yankee literary journals, and modeling itself after the best English miscellaneous weeklies, but, at the same time, being stamped with an independent, Southern tone, original with, and peculiar to itself."[58]

Turner promised that *The Countryman* would always be "fearless, independent, outspoken, and useful."[59] Outspoken it was. Turner despised Georgia Governor Joseph Brown and bitterly resented Brown's obstructionist opposition to Jefferson Davis, and he made it the special mission of *The Countryman* to denounce the Governor and all who supported him. To any "silly people" who might think that his paper was merely the organ of the Confederate president, however, he was quick to correct them: "The Countryman is the organ of another great man—J. A. Turner."[60]

Turner's editorial policies were markedly different from those of his fellow editors in that he refused to broaden *The Countryman's* appeal by catering to a mass audience. "Our object is to publish a journal of CHARACTER and STANDING. INFLUENCE will necessarily follow in the wake of these."[61] His aim was not necessarily to reach a large number of readers directly, but rather to reach the right "kind" of readers. *The Countryman* was intended for the "leading minds of the land," its editors, politicians, generals, intellectuals, and religious leaders. "Week by week, this journal sets in motion truth—original ideas," Turner boasted in October 1864. "Controlling minds take them up, and read them. They set those minds in motion. Those set others in motion. And though The Countryman may, perchance, be forgotten, or never known as the originator of the idea, still it travels on upon its mission of good, until every person, big and little, white and black, throughout the length and breadth of the land, feels its influence." Turner firmly believed in this trickle-down approach to the transmission of ideas. *The Countryman* was a particular favorite of the Confederate press, and many of Turner's columns addressed his fellow editors directly. They in turn reprinted and excerpted articles from *The Countryman* in their own journals (with or without attribution) and thus, Turner argued, his influence extended far beyond his own modest circulation. For the good of the nation, he vowed, "The Countryman must continue to be published," whatever the obstacles, and he somehow managed to maintain his journal's size and quality even as the Confederacy collapsed around him.[62]

Other voices, new and old, joined Turner in attempting to advance the cause of Confederate literature during the final year of the war. The *Southern Presbyterian*, the *Church Intelligencer*, *The Age*, and *De Bow's Review* (albeit briefly) all managed to resume after extended suspensions.[63] There were also a number of completely new journals. *The Illustrated Mercury* in Raleigh and the short-lived *Smith & Barrow's Monthly Magazine* in Richmond have already been discussed, but there were other new titles as well. In October, the Confederacy's first Catholic paper appeared. The arrival of *The Pacificator* (published weekly in Augusta) attracted a great deal of attention from the Confederate press, both for its novelty and for the unusual timing of its advent. The Protestant papers officially welcomed this new arrival, though their anti-Catholic fears were thinly veiled.[64] Also appearing in October 1864 was the Quaker *Southern Friend* in Richmond. In keeping with the Quakers' status as conscientious objectors, editor J. B. Crenshaw promised that when reporting current events his journal would give only a "concise statement of facts, from the most reliable sources within reach, without expressing any opinion thereon."[65]

Even 1865 witnessed the introduction of two new Confederate periodicals. In January, Raleigh publisher William Smith launched the impressively sized *The Key-Stone: A Monthly Masonic Magazine*. Not surprisingly, the journal contained Masonic news, lodge reports, and the like, but Smith also appealed to "the general as well as the Masonic reader" by varying "its contents with good original or selected sketches, essays, poems, etc., that may not have any more than an indirect bearing upon our Order."[66] The *Child's Banner*, first published on February 15, 1865, represented the final addition to the Confederate periodical press. Printed in Salisbury, North Carolina, the *Banner* was a conventional religious children's paper concerned with the state of young souls, the fate of "soldier's orphans," and the future of Confederate education.[67]

Confederate theater continued to exhibit signs of life. Even during the difficult summer of 1864, the *Magnolia Weekly* was pleased to report that the Richmond Theatre's audiences, "if not large, have, at least, been remunerative, and the efforts of the manager to please the public, in this clamorous time of war, have not failed of success."[68] The continued operation of the theaters contributed directly to the war effort, *Southern Punch* argued, by demonstrating to the southern people and the outside world that Union incursions had not broken their spirit or disrupted their culture. "One of the best evidences of the absence of 'scare,' is the fact that a crack place of amusement is . . . driving ahead as if Grant and Butler were a thousand miles from Richmond. Such a fact puzzles the enemy, and looks ominous when reflection follows the puzzle." For this reason, the temporary suspensions of the theater by Richmond authorities were "impolitic" to say the least.[69] The survival of the theaters and especially their staging of original Confederate productions bolstered the spirits of cultural nationalists during this difficult final year by providing "hopeful evidences of the growth of the Literature of Southern Drama."[70]

The perseverance of the Confederacy's book publishers and their ever-expanding list of titles also remained a source of pride. For the most part, Confederate publishing houses continued to operate up until the very end, or at least until their cities fell to Union forces. The Publication Committee of the Presbyterian General Assembly, for instance, reported in July 1864, "that nearly fourteen millions of pages have been distributed over the land through this agency alone."[71] For their part, the Episcopalians announced the creation of an entirely new religious publishing house, the Protestant Episcopal Church Publishing Association, in September 1864.[72] The accomplishments of the Confederacy's major secular publishing houses, like West & Johnston in Richmond; Evans & Cogswell in Columbia; Burke, Boykin & Co. in Macon; Sterling, Campbell & Albright in Greensboro; and Branson & Farrar in Raleigh, were particularly celebrated. While shortages and other hardships may have delayed the production and marred the physical appearance of Confederate books, they did not stop the presses, and southerners continued to be greeted by new Confederate titles up until the very last days of the war.

But while Confederate presses continued to roll, the question of the quality of their products' content became ever more urgent. Were these books, periodicals, poems, songs, and plays the embodiment, or even the basis, of the original national literature that intellectual independence required? In all frankness, and not without a great deal of disappointment, Confederate critics were forced to concede that they were not.

The tone of criticism changed during the final year of the war. The novelty of native fiction, poetry, and other literary forms had worn off, and cultural nationalists now approached such works with an increasingly critical eye. Whereas before, they had rejoiced at the flood of articles, poems, and books produced by new Confederate authors as a sign of the awakening of the southern mind, critics now saw such amateurish productions as a nuisance, serving only to hinder true growth. Impatient at the lack of intellectual progress, they advised the "young and inexperienced writers" of the South to " 'stop writing; not for your own amusement and improvement, but for publication.' . . . Lay your MSS. [manuscripts] carefully aside and when you have arrived at a greater degree of maturity of mind and cultivation, revise and correct them. You will be amazed at their imperfections, as well as your own temerity in desiring to 'rush into print' with such faulty and immature productions."[73] And for those temerarious authors who still rushed into print during the last year of the war, they met a far less forgiving critical reception. "It is our aim to erect a high standard of merit," *Southern Field and Fireside* explained in August 1864, "and to do so we must, as the Spartans did with their misshapen offspring, remorselessly cut off all those children of the brain that come before us not up to the mark."[74]

A few examples will suffice. Of Simon Spicewood's *Junaluskie. The Cherokee. A Story of the War*, the best one reviewer could say was that "typographically, it is very finely executed." "As a work of fiction," however, "it possesses neither plan, plot, combination, connection or completeness. Its greatest merit is its brevity—the less we have of it the better it is."[75] *The Illustrated Mercury* in Raleigh attacked the work of poet R. Lynden Cowper with a vehemence bordering on malice. Of Cowper's long poem "Confederate America" which appeared as a stand-alone publication in 1864, *The Mercury* was "in doubt which to pronounce the more striking, the frantic energy of the author's *effort* or the magnificence of his failure. . . . The poem—the *thing*, we mean—is feeble and farcical beyond any terms we can command to use upon it. . . . It is doggeral of the vilest type. We dismiss the whole subject with infinite pleasure and a feeling of grateful relief."[76] But the subject was not dismissed. When Cowper struck back with a satiric poem entitled "Mercurial Ointment," *The Mercury* was ready. Whether this new poem was "better or worse than Confederate America is difficult to determine," *The Mercury*'s critic scoffed, "because infinities cannot well be compared, except as equals; and both these productions are infinitely poor." *The Mercury* proceeded to print Cowper's entire poem over the course of two issues, all the while inserting snide comments, corrections, and biting criticisms in brackets amongst the stanzas.[77] The harshness of these reviews was exceptional in degree, but not in tone. The past indulgence that cultural nationalists requested and critics generally granted had evaporated. The rose-tinted glasses had been removed.

Even the South's most established authors were subjected to greater scrutiny. While they did not receive the chastisement meted out to the young and inexperienced, critics now attempted to give a more balanced assessment of their accomplishments and weigh their merits by more objective literary standards. James Wood Davidson's efforts in this regard have already been discussed. His "Litterateurs of the South," which appeared throughout the summer of 1864, simultaneously critiqued and praised the work of Augusta Jane Evans, Paul Hamilton Hayne, William Gilmore Simms, Henry Lynden Flash, and George Fitzhugh, among others. Similarly, a young Joel Chandler Harris published a long detailed review of Flash's poetry in *The Countryman*.[78]

This change in tone was best exemplified by the surprisingly critical reaction to Augusta Jane Evans's new Confederate novel, *Macaria; or, Altars of Sacrifice*. Appearing in 1864, *Macaria* was a tale of wartime heroism, martyrdom, and staunch patriotic devotion.[79] Above all, it was a story of Confederate women, following the travails of twin heroines, Irene Huntingdon and Electra Grey. Evans's motivations for writing the novel were explicitly patriotic and her inscription read:

To the
ARMY OF THE SOUTHERN CONFEDERACY,
Who have delivered the South from despotism, and who have won for
Generations yet unborn the precious guerdon of
Constitutional republican liberty:
TO THIS VAST LEGION OF HONOR,
Whether limping on crutches through
The land they have saved and immortalized,
Or surviving uninjured to share the blessings their
Unexampled heroism bought, or sleeping dreamlessly in nameless
Martyr-graves on hallowed battle-fields whose
Historic memory shall perish only with

The remnants of our language,

These pages are

GRATEFULLY AND REVERENTLY DEDICATED

By one who, although debarred from the

Dangers and deathless glory of the "tented field,"

Would fain offer a woman's inadequate tribute to the noble

Patriotism and sublime self-abnegation of her

Dear and devoted countrymen.[80]

The success of *Macaria* was phenomenal. It passed through at least two Confederate editions and at least 20,000 copies. "The novel of the season," *Macaria* was by far the most popular work of fiction to appear during the war.[81]

Ostensibly, the arrival of Evans's book should have been cause for universal celebration for Confederate cultural nationalists. Here was a full-length novel written in elevated style by one of the South's most famous and respected authors (Evans had also penned the critically acclaimed antebellum best seller *Beulah*), published by its leading publishers (West & Johnston, and Evans & Cogswell), dedicated to the Confederate army, and shot through with Confederate nationalist sentiment. What was more, it was a tremendous success, proving that the Confederate reading public was capable of supporting its authors and supporting them well. Had *Macaria* appeared in 1862 or 1863, it would, no doubt, have been hailed as a major triumph, a serious blow struck against northern dominance, and a harbinger of Confederate intellectual independence. By the second half of 1864, however, when the book began to be seriously reviewed, the criteria for success had changed, and critics dissected Evans's work with a meticulousness heretofore unknown.

Southern Field and Fireside, the *Southern Illustrated News*, *Southern Punch*, *The Mercury*, *The Age*, and *The Countryman* all ran extended reviews of *Macaria*, and nearly every Confederate periodical carried at least a lengthy notice.[82] The sixteen-page review in *The Age* and Joel Chandler Harris's critique in *The Countryman* (both appearing in January 1865) were by far the most extensive. While there were a few celebrants, the general tone of the Confederate critical reaction was decidedly negative. Notwithstanding its immense popularity, and almost certainly driven by it, Confederate critics took great pains to explain to their readers why *Macaria* was flawed and, more importantly, why it could not be representative of the original national literature they envisioned.

The most common complaint lodged against the book was that its language was artificial, overwrought, pedantic, inappropriate for its subject matter, and full of obscure and, in some cases, impregnable allusions. Evans's "dangerous experiment" of writing about the Confederate experience in "an ultra classic and super-erudite style . . . has failed," *Southern Field and Fireside* concluded bluntly in October 1864. The essence of southern life could not be "written in Greecisms [*sic*] or told by all the recondite philosophizing of science," the reviewer explained. "We are neither a classic nor a profound people, and any attempt to portray us by a style appropriate to such must strike us with as painful an incongruity as those French melodrama where Hannibal wears red-heeled shoes, and Cato harangues in a *roquelaire*, and a tie wig." Such a "flashy show of erudition" on Evans's part only served to obscure her message and distance her readers.[83] Quoting a passage from *Macaria*, Joel Chandler Harris demanded "how many readers will understand such language as the following? 'Perish the microcosm in the limitless macrocosm, and sink the feeble earthly segregate, in the boundless, rushing, choral aggregation!' " Even if the reader managed to decipher "the meaning of the 'hard words,' " Harris continued, "their connection with what goes before, is so indistinctly seen, he does not know how to apply the sentences."[84] The reviewer for *The Age* believed that Evans's style was so "excessively elaborate . . . as to be indicative of a strain upon the mind, which seems reaching after something higher than it can attain, and breaks down in the effort."[85] But whatever their interpretations as to the cause, nearly all reviewers agreed that Evans's overwrought style and convoluted language inhibited the book and limited its utility as an expression of southern character.

Some criticized the plot, or lack thereof. "Indeed the work before us can scarcely be said to have any plot at all," *The Age* charged, or rather it "has no consistency . . . its parts do not cohere together."[86] Others like *De Bow's Review* and the *Southern Illustrated News* complained that *Macaria* lacked originality, and they accused Evans of simply cobbling together clichéd scenes from other works of sentimental fiction. She had "depended too much on her scrap-book, and too little upon her own rich imagination," the *Southern Illustrated News* concluded. "We sincerely trust that with 'Macaria' that scrap-book is entirely exhausted, and that when next we meet her in the walks of literature, she will have learned to eschew the tinkling of borrowed trinkets, and founded for herself a taste and a style based upon no less an idea than that of *Intellectual Independence* [emphasis added]."[87]

As for her characters, critics found them "not only unnatural but impossible."[88] Harris, in his review, carefully dissected the three major characters, Irene Huntingdon, Electra Grey, and Russell Aubrey, only to expose a mass of contradictions.[89] But what really bothered Harris and others was Evans's portrayal of southern women and the unladylike indelicacy of some of the opinions expressed and actions taken by her heroines. The "personages" of the novel "so constantly violate[d] the primal laws of humanity" as to render them utterly unbelievable, *The Age* charged.[90] Harris particularly objected to the character of Irene, who was "sometimes a mere woman, with a woman's heart and feelings—and sometimes as cold, and calm as the—'placid bust of Pallas'—a living contradiction of herself, as well as a contradiction of the feelings natural to a woman."[91] Likewise, *The Age*'s reviewer complained that Evans "too often places her heroine in the observatory, conning over the mysteries of the starry heavens, or tracing out the explorations of Newton, Kepler and Laplace, when she should be entertaining her visitors in her father's drawing-room."[92] Both critics agreed that Evans's "political disquisitions" were completely "out of place in a work of female art."[93] While not quite scandalous, Evans's violations of gender norms deprived the story and its characters of credibility, these critics argued, disqualifying it as a true exemplar of southern character and values.

The publication of *Macaria* and the reaction of cultural nationalists to it were significant for a number of reasons. *Macaria* was the single most substantial and popular Confederate literary work to appear during the war, and, as such, it was also the single most likely candidate for elevation into the realm of "literature of power." Given its success and potential significance to the movement for intellectual independence, *Macaria* received extensive critical attention from the southern press. What these frank and often harsh reviews revealed was an important shift during this final year. Whereas earlier in the war, such a work would have been hailed as the realization of their hopes, critics now approached the novel with apprehension and skepticism, lest they endorse a work of inferior merit or insufficient originality. Cultural nationalists had grown impatient at the lack of demonstrated intellectual progress, and their reaction to *Macaria* clearly evidenced this frustration. While they applauded Evans's patriotism and were gratified by the book's financial success, cultural nationalists were confident that this was not the great Confederate literature for which they had been waiting.

THIS FRUSTRATION STEMMED FROM a growing realization about the general state of Confederate literature. Southerners had been cut off from the North and its culture for over three years, and it was time for a frank assessment of what had been accomplished. Having remained silent for two years since the suspension of his journal, James De Bow reappeared in July 1864 to pass judgment on Confederate literature. The verdict was not good. Since the beginning of the conflict, he wrote, "little has appeared which is worthy either of the genius or attainments of our people." The war had not given birth to the great southern national literature that so many expected. "The glorious struggle has scarcely inspired one song which will live beyond the [present] generation," De Bow sadly observed. "Books we have had—not a few. Works upon the army, works upon the navy, treatises interesting to the medical staff, translations and digests, some attempts at history, occasional school-books, and now and then a work of romance. We are not doing injustice to these. Many are of great value, some of literary merit, and a few which deserve more than passing comment. Still, the truth with which we set out can not be gainsaid, and the development of Southern literature remains for the future."[94]

Others were inclined to agree. In critiquing the Confederacy's periodical literature, A. W. Dillard of Alabama found little to celebrate: "We have stories, which are absolutely destitute of probability, dished up in the inflated style of a schoolboy. We have cart loads of articles, which seem to be written only to prove that words may be hitched together. . . . The famishing public demands intellectual food—health-giving, nutritious food, and our periodicals set before them—what? The rhetorical inanities of school boys and girls. In place of bread they are put off with a stone."[95] Fabian, writing for *Southern Field and Fireside* in June 1864, complained that Confederate writers had demonstrated a deficiency "both in boldness of thought and fertility of invention; we have too many of the old plots with only a little change of scene and name. Do let us seek out some new subjects," he implored, or, at the very least, "present old ones in novel aspects!"[96] Thus far, critics could detect little in Confederate literature that was truly original and therefore truly and uniquely southern.

Although the Confederacy had produced an impressive volume of print material, established new periodicals and publishing houses, and generally met the day-to-day needs of its reading public, cultural nationalists were forced to admit that it had not created a national literature capable of vindicating Confederate nationality, impressing foreign critics, or even withstanding the test of time. "In the opinion of the world at large, we should be guilty of not a little arrogance, in making any pretension to a national literature, notwithstanding the evidence of intellectual activity which the war has evoked, and the number of publications which it has called into being," the editor of the *Southern Literary Messenger* conceded in May 1864.[97] A true national literature would have the power to "force its way abroad" and the merit to withstand the "crucible of foreign criticism."[98] Confederate literature thus far had failed on both accounts.

The admitted failure of Confederate literature to live up to the lofty expectations set by cultural nationalists raised disturbing questions: What did this say about southern character? Were southerners worthy of intellectual independence? Were they indeed as highly civilized a people as they had always claimed? As Confederate periodicals and publishers struggled to stay afloat and the quality of native works continued to disappoint, some began to voice their doubts publicly. "Are we a literary people?" *Southern Punch* asked. "No. We are a Spartan people, rude, uncultivated, capital fighters, giving harder blows than we receive, excellent cultivators of tobacco, rice, sugar, cotton, and embodiers of a certain sort of chivalry." They were not, however, an "Athenian" people. In truth, "There is nothing of the Athenian about us. Point to a Euripides, a Sophocles in authorship; a Praxiteles in art; a Parthenon in architecture," editor John Overall challenged. "Wipe us out tomorrow, and where be our monuments of parchment or of marble?" "Let us not deceive ourselves," he told his countrymen. "The cultivated world has long laughed at our pretensions," and Confederates had accomplished little thus far in the cultural realm that was likely to change many minds.[99]

So where did this leave cultural nationalists and their quest for Confederate intellectual independence? Coming at the end of the war as such admissions did, and in conjunction with a myriad of other crushing disappointments, they could have been the death knell for the movement for cultural autonomy. But the struggle did not end. Confederate editors, publishers, and educators remained as convinced as ever of the importance of their efforts and the absolute necessity of intellectual independence. They continued to believe, and constantly reiterated, that the key to true independence lay in the ability of southerners to cast off all foreign dependencies and think for themselves. "Independence, when won, must bring to us freedom of thought—intellectual liberty," *The Mercury* steadfastly maintained in late September 1864.[100] Neither the hard hand of war nor frustrations over the quality of Confederate literature up to that point had altered the convictions of cultural nationalists, and they continued to fight for the "literary enfranchisement of the South" and the "special cultivation of our nationality."[101]

But if the ultimate objective had not changed, the timeframe and methods for attaining it had. When a great Confederate literature failed to arise immediately, cultural nationalists simply scaled back their expectations and adopted a more gradual approach instead of scrapping their project. They recognized that the southern people required more preparation before they would be ready to seize their intellectual autonomy. Having answered its own question "Are We a Literary People?" in the negative, *Southern Punch* immediately posed a follow-up: "Will we become a literary people?" To which, it answered: "In time perhaps. Age may refine and cultivate us up to that high point of civilization."[102]

Further cultivation was the key. Southern talent and cultural appreciation "must be developed," *The Mercury* argued, and that "require[d] time, care and taste."[103] How much time was a matter of conjecture, for "what is in the womb of Time, its lapse only can disclose," but there was no doubt as to what ultimately would be born.[104] Editor Frank Alfriend predicted that "a long time will elapse before we have our Humes and Robertsons, Guizots and Gibbons to trace our national progress" and "centuries perhaps will elapse before . . . our Chaucers and Spensers, Miltons and Cowpers, Burns', Byrons and Wordsworths" would emerge.[105] But they would come. Hopes that the Confederacy would attain its intellectual independence concurrently with its political freedom necessarily had to be abandoned; but Confederate cultural nationalists retained their conviction that national legitimacy required intellectual autonomy, and their faith that southerners as a people were destined to achieve it. They remained convinced that the mental soil of the South was "an alluvial substratum, rich in the promise of abundant and varied and substantial stores, which may be confidently anticipated by reason of the depth, happy conformation, perfect balance and distinguished traits of the Southern mind."[106] It was to future generations that cultural nationalists now directed their efforts so that the foundation of a true national literature could be properly laid. "The FUTURE looms up grand and inviting," James De Bow wrote during a particularly dark period in the summer of 1864, "and our children's children, speaking to us from its depths, cry 'Worthy, worthy, oh noble race; see here the rewards of your toils and sorrows!'"[107] It was with these "children's children" in mind that Confederate cultural nationalists reconceived their project during the last year of the war.

The shortcomings of Confederate literature were seen to stem partly from the chaos of war, but mostly from the underdeveloped state of southern society. Cultural nationalists, turned amateur sociologists, speculated that perhaps, as a society, the South was not yet ready to embrace a high intellectual culture. "Certain sociological laws growing out of the existing status of our society" had hampered the growth of native literature. All societies had to pass through three stages of development—agricultural, industrial, and finally artistic, these thinkers argued. At best, "we have not reached farther than the second stage of progress of society; hence it could not be expected of us to be a literary people."[108] "Literature," *Southern Punch* agreed, "does not seem to flourish in a purely agricultural country. . . . Perhaps, hereafter, when the South becomes a commercial and manufacturing, as well as an agricultural country, the romancist and the poet, the painter and the sculptor may leap into living life."[109] Others placed less stock in sociological categorization and more faith in the intellectual potential of agricultural societies, but all agreed that Confederate writers and readers required more time and careful preparation before they would be ready to create and embrace a distinctive national literature.

Still, there were promising signs, and cultural nationalists believed that the war experience had significantly advanced the South toward intellectual independence. While much of Confederate literature had failed to meet expectations, there were a few creditable, if not immortal, works that gave Confederate critics a glimpse, "although as yet faintly and timidly," of "the struggling Star of Literature rising in the gloom of this desperate struggle for social and political existence."[110] The wartime compositions of Henry Timrod, "our Tennyson," as well as certain poems by Hayne, Hope, Thompson, Lamar Fontaine, and Asa Hartz were cited as examples.[111] Timrod himself could think of "at least a dozen fine lyrics" that were "likely to live beyond the present generation." Out of the thousands of pages printed during the Confederacy's lifetime, this was admittedly a very small proportion, and Timrod conceded that "the stormy emotions of the time have not found any very general expression in verse."[112] But he had no doubt that Confederate writers would emerge from the war "strengthened and elevated" and that within "the brain of every true poet of the Confederacy sleeps many a poem, which, though it may not burst into blossom until the return of peace, shall show in the color of all its petals that its roots are deep in the blood-enriched soil of the now pending revolution."[113]

The experience of war also promised to help prepare the general Confederate population to appreciate native literature in the future. As a number of commentators observed, the war and especially the army had created a nation of readers. According to the *Soldier's Visitor*,

Not a few of our soldiers have learned to read since entering the service; and the greater part of them have for the first time in their lives found interest and companionship and solace in the printed page. True it may have been but a newspaper or a tract; but it was still something to think of, and oftentimes to impart information; and though the stores may have been gathered little by little in the long run the aggregate must be no small addition of intelligence. The taste for reading once formed too, may be cultivated, and in the end the result may be a decided elevation of the mental character of the great body of our people.[114]

A similar phenomenon had occurred on the home front. Like the soldiers, civilians were crowded together, not on the tented field, but in the ever-growing towns and cities of their shrinking nation. Here, the printed word was far more accessible than in the countryside, and hunger for war news along with concern for their loved ones drove southerners to read. Cultural nationalists hoped that this taste for reading, properly encouraged, would lead to bigger and better things. As Emily Romeo reported for *The Mercury*,

> Those who never glanced at a paper before now eagerly desire to hear all the news connected with the army, and this leads them to become interested in the general affairs of the country, so that bye and bye when the excitement for the latest war news has passed, there will remain or be implanted a love for reading which, not content with a mere summary of events, will go on to full particulars, taking in its progress biographies and [histories], and where imagination and fancy abound, will glance off to poetry, eloquence, fiction and works of a miscellaneous nature.[115]

The experience of war had broadened southerners. In their travels and marches, "They have been brought in contact with men accustomed to other habits and modes of thought. . . . Their mental horizon has been vastly expanded."[116]

While certainly not offsetting the bitter disappointment felt over their failure to achieve intellectual independence during the war, these encouraging signs, coupled with the creation and continued survival of a native periodical press and book publishing industry, gave cultural nationalists reason to hope for the future. Having confronted the ugly truth that they would not witness the birth of a Confederate "literature of power" during the war, and probably not even during their lifetimes, cultural nationalists—crestfallen as they were—turned their attention to future generations and pondered how best to prepare southerners to become a "literary people."

THERE WERE STILL A number of things that southerners could do to pave the way for future Confederate intellectual autonomy even as the war raged, and cultural leaders urged their comrades to remain focused on their goal even as their nation collapsed around them. First and foremost, Confederates needed to safeguard the important gains that had been made. All sensed, and desperately hoped, that the war could not long continue. While cultural nationalists were confident—at least publicly—that the Confederacy would emerge triumphant, they feared that once the blockade was lifted, a flood of "sensational, bizarre, semi-atheistical Northern literature" would overwhelm the native periodicals and publishers to which the war had given life. "We are, it is true, at times afraid of some such relapse among our people," *Southern Field and Fireside* admitted in late January 1865. "For years, perhaps, to come, we will be unable to compete with their literary journals in the elegance of their typography, and the profusion of their illustrations, and it may be that many, seduced by glitter, by novelty, and by the glare may prefer the showy to the solid. Should such be the case, Southern letters must lose that proud vantage ground the war has given it and sink once more into a secondary position, where she will be, as of old, the despised handmaid of a gaudy mistress."[117]

To prevent such a "relapse" and to protect the Confederacy's hopes for intellectual independence, not to mention their own livelihoods, editors and other cultural nationalists called upon the Confederate and state governments to take steps to restrict free trade. More effective still, they hoped that the hatred generated by the war, the now overtly anti-southern tone of the Yankee press, and the inability of northern writers to comprehend or do justice to the Confederate war experience would cause southerners to recoil from northern publications even when available.[118] Confederates had not created a transcendent literature, but they had produced an everyday literature and a cultural infrastructure capable of carrying and distributing a great literature when it arose, and these things needed to be protected. Cultural nationalists continually reminded southern readers that their obligation to support native literature would not end when peace came.

But simply holding the line would not be enough. Separation by itself had not produced the original Confederate literature that cultural nationalists had expected and true independence required. Recognizing this, cultural leaders changed their tactics and adopted new methods to properly prepare the southern population for eventual intellectual independence as the war drew to a close. Confederate writers had been unable to construct a unique national literature, they reasoned, because the Confederate people lacked a common national history from which to draw inspiration and emotional power. As Frank Alfriend explained in May 1864, "Having virtually no history, and *par consequence*, comparatively few of those great landmarks of thought and reflection in the shape of grand events, . . . we shall necessarily find the earlier exhibitions of Southern genius imitative of others rather than creative of a type of our own."[119] Confederates were making that history now, and it was the sacred duty of the present generation to preserve a detailed record of those "grand events" and forge a link between the heroic sacrifices of today and the glorious literature of tomorrow. "Gather them [these southern heroes] up by writings, pictures, or any way, to make up for us our history, our identity, indeed, our *nationality*," *Smith & Barrow's Monthly Magazine* urged. "We must preserve them as we proceed, else we may lose many of them forever. We must dignify our character to the world with all such as these."[120]

In the eyes of cultural nationalists, this collective memory of the war would serve as the basis and inspiration for an original national literature. The experiences and emotions contained within the Confederacy's wartime publications would be transformed into a great literature by future southern authors. As one contributor to *Southern Field and Fireside* predicted, " 'When this cruel war is over,' every hilltop and heath, every river and lagoon, will teem with legends of high devotion and Spartan heroism. Then our necessities will call for some skillful harp to wake the genii of our 'Sleepy Hollows,' and send forth in full strain the record of the glorious dead who have poured out their blood, a free libation for the happiness of unborn millions."[121] In effect anticipating the "Lost Cause" literature of the postwar South, these cultural nationalists called upon all Confederates to help them commemorate, celebrate, and, most importantly, pass on the glorious history to which they had been both witness and participant. "The deeds of our heroes lying dead on the field of glory, need Southern pens to record their fame. Southern flowers to deck their honored corpses," *Southern Field and Fireside* demanded.[122] While not great literature in itself, these wartime writings would bequeath to subsequent generations a glorious legacy from which future writers would create an original Confederate national literature, thus finishing the work started by their fathers and grandfathers and completing the Confederacy's struggle for independence.

WHILE THESE LITERARY "MONUMENTS" would provide future southern authors and poets with the necessary materials to build a national literature, the question of how to improve the quality of native writing remained.[123] The war years had taught cultural nationalists that enthusiasm alone was not enough and that Confederate authors would require extensive training, practice, and discipline before they would be ready to dazzle the world with their words. Thus far, A. W. Dillard lamented, "the formation of our national literature, which is so interwoven with the rank our country is to assume" had been "surrendered almost entirely to the young and immature," writers who had "not studied the subject of style, not composed very much," and whose "diction" was "far more remarkable for ornateness and . . . redundancy than for either correctness or simplicity."[124] Criticism—"fearless and pungent criticism"—could correct some of this, and cultural nationalists continued to maintain that "careful circumspection" was essential to literary advancement. But Confederate thinkers now realized that criticism alone was not enough. What young writers most needed were "literary models of a high order" to study, absorb, and emulate.[125]

But where were they to find these models? The Confederacy had produced no such masterpieces, and antebellum southern literature, laudable as it was, was insufficient for reasons already discussed. Obviously, northern literature was out of the question. In order to produce their own national literature, Confederate authors needed to see what such a literature looked like, how it was composed, and what virtues and emotions it embodied. Of course, a Confederate national literature still had to be original, and, growing out of the unique character and experiences of the Confederate people, undoubtedly it would be; but for models, cultural nationalists admitted reluctantly, they had to look to Europe.

This was a radical turnabout, one that would have been considered heretical and unpatriotic just a year or two earlier, and European literature was still considered potentially dangerous. Fanatical notions and moral pitfalls were known to lurk in its pages, and the selection of proper and safe "models of style . . . will constitute one of the most important and delicate duties of Southern writers and journalists," editor Frank Alfriend advised. Without a great literature of their own, cultural nationalists planned to gradually elevate the tone and expectations of southern literary discourse by feeding the public mind a steady diet of carefully selected and particularly instructive works of European literature. Patience was required. "If we wish the people to read we must make our offerings suitable to their capacity and taste," Alfriend argued pragmatically. "That capacity and taste can be educated and developed, but not suddenly or by violent remedies. . . . The mass of men cannot be transformed in an instant into philosophers and *savans* [sic], and until the dream of Utopia is realized, when all men shall occupy one common footing of blissful equality, some concession must be made to degrees of intellectual advancement." The general population could not subsist on Milton, Chaucer, and Shakespeare alone, and if presented with only the most refined and highbrow literature, would naturally look elsewhere for its entertainment. What was wanted were authors with "the capacity to depict popular subjects in their true traits and colours, so that all classes of society may recognize their fidelity, and yet avoid offence to the refinements of cultivated taste." Along these lines, Alfriend suggested the work of Dickens, Thackeray, and Fielding.[126] Others likewise pointed to Addison, Hume, Gibbon, Macaulay, Scott, Bulwer-Lytton, Thomas Campbell, Thomas Moore, and Robert Hall as useful models that would entertain as well as elevate.[127]

Accordingly, the literary journals, many of which earlier had pledged to carry only original southern literature, now began to print serialized novels and stories by Dickens and Thackeray as well as essays from prominent British periodicals. As an "eclectic" magazine, *The Age* had been expressly created for this purpose, but the other Confederate literary journals also ran foreign items with increasing frequency during 1864 and 1865. Editors had always been eager to learn of recent European intellectual and literary developments, and the occasional inclusion of short foreign pieces was not uncommon. Since its inception, the *Southern Illustrated News* had sporadically presented its readers with "Our Selected Poem" from great European masters, and its drama critic had endeavored to stay abreast of English theater. Now these foreign importations became both longer and more regular. The *Magnolia Weekly*, for instance, assumed a decidedly eclectic character during the final year of the war. Charles Dickens, unknowingly, had become an occasional contributor in 1863, but under the new editorship of Charles Dimitry beginning in March 1864, the *Magnolia* ran Dickens's entire *A Tale of Two Cities* in weekly installments as well as a number of shorter pieces.[128] Dimitry also filled his columns with Thackeray stories including many selections from his *Roundabout Papers*.[129]

In large part, the need for such foreign material stemmed from a dearth of acceptable new southern pieces, for, as *Southern Field and Fireside* admitted, by 1864 "our Southern journalism moves almost entirely in a circle. We have republished each others['] articles and picked up old scraps, here and there, until it is getting to be a tiresome and uninteresting business."[130] But despite appearances, the decision to print foreign authors did not represent a surrendering of the cause, editors assured their readers. The pieces were not selected at random and not just any foreign author or article would do. These essays, stories, and poems were intended to be instructive and to prepare Confederates to create and appreciate a literature of their own. The *Magnolia* made its selections in view of exposing southerners to "the thoughts of the most polished writers in the language," and *Southern Field and Fireside*, somewhat defensively, justified publishing poems by Scott, Campbell, Moore, and "other standard authors" on the grounds that "there are very many of our readers who have been and still are excluded from literature of a high order—the books in which it is found being inaccessible to the common people. . . . We feel assured that in doing this we will be rendering an acceptable service to many of our readers."[131] Though an unpleasant necessity underscoring the failure of southerners to construct an original national literature of their own, the increasing eclecticism of the Confederate literary periodical press was not without purpose and in no way marked a capitulation in the struggle for intellectual independence—so cultural nationalists rationalized.

Confederate book publishers were even more active in injecting European content into their offerings. Between 1863 and 1865, Confederate publishers issued over twenty full-length works by major European authors, including Dickens's *Great Expectations*, George Eliot's *Silas Marner*, Victor Hugo's *Les Misérables*, and Thackeray's *The Adventures of Philip on his Way Through the World*. Confederate presses also republished five novels by popular English writer Mary Elizabeth Braddon.[132] Again, these selections were not without purpose. While demand and marketability were primary considerations for publishers, the merits of the works were also taken into account and lowbrow or otherwise unacceptable books were assiduously avoided.

Given Victor Hugo's known abolitionist sympathies, the publication of *Les Misérables* posed particular challenges for cultural nationalists. In preparing the Confederate edition, the editor excluded "several long . . . rather rambling disquisitions on political and other matters of a purely local character" as well as "a few scattered sentences, reflecting on slavery." He assured Confederates that "the extraneous matter omitted has not the remotest connection with the characters or the incidents of the novel," and that, in any case, "the absence of a few anti-slavery paragraphs will hardly be complained of by Southern readers."[133] Nevertheless, the censoring of *Les Misérables* touched off a minor controversy. One essayist in the *Southern Literary Messenger* found these "literary expurgations" to be "deplorable." While he too condemned Hugo's abolitionism, he warned that such excisions as well as recent denunciations of the novel in the southern press reflected badly on "our vaunted enlightenment" before the eyes of the world.[134] What Confederate readers thought of the censorship of *Les Misérables* is unknown, but, as a humorous story in the *Magnolia Weekly* suggested, they may have had other things on their minds. When an old lady entered West & Johnston's bookstore demanding "that book about Gen. Lee's poor, miserable soldiers faintin," the proprietor was dumbfounded. "You mean *Les Miserables (Fantine)* by Victor Hugo," he realized at last. " 'No I don't.' replied the old lady, 'I know nothing and care nothing about 'Lays Meseererabuls;' I want Lee's Miserables, faintin'." Unable to be convinced, she left the store empty-handed.[135]

In the case of Hugo's novel, most commentators agreed that its literary merits outweighed a few misguided antislavery intrusions, especially once the offending sections had been removed. More generally, cultural nationalists beseeched their publishers to exercise restraint and look to the public good when deciding what foreign books to publish, and they chastised those works and publishers that fell below their standards.[136] The admission that they needed European literature to fill their columns and guide their writers was painful, but, once made, cultural nationalists promised that only carefully selected and approved foreign works would reach the eyes of southern readers.

AS CULTURAL NATIONALISTS RELUCTANTLY abandoned their expectations for immediate intellectual independence and adopted a longer-term trajectory, education, inevitably, became even more central to their plans. If southerners were not yet a "highly civilized people," the responsibility for making them so lay in large part with Confederate educators. Before they would be ready to welcome an exalted national literature, Confederates first needed "an Education simple, earnest, truthful, worthy of the intellect and character of a free and uncorrupted people."[137] "A People's Education is a Nation's Best Defence," read the new motto of the *Southern Literary Companion*, and cultural nationalists came to place much of their hope for the future attainment of intellectual autonomy in educators' ability to properly prepare their people.[138] "Our duties do not all lie in the present," Henry Timrod wrote in May 1864. "We owe much to future generations," an obligation that could only be paid in the form of careful "moral and intellectual instruction."[139] After the war, Reverend J. L. Kirkpatrick agreed, southerners would have to "prove to the world" that the "separate national existence which we have purchased by the sacrifice of thousands of our best citizens on the field of battle, is yet held by us in such estimation that we are ready to make the further sacrifices necessary to preserve it . . . and transmit it unimpaired to our posterity." This, he argued, was and would remain the sacred duty of southern teachers.[140] It was a weighty obligation. "The stability, the prosperity, the moral tone and glory of our infant nation, all depend upon the manner in which you discharge your duties," the leaders of the Educational Association of the Confederate States of America urged their fellow teachers in January 1865. "It is your office to shape the mind and literature of our infant nation."[141]

As faith in the transformative power of education grew during the final year of the war, so too did the realization that Confederate education would have to be improved and expanded dramatically. In order to perform its vital function of preparing southern children for intellectual independence, Confederate education would have to become more rigorous and comprehensive. As with their literature, Confederate cultural nationalists now admitted that deficiencies in southern education stemmed in large part from the state of southern society and not simply from past Yankee dependence. "Being a full-blooded Georgian," William Turner was "permitted to say what would hardly be tolerated in a stranger: . . . that the standard of scholarship among us is very low." Southern education, he confessed, "lacks a great many things . . . above all, *thoroughness*." As a society, southerners had placed too little stock in their children's education and granted too little support to their educational institutions, and, as a result, expectations and standards were far below where they needed to be in order to guide the Confederacy toward true independence. "We aim too low," Turner complained.[142] Such soul-searching critiques were symptomatic of a larger trend guiding the collective thinking of cultural nationalists during the war's last year. The conclusions reached were the same: namely, that as with their literature, efforts at building a native system of education during the war had proved insufficient and that these failures were the result of internal deficiencies, not northern interference. Such inadequacies could be overcome, but it would take far more time and far more work than they had predicted at the beginning of the conflict. Education, in the future, would become the primary means for preparing the Confederate populace for cultural autonomy. Before that could happen, southern education itself would have to be improved, its tone elevated, and its goals and methods clearly mapped out.

For now, however, the bleak realities of 1864–65 meant that any and all improvements would have to wait until the war ended. Educators were less concerned with advancing southerners toward a higher state of civilization than with helping them cling to whatever intellectual culture they had. With teacher shortages, a collapsing economy, and invading Union armies threatening to halt Confederate education altogether, teachers and their supporters in the press rallied to keep their schools open and their hopes for the future alive. "Let retrenchment begin anywhere else than in school expenses," Joseph Turner cried in November 1864. "In coarse raiment, and upon simple food, our children may grow strong and fair, but deprived of the pabulum of the soul, they will be weak, and 'poor indeed.'"[143] Even after the last and most important Confederate educational journal, the *North Carolina Journal of*

Education, faltered in the summer of 1864, educators struggled on in their classrooms and through their organizations, and they urged all southerners to defend their schools to the end.

The recruitment of women as teachers reached a fever pitch during this final year. *"Our females must engage in the work of teacher. I say must*; for there is no other alternative," Reverend Kirkpatrick exhorted the students of Concord Female College.[144] To the many young southern ladies at home thinking " 'O, how I wish I could be a soldier! I'd glory in fighting the hateful Yankees,' " *Southern Field and Fireside* offered a reminder that the classroom was their "glorious battlefield." "Let not duty find you sleeping at your post."[145] While many southern women did come forward, there were never enough teachers to meet the demand, and Confederate education continued to lose valuable ground as a result.

Native textbooks were the one ray of light brightening the otherwise dismal Confederate educational landscape. The production of textbooks did not slacken during the final year of the war. In 1864 and the first four months of 1865, Confederate publishers issued over fifty new schoolbooks or subsequent editions of previously released titles. Remarkably, twenty of these books appeared in 1865, even as the Confederacy was drawing its last breath.[146] The productivity of Confederate textbook writers and publishers during the final year clearly demonstrated the importance placed on the creation of a native educational literature and marked one of the real wartime accomplishments of the cultural nationalists. While models borrowed from European literature had become an unpleasant necessity for guiding Confederate writers, cultural nationalists would not make similar concessions when it came to their schoolbooks. In view of their potential power in shaping future generations of southerners, it remained essential that such books came from southern pens. "Let our scholars prepare grammars, arithmetics, geographies, and all kinds of school books," *Southern Field and Fireside* demanded in March 1864. "Not mere reproductions . . . vamped and altered with a few names to secure Southern patronage. But *original works* in which, indeed, the excellencies of foreign works may be retained, but not their errors and nonsense perpetuated."[147] Firmly believing that a national literature must begin with its textbooks, the spokesmen for the Educational Association of the Confederate States of America warned their countrymen in January 1865, that "the republication of foreign books generally, will but corrupt the minds of our people, undermine the foundations of our nationality, and present us to the world as an ignoble and despicable people."[148] For this reason, textbooks remained a focal point in the campaign for Confederate intellectual independence and cultural nationalists never tired of stressing the vital importance of a native educational literature to the future independence of the southern nation.

The authors and publishers of these schoolbooks cited Confederate nationalism as their primary motivation for continuing to produce new works up until the last possible moment. In offering his *Southern Confederacy Arithmetic* to the public in 1864, Reverend Charles E. Leverett affirmed "that it will be a source of the deepest gratification to him, if, through his humble agency" northern textbooks "should be forever excluded from a Southern school."[149] John Neely's *Confederate States Speller and Reader* (dated 1864, but actually published in 1865) was intended not "merely to fill up a gap for a time, and to be thrown aside when other books of its class can be procured from our former literary emporium [the North]," publisher A. Bleakley told its readers. "It claims at least equality with the very best of these productions; and it is intended to hold its position *permanently* in the face of all such competitors."[150] If, by their own admission, Confederate writers of imaginative literature had failed to meet expectations, the same could not be said for the textbook authors. Encouraged by their accomplishments and the brisk sales that their books enjoyed, textbook authors and publishers defiantly issued new works right up until the bitter end.

"Are we a highly civilized people?" In 1861, Confederate cultural nationalists had had no doubt that they were. The failure of the South to develop its own self-supporting literature and fully assert its cultural identity during the antebellum period, they believed, had been the direct result of stifling northern competition and decades of Yankee cultural dominance. Once the two nations were separated, the unique character of the southern people would manifest itself in a brilliant efflorescence of literary and cultural achievement that would vindicate Confederate nationality, expose northern duplicity, and command international respect. By the final year of the war, however, cultural nationalists were not so sure. Increasing hardships and the generally disappointing quality of Confederate productions up to that point led Confederate nationalists to question whether southerners were indeed ready to embrace their intellectual independence. True, Confederates had created a sizable and diverse print literature, supplanting northern publications and generally meeting their day-to-day news, entertainment, and educational needs. But the essential "literature of power" remained beyond their grasp. A southern renaissance had not come to pass, and cultural leaders saw few indications that one was likely to blossom anytime soon. Frustrated and disillusioned, Confederate cultural nationalists were forced to admit that their earlier expectations for concurrent political and intellectual independence had been unrealistic. Confederates were not yet the "literary people" that they needed to become in order to make the Confederacy a complete and truly independent nation.

But the struggle for Confederate intellectual independence did not end there. If southerners were not yet a highly civilized and literary people, cultural leaders were determined that they would become so, even if it took generations to accomplish. With some notable exceptions, most Confederate periodicals and publishers survived, albeit with difficulty, until their hometowns fell to Union forces, and the ideas of the cultural nationalists continued to circulate in the ever-shrinking Confederacy. Having swallowed the bitter pill of disappointment over their failure to achieve cultural autonomy during the war, Confederate nationalists reconceived their project. Defiant to the end, they continued to fight for their dying nation's intellectual independence until the Union army and bitter defeat abruptly stilled their pens and stopped their presses.

CONCLUSION

INDEPENDENT IN NOTHING— NEUTRAL IN EVERYTHING

The collapse of the Confederacy came hard for cultural nationalists. Having staked their all on the attainment of complete Confederate independence, the shock and subsequent agony of defeat cut very painfully. "We are deeply mortified—chagrined beyond endurance at the failure of our cause— the striking of our colors," Joseph Turner lamented in May 1865. "Exceeding sorrowful, even unto death," Turner reported that "so far as any hope of having a country is concerned, this is the saddest period of our life."[1]

During the final months leading up to Appomattox, Confederate cultural nationalists had attempted to rally southerners behind the flag, dispel the growing despondency, and stave off all talk of defeat and reconstruction. Conceding nothing, publicly at least, Confederate editors continued to declare that victory was around the corner, that God would never forsake the South, and that southerners needed only to resolve to accept nothing less than national independence to make it so. "If our people will but stand firm, and *never* think of yielding, time and the extent of our territory will give us independence, if nothing else will," Turner promised in February 1865.[2] "For four years the gale has howled about us" and "the rolling, plunging, creaking and quivering of our little ship of State have become familiar sounds and scenes to us. But because the storm continues, because the wind becomes a whirlwind, . . . because the blue billows that have swept beneath us with a cradling rock suddenly tower above us mountain high, capped with a furious foam, are we to fold our arms in idiotic despair upon our breasts and let the glorious little craft go down?" No! *Field and Fireside* shouted. "Let the anchor be weighed, let the ship's flag be run to the main top mast, let the boat be trimmed and let every man lash himself to the bulwarks of Defiance." Maintaining this brave front, Confederate nationalists preached unrelenting resistance and resolved "in the name of God and man and in the face of the universe that we will know no peace but freedom and independence and the very earth beneath us will tremble under our steady tread as we move forward to victory or death."[3] Every day brought them closer to independence, they assured their countrymen, for "no nation worthy to enjoy freedom ever lost it."[4]

Confederate nationalists were dismayed by the signs of demoralization everywhere evident throughout the Confederacy during its final months. Already by July 1864, James De Bow sensed that "the springs which moved the revolution have in many cases rusted. The sufferings, the disappointments, the casualties of a protracted war have produced a feeling of depression in many quarters unknown in the earlier days of the struggle."[5] This grumbling did not reflect well on the southern people. Writing in 1865, Edward Pollard complained that "a large portion of our people have fallen below the standards of history, and hold no honourable comparison with other nations that have fought and struggled for independence."[6] Now, at their hour of supreme trial, Confederates must prove themselves worthy of nationhood, and these writers urged "the lukewarm and the listless" to "retouch their blood with a quickening flame" and for "every heart" to "nerve itself to the sternness of a rock."[7]

Fearful of growing peace sentiment, cultural nationalists insisted that reconstruction was impossible. Too much was at stake and too much blood had been spilt to ever allow the South to return to the Union, they argued. Absolute independence or absolute subjugation were the only options. "There is no half-way house," James De Bow declared. "We must succeed in this conflict, or all is lost. *Reconstruction* is but a dream of fools, traitors, or weak-minded men."[8] As one defiant Confederate poet scoffed:

Unite? How will you gather up
  The fragments of our broken laws?
Their hands have filled the bitter cup
  Of hate. The arm of vengeance draws
Its sword with a convulsive start,
To smite submission to the heart.

Re-union? Yes! when you can raise
   Pale thousands from their sleep of death,
When light, from sightless eyes, shall blaze,
   And rotting forms rejoice in breath:
When blood, that flecked a hundred plains,
Shall leap, again, through living veins.

Submit? To wrongs that needs must send
   A shudder through a tyrant's frame?
To deeds of reeking crime that blend
   Their lurid glare, beclouding fame?
Connive at outrage, shame, and guilt?
Ignore the blood that freeman spilt?

No! Heaven! like a thunder shout,
   Burst from each clotted battle plain—
From every wound-mouth gushes out,
   A curse that throbs through every vein
Of timid caitiff, who would frame
That fabric of eternal shame![9]

For these "caitiffs," these "fools, traitors, or weak-minded men" who voiced "the cravenly cry of peace," cultural nationalists had nothing but the bitterest scorn.[10] "Of all the mean, contemptible wretches of earth, surely none are so mean as the reconstructionists," Joseph Turner hissed. "We always think that such men are not good enough for us to even spit upon: for they court the saliva of the yankees, and we do not wish to degrade ourself by expectorating upon the same object that the yankee spits upon." These "southern submissionists" should be banished from the Confederacy forthwith. "Let the decks be cleared, let all dead weight be thrown overboard and if there be among us a man or a boy who will not fight for us, a woman who will not work and pray for us, let them leave us and be quick about it," Southern Field and Fireside demanded.[11] Talk of defeat or reunion was not to be tolerated. Given the choice, Edward Pollard preferred his fellow Virginians "going down to history, proudly and starkly, with the title of a subjugated people—a title not inseparable from true glory, and which has often claimed the admiration of the world—rather than as a people who ever submitted, and bartered their honour for the mercy of an enemy—in our case a mercy whose pittance would be as a mess of pottage weighed against an immortal patrimony!"[12]

WHEN DEFEAT FINALLY CAME, there were very few cultural nationalists left with the means, let alone the heart, to report it. Most of the new journals born with the Confederacy also died with it. The evacuation and subsequent destruction of much of Richmond silenced its literary and religious press. The *Southern Illustrated News* published its last issue on March 25, 1865, and the *Magnolia Weekly* made its final appearance on April 1st. The offices of the *Central Presbyterian*, the *Religious Herald*, the *Southern Churchman*, and the *Richmond Christian Advocate* were all destroyed in a fire on April 3.[13] In March, the Raleigh offices of William B. Smith & Co., publishers of *Southern Field and Fireside* and *The Key-Stone*, were "destroyed by the war."[14] Other major publishing centers like Columbia, South Carolina, were razed to the ground.[15] Defiantly, Confederate editors and publishers continued to issue their journals and books right up until their cities fell, but they could not resist the relentless advance of the Yankees. "The enemy is coming upon us like the 'breaking in of waters,'" the *Richmond Christian Advocate* wrote in desperation. "The dykes are giving way. First we had a crevice here and there—now the whole stream rushes upon us."[16]

It was left to the few surviving southern periodicals to confirm what everyone already knew: that the Confederacy was no more, that it had been "blotted out."[17] With the mails stopped, telegraphs inoperable, and most newspapers suspended, news traveled slowly through the remnants of the Confederacy. It was not until May 2, 1865, that *The Countryman* reported the sad news of General Lee's surrender at Appomattox. "The land is overspread with mourning and gloom," Turner cried. "The great heart of the nation has been paralyzed."[18] In the following week came reports that General Johnston had surrendered to Sherman and that "we are an overpowered, and, *for the present*, a conquered people."[19] "What is to be the fate of our beloved and unfortunate country we cannot, of course, tell," the *Church Intelligencer* wrote on April 20th. "We trust the faithful may be faithful still; and in this day of their calamity show the fortitude and patience which the religion of Christ through His Word and the Church so fully teaches."[20] Joseph Turner had no such comfort to offer his readers as he had rested his faith on the future of the Confederate nation. "No one can accuse us of want of fidelity to the confederate flag," he declared on May 16. "The only fault chargeable against us is, that we have been too zealous in its support. Would God that its folds were now our winding sheet upon some honored battle-field, and that our wife and our little ones slept by our side, covered by the same noble shroud."[21]

The collapse of the Confederacy brought an end to the struggle for intellectual independence. Political and intellectual independence could not exist without each other, and there could be no national literature without a nation. In June 1865, Joseph Turner abandoned the wartime motto of *The Countryman*: "Independent in Everything—Neutral in Nothing." It was "a living lie flying at our mast-head. Therefore we strike our old colors, and run up new ones more congenial to the times." The new motto, "Independent in Nothing—Neutral in Everything," marked the end and served as a fitting epitaph for the Confederate struggle for intellectual independence.[22]

That it failed does not mean that this wartime campaign for southern cultural autonomy was without significance. The goals, accomplishments, and disappointments of Confederate cultural nationalists reveal much about southern cultural development, life within the Confederacy, and the creation, substance, and shortcomings of Confederate nationalism. What is more, the manner in which it failed raises important questions about southern cultural distinctiveness that these nationalists would never have dared to ask.

Contrary to what has been generally assumed, material hardships and shortages did not stop Confederate presses or southern cultural life during the war. Only northern occupation and actual physical destruction had the power to compel these nationalists to halt their activities. While they did not succeed in achieving Confederate intellectual independence, their accomplishments were impressive nonetheless. In short order, Confederates had created a diverse native literature, supplanting northern publications and fulfilling many of the informational, educational, and entertainment needs of their people. The production of new wartime periodicals, books, and textbooks accelerated at an astonishing rate. Not content with their progress, cultural nationalists urged their writers and thinkers to reach for even greater heights and to create a transcendent literature that would exemplify southern character and vindicate Confederate nationality. As they fought to free the South from northern dominance and erect a uniquely Confederate national culture, these southerners promoted a grand vision of the Confederate nation, not as it was, but as it was supposed to be.

A close examination of the struggle for intellectual independence contributes to our understanding of southern cultural history, the Confederacy, and nineteenth-century nationalism in a number of important ways. For one, it shows that the impulse driving antebellum southern cultural nationalism did not diminish with secession. Separation and wartime isolation provided the "golden opportunity" for Confederates to escape northern dominance and create a print culture of their own. As such, secession marked a turning point, not an end point, and it sparked a dramatic expansion of southern literary production during the war. The cultural life of the Confederacy was not as moribund as has often been assumed. The coming of the war transformed southern cultural nationalists from a disparate band of disgruntled and continually disappointed editors, writers, and educators into a cohesive movement dedicated to achieving Confederate intellectual independence. By virtue of the captive market imposed by the war, they commanded public attention as never before.

The perceived necessity of intellectual independence reveals a great deal about Confederate nationalism as understood by Confederates themselves. During the war, southerners evinced a far more complex and nuanced understanding of the meaning and requirements of nationhood than many historians have subsequently acknowledged. This was a consciously and explicitly nationalistic movement. All of its various facets were recognized and celebrated as part of a broad campaign for national cultural autonomy that contributed directly to the larger war effort. Political freedom won on the battlefield would be meaningless, it was argued, without cultural independence. Southern nationalists conceded that the Confederacy was an incomplete nation at the start of the war. It lacked the necessary cultural and intellectual components to legitimate its nationality. Through the creation of their own unique literature and culture, Confederates would prove their distinctiveness as people along with their indisputable right to a separate national existence.

The Confederate experience presents a fascinating and tightly encapsulated case study of nineteenth-century cultural nation building. Following guidelines derived, if not directly absorbed, from European romantic nationalism, Confederates attempted to construct the cultural framework necessary to support their nationality, and in so doing revealed what they thought defined a nation. That the arguments and ideas of Confederate cultural nationalists did not approach the sophistication of their European counterparts is not surprising. The distractions of a devastating war necessarily precluded deep theoretical contemplation and innovation. By and large, Confederate cultural nationalists were not profound thinkers, nor did they claim to be. They were the facilitators of culture dedicated to fostering an intellectual environment and constructing a cultural infrastructure that would allow great southern thinkers to emerge, and then sustain them. Confident that the Confederacy possessed the necessary raw materials and mental talent, the nationalists endeavored to culturally elevate their people and to provide opportunities for the true poets and artists of the South to come to the fore and be heard.

But unlike cultural nationalist movements in Germany, France, England, or Italy, or indeed even the literary Young Americans of a few decades earlier, Confederates at the start of the war lacked the necessary apparatus and distribution networks to physically produce print literature on a large scale, let alone create an original and distinctive national literature. Thus, after freeing themselves from northern competition, Confederates still had two significant hurdles to cross. The first was creating and sustaining the every-day print literature that all self-supporting modern societies required: its newspapers, periodicals, textbooks, light fiction and poetry, religious litera-ture, history, drama, humor—in short its "literature of knowledge." It was this literature that southerners had looked to the North to provide in the past, the southern production of which would represent a major step toward intel-lectual independence. The second hurdle would be the creation of a "litera-ture of power," that higher literature of great originality and recognizable merit that would embody southern character and showcase its virtues for the world.

Confederates cleared the first hurdle with remarkable speed and dexterity, and despite the tremendous obstacles, managed to create a Confederate print literature surpassing in diversity and circulation anything before seen in the South. It was on the second hurdle that the movement for Confederate intel-lectual independence stumbled and ultimately fell. Frankly recognizing that the quality of their wartime literature was not sufficient or original enough to pass muster, Confederate cultural nationalists continually adapted their proj-ect and, toward the end, conceded that further preparation was required before southerners would be ready to produce and appreciate their true na-tional literature. Through it all, cultural nationalists sustained their staunch dedication to the cause of Confederate intellectual independence, and while their means and timeframes were flexible, their ultimate objective always remained the same.

While not great thinkers themselves, Confederate cultural nationalists did have influence, or at least readership. It was they, and they alone, who con-trolled the means of literary production and wrote what the rest of the Con-federacy read. Nearly every page of Confederate print literature was stamped with cultural nationalist sentiment. Indeed, the continued existence of a na-tive publishing industry was in itself a declaration of independence against northern dominance. That Confederate literature was a "hot-house litera-ture" is undeniable, but it was also a purposeful literature whose artificially accelerated growth was directed, carefully monitored, and pruned when nec-essary. Confederate writers produced little of lasting literary value, it is true, but this does not mean that Confederate literature lacks historical value, and the fact that southerners themselves recognized their own inadequacies is very significant.

Northern armies may have stopped Confederate presses but they were not the reason why the struggle for intellectual independence failed. Despite their repeated and forceful assertions of southern cultural distinctiveness, Confederate nationalists could not demonstrate it, even to their own satisfaction. According to their understanding of nationalism, a nation was defined by its people's character, and that character was expressed through its unique literature and culture. That southerners were unable to produce this unique culture necessarily cast doubt on the legitimacy of the Confederate nation. This is not to say that we today must accept this definition of nationalism or that this is the test that we should apply to Confederate nationalism, but it is the test that these Confederates applied. By their own criteria, they failed. The perception and reality of southern distinctiveness remain extremely contentious and hotly debated questions that surely cannot be answered based on such a short window of time during such extraordinary events.[23] However, it is notable that in this, the most forceful, conscious, and desperate attempt that southerners would ever mount to prove the distinctiveness of their culture, they failed.

This in no way suggests that Confederate nationalism did not exist. It most certainly did, and this entire book is a testament to that fact. It was nationalism that drove Confederates to try to create a native literature and to establish their own system of education amidst the fires of war. What their failure shows, however, is that these nationalists could not demonstrate the fundamental and unmistakable differences between northern and southern cultures that they believed their nationality required. In truth, for all their grand hopes and nearly limitless ambitions, their own vision of this great Confederate national culture remained amorphous and incomplete. They continued to rely largely on negative criteria, defining southern culture by what it was not. They knew that it must be different from that of the North; but what these cultural differences were, how they should manifest themselves, or what this great Confederate literature might look like, they could never quite articulate. More time and preparation were needed before this Confederate national culture could arise, they came to argue by the end of the war—and perhaps so—but their own wartime efforts and criticisms revealed that a southern renaissance had not been waiting to instantly emerge once the weight of northern dominance was lifted. Contrary to A. B. Stark's 1861 confident prediction, the Confederacy could not simply "spring into existence . . .

full panoplied, intellectually, religiously, morally, politically, and materially, a nation full-grown."[24] That Confederate nationalists thought it could seems hopelessly quixotic. Given the extent of their past dependence on the North, the Confederacy's short life, and the crippling obstacles they faced, it is not surprising that Confederates failed to win their intellectual independence. That they tried to achieve Confederate cultural autonomy, the ways in which they tried, and especially the reasons why they felt compelled to try, however, are as significant as their ultimate failure.

Confederate defeat may have forever crushed hopes of achieving southern intellectual independence, but the desire for a native literature and a distinctive southern culture remained. Southern nationalist spirit did not dissolve as quickly as did the Confederate armies, and while this study is concerned specifically with the war years, it is important to ask what happened to these sentiments in the wake of the Confederacy's destruction.

The years immediately following the war witnessed a resurgence of southern periodical production. The war had killed most of the Confederate journals, but a few, like *The Countryman* and the *Southern Cultivator*, managed to survive. Others, like *Field and Fireside*, *De Bow's Review*, and many of the religious weeklies, later resumed.[25] Having contemplated suspending *The Countryman* entirely in the wake of defeat, Joseph Turner soon resolved to renew publication with "vigor," arguing that though conquered, "our people [still] must have something to read that they can relish." "We survive our flag—we have outlived our country—and new duties devolve upon us, under our new relations."[26] The South still needed a native literature, and many of those who had labored for Confederate intellectual independence were still determined to provide it. When *Field and Fireside* resumed in mid-December 1865, the left side of its new header carried an engraving of a devastated South with the word "Resurgemus" underneath and William Smith pledged to continue to devote his efforts to the creation of "a pure and dignified [southern] literature."[27]

Joining these Confederate survivors was a crop of new periodicals that emerged during the early days of Reconstruction and jostled for southern patronage. Like their wartime and antebellum forebearers, new literary and quasi-literary journals like *Scott's Monthly Magazine*, the *Crescent Monthly*, *The Land We Love*, *Southern Opinion*, *The Banner of the South*, *Southern Review*, *Southern Home Journal*, *Home Monthly*, the *Richmond Eclectic* and its subsequent reincarnations, the *New Eclectic* and *Southern Magazine*, condemned northern publications, argued for the necessity of a uniquely southern litera-ture, and demanded vociferously that the southern people support them in their efforts.[28] In tone, format, and language, there was a strong continuity between these journals and those of the past. Nor were these similarities restricted to the periodical press. Certainly the preface to R. H. Crozier's 1866 novel *The Confederate Spy* struck a very familiar chord. He submitted the book "to the judgment of the patriotic southern public, with the hope that it may help to supplant the poisonous northern literature which has for so many years flooded the South, and vilified the southern people and their institutions. The time has now come when there ought to be change. The South must have a literature of her own."[29]

Now that military resistance was impossible—though Joseph Turner was quick to remind "our conquerors that if we could see any chance under heaven to further resist them successfully, we would certainly avail ourself of all the means in our power to do so"—southern editors, writers, and pub-lishers vowed to continue the cultural struggle "*in* the Union, since we cannot labor out of it."[30] Literary endeavors were one of the few arenas of action still open to white southerners in the wake of defeat. "Overthrown in our efforts to establish a political nationality by *force of arms*, we may yet establish an intellectual dynasty more glorious and permanent by *force of thought*," poet Paul Hamilton Hayne urged in *Scott's Monthly* in September 1866.[31] "All that is left the South is 'the war of ideas,'" Edward Pollard agreed, but "in such a war there are noble victories to be won, memorable services to be performed, and grand results to be achieved."[32]

Historians of the postwar South describe two distinct stages in the devel-opment of the myth and ideology of what is known as the Lost Cause. The first, commencing immediately after hostilities had ended and largely or-chestrated by the "diehards," as David Blight calls them, was a defiant cham-pioning of the Confederate cause that asserted southern moral, cultural, and martial superiority in order to reassure a defeated and disheartened white southern audience.[33] Thomas Connelly and Barbara Bellows have labeled this bitter and sectional reaction to defeat as the "Inner Lost Cause" and certainly Pollard's advocacy of a continuing "war of ideas" fits the bill.[34] "It would be immeasurably the worst consequence of defeat in this war that the South should lose its moral and intellectual distinctiveness as a people," he warned in 1866 in the book that popularized the term "Lost Cause." Con-quered as they were, Pollard worried that southerners would further suffer "the extinction of their literature, the decay of mind, and the loss of their distinctive forms of thought," and he urged them to resist. "It is not untimely or unreasonable to tell the South to cultivate her superiourity as a people; to maintain her old schools of literature and scholarship; to assert, in the forms of her thought, and in the style of her manners, her peculiar civilization, and to convince the North that, instead of subjugating an inferiour country, she has obtained the alliance of a noble and cultivated people." The South, as a distinctive cultural entity, must be preserved through a regional literature celebrating its past, its virtues, and its philosophy. "There may not be a political South," he conceded with regret, "Yet there may [still] be a social and intellectual South."[35] It was to the preservation of this "intellectual South" that Pollard and other former Confederate cultural nationalists devoted their efforts in the wake of defeat.

Historian Anne Sarah Rubin has argued that the activities of southern writers like Pollard and the editors of these postwar southern periodicals should be viewed within the context of a Confederate nationalism that had outlived its nation. Rather than the first manifestation of Lost Cause nostalgia, she maintains that such sentiments represented a continuing sense of difference and defiance that can best be understood as an extension of Confederate history into the postwar era.[36] Certainly there is much to recommend this view, and the arguments of these postwar writers bear a striking resemblance to those of Confederate cultural nationalists while their nation still lived.

But whether seen as the first phase of the Lost Cause or the final chapter of the war, there is no disputing the fact that such efforts were short-lived. This initial burst of southern literary activity dedicated to continuing the struggle through other means proved unsustainable. Without the possibility of a nation of their own, the old nationalist spirit was impossible to maintain, and southern periodicals quickly succumbed. Despite surviving the war, *The Countryman* did not last long after it. Joseph Turner's defiant statements quickly attracted the attention of local Union military authorities. He was arrested and briefly detained in June 1865, and *The Countryman* was suspended for six months.[37] The paper would resume, but it was clear that Turner's heart was no longer in it. In May 1866, he shut the paper down for good. *Field and Fireside* issued its last number in 1867. Many of the new southern journals had even shorter life spans than their Confederate predecessors, and only a few survived into the 1870s.

Postwar sectional publications and periodicals ran up against the age-old enemy of southern literature: apathy. Facing a renewed flood of northern literature, impoverished southern publishers were even less able to compete than before the war, and appeals to regional pride seemingly had little effect in convincing southern readers to shun northern products. What was more, starting in the 1870s, northern publishers began to welcome southern writers with open and remunerative arms. With the Confederacy defeated, slavery abolished, and the Old South destroyed, northerners were now eager to read about this world that had been lost. The major national magazines of the day, including *Scribner's Monthly*, its successor *Century Magazine*, *Lippincott's Magazine*, *Harper's Monthly*, *Cosmopolitan*, *McClure's*, and even the arch-Yankee *Atlantic Monthly*, ironically became the primary disseminators and financial supporters of southern literature.[38] As southern writers flocked to northern journals, warnings about the dangers and foreignness of the national press lost much of their relevancy and southern readers could now buy the latest northern publications guilt-free. As literary historian Jay Hubbell observed, "When the younger Southern writers discovered that they could write acceptably for *Lippincott's Magazine* and *Scribner's Monthly* without doing violence to their convictions—and be well paid for what they wrote—the day of the Southern sectional magazine was drawing to a close."[39]

This trend was even more pronounced when it came to books. The southern book industry never recovered after the war, and southern authors had little choice but to seek northern publishers. During the decade following Confederate defeat, there were a few northern publishers willing to produce southern books for southern audiences, but by the late 1870s, and especially the 1880s and 1890s, it was discovered that southern literature could be profitably marketed to northern readers, and the doors of the national book publishing industry opened wide before southern authors. As northern periodical and book publishers became increasingly receptive to southern writers, demands for an insular native southern literature—one written, published, and read exclusively in the South—lost much of their force.

Even so staunch a Confederate nationalist as Edward Pollard would change his tune in the years following the Confederacy's demise. The leading spokesman for continued defiance and southern separatism, Pollard's nationalism had survived the war seemingly unscathed, and if anything had intensified in the wake of defeat. But, as historian Jack Maddex has shown, by 1868, Pollard's thinking would shift radically. With slavery destroyed and hopes of a separate southern nation forever crushed, Pollard converted to unionism in order to help shape the future of the South and maintain the white racial order. He ceased to argue that northerners and southerners were two distinct and incompatible peoples and instead urged white southerners to unite with northern conservatives in order to defeat radical Republicans and facilitate reconciliation on southern terms. In his writings, he recast the history of the

Confederacy and the causes of the war so as to remake the struggle into one between radicals and conservatives, Republicans and Democrats, rather than between fanatical Yankees and proslavery Confederate nationalists as he had maintained previously. As Maddex observed, Pollard's opposition to Reconstruction "became that of a conservative within the context of Unionist politics instead of a Southern nationalist outside that context."[40]

Pollard, through his conversion, helped to usher in the reconciliationist phase of the Lost Cause that would come to dominate southern cultural life for the last quarter of the nineteenth century and beyond—what Connelly and Bellows have called the "National Lost Cause."[41] While the irreconcilables remained irreconcilable and various manifestations of the bitter "Inner Lost Cause" would continue to surface until the turn of the century, these diehards were soon superseded by other southerners more interested in winning the peace than refighting the war. Whereas the earlier, defiant literature was intended solely for domestic southern consumption, this new literature was distributed through the national press and directed primarily at a non-southern audience. Feeding their readers a steady diet of magnolias and moonlight, chivalrous southern gentlemen, refined southern belles, and, of course, loyal and contented slaves, the romancers of the Old South constructed a usable past around which northern and southern whites could unite. In this retelling, Confederates had fought gallantly for a noble cause and had lost through no fault of their own. The men and women who wrote and celebrated this glorious past were no less devoted to the South and the preservation of southern memory than were the diehards. But rather than preaching unrelenting defiance, they offered white northerners a path to reunion. The toll would be accepting and honoring this southern version of events, a price that by the late nineteenth century northern whites proved more than willing to pay.[42]

Through it all, echoes of the struggle for Confederate intellectual independence could be distinctly heard. Certainly much of the writing and rhetoric of the immediate postwar years borrowed directly from the cultural nationalists. But even in its later stages, the literature and ideology of the Lost Cause retained elements from that earlier movement. There was still much talk about the need for a distinctive southern literature, even if the reasons for it had changed. Southern culture and history needed to be perpetuated and protected, a task that only truehearted southern writers could perform. The war years had encouraged an increasing number of southerners to write for publication and that trend would continue and accelerate during the postwar era. Southern women writers, in particular, were emboldened to come forward, a development that historian Jane Turner Censer attributes directly to the experience and inspiring examples of Confederate women writing during the war.[43] Southern men, and especially women, also now joined the ranks of teachers in unprecedented numbers, albeit for reasons having much more to do with economic necessity than regional pride. As a result, the teaching profession in the South became southernized at last.[44] The various Confederate commemorative organizations and especially the United Daughters of the Confederacy, after its founding in 1894, opened additional avenues for women into the public sphere.[45] Indeed, southern women would be the primary keepers and guardians of the Lost Cause.

Although, by the 1880s, southern writers appeared regularly in northern periodicals and publishers' book lists, the old suspicion of northern writing and northern intentions remained among southerners, especially when it came to writing about the recent past—namely, the war. As always, such concerns were particularly acute when it came to children's literature and schoolbooks. The rhetoric of the textbook crusades launched by the UDC and veterans groups to protect southern children from the "long-legged Yankee lies" embedded within northern history texts could have been written forty years earlier with a few key word substitutions, as could demands that southern schoolbooks come only from native southern pens.[46]

In fact, some Confederate literature returned verbatim. Starting after the war and continuing well into the twentieth century, a string of Confederate poetry anthologies was presented to the American public. One of the first of these compilations would come from no less an eminent literary figure than William Gilmore Simms who, having lapsed into relative silence during the war, reemerged in 1867 to pass judgment on those who had not. He introduced his 480-page *War Poetry of the South* as a "valuable" illustration of "the degree of mental and art development which has been made, in a large section of the country, under circumstances greatly calculated to stimulate talent and provoke expression, through the higher utterances of passion and imagination." These poems and songs were "essential to the reputation of the Southern people, as illustrating their feelings, sentiments, ideas, and opinions—the motives which influenced their actions, and the objects which they had in contemplation, and which seemed to them to justify the struggle in which they were engaged." Such was the underlying emotion and historical significance of this literature, Simms argued, that readers (and future historians) must "forgive the muse who, in her fervor, is sometimes forgetful of her art." Above all, this wartime literature testified to southerners' determination and "ability in creating their own resources, under all reverses, and amidst every form of privation."[47]

The other postwar southern compilers of Confederate poetry expressed similar motivations, though they were far less willing than Simms to concede any literary deficiencies. Emily Mason's equally lengthy collection, *The Southern Poems of the War*, preserved the "hopes and triumphs and sorrows of a 'lost cause,'" and its proceeds were used "*to aid . . . the Education of the Daughters of our desolate land*" so that they could become southern teachers.[48] In 1939, Mary Flournoy, the "Historian-General" of the United Daughters of the Confederacy, declared that "there is something in this war poetry of the South that transcends all argument, and if it could really be known . . . the problem of bringing the World to understand the attitude of the South in 1861 would largely be solved. Such high and noble devotion as these poems exhibit is not given to unworthy causes."[49] Thus, Confederate literature would have a second life. Unable to achieve intellectual independence during the war, the literary efforts of the cultural nationalists would become the cherished keepsakes of the Lost Cause.

While it would be tempting to see postwar southern literary activity and especially the literature of the Lost Cause as a continuation of the Confederate struggle for cultural autonomy, such a view would be misleading. The campaign for Confederate intellectual independence may have shaped the rhetoric and inspired the activities of some postwar southerners, but the motivations and goals of Confederate cultural nationalists were fundamentally different from those who came after them. In part, it was a difference of trajectory. Whereas Confederate cultural nationalists had looked hopefully to the future, postwar southern writers looked regretfully back to the past. Confederate cultural nationalists had been dedicated to the creation of something new. The guardians of the Lost Cause were committed to the preservation of something old. Whereas the purpose of the campaign for intellectual independence had been to create a self-sufficient national literature that would explore the fullness of southern distinctiveness, the purpose of the Lost Cause was to perpetuate a backwards-looking regional literature that would cling to the distinctiveness of an imagined past.

The destruction of the Confederate nation had changed everything. Even in the days immediately following defeat, when wounds were rawest and rhetoric most bitter, when Pollard and others called for never-ending defiance, an unmistakable shift had taken place. The language and tone were similar to those of the cultural nationalists during the war, but the purpose was different. As R. H. Crozier revealed in his preface to *The Confederate Spy* dated May 27, 1865, the rationale for a native southern literature had changed instantly in the wake of Appomattox.

> Soon thousands of tales will come forth from the vile den of New England, containing scandalous caricatures of our beloved South, and of the misfortunes of our late Confederacy. Do not buy them, southern reader! Do not insult the memory of your noble dead by enriching northern writers, who make sport of their bloody graves! If you must read novels, we ask you, for the sake of your dead heroes, to read those which do not abuse and vilify your ancestors, yourselves, your institutions, your religion—all that you hold dear and sacred![50]

With the destruction of the Confederacy, white southern eyes had been turned 180 degrees. An 1872 editorial in the *Southern Review* captured this altered trajectory perfectly: "While the storm-cloud darkens the political heavens, we may turn to the past for consolation, for agreeable and heroic reminiscences. If we are mortified with the changes that have come over the face of American society; if we despair of reform, when the flood-tide of corruption is sweeping over the land with a continually accumulating force; if the present terrifies and alarms us with its prognostications and omens of worse times to come, we may still turn with pride and pleasure to the past."[51]

Thus, despite some clear carryovers, the Lost Cause was not a perpetuation of Confederate cultural nationalism. In the postwar years, southern intellectual self-sufficiency was no longer a possibility. What was more, the optimism and the quixotic hopes of the cultural nationalists were gone. They had believed that the Confederate war experience would be the basis for a collective southern culture, but they had hoped that it would lead to the creation of something new, something original. In the wake of defeat, such forward-looking optimism was abandoned, and the Lost Cause, in its exclusive obsession with a rigidly defined past, effectively stifled creativity rather than facilitated it.

The Confederate experience was unique. Never before and never again would southerners embark on such an intense and united effort to construct their own distinctive culture, nor would they ever again have the opportunity to produce a native print literature, free from outside competition and influence. While antebellum writers anticipated, and postwar southerners echoed, Confederate cultural nationalists, the nationalists' wartime labors and ambitions exceeded everything attempted, before or since. Not content with promoting intellectual parity or regional identity, the cultural nationalists had demanded nothing less than complete intellectual independence and the cultural legitimatization of a separate southern nation. Driven by the perceived demands of nationhood, their campaign for intellectual independence could not survive Confederate defeat.

At the point when the South became a conquered region within the United States rather than an independent nation outside of it, Confederate literature was reabsorbed back into American culture as a sort of literary spoils of war. This was certainly how William Gilmore Simms presented his volume of Confederate poetry to the American public: "Though sectional in its character, and indicative of a temper and a feeling which were in conflict with [American] nationality, yet, now that the States of the Union have been resolved into one nation, this collection is essentially as much the property of the whole as are the captured cannon which were employed against it during the progress of the late war."[52] It was a telling comparison.

IT IS IMPORTANT TO note that in the twentieth century the South would experience the literary renaissance that Confederate cultural nationalists had tried to manufacture, and Faulkner, Tate, Wolfe, Wright, Warren, Welty, Williams, O'Connor, Lee, Morrison, and others would create what could be considered a southern "literature of power," although now without its nationalistic implications. When this literature did arise, it did not come from the benign influences of white southern slave society, as Confederate cultural nationalists had expected, but rather from the ordeals of defeat, reconstruction, continuing racial tension, and collective guilt over slavery. It also came as a conscious reaction against the mental shackles of the Lost Cause. Confederate cultural nationalists would have been further shocked to find that much of this new southern literature flowed from the pens of the children and grandchildren of slaves.

NOTES

ABBREVIATIONS

CSMSJ   Confederate States Medical and Surgical Journal
CTM   The Countryman
DBR   De Bow's Review
DSC   Daily South Carolinian
ERFM   Educational Repository and Family Monthly
GCHJ   Gulf City Home Journal
MW   Magnolia Weekly
NCJE   North Carolina Journal of Education
NCP   North Carolina Presbyterian
Punch   Southern Punch
QRMECS   Quarterly Review of the Methodist Episcopal Church, South
RCA   Richmond Christian Advocate
SC   Southern Cultivator
SCA   Southern Christian Advocate
SFF   Southern Field and Fireside
SIN   Southern Illustrated News
SLM   Southern Literary Messenger
SM   Southern Monthly
SP   Southern Presbyterian
WC   Weekly Constitutionalist

1. The most influential works on nationalism remain Anderson, *Imagined Communities*; Gellner, *Nations and Nationalism*; Hobsbawm and Ranger, eds., *The Invention of Tradition*; Hobsbawm, *Nations and Nationalism since 1780*; and Geertz's essays in *The Interpretation of Cultures*: "Ideology as a Cultural System," and "After the Revolution: The Fate of Nationalism in the New States." See also Hobsbawm, "Some Reflections on Nationalism," in *Imagination and Precision in the Social Sciences*; Smith, *National Identity*; Smith, *Nationalism: Theory, Ideology, History*; Kohn, *The Idea of Nationalism*; Minogue, *Nationalism*; Hayes, *Essays on Nationalism*.

2. For comparative perspectives, see Doyle, *Nations Divided*; Doyle and Pamplona, eds., *Nationalism in the New World*; McPherson, *Is Blood Thicker than Water?* For the development, substance, and peculiarities of American nationalism generally, see Waldstreicher, *In the Midst of Perpetual Fetes*; Nagel, *This Sacred Trust*; Nagel, *One Nation Indivisible*; Parish, *The North and the Nation*; Parish, "An Exception to Most of the Rules"; Carp, "Nations of American Rebels"; Lepore, *A is for American*; Kohn, *American Nationalism*; Curti, *The Roots of American Loyalty*; Arieli, *Individualism and Nationalism in American Ideology*.

3. See Grant, *North over South*; Grant, " 'The Charter of Its Birthright' "; Lawson, *Patriot Fires*; Parish, *The North and the Nation*; Parish, "Abraham Lincoln and American Nationhood"; Blum, *Reforging the White Republic*.

4. Faust, *The Creation of Confederate Nationalism*; Potter, "The Historian's Use of Nationalism and Vice Versa."

5. Gallagher, *The Confederate War*; Bonner, *Mastering America*; Bonner, *Colors and Blood*; Bonner, "Roundheaded Cavaliers"; Bonner, "Flag Culture and the Consolidation of Confederate Nationalism"; Bonner, "Americans Apart"; Rubin, *A Shattered Nation*; Rubin, "Seventy-six and Sixty-one." See also Binnington, " 'They Have Made a Nation' "; Quigley, "Patchwork Nation."

6. For the continuing debate about the meaning, strengths, and failures of Confederate nationalism (in addition to the aforementioned works), see Stampp, "The Southern Road to Appomattox"; Escott, *After Secession*; Escott, "The Failure of Confederate Nationalism"; Channing, "Slavery and Confederate Nationalism"; Powell and Wayne, "Self-Interest and the Decline of Confederate Nationalism"; Beringer et al., *Why the South Lost the Civil War*; Kerby, "Why the Confederacy Lost"; Silver, *Confederate Morale and Church Propaganda*; Thomas, *The Confederate Nation*; Degler, *One Among Many*; Rable, *The Confederate Republic*; Davis, *Look Away!*.

Important recent contributions include Blair, *Virginia's Private War*; Robinson, *Bitter Fruits of Bondage*; Carmichael, *The Last Generation*; Campbell, *When Sherman Marched North From the Sea*; Sheehan-Dean, *Why Confederates Fought*; Gordon and Inscoe, eds., *Inside the Confederate Nation*; Walther, "Fire-eaters and the Riddle of Southern Nationalism."

7. Harwell, *Confederate Belles-Lettres*, 11.

8. Parrish and Willingham, *Confederate Imprints*.

9. The best account of antebellum southern cultural nationalism remains McCardell, *The Idea of a Southern Nation*. See also Craven, *The Growth of Southern Nationalism*; Hubbell, "Literary Nationalism in the Old South"; Ezell, "A Southern Education for Southrons"; Whitescarver, "School Books, Publishers, and Southern Nationalists."

10. Adams, *The Education of Henry Adams*, 57–58; O'Brien, *Conjectures of Order*; Fox-Genovese and Genovese, *The Mind of the Master Class*. See also Tate, *Conservatism and Southern Intellectuals*; Young, *Domesticating Slavery*. For a discussion of northern and southern cultural interconnectedness from a class perspective, see Wells, *The Origins of the Southern Middle Class*. For more on antebellum southern intellectual life, see O'Brien, *Rethinking the South*; O'Brien, ed., *All Clever Men, Who Make Their Way*; O'Brien, *A Character of Hugh Legaré*; O'Brien and Moltke-Hansen, *Intellectual Life in Antebellum Charleston*; Faust, *A Sacred Circle*; Cash, *The Mind of the South*; Doherty, "The Mind of the Antebellum South"; Eaton, *The Mind of the Old South*; Eaton, *Freedom of Thought in the Old South*; Hubbell, *The South in American Literature*; Osterweis, *Romanticism and Nationalism in the Old South*; Parrington, *The Romantic Revolution in America*; Simpson, *The Man of Letters in New England and the South*; Simpson, *Mind and the American Civil War*; Wyatt-Brown, *Hearts of Darkness*.

11. For the most influential articulation of this earlier view, see Cash, *The Mind of the South*.

12. Faust, *A Sacred Circle*.

13. Henry Timrod, "Literature in the South," *Russell's Magazine* 5 (August 1859), 385–95.

14. Reprinted as "Southern Enterprise—Southern Literature," *WC*, November 6, 1861, 8.

15. While there have been a few scholarly works dedicated to Confederate music, this important subject awaits a thorough and systematic study. See Harwell, *Confederate Music*; Abel, *Singing the New Nation*; Hoogerwerf, *Confederate Sheet-Music Imprints*; Rudolph, *Confederate Broadside Verse*.

CHAPTER 1

1. Smythe, *Our Own Primary Grammar for the Use of Beginners*, iii.

2. [William Falconer], "The True Question: A Contest for the Supremacy of Race, as between the SAXON PURITAN of the NORTH, and the NORMAN of the SOUTH," *SLM* 33 (July 1861): 21. Falconer is identified as the author by Bonner, "Roundheaded Cavaliers," 40–41.

3. Wiley et al., *Address to the People of North Carolina*, 10.

4. "Literary Independence," *SFF*, May 11, 1861, 404.

5. Reprinted as "A New Development of Southern Literature," *SLM* 33 (October 1861): 317.

6. Calvin H. Wiley, *"To the Boards of County Superintendents of Common Schools for the Several Counties of the State,"* *NCJE* 4 (November 1861): 346.

7. George W. Bagby, "Editor's Table," *SLM* 33 (December 1861): 467.

8. *Providential Aspect and Salutary Tendency of the Existing Crisis*, 24.

9. George W. Bagby, "Editor's Table," *SLM* 32 (April 1861): 322.

10. H. [Charles Wallace Howard], "The Future of the Confederate States," *SC* 19 (May 1861): 137.

11. I. N. Davis Sr., "An Appeal to Southern Men and Women," *Southern Literary Companion*, January 23, 1861, 2.

12. Wiley et al., *Address to the People of North Carolina*, 13.

13. "Now is the Time," *SC* 19 (November 1861): 291. It should be noted that the author here is speaking more generally about the need for Confederate manufacturing as well as intellectual self-sufficiency.

14. Wiley et al., *Address to the People of North Carolina*, 2.

15. A. B. Stark, "Southern Literature," *Home Circle* 7 (September 1861): 513.

16. Reprinted in "Literature in the South," *SFF*, Supplement to the Southern Field and Fireside, May 18, 1861, 3.

17. Reprinted in "The Times—Keep Your Eyes Open," *SP*, October 26, 1861, 4.

18. *Providential Aspect and Salutary Tendency of the Existing Crisis*, 22.

19. Wiley et al., *Address to the People of North Carolina*, 3.

20. H. [Charles Wallace Howard], "Report of Dr. Joseph Jones," *SC* 18 (December 1860): 361.

21. "Disenthralment of Southern Literature," *DBR* 31 (October and November 1861): 348.

22. "Our Contributors," *Southern Teacher* 2 (May 1861): 474.

23. For a discussion of the southern appetite for northern print literature, see Wells, *The Origins of the Southern Middle Class*, 41–57; Tyron, "The Publications of Ticknor and Fields in the South."

24. Reprinted in "The South on Northern Publications," *The Aurora* 4 (May 1861): 314.

25. "Education of Southern Women," *DBR* 31 (October and November 1861): 382.

26. *Providential Aspect and Salutary Tendency of the Existing Crisis*, 22.

27. C. H. Wiley, "Ninth Annual Letter of Instructions and Suggestions," *NCJE* 4 (May 1861): 157–58.

28. *Providential Aspect and Salutary Tendency of the Existing Crisis*, 19.

29. Wiley et al., *Address to the People of North Carolina*, 7.

30. Mrs. B. M. Z., "A Response to 'M. M. J.,' " *SFF*, September 28, 1861, 148.

31. Barrow, *Remarks on the Present War*, 4.

32. Worrell, *The Principles of English Grammar*, iii.

33. Moore, ed., *Spirit of the Pulpit*, 131.

34. Reprinted in "Editor's Table," *SLM* 33 (October 1861): 317–18.

35. "The Future of Our Confederation," *DBR* 31 (July 1861): 40–41.

36. "Future Revolution in Southern School Books," *DBR* 30 (May and June 1861): 609.

37. J., "A Lesson of the Times. The South Must be Independent!" *SC* 19 (January 1861): 15.

38. Reprinted as D. H. Hill, "Gone Over to the Enemy," *SP*, February 16, 1861, 3.

39. "Literary Independence," *SFF*, May 11, 1861, 404.

40. For an overview, see McCardell, *The Idea of a Southern Nation*.

41. "Southern Independence," *SP*, December 1, 1860, 2.

42. Ibid.

43. "Editor's Table," *SLM* 33 (September 1861): 237. George Bagby, the official editor, was serving briefly in the Confederate army during this time.

44. *Providential Aspect and Salutary Tendency of the Existing Crisis*, 23.

45. Reprinted from *SFF* in "Southern Enterprise—Southern Literature," *WC*, November 6, 1861, 8.

46. Wiley et al., *Address to the People of North Carolina*, 13.

47. Reprinted in "Southern Literature," *WC*, July 17, 1861, 8.

48. Although the Union blockade was quite porous at first, it would become increasingly effective as the war progressed. Even in the early years, however, the blockade helped to stem the flow of northern literature as southern smugglers generally prioritized other goods over northern periodicals and books.

49. "Editorial," *DBR* 31 (September 1861): 329–30.

50. "Our Next Volume," *QRMECS* 15 (October 1861): 631; "Our Next Number," *QRMECS* 15 (July 1861): 474.

51. Amicus, "Great Southern Book," *WC*, September 11, 1861, 6.

52. C. C. Pinckney Jr., "To the Friends of Southern Publications," *Southern Episcopalian* 8 (June 1861): 168.

53. Wiley et al., *Address to the People of North Carolina*, 13.

54. "Literary Independence," *SFF*, May 11, 1861, 404.

55. Ibid.

56. *SFF*, January 19, 1861, 276; "Literature in the South," *SFF*, May 4, 1861, 396.

57. Reprinted in "The South on Northern Publications," *The Aurora* 4 (May 1861): 314.

58. Wiley et al., *Address to the People of North Carolina*, 4.

59. Reprinted in "The South on Northern Publications," *The Aurora* 4 (May 1861): 314.

60. "Future Revolution in Southern School Books," *DBR* 30 (May and June 1861): 614.

61. Wiley et al., *Address to the People of North Carolina*, 1, 5.

62. Wiley, "Ninth Annual Letter of Instructions and Suggestions," *NCJE* 4 (May 1861): 157.

63. V. E. W. McCord, "President Jeff. Davis," *The Aurora* 4 (May 1861): 305.

64. Wiley et al., *Address to the People of North Carolina*, 5.

65. "The New Republic," *SLM* 32 (May 1861): 393. For more on reopening the slave trade, see W. Gilmore Simms, "Our Commissioners to Europe—What are the Facts?" *DBR* 31 (October and November 1861): 413; [William Falconer], "The African Slave Trade," *SLM* 33 (August 1861): 111; William Gregg, "Southern Patronage to Southern Imports and Domestic Industry," *DBR* 30 (February 1861): 222; W. T. Walthall, "Letters to an Englishman," *SLM* 34 (January 1862): 4.

66. Wiley et al., *Address to the People of North Carolina*, 11.

67. "Proceedings of the State Educational Association," *NCJE* 4 (November 1861): 333. These "isms" included abolitionism, womanism, free-loveism, Mormonism, atheism, transcendentalism, Fourierism, communism, agrarianism, and a whole host of other pernicious northern belief systems that are discussed at much greater length in Chapter 2.

68. Ibid.

69. Worrell, *The Principles of English Grammar*, iii.

70. Reprinted in "Literature in the South," *SFF*, Supplement to the Southern Field and Fireside, May 18, 1861, 2.

71. This concept of romantic cultural nationalism is most often associated with the writings of German philosopher Johann Gottfried von Herder. In the late eighteenth century, Herder maintained that each nation possessed its own unique national genius which was manifested primarily through its literature, art, music, laws, customs, education, and religion. Each nation, and especially Germany, Herder argued, needed to cultivate its own unadulterated national genius and stop attempting to imitate the achievements of other foreign cultures. Herder did not believe that one national culture was superior to another, merely that each must be unique and true to itself. For more on Herder's thought, see Berlin, *Vico and Herder*; Hayes, "Contributions of Herder"; Ergang, *Herder and the Foundation of German Nationalism*; and Barnard, *Herder's Social and Political Thought*.

72. Sybil, "Knowledge—Its Power," *SFF*, July 6, 1861, 52.

73. George Fitzhugh, "Thoughts Suggested by the War—The Past and the Future," *DBR* 31 (September 1861): 303.

74. "Literary Independence," *SFF*, May 11, 1861, 404.

75. John McCrady, "The Study of Nature and the Arts of Civilized Life," *DBR* 30 (May and June 1861): 603. McCrady was a noted scientist and mathematician from Charleston, South Carolina.

CHAPTER 2

1. Palmer, *A Vindication of Secession and the South*, 44.

2. "Disfederation of the States," *SLM* 32 (February 1861): 119. Although the article was unsigned, authorship is elsewhere attributed to "Mr. Reese" by editor George Bagby. See "Editor's Table," Ibid., 152.

3. George Fitzhugh, "The Message, The Constitution, and The Times," *DBR* 30 (February 1861): 165.

4. "The Union: Its Benefits and Dangers," *SLM* 32 (January 1861): 4.

5. Reprinted portion of letter from L. W. Spratt to John Perkins. "Editor's Table," *SLM* 32 (March 1861): 243–44. In the text the pages are misnumbered as 343–44.

6. Georgia, "Circular Letter," *SP*, January 26, 1861, 3. The open letter *"To the Clergy and Laity of Christian Churches in the Southern States of the Union"* was widely reprinted in the southern religious newspaper press. The northern clergymen who signed the

letter maintained that the sectional conflict was the result of "*misrepresentation*" by both sides. For the complete letter, see "An Earnest Appeal to Christians at the South," *Southern Churchman*, January 18, 1861, 2.

7. "Puritanism Perverted, A Cause of the Present Trouble," *Church Intelligencer*, August 2, 1861, 566.

8. "The New Republic," *SLM* 32 (May 1861): 398.

9. Benjamin M. Palmer, "Thanksgiving Sermon," reprinted in "Why We Resist and What We Resist. The Two Opposing Views of the Great Issues Between the North and the South," *DBR* 30 (February 1861): 230.

10. "A Nation of Soldiers!" *SC* 19 (June 1861): 184.

11. For a reasonably comprehensive list of the northern "isms," see A South Carolinian, *The Confederate*, 50.

12. An Alabamian, "The One Great Cause of the Failure of the Federal Government," *SLM* 32 (May 1861): 334.

13. J. D. B. De Bow, "The Non-Slaveholders of the South: Their Interest in the Present Sectional Controversy Identical with that of the Slaveholders," *DBR* 30 (January 1861): 73.

14. "The Future of Our Confederation," *DBR* 31 (July 1861): 37.

15. Atticus G. Haygood, "Southern Independence and Southern Literature," *ERFM* 2 (February 1861): 73.

16. "Northern Mind and Character," *SLM* 31 (November 1860): 343–44.

17. "Education of Southern Women," *DBR* 31 (October and November 1861): 387–88.

18. Fitzhugh, "The Message, The Constitution, and The Times," *DBR* 30 (February 1861): 162.

19. George Fitzhugh, "The Women of the South," *DBR* 31 (August 1861): 153. Whether southern female education did indeed lead to contentment with prescribed social roles as Fitzhugh and others claimed, is debatable and even doubtful. What is important for the purposes at hand, however, is that advocates of southern female education justified their project by praising the innate conservatism of southern womanhood and thereby assuaging fears that female education would undermine existing social roles. The debate over female education and educational reform in the Confederacy is covered in greater detail in Chapter 4.

20. Ibid., 150, 153. See also Samuel Cartwright, "The War Spirit Among the Women. *What is it! What has caused it?*" printed in "Editor's Table," *SLM* 33 (October 1861): 316–17.

21. George Fitzhugh, "One Idea," *DBR* 30 (March 1861): 311.

22. "The Union: Its Benefits and Dangers," *SLM* 32 (January 1861): 3.

23. George Bagby, "Editor's Table," *SLM* 32 (February 1861): 152.

24. It should be noted that these antidemocratic political theorists and critics were a small and self-consciously marginalized segment of southern society. Their work appeared almost exclusively in the elite, highbrow southern journals *De Bow's Review* and the *Southern Literary Messenger*. While most southerners shared their suspicion of agrarianism and other northern "isms," few were willing to go so far as these arch-

conservative writers, who denounced the cherished rights of suffrage and popular sovereignty, as discussed below.

25. J. Quitman Moore, "National Characteristics—The Issues of the Day," *DBR* 30 (January 1861): 49–50, 51.

26. "The Union: Its Benefits and Dangers," *SLM* 32 (January 1861): 3, 4. See also George Fitzhugh, "The Perils of Peace," *DBR* 31 (October and November 1861): 397.

27. [William Falconer], "The African Slave Trade," *SLM* 33 (August 1861): 113.

28. Fitzhugh, "The Message, The Constitution, and The Times," *DBR* 30 (February 1861): 164.

29. The literature on proslavery is immense. Important works include Davis, *The Problem of Slavery in Western Culture*; Davis, *The Problem of Slavery in the Age of Revolution*; Donald, "The Proslavery Argument Reconsidered"; Ericson, *The Debate Over Slavery*; Fox-Genovese and Genovese, *The Mind of the Master Class*; Genovese, *The Slaveholders' Dilemma*; Jenkins, *Proslavery Thought in the Old South*; Smith, *Debating Slavery*; Tise, *Proslavery*.

30. "South-Carolina and the Union," *Southern Episcopalian* 7 (December 1860): 489.

31. [Miles], *The Relation Between the Races at the South*, 10.

32. Stiles, *The National Controversy*, 76.

33. Religious proslavery also has a long historiography. Some key works include Genovese, *"Slavery Ordained of God"*; Daly, *When Slavery was Called Freedom*; Adams, "The Biblical Defense of Slavery in the Antebellum South"; Bailey, *Shadow on the Church*; McKivigan and Snay, eds., *Religion and the Antebellum Debate over Slavery*; Snay, *Gospel of Disunion*; Snay, "American Thought and Southern Distinctiveness"; Goen, *Broken Churches, Broken Nation*; Maddex, "Proslavery Millennialism"; Maddex, " 'The Southern Apostasy' Revisited"; Mathews, *Religion in the Old South*; Noll, *The Civil War as a Theological Crisis*; Smith, *In His Image*; Sparks, "Mississippi's Apostle of Slavery."

34. Palmer, "Thanksgiving Sermon," Reprinted in "Why We Resist and What We Resist. The Two Opposing Views of the Great Issues Between the North and the South," *DBR* 30 (February 1861): 230.

35. "The Great Day of Manassas," *DBR* 31 (September 1861): 285.

36. Palmer, "Thanksgiving Sermon," Reprinted in "Why We Resist and What We Resist. The Two Opposing Views of the Great Issues Between the North and the South," *DBR* 30 (February 1861): 231.

37. Stiles, *The National Controversy*, 79.

38. [J. Randolph Tucker], "The Great Issue: Our Relations to It," *SLM* 32 (March 1861): 177, 178.

39. George Bagby, "Editor's Table," *SLM* 32 (March 1861): 244. In the text itself, the page is misnumbered as 344.

40. [Tucker], "The Great Issue: Our Relations to It," *SLM* 32 (March 1861): 177.

41. "The Union: Its Benefits and Dangers," *SLM* 32 (January 1861): 4.

42. "The New Republic," *SLM* 32 (May 1861): 399.

43. An Alabamian, "The One Great Cause of the Failure of the Federal Government," *SLM* 32 (May 1861): 334.

44. "Northern Mind and Character," *SLM* 31 (November 1860): 343.

45. J. H. Thornwell, "Our National Sins," as published in Moore, ed., *Spirit of the Pulpit*, 55.

46. Palmer, *A Vindication of Secession and the South*, 13.

47. George Bagby, "Editor's Table," *SLM* 33 (December 1861): 466.

48. Stephen Elliott, "God's Presence with the Confederate States," as published in Moore, ed., *Spirit of the Pulpit*, 138.

49. John B. Adger, "Explanatory Note," *Southern Presbyterian Review* 14 (October 1861): 503.

50. J. H. Thornwell, "Our National Sins," as published in Moore, ed., *Spirit of the Pulpit*, 55–56.

51. "Our Position," *North Carolina Christian Advocate*, April 29, 1861, 2.

52. "The Present Juncture," *SP*, January 19, 1861, 2.

53. "The Future of Our Confederation," *DBR* 31 (July 1861), 38.

54. George Fitzhugh, "Superiority of Southern Races—Review of Count De Gobineau's Work," *DBR* 31 (October and November 1861): 372.

55. "Our Country," *SP*, December 8, 1860, 2.

56. "Editor's Table," *SLM* 33 (July 1861): 75.

57. Edward Alfred Pollard, "Hints on Southern Civilization," *SLM* 32 (April 1861): 309–10.

58. "Editor's Table," *SLM* 33 (July 1861): 75.

59. "Education of Southern Women," *DBR* 31 (October and November 1861): 383.

60. "Future Revolution in Southern School Books," *DBR* 30 (May and June 1861): 611.

61. As to what this abolitionist trigonometry might look like or how it might function, the author, unfortunately, did not elaborate. "Future Revolution in Southern School Books," *DBR* 30 (May and June 1861): 612.

62. George E. Naff, "Cleveland's Text-Books," *QRMECS* 15 (January 1861): 70.

63. Pollard, "Hints on Southern Civilization," *SLM* 32 (April 1861): 310.

64. Ibid., 310–11. By "divine right of murderers," Pollard referred to John Brown, his followers, and the public support they received from northern abolitionist leaders in the wake of their failed raid on Harper's Ferry.

65. [William Falconer], "The True Question: A Contest for the Supremacy of Race, as between the SAXON PURITAN of the NORTH, and the NORMAN of the SOUTH," *SLM* 33 (July 1861), 19.

66. William Henry Holcombe, "The Alternative: A Separate Nationality, or the Africanization of the South," *SLM* 32 (February 1861): 86.

67. Fitzhugh, "The Perils of Peace," *DBR* 31 (October and November 1861): 396–97.

68. George Fitzhugh, "Cuba: The March of Empire and the Course of Trade," *DBR* 30 (January 1861): 34.

69. " 'Boston Notions.' A Letter and Reply," *SLM* 33 (October 1861): 293.

70. Fitzhugh, "Cuba: The March of Empire and the Course of Trade," *DBR* 30 (January 1861): 34.

71. "Editorial Notes and Miscellany," *DBR* 30 (February 1861): 252.

72. The most recent and thorough study of this subject is Watson, *Normans and Saxons*. On the Confederate racial interpretation of the Civil War, see also Bonner, "Roundheaded Cavaliers." For the antebellum development of the Cavalier myth, see Taylor's classic *Cavalier and Yankee*, as well as Watson, " 'The Difference of Race' "; Osterweis, *Romanticism and Nationalism in the Old South*; Adams, *Our Masters the Rebels*. The idea of southern racial or ethnic distinctiveness still attracts attention to this day. For instance, see McWhiney's famous "Celtic Thesis" in *Cracker Culture*.

73. George Fitzhugh, "The Pioneers, Preachers, and People, of the Mississippi Valley," *DBR* 30 (March 1861): 260.

74. Fitzhugh, "The Message, The Constitution, and The Times," *DBR* 30 (February 1861): 162.

75. Fitzhugh, "The Pioneers, Preachers, and People, of the Mississippi Valley," *DBR* 30 (March 1861): 260.

76. J. Quitman Moore, "The Belligerents," *DBR* 31 (July 1861): 73.

77. [William Falconer], "The True Question: A Contest for the Supremacy of Race, as between the SAXON PURITAN of the NORTH, and the NORMAN of the SOUTH," *SLM* 33 (July 1861): 27.

78. William Archer Cocke, "The Puritan and the Cavalier; or, The Elements of American Colonial Society," *DBR* 31 (September 1861): 211–12.

79. George Fitzhugh, "The Huguenots of the South," *DBR* 30 (May and June 1861): 517.

80. [William Falconer], "The African Slave Trade," *SLM* 33 (August 1861): 106.

81. [William Falconer], "The True Question: A Contest for the Supremacy of Race, as between the SAXON PURITAN of the NORTH, and the NORMAN of the SOUTH," *SLM* 33 (July 1861): 21.

82. This popularity would fade as the war progressed, however, due to a strong intellectual backlash led by the Confederate religious press. To equate northerners with the English Puritans and southerners with the Cavaliers was not only historically inaccurate, critics argued, but an insult to the memory of the Puritans as well as undeserved praise for the Cavaliers. See Bernath, "Confederate Minds," 451 n. 55.

83. [William Falconer], "The True Question: A Contest for the Supremacy of Race, as between the SAXON PURITAN of the NORTH, and the NORMAN of the SOUTH," *SLM* 33 (July 1861): 23, 25.

84. George Fitzhugh, "Thoughts Suggested by the War—The Past and the Future," *DBR* 31 (September 1861): 298.

85. "Disenthralment of Southern Literature," *DBR* 31 (October and November 1861): 348.

86. "Southern Literature," *North Carolina University Magazine* 10 (December 1860): 300.

87. Reprinted in "Southern Literature," *NCJE* 4 (July 1861): 216.

88. Mrs. B. M. Z., "A Response to 'M. M. J.,' " *SFF*, September 28, 1861, 148.

89. Fitzhugh, "The Pioneers, Preachers, and People, of the Mississippi Valley," *DBR* 30 (March 1861): 264.

90. Haygood, "Southern Independence and Southern Literature," *ERFM* 2 (February 1861): 73.

91. A. B. Stark, "Southern Literature," *Home Circle* 7 (September 1861): 515.

92. "The Northern Press—'The Day Book,' " *DBR* 29 (December 1860): 792.

93. C. M. Irwin and S. Boykin, "Salutary," *Christian Index*, May 15, 1861, 2.

94. "Agricultural Journals, Southern vs. Northern," *SC* 19 (January 1861): 11.

95. "An Appeal to Southern Men and Women," *Southern Literary Companion*, January 23, 1861, 2.

96. Haygood, "Southern Independence and Southern Literature," *ERFM* 2 (February 1861): 72, 70.

97. "An Appeal to Southern Men and Women," *Southern Literary Companion*, January 23, 1861, 2.

98. For a discussion of the sensationalist tendencies of the antebellum northern press, see Lehuu, *Carnival on the Page*.

99. C. W., "Book Notices, Editorial, Etc.," *DBR* 29 (December 1860): 795.

100. Haygood, "Southern Independence and Southern Literature," *ERFM* 2 (February 1861): 70.

101. "Editor's Table," *SLM* 33 (September 1861): 237.

102. "Disenthralment of Southern Literature," *DBR* 31 (October and November 1861): 353.

103. "Southern Literature," *North Carolina University Magazine* 10 (December 1860): 301.

104. Mrs. B. M. Z., "A Response to 'M. M. J.,' " *SFF*, September 28, 1861, 148. Though southern-born, E. D. E. N. Southworth was generally considered a northern author by Confederate critics due to her advocacy of abolition.

105. Reprinted in "The South on Northern Publications," *The Aurora* 4 (May 1861): 314.

106. "Editor's Table," *SLM* 32 (April 1861): 326–27.

107. See Hubbell, *The South in American Literature*, 385–93.

108. "Disenthralment of Southern Literature," *DBR* 31 (October and November 1861): 354–55.

109. Ibid., 353.

110. V. E. W. McCord, "President Jeff. Davis," *The Aurora* 4 (May 1861): 306.

111. "Editor's Table," *SLM* 33 (July 1861): 75.

112. "Southern Literature," *North Carolina University Magazine* 10 (December 1860): 302–3.

113. "Future Revolution in Southern School Books," *DBR* 30 (May and June 1861): 610.

114. "Education of Southern Women," *DBR* 31 (October and November 1861): 382–83.

115. Octogenarian, *The Origin and End of the Irrepressible Conflict*, 2.

116. "Education of Southern Women," *DBR* 31 (October and November 1861): 383, 382.

117. H. [Charles W. Howard], "The Education of Our Daughters," *SC* 19 (November 1861): 282.

118. "Editor's Table," *SLM* 33 (December 1861): 467.

119. *Providential Aspect and Salutary Tendency of the Existing Crisis*, 22.

120. Ibid.

121. "Future Revolution in Southern School Books," *DBR* 30 (May and June 1861): 610.

122. "Resignation of our Late Editor, and the Future Management of the Repository and Monthly," *ERFM* 2 (January 1861): 60.

123. "Literary Independence," *SFF*, May 11, 1861, 404.

124. William A. Rogers, "Review of Text-books on Reading," *ERFM* 2 (January 1861): 19.

125. "Book Notices," *ERFM* 2 (April 1861): 241.

126. The actual extent of anti-southern bias in northern textbooks is a matter of interpretation, of course. Suspicious southern nationalists could find anti-southern slights and abolitionist propaganda in the most seemingly innocuous language. Still, there was some truth to their charges. In his survey of 78 antebellum northern textbooks, for instance, historian John Ezell discovered 35 that were, in his opinion, "obviously biased," 17 "prejudiced enough to be offensive," and only 26 that "appeared fair." Ezell, "A Southern Education for Southrons," 314–15.

127. Naff, "Cleveland's Text-books," *QRMECS* 15 (January 1861): 64–65.

128. "Education of Southern Women," *DBR* 31 (October and November 1861): 383; "Book Notices," *ERFM* 2 (April 1861): 241.

129. "Books Rejected in the South," *ERFM* 2 (May 1861): 278.

130. Rivers, *Elements of Moral Philosophy*, xv.

131. "Books Rejected in the South," *ERFM* 2 (May 1861): 278.

132. In the 1858 edition, Cleveland included only a handful of southern authors such as Jefferson, Washington, Madison, and Poe. In response to the outcry from southern critics, Cleveland added "a few more Southern writers" like William Gilmore Simms, St. George Tucker, and Philip Pendleton Cooke to the 1859 edition, but he also significantly increased the number of northern, and especially abolitionist, writers, so that the number of southern authors increased "numerically, but not more in proportion." Cleveland, *A Compendium of American Literature*, 3rd ed., 10.

133. "Future Revolution in Southern School Books," *DBR* 30 (May and June 1861): 606–14; "The Library," *Home Circle* 7 (February 1861): 127–28; D. S. Richardson, "Abolition Text Books," *NCJE* 4 (February 1861): 41–42; Naff, "Cleveland's Text-books," *QRMECS* 15 (January 1861): 63–75.

134. Cleveland's abolitionism was no secret. He had delivered antislavery speeches throughout the 1840s and 1850s and had published an abolitionist pamphlet in 1859 entitled *Slavery and Infidelity*. See Cleveland, *Anti-Slavery Addresses*; Cleveland, *Slavery and Infidelity*.

135. Richardson, "Abolition Text Books," *NCJE* 4 (February 1861): 41; Naff, "Cleveland's Text-books," *QRMECS* 15 (January 1861): 66.

136. Cleveland, *A Compendium of American Literature*, 3rd ed., 8–9.

137. Naff, "Cleveland's Text-books," *QRMECS* 15 (January 1861): 71.

138. "Future Revolution in Southern School Books," *DBR* 30 (May and June 1861): 613.

139. Naff, "Cleveland's Text-books," *QRMECS* 15 (January 1861): 71–72.

140. "Future Revolution in Southern School Books," *DBR* 30 (May and June 1861): 613.

141. Naff, "Cleveland's Text-books," *QRMECS* 15 (January 1861): 75.

142. *Providential Aspect and Salutary Tendency of the Existing Crisis*, 23.

143. "The Greensboro Female College," *SP*, January 26, 1861, 2.

144. J. C., "Teachers and Religion," *NCP*, March 2, 1861, 1.

145. "Education of Southern Women," *DBR* 31 (October and November 1861): 382.

146. "Northern Publications," *WC*, May 22, 1861, 4.

147. Reprinted in "The South on Northern Publications," *The Aurora* 4 (May 1861): 314.

148. "Our Contributors," *Southern Teacher* 2 (May 1861): 474.

CHAPTER 3

1. Reprinted in "Southern Enterprise—Southern Literature," *WC*, November 6, 1861, 8.

2. "Wants of the South," *ERFM* 2 (March 1861): 174.

3. A. B. Stark, "Southern Literature," *Home Circle* 7 (September 1861): 515.

4. Ibid., 515–16.

5. Reprinted from *SCA* in "Southern Literature," *WC*, July 17, 1861, 8.

6. Reprinted in "Literature in the South," *SFF*, Supplement to the Southern Field and Fireside, May 18, 1861, 2.

7. Atticus G. Haygood, "Southern Independence and Southern Literature," *ERFM* 2 (February 1861): 71.

8. For the sake of comparison, this total represented only 11 percent of the annual periodical production for the country as a whole. The state of New York alone boasted 542 titles with a total production run of 320,930,884 copies per year, and Pennsylvania and Massachusetts each printed over 100,000,000 copies annually. Kennedy, *Preliminary Report on the Eighth Census*, 211–13.

9. "Editor's Table," *SLM* 33 (August 1861): 160.

10. "A Native of the South—'Religious Newspapers,' " *SP*, August 24, 1861, 1.

11. "Editor's Table," *SLM* 31 (December 1860): 468–75.

12. For more on the *Southern Literary Messenger*, see Minor, *The Southern Literary Messenger*; Jacobs, "Campaign for a Southern Literature: The *Southern Literary Messenger*"; Jackson, *The Contributors and Contributions to the Southern Literary Messenger*; Jackson, "An Estimate of the Influence of 'The Southern Literary Messenger' "; Tucker,

"'A Rash and Perilous Enterprize'"; Rogers, "Four Southern Magazines," 92–114; Mott, *A History of American Magazines*, I, 629–57. See also Jonathan Daniel Well's introduction to the recent reprint of Minor's *The Southern Literary Messenger*. On George Bagby, see King, *Dr. George William Bagby*; Hubbell, *The South in American Literature*, 680–83; Bain and Flora, eds., *Fifty Southern Writers Before 1900*, 20–28.

13. For more on James De Bow and *De Bow's Review*, see Skipper, *J. D. B. De Bow*; Mott, *A History of American Magazines*, II, 338–48; Rogers, "Four Southern Magazines," 20–47; McMillen, ed., *The Works of James D. B. De Bow*; Paskoff and Wilson, eds., *The Cause of the South*; Aphornsuvan, "James D. B. De Bow and the Political Economy of the Old South"; Durden, "J. D. B. De Bow"; Weatherford, *Analytical Index of De Bow's Review*.

14. Both *Southern Literary Messenger* and *De Bow's Review* had circulations of approximately 4,000 issues per month. Jackson, "An Estimate of the Influence of 'The Southern Literary Messenger,'" 513; Skipper, *J. D. B. De Bow*, 135–36.

15. Always popular, *Southern Field and Fireside* obtained a large subscription base during the war. In March 1864, it announced that there were 13,000 subscriptions about to expire, suggesting that the overall subscription list was even larger. "To Our Subscribers and Friends," *SFF*, March 6, 1864, 5. For more on *Southern Field and Fireside*, see Flanders, *Early Georgia Magazines*, 136–48. For more on James Gardner, see Brown, "Augusta's Other Voice: James Gardner and the *Constitutionalist*."

16. In 1860, the *Companion* had about 1,200 subscribers. The *Crusader*'s circulation in 1850 was estimated at 5,000. See Flanders, *Early Georgia Magazines*, 157–64.

17. *Home Circle* was estimated to have "less, perhaps, than 10,000 subscribers," and *The Aurora*, while providing no specific number, claimed to have "reached a SELF-SUSTAINING CIRCULATION" by May 1861. "Literature, North and South," *Home Circle* 6 (December 1860): 755; Advertisement, *The Aurora* 4 (May 1861): back cover.

18. Although providing no hard numbers, Campbell claimed that by November 1861, "The circulation of the Journal is now sufficient to secure it against discontinuance, even in these trying times." "The Journal for 1862," *NCJE* 4 (November 1861): 350.

19. The circulations of these journals were never large, though *Southern Teacher*, in January 1861, did claim that it had "attained an extent of circulation never before accomplished by any Educational Periodical in the South and South-West." "Terms of Advertising," *Southern Teacher* 2 (January 1861): 281.

20. During the 1850s, the *Cultivator* had as many as 10,000 subscribers. See Demaree, *The American Agricultural Press*, 372–75.

21. For instance, see "Medical College of Georgia," *Southern Medical and Surgical Journal* 17 (June 1861): 511.

22. For a good overview of southern denominational periodical literature, see Stroupe, *The Religious Press in the South Atlantic States*, 3–37. On the role of the religious press in the Confederacy, see Silver, *Confederate Morale and Church Propaganda*. See also Berends, "'Wholesome Reading Purifies and Elevates the Man,'" and Stout and Grasso, "Civil War, Religion, and Communications."

23. "A Letter from 'Eunice' to 'Minnie,' " *SP*, April 20, 1861, 2.

24. See Stroupe, *The Religious Press in the South Atlantic States*, 122.

25. Although printed in Philadelphia at the start of the war, the *Christian Observer* began dating itself from Richmond in order to show its southern sympathies for the first seven months of 1861. In September, its owner and editor, Amasa Converse, permanently moved the paper to the Confederate capital.

26. The *Southern Presbyterian* had approximately 4,000 subscribers. The *North Carolina Presbyterian* printed 4,600 issues a week—3,000 for its subscribers and 1,600 free issues for Confederate soldiers. Likewise, the *Christian Observer* sent 3,000 free copies into the ranks every week. Stroupe, *The Religious Press in the South Atlantic States*, 53–54, 63–64, 93–95, 120–21. See also "The N.C. Presbyterian for 1861," *NCP*, December 15, 1860, 2; "A Hint," *NCP*, March 16, 1861, 2; "Our Resumption," *SP*, October 6, 1864, 2.

27. The *Southern Christian Advocate* had approximately 4,000 subscribers. The *North Carolina Christian Advocate* printed approximately 5,000 issues per week during the war—3,000 for subscribers and 2,000 for the troops. The *Richmond Christian Advocate* had about 4,000 subscribers, although it too sent "several thousand" additional issues to the camps. For more on these Methodist papers, see Stroupe, *The Religious Press in the South Atlantic States*, 65–66, 93, 108–9. For more on the *Southern Christian Advocate* specifically see Crum, *History of the Southern Christian Advocate*.

28. The *Home Circle* reported that the *Sunday-School Visitor* had "a circulation of, we believe, less than 40,000." "Literature, North and South," *Home Circle* 6 (December 1860): 755.

29. *Church Intelligencer*, December 6, 1861, 686.

30. At its height, the *Church Intelligencer* had "a little short of three thousand" subscribers, while the *Southern Churchman* had about 2,500. "Indefinite Suspension," *Church Intelligencer*, April 8, 1864, 305; Stroupe, *The Religious Press in the South Atlantic States*, 69–70, 111–13. For more on the Episcopalian periodicals and their role during the Civil War, see Cheshire, *The Church in the Confederate States*; London, "The Literature of the Church in the Confederate States."

31. The *Biblical Recorder* had 1,800 subscribers. The *Christian Index* had somewhere between 5,000 and 6,000 subscribers plus a "large number" sent to the troops. The *Banner and Baptist* had about 2,000 paying subscribers, and the *Religious Herald* had around 3,000 subscribers with another 3,200 issues sent to the soldiers. Stroupe, *The Religious Press in the South Atlantic States*, 48–49, 59–60, 84–85, 99–100.

32. "Retrospective," *ERFM* 1 (December 1860): 733–34.

33. "Editor's Drawer," *SFF*, September 14, 1861, 132.

34. "Southern Ink," *NCP*, September 14, 1861, 2.

35. W. S. Perry, "A Word to our Old Subscribers," *The Aurora* 4 (May 1861): 318.

36. "A Gigantic Publishing House," *CTM*, July 12, 1864, 376.

37. Thomas O. Summers, "First Stereotype Edition of the New Testament in the South," *SP*, October 26, 1861, 4.

38. In June 1861, editor George Bagby observed that "by the position that we took six

months since [in favor of secession], we suffered greatly—losing nearly all subscribers North, and many [Unionists] in our own section." "Editor's Table," *SLM* 32 (June 1861): 480.

39. *Southern Teacher* 2 (January, May 1861); "Editorial," *DBR* 31 (August 1861): 208.

40. The *North Carolina University Magazine* suspended publication following its May 1861 issue.

41. James Gardner, "Resigning the Pen for the Sword," *SFF*, May 11, 1861, 404.

42. "Editor's Table," *SLM* 32 (May 1861): 404.

43. "Editor's Table," *SLM* 32 (June 1861): 480.

44. W. H. C. Price, "Valedictory," *ERFM* 2 (February 1861): 120.

45. See "Editorial," *DBR* 30 (May and June 1861): 681–84; "Editorial," *DBR* 31 (August 1861): 206–8; "Editorial," *DBR* 31 (September 1861): 330–32.

46. King, *Dr. George William Bagby*, 95; [J. M. Wood], "The Banner," *Banner and Baptist*, July 5, 1862, 5.

47. "Editor's Table," *SLM* 33 (September 1861): 237.

48. "Agricultural Press of the South," *SC* 19 (December 1861): 307. Redmond was as good as his word. The *Southern Cultivator* did not once suspend publication during the war.

49. Ella Swan, "Southern Literature," *SFF*, Supplement to the Southern Field and Fireside, May 18, 1861, 2.

50. "An Appeal to Southern Men and Women," *Southern Literary Companion*, January 23, 1861, 2; Literary Section, *SFF*, January 19, 1861, 276.

51. Reprinted as "Southern Literature," *WC*, July 17, 1861, 8.

52. "Editor's Table," *SLM* 33 (September 1861): 237.

53. W. S. Perry, "A Word to our Old Subscribers," *The Aurora* 4 (May 1861): 318.

54. "Disenthralment of Southern Literature," *DBR* 31 (October and November 1861): 359.

55. "Our Next Number," *QRMECS* 15 (July 1861): 474.

56. "Editor's Table," *SLM* 33 (September 1861): 237; "Editor's Table," *SLM* 33 (August 1861): 160.

57. "Editorial Department," *ERFM* 2 (January 1861): 60.

58. For instance, see Advertisement for *Southern Field and Fireside*, *WC*, August 14, 1861, 8.

59. "To Our Subscribers," *SFF*, December 22, 1860, 244.

60. "A Flourishing Paper," *RCA*, February 14, 1861, 2.

61. "To Preachers' Wives and Daughters," *Home Circle* 7 (February 1861): 113; "Introduce Us to Your Friend," *Home Circle* 7 (February 1861): 113.

62. "An Earnest Appeal," *ERFM* 1 (November 1860): 674.

63. "Repository and Monthly Suspended," *ERFM* 2 (May 1861): 281.

64. "Editor's Table," *SLM* 33 (November 1861): 395.

65. For a detailed discussion of this mutual support network, see Bernath, "Confederate Minds," 190–99.

66. Reprinted in "The Field and Fireside," *SFF*, September 28, 1861, 148.

67. "Resuscitated," *Church Intelligencer*, December 6, 1861, 686.

68. Haygood, "Southern Independence and Southern Literature," *ERFM* 2 (February 1861): 74.

69. H. Hinkley, "Southern Resources," *SC* 19 (November 1861): 287.

70. "Literary," *SFF*, September 21, 1861, 140.

71. From *The Banner of Peace* reprinted in "The Times—Keep Your Eyes Open," *SP*, October 26, 1861, 4.

72. Haygood, "Southern Independence and Southern Literature," *ERFM* 2 (February 1861): 69.

73. Stark, "Southern Literature," *Home Circle* 7 (September 1861): 513.

74. Haygood, "Southern Independence and Southern Literature," *ERFM* 2 (February 1861): 75. Interestingly, these writers rarely cited specific examples to support such claims of postwar intellectual groundswells and instead asserted that these were simply well-documented and incontestable facts of history.

75. Reprinted as "Southern Enterprise—Southern Literature," *WC*, November 6, 1861, 8.

76. Ibid.

77. Stark, "Southern Literature," *Home Circle* 7 (September 1861): 513.

78. Reprinted from *SFF* as "A New Development of Southern Literature," *SLM* 33 (October 1861): 318.

79. "To Our Correspondents," *SP*, March 9, 1861, 2.

80. Reprinted as "Southern Literature," *WC*, July 17, 1861, 8.

81. Stark, "Southern Literature," *Home Circle* 7 (September 1861): 514.

82. Ibid., 514–15.

83. "The Future of Our Confederation," *DBR* 31 (July 1861): 41.

84. For instance, see "Southern Literature," *North Carolina University Magazine* 10 (December 1860): 301–2.

85. Reprinted as "Literature in the South," *SFF*, Supplement to the Southern Field and Fireside, May 18, 1861, 3.

86. Stark, "Southern Literature," *Home Circle* 7 (September 1861): 514.

87. Interestingly, George Bagby expressed concern as to what this newfound consensus might portend for the future of the Confederacy. Without a northern intellectual adversary to unite them, Bagby worried that southerners might begin to fight among themselves over far more petty matters. In October, he mused, "It is a question whether, in the absence of a legitimate quarrel over theories of government, our wrangles may not immediately seek a lower level and degenerate into sectional disputes waged on purely material issues." Bagby made this surprisingly astute observation in passing and did not again return to this line of inquiry. Other southern thinkers seem not to have shared his reservations and instead saw southern homogeneity as an unmixed blessing and source of strength. "Editor's Table," *SLM* 33 (October 1861): 317.

88. "Editor's Table," *SLM* 33 (September 1861): 238.

89. Editor's Note to W. S. Grayson's "The Legation of Thomas Jefferson: Is the

Declaration of Independence at War with the Institution of Domestic Slavery?" *DBR* 31 (August 1861): 136.

90. On the centrality of slavery to southern secession and Confederate nationalism, see Bonner, *Mastering America*; Sinha, *The Counterrevolution of Slavery*; Guterl, *American Mediterranean*; Dew, *Apostles of Disunion*.

91. See Mohr, *On the Threshold of Freedom*, 235–71; Faust, *The Creation of Confederate Nationalism*, 58–81.

92. H. [Charles Wallace Howard], "Serfs, Not Slaves; Or, The Relation Between the Races at the South," *SC* 19 (April 1861): 108.

93. "The Abuse of Slavery," *SP*, February 16, 1861, 3.

94. [William Falconer], "The True Question: A Contest for the Supremacy of Race, as between the SAXON PURITAN of the NORTH, and the NORMAN of the SOUTH," *SLM* 33 (July 1861): 26.

95. J. Quitman Moore, "The Belligerents," *DBR* 31 (July 1861): 73–74.

96. "Political Discussions," *SC* 19 (January 1861): 25.

97. For instance, see Samuel Cartwright, "Negro Freedom An Impossibility Under Nature's Laws: The Republican Caucasians of America the Natural Masters and Guardians of Nigrations," *DBR* 30 (May and June 1861): 648–59; Cartwright, "Abolitionism, a Curse to the North, and a Blessing to the South," *DBR* 32 (March and April 1862): 295–304.

98. "Editor's Table," *SLM* 32 (April 1861): 322.

99. R. [D. Redmond], " 'Platform' of the Cultivator; Agricultural and Political," *SC* 19 (January 1861): 26.

100. "A Nation of Soldiers!" *SC* 19 (June 1861): 184.

101. "Politics," *SP*, December 1, 1860, 2.

102. "Trust of the South in God," *SP*, February 2, 1861, 2.

103. "The Progress of Events," *SP*, April 13, 1861, 2.

104. "Too Much About the War," *SP*, September 21, 1861, 2.

105. "To the Editors of Religious Newspapers," *SP*, September 14, 1861, 2.

106. For instance, see "Our Position," *North Carolina Christian Advocate*, April 29, 1861, 2.

107. "Editorial," *DBR* 31 (August 1861): 208.

108. Haygood, "Southern Independence and Southern Literature," *ERFM* 2 (February 1861): 76.

109. Reprinted from *Charleston Courier* in "Literature in the South," *SFF*, Supplement to the Southern Field and Fireside, May 18, 1861, 2.

110. Reprinted as "Southern Enterprise—Southern Literature," *WC*, November 6, 1861, 8.

111. Stark, "Southern Literature," *Home Circle* 7 (September 1861): 516.

112. Reprinted in "The Times—Keep Your Eyes Open," *SP*, October 26, 1861, 4.

113. Reprinted in "Southern Literature," *WC*, July 17, 1861, 8.

114. Haygood, "Southern Independence and Southern Literature," *ERFM* 2 (February 1861): 75.

115. "Our Contributors," *Southern Teacher* 2 (May 1861): 474.

116. George Fitzhugh advocated government subsidies for native authors on the grounds that "no official whatever has a stronger or clearer claim to be paid for his services, by the public, than the author, who zealously and ably sustains his country's cause and his country's institutions." Fitzhugh, "The Perils of Peace," *DBR* 31 (October and November 1861): 398.

117. For instance, see W. S. Perry, "To Our Contributors," *The Aurora* 4 (May 1861): 319.

118. Stark, "Southern Literature," *Home Circle* 7 (September 1861): 517.

119. On the wartime writing and reading of elite southern women, see Faust, *Mothers of Invention*, 153–78.

120. Stark, "Southern Literature," *Home Circle* 7 (September 1861): 517.

121. Sybil, "Knowledge—Its Power," *SFF*, July 6, 1861, 52.

122. "Editor's Table," *SLM* 33 (September 1861): 238.

123. "Where Are Our Writers!" *SCA*, February 28, 1861, 34.

124. "To Our Correspondents," *SP*, March 9, 1861, 2.

125. "The Premiums," *NCJE* 4 (November 1861): 350; and "Advertisement for Premiums," Ibid., 352.

126. Emma Miot, "Our Little Annie," *SFF*, July 6, 1861, 49–50. This was not the first time that *Southern Field and Fireside* had offered prizes. In 1859, it had held a contest for the best southern tale, essay, long poem, and short poem. Flanders, *Early Georgia Magazines*, 139–40.

127. "The N.C. Presbyterian for 1861," *NCP*, December 15, 1860, 2.

128. "To Our Correspondents," *SP*, March 9, 1861, 2.

129. "Literary," *SFF*, September 21, 1861, 140.

130. Joan, of Columbia, "A National Song," *SP*, December 21, 1861, 3.

131. "Newspaper Poetry; Or, An Editor's Singing Birds," *RCA*, February 14, 1861, 2.

132. "Our Sanctum," *SM* 1 (October 1861): 146.

133. "Where are Our Writers!" *SCA*, February 28, 1861, 34.

134. For more on the Young America movement, see Widmer, *Young America*; Miller, *The Raven and the Whale*; Ziff, *Literary Democracy*; Kohn, *American Nationalism*; Stafford, *The Literary Criticism of Young America*; Kerrigan, "Young America!"; Harrison, "The Young Americans"; Spiller, "Emerson's 'The Young American.'"

135. "Disenthralment of Southern Literature," *DBR* 31 (October and November 1861): 361. For Sydney Smith's original indictment of American culture, see his review of Adam Seybert's *Statistical Annuals of the United States of America* in *Edinburgh Review* 33 (January 1820): 69–79. For the antebellum discussion of "Who reads a Southern book?," see McCardell, *The Idea of a Southern Nation*, 155.

136. "Where are Our Writers!" *SCA*, February 28, 1861, 34.

137. *Church Intelligencer*, December 6, 1861, 686.

138. Reprinted as "Southern Literature," *WC*, July 17, 1861, 8.

139. "Editor's Table," *SLM* 33 (October 1861): 315.

140. Three Sisters of South-Western Virginia, "Terrible," *SLM* 33 (November 1861): 396.

141. Incognito, "To the Poetical Editor of the Presbyterian," *SP*, October 5, 1861, 4.

142. "Editor's Table," *SLM* 33 (November 1861): 397.

143. Stark, "Southern Literature," *Home Circle* 7 (September 1861): 513–14.

CHAPTER 4

1. There is a sizable body of historical work on Confederate education, particularly on Confederate textbooks. The most comprehensive is Rachel Stillman's unpublished dissertation, "Education in the Confederate States of America." See also Albright, "Books Made in Dixie"; Clausen, "Some Confederate Ideas About Education"; Davis, "Textbooks for Confederate School Children"; Davis, "The Educational Association of the C.S.A."; Davis, "Textbooks for Virginia Schoolchildren During the Civil War"; Davis, "E. H. Cushing"; Davis, "Textbooks for Texans During the Civil War"; Davis and Davis, "Imported Yankee Textbooks for Confederate Texans"; Davis and Parks, "Confederate School Geographies"; Parks and Davis, "North Carolina's Textbooks"; Ezell, "A Southern Education for Southrons"; Ford, "Calvin H. Wiley and the Common Schools of North Carolina"; Kennerly, "Confederate Juvenile Imprints"; Marten, *The Children's Civil War*, 6–67; Whitescarver, "School Books, Publishers, and Southern Nationalists"; Wolcott, "The Southern Educational Convention of 1863"; Flynt, "Southern Higher Education and the Civil War."

2. "The Greensboro Female College," *SP*, January 26, 1861, 2.

3. H. [Charles Wallace Howard], "The Education of Our Daughters," *SC* 19 (November 1861): 281.

4. "The War," *NCJE* 4 (October 1861): 317.

5. As quoted in "Our Schools," *NCJE* 4 (July 1861): 222.

6. A. B. Stark, "Southern Literature," *Home Circle* 7 (September 1861): 515.

7. For more on Wiley, see Ford, "Calvin H. Wiley and the Common Schools of North Carolina"; Stillman, "Education in the Confederate States of America"; Whitescarver, "School Books, Publishers, and Southern Nationalists"; Braverman, "Calvin Henderson Wiley"; Braverman, "Calvin H. Wiley's North Carolina Reader"; Connor, *Ante-Bellum Builders of North Carolina*, 77–95; Knight, *Public School Education in North Carolina*, 159–90.

8. C. H. Wiley, *"To the Boards of County Superintendents of Common Schools for the Several Counties of the State,"* *NCJE* 4 (November 1861): 346.

9. Wiley et al., *Address to the People of North Carolina*, 1–2.

10. "Proceedings of the State Educational Association," *NCJE* 4 (November 1861): 332, 329.

11. "The Board of Editors," *NCJE* 4 (August 1861): 256.

12. Wiley et al., *Address to the People of North Carolina*, 5.

13. Wiley, *"To the Boards of County Superintendents of Common Schools for the Several Counties of the State,"* *NCJE* 4 (November 1861): 346.

14. Wiley et al., *Address to the People of North Carolina*, 8.

15. "Proceedings of the State Educational Association," *NCJE* 4 (November 1861): 330.

16. C. H. Wiley, "Ninth Annual Letter of Instructions and Suggestions," *NCJE* 4 (May 1861): 155. Wiley was ordained in 1866. Ford, "Calvin H. Wiley and the Common Schools of North Carolina," 279.

17. Ruffin, *Anticipations of the Future*.

18. Wiley et al., *Address to the People of North Carolina*, 8.

19. Stark, "Southern Literature," *Home Circle* 7 (September 1861): 515.

20. Reprinted as "Southern School Books," *WC*, November 6, 1861, 8.

21. Wiley et al., *Address to the People of North Carolina*, 11.

22. Ibid., 12.

23. D. S. Richardson and J. D. Campbell, "Meeting of Teachers," *NCJE* 4 (July 1861): 209.

24. Reprinted from *Southern Field and Fireside* as "Southern School Books," *WC*, November 6, 1861, 8.

25. There were exceptions of course. There were a few Virginia-centric textbook titles such as *The Old Dominion Speller* (1862), *The Virginia Speller and Reader* (1863), *The Virginia Primer* (1864), and *The Virginia Spelling and Reading Book* (1864). In Texas, Edward Cushing began publishing his "New Texas" series of schoolbooks in 1863, but these were the only specifically state-designated Confederate textbooks out of a total production of over one hundred titles during the war.

26. Richardson and Campbell, "Meeting of Teachers," *NCJE* 4 (July 1861): 209.

27. William A. Rogers, "Review of Text-Books on Reading," *ERFM* 2 (January 1861): 19.

28. "Future Revolution in Southern School Books," *DBR* 30 (May and June 1861): 614.

29. Reprinted in "Southern Literature," *WC*, July 17, 1861, 8.

30. A Young Teacher, of Granville, "Demand for Southern Literature," *NCJE* 4 (June 1861): 185.

31. For instance, as discussed in Chapter 3, the North Carolina State Educational Association offered premiums in 1861 for the best essays on various education-related topics.

32. For examples, see James De Bow's editorial comment on "Future Revolution in Southern School Books," *DBR* 30 (May and June 1861): 606; George Fitzhugh, "The Perils of Peace," *DBR* 31 (October and November 1861): 398–99; "Southern School Books," *Southern Teacher* 2 (March 1861): 378; "Southern School Books," *WC*, November 6, 1861, 8.

33. It is interesting to note, however, that efforts to involve the State in the cause of native textbook production did occasionally reach the floor of legislatures and state conventions. For instance, immediately following Georgia's secession, Representative Crawford from Greene County, Georgia moved that his state offer prizes of $400 each for a spelling book, an arithmetic, an English grammar, a geography, and two reading

books (beginner and advanced) "to be written or compiled by citizens resident in the Confederate States of America." "Southern School Books," *Southern Teacher* 2 (March 1861): 378.

34. Wiley et al., *Address to the People of North Carolina*, 13.

35. "Proceedings of the State Educational Association," *NCJE* 4 (November 1861): 330.

36. Gorn, ed., *The McGuffey Readers*, 2.

37. Monaghan, *A Common Heritage*, 219.

38. Stark, "Southern Literature," *Home Circle* 7 (September 1861): 515.

39. For a fascinating discussion of Berry's book, see Mohr, *On the Threshold of Freedom*, 58–64.

40. "School Books," *NCJE* 4 (June 1861): 191.

41. [Colby], *The World in Miniature*.

42. Parrish and Willingham, *Confederate Imprints*, 630–55.

43. Caldwell and Everett, *The Student's Arithmetic*; [Colby], *The World in Miniature*; Darby, *Text Book of Chemistry*; Poindexter, *Philological Reader*, Books 2–4; Rivers, *Elements of Moral Philosophy*; Scott, *A New Southern Grammar*; Sargent, *The Standard Speller*; Smythe, *Our Own Primary Grammar*; Whately, *Elements of Logic*; Whately, *Elements of Rhetoric*; Worrell, *The Principles of English Grammar*; *The Confederate Primer By An Association of Southern Teachers*; *The First Confederate Speller By An Association of Southern Teachers*; *The Second Confederate Speller By An Association of Southern Teachers*.

44. Smythe, *Our Own Primary Grammar*, iii–iv.

45. Worrell, *The Principles of English Grammar*, iii.

46. Scott, *A New Southern Grammar*, iv.

47. Although they certainly could be used for political and nationalist ends. See Lepore, *A is for American*.

48. Worrell, *The Principles of English Grammar*, 158–59.

49. The content of Confederate textbooks appearing later in the war would be even more consciously political. See Chapter 5.

50. "Our Own Primary Grammar for the use of beginners," *NCJE* 4 (October 1861): 320. The positive tone of this review was not surprising, given that the *Journal of Education*'s editor, J. D. Campbell, was also co-owner of the company that published Smythe's book.

51. "Book Notices," *ERFM* 2 (March 1861): 180; "Editor's Table," *SLM* 33 (October 1861): 320.

52. Richardson and Campbell, "Meeting of Teachers," *NCJE* 4 (July 1861): 210.

53. "Our Own Primary Grammar for the use of beginners," *NCJE* 4 (October 1861): 320.

54. "Editor's Table," *SLM* 33 (October 1861): 320.

55. The titles of the books in question were *The Southern Reader; or Child's First Reading Book*, *The Southern Reader; or Child's Second Reading Book*, and *The Southern Reader; or First Class Reader*. This series was published by Wm. R. Babcock and

M'Carter Co. of Charleston throughout the 1840s and 1850s. "Our Book Table," *Southern Teacher* 2 (March 1861): 383.

56. Richardson and Campbell, "Meeting of Teachers," *NCJE* 4 (July 1861): 207–12; "Proceedings of the State Educational Association," *NCJE* 4 (November 1861): 321–36.

57. Reprinted as "Keep Up the Schools," *NCJE* 4 (June 1861): 176.

58. "Education," *SP*, August 31, 1861, 2.

59. "Laurensville Female College," *SP*, February 9, 1861, 2.

60. "Proceedings of the State Educational Association," *NCJE* 4 (November 1861): 329.

61. "The Journal for 1861," *NCJE* 4 (January 1861): 29.

62. Reprinted in W. H. O., "To Parents," *NCJE* 4 (December 1861): 372.

63. The exemption of teachers from the Confederate draft is discussed in Chapter 6.

64. "How Can We Obtain Southern Teachers," *Southern Teacher* 2 (January 1861): 285.

65. "Our Frontispiece," *Southern Teacher* 2 (May 1861): 473.

66. Many observers at the time and many historians since blamed members of the wealthy planter class for hindering the development of public education, either through their indifference, or in some cases, their active hostility. For a recent discussion of the class dimensions surrounding antebellum southern education reform, see Wells, *The Origins of the Southern Middle Class*, 133–53.

67. *Providential Aspect and Salutary Tendency of the Existing Crisis*, 25.

68. Naff's remarks were reprinted in "Teachers' Agency," *ERFM* 2 (April 1861): 238.

69. The editor of the *Repository* readily agreed and offered advertisement space for teachers and schools seeking teachers at $2 for the first insertion and $1 for each continuance. An additional $1 would be charged to forward applications to interested parties. It was not uncommon for southern newspapers and magazines to advertise teaching positions, but Naff wanted the editors themselves to take a more active role in discreetly matching teachers and employers. For its part, the *North Carolina Journal of Education* also established a "Southern School Exchange" in May 1861, to facilitate teacher placement. "Teachers' Agency," *ERFM* 2 (April 1861): 238–40; Stillman, "Education in the Confederate States of America," 73.

70. The increasing feminization of the southern teaching profession is discussed later in this chapter and in Chapter 6. For more on the experience and ambivalence of Confederate female teachers, see Faust, *Mothers of Invention*, 82–88.

71. In North Carolina, Wiley had already established a system for monitoring teacher quality in the common schools. Each year, every teacher was rated by a county examining board on a scale of one to five in such areas as spelling, reading, writing, arithmetic, geography, and grammar. By 1861, there were 2,479 teachers working in North Carolina common schools, 99 percent of whom had been licensed by examining committees. While this system was designed to ensure a minimum level of competency, it was only a beginning. Effective teachers needed to know more than simply how to read and write themselves, and normal schools would provide them with the necessary teaching skills. Ford, "Calvin H. Wiley and the Common Schools of North Carolina," 157–61, 184.

72. "Our Frontispiece," *Southern Teacher* 2 (May 1861): 473.

73. Stillman, "Education in the Confederate States of America," 50, 53. On the New Orleans normal school, see Reinders, "New England Influences on the Formation of Public Schools in New Orleans," 188–89.

74. "Our Frontispiece," *Southern Teacher* 2 (May 1861): 473.

75. For a discussion of such proposals, see Bernath, "Confederate Minds," 281–83.

76. "Bogus Normal Schools," *Southern Teacher* 2 (January 1861): 285.

77. The creation and objectives of these Confederate normal schools are discussed in Chapter 6.

78. The formation of the Educational Association of the Confederate States of America and the Educational Association of Virginia are discussed in Chapter 6.

79. The *North Carolina Journal of Education* was the organ of the North Carolina State Educational Association, and the *Repository* spoke for the Educational Institute of the Methodist Church.

80. Stillman, "Education in the Confederate States of America," 103–4.

81. For instance, it was an "Association of Southern Teachers" that produced the *Confederate Primer* and *First* and *Second Confederate Readers.*

82. "Proceedings of the State Educational Association," *NCJE* 4 (November 1861): 330.

83. Ibid., 328–31.

84. "Editorial," *DBR* 31 (October and November 1861): 469.

85. "A General Educational Convention for the South," *ERFM* 2 (April 1861): 245. This proposed meeting, though endorsed by the editor, never took place. "The July Meeting of the Educational Institute," *ERFM* 2 (May 1861): 279.

86. Richardson and Campbell, "Meeting of Teachers," *NCJE* 4 (July 1861): 207–12.

87. "Sixth Annual Meeting of the State Educational Association," *NCJE* 4 (September 1861): 286.

88. *Washington (N.C.) Dispatch*, December 3, 1861, as quoted in Stillman, "Education in the Confederate States of America," 104.

89. Two committees on the status of education were appointed at the meeting: one, headed by Wiley, to examine the general interests of Confederate education, and the other to look more specifically at the state of common schools in North Carolina. See Stillman, "Education in the Confederate States of America," 105.

90. The most comprehensive study of elite southern female education is Farnham, *The Education of the Southern Belle*. See also Clinton, *The Plantation Mistress*, 123–38; McMillen, *Southern Women*, 77–85; Woody, *A History of Women's Education in the United States*; Rable, *Civil Wars*, 18–22.

91. R. N. Price, "Popular Objections to a High Standard of Female Education," *Home Circle* 7 (April 1861): 205.

92. "Education of Southern Women," *DBR* 31 (October and November 1861): 386.

93. Ibid., 389.

94. Ibid., 390.

95. For more on southern women's changing roles during the war, see Faust, *Mothers of Invention*; Rable, *Civil Wars*; Campbell and Rice, eds., *A Woman's War*; Clinton

and Silber, eds., *Divided Houses*; Edwards, *Scarlett Doesn't Live Here Anymore*; Massey, *Refugee Life in the Confederacy*; Massey, *Bonnet Brigades*; Racine, "Emily Lyles Harris"; Roberts, *The Confederate Belle*; Scott, *The Southern Lady*; Whites, *The Civil War as a Crisis in Gender*; Wiley, *Confederate Women*.

96. C. H. Wiley, "To the People of North Carolina," *NCJE* 5 (January 1862): 2.

97. "A New Volume," *NCJE* 5 (January 1862): 30.

98. "Our Prospects," *NCJE* 5 (February 1862): 62.

99. Price, "Popular Objections to a High Standard of Female Education," *Home Circle* 7 (April 1861): 206.

100. "Education of Southern Women," *DBR* 31 (October and November 1861): 384.

101. Price, "Popular Objections to a High Standard of Female Education," *Home Circle* 7 (April 1861): 203.

102. R. N. Price, "Popular Objections to a High Standard of Female Education," *Home Circle* 7 (June 1861): 360.

103. "Education of Southern Women," *DBR* 31 (October and November 1861): 388–89.

104. Ibid., 384.

105. George Fitzhugh, "The Women of the South," *DBR* 31 (August 1861): 147, 150, 153.

106. "Education of Southern Women," *DBR* 31 (October and November 1861): 390.

107. Ibid., 389; Price, "Popular Objections to a High Standard of Female Education," *Home Circle* 7 (April 1861): 205.

108. "Education of Southern Women," *DBR* 31 (October and November 1861): 390.

109. "The Board of Editors," *NCJE* 4 (August 1861): 256.

CHAPTER 5

1. I am not the first to make this claim. Richard Harwell has noted that in terms of "new literary works," the Confederacy "was almost entirely dependent on her own resources" by the end of 1862. But whereas Harwell limited his claim to belles lettres, I am expanding this contention to include nearly all facets of Confederate print literature. Harwell, *Confederate Belles-Lettres*, 17.

2. "Editor's Table," *SLM* 34 (November and December 1862): 689; "Editor's Table," *SLM* 37 (February 1863): 117, 119.

3. Reprinted as "Current Literature," *SIN*, January 16, 1864, 16.

4. "A Southern Publishing House," *SIN*, September 27, 1862, 4.

5. "Good Sign," *Punch*, October 24, 1863, 3.

6. Reprinted as "A Criticism," *SIN*, November 29, 1862, 4.

7. Reprinted as "Current Literature," *SIN*, January 16, 1864, 16.

8. "Southern Nationality," *DSC*, January 16, 1864.

9. J. A. Turner, "A Familiar Talk with My Readers," *CTM*, January 12, 1864, 1.

10. "Chances and Changes," *SIN*, December 13, 1862, 2.

11. "The Hot Iron," *SP*, October 11, 1862, 2.

12. "Salutatory," *SIN*, September 13, 1862, 4.

13. The *Southern Episcopalian* would resume again briefly in 1863. Stroupe, *The Religious Press in the South Atlantic States*, 112–13.

14. "Our Sanctum," *SM* 1 (November 1861): 231.

15. "Our Sanctum," *SM* 1 (February 1862): 467; "Southern Literature," *SM* 1 (September 1861): 5.

16. For instance, see "Southern Literature," *SM* 1 (September 1861): 1–5; "Our Sanctum," *SM* 1 (November 1861): 225–35.

17. "Our Sanctum," *SM* 1 (February 1862): 465.

18. "The Rambler," *SM* 1 (March 1862): 556.

19. "Our Sanctum," *SM* 1 (October 1861): 146.

20. "Our Sanctum," *SM* 1 (November 1861): 231.

21. The first installment of the novel was published as "Idlewild: A Tale of West Tennessee," Southern Monthly Novel Library, No. 1., Supplement to *SM* 1 (December 1861): 1–16; "Our Sanctum," *SM* 1 (December 1861): 308.

22. "Our Sanctum," *SM* 1 (February 1862): 465.

23. "Our Sanctum," *SM* 1 (April 1862): 626.

24. "To the Patrons of the Southern Monthly," *North Carolina Whig*, May 27, 1862, 2.

25. Turner adopted the byline "Independent in Everything—Neutral in Nothing" for the September 22, 1863, issue, replacing "Brevity is the soul of wit."

26. For more on Turner and Harris, see Turner, *Autobiography of "The Countryman"*; Turner, *The Old Plantation*; Harris, *On the Plantation*; Huff, "Joseph Addison Turner: Southern Editor During the Civil War"; Huff, "Joel Harris's Mentor, Joseph Addison Turner"; Huff, "'A Bitter Draught We have Had to Quaff'"; Flanders, *Early Georgia Magazines*, 164–77; Cousins, *Joel Chandler Harris*; Harris, *The Life and Letters of Joel Chandler Harris*; Brasch, *Brer Rabbit, Uncle Remus, and the "Cornfield Journalist"*; Hubbell, *The South in American Literature*, 783–86.

27. Cousins, *Joel Chandler Harris*, 52.

28. J. A. Turner, "A Familiar Talk with My Readers," *CTM*, January 12, 1864, 1.

29. Ibid.; Turner, *Autobiography of "The Countryman,"* 9–10, 17.

30. "Prospectus," *CTM*, September 29, 1862, 8.

31. "Vol. V.," *CTM*, April 7, 1863, 2.

32. "Stonewall and the Sacrament," *CTM*, October 20, 1862, 28; "Vol. V.," *CTM*, April 7, 1863, 2.

33. For instance, see Turner's notice of the *Baptist Banner*, *CTM*, September 20, 1864, 515, and *Banner* editor James Ells's response, reprinted as "The Countryman," *CTM*, October 11, 1864, 559.

34. "This War a Punishment," *CTM*, June 10, 1863, 45.

35. "Secular Newspapers on the Lord's Day," *CTM*, September 22, 1863, 89.

36. "Third Volume," *CTM*, September 29, 1862, 1.

37. Harris, *The Life and Letters of Joel Chandler Harris*, 28; Mott, *A History of American Magazines*, 2:111; Harris, *On the Plantation*, 21–22.

38. "Third Volume," *CTM*, September 29, 1862, 1.

39. "Vol. V.," *CTM*, April 7, 1863, 2.

40. "Enlarging," *CTM*, July 14, 1863, 12.

41. *CTM*, January 12, 1864.

42. Despite the fact that the *Southern Illustrated News* was the most popular and widest circulating periodical in the Confederacy, it has attracted surprisingly little historical attention. For the most recent treatment, see Binnington, "Promoting the Confederate Nation." See also Harwell, "A Confederate View of the Southern Poets"; Bryer and Schorr, "*The Southern Illustrated News*"; McCabe, "Literature of the War"; Fahs, *The Imagined Civil War*, 31–41.

43. "Our Paper," *SIN*, January 3, 1863, 2.

44. "Salutatory," *SIN*, September 13, 1862, 4; "A News and Literary Journal for Southern Families," *SIN*, October 4, 1862, 5; "Federal Falsehood and a Doctorate of Lying," *SIN*, March 14, 1863, 2.

45. M. Louise Rogers, "Glad Greetings We Send Thee," *SIN*, October 18, 1862, 3.

46. "A News and Literary Journal for Southern Families," *SIN*, October 4, 1862, 5.

47. McCabe, "Literature of the War," 200.

48. *SIN*, September 13, 1862, 1.

49. "Our Paper," *SIN*, January 3, 1863, 2.

50. "New Contributors and a New Novel," *SIN*, February 14, 1863, 3.

51. "Completion of the First Volume," *SIN*, June 27, 1863, 4; "Close of the Second Volume," *SIN*, December 26, 1863, 198.

52. "Writing for the Press," *SIN*, April 25, 1863, 7.

53. "Our Paper," *SIN*, January 3, 1863, 2.

54. It should be noted that this number referred to estimated readers, not subscribers. "The Drama," *SIN*, April 11, 1863, 8.

55. "Completion of the First Volume," *SIN*, June 27, 1863, 4; "Close of the Second Volume," *SIN*, December 26, 1863, 198.

56. See "A Criticism," *SIN*, November 29, 1862, 4; "Notice of the Press," *SIN*, July 11, 1863, 16; "Notice of New Works," *SLM* 34 (July and August 1862): 512.

57. "We Thank Thee, Jew," *SIN*, October 11, 1862, 5.

58. Bagby went on to credit the pictures and, implicitly, the lowbrow reading habits of the southern public for the *News*'s advantage over the *Messenger*. "Editor's Table," *SLM* 36 (September and October 1862): 581. See also "Editor's Table," *SLM* 37 (April 1863): 252. For a discussion of the contrasting fortunes of the *Southern Illustrated News* and the *Southern Literary Messenger*, see Fahs, *The Imagined Civil War*, 31–33.

59. *The Magnolia: A Southern Home Journal*, December 27, 1862, 50; "To Our Readers," and A. M. "Lines on the Death of Charles Bailie," *The Magnolia*, January 3, 1863, 54, 55; "The Close of the Volume," *MW*, September 26, 1863, 320.

60. *MW*, March 7, 1863.

61. "To the Public," *MW*, June 27, 1863, 216.

62. The paper would undergo two more ownership changes and one more change of

editor during its life. H. C. Barrow and J. S. Robertson would each become part owners of the magazine for a time. Charles P. J. Dimitry became editor when McCabe departed at the end of February 1864.

63. "The Close of the Volume," *MW*, September 26, 1863, 320.

64. "The Magnolia Stories," *MW*, April 11, 1863, 129; "Our Contributors," *MW*, June 13, 1863, 200.

65. As Alice Fahs has discovered, a few of the pieces that appeared in the *Magnolia* claiming southern authorship actually came from northern journals. However, it is doubtful that the editors themselves were aware of the deception. It was more likely the work of unscrupulous contributors seeking to cash in. Such practices, and their discovery, will be discussed in the next chapter. Fahs, *The Imagined Civil War*, 107.

66. "Our Contributors," *MW*, June 13, 1863, 200.

67. McCabe, "Literature of the War": 201.

68. W. Gilmore Simms, "Benedict Arnold: The Traitor. A Drama, in an Essay," *MW*, May 16–August 1, 1863.

69. "The Close of the Volume," *MW*, September 26, 1863, 320.

70. "The Magnolia Weekly Magazine," *The Magnolia*, January 31, 1863, 70.

71. James D. McCabe Jr., "To Our Readers," *MW*, July 4, 1863, 224; "The Close of the Volume," *MW*, September 26, 1863, 320.

72. "New Literary Enterprises," *MW*, June 20, 1863, 208.

73. For a more detailed discussion of the periodicals in the following section, see Bernath, "Confederate Minds," 340–51.

74. *GCHJ*, November 2, 1863, 7.

75. "To the Literati," and William B. Smith, "A Card," *The Mercury*, April 30, 1864, 4.

76. For more on Timrod's wartime writings and activities, see Hubbell, ed., *The Last Years of Henry Timrod*; Thompson, *Henry Timrod*; Timrod, *The Poems of Henry Timrod*; Timrod, *The Essays of Henry Timrod*; Timrod, *The Collected Poems of Henry Timrod*; Timrod, *The Uncollected Poems of Henry Timrod*; West, "A Southern Editor Views the Civil War."

77. *The Portfolio* was basically a compilation of the week's issues of the *Daily South Carolinian* with some additional fiction and poetry added.

78. "Southern Nationality," *DSC*, January 16, 1864.

79. "An Opening Address," *Smith and Barrow's Monthly Magazine* 1 (May 1864): 4.

80. In July, Smith and Barrow dissolved their partnership. Barrow sold his interest in the *Magnolia* and purchased Smith's share of *Smith and Barrow's*, intending to continue the journal as *Barrow's Monthly Magazine*, and even advertising for it, but no numbers seem to have been issued. *MW*, July 30, 1864, 284.

81. *The Bohemian* was another single-issue Richmond literary journal, launched in December 1863.

82. *The Record*, December 10, 1863, 237.

83. "The 'Record' Subscribers," *The Age* 1 (February 1864): 160.

84. "Our Frontispiece," *The Age* 1 (February 1864): 159.

85. The growing eclecticism of the Confederate periodical press in general during the final year of the war and its significance will be examined in Chapter 7.

86. "Traits of the Age," *The Age* 1 (January 1864): 4.

87. Beyond the fact that it continued to publish, run advertisements, and occasionally attract notice in the Confederate press, little is known about the *Southern Literary Companion* during this period. Only scattered issues exist.

88. "Double Numbers," *SC* 20 (March and April 1862): 80.

89. "Editorial," *DBR* 32 (May–August 1862): 96.

90. "The Journal for 1863," *NCJE* 6 (March 1863): 48.

91. "Beginning of Vol. 21," *SC* 21 (January and February 1863): 25.

92. "New Publications," *SFF*, January 31, 1863, 36; "To Our Readers," *SC* 20 (November and December 1862): 208. Inflation was a serious problem for periodical publishers, forcing them to raise prices frequently. *Southern Field and Fireside*, for instance, having raised its yearly rate to $3 in November 1862, increased it to $4 in February 1863, to $7 in May, and in January 1864 more than doubled it to $8 for six months. For a discussion of publishers' attempts to cope with inflation, see Bernath, "Confederate Minds," 355–56 n. 160.

93. "To Our Readers," *SFF*, November 15, 1862, 99.

94. In order to emphasize this transformation, Gardner discontinued the old numbering system and began his "New Series" afresh with Volume I, No. 1.

95. "A New Feature," *SFF*, May 23, 1863, 143.

96. "To Our Readers," *SFF*, November 15, 1862, 99; Flanders, *Early Georgia Magazines*, 141–42. Confirming that *Southern Field and Fireside* did indeed pay its contributors, William Gilmore Simms, in a letter dated May 8, 1864, urged Paul Hamilton Hayne to "contract with Field & Fireside" for some prose writing, for which, Simms promised, he would be paid "tolerably." Simms, *The Letters of William Gilmore Simms*, 4:452.

97. "Another Advance in Subscriptions," *SFF*, February 21, 1863, 60.

98. "The Field and Fireside—Suspension," *SFF*, April 11, 1863, 116. The destruction of the Bath paper mill was a major "calamity" for publishers in the Carolinas and Georgia. The *Southern Presbyterian*, *The Countryman*, and many others were forced to resort to half sheets, or to suspend briefly as they searched for a new source of paper. "The Bath Mills," *SP*, April 23, 1863, 2; "The Half Sheet," *SP*, April 16, 1863, 2; "Scarcity of Paper," *CTM*, April 21, 1863, 17.

99. Stockton & Co. would later sell the paper to William B. Smith and J. H. Bryahn Jr. of Raleigh. See Chapter 7.

100. "To Our Subscribers and Friends," *SFF*, March 6, 1864, 5.

101. "The Southern Literary Messenger," *The Age* 1 (February 1864): 160.

102. "Editor's Table," *SLM* 34 (April 1862): 266.

103. "Editor's Table," *SLM* 34 (November and December 1862): 689.

104. Robert R. Howison, "History of the War," *SLM* 34 (February and March 1862): 172–88. Howison's work and Confederate history writing generally are examined later in this chapter.

105. "Editor's Table," *SLM* 34 (September and October 1862): 581.

106. "Editor's Table," *SLM* 38 (January 1864): 61–62.

107. The unfortunate fate of the *Southern Literary Messenger* will be discussed in Chapter 7.

108. "Southern Presbyterian Review," *SP*, March 1, 1862, 2.

109. "A Half Sheet," *SP*, April 26, 1862, 2.

110. "Our Paper," *RCA*, June 26, 1862, 2.

111. Ibid.

112. "The Southern Presbyterian in the Army," *SP*, July 5, 1862, 2. For a discussion of religious reading in the ranks, see Berends, " 'Wholesome Reading Purifies and Elevates the Man.' "

113. "A Timely Warning," *NCP*, April 25, 1863, 2; "Close of the Volume," *NCP*, December 27, 1862, 2.

114. "Our Paper," *RCA*, June 26, 1862, 2.

115. "Ourselves," *SP*, November 12, 1863, 2.

116. For instance, both the *Southern Presbyterian* and the *Southern Lutheran* were suspended briefly from late 1863 to early 1864.

117. "Our Journal," *Church Intelligencer*, January 17, 1862, 705.

118. "Price of Paper," *Christian Advocate* (Raleigh), May 27, 1863, 2. When it resumed publication in 1863, the *North Carolina Christian Advocate* shortened its name to *Christian Advocate*.

119. "Ourselves," *SP*, March 12, 1863, 2; "The Rag Bag," *SP*, April 30, 1863, 2.

120. "The Fifth Volume," *NCP*, January 4, 1862, 2; "A Timely Warning," *NCP*, April 25, 1863, 2.

121. "Our Contemporaries," *SP*, January 28, 1864, 2. The *Southern Christian Advocate* had relocated in April 1862.

122. "Southern Presbyterian Review," *NCP*, January 31, 1863, 2.

123. See "The Southern Presbyterian Review," *NCP*, April 11, 1863, 2.

124. For instance, the *Christian Index*, the *North Carolina Presbyterian*, the *Southern Christian Advocate*, and the *Southern Presbyterian* all returned to their original formats after varying periods of printing half sheets.

125. Cushing, *The New Texas Reader*, iii.

126. "A Southern Publishing House," *SIN*, September 27, 1862, 4.

127. "A Gigantic Publishing House," *CTM*, July 12, 1864, 376.

128. "The Bugle Horn of Liberty," *CTM*, July 21, 1863, 22.

129. "Editor's Table," *SLM* 37 (February 1863): 118.

130. "Another Glorious Victory," *CTM*, November 3, 1862, 46.

131. "A Southern Publishing House," *SIN*, September 27, 1862, 5.

132. The belles lettres of the Confederacy have received some scholarly attention. See Harwell, *Confederate Belles-Lettres*; Fahs, *The Imagined Civil War*; Harwell, "Gone with Miss Ravenel's Courage"; Moss, *Confederate Broadside Poems*; Ellinger, *The Southern War Poetry of the Civil War*; Klein, "Wielding the Pen"; Riepma, *Fire and Fiction*;

Binnington, "'They Have Made a Nation.'" See also Drew Faust's introduction to Augusta Jane Evans, *Macaria*, xiii–xxvi.

133. [Shepperson], *War Songs of the South*, 3.

134. Samuel D. Davies, "Observations on Our Literary Prospects," *SLM* 37 (October 1863): 620, 624.

135. "Notices of New Works," *SLM* 34 (June 1862): 399.

136. Moss, *Confederate Broadside Poems*, 5.

137. [Shepperson], *War Songs of the South*, 4–5.

138. Many of these pieces were continued in subsequent issues. In the interest of space, only a single citation for each is provided here. J. D. M'Cabe Jr., "The Aid-de-Camp: A Romance of the War," *MW*, April 4, 1863, 117–19; S, "Nellie Graves: A Story of the Present War," *MW*, November 29, 1862, 1,3; Phil. Philo, "Played Sick; or, Furloughed for Ten Days," *MW*, January 3, 1863, 55; M. T. M., "The Story of a Refugee," *MW*, April 18, 1863, 139; "The Old Scout, or, Ben Phelps's Adventure in the Yankee Fleet," *MW*, August 1, 1863, 260; Refugitta [Constance Cary Harrison], "Until Death Do Us Part. A Story of this War," *MW*, August 29, 1863, 289–90; Ernest Linn, "Forcing the Pickets: A Reminiscence of the Present War," *MW*, September 5, 1863, 300; D, "The Fatal Spring: A Peninsula Episode," *MW*, September 12, 1863, 306; A, "Sam Simpkins' First and Last Night as Sentinel," *MW*, December 5, 1863, 78–79.

139. "A Prize Romance!" *MW*, June 13, 1863, 200; "The Prize Story," *MW*, December 5, 1863, 76.

140. "$1000 Premiums," *SFF*, March 26, 1864, 4.

141. *SIN*, July 4, 1863, 4; *SIN*, March 19, 1864, 84. See also "The Award of the 'Illustrated News' Prize," *MW*, March 19, 1864, 196. By the time the *News* published Haw's tale in late April 1864, the title was changed slightly to "The Rivals: A Chickahominy Story."

142. "The Prizes," *SFF*, January 10, 1863, 16.

143. [Shepperson], *War Songs of the South*, 3.

144. Hill, *Hesper and Other Poems*.

145. See "New Books," *Church Intelligencer*, January 31, 1862, 713.

146. On Confederate broadsheet poetry, see Moss, *Confederate Broadside Poems*. See also Ellinger, *The Southern War Poetry of the Civil War.*

147. [Shepperson], *War Songs of the South*, 5.

148. *The Southern Field and Fireside Novelette.*

149. Davis's *The British Partizan* was first published in 1839.

150. Tucker, *The Partisan Leader.*

151. The public and critical reception of *Macaria* will be discussed in Chapter 7.

152. On antebellum southern history writing, see O'Brien, *Conjectures of Order*, 591–682; Bonner, *Mastering America*, 149–83.

153. Besides Jamison's massive *The Life and Times of Bertrand Du Guesclin*, there were other non-war-related historical pieces, but, like the account of New England witch-burning that appeared in *The Bohemian* in December 1863, they often had ob-

vious current political implications. "Burnt at the Stake. A Tale of 1692," *The Bohemian* (Christmas 1863): 24–30.

154. Jackson, *Confederate Monitor and Patriot's Friend*, 6.

155. "Notices of New Works," *SLM* 34 (September and October 1862): 591.

156. *The War and Its Heroes*, iii.

157. For a complete list, see Parrish and Willingham, *Confederate Imprints*, 419–526.

158. The major biographies of Jackson to appear during the war were Cooke, *The Life of Stonewall Jackson*; Dabney, *Life of Lieut. Gen. Thomas J. Jackson*; Hallock, *A Complete Biographical Sketch of "Stonewall" Jackson*; McCabe, *The Life of Lieut. Gen. T. J. Jackson*. Given the tremendous demand, these books sold extremely well. In fact, they were so profitable that bitter debates erupted between competing publishers as to whose biography was the most accurate. See "A Scandalous Libel," *SIN*, July 4, 1863, 4.

159. Pollard, *The Southern Spy*; Pollard, *The First Year of the War*; Pollard, *The Second Battle of Manassas*; Pollard, *The Seven Days' Battles in Front of Richmond*; Pollard, *The Second Year of the War*; Pollard, *The Two Nations*; Pollard, *The Rival Administrations*; Pollard, *Observations in the North*.

160. The final volumes would not appear until after the war had ended and the Confederacy was but a memory.

161. Pollard, *The Two Nations*, 8.

162. "History of the War," *Religious Herald*, December 24, 1863, 99.

163. "Literary Notices," *SLM* 38 (April 1864): 254. Alfriend, *The Life of Jefferson Davis*.

164. Abrams, *President Davis and His Administration*, 9.

165. "Notices of New Works," *SLM* 34 (June 1862): 400.

166. "Literary Notices," *SLM* 38 (April 1864): 254.

167. As discussed in the conclusion, Pollard became one of the initial architects of the "Lost Cause." Pollard, *The Lost Cause*.

168. Robert R. Howison, "History of the War," *SLM* 34 (February and March 1862): 173.

169. Howison, "History of the War," *SLM* 34 (September and October 1862): 520.

170. Howison, "History of the War," *SLM* 37 (June 1863): 321.

171. Howison, "History of the War," *SLM* 38 (June 1864): 321–33.

172. "Editor's Table," *SLM* 37 (February 1863): 118–19.

173. "The Rambler," *SM* 1 (October 1861): 151.

174. "New Publications," *MW*, October 31, 1863, 36.

175. Taliaferro's contributions to the *Southern Literary Messenger* from 1860–63 have been reprinted in Taliaferro, *Carolina Humor*.

176. Skitt, "The 'Desperade,'" *SLM* 34 (June 1862): 398; Skitt, "Sketches by Skitt," *SLM* 34 (July and August 1862): 471–72.

177. For instance, see "Negro Representation. A Letter from Africa," *SLM* 37 (March 1863): 148–51; "Editor's Table," *SLM* 37 (July 1863): 447–48.

178. There were limits, however, as the fate of the *Bugle-Horn of Liberty*, discussed below, demonstrated.

179. Reprinted as "A Well-Digested Plan for the Relief of Richmond," *SLM* 37 (November and December 1863): 732.

180. Admittedly, Longstreet's book had already appeared in serialized form in *Southern Field and Fireside* in 1859. For more on Longstreet, see Wade, *Augustus Baldwin Longstreet*.

181. Subtitle from *Bugle-Horn of Liberty* 1 (October 1863): 1.

182. For more on the humor and wartime commentary of Bill Arp, see Christie, "Bill Arp"; Parker, *Alias Bill Arp*; Austin, *Bill Arp*. See also James Austin's entry on Smith in Bain and Flora, eds., *Fifty Southern Writers*, 416–26. For Arp's collected wartime letters, see Smith, *Bill Arp, So Called*.

183. Flanders, "*Bugle-Horn of Liberty*," 82–83.

184. The series concluded with the quip: "Can't some of you do as John has done, and raise yourselves to that prominence that will insure not only your name, but a full length engraving, being printed in the leading *Illustrated* paper of the country. Try to emulate his example, less his last grand splurge in Ohio." *Bugle-Horn of Liberty* 1 (October 1863): 9.

185. *GCHJ*, November 9, 1863, 4.

186. "Miscegenation: or, the 'Free American of African descent' enjoying his long-lost 'Freedom,' " *Confederate Spirit and Knapsack of Fun* 1 (May 1864): 16.

187. "New Publications," *SIN*, May 7, 1864, 144; *CTM*, May 17, 1864, 280; "New Publications," *SC* 22 (June 1864): 96.

188. For a brief overview of the publishing history and content of *Southern Punch*, see Linneman, "*Southern Punch*."

189. "Salutatory," *Punch*, August 15, 1863, 2.

190. "Punch and a Critic," *Punch*, August 22, 1863, 5.

191. Co-owner William Campbell served as *Punch*'s main engraver, at least until he absconded with funds in February 1864. "Notice," *Punch*, February 6, 1864, 4.

192. See untitled engraving, *Punch*, August 29, 1863, 5; "A Change of Masters," *Punch*, September 19, 1863, 8; "Fate of Contrabands," *Punch*, December 26, 1863, 8; "Yankee Idea of African Freedom," *Punch*, April 23, 1864, 5.

193. "Past, Present and Future," *Punch*, September 13, 1863, 2; "Some Words about Punch," *Punch*, October 10, 1863, 4.

194. "New England Brayeth," *Punch*, October 24, 1863, 4.

195. See "Attention Each Army Corps of Readers," *Punch*, August 22, 1864, 4; "Third Volume," *Punch*, November 8, 1864, 4.

196. *GCHJ*, August 17, 1863, 2.

197. "The Southern Punch," *CTM*, September 15, 1863, 82–83.

198. Mott, *A History of American Magazines*, II, 113.

199. Porcher, *Resources of the Southern Fields and Forests*.

200. "A Medical and Surgical Journal," *SIN*, October 24, 1863, 124.

201. "A Medical and Surgical Journal Again," *SIN*, October 31, 1863, 132; "The Medical and Surgical Journal," *SIN*, November 7, 1863, 140.

202. *SIN*, December 5, 1863, 176; "The Confederate States Medical and Surgical Journal," *SIN*, January 16, 1864, 12.

203. "Salutatory," *CSMSJ* 1 (January 1864): 13.

204. "The Prospect Before Us," *CSMSJ* 1 (May 1864): 78.

205. "To the Reader," *CSMSJ* 1 (September 1864): 140.

206. For more on these papers, see Berends, "'Wholesome Reading Purifies and Elevates the Man.'"

207. "The Army and Navy Messenger," *RCA*, May 7, 1863, 2.

208. *The Camp Jester*, iv.

209. By far, the most comprehensive work on Confederate children's literature is Kennerly, "Confederate Juvenile Imprints." See also Marten, *The Children's Civil War*; Fahs, *The Imagined Civil War*, 256–86.

210. Authorship of *For the Little Ones* is attributed to Althea Law Burroughs in Parrish and Willingham, *Confederate Imprints*, 537.

211. The *Child's Index*, a Baptist monthly from Macon, made its first appearance in September 1862, and began regular publication at the beginning of 1863. It continued until the end of the war. The *Children's Guide* was also published in Macon by the same publishers, and though edited by a Methodist minister, was non-denominational in tone. It began in July 1863, and published monthly throughout the war. The Presbyterian *Children's Friend* came from Richmond. It first appeared in August 1862, and continued, it seems, until the city's fall. The late-arriving *Child's Banner* was published in Salisbury, North Carolina, starting in February 1865. Not surprisingly, given this late date, it did not live long. *The Portfolio* and the *Sunday School Paper for the South* were both short-lived papers from Charleston founded in 1861. Published by the students of the North Carolina Institution for the Deaf and Dumb and the Blind, *Deaf Mute Casket* was the longest running Confederate juvenile periodical. Established in the fall of 1861, it ran through the end of the war. For more, see Kennerly, "Confederate Juvenile Imprints," 250–312.

212. Much to Joseph Turner's outrage, each denomination had its own children's paper advocating its own brand of Christianity. He specifically accused the Baptist *Child's Index* and the Presbyterian *Children's Friend* of poisoning "the minds of the infants with their sectarian prejudices, so as to render it as impossible to get an enlarged idea of religion into their cramped up minds and hearts, as it is to give proper shape to the craniums of the Flat-head Indians." "The Child's Friend," *CTM*, October 27, 1862, 38.

213. "Salutatory," *Child's Index* 1 (September 1862): 3.

214. "The Children's Friend," *NCP*, September 20, 1862, 2; "Subscription List," *Children's Friend* 1 (January 1863): 23; "The Children's Friend," *NCP*, January 31, 1863, 2; "Close of the Volume," *Children's Friend* 1 (July 1863): 47.

215. "10,000 copies," *Child's Index* 1 (February 1863): 2; "11,000," *Child's Index* 1 (November 1863): 42; "The Child's Index," *Christian Index*, May 20, 1864, 2; "Unfortunate—Pardon Asked," *Child's Index* 2 (December 1864): 46.

216. "War," *Child's Index* 1 (September 1862): 2.

217. "Editor's Monthly Letter," *Child's Index* 1 (June 1863): 22.

218. Samuel Boykin, "Our Negroes," *Child's Index* 1 (October 1863): 39.

219. Mrs. L. N. Boykin, "Nellie Lester," *Child's Index* 1 (February 1863): 1; Samuel Boykin, "The 'Raid,'" *Child's Index* 1 (October 1863): 37; Mrs. M. J. Mallary, "A War Picture (Founded on Fact)," *Child's Index* 1 (November 1863): 44.

220. Boykin, *The Boys and Girls Stories of the War*.

221. *Uncle Buddy's Gift Book for the Holidays*, 14–19.

222. *For the Little Ones*, 32–33.

223. *A Confederate Alphabet*.

224. "The Children's Friend," *NCP*, September 20, 1862, 2.

225. "Smith's Revised English Grammar," *The Age* 1 (January 1864): 49.

226. "Notices of New Works," *SLM* 37 (June 1863): 384.

227. "Publishers' Notice to Second Edition," dated June 1864, in Chaudron, *The First Reader*, 4.

228. Likewise, such was the demand for Samuel Lander's *Our Own Primary Arithmetic* that it had at least three print runs and two editions. John Neely's *Confederate States Speller and Reader* was printed twice, as was the revised Confederate version of *Smith's English Grammar*. There were three editions of Charles Smythe's *Our Own Primary Grammar*, three of Richard Sterling's *Our Own First Reader*, three of his *Our Own Primer*, two each of his *Our Own Second Reader* and *Our Own Third Reader*, and four of his *Our Own Spelling Book*. Parrish and Willingham, *Confederate Imprints*, 633, 638, 642, 647, 648, 649–50.

229. The second edition of Moore's geography was titled *Primary Geography*. See Davis and Parks, "Confederate School Geographies"; Parrish and Willingham, *Confederate Imprints*, 641–42.

230. Davis, "Textbooks for Texans During the Civil War," 20; Davis, "Textbooks for Confederate School Children," 17.

231. Parrish and Willingham, *Confederate Imprints*, 636–37.

232. Paedagogus, "Bingham's Latin Grammar," *NCP*, January 27, 1864, 1.

233. "Bays and Laurels—That Other Jackson," *SIN*, November 22, 1862, 2.

234. Bingham, *A Grammar of the Latin Language*, iv.

235. Rice, *A System of Modern Geography*, 3.

236. Cushing, *The New Texas Reader*, iii, 126–31. See also Thomas, "Rebel Nationalism: E. H. Cushing and the Confederate Experience."

237. Johnson, *An Elementary Arithmetic*, 44, 51, 38.

238. Moore, *The Dixie Speller*, 23.

239. Fleming, *The Revised Elementary Spelling Book*, 5, 97, 128, 166–68. In her dissertation, Sarah Kennerly documented at least nine other similar alterations to Webster's text. Kennerly, "Confederate Juvenile Imprints," 82–83.

240. Rice, *A System of Modern Geography*, 3.

241. Ibid., 12, 21.

242. Moore, *The Geographical Reader*, 14.

243. Ibid.

244. Rice, *A System of Modern Geography*, 51.

245. Moore, *The Geographical Reader*, 13–14.

246. Rice, *A System of Modern Geography*, 7. See also Moore, *The Geographical Reader*, 10–11.

247. Rice, *A System of Modern Geography*, 8, 21.

248. Moore, *The Geographical Reader*, 14, 21, 37.

249. Harwell, "Brief Candle: The Confederate Theatre," 42. Fortunately, there is a sizable body of secondary literature on Confederate theater. See Brockett and Brockett, "Civil War Theater: Contemporary Treatments"; Fife, "The Confederate Theater"; Fife, "The Confederate Theater in Georgia"; Harwell, "Civil War Theater: The Richmond Stage"; Hoole, "Charleston Theatricals During the Tragic Decade"; Reardon, "Civil War Theater: Formal Organization"; Reardon and Foxen, "Civil War Theater: The Propaganda Play"; Waal, "The First Original Confederate Drama"; Welsh, "Civil War Theater: The War in Drama"; Watson, *The History of Southern Drama*, 74–84.

250. Fife, "The Confederate Theater," 227.

251. For a discussion of these religious objections and the secular response to them, see Bernath, "Confederate Minds," 424–25 n. 380.

252. "The Drama—Its Regeneration," *The Magnolia*, October 11, 1862, 6.

253. For his poem, Timrod was paid $300 by theater manager Richard Ogden. "Notice of New Works," *SLM* 37 (March 1863): 192.

254. Henry Timrod, "Inaugural Poem," *SIN*, February 21, 1863, 8. See also "The Dedication of the Richmond Theatre," *MW*, February 14, 1863, 78; and *MW*, February 21, 1863, 82.

255. Harwell, "Brief Candle: The Confederate Theatre," 57.

256. Significantly, Waldon issued this call on a national level by running ads in the *Richmond Dispatch*, the *Southern Illustrated News*, the *Charleston Courier*, the *Savannah News and Republican*, the *Mobile Advertiser*, and *Southern Field and Fireside*. "To Southern Writers," *SFF*, February 28, 1863, 72.

257. "Notices of New Works," *SLM* 37 (March 1863): 192.

258. "The Local Drama," *MW*, August 27, 1864, 316.

259. There were many others. For a more complete list, see Brockett and Brockett, "Civil War Theater: Contemporary Treatments." See also *GCHJ*, July 6, 1863, 3; "Dramatic and Musical," *MW*, April 18, 1863, 136; "Dramatic," *SFF*, February 21, 1863, 60. *King Linkum the First: A Musical Burletta*, written by the prolific John Hill Hewitt, has been subsequently published by Emory University Publications.

260. Harwell, "Civil War Theater: The Richmond Stage," 297–98.

261. McCabe, *The Guerrillas: An Original Domestic Drama*. For reviews of *The Guerrillas*, see "The Varieties," *The Magnolia*, December 27, 1862, 50; "The Varieties—The Guerrillas," *The Magnolia*, January 3, 1863, 54; "The Drama," *SIN*, January 3, 1863, 8; "Notices of New Works," *SLM* 37 (March 1863): 192.

262. "The Drama," *SIN*, January 3, 1863, 8; McCabe, *The Guerrillas*, 3.

263. McCabe, *The Guerrillas*, 25, 37, 30.

264. "Notices of New Works," *SLM* 37 (March 1863): 192; McCabe, *The Guerrillas*, 3. See also Waal, "The First Original Confederate Drama."

265. Harwell, "Brief Candle: The Confederate Theatre," 69. For a particularly scathing review, see "The Drama," *SIN*, March 28, 1863, 8.

266. "The Local Drama," *MW*, August 27, 1864, 316.

CHAPTER 6

1. Reprinted as "Current Literature," *SIN*, January 16, 1864, 16.

2. A. B. Stark, "Southern Literature," *Home Circle* 7 (September 1861): 515–16.

3. Reprinted as Mary A. McCrimmon, "Speculation versus Literature," *Banner and Baptist*, March 22, 1862, 1.

4. M. B. Moore, "Our Literature," *Christian Advocate* (Raleigh), January 16, 1864, 1.

5. "A Home Literature," *MW*, November 7, 1863, 44.

6. "Our Literature," *MW*, July 11, 1863, 232.

7. "Current Literature," *MW*, June 20, 1863, 208.

8. "National Songs," *DSC*, January 24, 1864.

9. "National Ballads," *MW*, October 3, 1863, 4. See also "Not Written Yet," *Punch*, November 21, 1863, 5; "Song Writing," *Punch*, March 26, 1864, 7; "War Songs," *The Mercury*, September 3, 1864, 4.

10. "National Songs," *DSC*, January 24, 1864.

11. William Archer Cocke, "Sketches of Southern Literature," *MW*, November 28, 1863, 71.

12. "Editor's Table," *SLM* 38 (January 1864): 63–64.

13. Watchman, "Gossip Columns," *CTM*, September 22, 1863, 89.

14. "Southern Literature," *DSC*, January 14, 1864.

15. "Current Literature," *MW*, June 20, 1863, 208.

16. *The Education of Teachers in the South*, 17.

17. "Our Literature," *MW*, July 11, 1863, 232.

18. "The Drama," *SIN*, December 5, 1863, 176.

19. "Nationality in Literature," *DSC*, January 19, 1864.

20. "The Southern Punch," *CTM*, September 15, 1863, 83.

21. [George Bagby], "My Uncle Flatback's Plantation. A Rambling Summer Piece," *SLM* 37 (October 1863): 596.

22. "Southern Nationality," *DSC*, January 16, 1864.

23. "The Magnolia Stories," *MW*, April 11, 1863, 129.

24. Watchman, "Gossip Columns," *CTM*, September 22, 1863, 89.

25. "Yankee Literature," *SIN*, September 13, 1862, 5.

26. Davies, "Observations on Our Literary Prospects," *SLM* 37 (October 1863): 626.

27. "Revolution," *Confederate Baptist*, March 25, 1863, 2.

28. Hall, *The Historic Significance of the Southern Revolution*, 4–5, 41.

29. George Fitzhugh, "The Revolutions of 1776 and 1861 Contrasted," *SLM* 37 (November and December 1863): 723, 722.

30. "Southern Conservatism," *SFF*, January 23, 1864, 4. See also William A. Coleman, "Address," *NCJE* 6 (November 1863): 125; "Fogies and Fogydom," *Punch*, October 3, 1863, 2.

31. "Southern Conservatism," *SFF*, January 23, 1864, 4.

32. "Fogies and Fogydom," *Punch*, October 3, 1863, 2.

33. "Southern Conservatism," *SFF*, January 23, 1864, 4.

34. "Nationality in Literature," *DSC*, January 19, 1864.

35. [Bagby], "My Uncle Flatback's Plantation. A Rambling Summer Piece," *SLM* 37 (October 1863): 596.

36. "Nationality in Literature," *DSC*, January 19, 1864.

37. *The Education of Teachers in the South*, 5.

38. W. Gilmore Simms, "Sketches in Greece," *SIN*, October 11, 1862, 2.

39. Surveying the battles up to that point, *Punch* concluded that "Manassas, Malvern Hill, Chickamauga, will serve the ends of the poets. These names can be woven into ballad verse with some ease; so could Antietam, properly pronounced, had we wrested the name from the Yankees. But the balladist will pause at Fredericksburg, Sharpsburg, Gettysburg, Perryville and Chancellorsville. Punch verily believes that these names are lost to ballad verse. As for Gaines' Farm, Cross Keys, McDowell, (which should have been called Islington Hill, a poetical name,) the poet can do nothing with them." In the future, *Punch* advised generals that "whenever there is likely to be a battle, and you have selected your ground, see if the Indians have not given the spot one of their beautiful and significant baptismal names. If not, then invent a musical name for the encampment, and so go down to remote posterity through the poets." "Punch to the Generals of the Confederate Armies," *Punch*, November 21, 1863, 3.

40. "Current Literature," *MW*, June 20 1863, 208.

41. "The Southern Lyre," *SIN*, July 4, 1863, 5.

42. "Sketches of Southern Literature," *MW*, October 3, 1863, 4. Cocke, *The Constitutional History of the United States*.

43. "An Hour Among the Southern Poets," *Punch*, October 31, 1863, 2–3.

44. Davidson was a former professor of Greek and Latin at the College of South Carolina. During the war, he served as an adjutant in the 13th South Carolina Volunteers in Stonewall Jackson's Corps. William Moss, *Confederate Broadside Poems*, 9.

45. Paul Hamilton Hayne, "The Southern Lyre," *SIN*, July 4, 1863, 6.

46. "Literature of the South," *Punch*, December 12, 1863, 2.

47. "Bays and Laurels—That Other Jackson," *SIN*, November 22, 1862, 2.

48. "The Southern Lyre," *SIN*, July 4, 1863, 5.

49. "Bays and Laurels—That Other Jackson," *SIN*, November 22, 1862, 2.

50. Cocke, "Sketches of Southern Literature," *MW*, October 17, 1863, 22.

51. "Our Literature," *MW*, July 11, 1863, 232.

52. Cocke, "Sketches of Southern Literature," *MW*, October 17, 1863, 22.

53. "The Southern Lyre," *SIN*, July 4, 1863, 5.

54. Hayne, "The Southern Lyre," *SIN*, July 4, 1863, 6.

55. "The Southern Lyre," *SIN*, July 4, 1863, 5.

56. "An Hour Among the Southern Poets," *Punch*, October 31, 1863, 2–3; "An Hour Among the Southern Poets," *Punch*, November 7, 1863, 2; "An Hour Among the Southern Poets," *Punch*, November 14, 1863, 2.

57. Cocke, "Sketches of Southern Literature," *MW*, October 17, 1863, 23.

58. Cocke, "Sketches of Southern Literature," *MW*, October 31, 1863, 38.

59. Cocke, "Sketches of Southern Literature," *MW*, November 7, 1863, 47.

60. Cocke, "Sketches of Southern Literature," *MW*, October 24, 1863, 31; Cocke, "Sketches of Southern Literature," *MW*, October 31, 1863, 38; Cocke, "Sketches of Southern Literature," *MW*, November 7, 1863, 47.

61. These authors included Evans, Hayne, Simms, Flash, and Fitzhugh. I cannot provide a complete list of Davidson's figures as I have been unable to locate five issues of *The Mercury* in which his articles appeared. After the war, Davidson continued the series in the *Crescent Monthly* and later still reworked some of this material for his book *Living Writers of the South*.

62. Davidson, "Litterateurs of the South. No. I. Augusta J. Evans of Mobile, ALA," *The Mercury*, June 18, 1864, 5. The critical reaction to *Macaria* is discussed at length in Chapter 7.

63. Davidson, "Litterateurs of the South. No. 7 George Fitzhugh, of Richmond, VA," *The Mercury*, August 27, 1864, 5.

64. Davidson, "Litterateurs of the South. No. 2. Paul Hamilton Hayne of Charleston, S.C.," *The Mercury*, June 25, 1864, 5.

65. Davidson, "Litterateurs of the South. No. 5. William Gilmore Simms, LL.D., of South Carolina," *The Mercury*, July 30, 1864, 5; Davidson, "Litterateurs of the South. No. 5. William Gilmore Simms, LL.D., of South Carolina," *The Mercury*, August 6, 1864, 5.

66. The growing severity of criticism late in the war will be discussed in Chapter 7. In the case of Davidson, personal animosity also may have been a factor, at least when it came to critiquing Hayne and Simms. Timrod, Hayne, and Simms apparently harbored a strong dislike for Davidson and took a very dim view of his abilities as literary critic. Davidson was aware of this animosity and may have reciprocated it. See Hubbell, ed., *The Last Years of Henry Timrod*, 28–29; Simms, *The Letters of William Gilmore Simms*, 4:460–61.

67. "Southern Literature," *SM* 1 (September 1861): 5.

68. "Our Sanctum," *SM* 1 (November 1861): 230.

69. Cocke, "Sketches of Southern Literature," *MW*, November 28, 1863, 70.

70. Davies, "The Fine Arts at the South," *SLM* 34 (November and December 1862): 658.

71. Hayne, "The Southern Lyre," *SIN*, July 4, 1863, 6.

72. Davies, "Observations on Our Literary Prospects," *SLM* 37 (October 1863): 621.

73. "Southern Literature," *DSC*, January 14, 1864.

74. Amica, Letter to Editor, *GCHJ*, November 30, 1863, 7.

75. Quoted in "A Criticism," *SIN*, November 29, 1862, 4.

76. Davies, "Observations on Our Literary Prospects," *SLM* 37 (October 1863): 621.

77. "Blue Writing," *The Magnolia*, January 10, 1863, 58; "Writing for the Press," *SIN*, April 25, 1863, 7; "Editor's Table," *SLM* 38 (January 1864): 63; Amica, Letter to Editor, *GCHJ*, November 30, 1863, 7.

78. "Our Contributors," *MW*, June 13, 1863, 200.

79. Davies, "Observations on Our Literary Prospects," *SLM* 37 (October 1863): 624.

80. Watchman, "Gossip Columns," *CTM*, September 22, 1863, 89.

81. Davies, "Observations on Our Literary Prospects," *SLM* 37 (October 1863): 624.

82. "The Trials of an Editor," *MW*, January 16, 1864, 124.

83. "To Our Poetical Contributors," *DSC*, January 19, 1864.

84. "Writing for the Press," *SIN*, April 25, 1863, 7.

85. "Poetry," *Christian Advocate* (Raleigh), May 27, 1863, 2.

86. "Editor's Table," *SLM* 37 (July 1863): 447.

87. "To Correspondents," *SIN*, August 8, 1863, 40. To illustrate their point, Confederate editors occasionally printed particularly egregious examples of poor writing to vindicate their editorial decisions and show just how bad it could be. See Editorial Note to J. R. C., "The Stormy Perch," *GCHJ*, November 23, 1863, 5; "Editor's Table," *SLM* 34 (April 1862): 265–66.

88. "Literary Papers in the South," *CTM*, November 10, 1863, 4.

89. "New Works," *SIN*, May 16, 1863, 2.

90. "History," *MW*, October 10, 1863, 12.

91. "Mrs. Chaudron's First Reader," *GCHJ*, November 23, 1863, 4.

92. [Smith], *Smith's English Grammar*, 5.

93. "Smith's Revised English Grammar," *The Age* 1 (January 1864): 49–56.

94. "The Effect of Song," *Punch*, October 3, 1863, 3.

95. "New Publications," *MW*, November 21, 1863, 60.

96. "Southern Songs," *MW*, November 7, 1863, 44.

97. "Not Written Yet," *Punch*, November 21, 1863, 5; "New Publications," *MW*, November 21, 1863, 60.

98. "Dramatic Notices," *MW*, March 7, 1863, 88; "Dramatic Notices," *MW*, March 14, 1863, 96; "Dramatic Notices," *MW*, March 21, 1863, 104; "Dramatic Notices," *MW*, June 27, 1863, 216; "The Drama in Richmond," *MW*, April 16, 1864, 232; "The Drama," *SIN*, March 28, 1863, 8; "The Drama," *Bugle-Horn of Liberty* 1 (October 1863): 14.

99. "The Drama in Richmond," *MW*, April 16, 1864, 232.

100. "The Drama," *SIN*, December 5, 1863, 176.

101. "Dramatic Notices," *MW*, June 27, 1863, 216.

102. "The Drama," *SIN*, March 28, 1863, 8.

103. *GCHJ*, November 2, 1863, 7; "Dramatic Notices," *MW*, March 21, 1863, 104; "The Drama," *SIN*, January 3, 1863, 8; "The Drama," *SIN*, March 28, 1863, 8.

104. Editor A. G. Horn of the *Gulf City Home Journal* was the play's sole defender.

"Gulf City Home Journal and 'The Royal Ape,'" *GCHJ*, November 9, 1863, 6; *GCHJ*, October 19, 1863, 2; "The Royal Ape," *GCHJ*, May 25, 1863, 2.

105. "The Stage and its Critics," *Punch*, October 3, 1863, 8.

106. Watchman, "Gossip Columns," *CTM*, September 22, 1863, 89.

107. W. W. T., "Field and Fireside," *CTM*, February 9, 1864, 47; "Literary Papers in the South," *CTM*, November 10, 1863, 4; "Brief Items," *GCHJ*, September 26, 1863, 2.

108. S. A. W., "Uncle John on Poetry," *MW*, September 19, 1863, 316.

109. "Puffing," *MW*, November 14, 1863, 52.

110. "Punch Examining his Exchanges," *Punch*, November 21, 1863, 8; "To Our Exchanges," *SIN*, November 15, 1862, 3.

111. "An Explanation," *MW*, August 8, 1863, 264; "An Explanation," *MW*, August 29, 1863, 288; "A June Vigil," *SFF*, August 15, 1863, 200.

112. "Literary Papers in the South," *CTM*, November 10, 1863, 4.

113. "A Literary Theft," *MW*, October 10, 1863, 12. For a similar discovery involving an Oliver Wendell Holmes poem, see "Editor's Table," *SLM* 34 (November and December 1862): 690.

114. She also discovered at least one purportedly southern poem in *Magnolia Weekly* that had appeared in *Frank Leslie's Illustrated Newspaper* the year before. Alice Fahs, *The Imagined Civil War*, 132, 106–7.

115. Quoted in "Literary Papers in the South," *CTM*, November 10, 1863, 4.

116. "Plagiarism," *The Magnolia*, February 21, 1863, 82.

117. Amica, Letter to Editor, *GCHJ*, November 30, 1863, 7.

118. "Literary Papers in the South," *CTM*, November 10, 1863, 4.

119. "Yankee Literature," *SIN*, August 8, 1863, 36–37.

120. J.E.C.D., "The Future of our Country," *SP*, February 1, 1862, 1.

121. *The Education of Teachers in the South*, 3–4.

122. "What Are We To Do For School-Books?" *SFF*, April 4, 1863, 108.

123. Cocke, "Sketches of Southern Literature," *MW*, November 28, 1863, 71.

124. McCrimmon, "Speculation versus Literature," *Banner and Baptist*, March 22, 1862, 1.

125. J. C. J., "The Standard of Moral Character in Teachers," *NCJE* 7 (January 1864): 11.

126. "Teacher's Convention," *NCJE* 6 (March 1863): 47.

127. Edward S. Joynes, "Education After the War," *SLM* 37 (August 1863): 487.

128. "Extracts from Report of Gen. Sup. of Com. Schools," *NCJE* 7 (March 1864): 29.

129. *The Education of Teachers in the South*, 17.

130. Wiley, *Circular to the Authorities and People of North Carolina*; North Carolina General Assembly, *A Bill to Provide for the Establishment of Graded Schools*; Ford, "Calvin H. Wiley and the Common Schools of North Carolina," 181–83, 226–28, 235–39; Stillman, "Education in the Confederate States of America," 255–63; Knight, *Public School Education in North Carolina*, 183–84.

131. [Junius], *Conscription of Teachers*, 1.

132. "The Future of Our Youth," *DSC*, February 14, 1864.

133. A Teacher, "Not Extortioners," *CTM*, October 27, 1862, 38.

134. *The Education of Teachers in the South*, 6.

135. Ego, "Female Education," *NCP*, August 2, 1862, 1; "What Are We to do for School-Books?," *SFF*, April 4, 1863, 108.

136. "The Future of Our Youth," *DSC*, February 14, 1864.

137. "Education in the South," *MW*, December 12, 1863, 84.

138. "Danger Ahead," *MW*, August 1, 1863, 256.

139. Wiley, *Circular to the Authorities and People of North Carolina*, 7.

140. "New Publications," *SFF*, February 21, 1863, 60.

141. J. C. McLeod, F. H. Johnston, and Wm. M. Coleman, "Address to Parents and Teachers," *NCJE* 6 (July 1863): 91–92.

142. "Smith's Revised English Grammar," *The Age* 1 (January 1864): 49.

143. See Moore, *Conscription and Conflict in the Confederacy*, 53–55, 69; Stillman, "Education in the Confederate States of America," 151–59, 316–22.

144. Far more controversial was the "Twenty Negro Law," which exempted one white male on every plantation with twenty or more slaves.

145. Depending on the state in which they resided, male teachers could still be summoned for state militia duty. See Stillman, "Education in the Confederate States of America," 160–65.

146. *The Education of Teachers in the South*, 7.

147. F. H. Johnston, C. W. Smythe, and J. D. Campbell, "Address to Teachers and Friends of Education in North Carolina," *NCJE* 6 (July 1863): 88.

148. Joynes, "Education After the War," *SLM* 37 (August 1863): 486, 488–89.

149. "To the Ladies," *SP*, June 25, 1863, 1. There was some talk about training the ever-growing number of wounded and disabled Confederate soldiers to serve as teachers. Calvin Wiley was a major proponent of the idea, and some southern colleges offered to waive tuition for discharged veterans. Such proposals were much more concerned with providing a safety net for soldiers than advancing the educational interests of children, and, some writers worried, unintentionally undermined the respectability of the teaching profession by suggesting that those fitted for nothing else could always teach. For instance, see A. C. D., "The Education of Teachers," *Baptist Banner*, March 5, 1864, 2.

150. C. H. Wiley, "To the People of North Carolina," *NCJE* 5 (January 1862): 2.

151. "A New Volume," *NCJE* 5 (January 1862): 30.

152. In his annual report for 1863, Superintendent Wiley was pleased to note an impressive increase in the number of female teachers working in North Carolina's common schools. "Extracts from Report of Gen. Sup. of Com. Schools," *NCJE* 7 (March 1864): 28. See also Stillman, "Education in the Confederate States of America," 265–72. On the continued reluctance of some upper-class southern women to teach, and the ambivalence of those already doing so, see Faust, *Mothers of Invention*, 86–88.

153. "To the Ladies," *SP*, June 25, 1863, 1.

154. J. M. M. Caldwell, Letter to Editor responding to Knox's "Education in the Confederacy," *SP*, April 9, 1863, 1.

155. *The Education of Teachers in the South*; Stillman, "Education in the Confederate States of America," 276–80.

156. "Proceedings of State Educational Association," *NCJE* 5 (November 1862): 265; "Annual Meeting of the Association," *NCJE* 5 (November 1862): 282.

157. For more on the activities of the state educational association, see the *North Carolina Journal of Education*. As the public voice of the Association, the *Journal* recorded and reprinted all of its actions, circulars, public letters, and speeches. See also "Annual Meeting of State Educational Association of N.C.," *Biblical Recorder*, October 1, 1862, 2; "Educational Association," *NCP*, November 1, 1862, 2; "State Educational Association," *NCP*, September 5, 1863, 2; "To the Teachers of the South," *RCA*, March 12, 1863, 1; "To the Teachers of the South," *SCA*, March 12, 1863, 40–41; State Educational Association of North Carolina, *The Constitution[,] By-Laws and Act of Incorporation of the State Educational Association, of North Carolina*; Stillman, "Education in the Confederate States of America," 102–7.

158. "Teachers' Convention," *The Age* 1 (January 1864): 75–76; "Educational Interests—Teacher's Convention," *RCA*, December 10, 1863, 2; "Convention of Teachers of Virginia," *Richmond Enquirer*, November 24, 1863; Leavenworth, *To the Teachers*; Stillman, "Education in the Confederate States of America," 107–8; Davis, "The Educational Association of the C.S.A.," 77.

159. "Teacher's Convention," *NCJE* 6 (March 1863): 47. This resolution, or at least language from it, was reprinted in nearly every major Confederate newspaper and periodical.

160. John D. Wolcott, "The Southern Educational Convention of 1863," 354–55.

161. Educational Association of the Confederate States of America, *Proceedings of the Convention of Teachers of the Confederate States*, 8.

162. Ibid., 18.

163. "Resident Editor's Department," *NCJE* 6 (July 1863): 93; "Educational Convention Postponed," *SFF*, September 12, 1863, 233.

164. For more on the Educational Association of the Confederate States, see Davis, "The Educational Association of the C.S.A."; Wolcott, "The Southern Educational Convention of 1863"; Stillman, "Education in the Confederate States of America," 109–15.

CHAPTER 7

1. "Southern Literary Messenger," *Punch*, January 16, 1864, 6.

2. "Are We a Literary People," *Punch*, February 27, 1864, 2.

3. Reprinted as "Newspaper Expenses," *CTM*, August 2, 1864, 413.

4. Reprinted as "Printer's Glue," *CTM*, November 1, 1864, 605; Reprinted as "A Convention of Editors," *CTM*, March 28, 1865, 187; "Trouble Ahead—Change in Terms," *SCA*, February 18, 1864, 2.

5. "Take Notice," *RCA*, April 7, 1864, 2; "Prospects of the Advocate—Raising the Price," *RCA*, September 8, 1864, 2; *RCA*, January 12, 1865, 2.

6. From $5 a year to $10 for six months. *SP*, May 5, 1864, 1; "Our Resumption," *SP*, October 6, 1864, 2.

7. "Increased Price," *CTM*, May 3, 1864, 238; "Our Purpose," *CTM*, July 26, 1864, 394.

8. "Take Notice," *RCA*, April 7, 1864, 2.

9. In fact, the *Cultivator* remained one of the best bargains to be found in the Confederacy, so much so that Joseph Turner accused its proprietors of "giving their journal away." "To Our Old Patrons," *SC* 23 (February 1865): 24; "The Southern Cultivator," *CTM*, June 28, 1864, 350.

10. Reprinted in "Trials of the Religious Press," *Christian Observer*, July 21, 1864, 2.

11. Ibid.; "Advance in Terms," *Christian Observer*, September 15, 1864, 2.

12. Significantly, this list reveals not only the declining fortunes of the Confederacy, but also the truly national circulation of the *Cultivator*. " 'Refugee' Papers," *SC* 22 (April 1864): 65.

13. "The Mails—Irregular and Unsafe," *Christian Observer*, February 9, 1865, 2.

14. "Southern Cultivator," *SFF*, February 11, 1865, 8; " 'Monthly,' not 'Weekly,' " *SC* 23 (January 1865): 8; "To Our Old Patrons," *SC* 23 (February 1865): 24; Wm B. Smith and J. H. Bryahn Jr., "A Card," *SFF*, November 5, 1864, 4; "Our Resumption," *SP*, October 6, 1864, 2; "Temporary Suspension," *SCA*, April 13, 1865, 2.

15. "Journalists of Atlanta," *CTM*, September 13, 1864, 503.

16. "Apology," *Child's Index* 2 (December 1864): 46.

17. "What We Lost," *CTM*, December 6, 1864, 676; Harris, *On the Plantation*, 223–30.

18. "Incidents," *CTM*, November 29, 1864, 664.

19. "The Coming of the Yankees," *CTM*, December 6, 1864, 671–72. See also Huff, " 'A Bitter Draught We have Had to Quaff.' "

20. "Another Delay," *Christian Observer*, October 6, 1864, 2.

21. *DSC*, November 11, 1864.

22. See Moore, *Conscription and Conflict in the Confederacy*, 65–66, 89–113.

23. "To Our Subscribers," *MW*, June 11, 1864, 260; "To Our Subscribers," *MW*, July 9, 1864, 268.

24. "To Our Patrons," *Punch*, June 4, 1864, 2.

25. "Again Issued," *Punch*, June 11, 1864, 5.

26. "The Press," *DSC*, January 17, 1864.

27. "Exemptions and Other Matters," *SC* 23 (February 1865): 20.

28. "The Conscription in Alabama," *CTM*, November 22, 1864, 655.

29. "The Exempts," *CTM*, March 14, 1865, 150; *Official Records of the Union and Confederate Armies*, ser. IV, vol. III, 1099–1103. Confederate exemption statistics were notoriously inaccurate; these numbers are presented here only to establish a rough ratio and should not be taken as exact figures. See Moore, *Conscription and Conflict in the Confederacy*, 108.

30. "The Press," *DSC*, January 17, 1864.

31. "Detailed Printers," *CTM*, October 4, 1864, 542.

32. "The Southern Press," *DSC*, November 10, 1864.

33. "The Press," *DSC*, January 17, 1864.

34. "The Newspaper Press," *Punch*, November 28, 1864, 1; "The Newspapers," *Punch*, December 19, 1864, 1.

35. "Some Paragraphs in Senator Hill's Letter," *Punch*, November 14, 1864, 2.

36. "New Military Bill," *Punch*, February 13, 1864, 2; "The Press," *Punch*, February 13, 1864, 8.

37. "Suspension," *SIN*, June 11, 1864, 156; "The 'News,' " *SIN*, July 2, 1864, 162; "To Our Patrons," *Punch*, June 4, 1864, 2; "Third Volume," *Punch*, November 8, 1864, 4; "To Our Patrons," *Punch*, February 13, 1865, 2. For the *Magnolia Weekly*, see below.

38. "To Our Subscribers," *MW*, June 11, 1864, 260; "To Our Subscribers," *MW*, July 9, 1864, 268; "The 'Magnolia Weekly' and its Subscribers," *MW*, July 23, 1864, 276; "To Our Subscribers," *MW*, October 29, 1864, 13; "To Our Subscribers and Patrons," *MW*, December 10, 1864, 35; "To Our Readers," *MW*, March 25, 1865, 87.

39. "Editor's Table," *The Age* 1 (April 1864): 317; "Editor's Table," *The Age* 1 (January 1865): 399–400. Other journals suffered similar delays and reductions due to "military necessity." See "Our Paper Delayed," *Christian Observer*, July 21, 1864, 2; "The Observer Delayed Again," *Christian Observer*, September 8, 1864, 2; "Another Delay," *Christian Observer*, October 6, 1864, 2; "The Raiders!—Delay!" *SC* 22 (August 1864): 128; "Our Situation," *SC* 22 (September 1864): 144; *SC*, December 8, 1864, 196; "Editor's Table," *SLM* 38 (June 1864): 378; "Dear Children," *Child's Index* 2 (February 1864): 6.

40. "Third Volume," *Punch*, November 8, 1864, 4.

41. *CTM*, August 9, 1864, 425.

42. "Editorial," *DBR* 34 (July 1864): 97–98; *SFF*, November 12, 1864, 4.

43. "Another Journal Gone Under," *CTM*, November 29, 1864, 668; "Indefinite Suspension," *Church Intelligencer*, April 8, 1864, 305; "The Church Intelligencer Revived," *Church Intelligencer*, September 14, 1864, 2; "Our Resumption," *SP*, October 6, 1864, 2; "The Southern Presbyterian," *CTM*, October 23, 1864, 586.

44. Reprinted as "Literary," *SIN*, November 5, 1864, 232.

45. Stroupe, *The Religious Press in the South Atlantic States*, 35–36.

46. "The Drama," *SIN*, April 16, 1864, 120.

47. Harwell, *Confederate Belles-Lettres*, 18–19.

48. "The Quill-Drivers," *CTM*, March 7, 1865, 144.

49. "Enlargement," *Christian Index*, March 4, 1864, 10.

50. "Volume Twenty-Three!," *SC* 23 (January 1865): 1.

51. "To the Literateurs of the South," *SFF*, November 5, 1864, 4; Wm. B. Smith and J. H. Bryahn Jr., "A Card," *SFF*, November 5, 1864, 4; "Thinking About Our Readers," *SFF*, March 11, 1865, 4.

52. These new features generally involved the addition of engravings or the improvement of existing ones.

53. "Enlargement," *Christian Index*, March 4, 1864, 10; *Christian Index*, May 20,

1864; "Our Resumption," *SP*, October 6, 1864, 2; "Southern Presbyterian," *SC* 23 (April 1865): 56; *CTM*, September 20, 1864, 515. *Southern Churchman* began appearing as a half sheet in 1862. By 1865, however, it had returned to a four-page format.

54. Reprinted in *CTM*, November 15, 1864, 632.

55. "To the Reader," *CSMSJ* 1 (September 1864): 140; "Prospectus of the Confederate States Medical and Surgical Journal. Second Year," *CSMSJ* 1 (November 1864): 187; *CSMSJ* 2 (January 1865): 11.

56. "The Children's Friend," *SP*, January 28, 1864, 2.

57. "Our Weekly Cultivator," *SC*, November 3, 1864, 172; " 'Monthly,' not 'Weekly,' " *SC* 23 (January 1865): 8.

58. "Our Purpose," *CTM*, July 26, 1864, 394; J. A. Turner, "Niles' Register Revived," *CTM*, August 2, 1864, 406.

59. "A Specimen," *CTM*, July 26, 1864, 390.

60. "Silly People," *CTM*, April 4, 1865, 206.

61. "Character of The Countryman," *CTM*, July 5, 1864, 366.

62. "Detailed Printers," *CTM*, October 4, 1864, 542.

63. "Our Resumption," *SP*, October 6, 1864, 2; "The Southern Presbyterian," *Christian Observer*, October 27, 1864, 2; "Southern Presbyterian Revived," *NCP*, October 19, 1864, 2; "Southern Presbyterian," *SC* 23 (April 1865): 56; "The Church Intelligencer Revived," *Church Intelligencer*, September 14, 1864, 2; "Editor's Table," *The Age* 1 (January 1865): 399–400; "The 'Age,' " *MW*, September 24, 1864, 348; "The Age," *MW*, February 18, 1865, 71; "Editorial," *DBR* 34 (July 1864): 97–98.

64. "Roman Catholicism," *CTM*, September 13, 1864, 496; "The Pacificator," "A Little Paper," *CTM*, October 23, 1864, 584, 594; "Echoes from our Exchanges," *CTM*, November 22, 1864, 654; "The Pacificator," *CTM*, December 20, 1864, 706; "The Pacificator," *MW*, September 10, 1864, 332; "New Publications," *SC*, November 3, 1864, 173; "The Pacificator," *SC* 23 (April 1865): 57; "The Pacificator," *SFF*, September 17, 1864, 4; "The Pacificator," *The Mercury*, September 24, 1864, 2; "The Pacificator," *SP*, October 20, 1864, 2. See also Stroupe, *The Religious Press in the South Atlantic States*, 95–96.

65. "Prospectus," *Southern Friend* 1 (Tenth Month 1864): 5. See also Stroupe, 115.

66. "Our Eclectic Department," *The Key-Stone* 1 (February 1865): 63. For instance, the February issue carried a piece of war fiction entitled "The Soldier Mason," *The Key-Stone* 1 (February 1865): 33–37.

67. "The Soldier's Orphans," "Write to Us," *Child's Banner*, 15 February 1865, 1, 3. There were also a few new journals still in the planning stages when the Confederacy collapsed. In Richmond, a new daily, the *Richmond Herald*, was in preparation, as was a daily journal of Confederate congressional proceedings to be printed by Ayres & Wade. In Columbia, Felix De Fontaine was reported to be in the process of launching a new monthly illustrated literary journal. Prospectus of *Richmond Herald*, *Church Intelligencer*, January 18, 1865, 76; "New Daily Paper in Richmond," *SFF*, January 7, 1865, 8; "The Congressional Printer," *CTM*, November 22, 1864, 653; "Literary Gossip," *CTM*, December 27, 1864, 721; *CTM*, November 8, 1864, 626.

68. "The Richmond Theatre," *MW*, July 30, 1864, 288.

69. "The Drama," *Punch*, June 4, 1864, 5.

70. "The Local Drama," *MW*, August 27, 1864, 316.

71. Dr. Palmer, "The Publication Committee," *NCP*, July 13, 1864, 2.

72. "Protestant Episcopal Church Publishing Association," *Church Intelligencer*, September 14, 1864, 4.

73. "To Young Writers," *SFF*, August 6, 1864, 4.

74. "Answers to Correspondents," *SFF*, August 20, 1864, 4.

75. "Our Book Table," *SFF*, February 25, 1865, 4. According to the review, *Junaluskie* was published in 1864 by J. J. Bruner in Salisbury, N.C., but I have been unable to find any other record of this "little pamphlet," and it does not appear in *Confederate Imprints*.

76. "Poem," *The Mercury*, June 25, 1864, 4. Cowper, *Poem: "Confederate America."*

77. " 'Confederate America' Again," *The Mercury*, July 30, 1864, 4; "Mercurial Ointment," *The Mercury*, August 6, 1864, 6.

78. Joel C. Harris, "Henry Lynden Flash," *CTM*, June 14, 1864, 317–19.

79. A prior edition may have appeared in late 1863, but no copies have been found. See Evans, *Macaria; or, Altars of Sacrifice* (1992): xxvii. For more on *Macaria* and Augusta Jane Evans, see Faust's "Introduction: *Macaria*, A War Story for Confederate Women" in the above volume. See also Fidler, *Augusta Evans Wilson*; Riepma, *Fire and Fiction*; Bain and Flora, eds., *Fifty Southern Writers Before 1900*, 530–40; Hubbell, *The South in American Literature*, 610–16; Moss, *Domestic Novelists in the Old South*, 171–221. On Evans's earlier novel *Beulah*, see O'Brien, *Conjectures of Order*, 1162–70.

80. Evans, *Macaria*, 3.

81. "Literary Miscellanies," *The Age* 1 (April 1864): 318; "New Books," *Christian Observer*, November 17, 1864, 2; "Macaria," *MW*, December 3, 1864, 28; "Macaria," *SFF*, October 8, 1864, 4; "Macaria," *CTM*, October 18, 1864, 577.

82. *SFF*, October 15, 1864, 4; "New Publications," *SIN*, May 14, 1864, 148; "Macaria, or Altars of Sacrifice," *Punch*, June 4, 1864, 4; Hornet, "Miss Evans' Novels: Belulah [*sic*]. Macaria; Or, The Altars of Sacrifice," *The Mercury*, May 21, 1864, 6; James Wood Davidson, "Litterateurs of the South. No. 1. Augusta J. Evans of Mobile, ALA," *The Mercury*, June 18, 1864, 5; D. K. W., "Macaria; or the Altars of Sacrifice," *The Age* 1 (January 1865): 383–98; J. C. H. [Joel Chandler Harris], "Macaria," *CTM*, January 24, 1865, 42–43.

83. *SFF*, October 15, 1864, 4.

84. [Harris], "Macaria," *CTM*, January 24, 1865, 42.

85. D. K. W., "Macaria; or the Altars of Sacrifice," *The Age* 1 (January 1865): 393.

86. Ibid., 392.

87. "New Publications," *SIN*, May 14, 1864, 148; "Editorial," *DBR* 34 (July 1864): 99.

88. "New Books," *Christian Observer*, November 17, 1864, 2.

89. [Harris], "Macaria," *CTM*, January 24, 1865, 42.

90. D. K. W., "Macaria; or the Altars of Sacrifice," *The Age* 1 (January 1865): 392.

91. [Harris], "Macaria," *CTM*, January 24, 1865, 42.

92. D. K. W., "Macaria; or the Altars of Sacrifice," *The Age* 1 (January 1865): 393.

93. [Harris], "Macaria," *CTM*, January 24, 1865, 43; D. K. W., "Macaria; or the Altars of Sacrifice," *The Age* 1 (January 1865): 393.

94. "Editorial," *DBR* 34 (July 1864): 98.

95. A. W. Dillard, "The Importance of Style," *SFF*, February 27, 1864, 5.

96. Fabian, "A Bit of Fault-Finding," *SFF*, June 11, 1864, 7.

97. "Editor's table," *SLM* 38 (May 1864): 314.

98. J. R. R., "Literature at the South," *SFF*, March 6, 1864, 8.

99. "Spartan or Athenian," *Punch*, August 22, 1864, 2.

100. "Southern Periodical Literature," *The Mercury*, September 24, 1864, 2.

101. "Literary Notices," *SLM* 38 (March 1864): 189; O, "The Poet Laureate," *SFF*, February 25, 1865, 5.

102. "Are We a Literary People," *Punch*, February 27, 1864, 2.

103. "To the Literati," *The Mercury*, April 30, 1864, 4.

104. Sigma, "Southern Individuality," *SLM* 38 (June 1864): 373.

105. "Editor's Table," *SLM* 38 (May 1864): 314.

106. Heath, "Our Encouragement to Literary Pursuits," *SFF*, June 4, 1864, 4.

107. "Editorial," *DBR* 34 (July 1864): 100.

108. J. R. R., "Literature at the South," *SFF*, March 6, 1864, 8.

109. "Are We a Literary People," *Punch*, February 27, 1864, 2.

110. "The Local Drama," *MW*, August 27, 1864, 316.

111. Fabian, "A Bit of Fault-Finding," *SFF*, June 11, 1864, 7; "Editor's Table," *SLM* 38 (May 1864): 314.

112. *DSC*, September 15, 1864.

113. "War and Literature," *DSC*, February 28, 1864.

114. Reprinted as "The Moral Influences of the War," *NCP*, February 1, 1865, 2.

115. Emily J. Romeo, "Literature for the South," *The Mercury*, June 11, 1864, 6.

116. Reprinted as "The Moral Influences of the War," *NCP*, February 1, 1865, 2.

117. "Peace," *SFF*, January 28, 1865, 4.

118. See "Our Undeveloped Resources," *SC* 22 (June 1864): 95; "Are We a Literary People," *Punch*, February 27, 1864, 2; "Home Salt," *Punch*, April 23, 1864, 4; "Spartan or Athenian," *Punch*, August 22, 1864, 2; "Life of the Hon. Nathaniel Macon," *The Mercury*, June 11, 1864, 4; Romeo, "Literature for the South," *The Mercury*, June 11, 1864, 6–7; Southerner, "Northern Literature," *The Mercury*, August 27, 1864, 5; "Southern Periodical Literature," *The Mercury*, September 24, 1864, 2; "Terms of Peace," *CTM*, August 23, 1864, 450; [Harris], "Macaria," *CTM*, January 24, 1865, 42.

119. "Editor's Table," *SLM* 38 (May 1864): 314–15.

120. "A Plea for Monuments," *Smith and Barrow's Monthly Magazine* 1 (May 1864): 40.

121. Heath, "Our Encouragement to Literary Pursuits," *SFF*, June 4, 1864, 5.

122. "An Appeal to Our Friends and the Public," *SFF*, November 19, 1864, 4.

123. "A Plea for Monuments," *Smith and Barrow's Monthly Magazine* 1 (May 1864): 38–40.

124. Ironically (or perhaps the printer was having a bit of fun), the word "and"

was repeated twice before the word "redundancy." A. W. Dillard, "The Importance of Style," *SFF*, February 27, 1864, 5.

125. Ibid., 5; "Editor's Table," *SLM* 38 (May 1864): 314.

126. "Editor's Table," *SLM* 38 (May 1864): 315.

127. A. W. Dillard, "The Importance of Style," *SFF*, February 27, 1864, 5; *SFF*, April 30, 1864, 4; "Literary Gossip," *The Mercury*, May 21, 1864, 4. See also "The Genius of Thackeray," *Smith and Barrow's Monthly Magazine* 1 (May 1864): 35–37; Edith, "Some Friendly Hints," *SFF*, August 20, 1864, 7; "Thackeray and Dickens," *Punch*, February 27, 1864, 3.

128. Charles Dickens, "A Tale of Two Cities," *MW*, March 12, 1864, 185–87. Concluded in Dickens, "A Tale of Two Cities," *MW*, September 10, 1864, 329–31; Dickens, "Our Mutual Friend," *MW*, November 12, 1864, 19; Dickens, "A Chapter From 'Our Mutual Friend,'" *MW*, December 17, 1864, 38–39; Dickens, "A Christmas Dinner," *MW*, January 7, 1865, 50–51.

129. William M Thackeray, "A Mississippi Bubble," *MW*, July 23, 1864, 277–78; Thackeray, "On a Lazy, Idle Boy," *MW*, July 30, 1864, 285; Thackeray, "On Being Found Out," *MW*, August 6, 1864, 293–94; Thackeray, "On Two Children in Black," *MW*, August 13, 1864, 301; Thackeray, "Small-Beer Chronicle," *MW*, August 20, 1864, 309–10; Thackeray, "Tunbridge Toys," *MW*, August 27, 1864, 317; Thackeray, "Thorns in the Cushion," *MW*, September 10, 1864, 333–34; Thackeray, "On Some Late Great Victories," *MW*, October 1, 1864, 357 [5]; Thackeray, "On Ribbons," *MW*, October 29, 1864, 11–12; Thackeray, "Ogres," *MW*, November 12, 1864, 22–23; Thackeray, "On Letts's Diary," *MW*, February 18, 1865, 70; Thackeray, "On Screens in Dining-Rooms," *MW*, March 11, 1865, 82.

130. "Foreign Journals," *SFF*, March 6, 1864, 5.

131. "'The Magnolia' and its Future," *MW*, September 10, 1864, 332; *SFF*, April 30, 1864, 4.

132. The roster of European reprints included Braddon, *Aurora Floyd*; Braddon, *Darrell Markham*; Braddon, *Eleanor's Victory*; Braddon, *Lady Audley's Secret*; Braddon, *John Marchmont's Legacy*; Collins, *No Name*; Collins, *The Stolen Mask*; Dickens, *Great Expectations*; Dickens, *Charles Dickens's New Christmas Story*; Eliot, *Silas Marner*; Fane and Bulwer-Lytton, *Tannhauser*; Feuillet, *The Romance of a Poor Young Man*; Féval, *The Golden Daggers*; Hugo, *Les Misérables*; Bulwer-Lytton, *A Strange Story*; [Mundt], *Henry VIII. and his Court*; [Mundt], *Joseph II and His Court*; Thackeray, *The Adventures of Philip*; Wood, *East Lynne*; Wood, *Mrs. Halliburton's Troubles*; Craik, *Mistress and Maid*.

133. Hugo, *Les Misérables*, iv.

134. T. W. M., "Les Misérables—Fantine," *SLM* 37 (July 1863): 446.

135. "Lee's Miserables," *MW*, August 1, 1863, 255.

136. For instance, the *Southern Cultivator* found little of "any very permanent value" in Evans & Cogswell's new translation of the French novel *The Golden Daggers; A Romance of California*. "Will not our friends, the Publishers, give us some more 'attractive metal,'" the *Cultivator* scolded. "New Publications," *SC* 22 (July 1864): 113.

137. *The Education of Teachers in the South*, 9.

138. *Southern Literary Companion*, June 15, 1864, 1.

139. "Education," *DSC*, May 4, 1864.

140. J. L. Kirkpatrick, "The Duty of Females in Relation to the Future Educational Interests of Our Country," *NCJE* 7 (July 1864): 87–88.

141. Tilman R. Gaines, Washington Baird, and Richard Sterling, "To the Teachers of the Confederate States," *SP*, January 19, 1865, 1.

142. W. W. T. [William W. Turner,], "Thoughts on Education. No. 1," *CTM*, March 1, 1864, 100; W. W. T., "Thoughts on Education. No. 3," *CTM*, March 15, 1864, 128.

143. "Go to School!," *CTM*, November 8, 1864, 621.

144. Kirkpatrick, "The Duty of Females in Relation to the Future Educational Interests of Our Country," *NCJE* 7 (July 1864): 88.

145. Parker, "A Word to Southern Girls," *SFF*, September 17, 1864, 6.

146. Parrish and Willingham, *Confederate Imprints*, 630–55.

147. "Also," *SFF*, March 6, 1864, 5.

148. Gaines, Baird, and Sterling, "To the Teachers of the Confederate States," *SP*, January 19, 1865, 1.

149. Leverett, *The Southern Confederacy Arithmetic*, v.

150. Neely, *The Confederate States Speller and Reader*, 3.

CONCLUSION

1. "The Proper Course," *CTM*, May 16, 1865, 281; "The State of the Country," *CTM*, May 2, 1865, 266.

2. "Stand Firm," *CTM*, February 7, 1865, 69.

3. "The Roll of the Drum," *SFF*, February 18, 1865, 4.

4. James De Bow, "The War—Independence—Watchman, What of the Night?" *DBR* 34 (July 1864): 51.

5. Ibid., 47.

6. Pollard, *A Letter on the State of the War*, 6.

7. "The Roll of the Drum," *SFF*, February 18, 1865, 4.

8. James De Bow, "The War—Independence—Watchman, What of the Night?" *DBR* 34 (July 1864): 50.

9. "Reconstruction," *CTM*, April 4, 1865, 201.

10. "The Roll of the Drum," *SFF*, February 18, 1865, 4.

11. "The Reconstructionists," *CTM*, March 28, 1865, 194; "The Roll of the Drum," *SFF*, February 18, 1865, 4.

12. Pollard, *A Letter on the State of the War*, 8.

13. "Religious Journals Suspended," *Christian Observer*, June 1, 1865, 2.

14. "Close of the Volume," *The Key-Stone* 1 (December 1865): 157.

15. See "The Occupation and Destruction of Columbia," *Church Intelligencer*, March 16, 1865, 96; Simms, *Sack and Destruction of the City of Columbia*.

16. "Never Give up the Ship—One More Effort," *RCA*, February 23, 1865.

17. *Church Intelligencer*, August 31, 1865, 127.

18. "The State of the Country," *CTM*, May 2, 1865, 266.

19. "To my Patrons," *CTM*, May 9, 1865, 277.

20. *Church Intelligencer*, April 20, 1865, 116.

21. In his despair, Turner reduced *The Countryman* to a quarter sheet (4 pages) in the wake of Confederate defeat. "The Proper Course," *CTM*, May 16, 1865, 281.

22. "Our New Motto," *CTM*, June 6, 1865, 296.

23. The question of southern distinctiveness has always been at the heart of southern studies. For important perspectives on this debate, see Cobb, *Away Down South*; Brundage, *The Southern Past*; Degler, *Place Over Time*; Degler, "Thesis, Antithesis, Synthesis"; O'Brien, *Rethinking the South*; Genovese, *The Southern Tradition*; Gray, *Writing the South*; Sellers, ed., *The Southerner as American*; McWhiney, *Cracker Culture*; Weaver, *The Southern Tradition at Bay*; Weaver, *The Southern Essays of Richard M. Weaver*; Wells, *The Origins of the Southern Middle Class*; Current, *Northernizing the South*; Wyatt-Brown, *The Shaping of Southern Culture*; Goldfield, *Still Fighting the Civil War*; Griffin, "Southern Distinctiveness, Yet Again"; Kolchin, *A Sphinx on the American Land*.

24. A. B. Stark, "Southern Literature," *Home Circle* 7 (September 1861): 513–14.

25. On the resumption of southern denominational papers, see Stowell, *Rebuilding Zion*, 108–13.

26. "Our Paper," *CTM*, May 23, 1865, 286; "The Proper Course," *CTM*, May 16, 1865, 281.

27. "Resumed," *Field and Fireside*, December 16, 1865, 4.

28. On these postwar southern periodicals, see Atchison, "Southern Literary Magazines"; Hubbell, *The South in American Literature*, 716–26; Rubin, *A Shattered Nation*, 190–200; Mott, *A History of American Magazines*, Vol. III; Durant, "The Gently Furled Banner," 13–71.

29. Crozier, *The Confederate Spy*, 5.

30. "The Proper Course," *CTM*, May 16, 1865, 281; "Our Course," *CTM*, May 23, 1865, 286.

31. As quoted in Hubbell, *The South in American Literature*, 710.

32. Pollard, *The Lost Cause*, 750.

33. Blight, *Race and Reunion*, 258–64. For an excellent study of the ways in which this defiant Lost Cause manifested itself in South Carolina, see Poole, *Never Surrender*.

34. Connelly and Bellows, *God and General Longstreet*, 5–38.

35. Pollard, *The Lost Cause*, 750–52.

36. Rubin, *A Shattered Nation*.

37. Turner, *Autobiography of "The Countryman,"* 18.

38. See Hubbell, *The South in American Literature*, 726–33; Blight, *Race and Reunion*, 216–31; Connelly and Bellows, *God and General Longstreet*, 44–54; Osterweis, *The Myth of the Lost Cause*, 30–41.

39. Hubbell, *The South in American Literature*, 716–17.

40. Maddex, *The Reconstruction of Edward A. Pollard*, 43.

41. Connelly and Bellows, *God and General Longstreet*, 44–72.

42. On the Lost Cause and postwar reconciliation, see Blight, *Race and Reunion*; Foster, *Ghosts of the Confederacy*; Connelly, *The Marble Man*; Connelly and Bellows, *God and General Longstreet*; Silber, *The Romance of Reunion*; Buck, *The Road to Reunion*.

43. Censer, *The Reconstruction of White Southern Womanhood*, 210–12. See also Gardner, *Blood and Irony*; Censer, "Reimagining the North-South Reunion"; Wyatt-Brown, *Hearts of Darkness*, 181–230.

44. See Censer, *The Reconstruction of White Southern Womanhood*, 153–83.

45. On the early commemorative activities of southern women, see Janney, *Burying the Dead but Not the Past*.

46. McPherson, "Long-Legged Yankee Lies." See also Bailey, "The Textbooks of the 'Lost Cause;' " Wilson, *Baptized in Blood*, 139–60; Blight, *Race and Reunion*, 277–84; Osterweis, *The Myth of the Lost Cause*, 111–17.

47. Simms, *War Poetry of the South*, v–viii.

48. Mason, *The Southern Poems of the War*, 5. See also *War Lyrics and Songs of the South*; De Leon, *South Songs*; Davidson, ed., *Cullings from the Confederacy*.

49. Flournoy, *Side Lights on Southern History*, 91.

50. Crozier, *The Confederate Spy*, 5–6.

51. As quoted in Aaron, *The Unwritten War*, 243.

52. Simms, *War Poetry of the South*, v.

BIBLIOGRAPHY

CONFEDERATE PERIODICALS (INCLUDING LOCATION AND
YEARS OF WARTIME PUBLICATION)

Note: Periodicals marked with an asterisk (*) continued publication after the war.

The Age (Richmond, Va., 1864–65)

Army and Navy Herald (Macon, Ga., 1863–65)

The Aurora (Memphis, Tenn., 1861)

Banner and Baptist becomes *The Baptist Banner* (Atlanta and Augusta, Ga., 1861–65)*

Biblical Recorder (Raleigh, N.C., 1861–65)*

The Bohemian (Richmond, Va., 1863)

Bugle-Horn of Liberty (Griffin, Ga., 1863)

Central Presbyterian (Richmond, Va., 1861–65)*

The Children's Friend (Richmond, Va., 1862–65)*

The Child's Banner (Salisbury, N.C., 1865)

The Child's Index (Macon, Ga., 1862–65)

Christian Advocate (Memphis, Tenn., 1861–62?)

Christian Index (Macon, Ga., 1861–65)*

Christian Observer (Richmond, Va., 1861–65)*

Church Intelligencer (Raleigh and Charlotte, N.C., 1861–65)*

The Commission; or Southern Baptist Missionary Magazine (Richmond, Va., 1861)

Confederate Baptist (Columbia, S.C., 1862–65)

Confederate Spirit and Knapsack of Fun (Mobile, Ala., 1863–64?)

Confederate States Medical and Surgical Journal (Richmond, Va., 1864–65)

The Countryman (Turnwold, Ga., 1862–65)*

Daily Delta (New Orleans, La., 1861–63)

Daily South Carolinian (Columbia, S.C., Charlotte, N.C., 1861–65)*

Dayton's Baptist Monthly (Nashville, Tenn., 1861)

De Bow's Review (New Orleans, La., and Columbia, S.C., 1861–62, 1864)*

Educational Repository and Family Monthly (Atlanta, Ga., 1861)

Georgia Literary and Temperance Crusader (Atlanta, Ga., 1861–62)

Gulf City Home Journal (Mobile, Ala., 1862?–63)

Helena Weekly Note-Book (Helena, Ark., 1861–63?)

Home and Foreign Journal (Richmond, Va.; Marion, Ala.; and Nashville, Tenn., 1861)

Home Circle (Nashville, Tenn., 1861)

The Key-Stone: A Monthly Masonic Magazine (Raleigh, N.C., 1865)*

The Magnolia: A Southern Home Journal becomes *Magnolia Weekly* (Richmond, Va., 1862–65)

The Mercury aka *The Illustrated Mercury* merges with *Southern Field and Fireside* (Raleigh, N.C., 1864)

New Orleans Medical and Surgical Journal (New Orleans, La., 1861)*

North Carolina Christian Advocate becomes *Christian Advocate* (Raleigh, N.C., 1861, 1863–65)

North Carolina Journal of Education (Greensborough, N.C., 1861–64)

North Carolina Presbyterian (Fayetteville, N.C., 1861–65)*

North Carolina University Magazine (Chapel Hill, N.C., 1861)

North Carolina Whig (Charlotte, N.C., 1861–63)

The Portfolio (Columbia, S.C., 1861–65)

Quarterly Review of the Methodist Episcopal Church, South (Nashville, Tenn., 1861)

The Record of News, History and Literature (Richmond, Va., 1863)

Religious Herald (Richmond, Va., 1861–65)*

Richmond Christian Advocate (Richmond, Va., 1861–65)*

Richmond Dispatch (Richmond, Va., 1861–65)*

Richmond Enquirer (Richmond, Va., 1861–65)*

Richmond Examiner (Richmond, Va., 1861–65)*

Richmond Sentinel (Richmond, Va., 1863–65)*

Richmond Whig (Richmond, Va., 1862–65)

Smith and Barrow's Monthly Magazine (Richmond, Va., 1864)

The Soldier's Paper (Richmond, Va., 1863–65)

The Soldier's Visitor (Richmond, Va., 1863–65)

Southern Christian Advocate (Charleston, S.C., and Augusta, Ga., 1861–65)*

Southern Churchman (Alexandria and Richmond, Va., 1861–65)*

Southern Cultivator (Augusta and Athens, Ga., 1861–65)*

Southern Episcopalian (Charleston, S.C., 1861, 1863)

Southern Field and Fireside (Augusta, Ga., and Raleigh, N.C., 1861–65)*

Southern Friend (Richmond, Va., 1864)

Southern Illustrated News (Richmond, Va., 1862–65)

Southern Literary Companion (Newnan, Ga., 1861–65)

Southern Literary Messenger (Richmond, Va., 1861–64)

Southern Lutheran (Charleston and Columbia, S.C., 1861–65)

Southern Medical and Surgical Journal (Augusta, Ga., 1861)*

Southern Monthly (Memphis, Tenn., and Grenada, Miss., 1861–62)

Southern Presbyterian (Columbia, S.C., and Augusta, Ga., 1861–65)*

Southern Presbyterian Review (Columbia, S.C., 1861–64)*

Southern Punch (Richmond, Va., 1863–65)

Southern Teacher (Montgomery, Ala., 1861)

Weekly Constitutionalist (Augusta, Ga., 1861–65)*

Weekly Register (Lynchburg, Va., 1864–65)

CONFEDERATE BOOKS, PAMPHLETS, AND SERMONS

Abrams, Alexander St. Clair. *A Full and Detailed History of the Siege of Vicksburg.* Atlanta: Intelligencer Steam Power Presses, 1863.

——. *President Davis and His Administration: being a review of the "Rival Administrations," lately published in Richmond, and written by E. A. Pollard, author of the "First and Second Years of the War."* Atlanta: n.p., 1864.

——. *The Trials of the Soldier's Wife: A Tale of the Second American Revolution.* Atlanta: Intelligencer Steam Power Presses, 1864.

Addington, Joseph C. *Reds, Whites and Blacks, or the Colors, Dispersion, Language, Sphere and Unity of the Human Race, As Seen in the Lights of Scripture, Science and Observation.* Raleigh: Strother & Marcom Book and Job Printers, 1862.

Analytica. *The Problem of Government, in the light of the Past, Present and the Future. By Analytica. Is Respectfully Dedicated to the Rulers of the World, by the Author.* Richmond: n.p., 1862.

Anecdotes for our Soldiers. No.1. Charleston: South Carolina Tract Society; printed by Evans & Cogswell, 1862.

Armstrong, George Dodd. *"The Good Hand of God upon us." A thanksgiving sermon preached on the occasion of the victory of Manassas, July 21st, 1861, in the Presbyterian Church, Norfolk, Va.* Norfolk: J. D. Ghiselin, 1861.

Atkinson, Thomas. *"On the Causes of Our National Troubles." A sermon, delivered in St. James' Church, Wilmington, N.C.* Wilmington: "Herald" Book and Job Office, 1861.

[Bagby, George William]. *The Letters of Mozis Addums to Billy Ivvins.* Richmond: West & Johnston, 1862.

Barrow, Robert Ruffin. *A Miscellaneous Essay on the Political Parties of the Country, the Rise of Abolitionism and the Impolicy of Secession.* New Orleans: L. Marchand, 1861.

——. *Remarks on the Present War, by R. R. Barrow of Terrebonne. The Objects of the Abolition Party.* New Orleans, n.p., 1861.

——. *Valuable and Worth Preserving! Pertinent Questions. . . .* N.p., [1861].

[Barten, Otto Sievers]. *A Sermon Preached in St. James Church, Warrenton, Va., on Fast-Day, June 13, 1861.* Richmond: Enquirer Book and Job Press, 1861.

[Bartlett, Napier]. *Clarimonde: A Tale of New Orleans Life, and of the Present War.* Richmond: M. A. Malsby, 1863.

Berry, Harrison. *Slavery and Abolitionism, As Viewed by a Georgia Slave.* Atlanta: M. Lynch & Co., 1861.

Bilbo, William N. *The Past, Present, and Future of the Southern Confederacy: An oration delivered by Col. W. N. Bilbo, in the city of Nashville, Oct. 12, 1861.* Nashville: J. D. W. Green & Co., 1861.

Blackwell, Robert. *Original Acrostics; on some of the Southern states, and most eminent men of the Southern Confederacy; and on various other subjects, political and personal.* Loudoun Co., Va.: Z. F. Milbourn, 1863.

Boykin, Edward M. *The Boys and Girls Stories of the War.* Richmond: West & Johnston, [1863?].

Braddon, Mary Elizabeth. *Aurora Floyd.* Richmond: West & Johnston, 1863.

——. *Darrell Markham; or the Captain of the Vulture.* Richmond: Ayres & Wade, 1863.

——. *Eleanor's Victory.* Richmond: Ayres & Wade, 1864.

——. *John Marchmont's Legacy.* Richmond: West & Johnston, 1865.

——. *Lady Audley's Secret!* Mobile: S. H. Goetzel, 1864.

Bulwer-Lytton, Edward George Earle Lytton. *A Strange Story.* Mobile: S. H. Goetzel & Co., 1863.

Burrows, John Lansing. *Nationality Insured! Notes of a sermon delivered at the First Baptist Church, Augusta, Ga., September 11th, 1864.* Augusta: Jas. Nathan Ells, Baptist Banner Office, 1864.

——. *The New Richmond Theatre. A discourse, delivered on Sunday, February 8, 1863 in the First Baptist Church, Richmond, Va.* Richmond: Smith, Bailey & Co., 1863.

The Camp Follower containing the following stories: The cock fight, The wife's stratagem, How I coated Sal, The Champion, Whar no wood is, thar the fire goeth out, and many other humorous sketches, anecdotes, poetry, etc., designed for the amusement of the camp. Augusta: Stockton & Co., 1864.

The Camp Jester or, Amusement for the Mess. Augusta: Blackmar & Brother, 1864.

Cantrell, Oscar Alexander. *Sketches of the First Regiment Ga. Vols., together with the history of the 56th Regiment of Georgia Vols., to January 1, 1864.* Atlanta: Intelligencer Steam Power Presses, 1864.

Clarke, H. C. *Diary of the war for separation, a daily chronicle of the principal events and history of the present revolution, to which is added notes and descriptions of all the great battles, including Walker's narrative of the battle of Shiloh.* Augusta: Steam Press of Chronicle & Sentinel, 1862.

Collins, Wilkie. *No Name.* Richmond: West & Johnston, 1863.

——. *The Stolen Mask; or The Mysterious Cash-Box. A Story for a Christmas Fireside.* Columbia: F. G. DeFontaine & Co., 1864.

A Confederate Alphabet. 186[?].

Cooke, John Esten. *The Life of Stonewall Jackson. From Official Papers, Contemporary Narratives, and Personal Acquaintance.* Richmond: Ayres & Wade, 1863.

Cowper, R. Lynden. *Poem: "Confederate America;" by R. Lynden Cowper*. Raleigh: Book and Job Office Steam Power Press Print, 1864.

Craik, Dinah Maria (Mulock). *Mistress and Maid. A Household Story*. Richmond: West & Johnston, 1864.

Craven, Braxton. *Mary Barker*. Raleigh: Branson & Farrar, 1865.

Cross, Jane Tandy Hardin. *Duncan Adair: or, Captured in Escaping. A Story of One of Morgan's Men*. Macon: Burke, Boykin & Company, 1864.

Cross, Joseph. *Camp and Field. Papers from the portfolio of an army chaplain*. Macon: Burke, Boykin & Company, 1864.

Dabney, Robert Lewis. *Letter of the Rev. R. L. Dabney, D.D., of Union Theological Seminary, Virginia, to the Rev. S. J. Prime, D.D., One of the Editors of the New York Observer, on the State of the Country*. Richmond: Macfarlane & Fergusson, 1861.

——. *Life of Lieut. Gen. Thomas J. Jackson. Vol. I*. Greensboro: Sterling, Campbell, and Albright, 1865.

——. *True Courage: A Discourse Commemorative of Lieut. General Thomas J. Jackson*. Richmond: Presbyterian Committee of Publication of the Confederate States, 1863.

Davis, Mary Elizabeth Moragne. *The British Partizan: A Tale of the Olden Time. By a Lady of South Carolina*. Macon: Burke, Boykin & Company, 1864.

DeBow, James D. B. *The Interest in Slavery of the Southern Non-Slaveholder. The Right of Peaceful Secession. Slavery in the Bible*. Charleston: Evans & Cogswell, 1860.

Delchamps, J. J. *Love's Ambuscade; or The Sergeant's Stratagem; a War Drama, in three acts*. Mobile: A. G. Horn, 1863.

[——]. *W.B. Spiced Slaugh for Southern Digestion. Dish No. 3. For the Use of Members of the Order. By Order of the Publishing Committee. C. of G.A., Order of W.B.* Mobile: A. G. Horn & Co., 1862.

——. *W.B. Spiced Slaw for Southern Digestion, and Other Papers. Written for the Order of W.B. by J. J. Delchamps*. Mobile: A. G. Horn, 1863.

Dickens, Charles. *Charles Dickens's New Christmas Story*. Mobile: Office of the Daily Advertiser and Register, 1864.

——. *Great Expectations*. Mobile: S. H. Goetzel & Co., 1863.

Doggett, David Seth. *A Nation's Ebenezer. A discourse delivered in the Broad St. Methodist Church, Richmond, Virginia, Thursday, September 18, 1862: the day of public thanksgiving, appointed by the President of the Confederate States*. Richmond: Enquirer and Job Press, 1862.

——. *The War and Its Close. A discourse, delivered in Centenary Church, Richmond, Va., Friday, April 8th, 1864, by Rev. D. S. Doggett, D.D., pastor, on the occasion of the national fast. Published by the Soldiers' Tract Association, M.E. Church, South*. Richmond: Macfarlane & Fergusson, 1864.

[Duncan, James A.]. *Address to Christians throughout the World*. Richmond: n.p., [1863].

Eliot, George. *Silas Marner, the Weaver of Raveloe*. Mobile: S. H. Goetzel, 1863.

Elliott, Stephen. *Address of the Rt. Rev. Stephen Elliott, D.D., to the thirty-ninth annual* convention of the Protestant Episcopal Church, in the Diocese of Georgia. Savannah: John M. Cooper & Company, 1861.

——. *Ezra's Dilemma. A sermon preached in Christ Church, Savannah, on Friday, August 21st, 1863, being the day of humiliation, fasting and prayer, appointed by the President of the Confederate States.* Savannah: George N. Nichols, 1863.

——. *Gideon's Water-Lappers. A sermon preached in Christ Church, Savannah, on Friday, the 8th day of April, 1864. The day set apart by the Congress of the Confederate States, as a day of humiliation, fasting and prayer.* Macon: Burke, Boykin & Company, 1864.

——. *God's Presence with the Confederate States. A sermon preached in Christ Church, Savannah, on Thursday, the 13th June, being the day appointed at the request of Congress, by the President of the Confederate States, as a day of solemn humiliation, fasting and prayer.* Savannah: W. Thorne Williams, 1861.

——. *How to Renew our National Strength. A sermon preached in Christ Church, Savannah, on Friday, November 15th, 1861, being the day of humiliation, fasting, and prayer, appointed by the President of the Confederate States.* Richmond: Macfarlane & Fergusson, 1862.

——. *"New Wine not to be put in Old Bottles." A sermon preached in Christ Church, Savannah, on Friday, February 28th, 1862, being the day of humiliation, fasting, and prayer, appointed by the President of the Confederate States.* Savannah: John M. Cooper & Co., 1862.

——. *Our Cause in Harmony with the Purposes of God in Christ Jesus. A sermon preached in Christ Church, Savannah, on Thursday, September 18th, 1862, being the day set forth by the President of the Confederate States, as a day of prayer and thanksgiving, for our manifold victories, and especially of the fields of Manassas and Richmond, Ky.* Savannah: John M. Cooper & Co., 1862.

——. *"Samson's Riddle." A sermon preached in Christ Church, Savannah, on Friday, March 27th, 1863. Being the day of humiliation, fasting and prayer, appointed by the President of the Confederate States.* Macon: Burke, Boykin & Co., 1863.

——. *"Vain is the Help of Man." A sermon preached in Christ Church, Savannah, on Thursday, September 15, 1864, being the day of fasting, humiliation, and prayer, appointed by the Governor of the State of Georgia.* Macon: Burke, Boykin & Company, 1864.

Epitaph on the United States of America. Here lie the mutilated and disjointed remains of the noblest form of government ever contrived by the wisdom of man. . . . Charleston: Evans & Cogswell, 1861.

Evans, Augusta Jane. *Macaria; or, Altars of Sacrifice.* Richmond: West & Johnston, 1864.

Fane, Julian Henry Charles, and Edward Robert Bulwer-Lytton. *Tannhauser; or, The Battle of the Bards.* Mobile: S. H. Goetzel & Co., 1863.

Fanning, David. *The Narrative of Colonel David Fanning, (A Tory in the Revolutionary War with Great Britain;) Giving an Account of his Adventures in North Carolina, From 1775 to 1783, As Written by Himself, With an Introduction and Explanatory Notes.* Richmond: n.p., 1861.

Fentonhill, John. *Joan of Arc: an Opinion of her Life and Character, from Ancient Chronicles*. Richmond: J. W. Davies, 1864.

Feuillet, Octave. *The Romance of a Poor Young Man*. Richmond: West & Johnston, 1863.

Féval, Paul. *The Golden Daggers; A Romance of California*. Columbia: Evans & Cogswell, 1864.

[Fillmore, Millard]. *The Recognition of the Confederate States considered in a reply to the letters of 'Historicus' in the London Times. By Juridicus. Originally published in the Charleston Courier*. Charleston: Evans & Cogswell, 1863.

Folsom, James Madison. *Heroes and Martyrs of Georgia. Georgia's record in the revolution of 1861*. Macon: Burke, Boykin & Company, 1864.

For the Little Ones. Savannah: John M. Cooper & Co., 186[?].

Ford, Sally Rochester. *Raids and Romance of Morgan and His Men*. Mobile: S. H. Goetzel, 1863.

Gammage, W. L. *The Camp, the Bivouac, and the Battle Field. Being a history of the Fourth Arkansas Regiment, from its first organization down to the present date: "Its campaigns and its battles." With an occasional reference to the current events of the times, including biographical sketches of its field officers and others of the "Old Brigade." The whole interspersed here and there with descriptions of scenery, incidents of camp life, etc*. Selma: Cooper & Kimball, 1864.

Gordon, George Anderson. *"What will he do with it?" An essay, delivered in Masonic Hall, Savannah, on Thursday, October 27, 1863, and again by special request, on Monday, December 7, 1863. For the benefit of the Wayside Home, in Savannah. And repeated with slight alterations for similar objects in Augusta, Milledgeville, Macon, Atlanta, LaGrange and Columbus*. Savannah: George N. Nichols, 1863.

Gordon, John B. *Progress of Civil Liberty. An address delivered before the Thalian and Phi Delta societies of Oglethorpe University, Georgia at the last annual commencement*. Macon: Telegraph Steam Printing House, 1861.

Goulding, Francis Robert. *Robert and Harold; or the Young Marooners on the Florida Coast*. Rev. and enl. ed. Macon: Burke, Boykin & Co., 1863.

"Government or No Government," Or, The Question of State Allegiance. A Tract for Churchmen. Mobile: Farrow & Dennett, 1861.

Grayson, William John. *Reply to Professor Hodge, on the "State of the Country."* Charleston: Evans & Cogswell, 1861.

Great Expectations; or, Getting Promoted. A farce, in one act. Richmond: Chas. H. Wynne, 1864.

Hall, William A. *The Historic Significance of the Southern Revolution. A lecture delivered by invitation in Petersburg, Va., March 14th and April 29th, 1864. And in Richmond, Va., April 7th and April 21st, 1864*. Petersburg: A. F. Crutchfield & Co, 1864.

Hallock, Charles. *A Complete Biographical Sketch of "Stonewall" Jackson: giving a full and accurate account of the leading events of his military career, his dying moments, and the obsequies at Richmond and Lexington*. Augusta: Steam Power-Press Chronicle and Sentinel, 1863.

Harris, W. A. *The Record of Fort Sumter, from its occupation by Major Anderson, to its reduction by South Carolina troops, during the administration of Governor Pickens.* Columbia: South Carolinian Steam Job Printing Office, 1862.

[Haw, Mary Jane]. *The Rivals: A Chickahominy Story.* Richmond: Ayres & Wade, 1864.

Herrington, W. D. *The Captain's Bride, A Tale of the War.* Raleigh: William B. Smith & Co., 1864.

——. *The Deserter's Daughter.* Raleigh: William B. Smith & Co., 1865.

Hewitt, John H. *War: a poem, with copious notes, founded on the revolution of 1861– 1862, (up to the battles before Richmond, inclusive).* Richmond: West & Johnston, 1862.

Hill, Theophilus Hunter. *Hesper and Other Poems.* Raleigh: Strother & Marcom, 1861.

Hodgson, Joseph. *The Confederate Vivandiere; or, The Battle of Leesburg. A Military Drama in three acts.* Montgomery: John M. Floyd, 1862.

Hugo, Victor Marie. *Les Misérables.* Richmond: West & Johnston, 1863–1864.

Hurst, M. B. *History of the Fourteenth Regiment Alabama Vols.* Richmond: n.p., 1863.

An Introduction to a History of the Second American War for Independence or The Civil War in the United States Prefaced by A Treatise on the "Democratic Principle" and by An Essay on "Natural Government." N.p., 1863.

Jackson, Henry W. R. *Confederate Monitor and Patriot's Friend. Containing sketches of numerous important and thrilling events of the present revolution, together with several interesting chapters of history concerning Gen. Stonewall Jackson, Gen. Morgan, and other great men of a new nation her armor and salvation. . . .* Atlanta: Franklin Steam Printing House, 1862.

——. *Historical Register, and Confederates Assistant to National Independence.* Augusta: Office of the Constitutionalist, 1862.

——. *The Southern Women of the Second American Revolution. Their trials, &c. Yankee barbarity illustrated. Our naval victories and exploits of Confederate war steamers. Capture of Yankee gunboats, &c.* Atlanta: Intelligencer Steam-Power Press, 1863.

Jamison, David F. *The Life and Times of Bertrand Du Guesclin: A History of the Fourteenth Century.* 2 vols. Charleston: John Russell, 1864.

[Johnston, Richard Malcolm]. *Georgia Sketches.* Augusta: Stockton & Co., 1864.

Jones, Charles Colcock, Jr. *Monumental Remains of Georgia.* Savannah: John M. Cooper and Company, 1861.

Jones, John Beauchamp. *Wild Western Scenes; or, The White Spirit of the Wilderness.* Richmond: M. A. Malsby, 1863.

Jordan, Cornelia Jane. *Flowers of Hope and Memory: A Collection of Poems.* Richmond: A. Morris, 1861.

Judd, H. O. *Look Within for Fact and Fiction Consisting of Instructing Sketches and Thrilling Narratives.* Macon: n.p., 1864.

Lacy, Drury. *Address delivered at the general military hospital, Wilson, N.C., on the day appointed by the President as a day of fasting, humiliation and prayer.* Fayetteville: Edward J. Hale & Sons, 1863.

Life of James W. Jackson, the Alexandria hero, the slayer of Ellsworth, the first martyr in the cause of Southern independence; containing a full account of the circumstances of his heroic death, and the many remarkable incidents of his eventful life, constituting a true history, more like romance than reality. Richmond: West & Johnston, 1862.

Longstreet, Augustus Baldwin. *Fast-Day Sermon: delivered in the Washington Street Methodist Episcopal Church, Columbia, S.C., June 13, 1861*. Columbia: Townsend & North, 1861.

——. *Master William Mitten: or, A Youth of Brilliant Talents, who was Ruined by Bad Luck*. Macon: Burke, Boykin & Company, 1864.

——. *Shall South Carolina Begin the War?* Charleston: n.p., 1861.

[Lyons, James]. *Four Essays on the Right and Propriety of Secession by Southern States*. Richmond: Ritchie & Dunnavant, 1861.

MacMahon, T. W. *Cause and Contrast: An Essay on the American Crisis*. Richmond: West & Johnston, 1862 [c.1861].

Marshall, Alexander J. *Five Chapters of an Unpublished 'Book for the Times,' giving a Virginia view of the causes of the revolution in the border slave states, and demonstrating who were the true authors of the Civil War*. Richmond: James E. Goode, 1863.

Martin, Joseph Hamilton. *Smith and Pocahontas*. Richmond: West & Johnston, 1862.

McCabe, James Dabney. *The Aid-de-Camp; A Romance of the War*. Richmond: W. A. J. Smith, 1863.

——. *The Guerrillas: An Original Domestic Drama, in three acts*. Richmond: West & Johnston, 1863.

——. *The Life of Lieut. Gen. T. J. Jackson. By an ex-cadet*. Richmond: James E. Goode, 1863.

McDonald, William Naylor. *The Two Rebellions; or Treason Unmasked. By a Virginian*. Richmond: Smith, Bailey & Co., 1865.

McRae, Duncan K. *On Love of Country, an address, delivered before the young ladies of the Clio Society of Oxford Female College, June 2nd, 1864*. Raleigh: Strother & Marcom, 1864.

Meynardie, Elias James. *The Siege of Charleston; its history and progress. A discourse delivered in Bethel Church, Charleston, S.C., November 19, 1863*. Columbia: Evans & Cogswell, 1864.

Miles, James Warley. *God in History. A discourse delivered before the graduating class of the College of Charleston on Sunday evening, March 29, 1863*. Charleston: Evans & Cogswell, 1863.

[——]. *The Relation Between the Races at the South*. Charleston: Evans & Cogswell, 1861.

Moore, Thomas Verner. *God our Refuge and Strength in this War. A discourse before the congregation of the First and Second Presbyterian Churches, on the day of humiliation, fasting and prayer, appointed by President Davis, Friday, Nov. 15, 1861*. Richmond: W. Hargrave White, 1861.

[Mundt, Clara]. *Henry VIII. and his Court, or, Catherine Parr. A Historical Novel. By L. Muhlbach*. Translated by Rev. H. N. Pierce. 2 vols. Mobile: S. H. Goetze, 1865.

——. *Joseph II and His Court. An Historical Novel, by L. Muhlbach*. Translated by Adelaide De V. Chaudron. 4 vols. Mobile: S. H. Goetzel, 1864.

[Northrop, Claudian Bird]. *Political Remarks by "N" Numbers IX, X, XI*. Charleston: Evans & Cogswell, 1861.

Octogenarian. *The Origin and End of the Irrepressible Conflict*. Greenville, S.C.: G. E. Elford, 1861.

Palmer, Benjamin M. *A Discourse before the General Assembly of South Carolina, on December 10, 1863, appointed by the Legislature as a day of fasting, humiliation and prayer*. Columbia: Charles P. Pelham, 1864.

——. *A Discourse before the Legislature of Georgia, delivered on the day of fasting, humiliation and prayer, appointed by the President of the Confederate States of America, March 27th, 1863*. Milledgeville, Ga.: Boughton, Nisbet & Barnes, 1863.

——. *A Discourse Commemorative of the Life, Character, and Genius of the Late Rev. J. H. Thornwell, D.D., LL.D.* Columbia: Southern Guardian Steam-Power Press, 1862.

——. *National Responsibility before God. A discourse, delivered on the day of fasting, humiliation and prayer, appointed by the President of the Confederate States of America, June 13, 1861*. New Orleans: Price-Current Steam Book and Job Printing Office, 1861.

——. *The Oath of Allegiance to the United States, discussed in its moral and political bearings*. Richmond: Soldiers' Tract Association, M. E. Church, South, printed by Macfarlane & Fergusson, 1863.

——. *The Rainbow Round the Throne; or Judgment Tempered with Mercy. A discourse before the Legislature of Georgia, delivered on the day of fasting, humiliation and prayer, appointed by the President of the Confederate States of America, March 27th, 1863*. Milledgeville, Ga.: Boughton, Nisbet & Barnes, 1863.

——. *A Vindication of Secession and the South from the Strictures of Rev. R. J. Breckinridge, D.D., LL.D., in the Danville Quarterly Review*. Columbia: Southern Guardian Steam-Power Press, 1861.

Paris, John. *A Sermon: preached before Brig.-Gen. Hoke's Brigade, at Kinston, N.C., on the 28th of February, 1864, . . . upon the death of twenty-two men, who have been executed in the presence of the brigade for the crime of desertion*. Greensboro: A. W. Ingold & Co., 1864.

Peace-maker. *An Appeal to the Honest and Reasoning-minded People of the Northern and Southern States of North America*. Petersburg: n.p., 1863.

Pierce, George Foster. *The Word of God a Nation's Life. A sermon, preached before the Bible Convention of the Confederate States. Augusta, Georgia, March 19th, 1862*. Augusta: Office of the Constitutionalist, 1862.

Pinckney, Charles Cotesworth. *Nebuchadnezzars's Fault And Fall: A sermon, preached at Grace Church, Charleston, S.C., on the 17th of February, 1861*. Charleston: A. J. Burke, 1861.

Pollard, Edward Alfred. *The First Year of the War*. Richmond: West & Johnston, 1862.

——. *A Letter on the State of the War. By one recently returned from the enemy's country*. Richmond: n.p., 1865.

——. *Observations in the North: eight months in prison and on parole*. Richmond: E. W. Ayres, 1865.

——. *The Rival Administrations: Richmond and Washington in December, 1863.* Richmond: n.p., 1864.

——. *The Second Battle of Manassas: with sketches of the recent campaign in northern Virginia and on the upper Potomac.* Richmond: West & Johnston, 1862.

——. *The Second Year of the War.* Richmond: West & Johnston, 1863.

——. *The Seven Days' Battles in Front of Richmond. An outline narrative of the series of engagements which opened at Mechanicsville, near Richmond, on Thursday, June 26, 1862, and resulted in the defeat and retreat of the Northern army under Major-General M'Clellan.* Charleston: Evans & Cogswell, 1862.

——. *The Southern Spy. Letters on the policy and inauguration of the Lincoln war.* Richmond: West & Johnston, 1861.

——. *The Two Nations: a key to the history of the American war.* Richmond: Ayres & Wade, 1864.

Porcher, Francis Peyre. *Resources of the Southern Fields and Forests, Medical, Economical and Agricultural. Being also a medical botany of the Confederate States; with practical information on the useful properties of trees, plants, and shrubs.* Richmond: West & Johnston, 1863.

Preston, Margaret Junkin. *Beechenbrook; A Rhyme of the War.* Richmond: J. W. Randolph, 1865.

Providential Aspect and Salutary Tendency of the Existing Crisis. New Orleans: Picayune Office Print, 1861.

Ramsay, James G. *An Address Delivered by Hon. James G. Ramsay, M.D., before the young ladies of Concord Female College at Statesville, May 29th, 1863.* Statesville, N.C.: The Iredell Express, 1863.

Rea, D. B. *Sketches from Hampton's cavalry, embracing the principal exploits of the cavalry in the campaigns of 1862 and 1863.* Columbia: South Carolinian Steam Press, 1864.

[——]. *Sketches from Hampton's cavalry, in the summer, fall and winter campaigns of '62, including Stuart's raid into Pennsylvania, and also, in Burnside's rear.* Raleigh: Strother & Co., 1863.

Read, Charles Henry. *National fast: A discourse delivered on the day of fasting, humiliation and prayer appointed by the President of the United States January 4, 1861.* Richmond: Ritchie & Dunnavant, 1861.

Reid, Samuel Chester. *Great Battle of Chicamauga: a concise history of events from the evacuation of Chattanooga to the defeat of the enemy.* Mobile: F. Titcomb, 1863.

[——]. *A Full Account of the Capture and Wonderful Escape of Gen. John H. Morgan with Captain T. Henry Hines; thrilling and interesting incidents.* Atlanta: Intelligencer Steam Power Presses, 1864.

Remarks on Mr. Motley's Letter in the London Times on the War in America. Charleston: Evans & Cogswell, 1861.

Rogers, James Webb. *Lafitte. By a Soldier.* Selma: Mississippian Book and Job Office, 1864.

Rumney, B. W. *Address to the Laboring Men of Georgia.* N.p., 1861.

Schlesinger, S. *Southern Flowers (Fleurs du Sud) A Selection of Favorite Pieces Arranged for the Piano Forte and Respectfully Dedicated to the Young Ladies of the Sunny South.* Mobile: Joseph Bloch, [c. 1861].

Schley, John. *Our Position and Our True Policy.* Augusta: n.p., 1863.

Scott, John. *Letters to An Officer in the Army; proposing constitutional reform in the Confederate Government after the close of the present war. A supplement to "The Lost Principle."* Richmond: A. Morris, 1864.

Semmes, Raphael. *The Cruise of the Alabama and Sumter. From the private journals and other papers of Commander R. Semmes, C.S.N., and other officers.* Richmond: West & Johnston, 1864.

Shelton, William J. *Confederate Poems.* Lynchburg: Virginian Power Press Job Office, 1862.

[Shepperson, William G.]. *War Songs of the South.* Richmond: West & Johnston, 1862.

Simms, William Gilmore. *Sack and Destruction of the City of Columbia, S.C. To which is added a list of the property destroyed.* Columbia: Power Press of Daily Phoenix, 1865.

Slaughter, Philip. *A Sketch of the Life of Randolph Fairfax, a private in the ranks of the Rockbridge Artillery, attached to the "Stonewall Brigade" and subsequently to the 1st Reg. Va. Light Artillery, 2d corps, Army of Northern Virginia; including a brief account of Jackson's celebrated valley campaign.* Richmond: Tyler, Allegre & McDaniel, 1864.

Smith, Francis Henney. *Discourse on the Life and Character of Lt. Gen. Thos. J. Jackson (C.S.A.) late professor of natural and experimental philosophy in the Virginia Military Institute.* Richmond: Ritchie & Dunnavant, 1863.

Smith, Sallie M. *My Marriage and its Consequences.* Macon: Burke, Boykin & Co., 1864.

Smith, Robert H. *An Address to the Citizens of Alabama, on the Constitution and Laws of the Confederate States of America.* Mobile: Mobile Daily Register Print, 1861.

Smith, William Russell. *The Royal Ape: A Dramatic Poem.* Richmond: West & Johnston, 1863.

Smyth, Thomas. *The Sin and the Curse; The Union, the True Source of Disunion, and Our Duty in the Present Crisis.* Charleston: Evans & Cogswell, 1860.

South Carolinian. *The Confederate. By a South Carolinian.* Mobile: S. H. Goetzel & Co., 1863.

The Southern Field and Fireside Novelette, No. 1. Containing "Myra Bruce; or True Love Running Roughly," with illustrations; "Riverlands," a charming story of Southern life; and "Five Chapters of a History: A Georgia court, forty years ago." Augusta: James Gardner, [1863].

Spence, James. *The American Union; its effect on national character and policy, with an inquiry into secession as a constitutional right, and the causes of the disruption.* Richmond: West & Johnston, 1863.

Spratt, L. W. *The Philosophy of Secession; A Southern view, presented in a letter addressed to the Hon. Mr. Perkins of Louisiana, in criticism on the Provisional Constitution adopted by the Southern Congress at Montgomery, Alabama, by the Hon. L. W. Spratt, editor of the Charleston Mercury, 13th February, 1861.* [Charleston]: n.p., 1861.

Starnes, Ebenezer. *Rhymes, serious and humorous, for my children*. Augusta: Office of the Constitutionalist, 1862.

The Step-Sister. A Novelette. By a Southern Gentlemen. Richmond: Ayres & Wade, 1863.

Stiles, Joseph C. *National Rectitude the Only True Basis of National Prosperity: an appeal to the Confederate States*. Petersburg: Evangelical Tract Society, 1863.

St. Paul, Henry. *Our Home and Foreign Policy*. Mobile: Printed at the Office of the Daily Register and Advertiser, 1863.

[Swain, Margie P.]. *Mara: or, A Romance of the War*. Selma: Mississippian Steam Book and Job Office, 1864.

A Synopsis of the Art of War. Dedicated to the junior officers of the Confederate Army. Columbia: Evans & Cogswell, 1864.

Thackeray, William Makepeace. *The Adventures of Philip on his way through the world; showing who robbed him, who helped him, and who passed him by*. Columbia: Evans & Cogswell, 1864.

Thornwell, James H. *Our Danger and Our Duty*. Columbia: Southern Guardian Steam-Power Press, 1862.

——. *The State of the Country: an article republished from the Southern Presbyterian Review*. Columbia: Southern Guardian Steam-Power Press, 1861.

Thrasher, John B. *Slavery a Divine Institution. By J. B. Thrasher, of Port Gibson. A speech made before the Breckinridge and Lane Club, November 5th, 1860*. Port Gibson, Miss.: Southern Reveille Book and Job Office, 1861.

Troup. *To the People of the South. Senator Hammond and The Tribune*. Charleston: Evans & Cogswell, 1860.

Tucker, John Randolph. *The Southern Church Justified in its Support of the South in the Present War, delivered before the Young Men's Christian Association, of Richmond, on the 21st May, 1863*. Richmond: Wm. H. Clemmitt, 1863.

[——]. *A Southern Document. To the people of Virginia. The great issue! Our relations to it*. Wytheville, Va.: D. A. St. Clair, 1861.

Tucker, Nathaniel Beverly. *The Partisan Leader: A novel, and an apocalypse of the origin and struggles of the Southern Confederacy*. Richmond: West & Johnston, 1862.

[Turner, Joseph Addison]. *The Old Plantation*. Turnwold, Ga.: Countryman Print, 1862.

Tyree, Cornelius. *The Benefits of Affliction. A sermon on occasion of the death of General Philip St. George Cocke*. Richmond: Macfarlane & Fergusson, 1862.

Tyson, Bryan. *[Circular Letter]*. Brower's Mills, N.C.: n.p., 1862.

——. *A Ray of Light; Or, A Treatise on the Sectional Troubles, religiously and morally considered*. Brower's Mills, N.C.: n.p., 1862.

Uncle Buddy's Gift Book for the Holidays. Augusta: Blome & Tehan, 1863.

The War and Its Heroes. Richmond: Ayres & Wade, 1864.

Warder, T. B. *Battle of Young's Branch; or, Manassas Plain, fought July 21, 1861*. Richmond: Tyler, Wise, Allegre and Smith, 1862.

Warren, Ebenezer W. *Nellie Norton: or, Southern Slavery and the Bible. A Scriptural refutation of the principal arguments upon which the abolitionists rely. A vindication of Southern slavery from the Old and New Testaments*. Macon: Burke, Boykin & Company, 1864.

Warren, Kittrell J. *History of the Eleventh Georgia Vols., embracing the muster rolls, together with a special and succinct account of the marches, engagements, casualties, etc.* Richmond: Smith, Bailey & Co., 1863.

[West, Beckwith]. *Experience of a Confederate States Prisoner, being an ephemeris regularly kept by an officer of the Confederate States Army.* Richmond: West & Johnston, 1862.

[White, William Spottswood]. *Sketches of the Life of Captain Hugh A. White, of the Stonewall Brigade.* Columbia: South Carolinian Steam Press, 1864.

Wiley, Calvin Henderson. *Scriptural Views of National Trials: or the true road to the independence and peace of the Confederate States of America.* Greensboro: Sterling, Campbell & Albright, 1863.

Williams, James. *Letters on Slavery From the Old World: written during the canvass for the presidency of the United States in 1860. To which are added a letter to Lord Brougham on the John Brown raid; and a brief reference to the result of the presidential contest, and its consequences.* Nashville: Southern Methodist Publishing House, 1861.

Wood, Ellen. *East Lynne; or, The Earl's Daughter.* Richmond: West & Johnston, 1864.

——. *Mrs. Halliburton's Troubles.* 2 vols. Richmond: West & Johnston, 1865.

CONFEDERATE TEXTBOOKS AND EDUCATIONAL LITERATURE

Baird, Washington. *The Confederate Spelling Book: interspersed with choice reading lessons in poetry and in prose—at once to please and instruct—many of them conveying valuable information and well calculated to make a fine moral impression.* Macon: Burke, Boykin & Company, 1864.

Bingham, William. *A Grammar of the Latin Language for the use of schools with exercises and vocabularies.* Greensboro: Sterling, Campbell & Albright, 1863.

Branson, Levi. *First Book in Composition, applying the principles of grammar to the art of composing: also, giving full directions for punctuation; especially designed for the use of Southern schools.* Raleigh: Branson, Farrar & Co., 1863.

Browne, George Y. *Browne's Arithmetical Tables, combined with easy lessons in mental arithmetic, for beginners.* Atlanta: J. J. Toon, 1865.

Bullions, Peter. *An Analytical and Practical Grammar of the English Language.* Raleigh: N.C. Christian Advocate Publishing Company, 1864.

Burke's Picture Primer; or, spelling and reading taught in an easy and familiar manner. Macon: Burke, Boykin & Co., 1864.

Caldwell, M. P., and W. W. Everett. *The Student's Arithmetic; a collection of concise rules and abridged methods of calculation, adapted to the use of schools, farmers, mechanics, and business men generally.* Athens: J. H. Christy's Franklin Job Office Print, 1861.

Campbell, William A. *The Child's First Book. By Campbell and Dunn. Approved by the Educational Association of Virginia through their Committee.* Richmond: Ayres & Wade, 1864.

Carpenter, Thomas. *The Scholar's Spelling Assistant.* . . . Charleston: McCarter & Dawson, 1861.

Chaudron, Adelaide De Vendel. *Chaudron's Spelling Book, carefully prepared for family and school use.* Mobile: S. H. Goetzel, 1864.

——. *Chaudron's Spelling Book, carefully prepared for family and school use.* 5th ed. Mobile: S. H. Goetzel, 1865.

——. *The First Reader, designed for the use of primary schools.* 2nd ed. Mobile: W. G. Clark, 1864.

——. *The Second Reader, designed for the use of primary schools. Adopted for use in the public schools of Mobile.* Mobile: Office of the Daily Advertiser and Register, 1863.

——. *The Second Reader, designed for the use of primary schools. Second edition. Adopted for use in the public schools of Mobile.* Mobile: W. G. Clark & Co., 1864.

——. *The Third Reader, designed for the use of primary schools. Adopted for use in the public schools of Mobile.* Mobile: W. G. Clark & Co, 1864.

Colburn, Warren. *Intellectual Arithmetic, upon the inductive method of instruction.* . . . *Revised and adapted to the use of schools in the Confederate States. By Thos. O. Summers.* Nashville: Southern Methodist Publishing House, 1862.

[Colby, Charles Galusha]. *The World in Miniature; or, Diamond atlas of every nation and country both ancient and modern, embracing of the Confederate States, United States and Canadas of North America.* New Orleans: William F. Stuart, 1861.

The Confederate Primer. . . . *By an association of Southern teachers.* Nashville: n.p., 1861.

The Confederate Rhyming Primer; or, First Lessons Made Easy. Designed as an introduction to the Confederate Spelling Book. Richmond: George L. Bidgood, 1863.

The Confederate Spelling Book, compiled principally from the National Speller. A new and revised edition, to which is added short and easy reading lessons for beginners, comprising in the same book, a complete speller and primer. Austin: D. Richardson & Co, 1864.

Cushing, Edward H. *The New Texas Primary Reader for the Use of Primary Schools.* Houston: E. H. Cushing, 1863.

——. *The New Texas Reader. Designed for the use of schools in Texas.* Houston: E. H. Cushing, 1864.

Dagg, John Leadley. *The Grammar of the English Language.* Macon: Burke, Boykin & Company, 1864.

Darby, John. *Text Book of Chemistry . . . Designed for schools, academies, and colleges.* Savannah: John M. Cooper & Co., 1861.

The Dixie Speller and Reader, designed for the use of schools; by a lady of Georgia. Macon: J. W. Burke, 1863.

The Education of Teachers in the South: embracing a letter from Prof. Edw'd S. Joynes to Geo. P. Tayloe, Esq., and a plan for the foundation of a normal school in Hollins Institute, Virginia; to which is added a catalogue of the Institute, for the session 1863–4. Lynchburg: Virginian Power-Press Book and Job Office, 1864.

Educational Association of the Confederate States of America. *Proceedings of the*

Convention of Teachers of the Confederate States, Assembled at Columbia, South
Carolina, April 28th, 1863. Macon: Burke, Boykin & Co., 1863.

Exercises de Cacographie. . . . New Orleans: Propagateur Catholique, 1861.

The First Confederate Speller: on a strictly philosophical and progressive plan. . . . By an
association of Southern teachers. Nashville: n.p., 1861.

The First Reader, edited by a distinguished Southern teacher. Richmond: A. Morris,
1864.

The First Reader for Southern Schools. Raleigh: Christian Advocate Publishing
Company, 1864.

Fleming, Robert. The Revised Elementary Spelling Book. The elementary spelling book,
revised and adapted to the youth of the Southern Confederacy, interspersed with Bible
reading on domestic slavery. Atlanta: J. J. Toon & Co., 1863.

Fowler, Abijah. The Southern School Arithmetic; or, Youth's Assistant. . . . Revised by
M. Gibson. Richmond: West & Johnston, 1864.

Johnson, Lemuel. An Elementary Arithmetic, designed for beginners: embracing the first
principles of the science. Raleigh: Branson & Farrar, 1864.

Joynes, Edward Southey. Education After the War. A letter addressed to a member of the
Southern Educational Convention, Columbia, S.C., 28th April, 1863. Richmond:
Macfarlane & Fergusson, 1863.

[Junius]. Conscription of Teachers, 186[?].

Lander, Samuel. Our Own Primary Arithmetic. 2nd ed. Greensboro: Sterling, Campbell
and Albright, 1863.

——. Our Own School Arithmetic. Greensboro: Sterling, Campbell & Albright, 1863.

——. The Verbal Primer. Greensboro: Sterling, Campbell & Albright, 1865.

Leavenworth, Abner Johnson. To the Teachers and Others Identified with the Cause of
Education, in Virginia. Petersburg: n.p., 1863.

Leverett, Charles Edward. The Southern Confederacy Arithmetic, for common schools
and academies, with a practical system of book-keeping by single entry. Augusta: J. T.
Paterson & Co., 1864.

Moore, Marinda Branson. The Dixie Primer, for the Little Folks. 3rd ed. Raleigh:
Branson, Farrar & Co., 1863 [1864].

——. The Dixie Speller. To follow the First Dixie Reader. Raleigh: Branson & Farrar, 1864.

——. The First Dixie Reader; Designed to Follow the Dixie Primer. Raleigh: Branson,
Farrar & Co, 1863.

——. The First Dixie Reader; Designed to Follow the Dixie Primer. 2nd ed. Raleigh:
Branson & Farrar, 1864.

——. The Geographical Reader, for the Dixie Children. Raleigh: Branson, Farrar & Co.,
1863.

——. Primary Geography, Arranged as a Reading Book for Common Schools, with
questions and answers attached. 2nd ed. Raleigh: Branson & Farrar, 1864.

Neely, John. The Confederate States Speller and Reader: containing the principles and
practice of English orthography and orthoepy systematically developed. Designed to

accord with the "present usage of literary and well-bred society." In three parts. For the use of schools and families. Augusta: A. Bleakley, 1864 [1865].

North Carolina General Assembly. House of Commons. *A Bill to Provide for the Establishment of Graded Schools in North-Carolina, and for other Purposes.* Sess. 1863, House Bill No. 20.

The Old Dominion Speller. Richmond: J. R. Keiningham, 1862.

The Old Dominion Speller. Richmond: A. Morris, 1863.

The Pictorial Primer; Designed for the Use of Schools and Families. Embellished with fine engravings. Richmond: West & Johnston, 1863.

The Pictorial Tract Primer. Petersburg: The Evangelical Tract Society, 1864.

Poindexter, Mrs. S. A. *Philological Reader. A Southern Series. "Second Book."* Nashville: South-Western Publishing House; Southern Methodist Publishing House, 1861.

——. *Philological Reader. A Southern Series. "Third Book."* Nashville: South-Western Publishing House; Southern Methodist Publishing House, 1861.

——. *Philological Reader. A Southern Series. "Fourth Book."* Nashville: South-Western Publishing House; Southern Methodist Publishing House, 1861.

Rambaut, Thomas. *The Child's Primer.* Atlanta: J. J. Toon & Co., 1863.

Rice, John H. *A System of Modern Geography, compiled from various sources and adapted to the present condition of the world; expressly for the use of schools and academies in the Confederate States of America.* Atlanta: Franklin Printing House; Wood, Hanleiter, Rice & Co., 1862.

Rivers, Richard Henderson. *Elements of Mental Philosophy.* Edited by Thomas O. Summers. Nashville: Southern Methodist Publishing House, 1862.

——. *Elements of Moral Philosophy.* Edited by Thomas O. Summers. Nashville: Southern Methodist Publishing House, 1861.

Sargent, Epes. *The Standard Speller; containing exercises for oral spelling; also, sentences for silent spelling by writing from dictation.* Macon: J. W. Burke, 1861.

Scott, Allen M. *A New Southern Grammar of the English Language, designed for the use of schools and private learners.* Memphis: Hutton & Freligh, 1861.

The Second Confederate Speller. . . . By an Association of Southern Teachers. Nashville: Southern Methodist Publishing House, J. B. M'Ferrin, 1861.

[Smith, Richard McAllister]. *The Confederate First Reader: containing selections in prose and poetry, as reading exercises for the younger children in the schools and families of the Confederate States.* Richmond: George L. Bidgood, 1864.

——. *The Confederate Primer.* 3rd ed. Richmond: George L. Bidgood, 1863.

——. *The Confederate Primer.* 4th ed. Richmond: George L. Bidgood, 1864.

——. *The Confederate Rhyming Primer; or, First Lessons Made Easy. Designed as an introduction to the Confederate Spelling Book.* Richmond: George L. Bidgood, 1863.

——. *The Confederate Spelling Book with Reading Lessons for the Young, adapted to the use of schools or for private instruction.* 3rd ed. Richmond: George L. Bidgood, 1863.

——. *The Confederate Spelling Book with Reading Lessons for the Young, adapted to the use of schools or for private instruction.* 4th ed. Richmond: George L. Bidgood, 1864.

——. *The Confederate Spelling Book with Reading Lessons for the Young, adapted to the use of schools or for private instruction.* 5th ed. Richmond: George L. Bidgood, 1865.

[Smith, Roswell Chamberlain]. *Smith's English Grammar, on the productive system. Revised and improved, and adapted to the use of schools in the Confederate States.* Richmond: George L. Bidgood, 1863.

——. *Smith's English Grammar, on the productive system. Revised and improved, and adapted to the use of schools in the Confederate States.* 2nd ed. Richmond: George L. Bidgood, 1864.

Smythe, Charles W. *Our Own Elementary Grammar, intermediate between the primary and high school grammars, and especially adapted to the wants of the common schools.* Greensboro: Sterling, Campbell & Albright, 1863.

——. *Our Own Primary Grammar for the Use of Beginners.* Greensboro: Sterling and Campbell, 1861.

——. *Our Own School Grammar, designed for our schools and academies, as a sequel to the "Primary Grammar."* Greensboro: Sterling, Campbell & Albright, 1862.

The Southern Pictorial Primer; combining instruction with amusement, and designed for use in schools and families. Embellished with numerous engravings. Richmond: West & Johnston, 1864.

State Educational Association of North Carolina. *The Constitution[,] By-Laws and Act of Incorporation of the State Educational Association, of North Carolina.* Greensboro: James W. Albright, 1862.

[Sterling, Richard]. *Our Own Primer. For the children.* Greensboro: Sterling, Campbell and Albright, [c. 1862].

Sterling, Richard, and J. D. Campbell. *Our Own First Reader; for the use of schools and families.* Greensboro: Sterling, Campbell & Albright, 1862.

——. *Our Own First Reader; for the use of schools and families.* Greensboro: Sterling, Campbell & Albright, [1864? c. 1862].

——. *Our Own Second Reader: for the use of schools and families.* Greensboro: Sterling, Campbell, and Albright, [c. 1862].

——. *Our Own Spelling Book: for the use of schools and families.* Greensboro: Sterling, Campbell, and Albright, [c. 1862].

——. *Our Own Third Reader: for the use of schools and families.* Greensboro: Sterling, Campbell & Albright, [1863, c. 1862].

Stewart, Kensey Johns. *A Geography for Beginners.* Richmond: J. W. Randolph, 1864.

Taylor, J. C. R. *The Southern Primer, or the Child's First Book.* Charleston: A. E. Miller & Co., 1864.

The Virginia Primer. Richmond: J. R. Keiningham, 1864.

The Virginia Speller and Reader. Richmond: J. R. Keiningham, 1863.

The Virginia Speller and Reader. Richmond: J. R. Keiningham, 1865.

Virginia Spelling and Reading Book, adapted to the use of public schools, and private or family instruction. Arranged after the plan of John Comly. Richmond: A. Morris, 1864.

[Walker, John]. *The Palmetto Dictionary; in which the meaning of every word is clearly explained and the sound of every syllable distinctly shown; exhibiting the principles of a pure and correct pronunciation. A new edition, carefully revised, corrected, and enlarged.* Richmond: J. W. Randolph, 1864.

Webster, Noah. *The Elementary Spelling Book, being an improvement on "The American Spelling Book."* "Southern" ed. Macon: Burke, Boykin and Co., 1863.

——. *The Elementary Spelling Book, being An improvement on "The American Spelling Book."* Third "Southern" ed. Macon: J. W. Burke and Company, 1865.

——. *The Elementary Spelling-Book, revised from Webster, and adapted to Southern schools, by the publishers.* Raleigh: Branson, Farrar & Co., [1863?].

Whately, Richard. *Elements of Logic.* Nashville: Southern Methodist Publishing House, 1861.

——. *Elements of Rhetoric.* Nashville: Southern Methodist Publishing House, 1861.

Wiley, Calvin Henderson. *Circular to the Authorities and People of North Carolina.* Greensboro: Sterling, Campbell & Albright, 1863.

Wiley, Calvin Henderson, et al. *Address to the People of North Carolina.* Raleigh?: n.p., [1861].

Worrell, Adolphus Spalding. *The Principles of English Grammar.* Nashville: Graves, Marks & Co.; South-Western Publishing House, 1861.

York, Brantley. *York's English Grammar, revised and adapted to Southern schools.* 3rd ed. Raleigh: Branson, Farrar & Co., 1864.

OTHER PRIMARY SOURCES

Adams, Henry. *The Education of Henry Adams.* New York: The Modern Library, 1931.

Berlin, Ira, Barbara J. Fields, Steven F. Miller, Joseph P. Reidy, and Leslie S. Rowland, eds. *Free at Last: A Documentary History of Slavery, Freedom, and the Civil War.* New York: The New Press, 1992.

Chesebrough, David B., ed. *"God Ordained This War": Sermons on the Sectional Crisis, 1830–1865.* Columbia: University of South Carolina Press, 1991.

Chesnut, Mary Boykin. *A Diary from Dixie.* Edited by Ben Ames Williams. Cambridge: Harvard University Press, 1980.

Cleveland, Charles D. *Anti-Slavery Addresses of 1844 and 1845 by Salmon Portland Chase and Charles Dexter Cleveland.* London: S. Low, Son, and Marston, 1867.

——. *A Compendium of American Literature.* Philadelphia: E. C. & J. Biddle, 1858.

——. *A Compendium of American Literature.* 3rd ed. Philadelphia: Parry & McMillan, 1859.

——. *Slavery and Infidelity.* Philadelphia?: n.p., [1859?].

Cocke, William Archer. *The Constitutional History of the United States: from the Adoption of the Articles of Confederation to the Close of Jackson's Administration.* Philadelphia: J. B. Lippincott, 1858.

Crozier, R. H. *The Confederate Spy: A Story of the War of 1861.* Gallatin, Tenn.: R. B. Harmon, 1866.

Daniel, John M. *The Richmond Examiner During the War:* Arno & The New York Times, 1868. Reprint, 1970.

Daniel, Lizzie Cary. *Confederate Scrap-Book: Copied from a Scrap-book kept by a young girl during and immediately after the war, with additions from war copies of the "Southern Literary Messenger" and "Illustrated News" loaned by friends, and other selections as accredited.* Richmond: J. L. Hill Printing Company, 1893.

Davidson, James Wood. *The Living Writers of the South.* New York: Carleton, 1869.

Davidson, Nora Fontaine M., ed. *Cullings from the Confederacy. Southern Poems Popular During the War 1861–5 Including the Doggerel of the Camp.* Washington, D.C.: Rufus H. Darby Printing Co., 1903.

Davis, William C., ed. *A Fire-Eater Remembers: The Confederate Memoir of Robert Barnwell Rhett.* Columbia: University of South Carolina Press, 2000.

De Leon, T. C. *Belles, Beaux and Brains of the 60's.* New York: G. W. Dillingham Company, 1907.

——. *South Songs: From the Lays of Later Days.* New York: Blelock & Co., 1866.

Dumond, Dwight Lowell, ed. *Southern Editorials on Secession.* New York: The Century Co., 1931.

Ellinger, Esther Parker. *The Southern War Poetry of the Civil War.* Philadelphia: Hershey Press, 1918.

Emerson, Ralph Waldo. *Ralph Waldo Emerson: Essays and Lectures.* Edited by Joel Porte. New York: Library of America, 1983.

Evans, Augusta Jane. *Macaria; or, Altars of Sacrifice.* Edited by Drew Gilpin Faust. Baton Rouge: Louisiana State University Press, 1992.

Fagan, W. L. *Southern War Songs.* New York: M. T. Richardson & Co., 1890.

Farrar, C. C. S. *The War: Its Causes and Consequences.* Cairo, Ill.: Blelock & Co., 1864.

Fast Day Sermons: or The Pulpit on the State of the Country. New York: Rudd & Carleton, 1861.

Fitzhugh, George. *Cannibals All! or, Slaves Without Masters.* Edited by C. Vann Woodward. Cambridge: Belknap Press of Harvard University Press, 1960.

Harris, Joel Chandler. *On the Plantation: A Story of a Georgia Boy's Adventures During the War.* New York: D. Appleton and Company, 1892. Reprint, Athens: University of Georgia Press, 1980.

Harris, Julia Collier. *The Life and Letters of Joel Chandler Harris.* Boston: Houghton Mifflin Company, 1918.

Hayne, Paul Hamilton. *A Man of Letters in the Nineteenth-Century South: Selected Letters of Paul Hamilton Hayne.* Edited by Rayburn S. Moore. Baton Rouge: Louisiana State University Press, 1982.

Hewitt, John Hill. *King Linkum The First: A Musical Burletta.* Edited by Richard Barksdale Harwell. Reprint, Atlanta: Emory University Publications. Sources and Reprints. Series IV, 1947.

Hill, Alfred C. *MacPherson, the Confederate Philosopher.* New York: J. Miller, 1864.

Hubbell, Jay B., ed. *The Last Years of Henry Timrod 1864–1867.* Durham: Duke University Press, 1941.

Hubner, C. W. *War Poets of the South and Confederate Camp-Fire Songs.* Atlanta: U. P. Byrd, 1896.

Kennedy, Joseph C. G. *Preliminary Report on the Eighth Census, 1860.* Washington: Government Printing Office, 1862.

Lacon. *The Devil in America: A Dramatic Satire.* Mobile: J. K. Randall, 1867.

Lays of the South: Verses Relative to the War Between the Two Sections of the American States. N.p., 1864.

Mason, Emily V. *The Southern Poems of the War.* Baltimore: John Murphy & Co., 1867.

——. *The Southern Poems of the War.* 3rd ed. Baltimore: John Murphy & Co, 1869.

Moore, Frank, ed. *Rebel Rhymes and Rhapsodies.* New York: George P. Putnam, 1864.

——. *Songs and Ballads of the Southern People. 1861–1865.* New York: D. Appleton and Company, 1886.

——. *Spirit of the Pulpit, with Reference to the Present Crisis.* New York: G. P. Putnam, 1861.

O'Brien, Michael, ed. *All Clever Men, Who Make Their Way: Critical Discourse in the Old South.* Fayetteville: University of Arkansas Press, 1982.

——. *An Evening When Alone: Four Journals of Single Women in the South, 1827–67.* Charlottesville: University Press of Virginia, 1993.

Palmer, Benjamin M. *The Life and Letters of James Henley Thornwell.* Richmond: Whittet & Shepperson, 1875.

Paskoff, Paul F., and Daniel J. Wilson, eds. *The Cause of the South: Selections from De Bow's Review, 1846–1867.* Baton Rouge: Louisiana State University Press, 1982.

Pollard, Edward Alfred. *The Lost Cause: A New Southern History of the War of the Confederates.* New York: E. B. Treat & Co., 1866.

Ruffin, Edmund. *Anticipations of the Future, to Serve as Lessons for the Present Time.* Richmond: J. W. Randolph, 1860.

Simms, William Gilmore. *The Letters of William Gilmore Simms.* Edited by Mary C. Simms Oliphant, Alfred Taylor Odell and T. C. Duncan Eaves. 5 vols. Columbia: University of South Carolina Press, 1955.

——. *War Poetry of the South.* New York: Richardson & Company, 1867.

Smith, Charles Henry. *Bill Arp, So Called.* New York: Metropolitan Record Office, 1866.

Stiles, Joseph C. *The National Controversy, or, The Voice of the Fathers upon the State of the Country.* New York: Rudd & Carleton, 1861.

Stone, Kate. *Brokenburn: The Journal of Kate Stone 1861–1868.* Edited by John Q. Anderson. Baton Rouge: Louisiana State University Press, 1995.

Taliaferro, Harden E. *Carolina Humor: Sketches by Harden E. Taliaferro.* Richmond: The Dietz Press, 1938.

Throp, Willard, ed. *A Southern Reader.* New York: Alfred A. Knopf, 1955.

Timrod, Henry. *The Collected Poems of Henry Timrod.* Edited by Edd Winfield Parks and Aileen Wells Parks. Athens: University of Georgia Press, 1965.

——. *The Essays of Henry Timrod.* Edited by Edd Winfield Parks. Athens: University of Georgia Press, 1942.

——. "Literature in the South." *Russell's Magazine* 5 (August 1859): 385–95.

——. *The Poems of Henry Timrod.* Edited by Paul H. Hayne. New York: E. J. Hale & Son, 1873.

——. *The Uncollected Poems of Henry Timrod*. Edited by Guy A. Cardwell Jr. Athens: University of Georgia Press, 1942.

Turner, Joseph Addison. *Autobiography of "The Countryman" 1866*. Edited by Thomas H. English. Atlanta: Emory University Library, 1943.

——. *The Old Plantation: A Poem by Joseph Addison Turner 1862*. Edited by Henry Prentice Miller. Atlanta: Emory University Library, 1945.

United States War Department. *The War of the Rebellion: A Compilation of the Official Records of the Union and Confederate Armies*. 127 vols. Washington, D.C.: Government Printing Office, 1880–1901.

Wakelyn, Jon L., ed. *Southern Unionist Pamphlets and the Civil War*. Columbia, Mo.: University of Missouri Press, 1999.

War Lyrics and Songs of the South. London: Spottiswoode & Co, 1866.

West, William Franciscus, Jr. "A Southern Editor Views the Civil War: A Collection of Editorials by Henry Timrod and Other Editorial Materials Published in the *Daily South Carolinian*, January 14, 1864, to February 17, 1865." Ph.D. diss., Florida State University, 1984.

Wharton, H. M. *War Songs and Poems of the Southern Confederacy 1861–1865*. Philadelphia: The John C. Winston Co., 1904.

SECONDARY SOURCES AND BIBLIOGRAPHIC AIDS

Aaron, Daniel. *The Unwritten War: American Writers and the Civil War*. New York: Alfred A. Knopf, 1973.

Abel, E. Lawrence. *Singing the New Nation: How Music Shaped the Confederacy, 1861–1865*. Mechanicsburg, Pa.: Stackpole Books, 2000.

Adams, Eldon. "The Biblical Defense of Slavery in the Antebellum South." *The Mirror* 5 (May 1983): 1–29.

Adams, Michael C. C. *Our Masters the Rebels: A Speculation on Union Military Failure in the East 1861–1865*. Cambridge: Harvard University Press, 1978.

Ahlstrom, Sydney. *A Religious History of the American People*. New Haven: Yale University Press, 1972.

Albright, James W. "Books Made in Dixie." *Southern Historical Society Papers* 41 (September 1916): 57–60.

Alfriend, Frank H. *The Life of Jefferson Davis*. Cincinnati: Caxton Publishing House, 1868.

Anderson, Benedict. *Imagined Communities: Reflections on the Origin and Spread of Nationalism*. Rev. ed. London: Verso, 1991.

Andrews, J. Cutler. "The Confederate Press and Public Morale." *Journal of Southern History* 32 (November 1966): 445–65.

——. *The South Reports the Civil War*, 1970. Reprint, Pittsburgh: University of Pittsburgh Press, 1985.

Aphornsuvan, Thanet. "James D. B. De Bow and the Political Economy of the Old South." Ph.D. diss., State University of New York at Binghamton, 1991.

Arieli, Yehoshua. *Individualism and Nationalism in American Ideology*. Cambridge: Harvard University Press, 1964.

Atchison, Ray Morris. "Southern Literary Magazines, 1865–1887." Ph.D. diss., Duke University, 1956.

Austin, James C. *Bill Arp*. New York: Twayne, 1969.

Ayers, Edward L. *In the Presence of Mine Enemies: War in the Heart of America 1859–1863*. New York: W. W. Norton & Company, 2003.

——. *The Promise of the New South: Life After Reconstruction*. New York: Oxford University Press, 1992.

Bailey, David T. *Shadow on the Church: Southwestern Evangelical Religion and the Issue of Slavery, 1783–1860*. Ithaca: Cornell University Press, 1985.

Bailey, Fred Arthur. "The Textbooks of the 'Lost Cause': Censorship and the Creation of Southern State Histories." *Georgia Historical Quarterly* 75 (Fall 1991): 507–33.

Bain, Robert, and Joseph M. Flora, eds. *Fifty Southern Writers Before 1900*. New York: Greenwood Press, 1987.

Bain, Robert, Joseph M. Flora, and Louis D. Rubin Jr. *Southern Writers: A Biographical Dictionary*. Baton Rouge: Louisiana State University Press, 1979.

Baker, Thomas Harrison. *The Memphis Commercial Appeal: The History of a Southern Newspaper*. Baton Rouge: Louisiana State University Press, 1971.

Barnard, Frederick M. *Herder's Social and Political Thought from the Enlightenment to Nationalism*. Oxford: Clarendon, 1965.

Baro, Gene, ed. *After Appomattox: The Image of the South in its Fiction 1865–1900*. New York: Corinth Books, 1963.

Bartlett, Irving H. *The American Mind in the Mid-Nineteenth Century*. 2nd ed. Arlington Heights, Ill.: H. Davidson, 1982.

Bartley, Numan V., ed. *The Evolution of Southern Culture*. Athens: University of Georgia Press, 1988.

Baxter, Charles N., and James M. Dearborn. *Confederate Literature: A List of Books and Newspapers, Maps, Music, and Miscellaneous Matter Printed in the South during the Confederacy, Now in the Boston Athenaeum*. Boston: Boston Athenaeum, 1917.

Beals, Carleton. *War Within a War: The Confederacy Against Itself*. Philadelphia: Chilton Books, 1965.

Beckett, Ian F. W. *The American Civil War: The War Correspondents*. Dover, N.H.: Alan Sutton, 1993.

Bensel, Richard Franklin. *Yankee Leviathan: The Origins of Central State Authority in America, 1859–1877*. Cambridge: Cambridge University Press, 1990.

Berends, Kurt O. " 'Wholesome Reading Purifies and Elevates the Man': The Religious Military Press in the Confederacy." In *Religion and the American Civil War*, edited by Randall M. Miller, Harry S. Stout and Charles Reagan Wilson. New York: Oxford University Press, 1998.

Beringer, Richard E., Herman Hattaway, Archer Jones, and William N. Still Jr. *Why the South Lost the Civil War*. Athens: University of Georgia Press, 1986.

Berlin, Ira. *Generations of Captivity: A History of African-American Slaves*. Cambridge: Belknap Press of Harvard University Press, 2003.

——. *Many Thousands Gone: The First Two Centuries of Slavery in North America*. Cambridge: Belknap Press of Harvard University Press, 1998.

Berlin, Ira, Barbara J. Fields, Steven F. Miller, Joseph Reidy, and Leslie S. Rowland. *Slaves No More: Three Essays on Emancipation and the Civil War*. Cambridge: Cambridge University Press, 1992.

Berlin, Isaiah. *Vico and Herder: Two Studies in the History of Ideas*. London: Hogarth Press, 1976.

Bernath, Michael T. "Confederate Minds: The Struggle for Intellectual Independence in the Civil War South." Ph.D. diss., Harvard University, 2005.

Binnington, Ian. "Promoting the Confederate Nation: The *Southern Illustrated News* and the Civil War." In *Virginia's Civil War*, edited by Paul Wallenstein and Bertram Wyatt-Brown. Charlottesville: University of Virginia Press, 2005.

——. " 'They Have Made a Nation': Confederates and the Creation of Confederate Nationalism." Ph.D. diss., University of Illinois at Urbana-Champaign, 2004.

Blair, William. *Cities of the Dead: Contesting the Memory of the Civil War in the South, 1865–1914*. Chapel Hill: University of North Carolina Press, 2004.

——. *Virginia's Private War: Feeding Body and Soul in the Confederacy, 1861–1865*. Oxford: Oxford University Press, 1998.

Bleser, Carol. *The Hammonds of Redcliffe*. New York: Oxford University Press, 1981.

Blight, David W. *Race and Reunion: The Civil War in American Memory*. Cambridge: Belknap Press of Harvard University Press, 2001.

Blum, Edward J. *Reforging the White Republic: Race, Religion, and American Nationalism, 1865–1898*. Baton Rouge: Louisiana State University Press, 2005.

Boles, John B., ed. *Masters and Slaves in the House of the Lord: Race and Religion in the American South, 1740–1870*. Lexington: University Press of Kentucky, 1988.

Boles, John B., and Evelyn Thomas Nolen, eds. *Interpreting Southern History: Historiographical Essays in Honor of Sanford W. Higginbotham*. Baton Rouge: Louisiana State University Press, 1987.

Bonner, Robert E. "Americans Apart: Nationality in the Slaveholding South." Ph.D. diss, Yale University, 1997.

——. *Colors and Blood: Flag Passions of the Confederate South*. Princeton: Princeton University Press, 2002.

——. "Flag Culture and the Consolidation of Confederate Nationalism." *Journal of Southern History* 68 (May 2002): 293–332.

——. *Mastering America: Southern Slaveholders and the Crisis of American Nationhood*. Cambridge: Cambridge University Press, 2009.

——. "Roundheaded Cavaliers? The Context and Limits of a Confederate Racial Project." *Civil War History* 48 (March 2002): 34–59.

Boritt, Gabor S., ed. *Why the Confederacy Lost*. New York: Oxford University Press, 1992.

Brantley, Rabun Lee. *Georgia Journalism of the Civil War Period*. Contributions to

Education of George Peabody College for Teachers, no. 58. Nashville: George Peabody College for Teachers, 1929.

Brasch, Walter M. *Brer Rabbit, Uncle Remus, and the "Cornfield Journalist."* Macon: Mercer University Press, 2000.

Braude, Ann. *Radical Spirits: Spiritualism and Women's Rights in Nineteenth-Century America.* 2nd ed. Bloomington: Indiana University Press, 2001.

Braverman, Howard. "Calvin H. Wiley's North Carolina Reader." *North Carolina Historical Review* 29 (October 1952): 500–522.

———. "Calvin Henderson Wiley, North Carolina Educator and Writer." Ph.D. diss., Duke University, 1950.

Broadfoot, Winston. "Checklist of Confederate Imprints in the Duke University Library." *Library Notes: A Bulletin Issued for The Friends of Duke University Library*, no. 40 (September 1966).

Brockett, O. G., and Lenyth Brockett. "Civil War Theater: Contemporary Treatments." *Civil War History* 1 (September 1955): 229–50.

Brooks, Carlton P. "The *Magnolia*: A Literary Magazine for the Confederacy." *Virginia Cavalcade* 32 (Spring 1983): 150–57.

Brown, Russell K. "Augusta's Other Voice: James Gardner and the *Constitutionalist*." *Georgia Historical Quarterly* 85 (Winter 2001): 592–607.

Brown, Thomas J. "Civil War Remembrance as Reconstruction." In *Reconstructions: New Perspectives on the Postbellum United States*, edited by Thomas J. Brown. New York: Oxford University Press, 2006.

Brundage, W. Fitzhugh. *The Southern Past: A Clash of Race and Memory.* Cambridge: The Belknap Press of Harvard University Press, 2005.

Bryer, Morton, and Irwin Schorr. *"The Southern Illustrated News."* *Civil War Times Illustrated* 38 (March 1999): 46–53.

Buck, Paul H. *The Road to Reunion, 1865–1900.* Boston: Little, Brown and Co., 1937.

Butler, Leslie. "Reconstructions in Intellectual and Cultural Life." In *Reconstructions: New Perspectives on the Postbellum United States*, edited by Thomas J. Brown. New York: Oxford University Press, 2006.

Byrne, Frank J. "The Literary Shaping of Confederate Identity: Daniel R. Hundley and John Beauchamp Jones in Peace and War." In *Inside the Confederate Nation: Essays in Honor of Emory M. Thomas*, edited by Lesley J. Gordon and John C. Inscoe. Baton Rouge: Louisiana State University Press, 2005.

Calhoun, Richard J. "Literary Magazines in the Old South." In *The History of Southern Literature*, edited by Louis D. Rubin Jr., 157–63. Baton Rouge: Louisiana State University Press, 1985.

Calhoun, Richard James, and John Caldwell Guilds, eds. *A Tricentennial Anthology of South Carolina Literature 1670–1970.* Columbia: University of South Carolina Press, 1971.

Campbell, Edward D. C., Jr., and Kym S. Rice, eds. *A Woman's War: Southern Women, Civil War, and the Confederate Legacy.* Richmond: Museum of the Confederacy, 1996.

Campbell, Jacqueline Glass. *When Sherman Marched North From the Sea: Resistance on the Confederate Home Front*. Chapel Hill: University of North Carolina Press, 2003.

Carmichael, Peter S. *The Last Generation: Young Virginians in Peace, War, and Reunion*. Chapel Hill: University of North Carolina Press, 2005.

Carp, Benjamin L. "Nations of American Rebels: Understanding Nationalism in Revolutionary North America and the Civil War South." *Civil War History* 48 (March 2002): 5–33.

Carter, Dan T. "From the Old South to the New: Another Look at the Theme of Change and Continuity." In *From the Old South to the New: Essays on the Transitional South*, edited by Walter J. Fraser Jr. and Winfred B. Moore Jr. Westport, Conn.: Greenwood Press, 1981.

Carter, Hodding. *Their Words Were Bullets: The Southern Press in War, Reconstruction, and Peace*. Mercer University Lamar Memorial Lectures, No. 12. Athens: University of Georgia Press, 1969.

Cash, W. J. *The Mind of the South*. New York: A. A. Knopf, 1941.

Censer, Jane Turner. *The Reconstruction of White Southern Womanhood 1865–1895*. Baton Rouge: Louisiana State University Press, 2003.

——. "Reimagining the North-South Reunion: Southern Women Novelists and the Intersectional Romance, 1876–1900." *Southern Cultures* 5 (Summer 1999): 64–91.

Channing, Steven A. *Crisis of Fear: Secession in South Carolina*. New York: W. W. Norton & Company, 1974.

——. "Slavery and Confederate Nationalism." In *From the Old South to the New: Essays on the Transitional South*, edited by Walter J. Fraser Jr. and Winfred B. Moore Jr. Westport, Conn.: Greenwood Press, 1981.

Cheape, Kathleen Sophia Hambrough. "Confederate Book Publishing with Emphasis on Richmond, Virginia." M.A. Thesis, University of North Carolina, School of Library Science, 1960.

Cheshire, Joseph Blount. *The Church in the Confederate States*. New York: Longmans, Green, and Co., 1912.

Chielens, Edward E. *The Literary Journal in America to 1900. A Guide to Information Sources*. Detroit: Gale Research Company, 1975.

Christie, Anne M. "Bill Arp." *Civil War History* 2 (September 1956): 103–19.

Clarke, Frances. " 'Let All Nations See': Civil War Nationalism and the Memorialization of Wartime Voluntarism." *Civil War History* 52 (March 2006): 66–93.

Clausen, Christopher. "Some Confederate Ideas About Education." *Mississippi Quarterly* 30 (Spring 1977): 235–47.

Clebsch, William A. *Christian Interpretations of the Civil War*. Philadelphia: Fortress Press, 1969.

Clinton, Catherine. *The Plantation Mistress: Woman's World in the Old South*. New York: Pantheon Books, 1982.

Clinton, Catherine, and Nina Silber, eds. *Divided Houses: Gender and the Civil War*. New York: Oxford University Press, 1992.

Cobb, James C. *Away Down South: A History of Southern Identity*. New York: Oxford University Press, 2005.

Cobb, Jessie E. "Publications in Alabama during the Confederacy Located in the State Department of Archives and History." *Alabama Historical Quarterly* 23 (Spring 1961): 73–137.

Collins, Bruce. "Confederate Identity and the Southern Myth since the Civil War." In *Legacy of Disunion: The Enduring Significance of the American Civil War*, edited by Susan-Mary Grant and Peter J. Parish. Baton Rouge: Louisiana State University Press, 2003.

Conlan, Ann A. "A Preliminary Check List of Imprints, Charleston, South Carolina, 1858–1864, With a Historical Introduction." M.L.S. thesis, The Catholic University of America, 1958.

Connelly, Thomas L. *The Marble Man: Robert E. Lee and His Image in American Society*. Baton Rouge: Louisiana State University Press, 1977.

Connelly, Thomas L., and Barbara L. Bellows. *God and General Longstreet: The Lost Cause and the Southern Mind*. Baton Rouge: Louisiana State University Press, 1982.

Connor, R. D. W. *Ante-Bellum Builders of North Carolina*. Studies in North Carolina History No. 3. Greensboro: North Carolina College for Women, 1930. Reprint, Spartanburg, S.C.: Reprint Company, 1971.

Cooper, William J., Jr. *The South and the Politics of Slavery 1828–1856*. Baton Rouge: Louisiana State University Press, 1978.

Coulter, E. Merton. *The Confederate States of America, 1861–1865*. Baton Rouge: Louisiana State University Press, 1950.

Cousins, Paul M. *Joel Chandler Harris: A Biography*. Baton Rouge: Louisiana State University Press, 1968.

Craven, Avery O. *The Growth of Southern Nationalism: 1848–1861*. Baton Rouge: Louisiana State University Press, 1953.

Crum, Mason. *History of the Southern Christian Advocate*. Durham: Duke University Press, 1945.

Current, Richard N. "From Civil War to World Power: Perceptions and Realities, 1865–1914." In *Legacy of Disunion: The Enduring Significance of the American Civil War*, edited by Susan-Mary Grant and Peter J. Parish. Baton Rouge: Louisiana State University Press, 2003.

——. *Northernizing the South*. Athens: University of Georgia Press, 1983.

Curti, Merle. *The Roots of American Loyalty*. New York: Columbia University Press, 1946.

Dabbs, James McBride. *Who Speaks for the South?* New York: Funk & Wagnalls, 1964.

Daly, John Patrick. *When Slavery was Called Freedom: Evangelicalism, Proslavery, and the Causes of the Civil War*. Lexington: University Press of Kentucky, 2002.

Davis, David Brion. *The Problem of Slavery in the Age of Revolution, 1770–1823*. Ithaca, N.Y.: Cornell University Press, 1975.

——. *The Problem of Slavery in Western Culture*. Ithaca, N.Y.: Cornell University Press, 1966.

Davis, O. L., Jr. "E. H. Cushing: Textbooks in Confederate Texas." *The Library Chronicle of the University of Texas* 8 (Spring 1966): 46–50.

———. "The Educational Association of the C.S.A." *Civil War History* 10 (March 1964): 67–79.

———. "Textbooks for Confederate School Children: Pursuit of National Identity During the American Civil War." *American Educational History Journal* 28 (2001): 13–19.

———. "Textbooks for Texans During the Civil War." *Texas Outlook* 51 (August 1967): 20–21, 27.

———. "Textbooks for Virginia Schoolchildren During the Civil War." *Virginia Journal of Education* 69 (November 1965): 16–19.

Davis, O. L., Jr., and Joan E. Davis. "Imported Yankee Textbooks for Confederate Texans." *Journal of the West* 6 (April 1967): 321–28.

Davis, O. L., Jr., and Serena Rankin Parks. "Confederate School Geographies, I: Miranda Branson Moore's Dixie Geography." *Peabody Journal of Education* 40 (March 1963): 265–74.

Davis, William C. *"A Government of our Own": The Making of the Confederacy*. New York: The Free Press, 1994.

———. *Jefferson Davis: The Man and His Hour*. Baton Rouge: Louisiana State University Press, 1991.

———. *Look Away! A History of the Confederate States of America*. New York: The Free Press, 2002.

———. *Rhett: The Turbulent Life and Times of a Fire-Eater*. Columbia: University of South Carolina Press, 2001.

Degler, Carl N. *One Among Many: The Civil War in Comparative Perspective*. [Gettysburg, Pa.]: Gettysburg College, 1990.

———. *The Other South: Southern Dissenters in the Nineteenth Century*. New York: Harper & Row, 1974.

———. *Place Over Time: The Continuity of Southern Distinctiveness*. Baton Rouge: Louisiana State University Press, 1977.

———. "Thesis, Antithesis, Synthesis: The South, the North, and the Nation." *Journal of Southern History* 53 (February 1987): 3–18.

Dekker, George. *The American Historical Romance*. Cambridge: Cambridge University Press, 1987.

Demaree, Albert Lowther. *The American Agricultural Press 1819–1860*. Philadelphia: Porcupine Press, 1974.

Detlefsen, Ellen Gay. "Printing in the Confederacy, 1861–1865: A Southern Industry in Wartime." D.L.S. diss., Columbia University, 1975.

Deutsch, Karl W. *Nationalism and Social Communication: An Inquiry into the Foundations of Nationality*. New York: Technology Press of the Massachusetts Institute of Technology and John Wiley & Sons, 1953.

Dew, Charles B. *Apostles of Disunion: Southern Secession Commissioners and the Causes of the Civil War*. Charlottesville: University Press of Virginia, 2001.

——. *Bond of Iron: Master and Slave at Buffalo Forge*. New York: W. W. Norton & Company, 1994.

Diffley, Kathleen. *Where My Heart is Turning Ever: Civil War Stories and Constitutional Reform, 1861–1876*. Athens: University of Georgia Press, 1992.

Doherty, Herbert J., Jr. "The Mind of the Antebellum South." In *Writing Southern History: Essays in Historiography in Honor of Fletcher M. Green*, edited by Arthur S. Link and Rembert W. Patrick. Baton Rouge: Louisiana State University Press, 1965.

Donald, David. "The Proslavery Argument Reconsidered." *Journal of Southern History* 37 (February 1971): 3–18.

Doyle, Don H. *Nations Divided: America, Italy, and the Southern Question*. Athens: University of Georgia Press, 2002.

Doyle, Don H., and Marco Antonio Pamplona, eds. *Nationalism in the New World*. Athens: University of Georgia Press, 2006.

Durant, Susan Speare. "The Gently Furled Banner: The Development of the Myth of the Lost Cause, 1865–1900." Ph.D. diss., University of North Carolina, 1972.

Durden, Robert F. "J. D. B. De Bow: Convolutions of a Slavery Expansionist." *Journal of Southern History* 17 (November 1951): 441–61.

Durrill, Wayne K. *War of Another Kind: A Southern Community in the Great Rebellion*. New York: Oxford University Press, 1990.

Eaton, Clement. *Freedom of Thought in the Old South*. Durham: Duke University Press, 1940.

——. *The Growth of Southern Civilization 1790–1860*. New York: Harper & Brothers, 1961.

——. *A History of the Old South*. New York: Macmillan, 1949.

——. *Jefferson Davis*. New York: The Free Press, 1977.

——. *The Mind of the Old South*. Rev. ed. Baton Rouge: Louisiana State University Press, 1967.

——. "The Resistance of the South to Northern Radicalism." *New England Quarterly* 8 (June 1935): 215–31.

——. *The Waning of the Old South Civilization 1860–1880's*. Athens: University of Georgia Press, 1968.

Edwards, Laura F. *Scarlett Doesn't Live Here Anymore: Southern Women in the Civil War Era*. Urbana: University of Illinois Press, 2000.

Ellison, Rhoda Coleman. *History and Bibliography of Alabama Newspapers in the Nineteenth Century*. University, Ala.: University of Alabama Press, 1954.

Ergang, Robert Reinhold. *Herder and the Foundations of German Nationalism*. New York: Columbia University Press, 1931.

Ericson, David. *The Debate Over Slavery: Antislavery and Proslavery Liberalism in Antebellum America*. New York: New York University Press, 2000.

Escott, Paul D. *After Secession: Jefferson Davis and the Failure of Confederate Nationalism*. Baton Rouge: Louisiana State University Press, 1978.

——. "The Failure of Confederate Nationalism: The Old South's Class System in the

Crucible of War." In *The Old South in the Crucible of War*, edited by Harry P. Owens and James J. Cooke. Jackson: University Press of Mississippi, 1983.

Ezell, John S. "A Southern Education for Southrons." *Journal of Southern History* 17 (August 1951): 303–27.

Fahs, Alice. *The Imagined Civil War: Popular Literature of the North and South, 1861–1865*. Chapel Hill: University of North Carolina Press, 2001.

Farnham, Christie Anne. *The Education of the Southern Belle: Higher Education and Student Socialization in the Antebellum South*. New York: New York University Press, 1994.

Faust, Drew Gilpin. *The Creation of Confederate Nationalism: Ideology and Identity in the Civil War South*. Baton Rouge: Louisiana State University Press, 1988.

———. *James Henry Hammond and the Old South: A Design for Mastery*. Baton Rouge: Louisiana State University Press, 1982.

———. *Mothers of Invention: Women of the Slaveholding South in the American Civil War*. Chapel Hill: University of North Carolina Press, 1996. Reprint, New York: Vintage Books, 1997.

———. *A Sacred Circle: The Dilemma of the Intellectual in the Old South, 1840–1860*. Baltimore: Johns Hopkins University Press, 1977.

———. *Southern Stories: Slaveholders in Peace and War*. Columbia: University of Missouri Press, 1992.

———, ed. *The Ideology of Slavery: Proslavery Thought in the Antebellum South, 1830–1860*. Baton Rouge: Louisiana State University Press, 1981.

Feldman, Glenn, ed. *Reading Southern History: Essays on Interpreters and Interpretations*. Tuscaloosa: University of Alabama Press, 2001.

Fidler, William Perry. *Augusta Evans Wilson 1835–1909: A Biography*. University, Ala.: University of Alabama Press, 1951.

Fife, Iline. "The Confederate Theater." *Southern Speech Journal* 20 (1955): 224–31.

———. "The Confederate Theater in Georgia." *Georgia Review* 9 (Fall 1955): 305–15.

Finkelman, Paul. *Defending Slavery: Proslavery Thought in the Old South*. Boston: Bedford/St. Martin's, 2003.

———, ed. *Proslavery Thought, Ideology, and Politics*. New York: Garland, 1989.

Flanders, Bertram Holland. "*Bugle-Horn of Liberty*: A Confederate Humorous Magazine." *Emory University Quarterly* 9 (June 1953): 79–85.

———. *Early Georgia Magazines: Literary Periodicals to 1865*. Athens: University of Georgia Press, 1944.

Flournoy, Mary H. *Side Lights on Southern History*. Richmond: Dietz Press, 1939.

Flynt, Wayne. "Southern Higher Education and the Civil War." *Civil War History* 14, no. 3 (1968): 211–25.

Foner, Eric. *Politics and Ideology in the Age of the Civil War*. Oxford: Oxford University Press, 1980.

Ford, Lacy K., Jr. *Origins of Southern Radicalism: The South Carolina Upcountry 1800–1860*. New York: Oxford University Press, 1988.

Ford, Paul M. "Calvin H. Wiley and the Common Schools of North Carolina, 1850–1869." Ed.D. diss., Harvard University, 1960.

Foster, Gaines M. *Ghosts of the Confederacy: Defeat, The Lost Cause, and the Emergence of the New South, 1865 to 1913.* New York: Oxford University Press, 1987.

Fox-Genovese, Elizabeth. "The Fettered Mind: Time, Place, and the Literary Imagination of the Old South." *Georgia Historical Quarterly* 74 (Winter 1990): 622–50.

———. *Within the Plantation Household: Black and White Women of the Old South.* Chapel Hill: University of North Carolina Press, 1988.

Fox-Genovese, Elizabeth, and Eugene D. Genovese. *The Mind of the Master Class: History and Faith in the Southern Slaveholders' Worldview.* Cambridge: Cambridge University Press, 2005.

Fraser, Walter J., Jr., R. Frank Saunders Jr., and Jon L. Wakelyn, eds. *The Web of Southern Social Relations: Women, Family, and Education.* Athens: University of Georgia Press, 1985.

Fredrickson, George M. *The Inner Civil War: Northern Intellectuals and the Crisis of the Union.* New York: Harper & Row, 1965.

Freehling, William W. *Prelude to Civil War: The Nullification Controversy in South Carolina, 1816–1836.* New York: Harper and Row, 1965.

———. *The Reintegration of American History: Slavery and the Civil War.* New York: Oxford University Press, 1994.

———. *The Road to Disunion: Secessionists at Bay, 1776–1854.* New York: Oxford University Press, 1990.

———. *The Road to Disunion, Volume II: Secessionists Triumphant, 1854–1861.* New York: Oxford University Press, 2007.

———. *The South vs. the South: How Anti-Confederate Southerners Shaped the Course of the Civil War.* Oxford: Oxford University Press, 2001.

Freehling, William W., and Craig M. Simpson, eds. *Secession Debated: Georgia's Showdown in 1860.* New York: Oxford University Press, 1992.

Fritz, Karen E. *Voices in the Storm: Confederate Rhetoric, 1861–1865.* Denton, Tex.: University of North Texas Press, 1999.

Frost, Dan R. *Thinking Confederates: Academia and the Idea of Progress in the New South.* Knoxville: University of Tennessee Press, 2000.

Fuller, A. James. *Chaplain to the Confederacy: Basil Manly and Baptist Life in the Old South.* Baton Rouge: Louisiana State University Press, 2000.

Gallagher, Gary W. *The Confederate War.* Cambridge: Harvard University Press, 1997.

———. *Lee and His Army in Confederate History.* Chapel Hill: University of North Carolina Press, 2001.

———. *Lee and His Generals in War and Memory.* Baton Rouge: Louisiana State University Press, 1998.

Gallagher, Gary W., and Alan T. Nolan, eds. *The Myth of the Lost Cause and Civil War History.* Bloomington: Indiana University Press, 2000.

Gardner, Sarah E. *Blood and Irony: Southern White Women's Narratives of the Civil War, 1861–1937*. Chapel Hill: University of North Carolina Press, 2004.

Geertz, Clifford. *The Interpretation of Cultures*. New York: Basic Books, 1973.

Geimer, Alfred F. "A Check-List of Columbia, S.C., Imprints From 1861 through 1865 with a Historical Introduction." M.L.S. thesis, The Catholic University of America, 1958.

Gellner, Ernest. *Nations and Nationalism*. Ithaca, N.Y.: Cornell University Press, 1983.

Genovese, Eugene D. *A Consuming Fire: The Fall of the Confederacy in the Mind of the White Christian South*. Mercer University Lamar Memorial Lectures, No. 41. Athens: University of Georgia Press, 1998.

——. *The Political Economy of Slavery: Studies in the Economy and Society of the Slave South*. New York: Pantheon Books, 1965.

——. *The Slaveholders' Dilemma: Freedom and Progress in Southern Conservative Thought, 1820–1860*. Columbia: University of South Carolina Press, 1992.

——. *"Slavery Ordained of God": The Southern Slaveholders' View of Biblical History and Modern Politics*. Gettysburg, Pa.: Gettysburg College, 1985.

——. *The Southern Tradition: The Achievement and Limitations of an American Conservatism*. Cambridge: Harvard University Press, 1994.

——. *The World the Slaveholders Made: Two Essays in Interpretation*. New York: Pantheon Books, 1969.

Gerster, Patrick, and Nicholas Cords, eds. *The Old South*. Vol. 1 of *Myth and Southern History*. 2nd ed. Urbana: University of Illinois Press, 1989.

Gilmer, Gertrude C. *Checklist of Southern Periodicals to 1861*. Boston: F. W. Faxon Company, 1934.

Goen, C. C. *Broken Churches, Broken Nation: Denominational Schisms and the Coming of the American Civil War*. Macon: Mercer University Press, 1985.

Goldfield, David. *Still Fighting the Civil War: The American South and Southern History*. Baton Rouge: Louisiana State University Press, 2002.

Goode, James Moore. "The Confederate University: The Forgotten Institution of the American Civil War." M.A. Thesis, University of Virginia, 1966.

Gordon, Lesley J., and John C. Inscoe, eds. *Inside the Confederate Nation: Essays in Honor of Emory M. Thomas*. Baton Rouge: Louisiana State University Press, 2005.

Gorn, Elliott J., ed. *The McGuffey Readers: Selections from the 1879 Edition*. Boston: Bedford/St. Martin's, 1998.

Grant, Susan-Mary. " 'The Charter of Its Birthright': The Civil War and American Nationalism." In *Legacy of Disunion: The Enduring Significance of the American Civil War*, edited by Susan-Mary Grant and Peter J. Parish. Baton Rouge: Louisiana State University Press, 2003.

——. *North over South: Northern Nationalism and American Identity in the Antebellum Era*. Lawrence: University Press of Kansas, 2000.

Grantham, Dewey W., Jr. *The Democratic South*. Athens: University of Georgia Press, 1963.

Gray, Richard. *Writing the South: Ideas of an American Region*. Cambridge: Cambridge University Press, 1986.

Green, Jennifer R. "Networks of Military Educators: Middle-Class Stability and Professionalization in the Late Antebellum South." *Journal of Southern History* 73 (February 2007): 39–74.

Griffin, Larry J. "Southern Distinctiveness, Yet Again, or, Why America Still Needs the South." *Southern Cultures* 6 (Fall 2000): 47–72.

Griffith, Louis Turner, and John Erwin Talmadge. *Georgia Journalism 1763–1950*. Athens: University of Georgia Press, 1951.

Grimes, Maxyne Madden, and Patti Carr Black. "Confederate Imprints and Civil War Newspapers on File in the Mississippi Department of Archives and History." *Journal of Mississippi History* 24 (October 1961): 231–54.

Guterl, Matthew Pratt. *American Mediterranean: Southern Slaveholders in the Age of Emancipation*. Cambridge: Harvard University Press, 2008.

Hannum, Sharon Elaine. "Confederate Cavaliers: The Myth in War and Defeat." Ph.D. diss., Rice University, 1965.

Harris, William C. *North Carolina and the Coming of the Civil War*. Raleigh: North Carolina Division of Archives and History, 1988.

Harrison, Brady. "The Young Americans: Emerson, Walker, and the Early Literature of American Empire." *American Studies* 40 (Fall 1999): 75–97.

Harwell, Richard Barksdale. "Brief Candle: The Confederate Theatre." In *Proceedings of the American Antiquarian Society*, 41–160. Worcester, Mass.: American Antiquarian Society, 1971.

———. "Civil War Theater: The Richmond Stage." *Civil War History* 1 (September 1955): 295–304.

———. "Confederate Anti-Lincoln Literature." *Lincoln Herald* 53 (Fall 1951).

———. *Confederate Belles-Lettres: A Bibliography and a Finding List of the Fiction, Poetry, Drama, Songsters, and Miscellaneous Literature Published in the Confederate States of America*. Hattiesburg, Miss.: The Book Farm, 1941.

———. "The Confederate Hundred: A Bibliophilic Selection of Confederate Books." Portland, Maine: Anthoensen Press, 1964.

———. *Confederate Music*. Chapel Hill: University of North Carolina Press, 1950.

———. "A Confederate View of the Southern Poets." *American Literature: A Journal of Literary History, Criticism, and Bibliography* 24 (1952): 51–61.

———. *Cornerstones of Confederate Collecting*. Second ed. with an introduction by Clifford Dowdey, ed. Charlottesville: University of Virginia Press, 1953.

———. "The Creed of a Propagandist: Letter from a Confederate Editor." *Journalism Quarterly* (Spring 1951).

———. "Gone with Miss Ravenel's Courage; Or Bugles Blow So Red: A Note on the Civil War Novel." *New England Quarterly* 35 (June 1962): 253–61.

———, ed. *More Confederate Imprints*. 2 vols. Richmond: Virginia State Library, 1957.

Hayes, Carlton J. H. "Contributions of Herder to the Doctrine of Nationalism." *American Historical Review* 32 (1927): 719–36.

——. *Essays on Nationalism*. New York: Macmillan Company, 1926.

Heidler, David S. *Pulling the Temple Down: The Fire-Eaters and the Destruction of the Union*. Mechanicsburg, Pa.: Stackpole Books, 1994.

Hettle, Wallace. "The Minister, the Martyr, and the Maxim: Robert Lewis Dabney and Stonewall Jackson Biography." *Civil War History* 49, no. 4 (2003): 353–69.

Heyrman, Christine Leigh. *Southern Cross: The Beginnings of the Bible Belt*. New York: Alfred A. Knopf, 1997.

Hobsbawm, Eric. *Nations and Nationalism since 1780: Programme, Myth, Reality*. Cambridge: Cambridge University Press, 1990.

——. "Some Reflections on Nationalism." In *Imagination and Precision in the Social Sciences: Essays in Memory of Peter Nettl*, edited by T. J. Nossiter, A. H. Hanson, and Stein Rokkan. London: Faber & Faber, 1972.

Hobsbawm, Eric, and Terence Ranger, eds. *The Invention of Tradition*. Cambridge: Cambridge University Press, 1983.

Hodgson, Joseph. *The Cradle of the Confederacy; Or, The Times of Troup, Quitman and Yancey*. Mobile: Register Publishing Office, 1876.

Holden, Charles J. *In the Great Maelstrom: Conservatives in Post–Civil War South Carolina*. Columbia: University of South Carolina Press, 2002.

Holliday, Carl. *A History of Southern Literature*. New York: Neale Publishing Company, 1906.

Hoogerwerf, Frank W. *Confederate Sheet-Music Imprints*. I.S.A.M. Monographs, no. 21. Brooklyn: Institute for Studies in American Music, 1984.

Hoole, W. Stanley. "Charleston Theatricals During the Tragic Decade, 1860–1869." *Journal of Southern History* 11 (November 1945): 538–47.

——. *A Check-List and Finding-List of Charleston Periodicals 1732–1864*. Durham: Duke University Press, 1936.

——. *Vizetelly Covers the Confederacy*. Confederate Centennial Studies, no. 4. Tuscaloosa, Ala.: Confederate Publishing Company, 1957.

Hubbell, Jay B. "Literary Nationalism in the Old South." In *American Studies in Honor of William Kenneth Boyd*, edited by David Kelley Jackson. Durham: Duke University Press, 1940.

——. *The South in American Literature 1607–1900*. Durham: Duke University Press, 1954.

——. "Southern Magazines." In *Culture in the South*, edited by W. T. Couch, 159–82. Chapel Hill: University of North Carolina Press, 1934. Reprint, Westport, Conn.: Negro Universities Press, 1970.

——, ed. *The Last Years of Henry Timrod 1864–1867*. Durham: Duke University Press, 1941.

Huff, Lawrence. " 'A Bitter Draught We have Had to Quaff': Sherman's March Through the Eyes of Joseph Addison Turner." *Georgia Historical Quarterly* 72 (Summer 1988): 306–26.

——. "Joel Harris's Mentor, Joseph Addison Turner." *Atlanta History* 37 (Spring 1993): 5–16.

——. "Joseph Addison Turner: Southern Editor During the Civil War." *Journal of Southern History* 29 (November 1963): 469–85.

Hunt, Robert E. "Home, Domesticity, and School Reform in Antebellum Alabama." *The Alabama Review* 49 (October 1996): 253–75.

——. "Organizing a New South: Education Reformers in Antebellum Alabama, 1840–1860." Ph.D. diss., University of Missouri-Columbia, 1988.

Hunter, Lloyd Arthur. "The Sacred South: Postwar Confederates and the Sacralization of Southern Culture." Ph.D. diss., Saint Louis University, 1978.

Jackson, David K. *The Contributors and Contributions to the Southern Literary Messenger (1834–1864)*. Charlottesville, Va.: The Historical Publishing Company, 1936.

——. "An Estimate of the Influence of 'The Southern Literary Messenger' 1834–1864." *Southern Literary Messenger* 1 (August 1939): 508–14.

Jacobs, Robert D. "Campaign for a Southern Literature: The *Southern Literary Messenger*." *Southern Literary Journal* 2 (Fall 1969): 66–98.

Janney, Caroline E. *Burying the Dead but Not the Past: Ladies' Memorial Associations and the Lost Cause*. Chapel Hill: University of North Carolina Press, 2008.

Jenkins, William Sumner. *Proslavery Thought in the Old South*. Chapel Hill: University of North Carolina Press, 1935.

Jimerson, Randall C. *The Private Civil War: Popular Thought During the Sectional Conflict*. Baton Rouge: Louisiana State University Press, 1988.

Johannsen, Robert W. *Lincoln, the South, and Slavery: The Political Dimension*. Baton Rouge: Louisiana State University Press, 1991.

Johnson, Michael P. *Toward a Patriarchal Republic: The Secession of Georgia*. Baton Rouge: Louisiana State University Press, 1977.

Johnson, Vicki Vaughn. *The Men and the Vision of the Southern Commercial Conventions, 1845–1871*. Columbia, Mo.: University of Missouri Press, 1992.

Jones, H. G., and Julius H. Avant, eds. *Union List of North Carolina Newspapers, 1751–1900*. Raleigh: State Department of Archives and History, 1963.

Jones, Paul Christian. *Unwelcome Voices: Subversive Fiction in the Antebellum South*. Knoxville: University of Tennessee Press, 2005.

Jordan, Ervin L., Jr. *Charlottesville and the University of Virginia in the Civil War*. Virginia Civil War Battles and Leaders. 2nd ed. Lynchburg, Va.: H. E. Howard, 1988.

Joyner, Charles. " 'Forget, Hell!': The Civil War in Southern Memory." In *Legacy of Disunion: The Enduring Significance of the American Civil War*, edited by Susan-Mary Grant and Peter J. Parish. Baton Rouge: Louisiana State University Press, 2003.

——. *Shared Traditions: Southern History and Folk Culture*. Urbana: University of Illinois Press, 1999.

Kammen, Michael. *Mystic Chords of Memory: The Transformation of Tradition in American Culture*. New York: Alfred A. Knopf, 1991.

Kendrick, Benjamin Burks, and Alex Mathews Arnett. *The South Looks at its Past*. Chapel Hill: University of North Carolina Press, 1935.

Kennerly, Sarah Law. "Confederate Juvenile Imprints: Children's Books and

Periodicals Published in the Confederate States of America, 1861–1865." Ph.D. diss., University of Michigan, 1956.

Kerby, Robert L. "Why the Confederacy Lost." *The Review of Politics* 35 (July 1973): 326–45.

Kerrigan, William T. "Young America! Romantic Nationalism in Literature and Politics, 1843–1861." Ph.D. diss., University of Michigan at Ann Arbor, 1997.

Kimball, Gregg D. *American City, Southern Place: A Cultural History of Antebellum Richmond*. Athens: University of Georgia Press, 2000.

King, C. Richard. "Col. John Sidney Thrasher: Superintendent of the Confederate Press Association." *Texana* 6 (Spring 1968): 56–86.

King, Joseph Leonard, Jr. *Dr. George William Bagby: A Study of Virginian Literature 1850–1880*. New York: Columbia University Press, 1927.

King, William L. *The Newspaper Press of Charleston, S.C.* Charleston: Edward Perry, 1872.

Klein, Stacey Jean. "Wielding the Pen: Margaret Preston, Confederate Nationalistic Literature, and the Expansion of a Woman's Place in the South." *Civil War History* 49 (September 2003): 221–34.

Knight, Edgar W. "An Early Case of Opposition in the South to Northern Textbooks." *Journal of Southern History* 13 (May 1947): 245–64.

——. *Public School Education in North Carolina*. Boston: Houghton Mifflin Company, 1916.

Kobre, Sidney. *Foundations of American Journalism*. Tallahassee: Florida State University, 1958.

Kohn, Hans. *American Nationalism: An Interpretative Essay*. New York: Macmillan, 1957.

——. *The Idea of Nationalism: A Study of Its Origins and Background*. New York: Macmillan, 1946.

Kolchin, Peter. *A Sphinx on the American Land: The Nineteenth-Century South in Comparative Perspective*. Baton Rouge: Louisiana State University Press, 2003.

Landrum, Grace Warren. "Sir Walter Scott and His Literary Rivals in the Old South." *American Literature: A Journal of Literary History, Criticism, and Bibliography* 2 (November 1930): 256–76.

Lawson, Melinda. *Patriot Fires: Forging a New American Nationalism in the Civil War North*. Lawrence: University Press of Kansas, 2002.

Lee, James Melvin. *History of American Journalism*. Rev. ed. Garden City, N.Y.: Garden City Publishing Co, 1923.

Lehuu, Isabelle. *Carnival on the Page: Popular Print Media in Antebellum America*. Chapel Hill: University of North Carolina Press, 2000.

Lepore, Jill. *A is for American: Letters and Other Characters in the Newly United States*. New York: Alfred A. Knopf, 2002.

Link, Arthur S., and Rembert W. Patrick, eds. *Writing Southern History: Essays in Historiography in Honor of Fletcher M. Green*. Baton Rouge: Louisiana State University Press, 1965.

Linneman, William R. "*Southern Punch*: A Draught of Confederate Wit." *Southern Folklore Quarterly* 26 (June 1962): 131–36.

Lloyd, Arthur Young. *The Slavery Controversy, 1831–1860*. Chapel Hill: University of North Carolina Press, 1939.

London, Lawrence F. "Confederate Literature and its Publishers." In *Studies in Southern History*, edited by J. Carlyle Sitterson, 82–96. Chapel Hill: University of North Carolina Press, 1957.

——. "The Literature of the Church in the Confederate States." *Historical Magazine of the Episcopal Church* 17 ([1947]): 345–55.

Luraghi, Raimondo. *The Rise and Fall of the Plantation South*. New York: New Viewpoints, 1978.

Maddex, Jack P., Jr. "Proslavery Millennialism: Social Eschatology in Antebellum Southern Calvinism." *American Quarterly* 31 (Spring 1979): 46–62.

——. *The Reconstruction of Edward A. Pollard: A Rebel's Conversion to Postbellum Unionism*. The James Sprunt Studies in History and Political Science, vol. 54. Chapel Hill: University of North Carolina Press, 1974.

——. " 'The Southern Apostasy' Revisited: The Significance of Proslavery Christianity." *Marxist Perspectives* 2 (Fall 1979): 32–41.

Marten, James. *The Children's Civil War*. Chapel Hill: University of North Carolina Press, 1998.

Massey, Mary Elizabeth. *Bonnet Brigades*. New York: Alfred A. Knopf, 1966.

——. *Ersatz in the Confederacy*. Columbia: University of South Carolina Press, 1952.

——. *Refugee Life in the Confederacy*. Baton Rouge: Louisiana State University Press, 1964.

Mathews, Forrest David. "The Politics of Education in the Deep South: Georgia and Alabama, 1830–1860." Ph.D. diss., Columbia University, 1965.

Mathiessen, F. O. *American Renaissance: Art and Expression in the Age of Emerson and Whitman*. London: Oxford University Press, 1941.

Mathis, Robert Neil. "Freedom of the Press in the Confederacy: A Reality." *The Historian* 37 (August 1975): 633–48.

Mathews, Donald G. *Religion in the Old South*. Chicago: University of Chicago Press, 1977.

McCabe, James D. "Literature of the War." *Southern Historical Society Papers* 42 (October 1917): 199–203.

McCardell, John. *The Idea of a Southern Nation: Southern Nationalists and Southern Nationalism, 1830–1860*. New York: W. W. Norton, 1979.

McCurry, Stephanie. *Masters of Small Worlds: Yeoman Households, Gender Relations, and the Political Culture of the Antebellum South Carolina Low Country*. New York: Oxford University Press, 1995.

McDonald, Forrest. *States' Rights and the Union*. Lawrence: University Press of Kansas, 2000.

McKitrick, Eric. *Slavery Defended: The Views of the Old South*. Englewood Cliffs, N.J.: Prentice-Hall, 1963.

McKivigan, John R. *The War Against Proslavery Religion: Abolitionism and the Northern Churches, 1830–1865*. Chapel Hill: University of North Carolina Press, 1984.

——, ed. *Abolitionism and American Religion*. New York: Garland, 1999.

McKivigan, John R., and Mitchell Snay, eds. *Religion and the Antebellum Debate over Slavery*. Athens: University of Georgia Press, 1998.

McMillen, James A., ed. *The Works of James D. B. De Bow. A Bibliography of De Bow's Review with a Check List of His Miscellaneous Writings Including Contributions to Periodicals and a List of References Relating to James D. B. De Bow*. Hattiesburg, Miss.: The Book Farm, 1940.

McMillen, Sally G. *Southern Women: Black and White in the Old South*. Arlington Heights, Ill.: Harlan Davidson, 1992.

McPherson, James M. *Is Blood Thicker than Water? Crises of Nationalism in the Modern World*. Toronto: Vintage Canada, 1998.

——. "Long-Legged Yankee Lies: The Southern Textbook Crusade." In *The Memory of the Civil War in American Culture*, edited by Alice Fahs and Joan Waugh, 64–78. Chapel Hill: University of North Carolina Press, 2004.

McWhiney, Grady. *Cracker Culture: Celtic Ways in the Old South*. Tuscaloosa: University of Alabama Press, 1988.

Meriwether, James B., ed. *South Carolina Journals and Journalists*. Spartanburg, S.C.: Southern States Program, University of South Carolina, 1975.

Miller, James David. *South by Southwest: Planter Emigration and Identity in the Slave South*. Charlottesville: University of Virginia Press, 2002.

Miller, Perry. *The Raven and the Whale: The War of Words and Wits in the Era of Poe and Melville*. New York: Harcourt, Brace, & World, 1956.

Miller, Randall M., Harry S. Stout, and Charles Reagan Wilson, eds. *Religion and the American Civil War*. New York: Oxford University Press, 1998.

Minogue, Kenneth R. *Nationalism*. London: B. T. Batsford, 1967.

Minor, Benjamin Blake. *The Southern Literary Messenger: 1834–1864*. New York: Neale Publishing Company, 1905.

Mitchell, Eleanor Drake. *A Preliminary Checklist of Tennessee Imprints, 1861–1866*. Charlottesville: Bibliographical Society of the University of Virginia, 1953.

Mohr, Clarence L. *On the Threshold of Freedom: Masters and Slaves in Civil War Georgia*. Athens: University of Georgia Press, 1986.

Monaghan, E. Jennifer. *A Common Heritage: Noah Webster's Blue-Back Speller*. Hamden, Conn.: Archon Books, 1983.

Moore, Albert Burton. *Conscription and Conflict in the Confederacy*. New York: Macmillan, 1924. Reprint, Columbia: University of South Carolina Press, 1996.

Moss, Elizabeth. *Domestic Novelists in the Old South: Defenders of Southern Culture*. Baton Rouge: Louisiana State University Press, 1992.

Moss, William. *Confederate Broadside Poems: An Annotated Descriptive Bibliography*. Westport, Conn.: Meckler, 1988.

Mott, Frank Luther. *American Journalism: A History of Newspapers in the United States Through 250 Years 1690 to 1940*. New York: Macmillan, 1941.

——. *A History of American Magazines.* 5 vols. Cambridge: Harvard University Press, 1957–1968.

Muhlenfeld, Elisabeth. "The Civil War and Authorship." In *The History of Southern Literature,* edited by Louis D. Rubin Jr., 178–87. Baton Rouge: Louisiana State University Press, 1985.

Nagel, Paul C. *One Nation Indivisible: The Union in American Thought 1776–1861.* New York: Oxford University Press, 1964.

——. *This Sacred Trust: American Nationality 1798–1898.* New York: Oxford University Press, 1971.

Neely, Mark E., Jr. *Southern Rights: Political Prisoners and the Myth of Confederate Constitutionalism.* Charlottesville: University Press of Virginia, 1999.

Neely, Mark E., Jr., Harold Holzer, and Gabor S. Boritt. *The Confederate Image: Prints of the Lost Cause.* Chapel Hill: University of North Carolina Press, 1987.

Nichols, Roy F. *Blueprints for Leviathan: American Style.* New York: Atheneum, 1963.

Noll, Mark A. *The Civil War as a Theological Crisis.* Chapel Hill: University of North Carolina Press, 2006.

Oakes, James. *The Ruling Race: A History of American Slaveholders.* New York: Knopf, 1982.

O'Brien, Michael. *A Character of Hugh Legaré.* Knoxville: University of Tennessee Press, 1985.

——. *Conjectures of Order: Intellectual Life and the American South 1810–1860.* 2 vols. Chapel Hill: University of North Carolina Press, 2004.

——. *Rethinking the South: Essays in Intellectual History.* Baltimore: Johns Hopkins University Press, 1988.

O'Brien, Michael, and David Moltke-Hansen. *Intellectual Life in Antebellum Charleston.* Knoxville: University of Tennessee Press, 1986.

Orians, G. Harrison. "Walter Scott, Mark Twain, and the Civil War." *South Atlantic Quarterly* 40 (October 1941): 342–59.

Osterweis, Rollin G. *The Myth of the Lost Cause, 1865–1900.* Hamden, Conn.: Archon Books, 1973.

——. *Romanticism and Nationalism in the Old South.* New Haven: Yale University Press, 1949.

Owsley, Frank Lawrence. *Plain Folk of the Old South.* Baton Rouge: Louisiana State University Press, 1949.

——. *State Rights in the Confederacy.* Chicago: University of Chicago Press, 1925.

Page, Thomas Nelson. *The Old South: Essays Social and Political.* New York: Charles Scribner's Sons, 1900.

Parish, Peter J. "Abraham Lincoln and American Nationhood." In *Legacy of Disunion: The Enduring Significance of the American Civil War,* edited by Susan-Mary Grant and Peter J. Parish. Baton Rouge: Louisiana State University Press, 2003.

——. "An Exception to Most of the Rules: What Made American Nationalism Different in the Mid-Nineteenth Century?" *Prologue: Quarterly of the National Archives* 27 (Fall 1995): 219–29.

——. *The North and the Nation in the Era of the Civil War*. Edited by Adam I. P. Smith and Susan-Mary Grant. New York: Fordham University Press, 2003.

Parker, David B. *Alias Bill Arp: Charles Henry Smith and the South's "Goodly Heritage."* Athens: University of Georgia Press, 1991.

Parks, Serena Rankin, and O. L. Davis Jr. "North Carolina's Textbooks." *North Carolina Education* 29 (January 1963): 14–15, 32–33.

Parrington, Vernon Louis. *The Romantic Revolution in America 1800–1860*. Vol. 2 of *Main Currents in American Thought: An Interpretation of American Literature from the Beginnings to 1920*. New York: Harcourt, Brace and Company, 1927.

Parrish, T. Michael, and Robert M. Willingham Jr. *Confederate Imprints: A Bibliography of Southern Publications from Secession to Surrender*. Austin: Jenkins Publishing Company, [1987].

Phillips, Jason. *Diehard Rebels: The Confederate Culture of Invincibility*. Athens: University of Georgia Press, 2007.

Phillips, Ulrich Bonnell. *The Course of the South to Secession*. Edited by E. Merton Coulter. Gloucester, Mass.: Peter Smith, 1958.

Piehler, G. Kurt. *Remembering War the American Way*. Washington: Smithsonian Institution Press, 1995.

Poole, W. Scott. *Never Surrender: Confederate Memory and Conservatism in the South Carolina Upcountry*. Athens: University of Georgia Press, 2004.

Potter, David M. "The Historian's Use of Nationalism and Vice Versa." In *The South and the Sectional Conflict*. Baton Rouge: Louisiana State University Press, 1968.

——. *The South and the Concurrent Majority*. Edited by Don E. Fehrenbacher and Carl N. Degler. Baton Rouge: Louisiana State University Press, 1972.

Powell, Lawrence N., and Michael S. Wayne. "Self-Interest and the Decline of Confederate Nationalism." In *The Old South in the Crucible of War*, edited by Harry P. Owens and James J. Cooke. Jackson: University Press of Mississippi, 1983.

Purifoy, Lewis. "The Southern Methodist Church and the Proslavery Argument." *Journal of Southern History* 32 (August 1966): 325–41.

Quigley, Paul D. H. "Patchwork Nation: Sources of Confederate Nationalism, 1848–1865." Ph.D. diss., University of North Carolina, 2006.

Quist, John W. *Restless Visionaries: The Social Roots of Antebellum Reform in Alabama and Michigan*. Baton Rouge: Louisiana State University Press, 1998.

Rable, George C. *Civil Wars: Women and the Crisis of Southern Nationalism*. Urbana: University of Illinois Press, 1989.

——. *The Confederate Republic: A Revolution Against Politics*. Chapel Hill: University of North Carolina Press, 1994.

Racine, Philip N. "Emily Lyles Harris: A Piedmont Farmer during the Civil War." *South Atlantic Quarterly* 79 (Autumn 1980): 386–97.

Ransom, Roger L. *Conflict and Compromise: The Political Economy of Slavery, Emancipation, and the American Civil War*. Cambridge: Cambridge University Press, 1989.

Reardon, William R. "Civil War Theater: Formal Organization." *Civil War History* 1 (September 1955): 205–27.

Reardon, William R., and John Foxen. "Civil War Theater: The Propaganda Play." *Civil War History* 1 (September 1955): 281–93.

Reinders, Robert C. "New England Influences on the Formation of Public Schools in New Orleans." *Journal of Southern History* 30 (May 1964): 181–95.

Reynolds, David S. *Beneath the American Renaissance: The Subversive Imagination in the Age of Emerson and Melville.* Cambridge: Harvard University Press, 1988.

Reynolds, Donald E. *Editors Make War: Southern Newspapers in the Secession Crisis.* Nashville: Vanderbilt University Press, 1970.

Ridgely, J. V. *Nineteenth-Century Southern Literature.* Lexington: University Press of Kentucky, 1980.

Riepma, Anne Sophie. *Fire and Fiction: Augusta Jane Evans in Context.* Costernus New Series, no. 125. Amsterdam: Rodopi, 2000.

Riley, Susan B. "The Hazards of Periodical Publishing in the South During the Nineteenth Century." *Tennessee Historical Quarterly* 21 (December 1962): 365–76.

——. "The Southern Literary Magazine of the Mid-Nineteenth Century." *Tennessee Historical Quarterly* 23 (September 1964): 221–36.

Ringold, May Spencer. *The Role of the State Legislatures in the Confederacy.* Athens: University of Georgia Press, 1966.

Risley, Ford. "The Confederate Press Association: Cooperative News Reporting of the War." *Civil War History* 47 (September 2001): 222–39.

Roberts, Giselle. *The Confederate Belle.* Columbia, Mo.: University of Missouri Press, 2003.

Robinson, Armstead L. *Bitter Fruits of Bondage: The Demise of Slavery and the Collapse of the Confederacy, 1861–1865.* Charlottesville: University of Virginia Press, 2005.

Rocker, Rudolf. *Nationalism and Culture.* Translated by Ray E. Chase. New York: Covici, Friede, 1937.

Rogers, Edward Reinhold. "Four Southern Magazines." Ph.D. diss., University of Virginia, 1902.

Rogers, Tommy W. "Dr. F. A. Ross and the Presbyterian Defense of Slavery." *Journal of Presbyterian History* 45 (June 1967): 112–24.

Romero, Sidney J. *Religion in the Rebel Ranks.* Lanham, Md.: University Press of America, 1983.

Rose, Willie Lee. *Rehearsal for Reconstruction: The Port Royal Experiment.* London: Oxford University Press, 1964.

Rubin, Anne Sarah. "Seventy-six and Sixty-one: Confederates Remember the American Revolution." In *Where These Memories Grow: History, Memory, and Southern Identity,* edited by W. Fitzhugh Brundage. Chapel Hill: University of North Carolina Press, 2000.

——. *A Shattered Nation: The Rise and Fall of the Confederacy, 1861–1868.* Chapel Hill: University of North Carolina Press, 2005.

Rubin, Louis D., Jr. *The Edge of the Swamp: A Study in the Literature and Society of the Old South*. Baton Rouge: Louisiana State University Press, 1989.

——. *The Writer in the South: Studies in a Literary Community*. Athens: University of Georgia Press, 1972.

——, ed. *A Bibliographical Guide to the Study of Southern Literature*. Baton Rouge: Louisiana State University Press, 1969.

Rudolph, E. L. *Confederate Broadside Verse. A Bibliography and Finding List of Confederate Broadside Ballads and Songs*. New Braunfels, Tex.: The Book Farm, 1950.

Sass, Herbert Ravenel. *Outspoken: 150 Years of The News and Courier*. Columbia: University of South Carolina Press, 1953.

Schivelbusch, Wolfgang. *The Culture of Defeat: On National Trauma, Mourning, and Recovery*. Translated by Jefferson Chase. New York: Henry Holt and Company, 2003.

Scott, Anne Firor. *The Southern Lady: From Pedestal to Politics, 1830–1930*. Chicago: University of Chicago Press, 1970.

Sellers, Charles Grier, Jr., ed. *The Southerner as American*. Chapel Hill: University of North Carolina Press, 1960.

Shafer, Boyd C. *Nationalism: Myth and Reality*. New York: Harcourt, Brace and Company, 1955.

Sheehan-Dean, Aaron. *Why Confederates Fought: Family and Nation in Civil War Virginia*. Chapel Hill: University of North Carolina Press, 2007.

Silber, Nina. *The Romance of Reunion: Northerners and the South, 1865–1900*. Chapel Hill: University of North Carolina Press, 1993.

Silver, James W. *Confederate Morale and Church Propaganda*. Confederate Centennial Studies. Edited by W. Stanley Hoole. Tuscaloosa, Ala.: Confederate Publishing Company, 1957.

Simkins, Francis Butler, and Charles Pierce Roland. *A History of the South*. 4th ed. New York: Alfred A. Knopf, 1972.

Simpson, Lewis P. *The Dispossessed Garden: Pastoral and History in Southern Literature*. Mercer University Lamar Memorial Lectures, no. 16. Athens: University of Georgia Press, 1975.

——. *The Man of Letters in New England and the South: Essays on the History of the Literary Vocation in America*. Baton Rouge: Louisiana State University Press, 1973.

——. *Mind and the American Civil War: A Meditation on Lost Causes*. Baton Rouge: Louisiana State University Press, 1989.

——. "The Mind of the Antebellum South." In *The History of Southern Literature*, edited by Louis D. Rubin Jr. Baton Rouge: Louisiana State University Press, 1985.

Sinha, Manisha. *The Counterrevolution of Slavery: Politics and Ideology in Antebellum South Carolina*. Chapel Hill: University of North Carolina Press, 2000.

Skipper, Ottis Clark. *J. D. B. De Bow: Magazinist of the Old South*. Athens: University of Georgia Press, 1958.

Smith, Anthony D. *National Identity*. London: Penguin Books, 1991.

——. *Nationalism: Theory, Ideology, History*. Malden, Mass.: Polity Press, 2001.

Smith, H. Shelton. *In His Image But . . . : Racism in Southern Religion, 1780–1850*. Durham: Duke University Press, 1972.

Smith, Mark. *Debating Slavery: Economy and Society in the Antebellum American South*. London: Cambridge University Press, 1999.

Snay, Mitchell. "American Thought and Southern Distinctiveness: The Southern Clergy and the Sanctification of Slavery." *Civil War History* 35 (December 1989): 311–28.

——. *Gospel of Disunion: Religion and Separatism in the Antebellum South*. Cambridge: Cambridge University Press, 1993.

Snowden, Yates. *Confederate Books. The Titles of Many of Them and How They were Made*. Charleston: Daggett Printing Co., [1900–1909?].

——. *South Carolina School Books 1795–1865*. Columbia: n.p., 1910.

——. *War-Time Publications (1861–1865) from the Press of Walker, Evans & Cogswell Co.* Charleston: Walker, Evans & Cogswell, 1922.

Snyder, Louis L. *The Meaning of Nationalism*. New Brunswick, N.J.: Rutgers University Press, 1954.

Sparks, Randy. "Mississippi's Apostle of Slavery: James Smylie and the Biblical Defense of Slavery." *Journal of Mississippi History* (Fall 1989): 89–106.

Spiller, Robert E. "Emerson's 'The Young American'." *Clio* 1 (October 1971): 37–41.

Stafford, John. *The Literary Criticism of Young America*. Berkeley: University of California Press, 1952.

Stampp, Kenneth M. *And the War Came: The North and the Secession Crisis 1860–1861*. Baton Rouge: Louisiana State University Press, 1950.

——. *The Peculiar Institution: Slavery in the Ante-Bellum South*. New York: Alfred A. Knopf, 1956.

——. "The Southern Road to Appomattox." In *The Imperiled Union: Essays on the Background of the Civil War*. Oxford: Oxford University Press, 1980.

Stillman, Rachel Bryan. "Education in the Confederate States of America, 1861–1865." Ph.D. diss., University of Illinois at Urbana-Champaign, 1972.

Stout, Harry S., and Christopher Grasso. "Civil War, Religion, and Communications: The Case of Richmond." In *Religion and the American Civil War*, edited by Randall M. Miller, Harry S. Stout and Charles Reagan Wilson. New York: Oxford University Press, 1998.

Stowell, Daniel W. *Rebuilding Zion: The Religious Reconstruction of the South, 1863–1877*. New York: Oxford University Press, 1998.

Stroupe, Henry Smith. *The Religious Press in the South Atlantic States*. Durham: Duke University Press, 1956.

Tate, Adam L. *Conservatism and Southern Intellectuals 1789–1861*. Columbia: University of Missouri Press, 2005.

Taylor, William R. *Cavalier and Yankee: The Old South and American National Character*. Cambridge: Harvard University Press, 1979.

Thomas, Emory M. *The Confederacy as a Revolutionary Experience*. Englewood Cliffs,

N.J.: Prentice-Hall, 1971. Reprint, Columbia: University of South Carolina Press, 1991.

——. *The Confederate Nation: 1861–1865*. New York: Harper & Row, 1979.

——. "Rebel Nationalism: E. H. Cushing and the Confederate Experience." *Southwestern Historical Quarterly* 73 (January 1970): 343–55.

Thompson, Henry T. *Henry Timrod: Laureate of the Confederacy*. Columbia, S.C.: The State Company, 1928.

Tise, Larry. *Proslavery: A History of the Defense of Slavery in America, 1701–1840*. Athens: University of Georgia Press, 1987.

Todd, Emily B. "Walter Scott and the Nineteenth-Century American Literary Marketplace: Antebellum Richmond Readers and the Collected Editions of the Waverley Novels." *The Papers of the Bibliographical Society of America* 93 (December 1999): 495–517.

Tucker, Edward L. " 'A Rash and Perilous Enterprize' The Southern Literary Messenger and the Men Who Made It." *Virginia Cavalcade* 21 (Summer 1971): 14–21.

Twelve Southerners. *I'll Take My Stand: The South and the Agrarian Tradition*. New York: Harper & Brothers, 1930.

Tyron, Warren S. "The Publications of Ticknor and Fields in the South, 1840–1865." *Journal of Southern History* 14 (August 1948): 305–30.

Waal, Carla. "The First Original Confederate Drama." *Virginia Magazine of History and Biography* 70 (October 1962): 459–67.

Wade, John Donald. *Augustus Baldwin Longstreet: A Study of the Development of Culture in the South*. New York: Macmillan, 1924.

Wade, Richard C. *Slavery in the Cities: The South 1820–1860*. London: Oxford University Press, 1964.

Waldstreicher, David. *In the Midst of Perpetual Fetes: The Making of American Nationalism, 1776–1820*. Chapel Hill: University of North Carolina Press, 1997.

Walther, Eric H. "Fire-eaters and the Riddle of Southern Nationalism." *Southern Studies* 3, no. 1 (1992): 67–77.

Warren, Robert Penn. *The Legacy of the Civil War: Meditations on the Centennial*. New York: Random House, 1961.

Waters, Willard O. *Confederate Imprints in the Henry E. Huntington Library Unrecorded in Previously Published Bibliographies of Such Material*. Chicago, 1930.

Watson, Charles S. *The History of Southern Drama*. Lexington: University Press of Kentucky, 1997.

Watson, Ritchie. " 'The Difference of Race': Antebellum Race Mythology and the Development of Southern Nationalism." *Southern Literary Journal* 35 (Fall 2002): 1–13.

Watson, Ritchie Devon, Jr. *Normans and Saxons: Southern Race Mythology and the Intellectual History of the American Civil War*. Baton Rouge: Louisiana State University Press, 2008.

Weatherford, Willis Duke. *Analytical Index of De Bow's Review*, 1952.

Weaver, Richard M. *The Southern Essays of Richard M. Weaver*. Edited by George M. Curtis III and James J. Thompson Jr. Indianapolis: Liberty Press, 1987.

——. *The Southern Tradition at Bay: A History of Postbellum Thought*. Edited by George Core and M. E. Bradford, 1968. Reprint, Washington D.C.: Regnery Gateway, 1989.

Webb, William A. "Southern Poetry: 1849–1881." *South Atlantic Quarterly* 2 (January 1903): 35–50.

Weeks, Stephen B. *Confederate Text-Books. A Preliminary Bibliography*. Washington D.C.: Government Printing Office, 1900.

Wells, Jonathan Daniel. Introduction to *The Southern Literary Messenger, 1834–1864*, by Benjamin Blake Minor. Reprint, Columbia: University of South Carolina Press, 2007.

——. *The Origins of the Southern Middle Class, 1800–1861*. Chapel Hill: University of North Carolina Press, 2004.

Welsh, Willard. "Civil War Theater: The War in Drama." *Civil War History* 1 (September 1955): 251–80.

Whites, LeeAnn. *The Civil War as a Crisis in Gender: Augusta, Georgia, 1860–1890*. Athens: University of Georgia Press, 1995.

Whitescarver, Keith. "School Books, Publishers, and Southern Nationalists: Refashioning the Curriculum in North Carolina's Schools, 1850–1861." *North Carolina Historical Review* 79 (January 2002): 28–49.

Widmer, Edward L. *Young America: The Flowering of Democracy in New York City*. New York: Oxford University Press, 1999.

Wight, Willard Eugene. "Churches in the Confederacy." Ph.D. diss., Emory University, 1957.

Wiley, Bell Irvin. *Confederate Women*. Westport, Conn.: Greenwood Press, 1975.

Wilson, Charles Reagan. *Baptized in Blood: The Religion of the Lost Cause 1865–1920*. Athens: University of Georgia Press, 1980.

Wilson, Edmund. *Patriotic Gore: Studies in the Literature of the American Civil War*. New York: Farrar, Straus and Giroux, 1962.

Wolcott, John D. "The Southern Educational Convention of 1863." *South Atlantic Quarterly* 8 (October 1909): 354–60.

Woodward, C. Vann. *The Burden of Southern History*. 3rd ed. Baton Rouge: Louisiana State University Press, 1993.

Woody, Thomas. *A History of Women's Education in the United States*. 2 vols., 1929. New York: Octagon Books, 1966.

Wright, Gavin. *The Political Economy of the Cotton South: Households, Markets, and Wealth in the Nineteenth Century*. New York: W. W. Norton & Company, 1978.

Wyatt-Brown, Bertram. *Hearts of Darkness: Wellsprings of a Southern Literary Tradition*. Baton Rouge: Louisiana State University Press, 2003.

——. *The Shaping of Southern Culture: Honor, Grace, and War, 1760s–1890s*. Chapel Hill: University of North Carolina Press, 2001.

——. *Southern Honor: Ethics and Behavior in the Old South*. Oxford: Oxford University Press, 1982.

Yearns, W. Buck, ed. *The Confederate Governors*. Athens: University of Georgia Press, 1985.

Young, Jeffrey Robert. *Domesticating Slavery: The Master Class in Georgia and South Carolina, 1670–1837*. Chapel Hill: University of North Carolina Press, 1999.

Ziff, Larzer. *Literary Democracy: The Declaration of Cultural Independence in America*. New York: Viking Press, 1981.

INDEX

Cooke, Philip Pendleton, 101, 222, 223, 312 (n. 132)

Countryman, The, 153, 156–59, 167, 329 (n. 98); Joel Chandler Harris and, 156, 157; readership of, 159; literary standards of, 228, 229; criticism of other periodicals by, 233, 235; on importance of education, 240–41; in later years of war, 251, 253, 256, 259–61, 264, 265, 286; in postwar years, 287, 291, 293, 351 (n. 21)

Cowper, R. Lynden, 263–64, 265

Crafts, William, 222

Crenshaw, John Bacon, 261

Crescent Monthly, 291–92

Criticism, 117, 185, 212–15, 217–24; of textbooks, 132–33, 230–31; role of, in quest for intellectual independence, 215, 227–37; in last year of war, 263–69, 275. *See also* Theater criticism

Cross, Jane T. H., 184

Crozier, R. H., 292, 298

Cultural nationalism, 306 (n. 71); in antebellum South, 6, 22–23, 26. *See also* Confederate cultural nationalism

Currency. *See* Confederate currency

Cushing, Edward H., 179, 199, 200–201, 321 (n. 25)

Dabney, Robert Lewis, 186

Daily South Carolinian, 153, 168, 214, 328 (n. 77)

Darby, John, 132

Dargan, Clara, 111

Davidson, James Wood, 220, 224–25, 264, 338 (n. 44), 339 (nn. 61, 66)

Davies, Samuel, 181, 216, 225, 227, 228

Davis, I. N., Sr., 62, 85. *See also Southern Literary Companion*

Davis, Jefferson, 245, 254–55; southern writers on, 3, 186–87, 189, 201, 260

Davis, Mary E. M., 184

Dayton, A. C., 89. See also *Dayton's Baptist Monthly*

Dayton's Baptist Monthly, 89, 154

Deaf Mute Casket, 195, 334 (n. 211)

De Bow, B. F., 93

De Bow, James Dunwoody Brownson, 4, 25, 83–84, 93, 102–3, 170–71; southern pride of, 39, 56–57; on intellectual independence, 93, 107; in later years of war, 267–68, 270, 284. See also *De Bow's Review*

De Bow's Review, 49, 61, 83–84, 93, 112, 156–57, 170, 266; on need for intellectual independence, 20, 27, 114, 127–28; on influence of northern literature, 20, 61, 63, 64, 71, 72; on North-South differences, 46, 49, 52, 53; on importance of textbooks, 71, 127–28; readership of, 84, 314 (n. 14); wartime difficulties of, 92, 170–71, 257, 261; changing topics in, after secession, 104; on women's education, 143, 145; in postwar years, 291

Deen, Ethel, 234

De Fontaine, Felix G., 168, 346 (n. 67). See also *Daily South Carolinian*

Delchamps, J. J., 209, 232

De Vere, M. Schele, 165

Dew, Thomas, 222

Dickens, Charles, 276, 277

Dillard, A. W., 268, 274–75

Dimitry, Charles P. J., 183, 276

Duncan, James, 176, 251. See also *Richmond Christian Advocate*

"Eclectic" magazines, 169–70, 276, 277. See also *Age, The*; *Record of News, History and Literature, The*

Education, 52–55, 127, 133–35, 237–41, 278–80; for women, 142–47, 243, 307 (n. 19); higher (*see* Colleges and universities). *See also* Educational independence; Teachers; Textbooks

Gulf City Home Journal, 167, 192, 227, 257; criticism in, 207, 227, 230, 235, 340 (n. 104); suspension of publication by, 257

Haines, Oakley P., 164–65, 167
Hall, William A., 216
Hard Tack, 190
Harper's Monthly, 23, 294
Harper's Weekly, 61–62, 91, 160, 235
Harris, Joel Chandler, 156, 157, 264, 265, 266–67
Hartz, Asa, 271
Harwell, Richard, 5, 258, 325 (n. 1)
Haygood, Atticus, 63, 108; cultural nationalism expressed by, 39–40, 61, 98, 99, 107
Haygood, G. B., 71, 95, 97. See also *Educational Repository and Family Monthly*
Hayne, Paul Hamilton, 4, 101, 184, 224, 264; in Confederate periodicals, 113, 161, 165, 220–22, 226–27, 271; in postwar years, 292
Herrington, W. D., 184
Hewitt, John Hill, 183, 208
Hill, Daniel Harvey, 21
Hill, Theophilus Hunter, 193
Hill & Swayze publishers, 179, 180, 190
Hodgson, Joseph, 209
Holcombe, Dr. William H., 113, 184
Home Circle, 71, 85, 142, 154, 155; A. B. Stark and, 16, 80; as Methodist magazine, 16, 88, 89; on women's education, 142, 145; readership of, 314 (n. 17)
Home Journal, 62
Home Monthly, 291–92
Homogeneity, southern, 56–57, 317 (n. 87)
Hope, James Barron, 101, 161, 165, 184, 222, 271
Horn, A. G., 167, 179, 230, 340 (n. 104). See also *Gulf City Home Journal*

Howard, Charles Wallace, 15, 17, 68, 86, 103. See also *Southern Cultivator*
Howison, Robert R., 174, 186, 187–88, 230
Hubbell, Jay, 294
Hugo, Victor, 277–78
Humor, 188–93

Illustrated Mercury, 167–68, 184, 220, 224, 263–64, 272
Intellectual independence (quest for), 15–16, 26–27, 75–76, 80–81, 246, 286–91; as vital component of war effort, 2, 9, 15; and nationalist ideology, 6, 30–33; continuing, in war's last stages, 6, 257–62, 269–74, 282, 289; as justification for secession, 23–24; central role of periodicals in, 81–89, 93, 96–97; and literary standards, 94–95, 113–17, 174–75, 211–12, 227–37, 289; women's role in, 109–10; importance of education to, 119–20, 147, 246, 278–79; high point of, in middle years of war, 159, 167, 179–81, 188, 209–10; role of criticism in, 215, 227–37, 275; dooming of, 249–50, 281–82, 286–87, 289, 290–91; echoes of, in postwar years, 295–97. *See also* Educational independence; Literary independence

Jackson, Henry J., 222
Jackson, Henry W. R., 185
Jackson, Thomas "Stonewall," 176, 198, 200, 202; literary responses to death of, 113, 186; drawings of, 161, 162, 163; wartime biographies of, 332 (n. 158)
Jamison, D. F., 185
Johnson, Lemuel, 201
Johnston, F. H., 242
Johnston, Richard Malcolm, 184
Jordan, Cornelia J. M., 183

Mercury, The. See *Illustrated Mercury*

Methodist periodicals, 88, 106. See also *Christian Advocate* weeklies; *Educational Repository and Family Monthly*; *Home Circle*; *Quarterly Review of the Methodist Episcopal Church, South*

Military service, 240, 254–57; effect of, on southern colleges, 86, 127, 143, 242; teachers and, 127, 135, 241–42, 342 (n. 145). *See also* Conscription; Soldiers

Miot, Emma, 111

Moore, J. Quitman, 43, 58–59, 84, 104

Moore, Marinda Branson, 199, 201, 202, 203–4, 212

Morgan, John Hunt, 190

Mott, Frank, 193

Mott, T. S. W., 88, 114

Naff, George E., 54, 70, 72–73, 136–37

Nationalism, 2–4, 55, 288–89, 290; definitions of, 2, 3–4; and "character," 2, 55; Confederate (*see* Confederate nationalism); cultural (*see* Cultural nationalism)

Nazarene Banner, 178

Neely, John, 281

New Eclectic, 291–92

New England, 37–38, 52–53, 65, 66, 241, 298. *See also* Puritans

New Orleans Crescent, 60

New Orleans Daily Delta, 14, 20, 100, 190

New Orleans Medical and Surgical Journal, 86, 154

Niles' Weekly Register, 260

Normal schools, 137–38, 239, 243, 323 (n. 71)

Norman versus Saxon dichotomy, 57–59

North Carolina, state educational association of. *See* State Educational Association of North Carolina

North Carolina Christian Advocate. See *Christian Advocate* (Raleigh, N.C.)

North Carolina Journal of Education, 49, 170, 171; on educational independence, 28, 71, 119–20, 122, 171; and State Educational Association of North Carolina, 28, 85, 138, 139, 141; on textbooks, 71, 122, 132; readership of, beyond state's borders, 85, 141; wartime difficulties of, 171, 257

North Carolina Presbyterian, 74, 88, 111, 178; on dangers of northern culture, 21, 74; on importance of education, 135; wartime difficulties of, 177; readership of, 178

North Carolina University Magazine, 64, 67, 86, 92, 154, 316 (n. 40)

Novels, 184, 264–67

O'Brien, Michael, 6

Odgen, Richard, 207–8

Originality, 165, 215–16, 232, 234–36

Overall, John, 190–92, 269. See also *New Orleans Daily Delta*; *Southern Punch*

Palmer, Benjamin M., 4, 35–36, 38, 46–47, 87

Paper, 252; shortage of, 90, 170, 173, 174, 177

Peck, William, 15, 17, 23, 69, 73–74

Periodicals: northern, 61–64, 111, 161 (see also *Frank Leslie's Illustrated Newspaper*; *Harper's Magazine*); southern (*see* Confederate periodicals)

Perry, W. S., 91, 95

Peterson's Ladies' National Magazine, 62

Pike, Albert, 222

Pinckney, Edward C., 222

Plagiarism, 235–36

Poe, Edgar Allan, 101, 222, 223

Poetry, 181–82, 206, 222–23, 263–64, 284–85; northern, 65; by new Confederate writers, 112–13, 114, 115–17, 181; and literary standards, 114–17, 182, 228–29; by women, 115–17, 222;

Southern Presbyterian, 22, 87, 88, 100; on North-South hostility, 22, 37, 51, 52; on slavery, 104–5; and secession, 105–6; encouragement of southern writers by, 111, 112; literary standards of, 116–17; on importance of education, 119, 134, 242, 243; cultural nationalism of, 153–54; wartime difficulties of, 176, 177, 178, 251, 253, 257; readership of, 176, 177–78; revival of, in final year of war, 178, 257, 259, 261

Southern Presbyterian Review, 49, 87, 88, 178, 257; high standing of, 49, 87, 112, 178; and secession, 50, 87; readership of, 87–88, 178

Southern Punch, 152, 190–93, 219, 269, 333 (n. 191), 338 (n. 39); quality of humor in, 192; success of, in middle years of war, 192; readership of, 192, 195; and Confederate theater, 207, 232–33, 262; on southern literature, 217, 220, 221, 222–23, 265, 269, 270, 271; on originality, 217, 231; on conscription, 254, 255, 256, 257

Southern Review, 291–92, 298

Southern Teacher, 18, 85, 97, 109, 132–33, 154, 314 (n. 19); cultural nationalism expressed by, 18, 97; wartime difficulties of, 92, 154; on textbooks, 132–33; on teacher training, 136, 137–38

Southworth, E. D. E. N., 65, 311 (n. 104)

Spicewood, Simon, 263

Spratt, Leonidas W., 36

Sprigg, D. Francis, 89. See also Southern Churchman

Stark, A. B., 61, 100, 121, 290; cultural nationalism expressed by, 16, 80–81, 99, 100, 101, 108, 117–18; on "literature of knowledge" and "literature of power," 80–81, 211–12; on women's role, 109–10

State Educational Association of North Carolina, 111, 124, 129, 138, 141, 244; cultural nationalism expressed by, 30, 122, 139–40; and educational independence, 122, 139–40, 141–42; wider influence of, 141–42, 244. See also North Carolina Journal of Education

States' rights, 102, 104–5

Stiles, Joseph C., 45–46, 47

Stilling, Margaret, 161, 165, 184

Stowe, Harriet Beecher, 65

Stroupe, Henry, 258

Subscription prices, 91–92, 171, 177, 251, 329 (n. 92)

Summers, Thomas O., 25, 88. See also Quarterly Review of the Methodist Episcopal Church, South

Sunday School Paper for the South, 195, 334 (n. 211)

Sunday School Visitor, 88

Swain, Margie, 183

Swan, Ella, 94

Taliaferro, Harden E., 189

Talladega Watchtower, 232

Talley, Susan Archer, 113, 161, 165, 184

Teachers, 111, 121, 279–80, 296, 323 (n. 71), 342 (n. 149); recruitment of women as, 9, 137, 144, 238, 242–43, 280, 296, 342 (n. 152); northern, in antebellum South, 17, 53–54, 67–69, 74, 134; wartime shortage of, 69, 120, 125, 127, 133, 134–37, 144, 241–43, 279–80; and importance of textbooks, 126; and military service, 127, 135, 241–42, 342 (n. 145); social standing of, 135–37; training of, 137–38, 239, 243 (see also Normal schools); advertisements for, 323 (n. 69)

Teachers' organizations, 133, 138–42, 147, 243–46. See also State Educational Association of North Carolina

Textbooks, 125–33, 199–205, 280–81; cultural nationalism expressed in, 13, 19–20, 31, 126–27, 130–31, 200–205,

281; northern, 24, 25, 53–54, 60, 67–73, 126, 129, 201–2, 312 (n. 126); Confederate periodicals and, 120, 132–33, 200, 230–31; southern, as high priority, 121, 125–27, 140, 199, 204–5, 241, 280–81; in North Carolina, 121, 126, 128–29, 130, 132; importance of, in nineteenth-century classrooms, 126; teachers' organizations and, 126, 128–29, 132, 244; wartime production of, 129–32, 195, 199–200, 241; and slavery, 131, 204; postwar controversies over, 296

Thackeray, William Makepeace, 276, 277

Theater. *See* Confederate theater; Theater criticism

Theater criticism, 207, 209, 232–33, 276, 340 (n. 104)

Thompson, John Reuben, 101, 169, 184, 214–15; high reputation of, 101, 222; wartime writing by, 113, 161, 207, 271

Thompson, William Tappan, 102

Thornwell, James H., 4, 49, 50–51, 87, 101, 222

Ticknor, Dr. Francis O., 113, 184

Timrod, Henry, 4, 7, 13, 222, 224, 339 (n. 66); cultural nationalism expressed by, 7, 153, 168, 214, 215, 218; wartime poems by, 113, 161, 184, 212, 271; and *Daily South Carolinian*, 153, 168, 214, 228; on quality of Confederate literature, 213, 214, 215, 218, 271; on literary standards, 215, 218, 228; on importance of education, 239, 278; on threat posed by conscription, 254–55, 256

Trescot, William, 222

Tucker, George, 222

Tucker, J. Randolph, 47, 48

Tucker, Nathaniel Beverly, 101, 184, 222

Tucker, St. George, 101, 184, 222

Turner, Joseph Addison, 153, 156–59, 183, 256, 283; as editor of *The Countryman*, 153, 156–59, 229, 251, 253–54, 256, 259–61, 326 (n. 25), 351 (n. 21); cultural nationalism expressed by, 153, 180–81, 192–93, 235–36; plantation owned by, 156, 253; on religion, 158–59, 334 (n. 212); on literary standards, 229, 235–36; on importance of education, 279; and Confederacy's collapse, 283–84, 285, 286–87, 291, 292, 293, 351 (n. 21)

Turner, William Wilberforce, 157, 233, 279

Uncle Tom's Cabin (Stowe), 65

Union armies, 252, 253, 259, 286

United Daughters of the Confederacy, 296, 297

Universities. *See* Colleges and universities

Upshur, Abel, 222

Vance, Zebulon, 245

Wade, W. H., 160–64, 193, 259. See also *Southern Illustrated News*

Waldon, Alfred, 207

Wallis, Severn, 222

Warren, Ebenezer W., 184

Washington, Augusta, 165

Watchman and Harbinger, 178

Wedderburn, Alexander, 175

Webster, Noah, 200, 202

Weekly Constitutionalist, 25, 86

Weekly Register, 169

West & Johnston publishers, 169, 179–80, 183, 184, 262, 265, 277–78

Whately, Richard, 130

Wilde, Richard H., 222

Wiley, Calvin Henderson, 24, 28, 29, 85, 121–25; on educational independence, 14, 17, 19, 28, 85, 121–22, 123, 124, 125, 128–29; and State Educational Association of North Carolina, 85, 139; as state school superintendent, 85, 323 (n. 71),

342 (n. 149); on need for Confederate textbooks, 128–29, 140–41; on recruitment of teachers, 144, 243, 342 (nn. 149, 152); in later stages of war, 238–39, 240–41, 243, 244

Wirt, William, 102, 222

Women, 40–42, 109–10, 257; and cultural nationalism, 9, 109–10, 242–43; recruitment of, as teachers, 9, 137, 144, 238, 242–43, 280, 296, 342 (n. 152); northern, 40–41, 188; and secession, 41–42, 145–46; as writers, 109–10, 115–17, 181, 295–96 (*see also* Evans, Augusta Jane); education for, 142–47, 241, 307 (n. 19); and "Lost Cause," 296

Women's rights, 40–41

Worrell, Adolphus Spalding, 19–20, 30–31, 130, 131

Young America literary movement, 114, 289